INVESTING AT THE RACETRACK

William L. Scott

FOREWORD BY **Tom Ainslie**

A FIRESIDE BOOK
PUBLISHED BY SIMON & SCHUSTER, INC.
NEW YORK

Copyright © 1981 by William L. Scott
Foreword copyright © 1981 by Tom Ainslie
First Fireside Edition, 1986
Published by Simon & Schuster, Inc.
Simon & Schuster Building
Rockefeller Center
1230 Avenue of the Americas
New York, New York 10020

FIRESIDE and colophon are registered trademarks of Simon & Schuster, Inc.
Designed by Irving Perkins Associates

Manufactured in the United States of America

					6	7	8	9	10
Pbk.		3	4	5	6	7	8	9	10

Library of Congress Cataloging in Publication Data

Scott, William L.
Investing at the racetrack.
Includes index.
1. Horse race betting.   I. Title.
SF331.F49   798.4′01   81-9261
AACR2
ISBN 0-671-43152-8
ISBN 0-671-63017-2 Pbk.

Contents

Foreword

BY TOM AINSLIE

Among the sportive millions who enjoy betting on horse races, those who try to pick their own winners have much more fun than those who depend on the advice of others. That is perfectly reasonable. The person who knows how to read a menu is likely to obtain a more satisfactory meal.

Handicapping, as we call the informed effort to select winning horses, is a great game. It presents endlessly variable challenges to intellect and ego. Because it cannot be mastered overnight yet is so obviously worth learning, some author or other is forever trying to reduce it to its essentials, simplifying it for more rapid absorption by the needful. I have made some attempts of that kind and shall not apologize for them, even though they fell short of their goals and left me convinced that real handicapping could not be fully systematized.

Ah, but it can. And in this book it is. William Scott (an exceedingly smart lawyer operating here under a pen name) has brought a fresh eye to the old game and has found truths that were there all the time but had gone unnoticed by the rest of us. The resulting book is an absolutely phenomenal achievement, a race-selection system that not only works but works more often than not and works at all tracks and does so without a lot of infuriating detail.

If your mail resembles mine, it has for years contained an overabundance of solicitations from charlatans promising to teach you how to beat the races. Their systems, they say, require no judgment, offer a play in almost every race, and are so simple and unambiguous that every customer plays the same horse. But William Scott's is the first system I have ever seen that fills the prescription.

It supplies all the activity that anyone could want—sound selections in upwards of eight races per average nine-race program. Yet it demands nothing of the user beyond faithful adherence to the rules, which include at least two of the most brilliant handicapping innovations of the past half century. Experienced racegoers will be dazzled by the "ability ratings" with which Scott appraises Thoroughbred class and by the logic with which he narrows contention to not more than five and usually only three horses.

His procedures are so strikingly clever, and so faithful to the fundamental realities of the game, that I expect the system to perform well for many years. Which is to say that anybody motivated to read this book and follow its instructions can count on success as outstanding as Scott enjoyed during the week in June 1980 which he documents in these pages. All he accomplished during that test week was to beat every major U.S. track in operation at the time. As those who know me will understand without my making a big fuss of it, I have checked out that week for myself and have subjected the system to my own independent tests with real money. As I was saying, it works.

Enough of this. Let Scott tell you what he has found. With my profoundest congratulations on a first-rate piece of work which will surely have a permanent effect on racing and handicapping, I now yield the floor.

THE SEARCH FOR SOUND INVESTMENT IN HORSE RACING

Playing the horses, betting on Thoroughbreds, following the ponies, or whatever society wishes to call it, has never made an impression as a sound investment opportunity. Most people, even those who enjoy the racetrack, pass it off as a form of gambling. Much of it is, perhaps even an overwhelming portion. On the other hand, another popular form of gambling, playing the stock market, has acquired the socially respectable label of "investing."

You can make money in the stock market, they say, but playing the horses leads to a certainty of losses as truly inevitable as death and taxes. And when you lose at the track, you are gambling. Oh, if you lose in the stock market, you made "bad investments," of course.

But if, buried somewhere in the myths that surround the racetrack, there is indeed a method of putting money on horses that will produce a steady, consistent profit, that would be investing, wouldn't it? Perhaps even safer than the stock market, where your fate is totally in the hands of forces far outside your own control. What if it could indeed be done, steadily and consistently, day after day, or enough days in the week to make it beautifully worthwhile?

Is man's ingenuity keen enough to cope with a problem like this, produce a solution, and put it into play? Or is it impossible, as common knowledge would have you believe—destined to be filed among the shambles left by dreamers and charlatans?

If it could be done, why, it might even be safer than the stock market, mightn't it? While the market is a revered institution, the investor there is engaging in gambling as surely as is the bingo player at a church supper. No one ever guaranteed you a profit in the stock market. Bad economic news, changes in the prime rate of interest, unknown adversity in the company where your money resides, and a hundred other factors can punish your pocket as surely as a losing ticket on a slow horse at a racetrack.

But this book will demonstrate to you that there is a method of investing money in racehorses that is even safer than investing it in common stocks, that will return a far greater percentage on investment, and that requires so little initial capital that almost anyone can engage in it.

I became convinced several years ago that it was possible, once I learned how playing the races works. All it took was the recognition that when you bet on horses at the racetrack, you are competing in skill and knowledge not against the house as in a gambling casino, but against your fellow player. That being so, the wisest, the most skilled, the most knowledgeable would surely emerge on top. Once I became fascinated with the sport and began to attend the track, read books, experiment, do research that I enjoy doing, and understand the nature of the challenge itself, I became determined to prove it to myself, always accepting the premise that it could be done.

It can, is, and has.

It was a long time coming, filled with work, sweat, frustration, paying my dues at the windows, learning endlessly about the intricacies of evaluating animals and the people who attend them, and generally maintaining the hopeful belief not only that it was possible, but that I was making progress in achieving it. I promised myself that I would never claim that it could be done until I could actually do it myself, and look any man in the eye when I said that I could do it.

I am ready to do that now.

In this book, experienced horse players will learn new methods of rating horses. The major approach of the book has been called revolutionary, which it is. The novice will grapple for a while with concepts and mathematics, but will find shortly that it is indeed so simple that anyone who can read and perform the basic skills of addition and subtraction can do it.

When these methods of play were finally and fully developed in 1980, I undertook to test them by applying them to six successive days of racing at Belmont Park in New York in the first week of June 1980. The week was chosen because I was ready by then, and primarily because I was able to be in New York that entire period. In the last portion of this book, you will see the method of play applied under the precise rules set forth.

Here is what happened.

Every single one of the six successive racing days resulted in a net profit!

In all the six days combined, net profits were at a return on money invested of 55%. This was for one week, and where in the world can anyone reap that kind of return on money invested in one week?

And, immediately, I can hear the first skeptic saying, "Oh, just a lucky week. Anyone might stumble on any one particular week, make a killing, and claim a new miracle has been discovered."

Before he can be answered, I can hear the second skeptic saying, "One week? Are you out of your mind? One week isn't a long enough period to prove anything. Do it for fifty-two weeks, come back with proof, and then maybe I'll believe it, and maybe I won't."

These are the two most legitimate questions about what is demonstrated here. They deserve serious, sound answers before we go an inch further.

No, it wasn't just a lucky week. The selections you will read about are made upon sound principles, not chance and circumstance. A method of selection, if it has intrinsic value, must stand the test of time and misfortune, week after week, month after month. If it can do that, it can become a method of investing, not sheer gambling. My first response, therefore, to the skeptic is that what will be set forth here is so inherently sound that it will win at any major racetrack in the United States and Canada, on a regular, demonstrable basis.

But to test the principles of this book beyond one week at Belmont in the summer of 1980, I decided, after the Belmont week was recorded, to run similar tests at tracks all across the United States. I decided to use the same days that were played at Belmont. Could this method of play produce a profit at each of those other tracks just as it did at Belmont? If it was not as solid and sound as I proclaimed, surely cracks would emerge and another good "system" (which this is not) would go down the drain.

The other test tracks were selected on the basis of geography, prominence, and availability of back issues of the *Daily Racing Form* that would enable me to apply precisely the same rating methods and rules of selection that I used at Belmont. I chose two more Eastern tracks, Suffolk Downs in Boston and Monmouth Park in northern New Jersey. Then in the Midwest, I chose Arlington Park in Chicago, the leading track, and Churchill Downs in Louisville, the historic home of the Kentucky Derby, still running in the first week of June 1980. On the West Coast, I chose Hollywood Park in Los Angeles, one of the two great tracks in California that rival the best that New York can offer, and Golden Gate Fields, in the San Francisco Bay area.

I decided to consider every possible race for three successive days at these tracks, since it is one of the themes of this book that you should be able to make a profit in any three-day period at any racetrack.

And how did we fare? Suffolk, Monmouth, Arlington, Churchill, Hollywood, and Golden Gate, all well known to horse players of their areas—yes, for each period at each track, there was indeed a net profit! The details and amounts will be set forth in a later chapter when I discuss the play at these tracks.

If this method is so good, why not win every day? You will see, when its statistical base is revealed, that on some days a slight loss is inevitable. You will also learn that a "break-even" day is a bad day, along with the "slight-loss" day. What I consider a slight loss will be explained later also. Because there is such a sound, unassailable statistical base for the investment program set out in this book, you will rarely lose two days in a row, although it can happen. But the profits on the other days surrounding the "bad days" will exceed the losses, and lead you into periods of profit over and over again. In all the research, experimentation, going to the track, and study that I have done, I have not found any three-consecutive-day period that has failed to produce a profit.

The best exposition of the premise of this book is that you cannot attend any racetrack in North America for a consecutive week and not return a net profit on your investment. If you fail to do so, you are not likely to be applying with exactitude what is set forth here. Or else you are laboring under a cloud of misfortune rarely known to man, one that would rival that of the old comic-strip character Joe Bfslptfk.

These claims of profits in investment at the racetrack have a statistical foundation which is set forth in the next chapter. You will then begin to understand the basic logic of it. After that comes a method of rating horses which is necessary to establish a formula for final selection. When you complete your reading of those portions of this book, you will see the soundness of the method, its stability, and its continuing likelihood of success. When a method is based on a secure, logical, orderly scheme of events, it ought to work over any demonstrably fair period of time, whether it is the three days I believe sufficient, or a week, or a month, or a year.

And there isn't even any luck to it. Luck connotes gambling; this is a program for investing, not gambling, as you will read over and over again. Admittedly, there is some chance involved in it, just as there is some chance involved in everything you do, from walking across the street to investing your money in the stock market. But the chance is overcome by numbers of happenings based upon logical findings, just as insurance companies retain their solvency by the expectancies of statistical happenings that occur over and over again with consistency.

The racetrack, of course, is indeed a magnificent place in which to gamble, and almost everyone who goes there engages in gambling. It offers thrills, excitement, disappointment, dismay, ups and downs, horses that do not live up to your expectations, and an unusual variety of ways in which you can lose your money. But it doesn't have to be that way, if you learn how to do otherwise.

The market, of course, is an arena for gambling on a slightly different scale. If a stock in which an "investment" is made goes down in value, the player may lose only a part of his money. If a horse fails to win, the entire wager is lost. The stock-market player may hold his investment for a long period of time and watch it go up and down. The horse player holds his investment usually for minutes only, and there is no seesawing. It is quickly won or lost.

The speculator, or investor, at the bourse is willing to risk his money in the hope that it will turn into even more money. And if good fortune occurs and the stock he purchases rises in value, he has made a "good investment." The investor in the stock market may carefully study the daily newspaper of the mart, the *Wall Street Journal,* he may closely follow other publications, he may seek inside information, and in the end, his backing of his opinion with money relies largely on the performance of other persons and public events over which he has little control.

The speculator, or investor, at the racetrack is also willing to risk his money in the hope that it will turn into even more money. He too carefully studies his daily newspaper, the *Daily Racing Form,* one of the world's most remarkable publications, and he may read other things as well, seek inside information, and finally make a decision whose outcome will soon be known in ultimate results.

But the horse player, if he fully understands how to apply it, has more sound information at his disposal than does the market investor, because past performances of horses in the *Daily Racing Form* are inherently a more reliable indicator of what they might do than any comparable business indicia that will enable the market investor to "know" how his stock will perform.

Heretofore, the horse player has been far more readily disposed to gambling. There are various exotic bets offered at the racetrack—exactas, quinellas, trifectas, pick six, and that old standby, the daily double. You can go there to play numbers off your license plate, your grandmother's birthday, the cute name of a jockey, a tip from your bartender's cousin, or just plain old dreams or guesswork. And there will be occasional days, of course, when good fortune indeed deposits its blessings—and that's what keeps gamblers going. But in the end, this kind of player will surely lose, and that, too, is truly as inevitable as death and taxes.

And in passing, let me say that I have absolutely nothing against gambling. Taking a chance, wagering, risking money, or whatever you wish to call it is as old as the human race. All our cultures engage in it, from the casinos that flourish in the Orient, in the Mediterranean, the Caribbean, and in the good old U.S.A., on to all other kinds of games and enterprises known to every student of anthropology. Most all of us have participated in it in some form or another, from pitching pennies as children to office pools, bingo games, drawings, lotteries, card games, carnivals, and, yes, the stock market and the racetrack.

What I find distasteful about it is the effect of losing.

The joy of winning is so much greater. I simply do not like to lose, and I will not continue to do so. After some experience and observation, for example, I will not shoot dice in an American casino. Because I understand the odds perfectly, I know that I am destined to lose. Pure luck does strike on occasions, and has, but if I continued to play, I would lose as surely as the sun will rise tomorrow.

Because I see nothing to be gained by losing (not even the occasional thrill of a chance winning), I therefore choose not to play. That is my right just as much as it is the right of the risk taker to roll the dice or purchase a fluctuating stock.

Horse racing, fortunately, is a far different kind of enterprise. There are no house odds inexorably weighted against the player. The pari-mutuel system of betting makes the racetrack a mere stake holder, extracting its percentage of the total amount of money wagered, and returning the remainder to the players. As I said a few pages ago, when you play the races, you are competing against your fellow players, seeking to win money that they will lose.

This is competition, pure and simple, and that I can relish. It is, in the long run, if you are serious enough about it to forgo the gambling opportunities that attract so many others, an ultimate test of skill, perception, fortitude, and, yes, courage. In my professional work, I have had to be competitive all my life—and this is nothing different, except the game is played in a different arena.

When you understand that playing, or investing in, horse races is essentially a contest between those who are determined to win and those who are destined to lose, it is not surprising that there are persons who do win money at the racetrack, and therefore stand as living refutations to the bromide "You can't beat the races." Many of these winners want to remain anonymous, and many of them are actually very good gamblers, which I am not.

One notable published example of winning came from the newspaper writer and racing authority Andrew Beyer, whose book *My $50,000 Year at the Races* (Harcourt, Brace, Jovanovich, 1978) passed on fascinating stories of how he won big sums over the course of a year. A previous book by Beyer, *Picking Winners* (Houghton Mifflin, 1975), revealed the selection method he would use to reap his rewards and established him as a first-rate analyst of speed of the breed. But even Beyer's $50,000 year was filled with gambling adventures and chance-taking of a high order, as I am sure even Mr. Beyer would admit. I am not asking for the élan of a riverboat gambler to fortify one for the grand adventure. I, and you, want a method of play that essentially eliminates gambling, and turns playing the races into what will be revealed here—sound investment.

I was never concerned about horse racing, or investment in it, until a few recent years back. Although a devoted sports fan from boyhood, I paid relatively little attention to the horses. Baseball was my game, with football and basketball for added off-season watching, and tennis for leisure-time play. Oh, sure, I followed the Kentucky Derby like everyone else, and I knew that Willie Shoemaker was the top jockey in the country. As a regular reader of the sports pages, I also knew the names of some of the champion horses like Kelso and Citation and others that came and passed from the scene. I had even attended one Kentucky Derby in the distant past, thanks to an invitation from friends.

Then I began to learn about racing in an unusual way. My teenage son found a summer job walking horses at a nearby track. His bright young sister learned to ride, and from her close companionship with her brother, she began to pay attention to such things as the *Daily Racing Form* and the business of picking winners at racetracks, hardly the normal recommended daily fare for schoolchildren. But their straight A's and outstanding classroom performances indicated that their diversions weren't harming them. The two of them began to importune their father to take them to the Kentucky Derby in 1968. They succeeded. Out of this, a new hobby world of fascination was quickly revealed.

In those now-halcyon years, one could actually buy tickets to the Derby by ordering through the mail. We secured our three, luckily found motel space in southern Indiana some forty miles from Louisville, pulled the two top students out of their classes a day early (excuse: going on trip with Father; the other way around might have been more accurate), and set out on the long drive.

We talked horses. Oh, how they began to educate me. First and foremost was learning about the bible for all players, the *Daily Racing Form*. From looking at it a time or two on those social visits in the past, I found that it was relatively easy to grasp a superficial understanding of what it contained and what it meant.

The joy and excitement of the children, fueled by their incredible knowledge, turned the trip into one of the half-dozen most pleasurable travel experiences of a lifetime. Churchill Downs in the first days of May is not only the center of American sports excitement for that time of year, but is blessed with a special kind of Kentucky beauty to go along with it. There is the spectacle of the swiftest, most graceful animals in the world, the spring finery of the land's most lovely ladies, color and pageantry. The sunshine and beds of tulips with reds and yellows more resplendent than you have ever seen make the old track a delightful fairyland sanctuary from the corruption and conflict in the world outside—at least until massive crowds of people have begun to push into it to convert it partially into a horrendous crush. But even so, it seizes one with a frenzy of interest and excitement, making it surely one of the more fascinating places in the world to be in that first week in May.

We walked the old grounds at Churchill, among the tulip beds and the saddling stalls, where one could almost reach out and touch the horses. We stared at their lines of conformity, the colors of their gleaming hides, their finely shaped heads. All Thoroughbreds are beautiful, it seems, from the great champions down to the painfully slow runners that perform at the cheaper tracks scattered around the country.

We studied the names of past winners of the Derby painted around the white wooden moldings above the entranceways and window levels. I recalled Assault and Citation and Whirlaway. It brought back boyhood memories of the radio voice of the famed announcer Clem McCarthy, whose gravelly barks of the calls of Derby after Derby became an American institution.

The night before, we sat in our motel room and watched a long Derby preview television program. The big races of the leading 1968 contenders were rerun. With little knowledge, I watched the surge of Dancer's Image down the stretch in the Wood Memorial and said to my children, "I'm going to bet on that horse tomorrow." And I did.

We sat in the extended bleachers where the far turn heads into the long stretch at Churchill Downs. From that point, Dancer's Image began his powerful move, accelerating with a flow of graceful drive that consumed his competitors in the run to the wire. When he began that magnificent effort, even though a long way from the finish, with several horses still ahead of him, I was sure then we had the winner. It was a triumphant day, a profit in the pocket, and a new pursuit was begun. (Of course, we didn't know then that Dancer's Image would subsequently be disqualified, in the only incident of its kind in Derby history, because a urine test found traces of the drug Butazolidin, a mild painkiller. But the cashier's windows paid off on Dancer's Image, and no matter what the record books say, I know who won the 1968 Kentucky Derby.)

With a new interest fueled, I began to read. I learned from the vast amount of knowledge that my son and daughter were able to impart. I discovered there were many books about horse racing. I began to make other trips to the track with my children. But I was never so naive as to believe that winning was easy. A lot of uncashed tickets were torn up in the process. But there were winners, too, as the new knowledge was rapidly applied. It was not even too difficult to learn enough to stay within shouting distance of the break-even point. And as I progressed, it was easy enough to rationalize that my occasional visits to the track cost no more than tickets for two or three or four at a football game, or dinner and the theater, and other forms of entertainment. I was even able to rejoin to a critical spouse that gross outlay in a year was far less than she spent on cigarettes (especially since I was unsuccessfully appealing to her to kick the habit even then).

As I began to go to the track fifteen or twenty times a year, attending some of them in various parts of the country while on business trips, I began to seriously confront the Big Question. Could anyone really make money at this game? Who were the winners? How did they get that way? What were their techniques? How could they be so disciplined as to come out ahead week after week, if they did so? Or was it all just a gambling game, as I had been taught by society to believe?

And I also observed that thousands of people who go to the races are careless gamblers. There was even a term, "Hatpin Annie," which connoted a blindfold and a stab of a pin into a program to make a selection. Many people might as well do that. There were spectators who did bet on names and numbers and colors and birthdays. Their contributions to the mutuel pools were enough to start a cushion of comfort for the serious player. Bless them all, and may their tribe increase! You who will be winners should always be respectful of those who will be losers, for it is upon their base of financial support that you can begin to build your investment program.

Not only did I devour every book on the subject of racing, but I even began to purchase mail-order offerings from system sellers, whose sales pitches always promised an immediate land of riches. Most of them border on outright fraud. But all of them, in one form or another, offer money-back guarantees, with the knowledge that most people may never bother. I returned one after another, and received my purchase price back every time. Only one put up resistance, requiring two threatening letters, but my money did come back. In the process, I did adopt a rule of operation. If I learned just one useful thing from the mail-order offering to add to my growing repertoire of knowledge, I would keep the method and pay the price. And from some of them I did acquire some useful ideas.

There were also gadgets, calculators, slide rules, plastic wheels, all designed to open the door to fabulous wealth. One gadget calculates the class of a horse based on earnings, and has some limited utility. But I learned quickly that the same calculation could be done with pencil and paper, and if one can do basic arithmetic with any degree of quickness, it is easier than bothering with the slide rule or calculator. These devices, in the long run, do very little for your welfare.

I continued to apply the new learning. Long experiments were run, based upon the speeds of horses. Class was studied, in hundreds of races. Various combinations of handicapping factors were tried, such as pace, fractional times, recent races, and dozens of other permutations. Many of these went through the window at the track, where it counted. There were some days of success, but by and large, I was still in the process of paying my dues, and I knew it.

I began to do careful research, constantly casting aside methods that faltered over a long run. On my many business trips, I often took with me back issues of the *Daily Racing Form,* good reading for lonely motel rooms at night, or on an airplane. Several approaches had promise, but there was nothing in which I could place complete confidence.

Probably the most frustrating part of those years was in how close I was actually coming to breaking through, even almost from the first year. Several of the methods that I developed, some of which were highly original, would show strings of paper profits for a while, and then run aground. A promise of profit was not good enough. I was still locked in with that great admonition "You can't beat the races."

But my losses were so low that at the end of each year, in reviewing my visits to the track, I kept believing that it could be done. In fact, many of my losing days were caused by wagers that were forgetfully foolish, after some post-race reflection (always a sobering event). There were mistakes and oversight and betting too much on a losing horse and not enough on a winning horse— breaches of discipline. All this had to be corrected.

All through this period, from 1969 to about 1976, I had begun to formulate some very solid theories about some elements of the game. I would often read running lines of winning horses, to try to determine what it was that brought them home first. I learned about some of the telltale signs that a horse might win his race, and some of that is contained in this book when I discuss a horse's current form. But most of all, I learned the importance of speed as the single most important handicapping factor. This may appear obvious to the newcomer, but old hands still debate it, mixing it with the concept of class. Part of the problem revolves around what is true speed, and I have tried to do something about that in this book.

But still the search had to go on. By 1977, I had, through further hours of painstaking research into back issues of the *Form,* developed a method of elimination of horses that is one of the key formulations of this book, insofar as investment is concerned. And in the calendar year of 1977, when I totaled up my results for the preceding twelve months, I realized that I had made a profit at last! Not a great one, but I had gone to the track more often that year than in any other, and for the first time had won more money than I had lost.

Yet I knew that I had hardly reached the promised land. There were still too many losing days. Some of my gains had been won from a mild form of progression betting, far too dangerous for building a safe plan of playing the races. I was still searching for a method that could win by betting the same amount of money on every playable race.

In 1978, ten years after I had begun to seriously follow horse racing, I made another trip to the Kentucky Derby, this time with a younger son who was not quite old enough to accompany us on the 1968 trip. We went with a group of racing fans, which had obtained tickets as an organization. We devoted a week to it, with attendance at the track every day as a part of the ritual. This was my first critical test. Could I win over a sustained period of time, having no excuse whatever except for my own deficiencies? It was the kind of examination I face with relish.

Six days in a row resulted in five winning days, and the one that produced a loss was by a narrow number. Had I made it now? Not quite, and I knew it. There were still too many holes, too many errors, too many decisions made with discomfort. After departing from Churchill, there were some losing days that really shook my confidence. This was depressing. What more did I need? What was I overlooking? Was there a better way of rating horses than I was using, and if so, where the hell was it? Come on, research man, probe deeper—a little more now was all that was needed.

Why was it so difficult for even a knowledgeable person to win at the racetrack? This inquiry was striking home toward the theory of impossibility, which I was not going to accept.

But I saw answers all around me. There is first of all the sheer complexity of the sport itself. The variables found in the past performances in the *Daily Racing Form* are as challenging as the incredible varieties of moves on a chessboard. Competing horses often come into a race having run different distances in the past. Their speeds vary up and down the scale. They run on different track surfaces, such as dirt and grass. The always variable condition of the surface on the day they ran might affect the speed at which they could move.

And, of course, there are elements of racing luck, which can affect any horse. An animal might get bumped coming out of the gate, which happens every now and then. He may get caught in a wall of horses and have no running room. He could be forced wide around turns, losing valuable ground. I have even wagered on some horses in my time and watched them turn lame and limp home badly beaten.

There is always the human element as well. The trainer of a horse is far more of a key figure than even the jockey. Like the manager or coach of a team, the trainer is responsible for having the horse ready to run his best race. He is the man who decides what level of competition his runner will face. And if he errs, woe ensues. Jockeys, too, even the best of them, can and do make mistakes that cost their horses dearly and frustrate those of us who bet on them.

Those who plan the races, the racing secretaries at each of the tracks, strive to match horses of as nearly equal ability as they can. While they generally do an excellent job of it, fortunately for us they are not always totally successful. But the point is—and you will see it unfold in the Big Week at Belmont I describe later in this book—there are many races where horses are so evenly matched that making a sound selection becomes highly risky.

To cope with these enormous complexities, one needs to acquire a great deal of knowledge, and perhaps even more discipline. And sometimes it has seemed that the more one learns, the more self-defeating it becomes. One does search repeatedly for the key factors that lead to victory for a particular horse, whether it be sheer speed, class, track condition, trainer intention, distance, running style, or any combination of these mysteries.

Perhaps we can pause in the search and look closely at what does confront us. Old horse players will consider the next few pages too elementary, except that I have always found the histories of horses full of fascination. But those who know little of the intricacies of the *Racing Form* will want to see what beckons, and perhaps the regular, if he stays with us, might even gain a new insight or two.

Any example will do, and I have taken the past performance of one horse, Free The Spirit, from the *Daily Racing Form* of January 29, 1980, where he was entered in the tenth race at Hialeah that day.

Free The Spirit — **B. g. 5, by Explodent—Ring of Steel, by Assagai**

Own.—Allen H — **$10,000** — **Br.—Ocala Stud Farms Inc (Fla)** — **Tr.—Jacobs Eugene** — **117**

Turf Record St.	1st	2nd	3rd		St.	1st	2nd	3rd	Amt.
3	0	1	0	1980	1	1	0	0	$3,300
				1979	10	0	3	1	$7,235

12Jan80- 4Crc	fst	$1\frac{1}{16}$	$:47\frac{4}{5}$	$1:13\frac{2}{5}$	$1:47\frac{1}{5}$		Clm 9000	6	9	9^{15}	$5^{9\frac{1}{2}}$	$2^{\frac{1}{2}}$	$1^{4\frac{1}{2}}$	Vasquez J		114	*2.50	83-21	Free The Spirit $114^{4\frac{1}{2}}$HolmeFlash116^{5}OrangeAmber118^{1}	Ret. sore	10
29Dec79- 2Crc	fst	1^{70}	$:48\frac{2}{5}$	$1:13\frac{4}{5}$	$1:44\frac{3}{5}$	3↑	Clm 18500	4	2	2^{1}	2^{1}	1^{hd}	$2^{\frac{3}{4}}$	Vasquez J	b	116	4.70	86-15	King Oasis $113^{\frac{3}{4}}$ Free TheSpirit$116^{1\frac{1}{2}}$Lead'mHome116^{nk}	Ret. lame	10
13Dec79-10Crc	fst	$6\frac{1}{2}$f	$:22\frac{3}{5}$	$:45\frac{4}{5}$	$1:19\frac{1}{5}$	3↑	Clm 21500	11	2	$8^{3\frac{1}{2}}$	6^{2}	$3^{1\frac{1}{2}}$	$5^{1\frac{1}{2}}$	Vasquez J		114	4.40	87-16	Big Moses$116^{1\frac{1}{2}}$HolidayCrossing114^{nk}NeverBurnACopi116^{no}	Hung	11
3Dec79- 8Crc	fst	6f	$:22\frac{4}{5}$	$:46\frac{3}{5}$	$1:13\frac{2}{5}$	3↑	Clm 17500	5	7	$7^{5\frac{3}{4}}$	$7^{9\frac{3}{4}}$	5^{4}	2^{nk}	Vasquez J		116	6.60	85-20	LordTresurer118^{nk}FreeTheSpirit116^{hd}NevrBurnACopi116^{1}	Rallied	8
12Oct79- 7Key	sly	7f	:23	$:46\frac{1}{5}$	$1:25\frac{4}{5}$	3↑	Allowance	7	10	$10^{5\frac{1}{2}}$	$7^{4\frac{3}{4}}$	6^{8}	5^{9}	Ruane J		119	3.70	69-23	Richiejim 119^{4} Big Greg $119^{1\frac{1}{2}}$ Blazing Eagle 119^{2}	Wide	12
2Oct79- 7Key	gd	6f	$:22\frac{2}{5}$	$:45\frac{2}{5}$	$1:10\frac{4}{5}$	3↑	Clm 17500	7	5	3^{1}	$2^{1\frac{1}{2}}$	$2^{1\frac{1}{2}}$	$2^{1\frac{1}{2}}$	Tejeira J		116	2.40	86-17	Lymond $116^{1\frac{1}{2}}$ Free The Spirit 116^{2} Native Cousin 120^{3}	Gamely	9
19Sep79- 9Bel	fst	1	$:46\frac{3}{5}$	$1:11\frac{4}{5}$	1:37	3↑	Clm 20000	6	7	4^{3}	$3^{\frac{1}{2}}$	2^{hd}	$3^{3\frac{3}{4}}$	Cruguet J		117	8.30	79-21	Gitche Gumee $113^{\frac{3}{4}}$ ScampBoy106^{3}FreeTheSpirit$117^{1\frac{1}{2}}$	Weakened	10
9Sep79- 2Bel	fst	6f	$:22\frac{3}{5}$	$:46\frac{1}{5}$	$1:10\frac{4}{5}$	3↑	Clm 35000	2	4	$4^{3\frac{1}{2}}$	$4^{3\frac{1}{2}}$	6^{5}	$7^{8\frac{1}{4}}$	Cruguet J	b	117	22.40	80-17	Mr. Ed 117^{hd} Morvan $113^{1\frac{1}{4}}$ Siwash Chief $113^{1\frac{1}{4}}$	Tired	8
17Feb79-10GP	fm	$1\frac{1}{16}$	Ⓣ$:46\frac{4}{5}$	$1:11\frac{1}{5}$	$1:42\frac{1}{5}$		Allowance	5	3	$3^{1\frac{1}{2}}$	3^{2}	10^{14}	10^{11}	Venezia M	b	122	8.40	79-10	Stage Fool 122^{3} Hazy Sun 116^{3} Garneray 116no	Tired	12
3Feb79- 5GP	fm	$1\frac{1}{16}$	Ⓣ$:46\frac{2}{5}$	$1:10\frac{3}{5}$	$1:42\frac{1}{5}$		Allowance	2	3	3^{3}	3^{1}	2^{1}	$4^{1\frac{3}{4}}$	Venezia M	b	114	3.90	88-10	Hand Canter 114^{nk} Lunar Lanvin $114^{\frac{1}{2}}$ Svelto 114^{1}	Weakened	9

LATEST WORKOUTS **Dec 11 GP 4f fst :51 b** **●Dec 1 GP 4f fst $:47\frac{2}{5}$ h**

Across the top, in the middle portion of the line, you will see "B.g.5, by Explodent—Ring of Steel, by Assagai." The "B" is for his color, bay, the "g" tells us he is a gelding ("c" for colt, "f" for filly, "m" for mare, "h" for horse, after a colt passes the age of four). His sire was Explodent and his dam was Ring of Steel, who in turn was sired by Assagai, a rather formidable runner in his day. These pedigrees and bloodlines mean a great deal to some handicappers, and I would never say they are not important. I am compelled to look more to actual performance than to lineage. In the next line below, we see that Free The Spirit was bred on the famed Ocala Stud Farms in Florida, and below that, his trainer is listed as Eugene Jacobs, who is well known as a competent handler of horses.

Under the designation "B.g.5," there is the larger figure of $10,000. This means that Free The Spirit was entered that day for a claiming price of $10,000, and could be claimed or purchased by any authorized person willing to deposit that amount of money in the claiming box before the race began. Claiming races with appropriate prices for horses entered are an essential part of the leveling of competition, since while a $20,000 horse might well defeat $10,000 animals, an owner would not dare enter him at that level of competition, because the $20,000 horse would quickly be claimed by some owner or trainer looking for a bargain.

On the other side of the top level of figures, the "117" represents the weight the horse must carry in the race. His "Turf Record" deals with all his lifetime starts on the grass. In the "money box" in the right-hand portion, you see the number of times he started in 1980 and 1979, the number of times he finished first, second, or third, and the amount of money he earned for his owners. Free The Spirit failed to win a race in 1979, and brought in far less than it cost to feed and care for him.

With these statistics out of the way, the interesting reading can now begin. The top line, showing the last race, is probably the most important, but every one of the ten lines tells you something of the story of Free The Spirit. In his last outing, he ran on January 12, 1980, at "Crc," which is the abbreviation for Calder Race Course in Miami. His event was the fourth race, on a fast track, at a distance of a mile and one-sixteenth. The symbols "4Crc fst 1 1/16" quickly tell us this information. Then, you see three times set forth. Pay close attention now, for you will see these lines many times in this book. The listed times represent "calls" of the race, and are taken when fixed points are reached. In races of one mile up to a mile and a quarter, the first call time is taken when a half-mile, or four furlongs, has been completed by the leading horse. The second figure represents the time of the leading horse (which was not Free The Spirit in that race) at the second point of call, at three-quarters of a mile, or six furlongs. The final time listed is the time of the winning horse, which in this case did happen to be Free The Spirit.

The next listing, "Clm 9000," means that the race was another claiming race, and that Free The Spirit was entered at the claiming price of $9,000. Following across the line is a row of figures, the first two of which represent the starting position in the gate and the next figure the position at the official "start" of the race. The *Daily Racing Form* published in the Midwest and on the West Coast does not carry these two figures in this row. The next four numbers, with smaller numbers raised beside them, are far more important. The first number, "9^{15}," shows that at the first call of the race, which is the same half-mile, or four-furlong, point represented by the time of :47 4/5, which means forty-seven and four-fifths seconds, Free The Spirit was running in ninth position and was 15 lengths behind the leading horse at that time.

The next numbers, "$5^{9½}$," mean that at the second call of the race, at three-quarters of a mile, or six furlongs, Free The Spirit had moved up to fifth in the field and was at that moment 9½ lengths behind the leader. The third numbers, "$2^{½}$," are placed at the "stretch call," which is one furlong from the finish line, but is not timed in the listing of the three times shown previously in the running line. Free The Spirit had now moved forward to second in the race, and was only a half-length behind the leader. The final figures, "1⁴½," tell us that Free The Spirit won nicely, finishing first by 4½ lengths ahead of his nearest pursuer.

The remaining data in the line show "114," as the weight that Free The Spirit carried; the "*2.50" shows by the asterisk that he was the favorite in the race, and his odds were 2.50 to 1. The "83-21" represents the speed rating (83) and track variant (21) that were recorded that day. (More about these figures later in this book.) The names show the first three finishers and their margins. Free The Spirit was first, of course, and the 114⁴½ repeats his weight and the fact that he was 4½ lengths ahead of the second horse, which was Holme Flash, who carried 116 pounds and finished 5 lengths ahead of the third-place horse. Orange Amber finished third, carrying 118 pounds, and was 1 length ahead of the unknown fourth-place finisher. The words "Ret. sore" are a part of what is known as the comment line, and mean that Free The Spirit, despite his victory, "returned sore." The final "10" means that ten horses ran in the race. All these figures are explained in the materials frequently published in the *Daily Racing Form*.

Once you learn to read and understand these figures, the other important information must be studied. The date on which a horse ran and the track where he competed are vital to know, as well as the distance of the particular race involved, and especially the caliber of the horses running.

This is where you can best trace the history of the horse. Start on the bottom line, where Free The Spirit ran on 3Feb79, or February 3, 1979, at GP, which means Gulfstream Park in Florida, in the fifth race. The "T" in the circle means that it was a grass, or turf, race, and Free The Spirit was running under allowance conditions, which means that he was not subject to be claimed at any price, since horses running in allowance races are not eligible to be claimed.

Following your dates upward, you will note that Free The Spirit had a long vacation from February to 9Sep79, when he was in New York to compete at Belmont. His absence for such a prolonged period would mean to the student that he was too besieged by aches and pains to be able to compete. This time, he was running in a claiming race, at the high figure of $35,000. He ran poorly and on 19Sep79, Jacobs entered him against $20,000 stock, perhaps in the belief that in weaker competition, he might win. On 2Oct79, Free The Spirit was shipped down the pike to Keystone outside Philadelphia and entered against horses at $17,500, which is approximately the same value as a $20,000 animal. He ran well, too, finishing second.

This no doubt encouraged Jacobs to take him off the claiming block, since he was raised into an allowance race still at Keystone on 12Oct79, where he was a badly beaten fifth. We see another vacation and Free The Spirit is returned to Florida to run on 3Dec79 against claiming horses at Calder in the $17,500 category. A good second caused him to rise slightly to $21,500 in his next race on 13Dec79, but again there was no victory. A slight drop again to $18,500 on 29Dec, and Free The Spirit ran a handsome second. But trouble was revealed when the comment said, "Ret. lame," as this horse, once a valuable property, was apparently struggling with severe leg problems.

Despite all this, Jacobs ran him back quickly on 12Jan80, surely patching him up enough to make him competitive. But he drastically lowered the price tag, entering his horse all the way down to $9,000. The bettors, apparently impressed by this drop, and unconcerned about a sore horse, made Free The Spirit the favorite in this race, and he rewarded the patience of Jacobs with a victory at last. You might inquire what he did on January 29, 1980. He won again, although more than that about the saga of Free The Spirit I cannot tell you.

What I have given here is an elementary run through of some of the data that you will see constantly. You will become very familiar with it and its significance, and will learn to quickly grasp the history of a horse by learning about his efforts, his times, his finishes, his competition, his earnings, and even more as these small numbers begin to take on even greater importance the more you learn about them.

Some of these complexities are what defeat even knowledgeable players from time to time. And with these complexities that I began to understand and appreciate, I continued my search into 1978 and 1979, certain that I was coming closer and closer to the goal I had set out to attain. I was still enjoying visiting tracks around the country, especially in California, at Santa Anita and Hollywood Park. I admired the beauty of Hialeah in Florida, stopped off at Arlington in Chicago, tried the Maryland circuit every now and then, went to Aqueduct and Belmont, and on to every fan's Eastern favorite, gorgeous old Saratoga. I could loll among the elms and the lawns, listen to the talk of the spectators, watch the horsemen and jockeys pass by, gather for breakfast on the porch while watching the morning runs of the horses, and drink in the majesty of the place. There is a liveliness and spirit about Saratoga in August, as the lovely village takes on a new urgency. Summer orchestra, arts, nearby theater, and other tourist delights are there, too, but the center of the town's life is the racetrack. It is the heartbeat of Saratoga, and when the four-week meet is ended and the horses go back to New York, the town relaxes and declines back into the upper New York State village that makes it a pleasant place to live all the rest of the year—but quiet.

As I went on working at my evaluations while enjoying these peregrinations,

I was constantly checking speed, time, and class to rate a horse's true ability, if I could find it. Was there any one figure that would encompass all of it, or would I have to retreat to rows of cumbersome calculations, which I had tried on several occasions? As always, there was the corresponding question: How would the horse, assuming his ability was defined, run in today's race? What was his readiness level, or form?

While some students of racehorse handicapping have standards for many indicia, such as weight, pace, recentness of last race, class, and even the jockey, I became satisfied by early 1979 that only two things really mattered: basic ability, and form, or readiness. Every element of the game would fit somewhere within those two broad categories. If I could redefine and reshape those two central ingredients, I might have something at last.

It was then that I began to try something entirely new. I had been relying on final times of horses in all my years of handicapping. But these times, and everything about them, were always subject to some adjustment. One adjustment led to another, and I began to experiment with a piece of a horse's race as an indicator of what his ability might be.

This required testing and retesting, almost as if I were starting over again. By the fall of 1979, I was satisfied that I had, at last, extracted a measure for rating a horse's ability that was better than anything I had ever seen or heard about. It was entirely original, used by no one, nor hardly even suggested in anything I had read. I noted its potency in race after race. And, of course, I struggled with race after race where a horse with apparent greater ability failed to defeat his weaker rivals. Readiness, or form, still had to be placed into perspective with ability. But it was beginning to fall into place.

Something else was happening, too. I was going to the track with greater confidence than ever before. Winning days were repeating themselves, over and over. Losing days were becoming rare, and when they did show up, I found mistakes that accounted for them. I would add and take away rules, after testing.

I began to work harder and harder, convinced that the methods I was now applying were so sound and so reliable that only egregious misfortune could prevent me from producing a profit every time at the track. I had a statistical foundation on which to base my efforts, which you will see in the very next chapter.

Then, by early 1980, I realized that I had indeed developed a method of play that would turn horse racing into investment, not gambling. It had to be sound enough that an ordinarily intelligent sporting person could take it to the track and win consistently with it. The weekend horse player should be able to go to the races and return home with enough money to take the family to dinner. The retired citizen who wanted some pleasant afternoon hours at the track would not only not be blowing his Social Security, but would be picking up some welcome extra purchasing power. The part-time housewife or office worker or factory hand, butcher or baker, could learn from this book how to make investments at the racetrack, and enjoy the process as well.

And finally, I demanded of myself that this program of racetrack investing had to be so secure that I could honestly proclaim it as being safer than the stock market. How much would be won was not nearly as important as consistent winning itself. If a player could win every day, or nearly every day, he could regulate his own amounts of investment. One could even begin with just a few dollars, not the hundreds that are required for market or real estate investment. The price of a *Racing Form* and a program, admission to the track, and transportation would be the only constant daily expense.

How well does it work? Have I really accomplished all this? You will soon see the logic of it, as you move into the next chapter. When its realities are grasped, and you begin to understand the reasoning behind the ratings of the horses, your skepticism will begin to fade. You will still not be totally convinced until you put it into play and succeed.

In this process, you will surely find interest and excitement and challenge. And, yes, even some frustration and failure intermingled with the error and miscalculation that will sometimes occur. You may be surprised at how much discipline is required, and unless you apply it, you will surely run into trouble. But that can also be one of the most valuable learning processes you will encounter in this book. It will bring you to the ultimate place we have sought from the beginning—an investment program at the racetrack that works.

We are now ready to begin.

HOW RACETRACK INVESTING
WORKS

Life insurance companies deal in predictability based on statistics. The entire foundation for their survival is based on these figures. They are rarely concerned with whether any individual will live to any certain age; they are only concerned about the mass expectancies of numbers of people dying over any given period of time.

If we are to turn playing the races into investment rather than gambling, we must look to some kind of statistical probability which is reliable, consistent, predictable. Many players may ponder if any such thing exists. But we all know that it does. It has a kind of established predictability that is remarkable in an industry where there is so much individual uncertainty in every single race.

Yes, there are indeed statistics on which we can rely—today, tomorrow, next week. These figures have remained consistent as long as there has been a pari-mutuel system of wagering in the United States. Every veteran horse player knows about them generally, but few have actually gone into any kind of analysis of what these figures mean, for reasons that will soon be apparent.

The first important statistic is that favorites in the betting win approximately one-third of all races run. This has been true year after year, and it applies to all tracks throughout the United States. For particular racing meets, one track's figures may fall as low as 30% or 31%, while others may rise to 34% or 35%. There may be some fluctuation from time to time throughout a racing meet, but when all the totals are compiled, the number of winning favorites will always approximate 33% of all winning horses.

This well-known figure has been disdained by the racing public for the most part for one reason only. If you wagered on every favorite in every race, you would always wind up losing money. Horses favored in the betting simply do not return enough to make it profitable to play them. Once this cardinal fact is known, most players appear to ignore what other possibilities may exist in this fact, and turn elsewhere to find better bargains. Which, of course, do not exist.

There are other figures that parallel this fact of racing life with similar consistency. Second choices in the betting win something in the nature of 20% of all races run. Third choices in the betting win approximately 14% of all races run.

As these figures remain constant, you will find that the first three choices in the betting will win two out of three races run, or 67% of all races!

Now we are beginning to get somewhere.

This percentage has remained on approximately this same level year after year. Not only does the first betting choice win more races than any other number in the betting, but the second choice wins the second-highest percentage of races, and the third choice follows in perfect order behind them. And what choice in the betting wins the fourth-highest number of races? You may now go to the head of the class. The fourth choice, of course. And it follows by the numbers thereafter, more and more remarkable as you ponder over it.

Now we come to another extremely important set of figures. That same favorite that wins one-third of all races will finish first or second in approximately one-half, or 50%, of all races run. The second choice in the wagering will run first or second more often than any other number in the wagering, and this follows down the line in perfect order with the other choices in the wagering.

Since these percentages have been known for a number of years, racing scholars undertake to test them from time to time to see if they continue to occur in this order. The last published set I have seen came from Robert V. Rowe, a veteran racing authority, in 1974, in a monograph where he compiled results for some 10,466 races. That was an enormous number of races to study. He found that favorites won 32.6% of these races. Any player who placed a wager on every one of those favorites would have sustained a loss of 10.3%, which is considerably less than the track's takeout. This makes playing favorites the best percentage bet in racing, day in and day out, week in and week out. But, as has been said too many times already, it will never produce a profit over any sustained period of time.

Rowe's study showed that second favorites won 19.9% of these races, with a net loss of 13.8%. Third favorites won 14.4% with a net loss of 15.6%.

The top three choices in the wagering won 66.9% of all races, which is the central theme on which I will rely in this book.

Rowe, in further testing the continuing realities of these remarkable figures, also made another study of the results of 4,960 other races. Favorites won exactly 33% of these, and finished first or second 51% of the time. Second favorites won 20% and third choices won 13%, adding up to 66% of all the races in the survey.

Other analysts have come up with similar figures, over and over again.

When I first began to appreciate the significance of these figures, I began to do my own testing. I am skeptical enough about any "accepted truths" (remember, "You can't beat the races") to want to see for myself before believing, no matter what anyone else tells me. I have not undertaken any long, detailed tallies like those performed by Rowe and others, but I have run tests of up to 1,000 races from time to time. Furthermore, I keep on watching, even as I read newspapers from day to day, glancing at results to see how well this trend holds up.

The results are always the same. Favorites win approximately one-third of the races, and the first three betting choices combined regularly win approximately six of the nine races run on the average daily card.

Try it yourself. Pick up any paper where racing charts are printed that show the odds on the horses in each race. There will be days when eight of the nine races are won by one of the first three choices in the betting. I have seen several days when all nine races are won by one of the first three favorites. Other days show six and five with great regularity. Four of the nine for the first three betting choices is a rarity, although it can happen.

I have never seen a day when as few as three of the races were won by one of the first three betting choices! I am sure there many have been such days, and a number of readers may rush to point them out. All I can do is repeat that I cannot recall ever seeing the results of a nine-race card where as few as three races were won by the first three betting choices.

In mid-1980, I was amused when I read about and saw advertisements for a new "handicapping calculator" produced by a reputable manufacturer and sold to the public for $100. Its primary advertising claim was that, following its instructions, it would reveal four horses in a race from among which the winner was found 60% of the time. The simple reality I am talking about here is far more effective, and it will not only not cost you $100, but you will not have to spend valuable time in intricate calculations to arrive at a result. You need only look at the tote board at the track.

There is yet another figure that has even more possibilities. One of the first three favorites in a race will run second or better 90% of the time! I think this is more potent than any other of these remarkable facts of life.

There are a great many days when one of these betting favorites runs second or better in all nine races run. It seems as if they do so eight times out of nine with reliable consistency. Try this one yourself also for three or four days in a row, looking at the odds figures in results charts, and checking only the three horses with the lowest odds. Of course, there are some days when there are only seven races where one of these three places second or better, but these are few. To find only six such races on a card is nearly unbelievable. I cannot recall when I last saw it happen, if ever. And as few as five, I cannot imagine.

This 90% place statistic is all the more remarkable when you consider that very few deviations can occur or else a figure that high would not remain. But it does, over and over again.

When you view these findings analytically, you can see why it is so difficult for long-shot players to win at the races, even though they do make occasional scores. The realities run against them. Of course, sharp handicappers every now and then can find extremely good selections among horses that are over-looked in the betting, and who are quite underplayed. The temptation to look for such bonanzas is always around, but remember, the risk overcomes the re-turn in the long run.

Why does this happen? How can such a set of statistics in an enterprise like horse racing remain so consistent year after year? Is the betting public, so largely disdained by the commentators, really that reliable when it comes to putting money on the line? Despite what I have said, can you count on those figures continuing in the same framework next month, next year? Why?

There are several sound reasons for this, and most of them begin with the vast supply of knowledge around the racetrack.

The information available to the industry in the *Daily Racing Form* provides so much data about the capabilities of horses that most players soon learn what to generally expect. Not specifically, mind you, for that is what makes the game so fascinating. But this general array of knowledge, spread out over a great number of people, who react to it, produces monetary trends at the bet-ting windows. It requires very little acumen to know that a Spectacular Bid or an Affirmed or a Seattle Slew is more likely to win a race than any of his com-petitors. The return is usually commensurate with the risk—low risk, low re-turn; high risk, higher return. However, as you learn more about the statistics of the sport, the solid low return for the low risk is infinitely superior to the high-risk high return.

There is also a vast army of selectors to aid the racing public in choosing a likely winner. Every sports page of every newspaper where there is racing has one or more selectors. The *Daily Racing Form* provides a corps of them, bear-ing such standard names as Trackman, Clocker, Sweep, Analyst, Hermis, and so on. All their choices are combined into a Consensus rating, and frequently the horse with the highest number of points among the *Form* selectors winds up as the betting favorite when the horses go to the post.

Racing programs contain selections in many states, and in others, such as New York, they list probable odds (or morning line) which provide a fair idea of how the final odds might go. Thus, this information on your program will often point out the betting favorites in most races. Over the years, and particularly at some tracks, I have found them to be more reliable than the choices set out in the *Daily Racing Form.*

At every track, there are tip sheets that are sold on the outside, promising great riches to those who purchase them. This is a business to the persons who provide them, and if they were not reasonably productive, the marketplace would likely drive them away. In California, for example, where the trackside sellers are licensed by the state, they are of very high quality. Many of the men who make these selections are sincere and conscientious racing scholars. I am not recommending any of them; in fact, I have never bought a tip sheet in my life, and never intend to do so. I will make my own decisions based upon what I know.

Another powerful influence on odds at the racetrack comes from inside the industry itself. Owners and trainers and stablehands talk horses day in and day out, and when powerful contenders are ready to go for the money, the word often circulates around the backside. The residents of that world pour a considerable amount of money through the windows every racing day, and it has a considerable impact on the tote board.

Then there are knowledgeable players, like you and me. We learn what indicators are decisive, we know about speed and class and form, and we are not likely to bet on Aunt Emma's name or the silks of any jockey or even sentiment. We are looking for winners, pure and simple.

From out of this crowd of players, this mass of competitors day in and day out, who march to the windows and put their money down, there emerges a number of dollars that establishes the betting odds. There is always a first choice, for better or for worse, and a second choice, and so on down the line. Thus, this great conglomeration of wisdom and knowledge and choice and chance, intermingled with the ignorance that always exists within it, combines to produce that incredibly consistent result—favorites win one-third of the time and the first three choices in the betting win two-thirds of all races run.

It really is not too surprising that this does occur. While no one person may be right, there is a sufficient mass number that combines to produce a series of consequences that remain on an even, predictable base. Because all betting money goes into a pool and odds are established by the amounts bet on each horse, this consistent percentage figure is not likely ever to change. It is simply logical that the most money should be placed on the horse that "appears" to be the most likely to win, and the second most money should be placed on the horse that "appears" second most likely to win. These appearances occur often enough, percentagewise, to remain rather constant.

If you were to believe that horse racing was totally a game of chance and that one animal had as much chance to win as any other, then these figures would not make any sense. But when you realize that ability is involved and that Spectacular Bid is indeed superior as an athlete to some steed of lesser potential, then you recognize that Spectacular Bid is more likely to win, and he, therefore, has more money bet on him than on his less talented rival. The same phenomenon goes on down the scale of racing performers, as the public, by and large, gravitates to the animal whose history affords a higher expectation, and histories are often quite reliable even in an unsettled world.

The fact that the more talented horse does not always win means no more than it does in similar consequences in other sporting endeavors. An old Yankee Murderers' Row was likely to obliterate the Chicago White Sox almost every time they played, but not always. The Yankees of Ruth and Gehrig and later editions of DiMaggio and Dickey and Mantle and Yogi Berra would suffer their defeats too, just as champion horses are sometimes beaten. But percentagewise, the champions will emerge, whether they be baseball teams or Secretariats.

The reason, therefore, for the remarkably consistent percentages in racing results as far as odds are concerned comes from the ability and knowledge of those who participate in the sport. It is not likely ever to change, because we are dealing with mathematical probabilities based upon outcomes that are reasonably (but never precisely) foreseeable over a general period of time.

And, as has been stated, reliance on any one particular betting choice will never return a profit at any time. Just as third choices return higher payoffs than first choices, they win less fequently, and the player will, in the end, lose less money by playing the shortest-priced horse.

But now the foundation for an investment program at the racetrack begins to emerge.

Since we know that one of the first three betting choices wins two out of every three races, even though we do not know which one it will be, if we were able to select the most likely winner among these three with some degree of consistency, we would begin to show an established profit. To be more specific, if we were able to select the one horse among the three top betting choices that would finish ahead of the other two not one time out of three (because drawing by lot might produce that outcome), but two times in three occasions, we would have made remarkable progress. An ability to select the one among three that will defeat the other two twice in three contests would, on a percentage basis, result in four winning selections on a nine-race card.

If you are able to produce four winning selections on a nine-race card, you will show a profit every single day of your life. Our goal in this book is to do better than that.

Prospects for place betting are even more secure, although the returns are much lower. Now that you know that one of those three top betting choices finishes second or better 90% of the time, and if you are able to select the one that will defeat his two rivals in two of three contests, you will attain a success percentage of 60% or more. And here you have a further advantage. If the one among the three that you select does not defeat another of his rivals, your selection might very well, and often does, wind up running second and you will still be able to cash a winning ticket. A 60% return in place betting will produce a small profit on a consistent basis. We will also expect to do better than that.

At this point, I will tell you one further piece of knowledge that will fortify what we are trying to do. Quite frequently, no matter what kind of rating method you use, you will see that one of the three contenders falls considerably short of being as strong as the other two. There are a great many occasions, therefore, when you can safely disregard the weaker member of the three favorites and confine your analysis, and your hopes, to two horses only. This narrows the risk considerably. In this book, and particularly in the chapters on the week at Belmont, you will observe, over and over again, how one of the three betting choices in reality has little chance at all. This is not always the case, as you can imagine, since sometimes you will see all three horses so closely matched that it is extremely difficult to choose between them. You will learn to deal with that situation also.

Thus, we come to Rule One in this book: You will restrict your investment in each race to one of three horses only, and that horse must be one of the first three choices in the betting.

No matter how good a betting outsider may appear, no matter how much your friends or your information sources may proclaim the virtues of an animal that is not one of those three choices, you will steadfastly, resolutely, determinedly, unflinchingly, confidently look at three horses, three only, and no more. This is inviolate.

There is but one logical minor addition to this rule. Sometimes the third and fourth choices in the betting are so equal in the amount of dollars wagered on them that they appear to be co-choices. You may look at the tote board and see that Horse C has $9,381 to win and Horse D has $9,148, and technically, of course, C is the third favorite, but the difference is insignificant. The dollar odds will usually show both horses with the same figure.

When this occurs, you will first compare the third and fourth choices in the betting. One of them will rank ahead of the other. You will then discard the weaker of the two as an improper choice, and then compare the survivor with the first two choices in the betting, where you are back to dealing with the first three favorites only.

Our primary approach will be to make win and place bets only. You will never bet to show. You will never play daily doubles, exactas, trifectas—at least not on this investment program. You will always bet the same amount of money on every race.

Now we come to the days when you are likely to lose. Since this entire investment program is based upon statistical performances of the first three favorites in a race, and only those three, there will be the occasions that I mentioned earlier when our remarkably consistent percentages do not hold. If you visit the track on a day when only four of the nine races are won by one of the first three betting choices, your chances of losing become relatively strong, since our investment horses have failed to come through. Betting to place may bail you out unless the first three betting choices are so off that day that only as many as six wind up in second.

And if you should hit that rare day, which I have not yet seen, when only three of nine races are won by one of the first three betting favorites, you are almost sure to lose.

This brings me to the reason why for any fair test of this investment program, you have to use it on consecutive days. Repeatedly, I have seen a "bad day" followed by a remarkably good day of profits. When you come to the chapter that provides the results of the tests at Arlington Park, you will see a day when losses substantially exceeded what you would expect, and then, on the following day, I recorded the highest profit that I have seen at any track on any test day. The bottom line, of course, was a solid profit, which is the name of our game.

There is another remarkably interesting feature about this investment program. You will find, as you learn the rules in this book, that although we strive to play every single race on the program, it is not always possible. Some races have to be passed altogether, and others occur where you are able to make but one bet to place only. You will have more investment opportunities in the early part of a racing year and in the autumn months when horses have compiled reasonable records. In the summer months, when two-year-old horses begin to run for the first time, and many tracks begin to schedule races on the turf, where many horses have had little or no experience, your investment opportunities will be fewer. The week at Belmont illustrates this quite clearly.

This general approach is another variance from much of the conventional wisdom about how to win at the races. Many astute players proclaim that the only way to win is to be very selective, wagering on those few races where chances look exceptionally good and odds are sufficient to make the risk worthwhile. I much prefer volume and percentage, with sound selections, to produce the results that will turn a consistent profit.

The difficulties with the occasional wager are several. First of all, there are not enough of them. Most players require frequent action, even when they learn they don't have to play every race. Second, and more important, is that the great advantage is too elusive for real reliance when you select only isolated plays. Your prime selection may not win, and then your day is fairly well lost. The volume player, relying on established percentages, can afford to lose a race even when his choice looked nearly invincible, because the next play on the card will usually redeem the lost situation.

The most vivid lesson of all is that there is no "sure thing" in racing. That is why varying the size of your wagers up and down in accordance with your opinion of the prospects of your choice contains so much peril. That lesson was brought home vividly to me in my earlier years of going to the track. In 1969, I went with my son to gracious, beautiful little Delaware Park, one of my favorite tracks in the East. The greatest filly of that era, Shuvee, was there to run in the Delaware Oaks. Shuvee was so consistent that New York players had likened her to death and taxes for inevitability. She was a remarkable animal, who later destroyed all her male rivals in the Jockey Club Gold Cup in New York two years in a row. She was practically unbeatable in any distance race, the longer the better.

Shortly after the windows opened in the Delaware race, a roar from the crowd attracted my attention. On the tote board, there was a single $20,000 flash in the show pool on Shuvee. It was the typical story of the "lady in red," with her black bag of cash, dumping it all on a sure thing. Shuvee was nearly certain to win, and it was inconceivable that she would not finish at least third or better. The owner of the $20,000 would merely "loan" the money to the track for a few minutes and collect the obligatory 5% minimum that the track was required to pay on wagers. Thus there seemed to be no easier way to make a sure $1,000 profit in less than half an hour.

There was but one problem, as you may have guessed by now. As the horses went into the backstretch, Shuvee was trailing badly. That wasn't so serious, but she was showing no signs of the great movement that characterized all her races. I shouted to my son, "She's not going to make it!" It was unbelievable, as Shuvee struggled in the back half of the field, picking up only enough momentum in the stretch to finish a badly trailing fourth, out of the money. What could never happen did happen.

The $20,000 bet in the show pool went down the drain. The "sure thing" was gone, and the investor who placed the $20,000 would have a long time recouping it in small pieces, if ever. I have never seen a wager I considered more certain to be successful than a show bet on Shuvee, yet it lost. Loading heavily on any one horse, be it Shuvee or even Spectacular Bid, carries far too great a risk to be considered anything other than gambling. This is not what we are here for.

Therefore, the percentages that we now recognize are certain to produce an investment profit if we can surmount the last and most demanding problem of all—picking the right horse. And even when you have chosen the "best" horse, he may not beat his rivals, just as there are numerous reasons why a championship baseball team may lose fifty or sixty games over a season. Your selection may be "off his feed" that day, running as unexplainedly poorly as did Shuvee on that one occasion at Delaware Park. Or he may run into bad racing luck, not able to escape from a box of surrounding horses to break free to have the running room he requires. He may lose a fraction of time in getting out of the gate, which can be nearly fatal among good sprinters. He may be nervous or anxious or act as do human competitors who have their good days and their bad days, performing far better on some occasions than on others.

But even though we know that we cannot win every race, or even always choose the "best" horse among the three, our objective is to do it often enough, with sound consistency and expectancy, to produce an investment profit, day after day. You will learn how it can be done, and how to apply it.

We shall now start at the beginning of the selection process, learning about the most important element in it.

BASIC ABILITY TIMES

1. HOW DO YOU MEASURE A HORSE'S BASIC ABILITY?

If we are to try to select one of three horses to defeat the other two among the first three favorites in any given race, it is obvious that we must have some method for rating the competitors to be able to compare them and choose one. There are actually a great many ways to do it. This is the essence of handicapping the races, a subject that has beguiled followers of the sport since wagering became established. Cutting through the volumes that have been written and the discussions of a thousand "experts," the two major measuring indicia have always been known as "speed" and "class." Speed, of course, is how fast a horse can run, and that is judged by time. Class is something different, and has never been as easy to define as a mathematical figure shown on a stopwatch or on a board. Class speaks of ability to perform at a certain level of competition, and exponents of the class theory of handicapping often argue that a "class horse" will defeat a "speed horse" every time.

But the two ingredients actually go together. The more class a horse possesses, the greater speed he will demonstrate. Spectacular Bid does not demonstrate his class by loafing around the racetrack—he demonstrates it with burning speed that equals or breaks track records all across the country. Of course he defeats his rivals—by running faster. Carrying this a step further, innumerable studies have shown, over and over again, that the higher-priced a horse is, the faster he will run. An animal valued and raced at $20,000 in claiming price, for example, will invariably run faster and defeat an animal valued and raced at $10,000 in claiming price.

36

The "faster he will run" is measured by time. The winning time at each distance in every race is posted and reported and evaluated. On these mathematical figures, shaved to a fifth of a second, called "ticks" by the cognoscenti, because the automatic timer at the track ticks off the fifths of seconds as the horses race over the surface, many handicapping methods and selection devices are based.

And it is always final time that is used. Let us illustrate by extracting from the *Daily Racing Form,* West Coast edition, of Thursday, February 14, 1980, the past performances in the first race at Santa Anita of a horse named Potomac Pride.

Potomac Pride			Dk. b. or br. g. 6, by Mr Washington—Heavy Burden, by Prince John					
			Br.—Robertson C (Ky)		1980	2 1 0 0		$4,875
Own.—Ustin & Ustin		119	Tr.—Mitchell Mike	$8,000	1979	9 1 3 0		$11,885
					Turf	1 0 0 0		$990

6Feb80-1SA	6f :21³ :44⁴ 1:10¹ft	*2½ 114	1³ 11½ 14½ 15	Hawley S¹¹	8000 88 PotomcPrd,SportngAround,BvrLk 11
1Feb80-1SA	6f :21³ :44³ 1:09⁴ft	*2½ 114	62½ 42½ 43¾ 44½	Hawley S⁷	9000 85 BlSrocco,OrntlDoctor,BootsFwctt 10
28Dec79-1SA	6f :21⁴ :45 1:09³ft	*6-5 115	3² 31½ 21½ 42	Hawley S⁸	8000 89 BootsFwcett,Lniffur,AnySizeAndy 12
22Jly79-1Hol	6f :22¹ :45² 1:10²ft	*4-5 120	4¾ 2ʰᵈ 1ʰᵈ 42½	Pincay L Jr⁷	8000 83 Windy'sIndin,ChiefFillmor,Nscinto 9
28Jun79-6Hol	6f :22¹ :45 1:10 ft	2½ 117	51¾ 21 1ʰᵈ 2ⁿᵒ	Pincay L Jr⁸	12500 87 ReignngNtiv,PotomcPrid,Rkindld 10
17Jun79-4Hol	6f :22² :45³ 1:10⁴ft	*8-5 117	1ʰᵈ 2ʰᵈ 2ʰᵈ 21	Pincay L Jr¹	16000 82 A Tony, Potomac Pride, Mr R. T.F. 7
1Jun79-9Hol	1¹ₜₒ :47 1:11¹ 1:43 ft	2½ 117	1½ 1½ 3ⁿᵏ 69½	Pincay L Jr⁷	16000 71 GoldenDocRy,SiSiMjsty,FuturofPc 7
19May79-3Hol	7f :21⁴ :44¹ 1:22³ft	*8-5 116	2ʰᵈ 2¹½ 6¹¹ 7¹⁵	DelahoussyeE³	25000 71 NrrowWy,Sm-Conscos,RomntcRvlr 8
3May79-5Hol	7f :22 :44² 1:21³ft	5½ 116	1½ 1ʰᵈ 2ʰᵈ 23½	Pincay L Jr³	25000 88 CrmsnCmmndr,PtmcPrd,AndrFny 10
26Apr79-5Hol	6f :22¹ :45¹ 1:09⁴ft	4½ 119	52½ 41¾ 63½ 85½	Pierce D⁶	c20000 83 AndrwFny,PrfctHittr,SwngThHrbor 9

Jan 26 SA 5f ft 1:00 h   Jan 19 SA 6f sl 1:17¹ h   Jan 5 SA 4f ft :46⁴ hg   Dec 15 SA 6f ft 1:11³ h

In the first chapter, I told you how to read running lines in the horse's record. Note that running lines above are somewhat different from those in the Eastern edition of the *Daily Racing Form* when you saw the record of Free The Spirit. But essentials are the same, and our concern now is only with time. Potomac Pride's last race, on 6Feb80, was at the distance of six furlongs, shown as "6f." When I told you about the recorded times at the three time calls of the race, the contest under review was a distance race of a mile and one-sixteenth. In sprint races, which are all races less than a mile in distance, the first call time is recorded after the first quarter of a mile, or two furlongs. The second call time is recorded at the end of a half-mile, or four furlongs, which is the second equal segment of a six-furlong race. The third time figure, of course, represents the time posted by the winning horse, which in this example was Potomac Pride.

The printed times are always the recorded time of the horse that was in the lead, for it is he whose nose breaks the light beam on the automatic timing device at the track at each of the points of call. The first time is ":21³," which means that the lead horse, Potomac Pride, ran the first two furlongs in twenty-one and three-fifths seconds, which we will give hereafter in the form :21.3. Remember, the number after the dot does not mean *tenths* of a second; the racetrack deals in *fifths,* or ticks, and that is what this method of recording indicates.

The second call time of the lead horse, still Potomac Pride, was :44⁴, or :44.4.

The third and final figure is $1:10^1$, which means that the winner, Potomac Pride, ran the six furlongs in 1:10.1. When analysts evaluate the times of the horses in the race, they will always work off the final time of 1:10.1 as a rating device. Speed ratings, for example (the speed rating was 88 in this race, as you can see in the column which states the speed rating), are always based on final time.

You have been informed previously about the position calls across the running line, where we see that Potomac Pride was in the lead at every call in the race.

But the point we stress again is that almost everyone in racing relies on the final time to make whatever ratings they use. Andrew Beyer's brilliant book *Picking Winners* erects his fascinating speed theories upon final times, using them as comparative ratings at varying distances for all horses. Track records are gauged on final times, as they perhaps must be. This is the accepted and dutiful foundation for the rating of the speed of racehorses.

In all the years I followed racing, until late 1979, I too relied almost exclusively on final times. That was how I had learned, and it was the only method that really made sense to me up to that time. And I did reasonably well with it, as I developed my own techniques for adjustments and variations and evaluations. Thousands of able horse players do extremely well with final times, and will surely continue to do so. But try as I did, I was never quite able to work out a consistent method of play based upon adjusted final times that gave me the confidence to believe that I could win consistently enough to turn playing the races into investment, not gambling.

I began to see inherent problems in total reliance on final time to such an extent that I began the search for a better way, which produced the method of rating ability that is the heart of this book.

What are these problems that make final time, in my judgment, not reliable enough on which to formulate an ability rating for horses?

Final times, for one thing, are perilous because of differences in distances. A horse may race at the most common sprint distance of six furlongs, and other occasions, run at six and a half furlongs, or seven furlongs, or even down to five and a half furlongs. If Horse A last ran at 7f, how do you compare his final time with Horse B, who last ran at 6f? We have to deal with that problem, as does every handicapper, and the usual way is by using parallel time charts. But horses also race at a mile, a mile and sixteenth, a mile seventy yards, a mile and an eighth, one and a quarter (the Kentucky Derby distance), one and three-eighths, a mile and a half (the distance of the Belmont), even one and three-sixteenths (the Preakness distance), and in longer marathons still. These races, because of the variations in distance, are run in slightly different styles, demanding more of horses at different points in the race, and in the long run, influencing final times to a degree that may make them somewhat deceptive.

But differences in distances, while posing difficulties, are not really the most troublesome factor. The surface of a racetrack may vary from day to day. When the surface is hardened, a horse may be expected to run faster than when there is deep mud underfoot. But even a "fast track" on Monday may be far faster or slower than a "fast track" on Tuesday, and even more so from January to June. Thus, a horse that runs six furlongs in 1:10.2 on Tuesday or in June may not be running any faster in terms of true effort than the horse who runs 1:11.1 on Monday and in January.

Furthermore, I have discovered that the farther a horse runs on a tiring track, the more his final time will be affected. In earlier portions of the race, when his reserve of energy is more intact, he will run nearer to his true ability for this segment of the race. In other words, his fractional time will not be so severely affected. This discovery, out of constant observation and experience (which I will illustrate shortly), is one of the key theories in the adjusted ability times that I will use in this book.

Consequently, if this is true, it follows that final time, even when adjusted by track variants, may not be as reliable an indicator of a horse's basic ability as the time compiled during a period of a race where track conditions have a lesser effect.

Besides varieties of distance and varieties of track surface, we also have varieties of racetracks as well. A horse who last ran at Monmouth in New Jersey may be running at Belmont in New York, or a horse that ran at Churchill Downs in Kentucky may be racing at Arlington Park in Chicago, or another animal may be shipping east from Hollywood Park. How does the final time at Monmouth compare with the final time at Belmont or Arlington or Hollywood Park? Racing writers have developed theories and charts and "track equalization" data to be applied everywhere. I do not believe they have totally succeeded, even though I am compelled to do it also to a certain extent.

There is also another problem that influences final time in a race. It also concerns the speed at which portions of a race are run, even apart from how the track's surface affects the horses. If a horse gallops easily in the first quarter of a race, not extending himself and not using up precious energy, he may come roaring home in a faster final time than anyone would have a right to expect. On the other hand, if all the contenders zoom out of the starting gate and travel at a lightning pace, they may slow down so dramatically in the last phase of the contest that their final time may even be slower than expected. How do you determine whether the race is being run in its earlier stages too fast or too slow? Or how the surface that day affects any of the running? Or how the strategy of the riders in the urging of their animals affects the final time?

All these questions baffled me for years, and they continue to do so to a certain extent, although I believe what I have set forth here partially resolves some of them. It is not possible, it seems, to extract an absolutely perfect rating method. But the question that concerned me was whether final time was the best that we had, or whether a better way could be found.

What I wanted was some rating method that would combine both time and class and tell me which horse had the most basic ability. Since I was not sure that final time was the best method available, despite its universal use, I set out to try to find another way. This book would not have been written if I did not believe that I had and that it works.

2. CONSTRUCTING ABILITY TIMES

From this point on in this book, we will be using the term *ability time*. I will define ability time in this fashion: It is an artificially constructed time element out of a portion of a race, *designed to represent both speed and class.* It is not actual time, although occasionally it will turn out to be. It is artificial because many adjustments are made to try to establish a figure that represents, as accurately as can be done, a comparative rating of a horse that will reflect his basic ability in terms of speed and class.

This is entirely new in the handicapping of horse races. It has never been used by anyone ever before in rating horses. It is totally original, put together out of my own research, experimentation, and testing at the racetrack. It is strikingly different from anything you have ever seen.

No claims are made for its perfection. Some of you may soon find ways to improve upon it. But for our purposes here, only one question is pertinent: Does it work?

I am now quite sure that it does. It has become the foundation of a new method of rating horses to allow the player to make selections that will produce an investment profit from the first three betting choices in a race.

To demonstrate how we arrive at these ability times, it is necessary to go through the search that brought us to this point, explaining what was observed and how it translates into a rating first expressed in terms of time. I shall begin with an examination of the six-furlong race, the most common event at most tracks. We are provided in the *Daily Racing Form* with times at which the lead horse reaches three points: the first two furlongs, the first four furlongs, and the final six furlongs. By the process of subtraction, you can determine the actual lead times of the two middle furlongs and the two final furlongs of the race. Thus, three separate time figures are available if we want to take the trouble to calculate them.

The next portion of the inquiry comes in how a sprint race is run. Because it is a reasonably short distance, speed from start to finish is usually required.

The horse that gets out of the gate the quickest and establishes an early lead is usually in a strong position. Because early speed is so important, horses in sprint races usually burn it up. To show you the pattern of how sprint races are run, let's look again at Potomac Pride's last race.

Turn back a few pages to his past performances. Now note that the first two furlongs were run in :21.3 seconds. The second-call lead time was :44.4. If we subtract :21.3 from :44.4, we get 23.1, which was the actual running time between the first and second call. The final time was 1:10.1, and we can subtract the four-furlong time of :44.4 from this figure and obtain 25.2 as the time in which the last two furlongs were run.

Here are the actual times for each of the three two-furlong segments of the race: :21.3, :23.1, and :25.2.

Potomac Pride was obviously running faster in the first third of the race. He slowed down a bit in the second third of the race, and in the final third portion of the contest he had slowed down considerably. And this is typical in sprint races, almost everywhere, since races are run this way. You may think a stretch runner is really flying when he passes tired animals near the end of the race, but he is only running less slowly than his competitors, since none of them is moving as fast as during the first two furlongs of the race. If you want to test this now, compute the various portions of every six-furlong race in Potomac Pride's past performances, and you will see the same phenomenon. This is the reality of descending speed, as horses run faster in the first portion of a sprint race than in later portions. Only rarely will you find a deviation. I did notice one at Pimlico on Preakness Day, 1980, as horses ran faster in the second segment of the race than in the first, which may have had something to do with the condition of the backstretch.

But something else about this caught my eye, even more important. It was when I began to compare fractional times and final times of California horses with Eastern horses that I began to realize that something more than track surface was involved, that the reality of descending speed might lead to further knowledge about inherent ability, and that a particular segment of a sprint race might be of even greater importance than final time.

Take Potomac Pride's last race as an example. As an $8,000 horse, he turned in a final time of 1:10.1 for six furlongs. In the East and Midwest, where racing surfaces are not nearly as fast as they are in Southern California, an $8,000 winner will rarely turn in a time as fast as 1:10.1. Because California tracks are inherently faster, this is to be expected.

Remember again, Potomac Pride's final quarter time was :25.2. Eastern horses valued at $8,000 can often equal that figure in their own last quarters, even though they would not run the final time in anything near 1:10.1.

We can see this by turning to the *Daily Racing Form* of April 19, 1980, third

Princely Heir * Ch. c. 4, by Berkley Prince—Bet Before Buy, by Popsaysno

Own.—Donovan & Gorman **$8,500** Br.—Cohen Jerome (Md) Tr.—Gorman John **116**

	St.	1st	2nd	3rd	Amt.
1980	7	1	1	2	$6,854
1979	22	2	4	2	$11,177

9Apr80-	9Key	sly	6f	:22⅖	:45⅖	1:10⅘	Clm 13000	10	2	5^3	$6^{6\frac{3}{4}}$	6^9	6^9	Morales J A	b	114	13.70	79–24	My Resolve 107^5 Blue Flag Day $109^{2\frac{1}{2}}$ More Than Fleet116^1	Wide	12
1Apr80-	9Key	my	6f	:22⅖	:45⅘	1:11⅖	Clm 8500	2	9	$7^{9\frac{1}{2}}$	5^4	2^2	3^1	Rodriguez J J^5	b	111	6.20	84–23	Wig In $109^{\frac{1}{2}}$ Navel Stone $119^{\frac{1}{2}}$ Princely Heir 111^4	Wide	9
24Mar80-	6Key	fst	6f	:22⅘	:45⅗	1:11⅘	Clm 8500	2	3	2^{hd}	3^1	3^3	3^5	Rodriguez J J^5	b	115	7.80	78–26	Navel Stone 116no Silver Gallant 116^5 Princely Heir 115^1	Tired	6
17Feb80-	6Key	fst	6f	:23	:46⅗	1:12⅖	Clm 11000	8	7	6^4	$7^{7\frac{1}{2}}$	9^{11}	9^{13}	Morales J A	b	116	9.30	67–25	Espier 116^{nk} Judge Pine 116no Fight at Night $116^{2\frac{1}{2}}$	Tired	9
2Feb80-	5Key	fst	6f	:23⅕	:47⅖	1:12⅗	Clm 8000	3	4	2^{hd}	1^3	1^4	1^8	McMahon W G	b	112	6.30	79–26	Princely Heir 112^8 Prince Lenso $108^{\frac{3}{4}}$ Iberian Ingot 102^{nk}	Driving	7
23Jan80-	1Key	sly	6f	:23	:46⅗	1:12⅖	Clm 6500	3	8	4^3	$3^{3\frac{1}{2}}$	2^3	$2^{\frac{1}{2}}$	McMahon W G	b	116	15.50	79–29	Silver Gallant $116^{\frac{1}{2}}$ Princely Heir 116^3 Ceara's Lad 116^2	Game	10
12Jan80-	5Pen	fst	6f	:22	:46⅕	1:11⅖	Clm 7000	7	8	6^4	$3^{2\frac{1}{2}}$	4^4	4^6	McMahon W G	b	113	5.20	81–15	Finance Prince111^1Ragan'sNail117^3MagicalRullah115^2	Slow start	9
31Dec79-	5Med	fst	6f	:23⅖	:47⅕	1:13⅗	Clm 6250	6	7	4^2	$3^{1\frac{1}{2}}$	3^3	$4^{2\frac{1}{2}}$	Miceli M	b	115	7.70	74–25	Sabatino 110^2 Vote for Mike $115^{\frac{1}{2}}$ Wig In 113^{hd}	Lacked rally	10
17Dec79-	9Med	fst	6f	:22⅘	:46	1:11⅘	Clm 6250	7	6	$9^{3\frac{3}{4}}$	$8^{5\frac{1}{2}}$	$5^{5\frac{1}{2}}$	5^4	Wacker D J^5	b	110	4.90	82–11	BrbertownIdle110^3MonteryRod115^{hd}WoodbournPrinc113^{no}	Wide	10
29Nov79-	3Med	fst	6f	:23⅖	:47⅖	1:13⅕	Clm 6000	7	2	3^{nk}	1^{hd}	1^{hd}	2^4	Lopez C C^5	b	108	3.70	75–26	Lion Honey 110^4 Princely Heir 108^1 Raise The Rhythm114^4	Wide	7

LATEST WORKOUTS **Mar 21 GS** 4f sly :53 b

race at Keystone outside Philadelphia, where we study the past performances of Princely Heir.

We are looking for races at approximately the same class as in the Santa Anita races of Potomac Pride. Look at the second line at the race of 1Apr80, with an $8,500 claiming price. Despite the muddy track, the lead time was :25.3 (subtract :45.4 from 1:11.2). Yet the winner's final time was 1:11.2, some six ticks slower than the winning time at Santa Anita. Next, drop down to the race of 2Feb80 at Keystone, where the winning time of Princely Heir was 1:12.3, some twelve ticks slower than the comparable Santa Anita time. Yet, the last quarter lead time was :25.1. Of course, there are other time variations in the listed races, as there will always be, but for the moment, let's compare from the races we have extracted.

Date	Race/Track	2d Call	Finish	Final Quarter
8Feb80	1SA	:44.4	1:10.1	:25.2
2Feb80	5Key	:47.2	1:12.3	:25.1
1Apr80	9Key	:45.4	1:11.2	:25.3

This is extremely significant. When I first began to see the phenomenon that the last quarter of a mile in a six-furlong race was more similar between fast California and normal East than I had previously thought possible, I was somewhat puzzled. Then I began to check many examples, taken from Western and Eastern copies of the *Racing Form.* While California final times were always faster, the final quarter times in sprint races were not nearly so far apart.

The comparison taken from the records of Potomac Pride and Princely Heir is meant only to illustrate that point in general. Not every race at the same class shows the same identical last quarter mile time, no matter where the horses may have run. You can find all kinds of variations in times between horses of the same class at every racetrack. But what I did find was a trend.

That trend, steadily and unmistakably, began to reveal a narrowing between the differences between last quarter times and final times, no matter what tracks were examined. While one could not maintain that this would even out, I began to notice this characteristic: When a California final time was four ticks faster than an Eastern time at the same distance among horses of the same class, the last quarter time at the fast California track might usually be only two ticks, or even one tick, faster than the comparable final quarter time at the slower Eastern track.

You can test this if you are able to compare California and Eastern copies of the *Racing Form.*

But I wanted to test it further. I began to compare slow Calder Race Course in Miami with much faster Hialeah and even faster Gulfstream Park in the same area. Final times for horses of the same class were obviously faster at Gulfstream and Hialeah than at Calder. And once again, I found the same parallel that I had discovered in the California comparisons. The last quarter times at Hialeah were sometimes no faster at all than those at Calder, and in other instances, there was a lesser difference than in final times.

Once again, I will use an example, not for proof of the thesis itself, but merely to illustrate how this actually works. From the Eastern *Daily Racing Form* of April 4, 1980, the record of Bombay Flight in the fourth race at Gulfstream, an allowance event for three-year-olds, is highly instructive. Note also that this youngster ran in California before moving to Florida to compete at all three of Miami's tracks.

Bombay Flight B. c. 3, by Bombay Duck—Stride, by Ambiorix
Own.—Cashman E C Br.—Casse J & M (Fla) Tr.—Fabry William A **114**

	St.	1st	2nd	3rd	Amt.
1980	3	1	0	0	$6,495
1979	5	M	0	1	$2,300

22Mar80-	2GP	fst	6f	:22⅗	:45⅘	1:12	Allowance	1	9	$2^{\frac{1}{2}}$	2^{2}	4^{6}	7^{11}	Vasquez J	118	14.50	68-21	Imaromeo 114no Rufame $114^{4\frac{1}{2}}$ Hadden Hall 114^{2}	Off slow	9
9Feb80-	1Hia	fst	6f	:22⅘	:46⅘	1:13	Md Sp Wt	10	3	$1^{\frac{1}{2}}$	1^{1}	$1^{1\frac{1}{2}}$	1^{1}	Cordero A Jr	120	3.30	78-28	Bombay Flight 120^{1} Far Out East $120^{1\frac{1}{2}}$ValiantOrder$120^{3\frac{1}{2}}$	Driving	12
17Jan80-	4Hia	fst	6f	:22⅕	:45⅘	1:11⅘	Md Sp Wt	1	3	2^{1}	$3^{3\frac{1}{2}}$	3^{4}	4^{4}	Gavidia W	120	39.70	80-22	Kcaj $120^{2\frac{1}{2}}$ Robesphere $120^{\frac{1}{2}}$ Bombay Quest 120^{1}	Needed closing	12
24Dec79-	4Crc	fst	6f	:23	:47⅕	1:13⅗	Md Sp Wt	9	8	$8^{3\frac{1}{2}}$	$8^{7\frac{3}{4}}$	$6^{6\frac{1}{2}}$	$4^{8\frac{1}{2}}$	Morgan M R	120	15.10	75-22	Pitch Game $120^{5\frac{1}{2}}$ GentlemanJeff115^{no}LegalTradition120^{3}	Rallied	11
17Dec79-	4Crc	fst	6f	:23⅕	:47	1:12⅘	Md Sp Wt	6	4	$5^{2\frac{1}{2}}$	4^{4}	4^{7}	4^{9}	Morgan M R	120	50.20	79-15	Fast Fast Freddie 120^{1}FortyOaks$120^{1\frac{1}{2}}$WhatADancer$120^{6\frac{1}{2}}$	Evenly	11
1Dec79-	4Crc	fst	6f	:23	:46⅗	1:12⅘	Md Sp Wt	11	7	$7^{5\frac{1}{2}}$	8^{11}	9^{14}	8^{14}	Verardi F	120	22.00	74-15	Superbity $120^{\frac{3}{4}}$ Fast Fast Freddie 120^{9} Orate 120^{hd}	Outrun	12
20Oct79-	3SA	my	6f	:22⅖	:46⅘	1:14⅕	Md Sp Wt	6	10	10^{15}	10^{17}	9^{23}	9^{29}	Olivares F	118	3.30	39-33	First Albert 118^{hd} Taiyo 113^{nk} Cinco Banditos $118^{1\frac{1}{2}}$	Outrun	10
25Aug79-	6Dmr	fst	6f	:22⅖	:45⅗	1:10⅕	Md Sp Wt	6	2	1^{1}	$1^{\frac{1}{2}}$	1^{hd}	$3^{5\frac{1}{2}}$	Sim M C	118	16.20	81-10	Idyll $118^{\frac{1}{2}}$ Rumbo 118^{5} Bombay Flight 118^{1}	Tired	6

LATEST WORKOUTS **Mar 20 Hia 4f fst :51 b** **Mar 6 Hia 4f fst :51 b** **Feb 28 Hia 5f fst 1:02 b** **Feb 23 Hia 4f fst :53 b**

In the last race at Gulfstream, on 22Mar80, the final quarter lead time was :26.1 (again, we are not at this moment concerned about Bombay Flight's times, since we are dealing only with lead times). In the 9Feb80 race at Hialeah, the lead time was the same :26.1. At Calder, on 1Dec79, we again have the same :26.1 lead time. Races at Calder on 17Dec79 and 24Dec79 produced times of :25.4 and :26.2.

Since we can even compare California off this record, we glance at those races also. The 20Oct79 race at Santa Anita in the mud is not representative.

But look at the 25Aug79 race at very fast Del Mar, where Bombay Flight finished third behind Rumbo, one of California's best, who competed in two of the three Triple Crown races in 1980. The lead time there was :24.3, which you might expect at Del Mar, but notice that Bombay Flight's last quarter time was :25.4, only two ticks superior to the :26.1 he turned in on 9Feb80 at Hialeah where he won the race.

All this begins to show how these times come together to a certain degree. Without establishing any detailed statistical comparison, I had begun to see enough to attach some validity to what I was doing. After that, it was test and test again to see if it worked in practice. The more I tested and experimented, the more I became satisfied with their validity. This led logically to the conclusion that I finally adopted, that final quarter times in a sprint race (if we could arrive at a reliable version of what those true times were) would be perhaps more useful as an indicator of a horse's basic ability than final times.

There is a logic about its reliability when one considers how sprint races are run. Horses are compelled to run as hard and fast as they can in the first portions of the race, or else fall so hopelessly far behind that they will have no chance to win. Because they run that way, they will have a minimum of energy remaining in the last portion of the race. Our theory thus gains support: The horse that can maintain the best speed in the last one-third of a sprint race is demonstrating inherent class when the going gets tougher, and this becomes a strong indicator of his basic comparative class and ability.

This now is my basic fundamental starting point for rating ability. The final quarter time in a sprint race (which is the last one-third of a six-furlong race) becomes our actual ability rating. But what sprint race, how many sprint races, when were they run, what are true times, and many other questions emerge, all of which must be addressed and resolved. As a final example, going back to Potomac Pride, his last quarter time of :25.2 would be the one on which he would be rated in his last race, not the 1:10.1 that you see in the running line. We will deal with other races as we proceed.

3. WHAT IS TRUE TIME AND HOW IS IT FOUND?

No matter what portion of a race one uses to evaluate time, there is only one true time in a race. That is the time between points of call when the horse that is in the lead breaks the light beam on the automatic timer. For example, going back to our friend Potomac Pride again, the times at each point of call for him were actual true times, since he was in the lead all the way, and was the actual horse that broke the beam at every point. But in the race of 6Feb80 at Santa Anita, there were eleven horses running. What were their true times?

We don't know the answer. But every one of those ten other horses in the race will be rated in the future, and the race of February 6 must be evaluated as to them also. Because we can learn a great deal more from studying Potomac Pride's past performances, let's look once again.

Potomac Pride — Dk. b. or br. g. 6, by Mr Washington—Heavy Burden, by Prince John

Br.—Robertson C (Ky) — 1980 2 1 0 0 $4,875

Own.—Ustin & Ustin 119 — Tr.—Mitchell Mike $8,000 — 1979 9 1 3 0 $11,885

Turf 1 0 0 0 $990

6Feb80-1SA	6f	:21^{3}	:44^{4}	1:10^{1}ft	*2½	114	1^{3}	1^{1½}	1^{4½}	1^{5}	Hawley S^{11}	8000	88	PotomcPrd,SportngAround,BvrLk	11
1Feb80-1SA	6f	:21^{3}	:44^{3}	1:09^{4}ft	*2½	114	6^{2¼}	4^{2½}	4^{3¾}	4^{4½}	Hawley S^{7}	9000	85	BlSrocco,OrntlDoctor,BootsFwctt	10
28Dec79-1SA	6f	:21^{4}	:45	1:09^{3}ft	*6-5	115	3^{2}	3^{1½}	2^{1½}	4^{2}	Hawley S^{8}	8000	89	BootsFwcett,Lniffur,AnySizeAndy	12
22Jly79-1Hol	6f	:22^{1}	:45^{2}	1:10^{2}ft	*4-5	120	4^{¾}	2^{hd}	1^{hd}	4^{2¼}	Pincay L Jr^{7}	8000	83	Windy'sIndin,ChiefFillmor,Nscinto	9
28Jun79-6Hol	6f	:22^{1}	:45	1:10 ft	2¼	117	5^{1¾}	2^{1}	1^{hd}	2no	Pincay L Jr^{8}	12500	87	ReigningNtiv,PotomcPrid,Rkindld	10
17Jun79-4Hol	6f	:22^{2}	:45^{3}	1:10^{4}ft	*8-5	117	1^{hd}	2^{hd}	2^{hd}	2^{1}	Pincay L Jr^{1}	16000	82	A Tony, Potomac Pride, Mr R. T.F.	7
1Jun79-9Hol	1$\frac{1}{16}$	:47	1:11^{1}	1:43 ft	2½	117	1^{½}	1^{½}	3^{nk}	6^{9¼}	Pincay L Jr^{7}	16000	71	GoldenDocRy,SiSiMjsty,FuturofPc	7
19May79-3Hol	7f	:21^{4}	:44^{1}	1:22^{3}ft	*8-5	116	2^{hd}	2^{1½}	6^{11}	7^{15}	DelahoussyeE^{3}	25000	71	NrrowWy,Sm-Conscos,RomntcRvlr	8
3May79-5Hol	7f	:22	:44^{2}	1:21^{3}ft	5¼	116	1^{½}	1^{hd}	2^{hd}	2^{3¼}	Pincay L Jr^{3}	25000	88	CrmsnCmmndr,PtmcPrd,AndrFny	10
26Apr79-5Hol	6f	:22^{1}	:45^{1}	1:09^{4}ft	4½	119	5^{2½}	4^{1¾}	6^{3¼}	8^{5¼}	Pierce D^{6}	c20000	83	AndrwFny,PrfctHittr,SwngThHrbor	9

Jan 26 SA 5f ft 1:00 h   Jan 19 SA 6f sl 1:17^{1} h   Jan 5 SA 4f ft :46^{4} hg   Dec 15 SA 6f ft 1:11^{3} h

The *Daily Racing Form* and every student of horse racing has adopted the rule of 1 length as equivalent to a fifth of a second in assessing times of horses that are not in the lead. Since only one horse can lead in a race, every other animal competing is evaluated by the 1-length-per-fifth-of-a-second formula. But, as every scholar who has studied time and distance readily acknowledges, this is simply not accurate. A horse can run the distance of a length of an animal in less than a fifth of a second!

That's Right!

But yet the 1-length formula has continued to be used, as if inscribed in stone, even if everyone knows it is faulty. It is used for one reason only—because it is easy. It fits. It requires nothing complicated. One equals one. And that, of course, is a major reason why any time evaluation, whether final or fractional, is not always reliable when the horse was not leading at each call that was timed. When a horse is given credit for lengths gained and his time is reduced accordingly, his comparison with the time of a horse that was in the lead (and thus acquired a truly accurate time) is distorted. That distortion can cost the horse player money.

But the time comparisons of lengths and fifths of seconds are only one part of the serious problem facing us. Who determines how many lengths? Look down at the second line for Potomac Pride in his race of 1Feb80 in the first at Santa Anita. At the first call, he was shown as running sixth in a field of ten horses, some 2¼ lengths behind the leader, whoever he was. Why not 2½ or 2¾ lengths behind? How accurate is the measurement of a quarter of a length, up or down, when horses are traveling at great speed, constantly moving up and back? Who measures this, and how? At the second call, he is shown 2½ back, and at the stretch call, 3¾ back. Again, why not 3½, or even 4 lengths? At the finish, he is shown as 4½ lengths behind the winner, as we read the line through to its final listing.

These fractions are critically important in rating times of horses. The *Racing Form* and others consider a half-length as a full fifth for rating time, and a quarter-length as reverting back to the lesser figure. In the 1Feb80 race of Potomac Pride, the final time of the winner was listed at 1:09.4 (precisely accurate), and since Potomac Pride was shown as 4½ lengths back, his time would be considered five fifths of a second slower, or 1:10.4. But what if the 4½ lengths at the finish had really been 4¼ instead? Then, Potomac Pride would have been credited with a final time of 1:10.3, and these slender fifths make an enormous difference in rating horses.

The person who decides how many lengths a horse is behind is an official known as the chart caller, who surely has one of the most difficult tasks known to man. My respect is unbounded for these unknown souls who sit high above the track and are responsible for cataloguing every horse in the race in lightning time. But they are human.

And humans err.

When horses pass the first point of call in a race (two furlongs in a sprint) and are strung out, the chart caller must assess how far behind each horse is running. Correctly placing the second horse is usually reasonably easy, and the third not so difficult, but as one's eye, as quickly as it can move, runs back into the field, with fifths of seconds flashing and with horses moving up and back, it becomes extremely difficult to make an accurate assessment of the actual number of lengths that are involved. He must do this four times in every race at each of the four points of call, which includes the finish line as the last point. Even though there are video replays now at each point to assist him after the race is run, he still is subject to error in making such fine-line judgments. But these judgments are relied upon by hundreds of thousands of people every day who go to the races, including you and me. If he errs by even a quarter of a length, it can affect the time at which a horse is rated! And when horses are strung out in a big field, I have to believe it is simply impossible to make an accurate evaluation of the precise number of lengths a horse is trailing any other horse in the race.

The final point is that we are always dealing with estimates. Good ones, to be sure, but estimates just the same. Every calculated time of every horse in a race except the leading horse is subject to estimation, judgment, and error. And when the lead horse changes between calls, we cannot be sure of the true time of either of the two horses that broke two separate time markers, since both their speeds varied.

These are some of the difficulties that befall all of us in evaluating race-horses. I, too, have to rely on estimations derived from the judgment of the chart makers. All I can do is try to find a better estimation than the one currently in use, and to that we now turn.

4. ADJUSTMENT OF TIME RATINGS

A horse, instead of running five lengths in five-fifths, more likely runs six lengths and slightly more, in five-fifths, or one second, or even five lengths in four-fifths of a second. The "slightly more" is important. It is also important that a horse may run these lengths faster in the first two furlongs than he will in the last two furlongs. But somewhere we have to reach out and establish a formula that is different from the one-length-one-fifth formula that is simply not accurate.

Bear in mind now that we are not trying to be as precisely accurate as the automatic timer. We want a figure for comparison basis only, even if it is a method that is better than the 1-for-one that has led to so much miscalculation over the years.

The reason why this is so essential is that we rate some horses' times off actual clock time, as when a horse led at the second call and finished first. But the trailing horse, whose time is calculated by giving a fifth of a second credit for every length gained, when that is not an accurate clock version, is thus getting an advantageous rating as compared to the lead time off the clock.

Once again, a quick review of the process may be helpful. Final quarter time in six-furlong sprints is calculated by subtracting the time at the half-mile point, or second call, from final time. Perhaps your quickest calculation is to subtract the half-mile time from 60, such as :46.4 from 60 equals 13.1. Then add the final time figure past the 1-minute number (which may be 1:12.1, or :12.1 for the final number) to get your final quarter time (in the example, 13.1 + 12.1 becomes an easy :25.2).

The problem occurs only when a horse gains lengths between the second call and the finish. If a 5-length gain is not worth five ticks off the clock, we would be making a mistake in crediting a full second off the final quarter time for the gaining horse.

Therefore, we now adopt a 5-for-four formula for lengths gained as converted to fifths of seconds. We shall equate 5 lengths with four fifths of a second. We can also deal with fractional lengths with more flexibility, and these fractional lengths will embrace slight shadings of error and leave us with a more realistic rating all around. Here is a simple table showing how we will treat lengths behind in terms of fifths of a second where a gain is involved.

Gain in Lengths	Gain in Fifths of Seconds
Less than 1	None
1 to 1¾	One
2 to 2¾	Two
3 to 3¾	Three
4 to 4¾	Three
5 to 5¾	Four
6 to 6¼	Four
6½ to 7¼	Five
7½ to 8	Six
8 and more	Six

Using .15 is simpler + more accurate

Compare with mine

This is one of the most important tools to be applied in rating horses. You must learn this formula, accept it, apply it. It is relatively easy to learn, even though it may look difficult. As soon as you use it a few times, it will become much easier. Surrounding 5-for-four, it flows up and down in proper sequence. You may question the 6-for-four allocation, but since we will apply it universally, and since we also know we are dealing with estimates and human error, we prefer to hold back a horse's rating in doubtful areas rather than making too much of it.

There is one further rule to apply here. You will note that I have stated for 8 lengths and more, the subtraction of six fifths is the maximum allowed. This may be one of the most arbitrary rules in our entire method, but it is founded on hard, realistic experience, and has a critical purpose behind it. Thus, if a horse gains 10, 12, or 15 lengths, no matter how many over 8, I will not give him ability-time credit for any more than a reduction of six ticks. This rule may not accurately reflect actual clock time to any realistic degree—it is not made for that purpose. It is for the purpose of comparative ability of horses, and experience has taught that a horse coming from far behind is a much weaker investment proposition than a horse that runs near the front.

Time after time over the years, I have backed horses that traditionally come from far back. And I have seen them come barreling down the stretch, flying past tired rivals, and finish a glorious second or frequently third. They seldom seem to get to the finish line first. Oh, certainly they win now and then, but for consistency, their records are abysmal. The front runner, on the other hand, is far more reliable. His true times are more accurate. He stays out of trouble. He is a far more reliable investment than the Silky Sullivan type who somehow seldom starts to move until it is too late.

The come-from-far-behind horse engages in a form of deceptive advertising.

In my analysis of races, I saw this phenomenon over and over again. A horse with a :24.4 ability time calculated off a 12-length gain was likely to lose to a front-runner with a :25.1 ability time with no gain involved. I first drew my arbitrary line at 10 lengths and suffered even under that. Then I made the adjustment to the arbitrary line of 8 lengths, upon which I now stand, confidently.

5. ADJUSTMENTS FOR SLOWER INTERNAL TIMES

You have now learned to make adjustments in ability times to allow for more accurate calculations when a horse has gained lengths on his competitors. There is one more vital adjustment to make which deals with dissipation of energy. Let's illustrate the problem in this fashion:

Horse	4f Time	6f Time	Ability Time
A	:46.1	1:12.1	:26.0
B	:48.1	1:14.1	:26.0

Both horses have the same unadjusted ability time. But which one would you choose for an investment? Anyone even remotely familiar with racing would choose Horse A. Of course, it may be said that because A's final time is so much better, one has to choose A. But that is not the full reason. A ran much faster for the first four furlongs, and had enough energy left to complete his sprint distance with an additional :26.0 seconds. Horse B ran the first four furlongs in very slow time, and because his expenditure of energy was much less, he was able to complete his distance with the same :26.0 seconds added on.

Therefore, if we are going to rely on final quarter time as the decisive ability time in sprint races, it would be not only unfair but patently ridiculous to consider A and B equal because they both compiled an actual final quarter time at the same figure. There must be a method, therefore, to adjust these times to compensate for expenditure of energy.

The theory again rests on the speed at which the first portion of the race was run. Horse A had to work extremely hard to travel his first four furlongs in :46.1, and thus had little energy remaining for the final run to the wire. Horse B was not required to work hard at all, as he eased along slowly in :48.4, and thus had a great deal of energy remaining for the final run to the finish. To deal with this, I have developed what I call an *energy adjustment*.

The line is drawn at less than 47 seconds for four furlongs on tracks of one mile and longer in circumference. If a horse ran the first four furlongs in :46.4

or less, we will make no adjustment at all. But if he ran the first four furlongs in :47.0, or more, I will begin to add fifths to his final quarter time as an energy adjustment. The slower he runs the first four furlongs, the more we will add on to him.

Once again, I have developed a formula for you to follow. I admit it is arbitrary line-drawing, but once again, it has been tried and tested over and over again, and no matter how you may label it, its final judgment must come on how well it works. Here is the energy-adjustment formula.

Four furlongs from :47.0 to :47.4—add one tick to ability time.
Four furlongs from :48.0 to :48.4—add two ticks.
Four furlongs from :49.0 to :49.4—add three ticks.
Four furlongs from :50.0 to :50.4—add four ticks, and so on.

Two versions?
His way
+ in ??
real time
a rating for both, relative
to averages, then added
together.

This is an easy formula to remember. Race trackers speak of time in seconds and "change," such as "47 and change," for anything from :47.1 through :47.4. Once you learn that anything in the 47's requires the addition of one tick, and for every second and "change" thereafter, one additional tick will be added on, you will be able to make these adjustments at a glance.

Why use such a wide span of a full second in time for making energy adjustments? Why not one tick, or two, or some other figure not nearly so wide as a whole second? Is this so much that it will detract from the accuracy of all our adjustments?

There are two major reasons why we use such a wide span as a full second before adding an additional tick.

The first is that the recorded time and lengths behind may very likely be affected by the condition of the surface of the track. It usually is. In a later chapter, I will deal more extensively with the problem and explain how I have handled it in the overall search for ability times. But because it is an element of some importance, there must be some allowances wherever practical for varieties of surface condition, and the use of the wide span of a full second is one way of taking this into account.

The second major reason falls within the recognition of what I call *varieties of individual performances.* A horse's competitive output may be vastly different from race to race, even though the animal has the same basic ability. Just as your tennis game may be on or off from day to day, with a booming twisting service inside the lines on Tuesday and a bundle of double faults on Wednesday, even though you may have the same basic ability at all times, so it is with race horses. That, too, will be illustrated when I come to dealing with track variants in the later chapter. But it is in recognition of this reality that I have broadened the span as I have. When the two vital ingredients, varieties of track surfaces and varieties of individual performances, are considered, the span of a full second seems quite reasonable.

And it works, as you will see. In our earlier example of Horse A and Horse B, where both had unadjusted ability times of :26.0, I would add two ticks to B's time because his 4f time was :48.1. This would make his adjusted ability time :26.2 against A's time of :26.0.

We are now ready to put into practice what we have learned about computing ability times, using the two major adjustments for lengths gained and energy used.

6. PRACTICING ABILITY-TIME COMPUTATION

We can use the record of almost any horse to illustrate these rules and concepts. From the *Daily Race Form* of May 29, 1980, from the fifth race at Bowie, I have extracted the past performances of Telly's Nade, which we will now use to run a series of examples on how to calculate and adjust ability times in six-furlong races.

Telly's Nade — **Own.—Remakis J**
Ch. c. 4, by Dream of Kings—Telly's Girl, by Nade — **$23,500** — **Br.—Taub J (Md)** — **Tr.—Bullock Alec J** — **110^{7}**

Turf Record	St.	1st	2nd	3rd		St.	1st	2nd	3rd	Amt.
	2	0	0	0	1980	8	1	0	0	$8,340
					1979	21	3	3	1	$27,610

17May80- 8Pim	fst	6f	:23	:45⅗	1:11⅕	Allowance	5	7	$7^{9\frac{1}{4}}$	7^{14}	6^{11}	$6^{7\frac{3}{4}}$	Purdom M D^{5}	b	114	28.80	82–12	Storm Watch 115$^{4\frac{3}{4}}$ Fuzzbuster 122$^{1\frac{1}{4}}$ NoScrupples112$\frac{1}{2}$	No factor	10
26Apr80- 8Pim	sly	6f	:23⅗	:46⅘	1:12⅗	Allowance	3	5	$5^{1\frac{3}{4}}$	7^{8}	6^{9}	6^{7}	Purdom M D^{5}	b	114	6.10	76–23	Ransack 119$\frac{3}{4}$ Fortent 115$\frac{1}{2}$ Walt's Hereford 122$^{1\frac{1}{2}}$	Tired	7
15Apr80- 8Pim	gd	6f	:23⅖	:46⅘	1:12⅕	Allowance	4	6	$6^{2\frac{1}{4}}$	$4^{3\frac{1}{4}}$	$1^{\frac{1}{2}}$	$1^{3\frac{1}{2}}$	Purdom M D^{5}	b	108	7.30	85–24	Telly's Nade108$^{3\frac{1}{2}}$SteppinShoes122$^{1\frac{1}{2}}$GalaDecade115$^{1\frac{1}{4}}$	Drew clear	7
3Apr80- 4Pim	fst	6f	:23⅕	:46⅕	1:11	Allowance	5	5	5^{5}	$5^{4\frac{1}{4}}$	$5^{3\frac{1}{2}}$	$4^{3\frac{1}{4}}$	Purdom M D^{5}	b	108	15.00	88–18	Mr.Doughnut119$^{2\frac{1}{4}}$[DH]MorePleasure112[DH]GalaDecde115^{1}	Mild bid	6
15Mar80- 8Pim	fst	6f	:22⅗	:45⅘	1:10⅘	Allowance	4	4	$4^{4\frac{1}{2}}$	$5^{4\frac{1}{2}}$	$4^{3\frac{1}{2}}$	$5^{3\frac{1}{4}}$	Guerra W A	b	112	38.90	89–14	Bolductive 119^{nk} Cephalonian 115$\frac{3}{4}$ Bright AndBrave112$^{1\frac{1}{2}}$	Evenly	8
30Jan80- 8Bow	fst	7f	:22⅖	:45⅖	1:26	Allowance	7	2	$5^{4\frac{1}{2}}$	4^{7}	$8^{9\frac{1}{2}}$	$8^{8\frac{3}{4}}$	Kupfer T	b	112	12.20	66–34	Toot Twice 113$\frac{1}{2}$ Looms The Star 119$\frac{3}{4}$ Northern Baron112^{4}	Tired	8
18Jan80- 8Bow	sly	6f	:22⅗	:46⅕	1:12⅗	Allowance	2	5	5^{5}	6^{6}	$6^{6\frac{1}{4}}$	5^{6}	Mackaben B W	b	112	19.00	71–32	Ambitious Ruler 115^{3} Toot Twice 114$^{1\frac{1}{4}}$Bolductive112^{1}	No factor	7
8Jan80- 6Bow	gd	6f	:22⅗	:45⅗	1:12⅗	Allowance	5	6	$6^{3\frac{3}{4}}$	6^{9}	$6^{9\frac{1}{2}}$	$4^{4\frac{1}{2}}$	Fazio J J	b	112	9.80	72–32	Skipper's Friend 116^{3} Bolductive 112$\frac{3}{4}$AmbitiousRuler119$\frac{3}{4}$	Rallied	6
28Dec79- 7Lrl	fst	7f	:22⅘	:45⅘	1:24⅖	3↑ Allowance	7	4	3^{hd}	3^{2}	3^{2}	5^{3}	Adams J K		114	7.60	86–19	King of Classics 118$\frac{3}{4}$ Toot Twice 116$^{1\frac{1}{2}}$ Gala Decade 116no	Tired	7
19Dec79- 8Lrl	fst	1	:47	1:12⅗	1:37⅖	3↑ Allowance	6	3	$3^{1\frac{1}{2}}$	$4^{\frac{3}{4}}$	$6^{6\frac{1}{2}}$	$5^{8\frac{1}{2}}$	Ussery R A^{5}		108	18.50	77–17	Second Try 111$^{4\frac{1}{2}}$ Judgement Call 111^{2} Toot Twice 116^{2}	Tired	7

LATEST WORKOUTS May 24 Pim 4f fst :52 b May 15 Pim 3f fst :36 h May 10 Pim 5f fst 1:03⅖ b Apr 12 Pim 3f fst :38⅗ b

Let's start on the top row, in the race of 17May80. The lead times for the four- and six-furlong distances are :45.3 and 1:11.1 respectively. We subtract the :45.3 from the 1:11.1 and obtain :25.3 as the "lead time" for the final quarter. Now, let's find out how Telly's Nade fared. He was 14 lengths behind at the four-furlong, or second, call. Remember, in applying the rule that calculates lengths gained only from 8 lengths behind, we are not concerned about the stretch call at all. It is only from the second call, or half-mile point, that we begin our calculation. Thus, treat the 14 lengths behind at the second call as if it were only 8 lengths behind, and subtract the gain, if any, from 8. Telly's Nade finished 7¾ lengths behind, and accordingly, he is entitled to an ability time gain of only a quarter-length, not enough to warrant any reduction at all for Telly's Nade. Thus, his ability time at this point is calculated at :25.3, the same as the lead time.

Next, we must check for an energy adjustment. The 4f lead time was recorded at :45.3. Telly's Nade was 14 lengths behind. Using the full 5 lengths per second, or 1-for-one formula except when we are dealing with gains, we add fourteen fifths (:02.4) to the time of :45.3 to calculate Telly's Nade's time at four furlongs. This gives us a :48.2 to place Telly's Nade within 48 and change and require the addition of two ticks to the :25.3 we had previously calculated. We now wind up with an adjusted ability time for Telly's Nade of :26.0 for the race of 17May80.

You may be puzzled why I use the 5-for-four formula when a gain is involved and retain the 5-for-five formula in other situations, especially after stressing that the 5-for-five calculation is inaccurate. In situations of gain, one horse may be accelerating somewhat and another may be slowing down, thus bringing their lengths closer together at a slightly faster blink. On the other hand, in dealing with time at the 1-for-one formula when no gain is involved, the distortion for error is much less, and when applied uniformly, we are close enough to allow us to use it with a reasonable degree of confidence. You have seen that I am much more concerned about overrating a horse when a gain is involved, and that is why the 5-for-four formula for gains is so important.

Don't become discouraged at the calculations. It gets easier and easier every time you do it. Now, let's tackle the second line from Telly's Nade's past performances, the race of 26Apr80.

The lead time for the last quarter is calculated at :25.4, which is obtained by subtracting the reported :46.4 from 1:12.3. Telly's Nade gained 1 length on the leaders between these two calls, and we can subtract one tick from the :25.4 lead time to bring us down to :25.3. Now for the energy adjustment, where we add the 8 lengths, or eight ticks, to the reported :46.4 to obtain :48.2, which once again requires the adding of two ticks to what has become :25.3, and we obtain a :26.0 as the ability time for the race of 26Apr80.

The third line down shows the race of 15Apr80, where the lead time for the last quarter is calculated at :25.2 by the usual process of subtracting the :46.4 from the 1:12.1. Telly's Nade was 3¼ lengths behind at the second call, and then he went on to win the race by an enormous 3½ lengths. How much of a gain do we give him credit for? Only for 3¼ lengths, since that was the amount he was behind when the lead horse's nose reached the automatic timer, and that was the amount of his gain on the final time when Telly's Nade triggered the timing device when he hit the finish wire. In other words, when a horse gains lengths in coming from behind to win, we subtract only the gain in lengths behind, and do not give additional credit for any lengths in which he may be in the lead.

Consequently, we can deduct three ticks for the 3¼ lengths, and reduce Telly's Nade's final quarter time to :24.4. We must next look for actual second call time to see if an energy adjustment is required. To the :46.4 recorded, we add three ticks for 3 lengths behind, and bring Telly's Nade's time to :47.2.

This is in the 47-and-change bracket and requires us to add one tick for energy adjustment to the :24.4 and thus gives us a flat :25.0

Now that you are beginning to get the hang of it, let's skip the line for the race of 3Apr80 and drop one notch farther down to the race of 15Mar80. We get a lead time of :25.0 by the usual subtraction process. Telly's Nade gained 1¼ lengths, which allows a deduction of one tick down to :24.4. To the :45.4 second call time, we add five ticks for the 4½ lengths behind to obtain a :46.4. This is less than :47.0, and thus requires no addition for energy. Telly's Nade's ability time for the race of 15Mar80 is thus a very good :24.4.

We'll skip the races of 30Jan80 and 28Dec79 because they were run at the distance of seven furlongs. You have not yet learned how to make the seven-furlong adjustment, which will come along in a few more paragraphs. The race of 19Dec79 was at a mile, and since we are only doing six-furlong races here, we will pass it by also. For the race of 18Jan80, we get an ability time of :26.3 for Telly's Nade, much poorer than for the strong effort of 15Mar80. Let's run the calculation quickly: lead time :26.2, no adjustment for gain or loss, with one tick added for energy to get :26.3.

One last example and we'll go on to something else. In the race of 8Jan80, the lead time was :27.0 (subtract :45.3 from 1:12.3). Telly's Nade gained 3½ lengths, from the maximum of 8 behind, which allows us to subtract three ticks down to :26.2. His 9 lengths back of a :45.3 time pushes his time up to :47.2 and requires the addition of one tick to :26.3, which is his adjusted ability time.

You will also have observed the wide fluctuation in ability times, from a low of :24.4, which is reasonably good, to a high of :26.3, which is almost too poor to win anything. But more about that later, also.

You should now be able to calculate ability times in six-furlong races. As we proceed in this book to other examples, you will have repeated opportunities to observe and practice the calculation of ability times. In the last portion of the book, when I show you the races for an entire week at Belmont, you should be able to compute ability times fully and completely.

7. CONVERTING OTHER SPRINT DISTANCES TO SIX FURLONGS FOR ABILITY-TIME CALCULATIONS

Since ability calculations in sprint races are geared to last quarter times in six-furlong events, we are frequently confronted with the problem of rating a horse off races run at five and a half or six and a half or seven furlongs. For consistent comparison, we must adopt a time span that is similar. The only way we can do this is to convert other sprint times to six-furlong figures, and calculate off these converted times. I will assure you that this is less than perfect, perhaps even somewhat undesirable, but it is the only way I am able to do it.

And to accomplish it, there has to be a comparative time chart for constant use. Here it is:

COMPARATIVE TIME CHART FOR SPRINT RACES ONLY

what formula would produce these results?

5f	5½f	6f	6½f	7f
:57.2	1:03.2	1:09.2	1:15.3	1:21.4
:57.3	1:03.3	1:09.3	1:15.4	1:22.0
:57.3	1:03.4	1:09.4	1:16.0	1:22.1
57.4	1:04.0	1:10.0	1:16.1	1:22.2
57.4	1:04.0	1:10.1	1:16.2	1:22.3
58.0	1:04.1	1:10.2	1:16.3	1:22.4
58.0	1:04.1	1:10.2	1:16.4	1:23.0
:58.1	1:04.2	1:10.3	1:17.0	1:23.1
:58.2	1:04.3	1:10.4	1:17.0	1:23.2
:58.2	1:04.3	1:10.4	1:17.1	1:23.3
:58.3	1:04.4	1:11.0	1:17.2	1:23.4
:58.3	1:04.4	1:11.0	1:17.3	1:24.0
:58.4	1:05.0	1:11.1	1:17.4	1:24.1
:59.0	1:05.1	1:11.2	1:18.0	1:24.2
:59.1	1:05.2	1:11.3	1:18.1	1:24.3
:59.1	1:05.3	1:11.4	1:18.2	1:24.4
:59.1	1:05.3	1:12.0	1:18.3	1:25.0
:59.2	1:05.4	1:12.1	1:18.4	1:25.1
:59.3	1:06.0	1:12.2	1:19.0	1:25.2
:59.3	1:06.0	1:12.2	1:19.0	1:25.3
:59.4	1:06.1	1:12.3	1:19.1	1:25.4
1:00.0	1:06.2	1:12.4	1:19.2	1:26.0
1:00.0	1:06.2	1:12.4	1:19.2	1:26.1
1:00.1	1:06.3	1:13.0	1:19.3	1:26.2
1:00.2	1:06.4	1:13.1	1:19.4	1:26.3
1:00.2	1:06.4	1:13.2	1:20.0	1:26.4
1:00.3	1:07.0	1:13.3	1:20.1	1:27.0
1:00.4	1:07.1	1:13.4	1:20.2	1:27.1
1:00.4	1:07.2	1:14.0	1:20.3	1:27.2
1:01.0	1:07.3	1:14.1	1:20.4	1:27.3
1:01.1	1:07.4	1:14.2	1:21.0	1:27.4
1:01.1	1:07.4	1:14.2	1:21.0	1:28.0
1:01.2	1:08.0	1:14.3	1:21.1	1:28.1
1:01.3	1:08.1	1:14.4	1:21.2	1:28.2
1:01.3	1:08.1	1:14.4	1:21.3	1:28.3
1:01.4	1:08.2	1:15.0	1:21.4	1:28.4
1:02.0	1:08.3	1:15.1	1:22.0	1:29.0
1:02.1	1:08.4	1:15.2	1:22.1	1:29.1
1:02.1	1:09.0	1:15.3	1:22.2	1:29.2
1:02.2	1:09.1	1:15.4	1:22.3	1:29.3
	1:09.2	1:16.0	1:22.4	1:29.4
	1:09.2	1:16.0	1:23.0	1:30.0

Using Digest times, + "values", produce a chart or a formula.?
or
Simply use a value for both times/calls — or assign a value to actual final time, based on the average final time in 'Digest

These running times at different sprint distances are far from a guarantee that a horse running five furlongs in 1 minute flat will surely traverse the next furlong in :12.4, which is what you will read on the chart. These are average expectancy times on normal track surfaces for horses of reasonable value in class, such as a $10,000 claiming figure, which is often used. A cheaper horse, able to run five furlongs in as decent a time as 1 minute, might not be able to hold on to a :12.4 for the next furlong, since class, or lack of it, might do him in.

But if I attempted to do more than point this out, you might be left awash in more complexities and intricacies, with which this sport is filled. We shall use this parallel, or comparative, time chart for the sole and limited, but necessary, purpose, of adjusting times at different distances to a common distance for all competitors in the race.

But there are many other difficulties with such a chart, which you may readily observe, and these must be dealt with. The most obvious is the duplication of time figures. Take the six-furlong column, and drop down to the time of 1:11.0. You will see it listed twice. Running from the first listing to the comparable time for 6½f, you will see 1:17.2, and then off the second listing to 6½f, you will see 1:17.3. You will likewise see two different times for 7f comparisons with 1:11.0 at 6f.

Well, which is it?

There are many such duplications in the comparative time chart. They are necessary because we cannot split times to less than a fifth of a second. Some writers have tried to do it with tenths of a second, but I have found this to be difficult and more confusing than the duplications you will see in our preferred chart. Why are these duplications necessary? Why not have a standard comparable time chart across the board? That, too, was common in charts of this kind for many years, but it is even more erroneous than what we have here.

To decide what to do, we must first explain the reasons that get us into this kind of problem. Let's start with the top row, and use the listed times at some of the key distances shown. A horse that runs 5½f in 1:03.2 may be expected to run an additional half-furlong in 6 seconds flat. A horse that runs 6f in 1:09.2 may be expected to run the next half-furlong to the 6½f point in :06.1, as he begins to slow down slightly. A horse that runs 6½f in 1:15.3 may be expected to run the next half-furlong to the 7f point in perhaps another :06.1—and note that we say "perhaps."

Now, drop down midway in the page to the 5½f time of 1:05.4. The horse that runs the distance at this figure is moving much slower than the very speedy animal who does it in 1:03.2 at the top of the page. The fast 1:03.2 runner is expected to use 6 seconds for his next half-furlong. Will the slower horse at 1:05.4 be able to do it in the same 6 seconds? Not at all. We allow him :06.2 for the next half-furlong to a 6f time of 1:12.1. Then, extending the same time line another half-furlong to the 6½ point, we credit him with :06.3, as the slowing-down process continues. Then, extending the time another half-furlong to 7f, we use :06.2. This is an apparent reversal of the slowing-down process, but actually is no more than a shifting of varying times between distances in an effort to convert some kind of sense of regularity into the process. Also, if you will test these times, you will see a strong runner often whittling a fifth of a second off in the last half-furlong to the wire.

Now, go all the way down in the 5½f column to 1:08.0, where the horse is really slowing down. There is an extended time of :06.3 to 6f, another :06.3 to 6½f, and then an :07.0 to 7f.

Today's Racing Digest has!!

We are thus at all times trying to factor in slower times and their equivalents. Because horses ordinarily tail off the farther they go, we cannot provide an exact, accurate comparative time chart across the board. No one else has either, as far as I know.

All right, now, back to the question of what to do when there are two listings of the same time in one column and different listings in the next column. Frequently, fractional lengths, such as ¼ or ½ or ¾, will allow you to choose the time that most conveniently fits, and that solves some of the problems. But what if there are no fractional lengths involved? Then you are required to use some judgment in the selection, based on how the horse has been performing. If his performance looks strong, use the better figure, or if he is weakening, use the lesser figure. You will be able to make these determinations as you acquire experience in using the chart and the time conversions. In addition, you will not likely be confronted with this problem too often.

We are now ready for a few examples to show how the conversion process works in practice. From the *Daily Racing Form* of September 8, 1979, here is the record of Little Marker in the third race at Belmont.

Little Marker — B. c. 2, by Beau Marker—My Filly Mignon, by Porterhouse
Own.—May-Don Stable — $50,000 — Br.—Laurin Mrs L (Va) — Tr.—Marcus Alan B — **116**

	St.	1st	2nd	3rd	Amt.
1979	5	1	1	0	$3,400

19Aug79- 2Sar	sly	6½f	:22⅘	:46⅕	1:19⅕	Md 30000	8	2	2hd	1 1½	1 3	1 8½	Martens G	b	118	3.50	79-21	Little Marker 118 8½ Fred The K 118 2½ Bello Boy 114 2	Ridden out	10
19Jly79- 4Bel	fst	6f	:22⅘	:46⅗	1:12	Md c-30000	1	4	7 3¾	6 6	5 8½	4 12	Asmussen C B	b	114	*2.60	70-22	SonOfADodo118 10 AThousndMore114 1½ DremCbin118 nk	No excuse	12
5Jly79- 3Bel	fst	5½f	:22⅗	:46	1:05⅖	Md 35000	7	6	5 8	6 11	4 8	4 6¼	Gonzalez M A 7		111	*2.50	82-16	My Pal Jeff 118 5¾ Beforehand 118 nk Discordant113 nk	Closed well	10
8Jun79- 4Bel	fst	5½f	:22	:46⅖	1:06⅗	Md 30000	8	6	3 6½	3 5½	2 2½	2 1¾	Rolfe D L 5		113	*2.50	80-20	Sir Sizzling Nehoc 118 1¾ LittleMarker113 2½ TightGrip118 7	Gamely	8
10Apr79- 4Aqu	my	4½f	:24⅕	:49⅖	:56	Md 30000	2	5		6 13	6 8	5 4¾	Hernandez R		117	2.30	— —	AlfredG.113½Toopher'sDrums117 nk CougrFllow113 3	Steadied early	6

LATEST WORKOUTS Sep 7 Bel tr.t 3f my :37⅘ b (d) Aug 31 Bel tr.t 4f gd :50⅘ b Aug 11 Sar tr.t 5f fst 1:02⅗ b ● Aug 4 Sar tr.t 5f fst 1:01⅗ h

His last race at Saratoga was at 6½f, where he finished in 1:19.1. Using the conversion chart, this is comparable to a six-furlong time of 1:12.3. We can now compute the comparable lead time by subtracting the second call time of :46.1 from 1:12.3, where we obtain a :26.2 ability time for this young two-year-old.

Now, drop down to the race of 5Jly79 at Belmont, where he ran 5½f. The final time of the winner was 1:05.2. The final winning time is what we always use, not the final time of the horse that we are studying. From the chart, we see that 1:05.2 is equal to 1:11.3 at 6f. We now compute the lead time as :25.3 by subtracting :46.0 from 1:11.3. Now, we can begin to compute Little Marker's ability time off that race. Note that he was 11 lengths behind at the second call. We chop that to 8 lengths and compute a gain of 1¾ lengths, which enables us to give him credit for one tick to bring the ability time down to :25.2. But since he was 11 lengths behind, we add eleven ticks to the :46.0 to get :48.1 for his second call time, and then penalize him two ticks for energy adjustment to bring his final adjusted ability time to :25.4.

Using the same technique for the race of 8Jun79, we convert the 1:06.3 to 1:13.0, get a lead time of :26.3, observe a gain of 3¾ to allow the subtraction of three ticks to :26.0, and add one for energy up to :26.1.

Now, let's try one off the 7f distance. From the same race at Belmont on September 8, 1979, here is the record of Little Lenny.

Little Lenny — Ch. c. 2, by True Knight—No Escape, by In Reality — $60,000 — Br.—Kuehn Martha B & R P (Ky) — Tr.—Zito Nicholas P — 120
Own.—Double Cee Stable

Turf Record: St. 1st 2nd 3rd — 1 0 0 0

	St.	1st	2nd	3rd	Amt.
1979	4	2	1	0	$17,640

22Aug79- 2Sar	fm	1 1/16 Ⓣ	:46⅗	1:11⅖	1:43	Allowance	5	9	9^{15}	$9^{9½}$	$6^{7½}$	$5^{8¾}$	Hernandez R	114	7.50	74-13	Sportful 117^{nk} Capital Punishment $114^{3¾}$ BagdadChief 114^{2}	Outrun	10
12Aug79- 4Sar	sly	7f	:23	:46⅗	1:26⅕	Clm 45000	4	8	$6^{9½}$	$6^{8½}$	3^{2}	$1^{½}$	Hernandez R	120	3.30	71-25	Little Lenny $120^{½}$ Boomie Two $117^{6½}$ Dover Prince 115^{1}	Driving	8
1Aug79- 3Sar	fst	6f	:22⅖	:46⅕	1:11⅗	Md 35000	9	6	$5^{4½}$	$4^{1¼}$	$2^{1½}$	1^{nk}	Hernandez R	118	3.20	83-10	Little Lenny 118^{nk} A Thousand More $118^{3¼}$ Likeable $118^{2¼}$	Driving	12
20Jly79- 4Bel	fst	6f	:23	:47⅖	1:13⅕	Md 40000	4	3	2^{hd}	$5^{4¾}$	4^{3}	$2^{2½}$	Hernandez R	114	21.00	74-21	SelfPressured $118^{2½}$ LittleLenny $114^{1½}$ GiveItAChance $118^{¾}$	Came on	8

LATEST WORKOUTS Sep 1 Bel tr.t 3f fst :39⅗ b Jly 28 Sar 4f gd :49⅗ b Jly 16 Bel 4f fst :49 b Jly 9 Bel 5f fst 1:02 b

We will now calculate the 7f race of 12Aug79 at Saratoga. The final time of 1:26.1 is converted from the chart to a 6f time of 1:12.4. The lead time is :26.1, obtained by subtracting :46.3 from 1:12.4. Little Lenny gained a whopping 8½ lengths in the process, extending his gain all the way to the finish, which provides a six-tick subtraction to a :25.0 time figure. But his second call time shoots up to :48.2 when the 8½ lengths are added, and that requires a two-tick energy adjustment to a final :25.2 time for Little Lenny.

Every calculation is made in the same manner. We must always convert to a comparable 6f time and treat the horse's performance as if he were running that distance. But please bear in mind that in doing this, we are still dealing in *estimates,* the necessary evil that plagues us throughout this entire book. Other scholars may well improve on what we have done here, and we hope they succeed. But for now, because we are required to have a working tool, be it an old-fashioned hand saw when we would prefer a power blade, to deal with the problems we face, we are going to proceed with what we have. For, as you will see later, these methods do indeed work. I have no objection to making them work even better.

8. UNANSWERED QUESTIONS ABOUT TRACK SURFACE

Old racing hands will have by now noticed that we have not dealt with track surfaces in our ability calculations. Track variants, or how the surface differs in speed from day to day, remain one of the most puzzling problems to confront any handicapper of the races. Then there is also the recognition that many tracks are different from others in inherent speed, as I have earlier remarked about the California tracks. Santa Anita, Hollywood Park, and Del Mar especially are all well known to be considerably faster than the New York ovals at Aqueduct, Belmont, and Saratoga.

However, I shall defer discussing these important issues to a later chapter, when it is time to deal with distance races of a mile or more, as well as turf contests. After we extract our ability times in these races, we will return to track surfaces and set forth how we deal with that range of problems.

9. POINTS FOR ABILITY TIMES

Now that we have learned how to calculate ability times, what do we do with them? How are they put to use to lead toward a final rating that will result in a sound selection from among the three horses eligible for our investment consideration?

We shall always look for the two best ability times from among the ten, or fewer, races listed in a horse's past performances. In his eleventh race back, he may have done considerably better, but nearly all players will have to confine themselves to what they see in the *Daily Racing Form* they hold in their hands. Selection of two is a critical part of the rating method. One ability time might be distorted by an exceptional performance; a horse may have been running faster than he will ever be able to run again. The use of two is therefore a sound safety device and a broader, more reliable rating method than standing on one best performance.

Ordinarily, you will use all ten races listed in a horse's past performances. Some critics may object to using any race more than six months back in evaluating a horse. Some like to rate only off the last three or four races and ignore all others prior to that. But this begins to merge with "recent form," which I consider a separate element altogether. We are searching here only for a measurement for what a horse has been able to do in the past, at some time which is relevant for our purposes today.

This, of course, brings up the question of how far does one go. A horse that ran well in 1978, was held out during the entire 1979 year, and is coming back in 1980 may never run again with the élan that he displayed in 1978. Thus a rule must be made to rely only on races during the current year and the preceding one. Therefore, if you are playing in 1981, you can use 1980 races, but not those recorded in 1979, and so on.

But there are often gaps in a record within the same year. If you are at the track in October or November, a horse may have two or three recent races and prior to that may not have run since January. Are the races prior to a long layoff sufficiently representative to rely on? Ordinarily, yes, but here again, a worthwhile rule of caution is in order. From the ten races where ability times are computed, no more than one race may be used that was run more than six months ago. A horse may not have run more than one time in the past six months, which may force you to use old races as a rating standard, so this is a rule that will have to be tempered with occasional flexibility. So, to repeat, try to avoid using races of more than six months back whenever possible.

Extracting the two best ability ratings out of the ten races available is not terribly burdensome. Although we have practiced it previously, I want to run through a short exercise in how to get the two best and do it quickly. Let's use Dutch Ditty again from the *Racing Form* of February 18, 1980, and forget that she would not qualify off her last race under our form rules. We are only running through ability-time calculations and how to do them quickly.

***Dutch Ditty** — Ch. m. 5, by Dike—Tra La La, by Penhurst — $12,500 — Br.—Kilcoyne T B (Eng) — Tr.—Farro Michael — 112^5

Own.—Tiedemann R T

	St.	1st	2nd	3rd	Amt.
1980	1	0	0	0	$570
1979	7	4	1	1	$17,555

11Feb80- 9Aqu	fst	6f	⊡:22⅗	:47	1:13⅗	ⓕClm 10000	7	2	$7^{4\frac{1}{2}}$	$7^{4\frac{1}{2}}$	$4^{4\frac{1}{2}}$	$4^{5\frac{3}{4}}$	Lopez C C^5	b 112	10.10	71-23	SpnishDme$117^{2\frac{1}{2}}$WellTurnedAnkle$117^{1\frac{1}{2}}$OnThCrst113^2	No menace 12
18Jun79- 4Mth	gd	6f	:22⅗	:46⅗	1:12⅗	ⓕClm c-5000	8	2	$2^{\frac{1}{2}}$	$1^{\frac{1}{2}}$	$1^{1\frac{1}{2}}$	1no	Klidzia S^3	b 117	*.80	77-20	Dutch Ditty 117no Portage Path 109^3 Me Daisy 116no	Driving 11
6Jun79- 3Mth	gd	6f	:22⅕	:45⅘	1:11⅗	ⓕClm 7500	1	3	2^{hd}	$1^{1\frac{1}{2}}$	1^5	1^{12}	Klidzia S^3	b 115	*1.60	83-26	Dutch Ditty 115^{12} Red Lace 109^2 FunnySunset$111^{1\frac{1}{2}}$	Brisk urging 6
26May79- 6Key	fst	6f	:22⅗	:46⅗	1:12⅗	ⓕClm 11000	8	1	$7^{4\frac{1}{2}}$	$6^{3\frac{1}{2}}$	$6^{2\frac{1}{2}}$	5^5	Klidzia S^3	b 113	2.90	74-27	Turned Loco $120^{1\frac{1}{2}}$ My Chang 111^2 Morning Pet$116^{\frac{3}{4}}$	Forced wide 8
23Apr79- 4Key	fst	6f	:22⅗	:46⅕	1:12⅗	ⓕClm 10000	8	4	$7^{3\frac{1}{2}}$	$3^{2\frac{1}{2}}$	$3^{1\frac{1}{2}}$	$2^{1\frac{1}{2}}$	Klidzia S^3	b 111	7.30	77-19	Turned Loco $116^{1\frac{1}{2}}$ Dutch Ditty $111^{1\frac{1}{2}}$ Parting Now 120^{hd}	Gamely 12
16Apr79- 2Key	fst	6f	:22⅗	:46⅘	1:13⅗	ⓕClm 8500	3	11	$7^{4\frac{1}{2}}$	4^2	2^2	1^{hd}	Klidzia S^3	b 113	4.00	75-26	Dutch Ditty 113^{hd} Bimbo Lassie 116^3 Beaux Bet 112^1	Driving 12
1Apr79- 4Key	fst	6f	:22⅘	:46⅗	1:12	ⓕClm 6500	9	9	$6^{4\frac{1}{2}}$	$1^{\frac{1}{2}}$	$1^{1\frac{1}{2}}$	1^{hd}	Gomez M A	b 116	4.10	82-19	Dutch Ditty 116^{hd} NorthernVersion$114^{1\frac{1}{2}}$Matto'sBaby120^3	Lasted 12
23Mar79- 2Key	fst	6f	:22⅗	:46⅗	1:13⅗	ⓕClm 6500	2	11	7^4	$8^{5\frac{1}{2}}$	$4^{6\frac{1}{2}}$	$3^{4\frac{1}{2}}$	Klidzia S^3	b 113	9.20	71-31	MePlayJoke$116^{\frac{3}{4}}$DontnockTheRock$112^{3\frac{1}{2}}$DutchDitty113^1	Steadied 11
10Jly78- 2Mth	fst	1	:49	1:14⅗	1:42	ⓕClm 7500	2	6	$6^{2\frac{1}{2}}$	$3^{2\frac{1}{2}}$	3^{nk}	$5^{1\frac{1}{2}}$	Klidzia S^3	b 112	4.90	61-22	Duffy's In Town $118^{\frac{1}{2}}$ Nothings Free 115^{no}Disaca$108^{1\frac{1}{2}}$	Weakened 9
1Jly78- 1Mth	fst	6f	:22⅗	:46⅘	1:13⅕	ⓕClm 9500	1	9	5^5	$6^{5\frac{1}{2}}$	$6^{2\frac{1}{2}}$	$7^{5\frac{1}{2}}$	Klidzia S^3	b 108	5.50	68-20	D. J's Dynamite 110^2 Hypsipyle $112^{\frac{1}{2}}$ Classic Flight $117^{\frac{1}{2}}$	Tired 9

LATEST WORKOUTS Feb 8 Bel tr.t 3f fst :37⅘ h Feb 5 Bel tr.t 4f fst :51 b Jan 21 Bel tr.t 5f fst 1:05⅗ b Jan 14 Bel tr.t 3f fst :35⅗ b

When looking at a past performance listing, first try to find the best time. One way of doing it is by glancing up and down a horse's record to look at races where the horse finished first or second. That is the most likely source for the best ability time. You may also run your finger quickly down the speed rating column to check the highest rating there, for it may give you a clue as to which of the ten races may have the highest possibility (although not always).

We spot four victories for Dutch Ditty, and comparing the speed rating column, we see one with an 83 and another with an 82. We can thus start our calculations with these races in an effort to speed up the process and find a shortcut. In the race of 6Jun79 at Monmouth, Dutch Ditty had the lead time of :25.3 with no adjustments. That was an easy one. Then, next down to the 1Apr79 race at Keystone, where again she had the same lead time of :25.3 with no adjustments.

With these figures established—and I like to write them in my *Form,* usually in the space between the jockey's name and the weight listing—we next must run up and down the list of races to see if we can find better times than the two :25.3's. In looking for other ability times, you will quickly learn that a race where a horse lost ground in the stretch and yielded several lengths is not likely to produce a strong ability time. On the other hand, we can look for running lines where strong gains are shown, if they are not made too far back in the field. In Dutch Ditty's case, we must check each of her other winning races to see what they may reveal. The 18Jun79 victory is also easily calculated at :26.1 at a glance, since there are no adjustments. On 16Apr79, we get a lead time of :26.3, with a gain of two down to :26.1, and a required energy adjustment back up to :26.2.

After you do this for a time, you begin to learn the correlationship between numbers. Times showing 46 and change and 1:12 and change break into a :26.0 time area. You learn that :45.0 and 1:11.0 have the same relationship, and that 46 and 1:11 places you into the 25's. You will soon be able to do your lead times by merely looking at them, then applying lengths gained and lost, with the requisite number of ticks coming along easily thereafter. And back to Dutch Ditty, you will have seen that the two :25.3's are her two best, and you would enter those times as her ability ratings.

For easy comparative purposes, we will want to use point ratings for these ability times, which will also be supplemented by an occasional additional form factor for *Improving Horses* and horses off a *Big Win*. To make it easy, I have arbitrarily used :25.0 as a median time, and allocated 15 points to this figure. It is easy to remember by the device of a pair of 5's: :25.0 equals 15 points, both having a 5 on the end. All other points go up and down with successive fifths of seconds, or ticks. To simplify it, here is our point chart:

Time	Points	Time	Points	Time	Points
:23.0	25	:24.2	18	:25.4	11
:23.1	24	:24.3	17	:26.0	10
:23.2	23	:24.4	16	:26.1	9
:23.3	22	:25.0	15	:26.2	8
:23.4	21	:25.1	14	:26.3	7
:24.0	20	:25.2	13	:26.4	6
:24.1	19	:25.3	12	:27.0	5

When you see :25.1, quick as a flash, you will know that since :25.0 is a flat 15, you subtract 1 and get 14. And when you find a :24.3, you know that it is 2 more than :25.0, or 15, and thus obtain a quick 17. If you want to come down from :24.0 at 20, and subtract 3, then you have the same 17.

I can almost assure you that this will be the easiest chart in this book to apply. You will be able to write down the point figures after a short time by glance-knowledge, without even the necessity of calculating the simple addition and subtraction that would be otherwise required.

Once you have extracted the two best ability times and awarded the points that go with them, you will have two figures to be added for a total that will often fall into the 20 to 40 range. This point total will be the major accumulation that we will deal with, but it is not all.

There are still other important elements to be considered, but before we come to those factors, we must next deal with ability times and points in distance races and on the turf. But before we get there, I want to digress for a moment to put to rest some other elements in handicapping horse races.

You will notice that to this point, I have said nothing about weight as an influence on the outcome of races. It is simply not a factor to be considered in my method of evaluation of horses. Some years ago, in the midst of my heavy researching, I did many studies on the effect of weight and wound up concluding that no matter how I used it, one rating scale would offset another. Trainers may continue to pay great attention to it, and they are the ones that must choose the races where their horses run. If they enter a horse at the weight assigned, and if his ability times stack up, I will be happy to make my investment in him, regardless of what anyone else thinks.

Another factor considered highly important by some students is the jockey. I, too, agree jockeys are important. I would far rather have Shoemaker, Cordero, Pincay, or Velasquez than some green youngster up from Florida Downs. But jockeys cannot make horses run faster than they are able to run. There are some astute trainers who maintain that no jockey can win a race—he can only lose it. I have seen veteran riders who are highly skilled get their horses caught in heavy traffic with no place to move, and wind up losing a race that a half-intelligent ride would have won. But I cannot rate jockeys. And if I could rate the people, I would far rather rate trainers, who are vastly more important to the outcome of a race than jockeys. So I leave this factor to others, also.

There are handicappers who are called pace handicappers and speed handicappers and perhaps even other kinds of handicappers. I do not derogate their methods at all. I have tried nearly every one of them in past years, and what I have learned has come out in this book—the concept of ability times, with proper adjustments, is far superior, in my way of analyzing races, than any other method I have ever seen.

CHAPTER IV

ABILITY TIMES IN DISTANCE AND GRASS RACES

1. FINDING ABILITY TIMES IN DISTANCE RACES

Thus far, I have dealt only with sprint races of less than one mile to compile ability times. Since we must also confront distance races of a mile or more, it is imperative to develop a comparable method of computing ability times in these contests.

In sprint races, we used the final quarter time, as adjusted, out of six-furlong races (and other distances converted to six furlongs) to derive ability ratings for the horses to be evaluated. The immediate question arises: Can we use some final portion time in distance races in the same manner? One look at the past performances of Finney Finster, taken out of the ninth race at Aqueduct from the *Daily Racing Form* of March 24, 1980, provides an unhappy answer.

This old distance campaigner has run four separate and distinct distances

Finney Finster — B. g. 8, by Aristocratic—Last Slam, by Slam Bang — $7,500 — Br.—Polinger M (Md) — Tr.—Nocella Vincent — Own.—Ferrette M A — 119

Turf Record	St.	1st	2nd	3rd			St.	1st	2nd	3rd	Amt.
	1	0	0	0		1980	6	2	0	1	$10,560
						1979	6	0	1	1	$4,000

13Mar80- 9Aqu	fst	1 70	⊡:48⅗	1:14	1:45	Clm 7500	3	4	4^{6}	$4^{4\frac{1}{2}}$	$3^{1\frac{1}{2}}$	$1^{1\frac{3}{4}}$	Amy J	b 119	12.10	77-23	FinneyFinster$119^{1\frac{3}{4}}$Rumncoke$112^{1\frac{1}{4}}$SpringLodg$117^{2\frac{1}{4}}$	Clearly best	9
29Feb80- 1Aqu	fst	1 1/16	⊡:48⅖	1:15	1:48	Clm 7500	1	8	5^{5}	7^{9}	6^{11}	6^{11}	Dahlquist T C^5	b 114	5.90	63-24	Senor Riddle 117^{hd} All Our Hopes $117^{1\frac{3}{4}}$ Best Hour $112^{6\frac{1}{4}}$	Tired	10
20Feb80- 9Aqu	fst	1⅛	⊡:49⅕	1:14⅖	1:56	Clm 7500	8	6	$5^{2\frac{3}{4}}$	$4^{5\frac{1}{2}}$	$2^{\frac{1}{2}}$	1^{1}	Dahlquist T C^5	b 112	5.10	66-19	Finney Finster 112^{1} Peppercorn Fee 117^{nk} [D]Nim 117^{hd}	Driving	11
17Feb80- 9Aqu	gd	1 70	⊡:47⅘	1:13⅘	1:45⅕	Clm 7500	8	4	3^{7}	4^{7}	5^{8}	$3^{7\frac{1}{2}}$	Dahlquist T C^5	b 112	9.90	68-26	Disputed $107^{1\frac{1}{4}}$ Coup Stick $112^{6\frac{1}{4}}$ Finney Finster $112^{1\frac{1}{4}}$	Hung	10
10Feb80- 1Aqu	fst	1 70	⊡:48⅗	1:15⅗	1:46	Clm 7500	5	6	$6^{5\frac{1}{2}}$	6^{4}	4^{5}	$5^{6\frac{3}{4}}$	Borden D A	b 117	7.00	65-20	Cincelari 117^{nk}BackAgain112^{5}MotormouthEckman$110^{1\frac{1}{2}}$	NO rally	10
3Jan80- 9Aqu	fst	1 1/16	⊡:49⅕	1:13⅗	1:47	Clm 8500	9	5	6^{6}	7^{8}	6^{10}	$6^{9\frac{3}{4}}$	Borden D A	117	4.20	69-22	Nasquarade 117^{1} Dobrynin $119^{1\frac{1}{4}}$ Baba'sBetloBoy$112^{4\frac{1}{4}}$	No factor	10
14Dec79- 9Aqu	my	1⅛	⊡:49⅕	1:14⅕	1:53⅖	3↑ Clm 10000	4	4	$4^{1\frac{1}{4}}$	$3^{3\frac{1}{2}}$	3^{3}	$3^{1\frac{3}{4}}$	Borden D A	117	3.30	77-18	CliffChesney$110^{\frac{1}{2}}$ArtfulPretender$113^{1\frac{1}{4}}$FinneyFinster$117^{3\frac{1}{4}}$	Evenly	9
10Dec79- 1Aqu	fst	1 1/16	⊡:49⅗	1:14⅘	1:46⅕	3↑ Clm 12500	4	9	7^{6}	$7^{3\frac{3}{4}}$	$8^{6\frac{1}{2}}$	$7^{5\frac{3}{4}}$	Borden D A	117	8.00	77-13	Dancing Gun $117^{\frac{1}{2}}$ King's Parade $117^{3\frac{3}{4}}$ Cincelari 117^{nk}	Outrun	9
16Nov79- 9Aqu	fst	1	:47⅖	1:13	1:39	3↑ Clm 10000	4	9	9^{7}	$7^{4\frac{1}{4}}$	3^{2}	$2^{1\frac{3}{4}}$	Borden D A	117	8.30	69-26	Len's Back $117^{1\frac{3}{4}}$ Finney Finster 117^{nk} Searing 111^{nk}	Rallied	10
11Nov79- 9Aqu	my	1⅛	:48⅖	1:13⅗	1:53⅖	3↑ Clm 12500	8	5	5^{10}	$7^{7\frac{3}{4}}$	$5^{8\frac{1}{2}}$	$4^{7\frac{3}{4}}$	Borden D A	117	9.40	60-24	RoyalAppluse$117^{4\frac{1}{4}}$FrnkTlk$112^{\frac{1}{2}}$MotormouthEckmn117^{3}	No factor	8

LATEST WORKOUTS Feb 5 Bel tr.t 4f fst :49⅗ h Jan 29 Bel tr.t 6f fst 1:17⅗ h

among the ten races shown in his past performances—a mile, a mile seventy yards, a mile and a sixteenth, and a mile and and an eighth. (Other distance races are also conducted at one mile and three-sixteenths, one and one-quarter, one and three-eighths, one and one-half, one and five-eighths, and so on.) Try to make some sense out of final portion times from such an incredible mess of distances!

Looking at Finney Finster again, in his last race, from the second call to the finish (which is the comparable distance we use in sprint races), there is the distance of two furlongs, seventy yards. At a mile and a sixteenth, from the 29Feb80 race, from the second call to the finish is a distance of two and a half furlongs, and at a mile and one-eighth, a distance of three furlongs. In the one-mile race, the distance from the second call to the finish is the same two-furlong distance that we use in sprints, but the one-mile distance is not heavily used. When you bring other long-distance races into the picture, you get even more varieties from the second call to the finish line.

But can we somehow make conversions to obtain a standard two-furlong time for the last portion of a distance race, just as we have done with six and a half and seven furlongs in sprint races? I have tried it, and have not succeeded. Or, could we use the three-furlong distance from second call to finish in a race of a mile and one-eighth and convert other distances to three furlongs for comparison? I have tried this, too, and it is terribly cumbersome, mathematically difficult, frustrating, time-consuming, and ultimately just not workable.

So, what can we do?

We start with the recognition that distance races are run differently from sprints. In sprints, as I told you in the last chapter, horses come gunning out of the gate, running as hard and as fast as they can, trying to get to the lead or stay as near to the lead as they can, or else their chances of winning are made immeasurably more difficult (even though some of them do come from behind to win occasionally). The sprinter is down to guts and stamina when he gets to his last two furlongs, where class and remaining speed are indeed the best measurement of his true ability.

The distance runner, however, requires a quite different pattern in a race. If he gunned out of the gate like a sprinter, burning up his energy in the first few furlongs, he would become exhausted long before the finish and would wind up hopelessly beaten. The first stages of a distance race, therefore, become more devoted to position, strategy, and conservation of energy. A horse in an outside post position may be maneuvered toward the rail to get a favorable running position. Or his jockey may want to hold him far back from the leaders to wait for the propitious time to move. He will need to be rated for the proper drive to the front.

Now, look at the data available to us in distance races. Finney Finster's past performances show the first call in the distance races at four furlongs. In sprints, four furlongs are recorded at the second call. In the second call of the ordinary distance race, the automatic timer is fixed at six furlongs, which is the finish line in the usual sprint race. Thus, you have the same two-furlong distance span between the first and second calls in the usual distance race that you have between the second and finish calls of a sprint race. Can this be properly used, and if so, how, and why?

The way a distance race is run provides our answer. When a horse reaches the four-furlong first point of call, he has traversed a considerable portion of the race. In a race of a mile and an eighth, which is nine furlongs, a horse at the first call has run four-ninths of the race by that time. His time for maneuvering and searching for position and conserving energy is over. He is by this point well into the backstretch, and there, my friends, is where the real running must begin. If he is to win the race, the time for dilly-dallying is ended. Open up and start moving is what his jockey will be thinking and doing. Between the point of the first and second calls, from four furlongs to six furlongs, he will be expending a maximum of energy and effort, bringing himself up to a position when he can exert his contention in the final portion of the race to the wire.

After my experimentation with adjusted final portion times had bogged down, I gave long and serious consideration to the use of the time between the first and second calls in distance races. Would it really work? And then I began to try it, both at the track and in my research efforts. I found it far superior to any converted final portion time! I also noticed that class horses would invariably pick up faster times between the first and second calls than horses of lesser value and ability.

Yes, it is indeed workable, and I have adopted this formula for the ordinary distance race—that is, races where the first call is fixed at four furlongs and the second call is fixed at six furlongs. By now, I am almost convinced that it is even superior to the last quarter of the sprint race as a measuring device. Its consistency is almost a jewel.

I am still impressed by the importance of final portion times in distance races, if they could be computed properly. We can use some, as I will show you shortly, in some instances. But with the difficulties inherent in the varieties of distances, and taking into account the way these races are run, I am quite satisfied with the times between the first and second calls. Of course, I am fully aware that a horse that turns on the steam between four and six furlongs in a distance race must also demonstrate stamina and guts and enough fleetness in the final portion to win the race, and that would also be a further indication of his class and ability. But I have learned through this process that a horse that is able to run well from the first call to the second call is likely to be able to continue his good performance right to the wire where it finally counts.

And in computing ability times in distance races, I have also found that the same adjustments for lengths behind and for energy are as valid here as in sprint races, or possibly even more so. Therefore, to use the same comparable two-furlong piece of the race, with the same methods of adjustment, for each kind of race, we are fortunate to be able to rely upon a good degree of consistency. And there is one further additional bonus—horses frequently run in both sprints and distance races, and the ability times are indeed interchangeable and usable for both, as you will also learn.

At this point, let's do a few calculations off Finney Finster, which you should, by now, be able to do rather handily. Start with the top race of 13Mar80, where we have a lead time of :25.2 (subtracting :48.3 from 1:14.0 just as we do in sprint races). Finney Finster gained 1½ lengths, enabling us to reduce his time to :25.1. But we must add his 6 lengths behind at the first call to the recorded time of :48.3, raising his time to :49.4 and requiring the addition of three ticks for energy, making his ability time :25.4. You will also see that it is comparable to the sprint times that we extract in the same manner.

There is little need to do more. I do want to comment that the first call times in all the races shown in this horse's record are unusually slow, largely because of the dull winter running surfaces reflected in the dates of the races, even though seven of the ten races show a "fast" track. But you can calculate every one of his ability times off the first and second calls of each race.

However, there is one allowable deviation that we should take note of at this time. Drop down to the mile race of 16Nov79. The lead time between the first two calls was :25.3, and Finney Finster gets a reduction of two ticks for gain down to :25.1. Because of his 7 lengths behind at the first call, we convert his time to :48.2 and add two ticks for energy to obtain a :25.3 ability time. Now, we can also look at the final portion of the race, since there are exactly two furlongs from the 6f second call to the finish at one mile, or eight furlongs. You can obtain a figure by subtracting 1:13.0 from 1:39.0 for a :26.0 final portion time. There was a gain of 2½ lengths to allow us to deduct two ticks to get a :25.3 figure. What should we do about an energy adjustment, if anything? In distance races, from the second call, wherever it is, to the finish, a horse has not likely been loafing to get to the second call, and therefore an energy adjustment is not only hardly needed, but in my judgment not needed at all. Thus we shall make only the lengths and time adjustment and leave the figure at :25.3, which happens to be the same time as for the first to second call portion of the race.

My point is this: In any distance race where the final portion between the second call and the finish line is two furlongs and that segment of time is published, you are allowed an alternate calculation. My practice is to look at both figures, and use the best one of the two, because of the nature of distance races. This is particularly important in the longer races, as you will see later.

To this time, we have dealt with standard distance races where the second call is always at the six-furlong position. But we are required to also look at the longer races, where the second call is placed at different points. These races, where the second call is not at six furlongs, introduce new problems in the calculation of ability times. To deal with some of these difficulties, look at the past performances of Sunny Puddles, taken from the second race at Belmont from the *Daily Racing Form* of Saturday, May 31, 1980.

We are only concerned with the races of 19Apr80 and 1Mar80, since all the other distance races show second call times for six furlongs, and in those races, ability can be calculated in the normal way. On 19Apr80, the distance was a mile and three-eighths, and in any distance greater than a mile and three-sixteenths and less than a mile and a half, the second call time is recorded at the distance of one mile. This means that there are four furlongs between the first and second calls, and four furlongs is not a measurable distance in our calculations of ability times. The final time likewise is at an odd distance.

Therefore, in all situations where the second call time is shown at one mile, we are compelled to calculate the published four-furlong time and divide it by two. Here, the one-mile second call lead time is shown as 1:38.1. The first call 4f time is :48.3 and when that is subtracted from 1:38.1, you obtain a :49.3. Since there was no gain or loss, we make no adjustments in that department. But the :48.3 requires an energy adjustment of two ticks added on, bringing the 4f time to :50.0. In all cases where we are compelled to divide 4f time into two portions, we will adopt another new rule: We shall always calculate the first portion in slightly faster time than we use for the second portion. For example, the :50.0 has to be divided into two segments of :25.0 and :25.0. Since we require a lesser half, we must reduce the first :25.0 to :24.4 and use that figure as the ability time of Sunny Puddles in the race of 19Apr80. If the 4f time had been :50.1, we would have had two portions of :25.0 and :25.1 and would have used :25.0 as the appropriate figure.

We use the same method for every distance race where the second call is at the one-mile point.

Now, look down to the race of 1Mar80, which was run at the long distance of one and a half miles. The point for the <u>second</u> call is now fixed at one and a quarter miles, rather than the one-mile post for distance races of one and a quarter, one and three-eighths, and one and five-sixteenths. The distance from the second call at one and a quarter miles to the one-and-a-half-mile finish line is the same two-furlong quarter-mile distance that we ordinarily use for measuring ability. But do we use this last quarter time in races of one and a half miles? Because of the extremely long distance involved, a horse is normally slowing down quite noticeably as he approaches the finish, and it simply would not be fair to rate him off his final last effort when he is undoubtedly gasping to reach the wire. In the 1Mar80 race, you will note that the lead time for the final quarter is :26.1 (obtained by subtracting 2:07.0 from 2:33.1). That is surely not representative of the comparable ability for the horses that ran in that race.

On the other hand, if the last quarter time in a marathon race is low enough to warrant use, by all means use it, just as we would use the best of either times in the mile race. But ordinarily, we will have to seek out some other time measurement, and that is not too promising, either. In the 1Mar80 race, the distance between the first call at four furlongs and the second call at one and a quarter miles, or ten furlongs, is six furlongs. We can obtain the lead time by the usual method of subtraction, taking the published :49.1 from 2:07.0 to obtain the abysmally slow time of 1:17.4 (which is a time commonly expected in sprints of six and a half furlongs). This, of course, is a further demonstration of how horses are conserving their energy by running slowly in the inner portions of a long-distance race.

If you are compelled to do so, you could divide the 1:17.4 by three to represent two-furlong segments. You have essentially :77.4 seconds, which can be divided into three portions of :25.4, :26.0, and :26.0. Add them up and still have :77.4 seconds. If you take the :25.4 and leave off any adjustment for energy, because a horse is entitled to conserve himself at such a distance, you are still playing around in a big sea of guesswork.

The practical way to avoid this difficult problem is to rely on other races to establish representative ability times. You will note that Sunny Puddles has six distance races listed where the second call was at the normal six-furlong time, plus one sprint race that could also be used, making a total of seven races from which to select. (The turf race of 5May80 will not be used, as you will shortly learn, except when a grass race is involved; here, we are concerned about illustrating the problem for dirt races).

With Sunny Puddles, you have plenty from which to choose. In his race of 25Apr80, there was a lead time of :24.3 as he was out front, and when we add the two ticks for energy adjustment, we get a respectable :25.0. Down to 3Apr80, there is a lead time of :24.1 made by Sunny Puddles, and the addition of two ticks for energy makes it :24.3. Since Sunny Puddles is a high-priced animal running for a tag of $40,000, and had won an allowance race on 25Apr80, you would expect times like that out of a horse of his caliber.

In the race of 26Mar80, the lead time was :24.2. Sunny Puddles gained 3½ lengths to reduce this time by three ticks to :23.4. The first call time was the published :47.4, with Sunny Puddles following some 5½ lengths behind. While we ordinarily count the half-length as a full one for time purposes for lengths behind, the addition of six ticks to :47.4 would bring the horse's first call time to :49.0 and would require the addition of three ticks for energy. We are approaching a very fine line here, where if we add five and a half ticks, he would have :48.4½. We give the benefit of the doubt in cases of this kind, and require full lengths when lengths behind would break at another energy tick to be added on. Therefore, we will penalize Sunny Puddles by adding only two ticks for energy, bringing his adjusted ability time to :24.1 for the race of 26Mar80, which is excellent time.

But the point of all this is that in most cases, you will be able to use ability times from standard distances rather than engage in the calculating guesswork encompassed in the one-and-a-half-milers. You will use the divisions of portions of long races, therefore, only when you have no other alternative.

You now have the calculation capability for ability times in almost all kinds of distance races.

Of course, with the same portion of distance that is used in sprint ability times, all races can be compared, and all point ratings, of course, are based on precisely the same figures. This is another enormous advantage of using this reliable time extraction in distance races.

2. DEALING WITH GRASS RACES

Racing on the turf presents slightly different problems from dirt racing, but out method of calculation of ability times will be basically the same. Most grass races are run at a distance, and therefore we will ordinarily calculate our ability times by using the same two furlongs between the first and second calls that we use in distance races on the dirt. And when grass races are run at a longer distance, greater than a mile and three-sixteenths, we have the same calculation problems that we have in dirt races at such distances, and use the same techniques.

The one major rule to follow, however, when you are dealing with grass races, is that ability times must be taken from grass races _only_. Horses run differently on the grass than on the dirt. Some horses are powerful forces on the turf and perform poorly on dirt. Some strong dirt runners simply cannot do as well on the grass. Why this is so, I am not entirely sure, although I have read many explanations of it. For our purposes in this book, however, you are enjoined to follow the rule: For grass races, use ability times derived from grass races only. The corresponding rule for dirt races is the same: When you are dealing with a dirt race, you will calculate ability times only from races run on the dirt, and ignore altogether races run on the grass.

If you are handicapping a grass race and all the favored animals have no grass experience, but have run only on the dirt, let that race go. You are dealing with unknown factors, and if you still insist on rating them off their dirt performances, you will have descended into the gambling which is not a part of the investment program set forth in this book.

But the major message at this point is that ability times in grass races work just as well as in dirt races. They are just as reliable if applied to grass races only. They are computed and calculated in the same manner. To show you how this works, here are the past performances of Valiant Order in the seventh race at Belmont at one mile and a sixteenth on the turf, taken from the *Daily Racing Form* of May 29, 1980.

Valiant Order — B. c. 3, by Round Table—Let's Be Gay, by Bagdad
Br.—Nuckols Bros (Ky)
Own.—R L Reineman Stable Inc — Tr.—Stephens Woodford C — **108**

Turf Record: St. 3, 1st 1, 2nd 2, 3rd 0

	St.	1st	2nd	3rd	Amt.
1980	6	1	3	1	$17,800
1979	3	M	0	1	$1,800

19May80- 1Aqu	gd	1	Ⓣ	:48⅕	1:14	1:38⅗	Md Sp Wt	3 7	76¼ 54½ 31½ 12¾	Venezia M	b	122	*1.70	87-14	ValiantOrder122¾CabinCaptin122nkMischievous122no	Ridden out	10
4May80- 6Aqu	fst	7f		:23⅕	:47⅕	1:25⅕	3 ▲ Md Sp Wt	4 9	76¾ 63½ 53½ 45¾	Maple E	b	113	45.40	69-25	Solve 1092¼ In The Woodpile 1242 Kryptonite 1131½	Tired	9
21Mar80- 2GP	fm	*1 1/16	Ⓣ			1:46	Md Sp Wt	10 5	54 2½ 2hd 2nk	Vasquez J		120	*1.70	76-22	Hawaiian Fighter 120nkValiantOrder120nk[D]Observer1202½	Gamely	10
10Mar80- 2GP	fm	1	Ⓣ	:47⅗	1:11⅗	1:36⅘	Md Sp Wt	5 9	86½ 44 33½ 24½	Vasquez J		120	1.80	81-16	Sulcus 1204½ Valiant Order 120½ More Fudge 1201	Gained place	12
22Feb80- 7Hia	fst	6f		:22⅕	:45⅗	1:12⅕	Md Sp Wt	9 2	86¾ 68 44½ 2no	Maple E		120	*2.50	82-25	Pacific Fleet 120no ValiantOrder1201Heisaturkey120½	Just missed	12
9Feb80- 1Hia	fst	6f		:22⅘	:46⅘	1:13	Md Sp Wt	12 1	42½ 21 21½ 32½	Maple E		120	*3.10	75-28	Bombay Flight1201FarOutEast1201½ValiantOrder1203½	Weakened	12
3Sep79- 4Bel	fst	6½f		:23	:46⅘	1:18⅖	Md Sp Wt	12 7	1214 119¼ 99 87½	Maple E		118	7.30	76-17	Koluctoo Bay 1182 War of Words118hdRaiseACrown113nk	Outrun	13
18Aug79- 5Sar	sly	6f		:22⅗	:46⅗	1:12	Md Sp Wt	7 1	41¾ 43 42½ 36½	Maple S		118	5.50	73-16	Grandiloquent Guy 118½ Proctor 1186 Valiant Order 1181¾	Evenly	8
11Aug79- 2Sar	fst	6f		:21⅘	:45⅖	1:11⅖	Md Sp Wt	7 8	1120 1114 108½ 55½	Maple S		118	17.80	77-13	StormWave118¾ChmpgneMood1182LonelyGuy1182½	Belated rally	11

LATEST WORKOUTS May 25 Bel 4f fst :49 b May 17 Bel 4f fst :49⅕ b May 11 Bel 4f fst :47 h May 3 Bel 3f fst :36⅖ b

The top race on the line of 19May80 was a grass race, as illustrated by the "T" within a circle. The lead time was :25.4, calculated as always. The horse gained 1¾ lengths, which allows him a one-tick deduction to :25.3. His first call time ballooned up into 49 and change, and requires an add-on of three ticks for energy, making his ability time a :26.1. However, since we also have a race of one mile, with a measurable final quarter, we compare it also.

The lead time for the final quarter was :26.3. Valiant Order's gain of 4½ lengths allows a deduction of three ticks down to :26.0. We make no adjustment for energy when using the last quarter of distance races. We establish ability time for the last quarter as :26.0, and use it because it is better than :26.1.

Since we may consider only races run on the grass, we next look at the 21Mar80 contest at Gulfstream, where, to our disappointment, there are no fractional times given. The asterisk between the "fm," which means that the turf course was "firm," and the "1 1/16" distance indicates that the race was run at "about one and one-sixteenth miles." The reason for this is that grass courses are usually inside the main track, thus making the inner oval into a slightly shorter span. The race, therefore, must begin from a slightly different starting point, and where there is but one automatic timing device in use around the track, the point at which the lead horse breaks the beam is not always the same distance as it would be in a dirt race. Accordingly, when these races are run at "about distances," you will seldom find fractional times, since there is no capability for producing them.

There is nothing we can do about it. We have to ignore every turf race where there are no internal fractions, and look to other races where there are if we are to obtain the necessary ability times. But now look at the 10Mar80 race at Gulfstream at one mile, where we do have internal times, because of a synchronization of timing devices. You can now calculate the times in the 10Mar80 in the same manner as the race of 19May80 was calculated.

There is one other problem with grass races that does not exist on the dirt. In the past performances, after the track is listed, you will always see the condition of the track. Look back at Valiant Order. On the dirt, you see such abbreviations as "fst," for fast and "sly" for sloppy, and in other past performances you will see other designations of the condition of the track surface. In grass racing, the surface is rated with different abbreviations. The most usual one, comparable to the "fst" on the dirt, is "fm" for firm. You will find this grass condition occurring far more often than any other. But in Valiant Order's race of 19May80 at Aqueduct, you see the abbreviation "gd" for good. This same abbreviation is often used for dirt tracks as well. But a "gd" turf course is treated, for our purposes, exactly the same as a "fm" course.

It is only when you see a different condition of the turf that you are to make adjustments in grass racing. Another condition is "hd" for hard, which represents a packed, extremely fast grass surface. Grass times on a "hard" surface will usually run much faster than on the ordinary "firm" surface. Because ability times on hard grass surfaces will run so much faster, we are compelled to make an adjustment for hard surfaces. When a turf race is run on a "hd" surface, we will add one tick to whatever ability time is compiled. For example, if the ability time is :25.0 on a "hd" surface, we will add one tick to make it :25.1. This adjustment is necessary to give us a truer comparable time.

The other side of the coin is a slow grass surface. There are two designations which reveal this condition. One is "yl," for yielding. The other is "sf," for soft. I have never been sure of the difference between a yielding grass surface and a soft grass surface, but I do know that times on these surfaces are much slower. A horse cannot run nearly as fast on a mushy sinking surface as he can on a firm course, and slower still than on a hard surface. It is as if you ran on a beach alongside the water's edge on hard-packed sand as compared to running in the soft sand up the bank where you will have to struggle to put one foot in front of the other.

Accordingly, when a horse shows a grass race on a "yl" or "sf" surface, we will subtract one tick from his ability time. A recorded time of :25.0 would thus be adjusted to a :24.4 in this kind of situation. An example comes from the past performances of Memory Rock, taken from the *Racing Form* of May 29, 1980.

Memory Rock — **B. c. 4, by Forli—Rocked Ribbed, by Ribot** — **Br.—Templeton Stables (Ky)** — **Own.—Templeton Sta** — **Tr.—Smithwick D Michael** — **119**

Turf Record	St.	1st	2nd	3rd			St.	1st	2nd	3rd	Amt.
	4	1	1	0		1980	2	1	0	0	$5,610
						1979	5	M	2	0	$6,160

```
8May80- 5Pim yl  1    Ⓣ:49⅖ 1:14⅘ 1:40⅘ 3↑Md Sp Wt   9 7 65¾ 43  22  13¼ Pilar H    124  3.60  75-24 Memory Rock 1243¼ Bing 1125 Little Red Prose 1136  Drew clear 12
18Apr80- 4Pim fst 1 1/16 :48⅗ 1:13⅖ 1:45⅘ 3↑Md Sp Wt  5 2 22½ 2hd 22  45¼ Pilar H    124  3.10  71-18 Born Great 1193 Unison 1241¾ Black Chrome 124½       Tired 9
12Jly79- 2Bel fm  1½   Ⓣ:48⅕       2:31⅘ 3↑Md Sp Wt   6 5 53½ 32  32½ 32  Cruguet J  116  7.40  63-18 RightfulRuler116¾[D]Nitroglycerin1161¼MmoryRock1161¾ Impeded 8
     12Jly79-Placed second through disqualification
21Jun79- 5Pim fst 1 1/16 :47   1:11⅗ 1:45⅕ 3↑Md Sp Wt  5 6 54½ 32½ 43  42  Pilar H    112  1.90  77-18 Gallant Astron 112no Fell's Point 114hd Hone 1122       Hung 9
11Jun79- 4Pim sly 1 1/16 :47⅗ 1:12⅗ 1:45⅗ 3↑Md Sp Wt  4 5 53½ 44  41¾ 21  Pilar H    112  25.50 76-22 Armada Strike 1121 Memory Rock112noBoldBobby1122 Game try 9
2Jun79- 1Fai gd *1 5/16 Ⓣ          2:21⅖ 3↑Allowance    2 2 67½ 76  66¼ 49½ Rengert K3 135  4.00  -- Waltz 1532¾ Cortege 1532¼ Northern Giver 1404½                  12
28May79- 1Fai fm *7f  Ⓣ            1:32⅕ 3↑Md Sp Wt    5 7 62¾ 83  52¾ 417 Rengert K  139 *1.50e -- Last Waterloo 14212 Quixotic 1531½SunnyStreaker1503  No factor 12
```

In the 8May80 race at Pimlico, the surface was shown as "yl" for yielding. The lead ability time is a good :24.4. It is reduced by two for gain, down to :24.2. We make the usual adjustment for energy; four ticks are added for a :25.1. Now, we make the final necessary adjustment of subtracting one tick for the "yl" surface and finish with a :25.0 ability time.

You will also note the race of 12Jly79 at Belmont, where at the mile-and-a-half grass distance, there are no internal times, for the same reason you don't have them in Florida grass races, because the timer cannot be synchronized with the marking poles. Also note the races of 2Jun79 and 28May79, where there are no internal times. These are steeplechase events that may never be used for comparison. in flat races, even if you had internal times, which you will not have.

This quick tour of distance and grass races completes your initial training on computing ability times, subject to a lot of working experience that you will acquire later in this book. There is one other adjustment, only an occasional and relatively rare one, which you will be asked to make, and it will be explained in the next chapter when we deal with the controversial and important issue of how to cope with track surfaces.

3. SUMMARY OF DETERMINING ABILITY TIMES

How to Find and Record Ability Times in Sprint Races

1. Calculations in all races are based upon times at six furlongs, or times adjusted to comparative six-furlong times.
2. The portion of the sprint race used for ability times is the last one-third, or last quarter-mile, of the six-furlong race, or its equivalent.
3. The lead time is the difference between the actual time of the horse first reaching the half-mile point and the actual time of the horse first reaching

the finish point. It is a time equivalent to that used in running two furlongs, or a quarter-mile.

4. For any horse that leads at the second call and at the finish, the actual
clock time is his preliminary ability time for the race under review.

5. For any horse that does not establish the lead time, his preliminary ability
time is calculated in this manner:
   a. When he is the same number of lengths behind at the finish as he was
   at the second call, his preliminary ability time is the same as the lead
   time.
   b. When a horse loses lengths from the second call to the finish, a fifth of
   a second for each lost length (or any fraction of half a length or more)
   will be added to the lead time to obtain a preliminary ability time.
   c. When a horse gains lengths from the second call to the finish, his gain
   will be adjusted by fifths of seconds in accordance with the table on p.
   48 by subtracting the allowable number of fifths, or ticks, from the
   lead time to obtain a preliminary ability time.

6. Final ability times are calculated by making a second adjustment known
as an energy adjustment, which requires adding, when necessary, fifths of
seconds, or ticks, to the preliminary ability time. These additions are based
upon actual times plus fifths of seconds for any lengths, or fractional portions, behind. This is based upon a time allocation as set forth on p. 50.

7. From each past performance record, the two best ability times are selected.
Point totals are awarded these ability times based upon a point schedule
set forth on p. 60.

How to Find and Record Ability Times in Distance Races, Both on the Dirt and on the Grass

1. Most calculations, with exceptions hereafter noted, are based upon the
time between the first call at four furlongs and the second call at six furlongs, in those races where those two points are used to record times for
first and second calls.

2. Since this is a two-furlong distance between the same two distances that
are used in calculating ability times in sprint races, the same methods of
calculations are used, both to establish preliminary ability times and final
ability times based upon an energy adjustment, when pertinent. Point
totals for ability times are the same as those used in sprint races.

3. In races of exactly one mile, you may use the time between either the first
and second calls, or in the alternative, between the second call and the finish call, since they are the same distance. It is appropriate to select the best
time of the two.

4. In races of exactly one mile and a quarter, or in any race where the second call time is recorded at the mile point, compute the total time between the first and second calls and divide by two to establish an appropriate two-furlong time. When the time does not divide equally, use the lesser fraction. When the time does divide equally, subtract one tick from the portion in order to make sure that a lesser time is allowed for the first half of the distance.

   In the alternative, calculate the last quarter time between the second point of call at a mile and the final finish point, since it is the same two-furlong distance that is regularly used. If this time is better than the divided time, use it.

5. In races of a mile and three-eighths, compute the four-furlong time between the first and second calls, divide by two, and use the faster portion, just as you would do in the first portion of the mile-and-a-quarter race.

6. In races of a mile and a half, or longer, use the best two-furlong time available, either by dividing a half-mile time or from any other reasonable calculation. Because these longer marathons are not run too frequently, it is more reliable to try to obtain ability times from races at more traditional distances.

CHAPTER

V

DEALING WITH VARIANTS AND TRACK SURFACES

1. THE ENIGMA OF THE TRACK VARIANT

As you have read thus far into this book, and have viewed a number of past performances from the Eastern edition of the *Daily Racing Form,* you have seen a published number representing the track variant. It is used in conjunction with the computed speed rating of the winners of the day it was issued, and its purpose is to provide a level of information as to whether the track was fast or slow that day, or whether it had a "variant" from "normal." To show you these figures again and how they are used, we can look at the past performances of Promenade All, taken from the *Daily Racing Form* of March 17, 1980.

Promenade All — B. c. 4, by Go Marching—Miss Debutante, by Windy City II
Own.—Silver M H — Br.—Silver M (NY) — Tr.—Lake Robert P — **116**

	St.	1st	2nd	3rd	Amt.
1980	2	0	1	0	$8,400
1979	6	2	1	1	$44,520

27Jan80- 8Aqu	fst	1 70	⊡:46⅖	1:11⅘	1:42⅘		Ⓢ Handicap	4	7	6 12	4 5½	3 nk	2 hd	Castaneda M	116	3.60	88–17	Tiempo 122hd Promenade All 1162¼ Kim's Chance 1202	Sharp 11
10Jan80- 8Aqu	fst	6f	⊡:23⅕	:46⅘	1:11⅖		Ⓢ Handicap	7	5	4 3	3 2½	4 4	4 4¾	Asmussen C B	115	4.40	82–19	Kim's Chance 1181½ Sir Ack 1191¼ BaconandEggs1122	Weakened 7
31Dec79- 6Aqu	fst	1 70	⊡:48⅗	1:14⅕	1:43⅗	3↑	Ⓢ Handicap	4	2	3 3½	2 2	2 hd	2 hd	Castaneda M	113	9.00	84–19	Tiempo 117hd Promenade All 1132½ Mr. International1243½	Sharp 7
19Dec79- 8Aqu	gd	1 1/16	⊡:49⅕	1:14⅕	1:45	3↑	Ⓢ Alex M Robb	7	8	7 4¾	8 11	8 14	8 12	Fell J	116	16.40	77–19	Mr. International 122no Tiempo 1162 Kim'sChance1162½	Far back 8
2Dec79- 7Aqu	fst	1	:49	1:15⅕	1:41⅗	3↑	Ⓢ Allowance	5	4	4 2½	2 1½	1 hd	1 3	Cordero A Jr	114	*1.40	58–29	PromenadeAll1143BirthdyWitch114½WiseOldMike112¾	Drew clear 7
18Nov79- 5Aqu	fst	6f	:23⅕	:47	1:11⅖	3↑	Ⓢ Allowance	3	6	5 4½	5 4½	4 7½	3 3¾	Cordero A Jr	115	*1.40	82–18	Birthday Witch 1143¾ Roman Chef117noPromenadeAll1151¼	Wide 6
27Jly79- 8Bel	fst	7f	:23⅖	:46⅘	1:24⅕	3↑	Ⓢ Allowance	1	6	6 5½	6 4	4 3¼	4 2¼	Cordero A Jr	113	3.70	79–21	Furrow 119hd Tiempo 1132¼ Fabulous Fur 116no	Wide 6
14Jly79- 6Bel	fst	7f	:23⅕	:46⅘	1:24⅘	3↑	Ⓢ Allowance	8	7	5 3½	3 ½	2 hd	1 2½	Cordero A Jr	112	*1.60	78–19	PromenadeAll1122½Dr.AlliPup1132¾WiseOldMike1174¾	Ridden out 10
15Aug78- 8Sar	fst	6f	:22⅖	:46⅗	1:12⅗		Ⓢ Empire	1	7	5 7½	5 4	3 4	1 ¾	Gonzalez B	122	4.60	77–22	Promenade All 122¾ Perfect Turn 1193½ Sir Ack 122hd	Driving 7
7Aug78- 4Sar	gd	5½f	:22⅗	:46⅗	1:05⅗		Ⓢ Md Sp Wt	8	7	6 6½	4 2	1 1½	1 7½	Gonzalez B	122	*2.60	89–10	PromenadeAll1227½RichVnWinkle122nkHoHckett1222	Ridden out 11

LATEST WORKOUTS Mar 8 Aqu ⊡ 6f fst 1:19 b Feb 20 Aqu ⊡ 6f fst 1:17 b Jan 18 Aqu ⊡ 5f fst 1:04⅖ b

Look at the column of double figures under the heavy-type "116," which is the weight carried that day (immaterial to us). On the top line, you see "88-17." The 88 represents the speed rating, which means that the time for that particular race was twelve ticks slower than the track record for the distance. This leads to a calculation of track variants for each day. The winning time of each race each day is compared to the track record for the distance at which it was run, which results in an individual speed rating for each winner, based upon the 100 figure for the track record. These nine (if that is the appropriate number) ratings are averaged, and the resultant figure is subtracted from 100, which then provides the number of the variant for that day. If all speed ratings averaged 83, for example, the variant would be established at 17, and it would be used along with the speed ratings for each horse than ran that day.

The theory of the usefulness of the track variant for those who wish to compute "true speed" is that it enables the handicapper to make adjustments in his times based on the track variant. For many years, I relied on variants to aid me in the adjustments I made. Some of them worked, and some of them didn't. There was never any solid confidence in the use of variants.

Theoretically, track variants would be low on days when a track was fast, would be a little higher when a track was slightly off, such as "good," even higher when a track was "muddy," and still higher when it was rated as "heavy." But this is not always so, as you look down the line at the different variants on the days that Promenade All ran. Eight of the ten races shown say the track was "fast," yet the variants ranged from a low of 17 to a high of 29. On 7Aug78 at Saratoga, the track was listed as "gd," for good, which is not supposed to be as receptive to speed as a fast track, yet the variant was a very low 10, the lowest on the board.

Every scholar who has studied the subject has pointed out that track variants are influenced by the caliber of horses running on the particular day of computation. On Saturdays in New York, for example, where you will usually find a stakes race and one or more very high-priced allowance races, you will have a faster, classier breed of animals that will run much faster than those on some other day, when there are not likely to be any stakes races, and where the cheaper horses are performing. Caliber of horse rather than variation in the surface of the track thus may even exert a greater influence on a track variant. Variants on Saturdays, therefore, are expected to be lower than on other days, even when track surface is irregular.

Many thoughtful racing writers simply do not use published variants in the *Daily Racing Form*. In addition, the *Daily Racing Form* as published in Chicago, Los Angeles, and Canada does not print track variants, although it does provide speed ratings, as you will see if you look back to Potomac Pride in Chapter III.

But because most good handicappers still consider track variants of major importance, scholars like Andrew Beyer make their own. They do it by calculating the normal times that a horse of a certain value would be expected to run, based upon a large number of past examples, and if horses of $10,000 in value ran three ticks faster than their "norm" on a given day for $10,000 horses, the variant for that race would be calculated as three ticks fast. On the other hand, if the $10,000 winner's time was three ticks slower than the computed norm time for that level of animal, the track would be considered "off" by three ticks. At the end of each racing day, they would average the "offs" and the "ons," all drawn from the various comparisons with "normal" times for each class of horse running, and come up with a variant for that day that they consider more reliable than the one used in the *Daily Racing Form,* which it undoubtedly is.

Beyer and his followers then adjust final times by their own variants and rate horses accordingly—final times as adjusted by homemade variants to determine the horse's speed rating.

Perhaps the most scholarly effort to compute and publish "par" times for all classes of horses at all tracks is provided in the remarkable book *Winning at the Races: Computer Studies in Thoroughbred Handicapping,* by William L. Quirin, Ph.D. (Wm. Morrow & Co., 1979). Before I give you my disagreements with the practical aspects of the theory, let me say that this is surely one of the very best volumes ever published on racing, and is invaluable to anyone with any scholarly interest in the sport. I have learned a great deal from reading Dr. Quirin.

Beyer and Quirin and others can readily argue that the surface of a racetrack indeed does have a variant in that horses of the same caliber run faster on some days than on others. The reasoning follows that a rating of a horse's ability based on final time is not a true picture if that final time is affected by a variance in the surface of the track. Therefore, their theory runs that all times in all races should be adjusted by the track variant to attain a truer time for the rating of the horse.

And for years and years, I, too, accepting that theory, struggled with track variants. I developed my own adjustments from the published variants in the Eastern *Form.* I formulated theories and adopted figures to compute variants in the editions where no variants were published. I spent a lot of time adding track variants to published speed ratings to try to obtain rating figures, which have a degree of effectiveness, as Tom Ainslie has demonstrated. I could not make my own variants, as Beyer has done, because I have other things to do than devote my entire working life to horse racing. I cannot read the *Racing Form* every day, nor spend the untold hours required to make my own variants. Most other players likewise find it similarly impossible. After Quirin's book was published, there was a good workable tool to help do this, but the practical burdens are still too great for all of us who do not attend every day. There had to be a better way.

2. DISCARDING THE TRACK VARIANT ALTOGETHER

At long last, after much thought and much experimentation, I came to the conclusion that I would discard track variants altogether in rating the ability of horses. In this book, that is what I have done.

It may be the most controversial factor in this book—heretical, indeed. Racing writers and scholars may disagree, may dispute, and may well argue to the contrary, but I stand firmly by my position, just as I have adopted the totally new technique of using adjusted fractional times rather than final times to rate a horse's ability.

The reason why I have dropped track variants altogether is simple and sound. Sad experience drove me to it. I became convinced that so much error was built into them, even though no one was to blame, that they were misleading at least as often as they were helpful. And if the gain from their use is offset by an equal portion of error, then all of us have been wasting a lot of our time for many years. On this supposition alone, that variants mislead as often as they contribute to a more accurate rating, then there is no point in doing the work required to use them.

We can examine the thesis that variants, no matter how they are computed, lack essential accuracy, or consistent accuracy, in a number of ways.

Let's start with the published track variants. Despite the criticisms of them, they do stand for something. It is indisputable that on days when the *Form* shows a low variant, horses on the whole were running faster than on days when there is a high variant. The question is, what significance may we attach to this? Also, higher-class horses should in theory achieve better times on days when the variant is low than on days when the variant is high. Again, in our test, we need not press for precise accuracy, but only for a reasonable relationship.

Let's take a look at the past performances of Fannie's Eagle from the Eastern *Form* for May 31, 1980, since Fannie's Eagle has run all her races at Aqueduct and Belmont, where variants, if they follow a true pattern, ought to be reasonably consistent with track surface and class of horse.

Begin by comparing the top race of 25Apr80 at 7f with the third race down on 28Mar80 at 7f. In both races, fillies valued at $10,000 were competing against each other, and both tracks were labeled "fast." The track variant on 25Apr80 was 26 and the variant on 28Mar80 was 24, not very much different.

Fannie's Eagle — B. f. 4, by L'Aiglon—Fanfannie, by Our Love II — **$10,500** — Br.—Seba L E (Fla) — Tr.—Puentes Gilbert — **1105**
Own.—Garren M M

	St.	1st	2nd	3rd	Amt.
1980	6	0	0	0	$1,140
1979	13	1	3	1	$12,370

25Apr80- 1Aqu fst 7f	:23⅖	:47	1:25⅘	3↑ⒻClm 10500	1	5	2hd	24	712	720	Lovato F Jr5	b	112	12.00	52-26	Open Bar 1173 Lillian's Princess 1073FourSummers112 4¾	Used up	7
9Apr80- 4Aqu sly 6f	:22⅗	:46⅖	1:12⅘	ⒻClm 10500	1	1	1hd	21½	33	42½	Beitia E5	b	108	9.90	76-21	Miss L. And B. 117¾ Pearl's Pick 117½ Open Bar 1151¼	Tired	6
28Mar80- 1Aqu fst 7f	:23	:46⅗	1:26⅘	ⒻClm 10000	5	3	1½	2½	34½	88½	Fell J	b	117	4.40	58-24	Spring Training110¾FourSummers1131¼MelodiousMiss1132½	Tired	9
5Mar80- 2Aqu fst 6f	⊡:23	:46⅘	1:12⅖	ⒻClm 10000	7	6	43½	45	55½	611	Hernandez R	b	117	6.30	71-22	Spanish Dame 1196¾ On The Crest1131¼Where'sPappa1081½	Tired	10
11Feb80- 1Aqu fst 6f	⊡:22⅗	:46⅘	1:12⅗	ⒻClm 14000	4	6	54	66	89¼	910	Santagata N	b	113	16.80	71-23	Lace Pillow 112½ Bright Wings 1174½ Julias Cause 108½	Tired	10
2Feb80- 2Aqu fst 6f	⊡:23⅕	:48⅗	1:14⅗	ⒻClm c-10000	8	3	42½	44	53½	48¾	Santagata N	b	117	3.20	62-27	Bright Wings 1173 Peggy's Pleasure1174JuliasCause1171¾	Evenly	10
28Dec79- 9Aqu fst 6f	⊡:22⅗	:47⅘	1:14⅖	ⒻClm 13000	3	6	75½	54	32	31½	Castaneda M		114	28.80	70-26	Miss L.AndB.116¾ThoughtfulCarol116¾Fannie'sEagle114hd	Rallied	12
17Dec79- 4Aqu my 170	⊡:49⅗	1:16	1:47⅕	ⒻClm 14000	8	1	31½	54½	714	824	Dahlquist T C5		111	40.40	42-27	RhythmWriter1182¾AllHerCharms1161¼RowdieTreasure1142	Tired	8
5Dec79- 9Aqu fst 6f	⊡:22⅖	:46	1:11⅗	ⒻClm 14000	6	12	76½	912	1012	1114	Santagata N		118	16.50	72-13	Intentional Twist 1162½ Honey Tree 116nk Flouncy 1092¼	Outrun	12
24Nov79- 2Aqu fst 6f	:22⅘	:46⅖	1:12⅕	3↑ⒻClm 20000	6	2	32	56	711	712	Santagata N		117	11.60	70-18	Hit Woman 1172¾ Stevlove 1131¼ Honey Tree 114hd	Early ft.	7

LATEST WORKOUTS May 27 Bel 4f fst :48 b — May 20 Bel tr.t 4f fst :50 b — Apr 22 Bel tr.t 4f fst :50⅖ b — Apr 17 Bel tr.t 4f fst :49⅕ b

Both days were Fridays, when the same general class of horses should have been running. With horses of the same class, with published variants approximately the same (only a difference of 2), and with the same racing day involved, the final times of the winners should be approximately the same. On 25Apr80, the winning time was 1:25.4. On 28Mar80, the winning time was 1:26.4, five full ticks slower on a track rated 2 faster, if the variant means anything.

I have no way of knowing what Beyer's and Quirin's variants would have been on either of those days. But since they are based on class ratings, and since general class for the day should have been the same, how would they account for such a wide disparity as five ticks in the winning time? Five ticks can throw your handicapping off from here to Hoboken.

Or, take the race of 5Mar80 for $10,000 fillies with a variant of 22 and a final time of 1:12.2 and compare it with 11Feb80 where you have $14,000 fillies and a variant of 23, and the $10,000 winner ran one tick faster than the $14,000 winner.

You will find distortions like this in every past performance. Take Miss L. And B. from the same *Form.*

Compare the race of 11Feb80 with the race of 14Jan80. The track variant was the same 23 for both days. The difference in class price is inconsequential. The 11Feb80 race was four ticks faster. Both days were Mondays, again when the same class of horses should have been competing. The published variant, no matter what its defects may be, would not likely be that far off.

Miss L. And B. * — Ch. f. 4, by Vertex—Anker Wat, by Edmundo — **$11,500** — Br.—Frank-Anna Stable (Fla) — Tr.—Parisella John — **117**
Own.—Barbati C

Turf Record	St.	1st	2nd	3rd
	2	0	0	0

	St.	1st	2nd	3rd	Amt.
1980	7	1	1	2	$10,970
1979	11	4	1	1	$26,390

19May80- 4Aqu fst 6f	:22⅖	:45⅗	1:10⅘	ⒻClm 14000	3	2	1hd	21½	24	37¼	Martens G	b	113	5.60	82-19	Very Quaint 1154½ General J. 1082¾ Miss L. And B. 113nk	Drifted	8
9May80- 3Aqu my 6f	:22⅘	:46⅗	1:11⅗	3↑ⒻClm 12500	3	3	1½	2½	31½	66¼	Martens G	b	119	*1.80	79-17	Pearl's Pick 119nk My Rosebud 1144¾ General J. 114½	Tired	7
9Apr80- 4Aqu sly 6f	:22⅗	:46⅖	1:12⅘	ⒻClm 12500	4	3	2hd	11½	13	1¾	Martens G	b	117	*.90	79-21	Miss L. And B. 117¾ Pearl's Pick 117½ Open Bar 1151¼	Driving	6
18Feb80- 2Aqu fst 6f	⊡:22⅕	:46	1:12⅗	ⒻClm 12500	3	3	12	11½	11½	21	Martens G	b	117	2.70	80-19	Well Turned Ankle 1171MissL.AndB.1172DutchDitty112no	Gamely	7
11Feb80- 1Aqu fst 6f	⊡:22⅗	:46⅘	1:12⅗	ⒻClm 16000	10	2	31½	31½	33½	79¼	Martens G	b	117	6.00	72-23	Lace Pillow 112½ Bright Wings 1174½ Julias Cause 108½	Tired	10
27Jan80- 2Aqu fst 6f	⊡:22⅖	:46	1:12⅘	ⒻClm 16000	7	2	11	1½	2½	34¼	Martens G	b	119	3.10	76-17	Very Quaint 1063 Flouncy 1171¼ Miss L. And B. 119¾	Tired	10
14Jan80- 3Aqu gd 6f	⊡:23⅕	:47⅗	1:13⅖	ⒻClm 17000	11	5	53½	31½	1½	43¼	Martens G	b	115	5.70	74-23	Diane'sJewel1131¼PssingPtty1122ThoughtfulCrol115no	Weakened	12
28Dec79- 9Aqu fst 6f	⊡:22⅗	:47⅘	1:14⅖	ⒻClm 14000	7	7	32½	31	12	1¾	Martens G	b	116	*2.40	72-26	Miss L.AndB.116¾ThoughtfulCarol116¾Fannie'sEagle114hd	Driving	12
14Dec79- 3Aqu my 6f	⊡:22⅖	:46⅕	1:12⅕	ⒻClm 20000	3	3	21	33½	811	815	Martens G	b	113	4.40	68-18	Admirable Jo 116¾ Shieling 1161¾ Dee'sBallerina1151¼	Tired badly	8
12Nov79- 1Aqu my 6f	:23	:47⅕	1:12⅗	ⒻClm 14000	7	3	15	14	15	12¾	Fell J	b	116	*1.30	80-34	Miss L. And B. 1162¾ Wanena 117hd Honey Tree 1161½	Ridden out	9

LATEST WORKOUTS May 5 Bel tr.t 5f fst 1:03 b — May 1 Bel tr.t 3f my :37⅖ b — Apr 7 Bel tr.t 4f fst :49 b

None of this can take into account varieties of individual performances by horses of the same class and the strategies, or ebb and flow, of the races. These factors have nothing whatever to do with track surface, but the times turned in get involved in the computation. Riskiness and error are all around us.

Perhaps even better than comparing published variants with classes of animals, we can evaluate ratings for different tracks, since a great deal of scientific study has gone into that area, particularly by Dr. Quirin, along with several others. Any player in the East is likely to confront horses with records compiled at several different tracks. Dutch Ditty is an example, having run at Monmouth, Keystone, and Aqueduct, as her record from the March 5, 1980, *Form* reveals.

***Dutch Ditty** Ch. m. 5, by Dike—Tra La La, by Penhurst
$12,500 Br.—Kilcoyne T B (Eng) Tr.—Farro Michael 112[5]
Own.—Tiedemann R T

	St.	1st	2nd	3rd	Amt.
1980	1	0	0	0	$570
1979	7	4	1	1	$17,555

11Feb80- 9Aqu	fst	6f	⊡:22⅗	:47	1:13⅗	ⒻClm 10000	7	2	74¾	74¼	44½	45¾	Lopez C C[5]	b 112	10.10	71-23	SpnishDme1172¼WellTurnedAnkle1171¼OnThCrst1132	No menace	12
18Jun79- 4Mth	gd	6f	:22⅗	:45⅗	1:12⅗	ⒻClm c-5000	8	2	2½	1½	11½	1no	Klidzia S[3]	b 117	*.80	77-20	Dutch Ditty 117no Portage Path 1093 Me Daisy 116no	Driving	11
6Jun79- 3Mth	gd	6f	:22⅕	:45⅘	1:11⅘	ⒻClm 7500	1	3	2hd	11½	15	112	Klidzia S[3]	b 115	*1.60	83-26	Dutch Ditty 11512 Red Lace 1092 FunnySunset1111½	Brisk urging	6
26May79- 6Key	fst	6f	:22⅗	:46⅗	1:12⅗	ⒻClm 11000	8	1	74¼	63¾	62½	55	Klidzia S[3]	b 113	2.90	74-27	Turned Loco 1201½ My Chang 1112 Morning Pet116¾	Forced wide	8
23Apr79- 4Key	fst	6f	:22⅗	:46⅕	1:12⅗	ⒻClm 10000	8	4	73¾	32½	31½	21½	Klidzia S[3]	b 111	7.30	77-19	Turned Loco 1161½ Dutch Ditty 1111½ Parting Now 120hd	Gamely	12
16Apr79- 2Key	fst	6f	:22⅗	:46⅘	1:13⅗	ⒻClm 8500	3	11	74¾	42	22	1hd	Klidzia S[3]	b 113	4.00	75-26	Dutch Ditty 113hd Bimbo Lassie 1163 Beaux Bel 1121	Driving	12
1Apr79- 4Key	fst	6f	:22⅘	:46⅗	1:12	ⒻClm 6500	9	9	64½	1½	11½	1hd	Gomez M A	b 116	4.10	82-19	Dutch Ditty 116hd NorthernVersion1141½Matto'sBaby1203	Lasted	12
23Mar79- 2Key	fst	6f	:22⅗	:46⅗	1:13⅗	ⒻClm 6500	2	11	74	85½	46¾	34¼	Klidzia S[3]	b 113	9.20	71-31	MePlayJoke116¾DontnockTheRock1123½DutchDitty1131	Steadied	11
10Jly78- 2Mth	fst	1	:49	1:14⅗	1:42	ⒻClm 7500	2	6	62¾	32½	3nk	51¾	Klidzia S[3]	b 112	4.90	61-22	Duffy's In Town 118½ Nothings Free 115noDisaca1081¼	Weakened	9
1Jly78- 1Mth	fst	6f	:22⅗	:46⅘	1:13⅕	ⒻClm 9500	1	9	55	65½	62½	75¾	Klidzia S[3]	b 108	5.50	68-20	D. J's Dynamite 1102 Hypsipyle 112¾ Classic Flight 117¾	Tired	9

LATEST WORKOUTS Feb 8 Bel tr.t 3f fst :37⅘ h Feb 5 Bel tr.t 4f fst :51 b Jan 21 Bel tr.t 5f fst 1:05⅗ b Jan 14 Bel tr.t 3f fst :35⅗ b

Dr. Quirin in his monumental study has rated Monmouth and Keystone as exactly even for par times at the same class. Compare the race of 18Jun79 at Monmouth for $5,000 horses where the variant was 20 with the race of 23Apr79 at Keystone where $10,000 horses were competing, and where the variant was 19, only 1 different. The Monmouth track was rated as "good," which should not be as speedy as the "fast" rating for Keystone. Yet, $5,000 horses at Monmouth had a winning time of 1:12.3, the same winning time as the $10,000 winner had at Keystone. A horse at $10,000 should run much faster than a cheap $5,000 animal. Or compare this with the 1Jly70 Monmouth race, with the variant at the same 20, where $9,500 horses ran at 1:13.1, three ticks slower than the $5,000 animals a year later. Can you make sense of this?

Let's do just a bit more. Let's use the Maryland circuit, where horses run at Bowie, Pimlico, Laurel, and up into Delaware in the summer. You have comparable animals at comparable classes in a well-defined circuit. Dr. Quirin has rated Bowie the fastest of the four, and I used to make adjustments for Bowie with that in mind. Quirin rates Bowie four whole ticks faster than Pimlico, which is substantial; Bowie is labeled three faster than Laurel, and one faster than Delaware. All this would have to be calculated in to speed figures if differences in track surfaces were following according to class of horse and par times expected in each class. Now look at Jarett, a medium-price speedster

Jarett Dk. b. or br. h. 5, by Royal Consort—Dall Erin, by Laugh Aloud
Own.—Smith David G $16,500 Br.—Watriss J B (Md) Tr.—Dutrow Richard E **112**

Turf Record					St.	1st	2nd	3rd	Amt.
St.	1st	2nd	3rd	1980	3	0	1	1	$3,060
1	0	0	0	1979	25	3	6	4	$34,068

7Feb80- 7Bow	fst	6f	:22⅘	:46⅖	1:12	Clm 18500	7	2	68½	66	65	56¾	Pino M G	b 114	2.80e	73-32	Eternal Rock 114½ Time To Bid 1141¾ Percy's Game 1224½	Outrun	7
29Jan80- 6Bow	fst	6f	:23⅗	:47⅕	1:13⅕	Clm 18500	1	4	45	43½	45½	21½	Fann B	b 114	2.40e	72-32	Percy's Game 1221½ Jarett 114no Silver Mountain 1181½	Rallied	6
17Jan80- 7Bow	fst	6f	:23⅗	:47⅖	1:12⅗	Clm 16500	4	6	64	53½	46	36½	Pino M G5	b 109	*1.10e	72-30	Percy's Game 1176 Kimani 114nk Jarett 109½	Rallied	7
15Dec79- 2Lrl	gd	1	:47	1:12⅗	1:39	3↑Clm 16000	5	6	58½	57½	43½	42½	Fann B	b 115	2.60	76-18	Kishmere 112½ Alon 1151 Penn Peg 112¾	Evenly	8
6Dec79- 6Lrl	fst	1	:47⅕	1:12	1:37⅖	3↑Clm 16000	5	5	56	35	23	21½	Fann B	b 115	4.20	84-16	Penn Peg 1081½ Jarett 1151½ Mika Song 1152½	Gamely	10
26Nov79- 7Lrl	sly	1	:47⅕	1:12⅗	1:39⅖	3↑Clm 16000	4	4	44	34½	34	56	Fann B	b 115	*2.30	70-25	Restless Ryan 1155 Mika Song 115nk Penn Peg 113¾	Weakened	9
10Nov79- 1Lrl	sly	6f	:22⅘	:46⅖	1:11⅖	3↑Clm 19000	1	7	66	69	56½	57½	Bracciale V Jr	b 114	4.00	82-18	Quill's Turn 110¾ Bold andLucky1155EternalRock115nk	No threat	8
25Oct79- 7Pim	fst	6f	:23⅘	:47⅖	1:12	3↑Clm 16000	3	4	61¾	41	52¾	31½	Bracciale V Jr	b 115	*.60e	85-21	Bet the Limit 113½ Thunder O'Shay 115¾ Jarett 1151	Rallied	9
8Oct79- 3Lrl	fst	6f	:23⅕	:47	1:11⅗	3↑Clm 16000	2	5	52½	42	43	3½	Bracciale V Jr	b 116	*1.20e	87-17	Fiddle Fingers 114hd Kingbird 115½ Jarett 116½	Wide str'ch	9
15Sep79- 6Del	fst	6f	:22⅖	:45⅘	1:11⅕	3↑Clm 18500	1	4	58	57	53	42½	Bracciale V Jr	b 117	*2.40	87-14	Bold and Swift 112½ First Ambassador1101½HunterF.117nk	Rallied	7

LATEST WORKOUTS Jan 25 Bow 4f fst :50 b Jan 3 Bow 6f fst 1:19 b

trained by the formidable Richard E. Dutrow, whose past performance from the *Form* of February 18, 1980, shows races at all four tracks.

Bowie's "fast" track on 7Feb80 shows a :25.3 lead time with a final time of 1:12.0, while "slow" Pimlico on 25Oct79 for horses of slightly less value shows a lead ability time of :24.3 with a final time of 1:12.0. Where is Bowie's faster surface by 4? Then, to the 8Oct79 race at Laurel, with a :24.3 lead time and a 1:11.3 final time, and compare it with the 15Sep79 race at Delaware, with a :25.2 lead ability time and a 1:11.1 final time.

If you are further confused by now, you should be. Go ahead, try to rationalize it, or claim that the variants were vastly different. Who knows? But if you relied on those variants to adjust your times, you would have been entering a jungle of guesswork and supposition.

Now, recall our earlier discussion on comparison of California times and Eastern times, where internal fractions were more similar than final times. And since, in our method of rating ability, we are not using final times, the fractional times, without variants, begin to take on a greater glow of reliability.

While I must concede that differences in track surfaces do have *some* influence (without knowing how much) on ability times, I must stand on the assumption that no known method of computing variants can possibly take into account all the variables. In ignoring the surfaces that do affect times, we still have ten races in every horse's record from which to draw, and that number of races should permit us to get at least two that will reflect the horse's basic ability, which is all we are after.

3. ADJUSTMENT FOR VERY FAST AND VERY SLOW TRACKS

Despite my general adherence to no adjustments for differences between racetracks, insofar as ability times go, it is imperative to take into account the reality that some tracks are indeed extremely fast and some extremely slow. No one disputes that Southern California surfaces are always faster than New

York or Midwestern surfaces, and that horses at Santa Anita and Hollywood Park will ordinarily run both faster final times and faster internal times. When a California horse comes east to run, as in the Triple Crown races, or a New York horse goes west to compete for California gold, it becomes necessary to make some adjustment for inherent differences in track surfaces.

Likewise, there are some tracks that are pitiably slow. Detroit Race Course, for one, is notoriously dead. Calder in Florida is not nearly as resilient as other Eastern tracks. As you play various tracks, you will begin to recognize some of the differences. Dr. Quirin's studies reveal many such differences, but again, as much as I respect his pioneering work, there are many tracks where my own experience will not allow me to accept the validity of comparative time or speed ratings.

I have tried to do it in a different way, by dealing only in broad general classifications. To assist you, and to provide rules for my own work, I have been compelled to place all North American one-mile tracks into three general categories: very fast, reasonably normal, and very slow.

When a horse who has compiled a record at one of the very fast tracks is moving to another track with more normal surfaces, I will have to make allowances by adjusting his ability times downward to make a fair comparison with his rival who has run on an inherently slower surface. Likewise, when a horse moves from a slow track like Calder to a speedy surface like Gulfstream, an allowance upward must be made for the Calder horse.

Every track comparison list I have ever seen has produced disagreements with my own ratings. The one I am about to give will likely receive the same fate from many knowledgeable players. I have personally played a vast number of these tracks, but far from all. I have studied various editions of the *Daily Racing Form,* taken into account Dr. Quirin's estimable researches, and read published "track equalization" charts put out by many persons, and from all this, I have extracted a general summarized rating for use in my own ratings.

WARNING: What I have said in the above paragraphs and in the material immediately to follow is based entirely upon general conditions as I interpreted them in 1980. Speeds of track surfaces change from one season to another, as they did a few years back at Ak-sar-ben in Omaha when an alteration in the top layer of the surface was made. Weather conditions may change them, track superintendents may change them, and other events beyond the knowledge of a mere reader of the *Daily Racing Form* may change them.

Consequently, as you read this in later years, be alert for any changes in general speeds of the tracks listed here. You may find ways of making your own adjustments, but the general theory of classifying tracks in limited categories is what I believe is useful.

Thus, I am providing the following listing based on 1980 observations only, starting with tracks in the very fast category and the number of ticks of adjustment that are necessary when horses that have run on them go to a track that is rated "reasonably normal."

VERY FAST TRACKS AND THE NECESSARY ADJUSTMENT BY ADDITION

- Bay Meadows (BM)—add one tick
- Caliente (AC)—add three ticks
- Del Mar (Dmr)—add three ticks
- Fresno (Fno)—add three ticks
- Golden Gate (GG)—add one tick
- Gulfstream Park (GP)—add one tick
- Hollywood Park (Hol)—add two ticks
- Longacres (Lga)—add three ticks
- Penn National (Pen)—add one tick
- Pleasanton (Pln)—add two ticks
- Sacramento (Sac)—add three ticks
- Santa Anita (SA)—add two ticks
- Stockton (Stk)—add two ticks
- Turf Paradise (TuP)—add two ticks

You will immediately recognize that most of the speedy surfaces are in the Far West. Of the fourteen tracks listed above, only Gulfstream and Penn National are in the South and East. But even in the West, when a Caliente horse comes into Hollywood Park to try to steal a purse, you will have to make a one-tick adjustment.

On the other hand, the very slow tracks are found in the East and South. Here is how I rate the ones with slow surfaces and the adjustments that are necessary.

VERY SLOW TRACKS

Calder (CRC)—subtract one tick
Detroit Race Course (Det)—subtract two ticks
Finger Lakes (FL)—subtract one tick
Tampa Bay Downs (Tam)—subtract one tick
Latonia (Lat)—subtract two ticks
Louisiana Downs (LaD)—subtract one tick
Oaklawn Park (OP)—subtract one tick

All other one-mile tracks are rated "reasonably normal" and no adjustment of any kind need be made.

I am not able to provide calculations for tracks of less than one mile in circumference. Players who have to deal with Sportsman's Park, Hazel Park, Jefferson Downs, Charles Town, Timonium, and other similar ovals will have their problems with this part of the book. I only hope the ingenious among you will be able to apply the principles you learn here and make your own proportional adjustments accordingly.

To show further how this works, when a horse from Calder with an ability time of :25.2 competes with a Hialeah horse with an ability time of :25.1 compiled at Hialeah, the Calder horse would be adjusted by subtracting one tick, which would make his ability time equal to that compiled at Hialeah. Suppose a horse is running at Hialeah with a :25.3 ability time compiled at Calder, and his rival has a :25.1 ability time compiled at Gulfstream, with a third rival having a :25.0 time compiled at Hialeah. The Calder horse would be adjusted by subtracting one to make his comparative ability time :25.2, and the Gulfstream horse would be adjusted by adding one tick to his :25.1 to make his comparative time :25.2, the same as that of the horse at Calder. The horse who compiled :25.0 at Hialeah would require no adjustment, and would rate ahead of both his rivals.

When any horse compiles an ability time at one of the very slow tracks and competes against horses whose ability times were compiled at reasonably normal tracks, the horse from the slow track will have his ability time adjusted by subtracting the requisite ticks set forth above, which will always be one or two. When a horse from a very fast track competes against a horse from a reasonably normal track, the ability time of the horse from the speedier surface will be adjusted by adding the requisite number of ticks set forth here.

All this, of course, borders on the realm of the speculative that I otherwise abhor. I would prefer precise mathematical accuracy in every case, but I know this is simply not possible.

But we have to live with the problem in some way. Horses from Oaklawn do come north to run at Arlington in Chicago, which is reasonably normal. Animals from Latonia move on to Keeneland and Churchill Downs. Calder horses are always competing at other tracks, both in Florida and in the Northeast. I have been at Santa Anita and Hollywood Park on many occasions when horses from Caliente ship up to challenge their higher-priced brothers and sisters.

But all in all, just the recognition that some tracks have a high comparative surface speed brings with it the parallel recognition that horses will not be required to use up as much energy in compiling ability times as horses running on slower surfaces. For example, at "reasonably normal" tracks, we do not add ticks for energy adjustment until a horse's time reaches :47.0 and slower. But a

Caliente sprinter, or even one at Santa Anita, who did not at least turn in a second call time of under 47 seconds in a six-furlong race would be loafing indeed. Turn back to Chapter III and look at past performances of our old friend Potomac Pride. Of the ten races shown, nine of them reveal 4f times under :46.0. Only one, the race of 1Jun79, reached as slow as 47 even.

To use the :47.0 line to add ticks for energy adjustment is unrealistic for the very fast tracks. Therefore, we now modify our energy-adjustment rule. For those ten tracks rated by us as so very fast as to require a comparative adjustment of two or three ticks (but not one), we will draw the energy-adjustment line at :46.0. In other words, when a 4f time is at 46 and change, we add one tick for energy; at 47 and change, two ticks; at 48 and change, three ticks; and so on. The West Coast player will find this a consistent and easy adjustment, and will find it most beneficial to penalize the slow animals who travel 4f in an easy time (on their surfaces) of 46 and change and slower.

This same recognition applies in reverse to the very slow tracks that require a two-tick comparative adjustment. There are but two in my rating, Detroit and Latonia. For these two only, we will start our energy adjustment at 48 and change, by adding one tick. At 49 and change, we add two ticks, and so on. This enables us to treat ability times at these two tracks in a far more realistic way than if left to the normal energy adjustment at the overwhelming majority of tracks.

Thus we have it—the best we can make it at this time, but workable enough to afford a fair degree of confidence as we move on to other important aspects of how to select the investment horse among the first three favorites in any race.

EARLY SPEED AND ITS IMPACT UPON ABILITY

The concept of ability times, as you have seen by now, is one of the cornerstones of this book. It is the prime fundamental upon which ultimate ratings are based. Reliance upon ability times alone will produce, in my opinion, a successful investment experience at the racetrack. But there is a major ingredient, particularly in sprint races, that influences how a horse performs to such a considerable degree that it vastly increases the success of the ultimate selection process. It has an impact on the total point ratings that we intend to use, and therefore it must be employed for maximum gain.

After I had thoroughly explored and tested my ability times and saw how effective they were, I was still concerned why some horses lost consistently when their ability times were superior to those of the animals that were beating them. Likewise, why were certain other horses with strong ability times winning steadily when their margins were not any greater than those of the losers? While it was not realistic to expect the horse top-rated in ability time to win every race, if I could find a pattern separating the losers from the winners, I was sure that my whole method would benefit enormously.

Once I began to analyze the factors separating many winners from losers, it was apparent that the strong front-runners with good ability times were beating their rivals, while the come-from-behind horses, even with good ability times, were having difficulty getting there. Originally, I had thought that my maximum of 8 lengths behind as a base for making energy adjustments of ability times might take care of the lack of early speed, since the horse making up considerable ground would not get full credit for lengths gained. But further study revealed that this was far from sufficient in sprint races to properly evaluate the horse that was quick out of the gate and surging toward the front of the pack.

I had run a series of tests several years ago on early speed, limiting it to the last three races run, and confining it to the first three betting choices. The results were spectacular for a while, and then bogged down, but overall, the formula was still producing a profit when I began working on my ability-time concepts. I became so dazzled with my discovery of ability time that I relegated early speed to the back burner. Even when I read with great interest the findings of Dr. Quirin on the importance of early speed, I had not formulated any method of utilizing it in a rating plan.

But continued reflection, even after I was turning regular profits based upon a combination of ability times and form ratings (which will be taken up in the next chapter), began to reveal how early speed and ability times blended together in sprint races.

Since ability times in sprint races are calculated off the last portion of the race, an early-speed formula to take into account the vital first two furlongs would surely be a significant supplement to the ability-time concept. Thus, all the old research was resurrected, but only as a starting point. Could it be used successfully? There was a compelling logic about it. If a horse could run close to the front in the first two furlongs of the race and still finish with a final quarter time better than any of his rivals, he would be formidable indeed in any sprint race.

Then the next inquiry began on how to evaluate early speed in sprint races, and construct a workable formula for it. Some who have tried to do it have noted positions at the first two calls of a race, looking for 1's and 2's as a sign of early speed, which it is. But a horse running third or fourth by a head or a neck, or even a half-length, may be doing just as well. When the 3's and 4's are added, he looks not quite so good in comparing early speed. Some students who recognize the importance of early speed try to evaluate times, looking for first call sprint times of :22.3 and even :21.4 as signs of early speed, which they are, of course. A half-mile in :44.4 is impressive, as is time in the early 45's. But time is too influenced by the racing surface and racing strategies. A horse leading at the half-mile point in :47.0 might be showing early speed also.

I was more impressed with how close to the leader my horse would run. No matter what position he might be in and no matter how fast or how slow the clock, if he was up battling for the lead or so close to it that he could make his move, he was showing good early speed. He was keeping out of trouble. He was exerting an influence on the race. He was in position to move out ahead of his rivals if his form and good ability to do it were present.

The real test was to work up some kind of point rating for early speed that would properly reflect its place in an overall rating scheme. The old problem, not too much, not too little, was always there to haunt me. After some experimentation, I decided to divide all horses into three groups: (1) those possessing strong early speed, (2) those possessing some early speed in some kind of medium range, and (3) those with no early speed at all. For shorter sprint races, I began to conceive of allowing 6 points for strong early speed, 3 points for medium early speed, and 0 points for no early speed. So far, so good, but how to separate the contenders into these groups?

One way was to add all the lengths behind and find some common divisor, and try to construct a point rating out of it. While possible, something like this bogs down in complexity, and to make our method of play workable for everyone, it has to be something that you can use without carrying around computer, calculator, or slide rule.

To establish a firm early-speed category, a horse that is within 2 lengths of the lead at the first call is showing good early speed. If he does it enough times in his races, he is entitled to merit an early-speed rating of 6. What is enough? At least half of all races shown in his past performances ought to show good early speed to warrant the highest rating of 6. Therefore, if a horse is within 2 lengths of the lead in half his races (five out of ten in a full listing of past performances; two out of four if he has had but four races), he gets the rating of 6.

For medium speed, if a horse is within 5 lengths of the lead at the first call, he is far from out of the race, especially at that early stage. Thus, we can give 3 points for medium speed if a horse is within 5 lengths or less of the lead at half the first calls shown in his past performances.

And it of course follows that if a horse is not within 5 lengths of the lead at the first call in at least half his races in his past performances, he gets nothing for early speed, and scores 0.

This is enormously simple to apply. In fact, it requires hardly any arithmetic at all. Merely by glancing down the first calls in any past performance and counting, you can quickly ascertain whether a horse is sufficiently up front to obtain a score. After doing it a few times, you will become quite adept at it.

There are only a few other things to consider. We still must treat grass and dirt differently. If the race you are considering is on the dirt, you should omit all the grass races showing in a horse's record in counting for early speed. Likewise if you are evaluating a grass race, you should count lengths behind at first calls only in the grass races showing.

The other important consideration is that you not downgrade a horse in the early-speed department because of a troublesome record. A horse may show extremely poor early speed in races of some time period ago, and in his recent races, demonstrate rather convincingly that he has taken a new lease on life and is showing strong early speed. If you genuinely believe that some races are unrepresentative, you may want to eliminate them and try to judge the horse on what he appears to be at the present time, with emphasis on his more recent races.

One way in which I deal with this occurs when a horse shows an uneven number of ratable races, such as nine or seven. Suppose he has nine races on the dirt (with one on the turf to be ignored), and he shows early speed of within 2 lengths of the leader in four of the nine races. Four is obviously not half of nine, but when you look again, that horse in his last race was out in front at the first call. A horse showing early speed in his last race is likely to show it today. Therefore, when a horse's lengths behind at first call in an uneven number of races are within one-half of a rating, I will then look at the last race only. If it is a speed race, I will count it and give the horse the top speed points.

Let me repeat it again by example. Your horse has nine (or seven) races to evaluate. In four of the nine (or three of the seven) he was within 2 lengths of the leader. If he was within 2 lengths in his last race only, I will give him credit for the one-half needed to merit the full 6 points for early speed. That's all there is to it.

Let's do a few examples now to see how it works.

From the *Daily Racing Form* of September 21, 1979, in the second race at the Meadowlands, Royal Rainbow is entered in a six-furlong sprint.

Royal Rainbow — Own.—Lugovich R J — **Ch. f. 4, by Royal Trace—Eds Rainbow, by Royal Note** — **$12,500** — Br.—Miron Julie & Walker (Fla) — Tr.—Schwalben Eugene — **116**

Turf Record	St.	1st	2nd	3rd		St.	1st	2nd	3rd	Amt.
	6	1	1	0	1979	12	1	1	0	$7,157
					1978	13	3	3	0	$8,705

31Aug79- 2Bel	gd	1	:46⅗	1:11⅘	1:37⅘	3↑Ⓕ Clm 12500	5	4	79½	713	718	722	Brocklebank J	119	13.90	57–19	Gusty Nito 1171¼ Free Milady1064½RhythmWriter114hd	No factor	8
16Aug79- 4Mth	fm	1 1/16 Ⓣ	:48⅖	1:14	1:47⅕	3↑Ⓕ Clm 16000	2	7	75	64¾	69¼	77¾	Thomas D B	119	11.50	57–34	Vic'sBoldGal107noPaddockPaula1191½Hagley'sKitten113no	Outrun	10
9Aug79- 6Mth	fm	1 1/16 Ⓣ	:50⅖	1:14⅖	1:46⅗	3↑Ⓕ Clm 16000	3	3	33	41½	43½	44¾	Thomas D B	119	4.80	63–26	Mari Marcher 1192 Ching Mei 1142¼ Indecent 116½	No mishap	8
2Aug79- 5Mth	fm	1 1/16 Ⓣ	:48⅕	1:13	1:45⅗	3↑Ⓕ Clm 12500	1	3	34	31	1hd	11¼	Thomas D B	116	5.90	73–28	Royal Rainbow 1161¼ Brave Queen 108¾ProBello1161¾	Drew clear	7
26Jly79- 6Mth	sly	1 1/16	:47⅖	1:12⅗	1:47⅕	3↑Ⓕ Clm 10000	5	5	53	2½	1hd	2nk	Thomas D B	116	6.70	69–21	Seltrima 114nk Royal Rainbow 1169 Queen Selari 1141	Gamely	8
21Jly79- 9Bel	fst	7f	:23	:46⅘	1:25⅘	3↑Ⓕ Clm 12500	7	5	42½	45½	46½	512	Brocklebank J	117	15.50	61–24	Gusty Nito 1134 Kelly's Cat 117no Take MyBluesAway1176¼	Tired	9
1Jly79- 8FL	gd	6f	:23⅘	:47⅗	1:13	3↑ Allowance	2	6	65¾	66	46½	48¼	Cordero A E	111	17.10	81–17	Broadway Buck 112hd Angel Ahead 1228 Do It To It115hd	Rallied	8
24Jun79- 6FL	fst	1	:48⅖	1:14	1:40⅘	3↑ Allowance	2	5	76	52½	42	53¼	Cordero A E	112	8.30	77–16	Conciliere 117nk Pierre's King 115¾ Never Today 1151	Outrun	7
17Jun79- 4FL	fst	6f	:23⅗	:47	1:12⅘	3↑Ⓕ Allowance	3	2	77½	77½	67	34¾	Ayala L	116	30.60 [D]	85–12	SerenadedLady1153½NeverTody1151½[D]RoylRinbow1161½	Bore out	7
17Jun79–Disqualified and placed seventh																			
10Jun79- 5FL	fst	6f	:23⅖	:47⅕	1:12⅕	3↑ Allowance	5	5	55	78¼	711	714	Plotkin N	110	52.10	79–12	Arleno 122hd Modern Owl 1243 Top Jet 1191	Outrun	7

This is a dirt race, as most 6f events are, and this requires us to delete the grass races showing, leaving us with 7 ratable races. Run your finger down the first calls showing. In none of the races was she within 2 lengths of the leader. The 2½ lengths behind on 21Jly79 is not enough. Thus, no 6 early-speed points for Royal Rainbow. Now, run down the lines once more, checking for those races where Royal Rainbow was within 5 lengths of the leader. There are three, those of 26Jly79, of 21Jly79, and of 10Jun79. That makes three out of seven. And now we look at the last race to see how it rated. If Royal Rainbow had been within 5 lengths of the lead in her last race, we would have awarded her 3 points for medium early speed. But this was not the case, and Royal Rainbow gets a 0 rating in the early-speed department.

From the same Meadowlands race, here is another one, which is relatively easy, as we look at the record of Answer Is No.

Answer Is No *

Own.—Tronco W L JR

B. f. 3, by Staunch Avenger—Death March, by Bazaar

$12,500

Br.—Farish W S III (Tex)

Tr.—Tronco William L jr

112

									St.	1st	2nd	3rd	Amt.
								1979	14	2	2	3	$15,033
								1978	0	M	0	0	

7Sep79- 2Med fst 6f	:22⅖	:45⅗	1:11⅗	ⓕClm c-10000	5 5	5⁵	42½	21½	32½	Wacker D J⁵	109	*1.60	84–13 Luvinheriseasy 109² Golden Disc 114½ Answer Is No 109⁴	Hung 9
21Aug79- 2Mth fst 6f	:21⅖	:45	1:11⅛	ⓕClm 13000	1 6	41½	44½	46½	67½	Brumfield D	114	5.70	77–15 Miss Metric 115½ Bert Joann Be 115¼ Silver Limerick 115²	Tired 9
9Aug79- 5Mth fst 6f	:22	:45	1:10⅜	ⓕClm 15000	2 5	32½	33½	35½	54½	Brumfield D	114	5.00	82–15 Love's Pleasure 119 31 Bert Joann Be 1141½ Susie Sue112ⁿᵒ	Tired 7
30Jly79- 5Mth fst 6f	:22½	:45⅖	1:11	ⓕClm 15500	2 3	1ʰᵈ	11	2½	22½	Brumfield D	114	2.40	82–18 Susie Sue 1092¼ Answer Is No 1142½ Bert Joann Be 118³	2nd best 6
10Jly79- 3Mth fst 6f	:21½	:44⅗	1:09⅗	ⓕClm 15000	4 5	51¾	43½	2⁵	21⁰	Brumfield D	116	2.10	81–10 WillowBottomMiss110¹⁰AnswrIsNo116½SmokOnWtr115⁴	2nd best 6
28Jun79- 2Mth fst 6f	:21½	:45	1:11⅘	ⓕClm c-10000	9 6	5⁵	44	33	11½	Wacker D J⁷	110	*2.20	81–18 Answer Is No 110¹½Love'sPleasure119½BobbiSue107ⁿᵒ	Drew clear 10
12Jun79- 4Mth fst 6f	:22½	:46	1:12⅜	ⓕClm 12500	7 1· 31½	33	34	3ⁿᵏ	Mackaben B W⁵	113	5.20	78–16 Brothers Double 115ʰᵈBertJoannBe121ⁿᵏAnswerIsNo113⁴½	Evenly 10
1Jun79- 6Mth fst 6f	:21½	:45	1:10½	ⓕClm 20000	6 2· 2²	36½	41²	51⁴	Mackaben B W⁵	114	5.60	75–19 Dr. Renzi 114⁸ Secret Affair 114² Susie Sue 115²	Tired 6
23May79- 4Pim sly 6f	:23⅗	:47½	1:13⅗	3＋ⓂMd 25000	1 4· 2ʰᵈ	2ʰᵈ	11	1ʰᵈ	Pino M G⁵	107	*3.20	77–24 Answer Is No 107ʰᵈ Her Angel 114⁴ Curlew's Cry 1122½	All out 11
12May79- 2Pim fst 6f	:23½	:47½	1:12½	3＋ⓂMd 25000	2 3	2⁵	12½	12	2ⁿᵏ	Pino M G⁵	107	25.50Ⓓ	85–14 Cleverness 115ⁿᵏ ⒹAnswer Is No 1072½ Nice Choice113ⁿᵒ	Bore in 9

12May79-Disqualified and placed third

There are ten races for us to evaluate. Starting at the top of the first call position and running down, we can count six races where Answer Is No was within 2 lengths of the lead or better. We stop right there. This filly gets a 6 in the early-speed department.

After we calculate each horse's ability times, therefore, we will look down all the races in his past performances to find his early speed rating, using either 6, 3, or 0 points in races of six and a half furlongs or less. This early-speed credit will be added to the point total, along with any points for form (which will be discussed later), and the total will be the final rating for the horse.

[handwritten: ✗ if todays race is 6½ or less!]

But what about early-speed totals for distances longer than six and a half furlongs? The longer the distance involved in the race, the less impact early speed will have on the outcome. I have found that at races of seven furlongs and one mile, early speed is still important, but has a lesser effect on the race than at shorter distances. Therefore, for races of seven furlongs and one mile only, I will award 4 points for good early speed, 2 points for medium early speed, and 0 points for no early speed at all. We will use the same 2-lengths-or-less standard in one-half the races for early speed, and the same 5-lengths-or-less standard at the first call for medium speed.

[handwritten: ✗ Todays Race of 7 or 8 F.]

For races longer than one mile, we will not factor early speed in at all. At *[handwritten: ✗]* some tracks, races of a mile forty yards or even a mile seventy yards are not much longer than the mile race, but the line must be drawn somewhere, and beyond one mile, the rule is that early speed will not be factored in as a point ingredient in our ratings. Of course, I am aware that in some distance races, early speed can be an important advantage, particularly where distance races begin close to a turn and the horse able to get out in front possesses an excellent chance to win.

But on the whole, the use of the ability-time add-ons for energy, based upon slow first call times (which takes into account lengths behind), is sufficient to take care of the early-speed problem in distance races. More important, as all writers properly point out, the running style in distance races is different from that in sprints, and many powerful competitors regularly win by coming from off the pace.

Now, let's progress into blending early-speed points in with ability points, and see how it affects our ratings.

From almost any back issue of the *Daily Racing Form,* one may find examples of how early speed may influence both our selections and the outcome of a race. An excellent demonstration may be taken from the *Form* of September 13, 1980, in the seventh race at Bowie, where some rather fast reasonably priced claimers were competing at six furlongs. Some of the good animals in the race lacked recent form, which negated their chances. But the two top betting choices, Flashy Guy and Pappy's Catfish, appeared almost evenly matched. Flashy Guy was a slight favorite, with the board showing 2-1 odds for him and 5-2 for Pappy's Catfish. How could a good handicapper choose between these two tough contenders?

We'll first look at the favorite, Flashy Guy, to see how his ability rates and also to test his early speed.

Flashy Guy — **B. g. 7, by Distinctive—Flash Can, by Tuscany**
Own.—Branch R W — **$23,500** — **Br.—Helmore Farm (Md)** — **Tr.—Dutrow Richard E** — **117**

Turf Record	St.	1st	2nd	3rd		St.	1st	2nd	3rd	Amt.
	36	3	4	9	1980	12	4	1	2	$23,526
					1979	21	5	8	1	$45,470

24Aug80- 4Del	fst	6f	:22	:45	1:10⅖	3↑ Clm 23500	3	5	69½	613	511	34	Pino M G	b 122	3.60	89-10	PashanatReb117½OscarOrlando1193½FlashyGuy122hd	Alter course	6
6Aug80- 5Del	fst	6f	:22⅖	:45⅖	1:10⅕	3↑ Clm 23500	4	2	54¾	44	22	1hd	Pino M G	b 119	2.60	94-14	Flashy Guy 119hd Pashanat Reb 1172½ Elyse's Pride 1171	Driving	7
26Jly80- 8Del	fm	1 1/16 Ⓣ	:47⅗	1:12	1:44⅕	3↑ Allowance	9	6	74¾	54	57½	44½	Pino M G	b 117	9.70	78-12	Rolfson 1171½ Ad Infinitum 1171¾ Mod John 1081¼	Mild rally	10
10Jly80- 7Bow	fst	7f	:23⅕	:46⅖	1:24⅕	3↑ Clm 23500	6	4	32½	32	31½	11½	Pino M G	b 119	*.70	84-20	Flashy Guy 1191½ Eternal Rock 105nk Lord Louis1171½	Drew clear	7
2Jly80- 8Bow	fst	6f	:22⅘	:46	1:11	3↑ Allowance	5	6	86¾	56	45	42¼	Pino M G	b 117	*1.60	83-24	Gantlet Dancer 113hd Ed's Boy 117nk Bold Brawler 1172	Late bid	8
9Jun80- 6Bow	fst	6f	:23	:46⅕	1:11⅕	Clm 23500	5	6	74½	66½	52¼	1¾	Pino M G	b 114	3.30	84-28	Flashy Guy 114¾ Bold Brawler 1141 Recitalist 1122¼	Driving	7
28Apr80- 6Pim	my	1 1/16	:47⅕	1:12⅖	1:46⅕	Clm 23500	1	2	25	26	45	33	Bracciale V Jr	b 115	2.40	71-25	GreatCombination114½MajesticFlsh1182½FlshyGuy115½	Weakened	6
18Apr80- 7Pim	fst	1 1/16	:48⅖	1:13⅖	1:45⅗	Clm 23500	3	1	11	1hd	23	25	Bracciale V Jr	b 114	3.90	73-18	TimeForFun1195FlashyGuy1141MajesticFlsh1172¼	Best of others	7
2Apr80- 7Pim	fst	6f	:23⅖	:46⅘	1:12⅕	Clm 18500	4	7	66	57	47	1no	Kupfer T	b 114	3.40e	85-22	Flashy Guy 114no Polar Point 1192 Buckley 109½	Driving	10
6Feb80- 7Bow	fst	1 1/16	:49⅗	1:14⅕	1:46⅖	Clm 18500	4	1	11½	2hd	43½	45¼	Pino M G	b 114	3.70	69-31	FoolishTimes1122¼PortConwyLn1143J.P.Mommy114no	Weakened	7

LATEST WORKOUTS Sep 10 Bow 4f my :50⅖ h Aug 20 Del 5f gd 1:01 h Aug 3 Del 4f fst :47⅖ h ●Jly 20 Del 5f fst 1:01 h

This veteran gelding has been a strong, consistent winner for trainer Richard Dutrow, one of the outstanding handlers on the Maryland circuit. His last race was not quite up to his usual standard, but he closed powerfully, gaining enough to easily qualify him on form. In his race of 6Aug80, he had an ability time of :24.1, off a :24.4 lead time reduced by three ticks for gain. On 9Jun80, there was a :25.0 lead time in his race, which he reduced by four ticks off his gain, but the one tick added for energy left him with a :24.2, still very strong.

We now look up and down his first calls to see how his early speed functioned. One race on the grass is eliminated, leaving nine for us to consider. Twice among the 9 races he was better than 2 lengths from the lead, since in both he was the actual leader. But that is all, and that is not enough to warrant a 6-point early-speed rating. But we can quickly see four additional races where he was within 5 lengths or less of the lead at the first call, which awards medium early speed to him, and a rating of 3 points. Not bad.

How does Pappy's Catfish rate? As we look at his record, there is no need to do any calculation on early speed, for merely by glancing, you can tell that he was always on the lead or so near to it that he will merit the top rating of 6 points without any further looking. But what do his ability points show?

Pappy's Catfish — Ch. g. 6, by Berseemboro—Sena Vee, by Admiral Vee — $18,500 — Br.—Peppermint Farms Inc (N Mex) — Tr.—Wolfendale W H III — 1125

Own.—Wolfendale W H III

Turf Record: St. 7, 1st 4, 2nd 0, 3rd 1

	St.	1st	2nd	3rd	Amt.
1980	21	9	3	1	$34,320
1979	25	4	7	6	$18,810

5Sep80-	4Del	fm	5f	Ⓣ	:22⅗	:46⅖	:58⅗	3↑	Clm 17500	4	3	2hd	1½	12	11¼	Pino M G		118	*1.40	94-20	Pappy's Catfish 1181¼ Repop 1141 Elyse's Pride 1151¼	Driving	6
22Aug80-	8Tim	fst	*6½f		:22⅘	:46⅖	1:18⅕	3↑	Allowance	5	6	31	1hd	11½	2¾	Grove P		116	*.60	90-17	Vaskaan 116¾ Pappy's Catfish 1164 Starullah 113nk	Lugged in	6
15Aug80-	6Tim	fst	*6½f		:22⅗	:46⅖	1:17⅗	3↑	Clm 16000	6	3	1hd	14	14	13	Grove P		113	*.50	94-15	Pppy'sCtfish1133PiedmontPt1161ChristophrStrong1131½	Handily	6
9Aug80-	7Del	fm	5f	Ⓣ	:22⅗	:46⅘	:59⅕	3↑	Clm 11500	4	2	1hd	1½	12	15½	Pino M G		119	*.70	91-27	Pappy's Catfish 1195½ Degas III 1171¾ PampasVillain110¾	Driving	7
29Jly80-	6Tim	gd	*6½f		:22⅘	:46⅖	1:17⅕	3↑	Clm 10000	6	2	2hd	14	14	15	Ussery R A		113	*2.30	96-19	Pappy'sCatfish1135Hgley'sMgic1142½ChrlieRudolphi1134	Handily	7
18Jly80-	6Bow	fst	6f		:22⅗	:45⅗	1:10⅗		Clm c-6500	6	2	1hd	1½	12½	16	Lindberg G		114	*1.30	87-20	Pappy's Catfish 1146 Act Icy 1071¾ Sagara 1121½	Handily	6
14Jun80-	2Bow	fst	6f		:23	:46⅖	1:11⅘		Clm c-6500	8	1	2½	1hd	21	34½	Kupfer T		114	*2.20	76-19	VirginTerritory1091½FinncePrinc1193Pppy'sCtfish1141	Weakened	9
5Jun80-	6Bow	fst	6f		:23⅕	:46⅖	1:11⅘		Clm 6500	5	1	12	11	1hd	2hd	Kupfer T		117	2.30	81-21	LndLightly112hdPppy'sCtfish1173½VirginTrritory1051¼	Just failed	7
26May80-	2Bow	fst	6f		:22⅗	:46	1:12⅕		Clm 8500	2	8	1hd	2½	23	45¼	Black K7	b	112	3.80	74-21	What If 1144 Sonny Spears 1141 Bardo 114nk	Steadied	8
17May80-	2Pim	fst	6f		:23⅕	:46⅕	1:12		Clm 8500	5	1	3nk	33	24	42	Kupfer T		119	4.10	84-12	Cari's Champ 1122 Nyree 114no Gallant Patriot 107no	Tired	9

LATEST WORKOUTS Aug 19 Del 4f sly :52 b

You can readily see that this is a fast horse. But now certain problems arise, and one of the reasons I have selected this race is to show you how to deal with situations that are not ordinarily covered. You see several races run at Timonium, which happens to be a five-furlong track in the Baltimore area where Maryland horses compete in midsummer. Veteran players soon learn characteristics of most tracks and readily recognize that Timonium is not one of the major one-mile tracks in the country. Less familiar racegoers may not know this offhand, but if you encounter a track that is not within your immediate range of knowledge, you had better try to find out at least enough about it to know how ability times can be compared to those at other tracks. An excellent source book, largely overlooked by the racing public, is Tom Ainslie's *Encyclopedia of Thoroughbred Handicapping* (Wm. Morrow & Co., 1978), which provides some information on every racetrack in the country.

Let's look at the Timonium races, at six and a half furlongs. On 15Aug80, we adjust the time of 1:17.2 to 1:11.0 for 6f. This gives us a lead time of :24.3. In the 29Jly80 race, the 1:17.1 time comes out to 1:10.4 for 6f and gives us a lead time of :24.2, even better. These are true times, since Pappy's Catfish established them all by himself. But a horse running six and a half furlongs on a five-furlong track must go around two turns, which hampers his time as compared to a sprint race around one turn. So an adjustment must be made for the two turns. Because Timonium is a fairly fast track and my comparison of its times over the years with the other Maryland ovals shows that its times are not too far off, I make only a one-tick adjustment in favor of the Timonium times because of the two turns. Therefore, we will now reduce the two Timonium times for Pappy's Catfish by one tick each, leaving him with ability times of :24.1 and :24.2, which you will now see are exactly the same as those of Flashy Guy.

Odds	Horse	Ability		A Pts		ES	Total
2.3	Flashy Guy	:24.1	:24.2	19	18	3	40
2.8	Pappy's Catfish	:24.1	:24.2	19	18	6	43

Without the early-speed factor, these two horses would be tied in total points (assuming form was equally qualifying, which it is). It would be hazardous indeed to try to choose between them on ability points alone. But the use of early-speed points propels Pappy's Catfish into a higher total, and he would thus become our selection.

The chart of the race makes this choice look good.

SEVENTH RACE
Bowie
SEPTEMBER 13, 1980

6 FURLONGS. (1.08) CLAIMING. Purse $8,000. 3-year-olds and upward. Weight, 3-year-olds, 118 lbs. Older, 122 lbs. Non-winners of two races since August 9, allowed 3 lbs. A race 5 lbs. Claiming price $23,500; for each $2,500 to $18,500 1 lb. (Races where entered for $16,000 or less not considered).

Value of race $8,000, value to winner $4,800, second $1,760, third $960, fourth $480. Mutuel pool $62,125. Exacta Pool $91,235.

Last Raced	Horse	Eqt.A.Wt	PP	St	¼	½	Str	Fin	Jockey	Cl'g Pr	Odds $1
5Sep80 4Del1	Pappy's Catfish	6 112	6	2	2½	11	13	1nk	Black K5	18500	2.80
2Sep80 7Del6	Polar Point	5 117	9	1	41	53	4½	21¾	Bracciale V Jr	23500	5.80
24Aug80 4Del3	Flashy Guy	b 7 117	2	6	62	63	65	3¾	Pino M G	23500	2.30
30Aug80 8Tim3	Recitalist	b 6 119	1	7	55	3½	3½	42¾	Turcotte R L	23500	6.10
6Sep80 8Tim4	Piedmont Pete	4 119	8	5	1hd	22	2hd	51¾	Lindberg G	23500	5.90
5Sep80 8Del6	More Pleasure	b 4 117	5	4	31	42	51	6¾	McCarron G	23500	16.00
23Aug80 7Del6	Fierce Invader	5 117	3	9	9	9	9	7½	Wright D R	23500	11.20
20Jly80 7Pen5	Minideck	b 5 117	7	8	8½	8½	7½	8½	Iliescu A	23500	77.80
21Aug80 8Tim5	Ken's Turn	b 6 117	4	3	72	7hd	8hd	9	Gilbert R B	23500	31.30

OFF AT 4:01 EDT. Start good, Won driving. Time, :23, :46⅗, :58⅗, 1:12 Track fast.

$2 Mutuel Prices:

6-PAPPY'S CATFISH		7.60	4.00	3.00
9-POLAR POINT			5.80	4.00
2-FLASHY GUY				2.80

$2 EXACTA 6-9 PAID $65.00.

Ch. g, by Berseemboro—Sena Vee, by Admiral Vee. Trainer Wolfendale W H III. Bred by Peppermint Farms Inc (N Mex).

PAPPY'S CATFISH took the lead from the inside leaving the backstretch, opened a clear lead in mid stretch then was under strong handling to hold off POLAR POINT. The latter finished with a rush on the outside. FLASHY GUY rallied belatedly. RECITALIST finished evenly outside. PIEDMONT PETE set or forced the pace outside before tiring. MORE PLEASURE had position inside, lacked a rally.

You can see that Pappy's Catfish, with his strong early speed, was only a head behind another speedball, Piedmont Pete, at the first call. Then he roared off in front and built up a 3-length lead at the stretch call, which was good enough to hold off the challenge of Polar Point. Flashy Guy, in the comment below the chart, "rallied belatedly." These "rallied belatedly" horses are not for us. He didn't have the early-speed consistency to match Pappy's Catfish and despite his strong finish, could not beat his major rival.

It should be rather obvious that all races won't turn out this way. Sometimes the expected early speed will not be displayed, but that is because nothing is certain in this game. My point is that early speed will prevail *far more often than not,* and that you will profit greatly by factoring it into a point rating as we do in this book.

I will now demonstrate by another race how early speed, or lack of it, can be overpowering in another area, and obedience to its tenets will save you money in situations like the kind that faced racegoers back on Friday, September 21, 1979, in the ninth race at Belmont, where the *Daily Racing Form* of that date revealed no early speed among the three top betting choices.

The favorite that day, in a six-and-a-half-furlong sprint for two-year-olds, was Cabin Proof, showing on the board at 2-1.

9 BELMONT

6½ FURLONGS. (1.15⅕) CLAIMING. Purse $12,000. 2-year-olds. Weights, 120 lbs. Claiming price $25,000; for each $2,500 to $15,000 2 lbs.

Cabin Proof — Own.—Garren M M — **$25,000** — B. c. 2, by Cabin—Border Try, by Saidam — Br.—Hancock III & Peters (Ky) — Tr.—Puentes Gilbert — **120**

Turf Record St.	1st	2nd	3rd		St.	1st	2nd	3rd	Amt.
1	0	0	0	1979	12	2	1	2	$27,634

15Sep79- 3Bel	fst	6f	:22⅕ :45⅗ 1:11⅖	Clm 35000	1	5	$3^{6\frac{1}{2}}$	3^{5}	4^{4}	$4^{4\frac{1}{4}}$	Amy J	113	*2.50	81-11 SirSizzlingNehoc117^{3}SovereignRule115^{hd}LittleMarker$113^{1\frac{1}{4}}$	Tired	7
8Sep79- 3Bel	fst	6f	:22⅘ :46⅕ 1:12⅕	Clm 40000	3	5	$7^{4\frac{3}{4}}$	6^{5}	5^{4}	$3^{1\frac{1}{4}}$	Amy J	112	15.00	80-17 Little Lenny 116½ Beforehand 115¾ Cabin Proof 112^{hd}	Rallied	9
1Sep79- 3Bel	fst	6f	:22⅘ :46⅘ 1:13⅖	Clm 25000	7	6	$6^{7\frac{3}{4}}$	$4^{3\frac{1}{4}}$	1^{hd}	$1^{1\frac{3}{4}}$	Amy J	116	3.60	75-19 Cabin Proof $116^{1\frac{3}{4}}$ Coq Au Vin $120^{2\frac{1}{4}}$ Regal Roy 120^{nk}	Drew clear	8
22Aug79- 2Sar	fm	$1\frac{1}{16}$	Ⓣ:46⅗ 1:11⅖ 1:43	Allowance	7	6	$6^{6\frac{1}{2}}$	7^{6}	9^{13}	9^{21}	Amy J	114	17.90e	61-13 Sportful 117^{nk} Capital Punishment$114^{3\frac{3}{4}}$BagdadChief114^{2}	Outrun	10
12Aug79- 4Sar	sly	7f	:23 :46⅗ 1:26⅕	Clm 35000	6	3	$5^{6\frac{1}{2}}$	4^{3}	$4^{3\frac{1}{2}}$	4^{8}	Amy J	113	5.90e	63-25 Little Lenny 120½ Boomie Two $117^{6\frac{1}{2}}$ Dover Prince 115^{1}	Evenly	8
5Aug79- 2Sar	fst	6f	:22⅕ :45⅖ 1:10⅘	Allowance	6	5	$5^{4\frac{1}{2}}$	$6^{5\frac{1}{2}}$	$7^{7\frac{1}{2}}$	8^{9}	Maple E	b 113	20.70	77-14 Gratification $118^{1\frac{1}{4}}$ Self Pressured 113no Sportful $118^{2\frac{3}{4}}$	Tired	8
25Jly79- 8Bel	fst	6f	:22⅘ :46⅕ 1:11⅘	Tremont	6	5	$8^{4\frac{1}{2}}$	$7^{6\frac{3}{4}}$	$6^{6\frac{1}{2}}$	$6^{8\frac{1}{2}}$	Asmussen C B	115	42.90	74-17 I Speedup 115^{2} J. P. Brother 122no Blues Alley 122½	Outrun	8
15Jly79- 7Bel	fst	5½f	:22⅗ :46⅗ 1:06	Allowance	1	1	$5^{4\frac{1}{2}}$	$4^{2\frac{1}{4}}$	$3^{1\frac{1}{2}}$	$3^{1\frac{3}{4}}$	Asmussen C B	113	11.80	83-19 My Pal Jeff 114no Noble Ties $105^{1\frac{3}{4}}$ Cabin Proof $113^{2\frac{1}{2}}$	Bumped	6
18Jun79- 8Bel	gd	5½f	:22⅗ :45⅖ 1:05⅕	Youthful	5	2	$7^{6\frac{3}{4}}$	7^{5}	7^{10}	6^{9}	Amy J	117	27.60	80-16 Blues Alley $117^{2\frac{1}{4}}$ Dr. Maguire 117½ Stiff Sentence117^{4}	No factor	7
30May79- 8Bel	my	5½f	:22⅖ :46⅘ 1:05⅘	Novelty	3	4	$5^{6\frac{1}{2}}$	$5^{7\frac{1}{2}}$	5^{3}	2^{4}	Amy J	119	17.80	82-18 Encourage 119^{4} Cabin Proof $119^{1\frac{3}{4}}$BudasTime119^{nk}	Finished well	5

LATEST WORKOUTS Sep 14 Bel tr.t 3f fst :36 h — Aug 29 Bel tr.t 4f sly :49 h — Aug 18 Sar tr.t 4f fst :50 b — Aug 4 Sar 3f fst :37⅘ b

Leaving aside his qualifications on form, about which more will be said later, we first calculate ability times. Without taking you through the steps, there is a :25.1 for 30May79 and a :25.3 out of the 8Sep79 race. Now, let's do our work on early speed, eliminating the one grass race showing. There are no races where Cabin Proof was within 2 lengths of the lead at the first call. Checking for races where he was within 5 lengths of the lead at the first call, we are able to find four, which leaves us with four out of nine. We then look at the last race to see if there was early speed, and find none. Therefore, Cabin Proof gets 0 points for early speed.

The second betting choice was Coq Au Vin, and look at how far he usually trailed his field at the first call:

Coq Au Vin — Own.—Tayhill Stable — **$25,000** — Dk. b. or br. c. 2, by Chieftain—Lost In Paris, by Kauai King — Br.—Lin-Drake Farm (Fla) — Tr.—Peterson Douglas — **120**

Turf Record St.	1st	2nd	3rd		St.	1st	2nd	3rd	Amt.
2	0	0	0	1979	7	1	1	0	$9,160

15Sep79- 3Bel	fst	6f	:22⅕ :45⅗ 1:11⅖	Clm 35000	2	3	7^{11}	7^{10}	6^{12}	5^{8}	Lovato F[10]	103	5.70	77-11 SirSizzlingNehoc117^{3}SovereignRule115^{hd}LittleMrker$113^{1\frac{1}{4}}$	Outrun	7
8Sep79- 3Bel	fst	6f	:22⅘ :46⅕ 1:12⅕	Clm 40000	8	7	9^{11}	9^{10}	8^{6}	$7^{2\frac{1}{4}}$	Lovato F[10]	102	10.20	79-17 Little Lenny 116½ Beforehand 115¾ Cabin Proof 112^{hd}	Outrun	9
1Sep79- 3Bel	fst	6f	:22⅘ :46⅘ 1:13⅖	Clm 30000	3	4	$4^{3\frac{1}{2}}$	3^{3}	4^{2}	$2^{1\frac{3}{4}}$	Santiago A	120	*1.70	73-19 Cabin Proof $116^{1\frac{3}{4}}$ Coq Au Vin $120^{2\frac{1}{4}}$ Regal Roy 120^{nk}	2nd best	8
17Aug79- 4Mth	fst	6f	:22⅕ :46 1:11	Md 22000	8	5	$7^{6\frac{3}{4}}$	2^{1}	1^{3}	1^{8}	Bailey J D	118	*1.60	85-16 Coq Au Vin 118^{8} Finest Sterling$114^{1\frac{1}{2}}$DeanDavid107^{hd}	Ridden out	9
8Aug79- 3Sar	fm	1	[T]:47⅘ 1:12⅗ 1:38	Md Sp Wt	8	10	10^{10}	9^{12}	9^{14}	9^{15}	Santiago A	118	11.70	— — CurrntWnnr118^{no}FrnchCut118^{nk}LonsomCowboy118^{2}	Forced wide	10
30Jly79- 6Bel	fm	7f	Ⓣ:23⅕ :46⅗ 1:25⅕	Md Sp Wt	2	10	$7^{3\frac{3}{4}}$	$8^{8\frac{1}{4}}$	6^{6}	$5^{8\frac{1}{4}}$	Vasquez J	118	4.00	70-13 Joanie's Chief 118^{3} French Cut 118¾ I'mRegalToo$118^{2\frac{1}{4}}$	Stumbled	10
13Jly79- 4Bel	fst	5½f	:22⅘ :46⅘ 1:06⅕	Md Sp Wt	9	7	9^{14}	9^{13}	$9^{9\frac{3}{4}}$	$4^{5\frac{3}{4}}$	Vasquez J	118	13.20	78-16 Alla Breva 118^{hd} Foolscap 118^{2} Impressive Prince$118^{3\frac{3}{4}}$	Late foot	10

LATEST WORKOUTS Sep 14 Bel tr.t 3f fst :35⅘ h — Aug 16 Bel tr.t 3f fst :36⅖ h — Jly 26 Bel [T] 5f fm 1:03⅕ b

First of all, this colt has abysmal form and would be eliminated under the form rules you will read in the next chapter. But for now, we are concerned primarily with the use of the early-speed factor in our handicapping ratings. Ability times are strong here, as we compute a :24.4 in the 17Aug79 race and a

:25.3 for 8Sep79. To evaluate early speed, we omit the two grass races, leaving only five from which to determine how much early speed, if any, there was. In only one of these races was Coq Au Vin within 5 lengths of the lead at the first call. He, too, gets 0 for early speed.

The third betting choice is Sweeten, who shows 4-1 on the board. Another animal, Sunshine Sam, also shows 4-1, but since Sweeten has more money wagered in the win pool, we will consider him the third favorite momentarily, although, as previously indicated, when two horses are approximately tied in the odds, you will be compelled to rate both of them to determine which should be the true third favorite in our selection method. But let's look first at Sweeten.

Sweeten — Dk. b. or br. c. 2, by Tentam—Sweet and Low, by Double Jay
Own.—Schwartz B K — $25,000 — Br.—Mill House (Md) — Tr.—Trevato Joseph A — 113⁷

Turf Record: St. 1 1st 1 2nd 0 3rd 0 — 1979: St. 7 1st 1 2nd 2 3rd 0 Amt. $12,040

1Sep79- 3Bel	fst	6f	:22⅘	:46⅘	1:13⅖	Clm 30000	1	3	88¼	76¼	65½	64¾	Gonzalez M A7	113	5.30	70-19 Cabin Proof 1161¾ Coq Au Vin 1202¼ Regal Roy 120nk	Outrun	8
12Aug79- 4Sar	sly	7f	:23	:46⅗	1:26⅕	Clm 35000	5	2	35	53½	55	612	Fell J	116	4.30	59-25 Little Lenny 120½ Boomie Two 1176½ Dover Prince 1151	Tired	8
5Aug79- 2Sar	fst	6f	:22⅕	:45⅖	1:10⅘	Allowance	7	4	76½	86¾	87¾	79	Fell J	113	24.60	77-14 Gratification 1181¼ Self Pressured 113no Sportful1182¾	No threat	8
26Jly79- 2Bel	fm	7f	Ⓣ:23⅘	:46⅗	1:25⅖	Md 45000	7	3	66½	68¼	32	1hd	Fell J	116	*2.60	77-21 Sweeten 116hd Sun Party 1143 Pi's Guy 118¾	Driving	10
20Jly79- 4Bel	fst	6f	:23	:47⅖	1:13⅕	Md 50000	3	4	63	77¾	79½	79¾	Fell J	118	*1.50	66-21 SelfPressured1182¼LittleLnny1141½GivItAChnc118½	Bumped turn	8
28Jun79- 5Bel	fst	5½f	:22⅗	:46⅗	1:06⅖	Md 45000	2	5	56	55½	33½	2nk	Fell J	116	*2.00	83-22 Dover Prince 118nk Sweeten 1161SelfPressured116½	Finished fast	10
21Jun79- 6Bel	fst	5½f	:23⅕	:48	1:07⅗	Md c-35000	6	6	57	54½	23	21½	Maple E	118	*1.40	75-26 Regal Roy 1181½ Sweeten 1182¾ Duffys Brother 1183	Gamely	8

LATEST WORKOUTS Sep 17 Aqu 4f fst :48 h

We are truly besieged with slow starters. Sweeten's ability times are somewhat under those of his rivals, as we give him a :25.3 and a :26.0. Out of six races to check for early speed, he was within 5 lengths of the lead in only two, and he, too, is awarded the same 0 rating as Cabin Proof and Coq Au Vin.

Before we come to Sunshine Sam, I now want to establish a rule for elimination of an entire race. When all three of the first three favorites earn no early-speed points at all (i.e., all of them get a 0), you will next check to see if any other horse in the race has an early-speed rating of 6. If any other horse has a rating of 6, and the three top betting choices all have 0, the rule is that you will pass the race altogether. On the other hand, if no horse in the race has an early-speed rating of 6, you should play the race on the point totals that will be further discussed later in the book.

We can now look to see if any other horses in this race have sufficient early speed to warrant a 6. Sunshine Sam, in this case a co-third choice with Sweeten, easily gets this figure.

In his three races, Sunshine Sam was always up front, and thus gets a 6. His ability times are weak, however, as we get a :25.4 for his 23Aug79 effort and only a weak :27.2 for his last race. Looking further at the field, we can readily

Sunshine Sam — Ch. c. 2, by Toomuchholme—Flora Neff, by Rash Prince
Own.—Feiner I — $20,000 — Br.—Goff D C (Ark) — Tr.—Campo John P — 116

1979: St. 3 1st 1 2nd 0 3rd 0 Amt. $6,180

1Sep79- 3Bel	fst	6f	:22⅘	:46⅘	1:13⅖	Clm 25000	4	8	2hd	2hd	3½	44¼	Cordero A Jr	116	4.00	71-19 Cabin Proof 1161¾ Coq Au Vin 1202¼ Regal Roy 120nk	Weakened	8
23Aug79- 1Sar	fst	6½f	:23	:46⅖	1:18⅘	Md 18000	1	5	1hd	1½	13	15	Velasquez J	114	8.90	81-16 Sunshine Sam 1145 Napoleon Hill 1184½DallyHigh1143	Ridden out	9
23Jly79- 5Bel	fst	6f	:23⅗	:48	1:14⅕	Md 20000	2	5	1hd	52	78	912	Velasquez J	118	6.50	59-23 Fast And Gallant 1181 Hands Above 1181½ BelloBoy118¾	Stopped	10

LATEST WORKOUTS Sep 19 Bel 5f fst 1:03 b — Sep 16 Bel 4f fst :48⅗ hg — Sep 13 Bel tr.t 5f fst 1:02⅖ h — Aug 15 Sar Ⓣ 5f fm 1:02⅗ b

Regal Roy — B. c. 2, by Prince Dantan—You'N Me, by Intentionally — **$22,500** — Br.—Lee Estate Of Mr J M (Fla) — Tr.—Zito Nicholas P — **118**

Own.—Jablow M

	St.	1st	2nd	3rd	Amt.
1979	7	1	1	1	$10,200

15Sep79- 3Bel	fst	6f	:22⅕	:45⅗	1:11⅖	Clm 35000	3	1	1^{5}	1^{2}	2^{3}	$6^{8\frac{1}{2}}$	Maple S	b	115	9.90	76–11	SirSizzlingNehoc117^{3}SovereignRule115^{hd}LittlMrkr$113^{1\frac{1}{4}}$	Stopped	7
1Sep79- 3Bel	fst	6f	:22⅘	:46⅘	1:13⅖	Clm 30000	6	1	1^{hd}	1^{hd}	2^{hd}	3^{4}	Asmussen C B		120	8.60	71–19	Cabin Proof $116^{1\frac{3}{4}}$ Coq Au Vin $120^{2\frac{1}{4}}$ Regal Roy 120^{nk}	Weakened	8
12Aug79- 4Sar	sly	7f	:23	:46⅗	1:26⅕	Clm 45000	1	5	1^{hd}	2^{hd}	$6^{6\frac{1}{2}}$	7^{17}	Asmussen C B		117	13.90	54–25	Little Lenny $120\frac{1}{2}$ Boomie Two $117^{6\frac{1}{2}}$ Dover Prince 115^{1}	Tired	8
15Jly79- 7Bel	fst	5½f	:22⅗	:46⅗	1:06	Allowance	6	4	$2\frac{1}{2}$	1^{hd}	6^{3}	$6^{6\frac{3}{4}}$	Hernandez R		113	13.50	78–19	My Pal Jeff 114no Noble Ties $105^{1\frac{3}{4}}$ Cabin Proof $113^{2\frac{1}{2}}$	Tired	6
21Jun79- 6Bel	fst	5½f	:23⅕	:48	1:07⅗	Md 35000	2	1	$1\frac{1}{2}$	1^{1}	1^{3}	$1^{1\frac{1}{2}}$	Hernandez R		118	3.20	77–26	Regal Roy $118^{1\frac{1}{2}}$ Sweeten $118^{2\frac{3}{4}}$ Duffys Brother 118^{3}	Driving	8
1Jun79- 3Bel	fst	5½f	:22⅘	:46⅘	1:06⅖	Md 50000	1	1	$1\frac{1}{2}$	$1\frac{1}{2}$	2^{2}	$2^{4\frac{1}{2}}$	Fell J		118	5.10	78–19	Noble Ties $109^{4\frac{1}{2}}$ Regal Roy $118^{2\frac{3}{4}}$ Bon File $118^{1\frac{3}{4}}$	No match	7
21May79- 5Aqu	gd	if	:22⅗	:46⅕	:59	Md 50000	2	6	$6^{4\frac{1}{2}}$	$5^{5\frac{1}{2}}$	$5^{6\frac{1}{2}}$	5^{8}	Fell J		118	3.80	82–17	Ustay 115^{hd} Slash $118^{6\frac{1}{2}}$ Noble Ties $113^{1\frac{1}{4}}$	Greenly	7

LATEST WOI:KOUTS Sep 11 Bel tr.t 4f fst :48⅖ h Aug 5 Sar tr.t 5f fst 1:04 b Jly 26 Bel tr.t 4f fst :52⅗ b

spot another early speedball when we look at the record of Regal Roy, who is 6-1 on the board.

While this horse shows the poor ability times of :26.3 and :27.2, he was within 2 lengths or better of the lead in the last six out of his seven total races. You can be sure he will be up with Sunshine Sam scrapping for the lead in this race, with the other betting choices running back in the pack.

When you look at the chart, you can see that Sunshine Sam rushed out in front at the first call, with Regal Roy only 1 length behind, as Whambang, a rank outsider, temporarily squeezed between them. At the second call, Sunshine Sam's lead had dwindled to a half-length over Regal Roy, with Whambang beginning to fall back. These two battled for the lead all the way, with Regal Roy winning the race. Cabin Proof, the favorite, managed to get third, but never threatened the two early-speed horses.

NINTH RACE Belmont — **6 ½ FURLONGS. (1.15⅗) CLAIMING. Purse $12,000. 2-year-olds. Weights, 120 lbs. Claiming price $25,000; for each $2,500 to $15,000 2 lbs.**

SEPTEMBER 21, 1979

Value of race $12,000, value to winner $7,200, second $2,640, third $1,440, fourth $720. Mutuel pool $113,941, OTB pool $184,596. Track Triple Pool $139,676; OTB Triple Pool $303,676.

Last Raced	Horse	Eqt.A.Wt	PP	St	¼	½	Str	Fin	Jockey	Cl'g Pr	Odds $1
15Sep79 ^{3}Bel^{6}	Regal Roy	2 118	1	3	3^{2}	2^{1}	$1^{\frac{1}{2}}$	$1^{1\frac{1}{4}}$	Hernandez R	22500	6.10
1Sep79 ^{3}Bel^{4}	Sunshine Sam	2 116	2	5	1^{1}	$1^{\frac{1}{2}}$	2^{4}	2^{3}	Velasquez J	20000	4.40
15Sep79 ^{3}Bel^{4}	Cabin Proof	2 120	3	7	4^{hd}	$4^{\frac{1}{2}}$	$3^{1\frac{1}{2}}$	3^{nk}	Amy J	25000	2.40
15Sep79 ^{3}Bel^{5}	Coq Au Vin	2 120	6	4	$6^{1\frac{1}{2}}$	5^{2}	$4^{\frac{1}{2}}$	4no	Vasquez J	25000	3.90
1Sep79 ^{3}Bel^{6}	Sweeten	2 120	5	1	$5^{\frac{1}{2}}$	6^{4}	6^{14}	$5^{2\frac{1}{4}}$	Pincay L Jr†	25000	4.20
1Sep79 ^{3}Bel^{5}	Whambang	2 120	4	2	2^{hd}	3^{hd}	$5^{\frac{1}{2}}$	6^{18}	Santagata N	25000	11.20
	Flying Business	2 118	7	6	7	7	7	7	Brocklebank J	22500	13.00

OFF AT 5:02, EDT. Start good, Won driving. Time, :23⅕, :47⅗, 1:12⅖, 1:19 Track fast.

$2 Mutuel Prices:

2-(A)-REGAL ROY	14.20	7.60	3.80
1-(B)-SUNSHINE SAM		6.00	3.40
4-(E)-CABIN PROOF			3.00

In this case, Coq Au Vin had the highest ability times, with Cabin Proof not far behind. Even allowing 6 early-speed points for Sunshine Sam and Regal Roy, their total points would not nearly have equaled those of Cabin Proof, Coq Au Vin, or Sweeten.

Thus, you have seen the importance of a rule of passing a race altogether when none of the first three favorites has any early-speed points, as long as there is at least one other horse in the race with 6 early-speed points. If some other horse has only 3 early-speed points, do not pass the race if it otherwise qualifies. In races of seven furlongs and one mile, where early-speed points go up only to 4, you will follow the same rule and pass the race if none among the first three has any early-speed points and at least one other horse in the field has 4.

The reason for this rule should be readily apparent by now, even though the race we gave you showed Sunshine Sam, an early-speed horse, as a co-third favorite. When all three of the leading betting choices show no early speed and some other horse does, any one of the three betting favorites becomes a poor risk. We will not play any horse, of course, that is not among the first three in the betting. This is a rule of safety, designed to keep the player from losing in a race that becomes a gambling proposition when there is no early speed at all among the three from which we may choose and there is strong early speed on some outsider that may readily win the race, just as did Regal Roy in the example we have given.

Thus far, we have said little about grass racing. The early-speed rules are designed to apply according to the distance of a race, not the surface. Therefore, you will handle grass races in exactly the same way as you do dirt for the purposes of evaluation of early speed (still not mixing the two running surfaces as far as the first call is concerned.) If your grass race is a sprint, like some of the 5f dashes at tracks like Delaware Park, you can be sure that early speed is vitally important. On the other hand, most grass races are distance events, and when they are longer than a mile, as most of them are, you will not be factoring in early speed at all. In the one-milers, of course, you will use the same 4, 2, and 0 point ratings as on dirt races.

One final comment before we leave early speed. Some horses that barely make the one-half-of-their-races guideline may lag badly in the other half of their runs, while one of their rivals may show early speed in all ten of his races. Yet their early-speed points will be the same. The consistent early-speedster may be expected to be out ahead of the less consistent early-speedster. For the calculations in this book, however—for the sake of both simplicity and consistency—we will stick with the point ratings throughout. In your own private evaluations, where you see a wide disparity in early speed between two horses when their point totals are the same, you may want to tinker with some slight adjustment. But that is up to you. If you lack the seasoning to deal with this difficult game with complete confidence, you had better stick with the point ratings to the letter, as we have here.

EVALUATING FORM

Now that we have discovered a new method of rating a horse's ability, with early speed factored in for sprint races and for races of one mile, it is time to develop some measurable way of determining whether his form makes him a contender, or whether poor form should eliminate him from consideration altogether.

Frankly, this is one of the most difficult aspects of handicapping. A horse may look great on paper but actually be declining in form. Another horse may look terrible out of his last performance and yet surprise everyone with a strong victory. If we eliminate a horse from consideration and then watch him romp home in front, we may want to do more than chew up the program.

Let us therefore try to surmount the difficulties and cope with the problem of form. We shall begin by establishing three categories of form for all horses: (1) Q, or qualified; (2) NQ, or not qualified; and (3) U, or unknown. The only other additive is that for qualified horses, we shall award form points in two situations, which will be added to the ability points and the early-speed points, where applicable, to become the horse's final total points.

Once you become familiar with the use of rules for form, you may want to apply them to determine whether a horse gets a U, or a Q, or an NQ even before you begin the work of calculating ability times. When a horse is not qualified on form, you will not consider him as a contender in the race and will not have to compute his ability times. This can be a considerable work saver. I usually do this first, and once I have determined a form rating, I write it above the horse's past performance in my copy of the *Daily Racing Form*.

1. THE (UNKNOWN-FORM) HORSE

Unknown form is a quite different matter from unknown ability. If a horse's ability is unknown, his form will be also, and you will have no need to do further work in rating him. But a horse's ability may be quite apparent from the lines in his past performances while his recent form is totally unknown. This largely comes about from absence from the racing scene.

Thus, the first essential inquiry becomes: What period of time do we use from the last race before we can use it to evaluate form?

For claiming horses (except the high-priced $100,000 and $75,000 horses that you will sometimes see in New York and California particularly, where such animals are in reality equal to high-valued allowance horses or even some stakes racers) and most allowance horses, the last race must have been run within twenty-eight days of today's race or else form will be considered U—unknown.

But why twenty-eight days? Why not thirty, as many allow, or a shorter period of twenty-five or twenty-one days? Twenty-eight days is four full weeks. A racehorse must work if he is to earn his keep. If he has reasonably good form and is in condition, his owner and trainer will want to take advantage of it and enter him where he can earn some money for the stable to help pay the enormous bills that never cease—a lowly $1,500 claimer eats just as much hay as Secretariat.

A horse may not run for two or three weeks while nursing some minor ailment or soreness that does not greatly interfere with his ordinary good condition. His trainer may give him a few extra days to recover fully from his ache, and then may search several more days to find a race in which his steed has a chance to win. Any number of reasons can keep a horse out of action into his fourth week after a race, but if it goes beyond that time, then there is something more seriously wrong with the horse and he is not likely to be in formful condition. Experience and sheer experimentation have also taught that the twenty-eight-day rule is sound, more so than any other I know concerning days between races.

For horses that have competed in stakes races (even though the race you are considering today is an allowance event) and for allowance horses that have frequently competed against stakes animals (you can determine this by looking at the names of some of their competitors in the final portion of the running lines in their past performances), the rule is different. These horses are often kept out of racing for longer periods awaiting a proper season, or for some necessary rest between two hard series of races. They can usually return in good form off workouts, with their outstanding ability still blazing. Thus, a horse that has run in stakes races or has competed against stakes runners will not be rated as unknown in form if he has a series of four workouts, evenly spaced, within the last few weeks immediately prior to his return to competition. At least one of these four workouts should be a reasonably good one.

If this caliber of horse does not have four workouts, or not even one of his workouts rates as reasonably good, then his form, too, would be classed as unknown.

A good example of a horse away more than twenty-eight days whose form will not be classed as unknown is Protect Joyce, whose past performances are taken from the Western edition of the *Daily Racing Form* for February 14, 1980, the day of the race.

Protect Joyce						Dk. b. or br. f. 4, by Delaware Chief—Princess Pamela, by Prince John					
						Br.—Dansar Stables (Cal)		1979 13 4 4 2	$69,450		
Own.—Gann E			1105			Tr.—Frankel Robert		1978 4 3 0 0	$12,925		
								Turf 3 0 1 1	$6,050		

24.3
25.1

30Nov79-8BM	1¹⁄₁₆:46³ 1:11 1:42⁴ft	2½ 112	1½ 1ʰᵈ 1² 1²	McCrrnCJ⁸ ⒻSanFrn 85	Protect Joyce, Tourulla, LeCherro 10
31Oct79-7SA	1¹⁄₁₆:45² 1:09⁴ 1:42³ft	*7-5 115	5²½ 4⁴ 3⁶ 3⁴	McCrrnCJ⁴ ⒻMantaH 84	FlackFlck,GretLdyM.,ProtectJoyce 7
31Oct79—Run in two divisions, 7th & 8th races.					
11Oct79-5SA	6½f:21² :44¹ 1:15²ft	*3½ 116	8⁴ 7³½ 6¹³₄ 4³	McCarron CJ¹¹ ⒻAlw 90	Juanita's Girl, Gold Girl,HappyKin 12
7Sep79-8Dmr	1¹⁄₁₆:45³ 1:10 1:43 ft	6½ 113	3¹ 3²½ 2² 2¹	McCrrnCJ⁸ ⒻTryPns 84	DoubleDeceit,ProtectJoyce,Person 8
20Aug79-8Dmr	7½f ⒯:22 :45⁴1:30⁴fm	4½ 112	9¹³ 9¹² 4²½ 2¹	McCarron C J⁵ ⒻAlw 86	LeShonTov,ProtectJoyce,GoldGirl 10
8Aug79-9Dmr	1 ⒯:47¹1:11⁴1:36²fm	5½ 112	6⁵½ 6⁵½ 5³ 5⁴½	McCarron C J¹ ⒻAlw 88	DonaYsidr,ShineHigh,PecosPepper 7
11Jly79-7Hol	1 :46⁴ 1:11² 1:36²ft	3 111	1½ 1ʰᵈ 1½ 1¹½	McCarron C J³ ⒻAlw 84	ProtectJoyce,RuledbySpd,Extrvgnt 8
28Jun79-7Hol	1¹⁄₁₆ ⒯:46¹1:11²1:43 fm	4½ 116	2¹½ 2ʰᵈ 2ʰᵈ 3ʰᵈ	McCarronCJ⁸ Ⓕ 40000 84	Spost,ContinuousShow,ProtctJoyc 8
9Jun79-1Hol	7f :22² :45 1:22⁴ft	*2-3 116	1½ 1½ 1² 1ⁿᵒ	McCarronCJ⁵ Ⓕ 40000 85	ProtctJoyc,DncLdr,ContnuosShow 6
2Jun79-6Hol	6f :21⁴ :45¹ 1:10²ft	*1 119	2½ 2¹½ 1ʰᵈ 2³₄	McCrronCJ² Ⓕ c32000 84	DnceLeder,ProtctJoyc,ShllyBluEys 8
Feb 10 SA 5f ft 1:00² h		Feb 4 SA 5f ft :58⁴ h		Jan 31 SA 6f ft 1:16 h	Jan 26 SA 6f ft 1:15² h

Since Protect Joyce has not run since 30Nov79, she has obviously been idle far more than the twenty-eight days I use as a line of demarcation. Now look below the listed races to the workouts: four of them shown. The dates are February 10, February 4, January 31, and January 26. It does not particularly matter how fast they were, although at least one of them should be at an impressive figure (here, the February 4 workout at 5f was run in :58.4, and that, good friends, is moving). With the four workouts shown, evenly spaced (by that I mean within reasonably close periods; a workout in December would be too long ago to qualify), the remaining question concerns the filly's class. She not only shows three stakes races, despite having graduated from expensive claiming ranks, but she won her last race in stakes competition at Bay Meadows. Protect Joyce, therefore, would qualify on form for her 14Feb80 race at Santa Anita. You will see many comparable situations whenever expensive horses are competing.

You may have questions about what is considered a good workout. The *Daily Racing Form* places a heavy dot, called a "bullet," in the paper before any workout that is the fastest at its distance at the track on the day it was run. Therefore, any "bullet workout" is good enough to qualify. But other workouts that may not be the fastest of any at the distance may also be quite strong. It is difficult to draw a line here, or even rate the varieties of workouts under a variety of conditions without going into a long dissertation on the subject. But, in general, any workout that is run at a speed of 12 seconds per furlong is considered quite good, At five furlongs, I would consider any workout in less than 1:01.0 as being impressive. But again, this involves one in long explanatory judgments beyond the scope of what we're trying to do here, especially when times of workouts are not critical issues in our method of investing at the racetrack.

There is one more exception to the rule of twenty-eight days between races for unknown form. A horse that is a habitual fast starter, always showing early speed, is likely to return after a layoff with the same consistent early speed that he usually shows. But he has to rate more than just 6 points in your early-speed calculations. He must show in at least 80% of his races (with a minimum of five) that he was within 2 lengths or less of the lead. If he can demonstrate in four of every five starts that he is well up front, you may consider that his form today will not be unknown, and you can rate him otherwise.

But with these few exceptions, all horses that have not run in the last twenty-eight days will have a form rating of U, or unknown. Some special problems arise when a horse is moving from dirt to grass, or from grass to dirt, and we will deal with this a little later.

2.   FINDING THE QUALIFIED FORM HORSE

Ordinarily, to determine whether a horse merits a Q, or a qualified, form rating, we will look to the last race run within twenty-eight days from today's race. There are some few situations when we cannot rely on the last race, which will be fully set forth after we show you how a horse does qualify on form from the last race within twenty-eight days.

There are several specific ways in which a horse can qualify on form.

 Up Close at Two Calls in the Last Race

When a horse is up close to the leader at any two calls in his last race, he is qualified on form to compete in today's race. What does "up close" mean? When a horse is running *less than 3 lengths behind the leader* at any particular call of the race, this is considered "up close" for our purposes. If he is 3 lengths behind, where the line is drawn, then he is not sufficiently up close for our purposes. When he is up close at two or more calls, he is usually in good form. From the *Daily Racing Form* of March 24, 1980, Pass Deceiver shows the necessary qualifying signs.

In his last race on 8Mar80, he was within less than three lengths of the leader at each of the first three calls. Now drop down to his race of 1Mar80 where he

Pass Deceiver — Own.—Podolak S — $16,000 — 117

Dk. b. or br. c. 4, by Flush—Chicanery, by Pretense
Br.—Willcox Mr-Mrs A A (Fla)
Tr.—Tagariello Frank F

Turf Record	St.	1st	2nd	3rd		St.	1st	2nd	3rd	Amt.
	1	0	0	0	1980	7	1	2	1	$12,980
					1979	19	4	2	3	$24,275

8Mar80- 2Aqu	fst	1 70	⊡:48	1:13⅗	1:44⅘	Clm 16000	6	7	42½	32	1hd	33½	Asmussen C B	b 117	3.30	74-16	Happy Hour 117nk Ernie'sLad1153½PassDeceiver1173	Bothered st. 9
1Mar80- 1Aqu	fst	1⅛	⊡:48⅖	1:13⅗	1:52⅘	Clm 20000	1	1	12	1½	65¾	89¼	Wacker D J	b 117	11.00	73-17	Il Vagabondo 117½ Drums and Fife1173½SavingGround117hd	Tired 9
11Feb80- 5Aqu	fst	1¼	⊡:49⅖	1:41	2:07⅗	Hcp 12500s	4	1	21	911	1127	1132	Beitia E	b 114	19.10	48-23	Indeed Gallant 1124½ North Star 1152¾ Scamp Boy 1133¾	Stopped 11
6Feb80- 3Aqu	fst	1⅛	⊡:47⅘	1:13⅘	1:54⅕	Clm 25000	3	1	11½	1hd	41½	22	Beitia E5	b 112	22.20	73-22	Caraqueno1172PssDeceiver112nk[D]DrumsndFife1173¾	Drifted out 7
26Jan80- 9Aqu	fst	1⅛	⊡:47⅕	1:12⅖	1:52⅕	Clm c-18000	9	7	66½	65	811	816	Gribcheck S B5	b 108	5.30	69-17	Arctic Service 117½ Amano 117¾ No Sir 1132¾	Wide 11
19Jan80- 3Aqu	my	1 1/16	⊡:46⅘	1:12⅕	1:46	Clm 16000	4	1	11½	11½	1½	11¾	Gribcheck S B5	b 114	3.80	84-21	Pass Deceiver 1141¾ My Best Pie 1176 Len's Back 1136½	Driving 10
13Jan80- 1Aqu	fst	1⅛	⊡:47⅖	1:12⅖	1:52⅘	Clm c-12500	9	4	11½	13	21½	27½	Wacker D J5	b 114	6.50	74-17	North Star 1197½ PassDeceiver1141¾CliffChesney119nk	Went well 12
26Dec79- 9Aqu	gd	1⅛	⊡:48	1:14	1:56⅘	Clm 14000	7	1	13	16	16	11¾	Wacker D J5	112	4.50	62-36	PssDeceiver1121½PeppercornFe1131½RturnForGlory1133¾	Driving 10
24Nov79- 4Aqu	fst	1	:46⅗	1:11⅕	1:36⅗	Clm c-20000	1	2	21½	37	612	720	Hernandez R	b 117	11.10	63-18	MidnightRcer11710HereComesHerbert1133½OurChrlieG.1141	Tired 8
31Oct79- 3Crc	fst	7f	:22⅘	:45⅗	1:25⅕	Clm 22500	2	1	13	13	2½	22	Hilburn K D5	b 109	2.60	88-14	Gentle Wind 1142 Pass Deceiver 1094½ Georgealite 1112	2nd best 5

LATEST WORKOUTS Feb 25 Bel tr.t 5f fst 1:01⅗ h

led at both the first two calls only, and was thus obviously within less than 3 lengths of the leader again. His performance on 1Mar80 qualified him on form for the race of 8Mar80 also, even though he did not win on that occasion. He would also qualify on this same count out of his races of 6Feb80, 19Jan80, 13Jan80, 26Dec79, and 31Oct79.

This is a rather easy qualifying sign to pick out of any past performances.

Up Close at One Call in the Last Race Plus Drop in Class

If a horse was up close—meaning less than 3 lengths back of the leader—at any one of the four calls in his last race, and in addition is dropping in class by as much as 20% in today's race, his form is sufficient to qualify. A good example is revealed in the West Coast *Form* for February 14, 1980, in the first race at Santa Anita, where Copelino is entered.

In his last race on 1Feb80, Copelino was 1¾ lengths back at the first call. That qualifies for one "up close." He is also dropping in class from $10,000 in his last race to $8,000 in today's race, and that is exactly 20% in price value. This qualifies Copelino on form for the 14Feb80 contest.

1st Santa Anita

6 FURLONGS. (1.07⅘) CLAIMING. Purse $7,500. 4-year-olds and upward. Weights, 4-year-olds, 121 lbs.; older, 122 lbs. Non-winners of two races since November 5 allowed 3 lbs.; of a race since December 25, 5 lbs.; since November 5, 8 lbs. Claiming price $8,000.

***Copelino** — Own.—Mashek & Van Berg — 114

Ch. h. 9, by Resuello—Coppelia, by Timor
Br.—Haras Siasa (Arg)
Tr.—Van Berg Jack C — $8,000

1980	1	0	0	0		
1979	15	0	3	2	$13,175
Turf	1	0	0	1	$2,400

1Feb80-1SA	6f	:213	:443	1:094ft	5¼	116	51¾	53	54¼	65½	Valenzuela I9	10000	84	BlSrocco,OrntlDoctor,BootsFwctt	10
5Nov79-2SA	6f	:214	:444	1:094ft	4	117	55	56½	65¾	77	Jones K1	12500	83	Mr R. T. F., Cajoje, Grape Juice	8
28Oct79-1SA	6f	:213	:443	1:094ft	6¼	117	85½	77¼	66¾	58¾	Jones K2	16000	81	NrrowWy,ChiefFillmore,Prkinthdrk	9
5Oct79-1SA	6f	:212	:44	1:091ft	4¾	117	64¾	54¼	43¼	64	Campas R1	16000	89	BrnstormShdow,RlfPtchr,TqlSnrs	12
7Jly79-9Hol	6f	:222	:45	1:091ft	18	116	85½	86¾	87½	87¼	Campas R4	16000	84	BankerJohn,‡Mrsos,SpottedChrger	9
29Jun79-4Hol	6f	:214	:442	1:084ft	18	114	54	56	56½	68¼	Campas R6	18000	85	PddyWlk,WorldPlsur,Four-Dmonds	6
10Jun79-4Hol	6f	:222	:45	1:092ft	8	116	42¾	65	810	918	Campas R2	20000	72	Jeffrvscnt,PddyWlk,Four-Dimonds	9
26May79-2Hol	6f	:22	:443	1:091ft	4½	116	79¾	78¼	69½	46½	Shoemaker W2	20000	84	PrinceFlmer,PddyWlk,ColorMPurpl	8
12May79-3Hol	6f	:22	:451	1:092ft	8	116	77	75¾	64	42	Shoemaker W8	20000	88	WorldPleasure,NarrowWy,LoomJet	8
8Apr79-1SA	6f	:214	:45	1:10 ft	*3½e	115	53	21½	32	3¾	Cordero A Jr4	20000	88	RestlessHeritge,Jffrvscnt,Coplino	12

Feb 8 SA 3f ft :361 h   Jan 25 SA 5f ft 1:004 h   Jan 19 SA 5f sl 1:041 h   Jan 6 SA 5f ft 1:01 h

A Gain of Five in the Running Line Within Contention

When a horse in his last race makes a gain of five in his running line and is not too far back in the pack, this is significant enough to qualify him on form. A "gain of five" may be computed in either horses or lengths, and usually embraces both. If a horse shows a 6^4 and then a 3^2 (sixth in the race and 4 lengths behind the leader and third in the race and 2 lengths behind the leader), his advancement from sixth to third is a gain of three over horses, and his improvement from 4 lengths to 2 lengths behind is a gain of 2 lengths, which, when added to the three in horses, gives him the requisite "gain of five."

We have the further term, however, "within contention." A gain of five far back in the pack is meaningless. To be in contention when the gain is completed, a horse must be less than 6 lengths behind the leader at the completion of his gain. That means 5¾ lengths or less, for anything more than that may not be counted. From the *Daily Racing Form* of February 18, 1980, we can demonstrate from the past performances of Oaklawn (a horse, not the track):

Oaklawn — B. g. 4, by Riva Ridge—Elaine, by Round Table — $16,500 — Br.—Lasater Farm (Ky) — Tr.—Dutrow Richard E — **112**

Own.—Aisquieth Stable

Turf Record	St.	1st	2nd	3rd		St.	1st	2nd	3rd	Amt.
	1	0	0	0	1980	2	0	0	1	$1,200
					1979	21	3	1	4	$18,028

5Feb80- 7Bow	fst	7f	:23⅘	:47⅕	1:26⅖	Allowance	2	8	8^{9}	$8^{8\frac{1}{4}}$	7^{6}	$5^{3\frac{1}{4}}$	McCarron G	b 113	*2.20e	70-30	Steppin Shoes 119^{hd} Polar Point 112^{2} Hagley's Magic 112^{nk}	Outrun	8
15Jan80- 8Bow	fst	7f	:23	:46	1:25⅕	Allowance	1	7	$8^{6\frac{3}{4}}$	$7^{9\frac{1}{4}}$	4^{3}	$3^{3\frac{1}{4}}$	Pino M G^{5}	b 109	*1.00e	76-31	Buckley $108^{2\frac{1}{4}}$ Polar Point 115^{1} Oaklawn $109^{2\frac{1}{2}}$	Rallied	9
31Dec79- 5Lrl	fst	7f	:23	:46⅗	1:24⅗	3↑ Clm 15000	8	8	8^{10}	7^{6}	$6^{9\frac{1}{2}}$	$6^{5\frac{3}{4}}$	Kupfer T	b 111	*1.80e	82-19	Percy's Game $115^{\frac{3}{4}}$ Twivil 110^{2} Kingbird 115^{hd}	No factor	8
3Dec79- 5Lrl	fst	1	:46⅘	1:11⅘	1:37⅖	Clm 16000	5	7	$7^{7\frac{1}{4}}$	$8^{8\frac{1}{2}}$	$9^{8\frac{1}{2}}$	$9^{6\frac{3}{4}}$	Pino M G^{5}	b 110	*2.40e	79-12	Hightoria 108^{1} Sally Past $124^{1\frac{1}{4}}$ Another Paris 110no	No factor	10
26Nov79- 6Lrl	sly	1	:47	1:12⅘	1:39⅗	Clm 18000	3	6	$7^{8\frac{3}{4}}$	$7^{9\frac{1}{4}}$	6^{8}	$5^{8\frac{3}{4}}$	Fann B	b 113	5.40	66-25	Joshua Egan $110^{\frac{1}{2}}$ Ambold $115^{4\frac{1}{2}}$ Honest Wishes $110^{1\frac{1}{2}}$	Outrun	7
14Nov79- 5Lrl	hy	1	:48	1:13⅘	1:41	Clm 16000	8	5	$5^{2\frac{1}{4}}$	$4^{2\frac{1}{2}}$	$4^{2\frac{1}{2}}$	$4^{1\frac{1}{4}}$	Pino M G^{5}	b 110	*1.10e	67-30	Sally Past 115^{1} Hightoria 115^{nk} Bar Talk 115^{hd}	Bore in	8
18Oct79- 9Pim	fst	$1\frac{1}{16}$	:48	1:13⅘	1:47⅕	Clm 12500	5	8	$7^{7\frac{1}{4}}$	$4^{3\frac{1}{2}}$	$3^{2\frac{1}{2}}$	1^{1}	Bracciale V Jr	b 115	*2.10	69-27	Oaklawn 115^{1} Teegeeif $115^{1\frac{3}{4}}$ Not So Proud $115^{2\frac{3}{4}}$	Driving	12
9Oct79- 9Lrl	my	6f	:23⅕	:48⅕	1:14	Clm 12500	3	9	9^{11}	7^{7}	4^{3}	3^{3}	Pino M G^{5}	b 110	3.20	73-26	Kishmere $115^{2\frac{3}{4}}$ Irv 115^{nk} Oaklawn $110^{1\frac{3}{4}}$	Rallied	9
22Sep79- 2Del	my	6f	:22⅘	:46⅖	1:11⅗	Clm 14500	2	9	$9^{5\frac{3}{4}}$	$6^{4\frac{1}{4}}$	$2^{2\frac{1}{2}}$	$2^{\frac{3}{4}}$	Pino M G^{5}	b 114	3.50	86-13	Hawkeye King $112^{\frac{3}{4}}$ Oaklawn $114^{3\frac{1}{4}}$ Capt. Ridiculous $116^{2\frac{1}{4}}$	Gaining	10
14Sep79- 2Del	fst	6f	:22⅗	:46⅕	1:11⅖	Clm 14500	5	5	$6^{7\frac{1}{4}}$	6^{5}	$4^{1\frac{1}{2}}$	3^{1}	Bracciale V Jr	b 119	3.60	87-16	Cinder Luck $117^{\frac{1}{2}}$ Hightoria $119^{\frac{1}{2}}$ Oaklawn 119^{4}	Hung	6

LATEST WORKOUTS Jan 31 Bow 6f gd 1:20 b Jan 25 Bow 6f fst 1:17 b Jan 14 Bow 3f fst :38 b

At the stretch call, Oaklawn was seventh by 6 lengths. At the finish line, he had improved his position to fifth and trailed by 3½ lengths. From seventh to fifth is a gain of two in horses, and from 6 lengths down to 3¼ lengths is close enough to the necessary 3 lengths to make a total of five. If we extend the gain further back to the second call, which we can do, we see Oaklawn eighth by 8¼ lengths. But we will not give credit for anything over 8 lengths for the start of a gain, just as the completion must be under 6 lengths. But since Oaklawn's completed gain was under 6 lengths, he qualifies easily all around.

The "gain of five" is a good form factor, and whenever it occurs, the horse, if he has good ability times, is worth respectful attention.

A Gain of Three from One Call to the Next Plus a Drop in Class

A horse that scores some appreciable gain from one call to the next call is beginning to show some degree of liveliness. We will give him credit if he makes a gain of three, but it must be from one call to the very next call, and at its completion he must not be as many as 6 lengths behind the leader. That is one part of the qualifying requirement. The other is that he must also be dropping in class. From the *Daily Racing Form* of May 31, 1980, we can look at Ramnoctious in the sixth at Bowie:

Ramnoctious — Ch. g. 3, by Rambunctious—D's Dilemma, by Nasco
$23,500 — Br.—Scheidt Mrs M E (Md) — Tr.—Wilson Gregory L — 1145
Own.—Scheidt Mrs M Est of

	St.	1st	2nd	3rd	Amt.
1980	5	1	0	0	$4,650
1979	3	M	0	0	

21May80- 7Pim	sly	1 1/16	:47⅘	1:14	1:48⅗	Allowance	6	5	67½	55½	45½	56½	Black K7	105	16.30	55-30	Grumblethorpe 1201¼ NightDelta1124¼LyricCount112nk	No factor	7
8May80- 9Pim	fst	6f	:23⅗	:46⅘	1:12	Allowance	2	6	72½	73¾	45	45¼	Black K7	105	19.20	81-18	Wing to Wing 1201 HurryHomeDuc1123GameWinner1121¼	Rallied	11
1May80- 2Pim	sly	6f	:24	:48⅗	1:14⅖	3↑ Md 23500	1	2	1hd	13	12	12	Black K7	105	13.00	74-26	Ramnoctious 1052 Michael R. 11312 Gala Peg 1122½	Driving	9
21Apr80- 3Pim	fst	6f	:24	:48	1:14⅕	3↑ Md 23500	6	3	4¾	65¾	67½	64	Torre M J	114	9.30	71-25	Silent Heir 1121¼ St. Camillus 113½ Timbuktu 122no	Steadied	8
9Apr80- 5Pim	my	6f	:23⅗	:47⅗	1:13⅘	3↑ Md 23500	4	7	77¼	69½	511	512	Torre M J	113	4.30	65-26	WiseMen'sGift115noLordRichmond1152¼Brondsbury1123	Off slow	7
27Dec79- 5Lrl	gd	6f	:22⅘	:46⅘	1:12⅕	Md Sp Wt	4	9	65½	57	612	59½	Torre M J	118	31.80	75-22	Thomas Pepper 1133¾ Dr. Tipton 1184 Shane'sJewel1181	Even try	12
15Dec79- 9Lrl	gd	6f	:22⅘	:46⅗	1:11⅘	Md Sp Wt	12	8	96¼	56½	49½	810	Torre M J	118	9.10	77-18	Phoebe's Phancy 1105 Blue Ensign 1182 Wheelivright1112¼	Tired	12
6Dec79- 4Lrl	fst	6f	:23	:47⅕	1:13	Md Sp Wt	3	5	52¼	4nk	2hd	63¾	Torre M J	118	23.50	77-16	Mark Aye El 118hd Blue Ensign118noHonoredOfficer1182	Greenly	9

LATEST WORKOUTS Apr 2 Pim 5f gd 1:04 b

He is dropping in class from an allowance race to a claiming race at a $23,-500 tag. From the first call, where he was sixth at 7½ lengths behind, he advanced to fifth only 5½ lengths behind at the second call. Passing one horse and picking up 2 lengths is the requisite gain of three, not a great deal indeed, but sufficient, when coupled with a drop in class, to turn the horse into a contender in his next race. Also note that Ramnoctious was less than 6 lengths behind at the second call when his gain was completed, and that it did not start more than the arbitrary 8-length line we have drawn for coming from behind. These adjustments are of critical importance again, as a gain of three, like a gain of five, which is made back in the pack is of little value. Veteran players will understand this readily, and newcomers can appreciate the logic of it as well, since the critical movements must come as close to the front as possible.

A Finish of Second

When a horse finishes second in his last race, no matter how he got there, he is usually a bona fide contender in his next start. I hardly need to show you an example from past performances. Merely finishing second is enough. A horse may be 10 lengths behind and may have never been up close, but if he defeats every horse in the race except one, he is worthy of study in his next race. Frequently, when a horse does finish second and is many lengths behind, it is because the winner was simply outstanding that day. There is only one easy exception to this rule, which we will come to shortly.

A Race Where a Horse Neither Gains Nor Loses Any Significant Number of Lengths

A horse that is able to keep reasonably close to the lead at all points of call without gaining or losing more than 2 lengths between any two successive calls is often classed as running "Evenly" in the comment line of the Eastern edition of the *Daily Racing Form*. Once again, in defining what we mean here, a horse must never be more than 6 lengths behind the leader. A good example is provided in the last running line of Rhapsodist, entered in a six-furlong allowance race at Pimlico on May 14, 1980.

Rhapsodist B. g. 3, by Cyane—Lyrico, by Jet Action
Own.—Murray W F Br.—Schneider H G (La)
Tr.—Field Thomas E **112**

	St.	1st	2nd	3rd	Amt.
1980	4	1	0	1	$7,440
1979	4	3	0	0	$12,900

3May80- 5Pim gd 6f :23 :46⅖ 1:13 Allowance 3 3 23½ 35 36 34 Pino M G b 112 6.00 77–25 Icy Dial 1051½ Command Control 1142½ Rhapsodist 1127 Evenly 5
11Apr80- 7Pim fst 6f :22⅘ :46⅖ 1:11⅘ Clm 23500 3 5 32 42½ 4nk 1nk Pino M G b 114 3.70 87–25 Rhapsodist 114nk Make A Try 117no Another Llanton112½ Driving 7
4Apr80- 7Pim my 6f :23⅗ :47⅕ 1:12⅘ Allowance 3 6 31 815 824 826 Pino M G b 112 8.20 56–23 Hillbizon 117½ Native Moment112noKnightLanding120¾ Brief foot 8
15Mar80- 9Pim fst 6f :23 :45⅘ 1:10⅘ H. Jacobs 1 3 1hd 52¾ 55¾ 65¼ Pino M G b 116 24.40 87–14 AmberPass1161Pickett'sCharge116½PeaceForPeace1192½ Used up 8
19Oct79- 7Pim fst 6f :23⅗ :46⅘ 1:12⅖ Allowance 7 3 52½ 68¾ 79 77 Pino M G5 b 114 *1.60 77–21 Command Control 122nk [D]Cuchillo1194JustALope119¾ No threat 9
5Oct79- 6Lrl sly 6f :23 :47⅕ 1:13⅖ Allowance 1 7 43 21 1hd 1nk Pino M G5 b 114 5.10 79–24 Rhapsodist 114nk Peace For Peace 122¾ Cuchillo 1191 Driving 9
13Sep79- 8Del fst 6f :22⅘ :46⅖ 1:12⅕ Allowance 5 1 1hd 1hd 1hd 1hd Pino M G5 b 110 3.40 84–20 Rhapsodist 110hd Century Rollick 1202 Just A Lope 1151¾ Driving 6
4Sep79- 7Del fst 6f :22⅘ :47 1:13⅕ Md 25000 3 8 2hd 2½ 11½ 14¼ Pino M G5 b 115 7.70 79–17 Rhpsodist1154¼CrlBernstin1202½ShhOfHmingwy1201¼ Ridden out 9
LATEST WORKOUTS Apr 29 Pim 4f my :48 h Apr 25 Pim 4f my :52⅗ b Apr 21 Pim 4f fst :48 h Apr 9 Pim 5f my 1:02⅗ b

Notice that Rhapsodist was farther back at the first and final calls of his race on 3May80 than he was on 11Apr80. He was not up close at any call, within our definition, nor did he score an appreciable gain. He is not dropping in class either. But he held evenly with his field, always within striking distance. The comment line carries the word "Evenly," which you will not find in Midwestern and West Coast editions of the *Form.* But awareness of the nature of the running line will enable you to identify it whether there is a comment line or not. Rhapsodist was never more than 6 lengths behind, and the closest he ran was at 3½ and 4 lengths. You should note also that he was rising in class from a claiming race to an allowance event when he turned in his "Evenly" performance.

Any horse that shows any one or more of the six qualifying factors gets a Q in his form rating and will be rated as a contender, unless one of our few exceptions pulls him down to NQ—not qualified.

3. ELIMINATING THE NOT-QUALIFIED HORSE

While it may appear rather obvious at this point that Q horses are in and NQ horses are out, a few more things need to be said. First of all, you will be surprised at how many NQ horses wind up as favorites and frequently among the first three betting choices. A good example comes from the test run I made at Monmouth on Monday, June 2, 1980 (*Daily Racing Form,* Eastern edition, that date), in the first race at six furlongs, a not too spectacular maiden claiming event. Would you believe that this horse was actually the favorite?

Bank President Ch. g. 4, by Mr Leader—In Trust, by Buckpasser
Own.—Lacy P **$12,500** Br.—Taylor's Purchase Farm (Ky)
Tr.—Raymond William T **123**

	St.	1st	2nd	3rd	Amt.
1980	1	M	0	0	
1979	3	M	0	1	$990

24May80- 2Mth fst 6f :22⅗ :45⅗ 1:11 3↑Md Sp Wt 9 7 1014 1019 1021 1019 Thomas D B b 123 35.10 66–12 Socko 115nk Wind River Man 1153 Rita's Deal 1151 Trailed 10
12Mar79- 2Key fst 6f :23⅕ :47⅗ 1:13⅗ Md Sp Wt 6 6 77 812 915 813 Dufton E 121 8.70 61–33 Garth Road 1211½ Person To Person 1215 Pudkin 1211 No factor 11
2Mar79- 4Key gd 6f :22⅘ :47⅖ 1:14⅘ Md Sp Wt 1 10 710 77 65½ 64¾ Dufton E b 120 11.70 63–34 Gold Victor 120½ Poogie 115no Person To Person1203½ No factor 11
9Feb79- 6Key fst 6f :23⅘ :49 1:15⅗ Md Sp Wt 7 7 67½ 58½ 511 313 Dufton E7 b 113 29.20 51–41 IndianTreaty1203½PersonToPerson1209BankPresident113½ Rallied 9
LATEST WORKOUTS May 22 Mth 3f sly :36⅖ bg

You may say that this is too obvious for comment, because of such atrocious form, but who were all those people who made him the favorite? This surely had to be on the fact that he was dropping from a maiden special race down to a relatively cheap claiming race. There is also the recognition that when a horse comes back after a layoff, as did Bank President, and runs poorer than in his last race before the vacation, he is not likely to be improving in form.

Thus, when a horse, like Bank President, does not meet any of the six qualifying rules, he rates an NQ, and is eliminated from any further consideration in the race before you. But there are some horses that will meet some of the qualifying rules and still ought to be eliminated from further consideration. This is extremely important in dealing with form.

Even though a horse may meet some of the qualifying rules on form, he will be eliminated as not qualified, NQ, if he is dropping in class by 40% or more. This generally means he is carrying a "for sale" sign on his back and his trainer merely wants to get rid of him. But even here, there are exceptions. If a horse dropping 40% in money value was up close at two calls in his last race, he is showing signs of good form. And if he showed a gain of five in his last running line, which is one of the most powerful form signs of all, then he cannot be eliminated automatically off a 40% class drop.

An excellent illustration of how the 40% class drop can disqualify a horse comes in the same Monmouth race where Bank President showed such abysmal form. Right behind him in the betting as the second choice was Believe In Luck, also well backed by the crowd.

Believe In Luck — Ch. g. 3, by What Luck—Nothing Faster, by Prince Dare — **$12,500** — Br.—Voigt Mrs L L (Md) — Tr.—Murphy James W — **115**

Own.—Voigt Mr L L

	St.	1st	2nd	3rd	Amt.
1980	6	M	1	1	$3,280
1979	0	M	0	0	

1May80- 2Pim sly	6f	:24	:48⅗	1:14⅖	3↑ Md 23500	4	4	$4^{2\frac{3}{4}}$	6^{6}	$5^{8\frac{1}{2}}$	5^{18}	Passmore W J	b 113	2.90	56-26	Ramnoctious 105^{2} Michael R. 113^{12} Gala Peg $112^{2\frac{1}{2}}$	Tired	9
17Apr80- 3Pim fst	6f	:23	:46⅗	1:12	3↑ Md Sp Wt	8	3	$2^{\frac{1}{2}}$	$4^{2\frac{1}{2}}$	5^{9}	8^{12}	Edwards J W	b 115	6.40	74-21	Rye At Sea 112^{7} Flatter 112^{nk} Pukka Pukka $107^{1\frac{1}{4}}$	Tired	12
5Apr80-10Pim fst	6f	:23⅖	:47⅗	1:13⅖	3↑ Md Sp Wt	10	5	2^{hd}	1^{hd}	1^{hd}	$3^{1\frac{1}{4}}$	Pino M G	b 112	5.60	78-19	Wing to Wing 113^{nk}CigarStoreInjun112^{1}BelieveInLuck$112^{\frac{3}{4}}$	Tired	12
28Mar80- 6Pim fst	6f	:23⅕	:46⅖	1:12⅖	3↑ [S]Md Sp Wt	5	4	4^{2}	3^{2}	$3^{5\frac{1}{2}}$	2^{1}	Edwards J W	b 115	26.50	83-21	Starullah 114^{1} Believe In Luck 115no Rye At Sea 112no	Rallied	10
27Feb80- 5Bow fst	7f	:23⅖	:46⅘	1:26	Md Sp Wt	2	2	$6^{3\frac{1}{2}}$	$6^{4\frac{3}{4}}$	5^{9}	$6^{8\frac{1}{4}}$	Edwards J W	120	12.20	67-28	Dixie Market 120^{nk}MajesticSong120^{1}DaringRescue120^{2}	No threat	8
18Feb80- 2Bow fst	6f	:23⅕	:46⅗	1:12	Md Sp Wt	9	3	$8^{8\frac{3}{4}}$	8^{18}	7^{15}	7^{14}	Edwards J W	120	4.80	66-22	Abbasid 120^{7} Ragtime Jazz 120^{hd} Meadows Of Dan $120^{\frac{1}{2}}$	Greenly	11

LATEST WORKOUTS May 29 Mth 4f fst :52 b May 24 Mth 4f fst :48 h Apr 15 Lrl 3f my :36⅘ b (d) Apr 4 Lrl 3f sly :38⅖ bg(d)

This horse's claiming price was cut almost in half, thus exceeding the 40% formula. He had one call up close, and under our qualifying rules, one up-close call plus a drop in class would ordinarily qualify him. But when the class drop equals 40% or more, unless he has two up-close calls or a gain of five, out he goes. Believe In Luck looks like a loser the more you examine his record. He is coming back into action after laying off more than a month after a bad race. His trainer was surely offering him in the bargain market. Under our rule, there would be no hesitation in eliminating this horse.

Determining whether a class drop is 40% or more in money value is relatively easy when one measures one claiming price against another. But when a horse drops from an allowance race into a claiming race, how do you evaluate the financial value of the class drop? Look back at Bank President, who dropped from a maiden special race down to a $12,500 claimer. Was this more than 40% in value? Maiden special races, unless they involve outstanding animals, may not rate so high on the money scale, and with Bank President you would have to guess, unless there was other information to assist you in the search.

One important approach is to determine whether a horse has actually established a dollar class value. Bank President, in his few outings, had not, but fortunately, we could discard him on his wretched form. Where a horse has run as many as ten races, which are shown in his past performances, you can look back at prior runs before he was entered in allowance events to see if he had established a dollar class value, and use that for comparison. But when a horse is dropping from allowance races into a claiming event for the first time, you may simply be compelled to hazard a guess, which we don't like to do. If the problem gets serious enough, your only recourse may be to pass the race.

An example of what we mean by a horse not establishing his dollar class comes from that same first race at Monmouth on June 2, 1980, where we have already eliminated the first two favorites as not qualified. The third choice in the betting was Jaohar, a gelding brought over from France more than a year previous. Was he dropping more than 40% in class?

Jaohar		Dk. b. or br. g. 5, by Delta Judge—Rhetoric, by Jaipur			Turf Record	St. 1st 2nd 3rd	Amt.
Own.—Maggio C	$12,500	Br.—Nuckols Bros (Ky) Tr.—Mazza John F	123	St. 1st 2nd 3rd	1980 1 M 0 0		
				4 0 1 0	1979 1 M 0 0		

23May80- 5Mth fst 170 :47 1:11⅝ 1:42½ 3♦ Md Sp Wt	7 5 52¾ 87¾ 6¹³ 7¹⁷ Lopez C	b 124	23.10	68-16 Rube's Touch 114² Upendicular 124ⁿᵏ NaturalDancer117⁷	No factor 8
20Apr79♦5StCloud(Fra) sf*1 1:41 ⊕ Prix Transvaal	10¹⁴ Rivases G	119	78.00	— — PyjamaHunt128½ MadCaptin132² AmericnMoney123¹½	No factor 12
10Apr78♦2StCloud(Fra) gd*7½f 1:43½ ⊕ Prix Magister(Mdn)	9¹⁷ StMartin Y	123	5.50	— — Mazzaro 123¾ Archange d'Or 123³ Pandion 123¼	No factor 12
22Mar78♦2StCloud(Fra) sf*7½f 1:53½ ⊕ Prix Rieur(Mdn)	6¹⁷ Kessas J L	123	*1.50	— — Peloponnes 113³ Cottaro 113⁴ Fai Roi Sol 122¹	No factor 12
1Mar78♦2StCloud(Fra) sf*7½f 1:53¾ ⊕ Prix Northeast(Mdn)	2⁴ StMartin Y	123	2.50	— — Mannshour 123⁴ Jaohar 123⁸ Nitry 123⁸	Well pl,bid,wknd 5
LATEST WORKOUTS Apr 2 GS 3f my :36 b					

Again, we don't really know. But this time it doesn't matter. He is dropping in class, that we do know, and has one call up close, which would qualify him as a contender otherwise. But note that he has run but one race in this country, where his trainer entered him perhaps to do no more than take a look. Accordingly, on this record, there is no established class. The last race was not a true test of the horse's class value, and all we can glean from it is that in today's race he is dropping in some amount. He therefore would qualify on form as the only one of the first three betting choices who could do so. I might also tell you his ability time off his one race was good in comparison with the others in the race.

You might not even have to guess very hard at the outcome. Jaohar won nicely, paying $13.40. He simply was not nearly as bad as Bank President and Believe In Luck, and the standards we use on form demonstrate that quite well.

Yet, in this whole area of evaluating the significance of class drops as a handicapping factor, you may do well to rely upon some judgment and some flexibility, even though we strive to establish as sound a set of rules as possible. There are some trainers, for example, like the highly successful Frank "Pancho" Martin in New York, who will drop a horse drastically in price for the express purpose of winning first-place money, and care not at all if someone claims him. An ironclad rule against eliminating horses dropping in class 40% or more is a dangerous thing when Frank Martin drops a horse. I am sure there are trainers at other tracks around the country who maneuver in precisely the same fashion. Thus, judgments and exceptions to rules continue to plague us constantly.

To this point, we have talked primarily about the difficulty of ascertaining what is a true 40% drop in class value when a horse is moved down from allowance ranks into claiming races. But at all times the major inquiry is: What is established class dollar value, or true class value? For example, a trainer may raise a claiming horse in price by double his value and then drop him back in the following race, which would show a 100% class drop in dollar value from the preceding race. Would this then serve to disqualify the horse because he was dropping more than 40% in class dollar value from his previous race? Not at all, as you can readily appreciate, since the previous class race was not a true value at all, but one merely inflated for the moment to satisfy a trainer's yen for maneuverability. Therefore, in any suspicious dollar class drop, you will be compelled to look back down the previous running lines to determine if today's drop is real rather than artificial.

To this point, we have identified one exception to our qualifying form rules, which deals with class drops of 40% or more in value. Now we come to the second exception, which, when properly applied, should save you a great deal of money.

A horse whose form is declining, as shown by his last race, is usually one of the poorest wagering propositions in racing. If we can pick him out and determine that he is not likely to run well today, and safely eliminate him, we will have progressed mightily in our efforts to select from the first three favorites the most probable winner. Again, we are dealing only with horses that show at least one qualifying form signal, or else they would be eliminated as not qualified.

I call this a *Declining Horse*. How do we identify him?

A Declining Horse is one whose last race is "demonstrably weaker" than his next-to-last race, if run within 28 days, and provided he was not rising in class. If he rises in class and runs a poorer race, it may be due to being outclassed rather than declining in form. And what do we mean by "demonstrably weaker," since we are still dealing only with those races showing at least one qualifying form signal?

Demonstrably weaker: When a horse is <u>approximately the same</u> number of lengths behind at the first call in his last race as he was at the first call in his next-to-last race, *or farther behind,* <u>and finishes more than 1 length farther behind</u> than he did in the semifinal race, then he is declining off a demonstrably weaker race. This applies in every situation except where there was a gain of five.

An easy example of a Declining Horse is Sheba's Gold, out of the fifth race at Pimlico on April 23, 1980 (from the Eastern edition, *Daily Racing Form,* of that date). Even though she is dropping in class in today's race (we don't know how much), she is on her way to an NQ in our rating book.

5  **PIMLICO**

1 1-16 MILES. (1.41) CLAIMING. Purse $7,800. Fillies and Mares, 4-year-old and upward, weights, 122 lbs. Non-winners of two races at one mile or over since March 11, allowed 3 lbs. One such race, 5 lbs. Two races at any distance since March 4, 8 lbs. Claiming price $8,500 for each $500 to $7,500 1 lb. (Races where entered for $6,500 or less not considered).

Sheba's Gold

Own.—Pappagallo Kathleen
$8,500
B. m. 5, by I Find Gold—Beersheba, by Seven Chances
Br.—Rogers E Jr (Md)
Tr.—Caviness Thomas S

119

	St.	1st	2nd	3rd	Amt.
1980	7	1	1	2	$9,770
1979	3	0	0	1	$660

Date															
8Apr80- 8Pim fst $1\frac{1}{16}$	:48$\frac{2}{5}$ 1:13$\frac{1}{5}$ 1:45$\frac{4}{5}$	ⒻAllowance	3	4	41$\frac{1}{4}$	810	817	730	Iliescu A	b 115	20.70	46–25 Emma Hamilton 119$\frac{1}{2}$ Kittrell 119$\frac{2}{1}$ Northern Halo 119$\frac{2}{1}$			Tired 8
24Mar80- 7Pim fst $1\frac{1}{16}$	:48$\frac{2}{5}$ 1:13 1:45$\frac{2}{5}$	ⒻAllowance	6	1	1$\frac{1}{2}$	13$\frac{1}{2}$	12$\frac{1}{2}$	12	Iliescu A	b 112	23.10	78–19 Sheba's Gold 112^2 Devon Pal 115^7 Overwhelm 119$\frac{2}{1}$			Driving 7
5Mar80- 5Bow gd $1\frac{1}{16}$	:50 1:15$\frac{1}{5}$ 1:48$\frac{4}{5}$	ⒻAllowance	4	2	2$\frac{1}{2}$	23	33	38	Iliescu A	b 112	8.70	54–33 Pretty Vixen 107^3 Gyro Lite 108^5 Sheba's Gold 112^{nk}			Tired 6
26Feb80- 6Bow fst 6f	:22$\frac{1}{5}$:45$\frac{4}{5}$ 1:14$\frac{4}{5}$	ⒻClm 11500	3	3	58$\frac{3}{4}$	511	59	6$\frac{3}{4}$	Iliescu A	b 114	24.80	68–41 No No Baby 114$\frac{1}{4}$ Pity 114no Just Play 113^{nk}			No mishap 7
15Feb80- 6Bow fst 6f	:23$\frac{4}{5}$:47$\frac{4}{5}$ 1:13$\frac{4}{5}$	ⒻClm 11500	3	8	69$\frac{1}{2}$	79$\frac{1}{2}$	810	65$\frac{1}{2}$	Reantillo L J	b 114	4.20e	67–34 No No Baby 108$\frac{1}{4}$ Royal Re Re 114^1 Safely Home119$\frac{3}{4}$			No menace 8
2Feb80-10Bow fst 7f	:23$\frac{2}{5}$:47$\frac{1}{5}$ 1:27$\frac{4}{5}$	ⒻClm c–6500	11	1	3$\frac{1}{2}$	42$\frac{1}{2}$	22	2$\frac{1}{2}$	Kupfer T	b 114	7.50	65–37 Daughter of Devil 114$\frac{1}{4}$ Sheba's Gold 114^{3}AngelsKrown114^1			Wide 12
22Jan80- 3Bow fst 6f	:22$\frac{4}{5}$:45$\frac{3}{5}$ 1:12$\frac{3}{5}$	ⒻClm 6500	6	6	44	46$\frac{1}{2}$	35	34$\frac{1}{4}$	Kupfer T	b 114	13.20	72–26 Humlum 114^1 Daughter of Devil109$\frac{3}{4}$Sheba'sGold114$\frac{1}{4}$			Held show 8
12Feb79- 4Bow fst 6f	:23$\frac{4}{5}$:48$\frac{1}{5}$ 1:14$\frac{4}{5}$	ⒻClm 5000	2	5	75$\frac{1}{2}$	86$\frac{1}{2}$	56$\frac{1}{2}$	33$\frac{1}{2}$	Gilbert R B	b 115	9.40	62–34 Lady Allegro112$^1\frac{1}{2}$She'sHardToBeat110^{2}Sheba'sGold115^{hd}			Rallied 8
30Jan79- 2Bow fst 6f	:22$\frac{4}{5}$:45$\frac{4}{5}$ 1:12$\frac{1}{5}$	ⒻClm 5000	5	3	2^1	2^{hd}	31	52$\frac{3}{4}$	Gilbert R B	b 115	10.60	76–26 Startawave 105no Lady Allegro 112$\frac{2}{1}$ Cheer Me 115no			Weakened 11
15Jan79- 3Bow fst 7f	:23 :45$\frac{4}{5}$ 1:24$\frac{4}{5}$	ⒻClm 6500	7	2	51$\frac{3}{4}$	43$\frac{1}{2}$	89$\frac{1}{2}$	78$\frac{1}{2}$	Lages J A^5	b 109	6.30	73–16 Mink Coat 119$\frac{3}{4}$ Four Summers 110^3 Whirling Loom 114^{hd}			Tired 8

At her last first call, she was 3 lengths farther behind than in the previous race, where she was the leader. She trailed off badly, finishing far back. This was a walloping decline, but she was a strong second choice in the betting, one of the three you would have had to consider had you been at Pimlico that day. But even though she <u>would</u> have qualified on the form rules, her status as a Declining Horse would eliminate her. She finished dead last.

The next example is rather typical, because the horse is running back at the same class and shows an up close at two calls, which would otherwise qualify him. We examine the record of No See Um out of the ninth race at Keystone from the *Daily Racing Form* of May 31, 1980.

Note that at the first call of the last race of 25May80, No See Um was a half-length behind the leader, just as he was in his previous race on 16May80. But did he do as well in his last race? You can see how he steadily fell back and finished considerably farther behind than he did in the preceding contest. This is a classic pattern of a Declining Horse, unable to do as well in his last race as he did in his preceding event. ~~He is to be avoided,~~ and accordingly merits an NQ despite his up close at two calls in his last race.

This completes our form rules for qualifying and not qualifying.

9 KEYSTONE

START
6 FURLONGS
KEYSTONE
FINISH

6 FURLONGS. (1.08⅖) ALLOWANCE. Purse $10,000. 3- and 4-year-olds, which have never won three races. Weights, 3-year-olds, 114 lbs. 4-year-olds, 122 lbs. Non-winners of $6,000 allowed, 2 lbs. $5,400, 4 lbs. $5,100, 6 lbs. (Races where entered for $18,000 or less not considered in estimating allowances.)

No See Um — Ch. g. 3, by Up Spirits—Monarkiss, by Tompion
Br.—Buckner & Mitchell (Ky)
Own.—Nixon R — Tr.—Euster Eugene — **114**

	St.	1st	2nd	3rd	Amt.
1980	7	2	0	2	$12,718
1979	0	M	0	0	

25May80- 6Key	fst	6f	:22⅗	:45⅗	1:10⅗	3↑ Allowance	6	4	2½	$2^{2½}$	$3^{5½}$	$5^{7½}$	Brumfield D	b 115	7.90	81-16	DukeFstDncer108^{1½}Richiejim116^{3}Whtsthedifferenc116^2 Gave way	6
16May80- 8Key	fst	6f	:22⅖	:45⅘	1:12	Allowance	1	6	3½	3½	3^1	4^2	Mucciolo J	b 118⁴	2.00	80-23	AmbtousConsort116^{1}DkFstDncr116½TorsonsVrson114½ Weakened	6
16May80-Dead heat																		
2May80- 7Key	gd	6f	:22⅖	:45⅘	1:12⅗	Allowance	2	3	1^{hd}	1½	$1^{2½}$	1^3	Wilson R	b 122	7.50	79-21	No See Um 122^3 Jilter Bug 116^{2½} Draconic's Chick 122¾ Driving	9
20Apr80- 1Key	fst	6f	:22⅕	:46	1:13	Md Sp Wt	3	3	1^{hd}	$1^{3½}$	1^5	1^3	Wilson R	b 120	3.70	77-24	No See Um 120^3 Comin' Alive 115^{1½} Port O Let 120^1 Driving	9
11Apr80- 5Key	fst	6f	:22⅘	:47⅖	1:13⅘	Md 20000	5	2	1^{hd}	1^{hd}	1½	$3^{5¾}$	Black A S	b 120	3.00	67-28	Darker Valentine 120^{5}ProudChieftain120¾NoSeeUm120^4 Bore out	8
22Mar80- 2Key	my	6f	:23⅕	:48⅕	1:14⅖	Md Sp Wt	12	4	2½	2^{hd}	2^5	6^8	Black A S	b 121	*3.60	62-26	PheasantWarrior121^{4}Comin'Alive121^{1½}DonNtss116^{1½} Speed, tired	12
8Mar80- 1Key	fst	6f	:22⅗	:46⅘	1:14⅖	Md Sp Wt	7	8	$4^{3¼}$	3^2	2^2	$3^{2½}$	Black A S	b 121	*2.20	67-26	Exclusive Home 121^1 Flaming Royal 121^{1½} No SeeUm121^{1½} Wide	9

LATEST WORKOUTS May 10 Key 4f fst :49⅖ b Apr 5 Key 4f my :50⅖ b

How effective are they? You may want to test them yourself, which can be done out of any issue of the *Daily Racing Form.* Look at the winners and study their previous races. More than nine times out of ten, you will see that winners of all prices had one or more of the six qualifying form signs (except those winners whose form was rated U—unknown) and would not be eliminated because of a 40% drop in class or rate as a Declining Horse. Many of the winners who lacked one of the form signals, and would not have qualified on form, will come in with high odds, where you would not have selected them under our method of play in any event.

You will find occasional winners, of course, even among the first three favorites, that rate as NQ in our method of play, and when this occurs, your serenity will surely be ruffled. But, once again, you will eliminate so many losers by strictly applying these rules that your profit results will be enhanced enormously.

4. POINT ALLOWANCES FOR POWERFUL FORM

When a horse's form is not only within our qualifying range but shows positive signs of improvement, he can usually be expected to do well in the race before us. The method of identifying an *Improving Horse* is even more simple than picking out the decliner. If a horse ran *more than* 1 length nearer the lead at three of the four calls in his last race than he did in the previous race (within the allowable time frame of twenty-eight days, of course), and was not dropping in class in his last race, he can be called an Improving Horse. These three calls must be successive ones, either the first three, or the last three.

In addition, the horse must otherwise qualify on our form rules. Improvement from far, far back to merely far back is not sufficient. Any comparison of lengths behind must end within less than 6 lengths of the leader, as in other situations.

While identifying an Improving Horse is usually fairly easy, let's see what we can learn from Eternal Rock, who ran at Bowie on February 18, 1980, and whose record is taken from the *Racing Form* of that date:

Eternal Rock — B. h. 5, by Rollicking—Eternal Path, by Eternal Bull — $18,500
Own.—Wasserman Janice
Br.—Glade Valley Farms Inc (Md)
Tr.—Gaudet Dean
117 — Turf Record: St. 1st 2nd 3rd: 3 0 0 0

	St.	1st	2nd	3rd	Amt.
1980	4	1	0	2	$7,560
1979	5	0	0	1	$1,020

7Feb80- 7Bow	fst	6f	:22⅘	:46⅖	1:12	Clm 18500	6	1	5^{7}	5^{4}	3½	1½	Wright D R	114	5.60	80-32	Eternal Rock 114½ Time To Bid 1141¾ Percy's Game 1224½	Driving	7
1Feb80- 6Bow	fst	7f	:22⅗	:45⅕	1:24⅗	Clm 35000 •	3	8	8^{11}	8^{9}¾	8^{9}¾	8^{13}	Lindberg G	113	5.40e	69-37	Quill's Turn 113^{3} El Capo 114^{3} Call the King 115¾	No factor	9
10Jan80- 7Bow	fst	7f	:23⅗	:47⅖	1:25⅗	Clm 21000 •	2	5	5^{6}	4^{2}½	4^{5}	3^{2}½	Wright D R	113	5.70	75-27	Quill's Turn 114½ Nayob 114^{2} Eternal Rock 113^{hd}	Rallied	8
2Jan80- 7Bow	fst	6f	:22⅘	:46⅕	1:12⅗	Clm 18500	1	4	5^{9}½	5^{13}	5^{10}	3^{4}¾	Wright D R	112	12.80	72-36	NorthernBron113^{2}½BoldndLucky117^{2}½EternlRock112^{1}½	Late gain	6
29Nov79- 8Lrl	gd	1	:46⅗	1:11⅘	1:37⅘	3↑ Clm 22500	2	7	7^{7}¾	7^{6}	7^{3}½	7^{5}½	Wright D R	113	8.00	78-22	Judgement Call 110^{nk} Rhino 110½ Sea Defier 114^{1}	Outrun	8
17Nov79- 6Lrl	fst	1	:47⅖	1:12⅖	1:37⅘	3↑ Clm 25000	6	1	1^{hd}	1^{hd}	2^{hd}	5^{nk}	Wright D R	113	7.40	84-14	Zyder Z. 113no Sea Defier 114no Straight Sets 113^{hd}	Weakened	8
10Nov79- 1Lrl	sly	6f	:22⅘	:46⅖	1:11⅗	3↑ Clm 20000	5	8	8^{9}	7^{13}	7^{8}¾	3^{5}¾	Fell J	115	10.70	83-18	Quill's Turn 110¾ BoldandLucky115^{5}EternalRock115^{nk}	Stride late	8
24Oct79- 8Pim	fst	6f	:23⅗	:47	1:12⅗	3↑ Clm 20000	5	3	4^{3}	5^{3}½	5^{3}½	5^{2}½	Torre M J	115	15.80e	81-21	King of Classics 113^{hd}FiddleFingers115^{nk}HunterF.113^{1}	No factor	7
9Oct79- 8Lrl	my	6f	:22⅗	:47	1:12	3↑ Allowance	8	8	8^{12}	8^{12}	8^{12}	8^{12}	Wright D R	116	30.20	74-26	Convenient 114^{3} Bolductive 115^{hd} I Know Why 112^{1}¾	No speed	9
14Nov78- 5Lrl	fm	1	(T):47⅗	1:12	1:36⅗	3↑ Clm 25000	2	4	4^{3}½	4^{2}½	6^{4}¾	6^{4}¾	Wright D R	110	13.30	82-13	Hold Em Joe 110^{nk} Flight Arrival 113^{hd} Swan Flight 113^{2}	Tired	8

LATEST WORKOUTS Feb 14 Bow 4f fst :50 b Jan 17 Bow 4f fst :51⅗ b

Bear in mind we are not talking about qualifying on form, since Eternal Rock qualifies easily by winning his last race. But does this last race make him an Improving Horse? No, because his great improvement was shown in a drop in class down to $18,500 from his previous effort at $35,000. Against horses of lesser ability, he should have been much closer to the front in his last race.

While we are at it, you will note that in the 7Feb80 race, Eternal Rock was dropping more than 40% in class from his previous race, yet he emerged a victor. Would our rule on placing an NQ on a horse dropping more than 40% apply to Eternal Rock? Note that in his race of 10Jan80, he ran for a price tag of $21,000 and on 1Feb80, his trainer elevated him all the way up to $35,000. Now look back down his previous running lines and you will see that $25,000 is the highest price previously placed on him. You can omit the one allowance race on 9Oct70 at Laurel. You may conclude that $25,000 is a more reasonable claiming price, that the $35,000 of 1Feb80 was artificial, and that, accordingly, he was not dropping 40% in class on 7Feb80 when he was entered at $18,500 and returned as a winner.

As in many past performances there are other applications of lessons learned when we study Eternal Rock's record. Compare his race of 10Jan80 with his effort of 2Jan80. He was more than a length closer at every call in the 10Jan80 race even with a slight rise in class, and this made him an Improving Horse (for all the good it did when he jumped in class all the way up to $35,000).

Testing our skill a step further, compare the 29Nov79 race with the previous run of 17Nov79. Would the 29Nov79 race make him a Declining Horse when he went to the post on 2Jan80? No, because he was absent more than 28 days between races. He would have been listed merely as unknown in form. But for his race of 29Nov79, you would compare the 17Nov79 race against the 10Nov79 race, since they came in quick sequence. Because he ran better at every call on 17Nov79, he would have rated as an improving horse for the 29Nov79 effort. The fact that he ran poorly does not take away from the fact that he deserved an improved rating.

Now, we can apply another test in comparing the races of 10Nov79 and 24Oct79 to see how Eternal Rock would have rated when he went to the post on November 17, 1979. On 10Nov79, he was more than a length farther from the lead at every call. But he also scored better than a gain of five from the stretch call to the finish, even at the limit of 8 lengths back. Thus, he is not a Declining Horse and would qualify on form.

2 lengths
4 places
6

Now that we have identified the Improving Horse, what kind of point rating for form is adequate? Our line is 2 points for an Improving Horse, and whenever we find that development, these 2 points will be considered as form points, and added to his ability point total.

There is but one reservation on this addition. It should not be used to increase total points above what a horse's best ability time would rate, if it were doubled. For example, if a horse showed ability times of :25.0 and :25.2, for 15 and 13 points respectively, we would add 2 points if he was an Improving Horse. But if his ability times were :25.0 and :25.1, we would add only 1 point, so he would not exceed an ability plus form rating of 30, so it would not be more than twice what his best ability time would produce. And, of course, as does frequently happen, if the two ability times were :25.0 and :25.0, we would add nothing at all, even if there was an improved running line.

Now, we come to the second addition for good form, which is very strong indeed. A number of years ago, Tom Ainslie coined the phrase *Big Win,* which made such an impression on me that I began to use it as a matter of course, as a regular part of my handicapping language. A Big Win is a scintillating sign of a horse's readiness to run. If a horse won his last race (within the allowable twenty-eight days) by more than 3 lengths, and was not leading by more than 1 length at the first call, this is a Big Win for our purposes here, and I will award him 4 points, no matter what his ability times may be. This is an arbitrary award of points, which could as easily be 5 (and I sometimes wonder if it should not be), but for the purposes of our rating, it merits a 4.

The reason why a horse should not be leading at the first call by more than a length to rate a Big Win 4 points is that his early speed might discourage his competitors, who might let him run away with the race. The margin of victory would then be unrealistic. But when a horse fights off close rivals, or runs past them, and finishes more than 3 lengths in front, he is entitled to this rating.

There are numerous examples in every issue of the *Daily Racing Form.* Illustrative is Pink Bolero, from the West Coast edition of February 14, 1980, which shows how this filly demolished her opposition in her previous race on 31Jan80:

She ran away from her rivals and finished 3¾ lengths ahead of the second-place filly. She even shows two other Big Wins in her past performances, in the races of 8Nov79 and 22Jun79. You don't need to remind me that she did not win either of the two races following. No one ever said a Big Win was a guarantee of a victory next time out, but only that it is an enormously powerful form indicator. But after each of her previous Big Wins, she was raised drastically in class, which probably had something to do with her ultimate finish.

5. SUMMARY OF RULES ON FORM

Now that we have completed the essential rules on form, let's repeat them again in this summary for your handy reference.

1. All horses will receive a rating on form, either U for unknown, Q for qualified, or NQ for not qualified.

Unknown Form

2. A horse's rating for form will usually be based off his last race, which must have been run within twenty-eight days of today's race. If a horse has not run within the past twenty-eight days, he will usually receive a rating of U, with these exceptions: A stakes horse or high-priced allowance horse that shows four recent workouts, evenly spaced, can receive a Q rating, and a horse in a sprint race only that shows consistent early speed (with a total of 20 lengths or less behind at his ten first calls) can receive a Q rating.

Unknown and Known Form from Dirt to Grass and from Grass to Dirt

3. If today's race is on the grass, and the horse's last race was on the dirt, within the past twenty-eight days, his form will be judged as follows:

a. If the horse has never run on grass before, he will receive a U rating for both ability and form.

b. If the horse has run on grass before, and shows good grass form, such as 20% previous wins or 33% previous place finishes (unless he is lightly raced and shows some good form), he can be rated as Q on form if his last dirt race would merit a Q rating. If his last dirt race would not merit a Q rating, then the horse would have to be rated U for today's grass race.

c. If the horse has run on grass before, but does not show good grass form in the past, he will rate as unknown if his last race on the dirt within twenty-eight days was good. If his last dirt race was an NQ race, and without good grass form in the past, the horse must rate an NQ for today's grass race.

d. If the last dirt race was NQ on form, and if there was a preceding grass race within twenty-eight days of the last poor dirt race, then go back to the preceding grass race and rate for form off it.

4. If today's race is on the dirt and the last race within twenty-eight days was on the grass, the horse's form will be judged in this manner:

a. If the last grass race rated a Q for form, then rate him the same for today's dirt race.

b. If the last grass race rated an NQ on form, then rate him off a previous race on the dirt within twenty-eight days of the grass race. If there was no dirt race within twenty-eight days of the previous grass race, his form will be rated U.

When the Last Race Was Not Representative

5. The last race may not have been representative, as far as true form is concerned, if the horse ran at a higher class than he was accustomed to and is dropping back today to a more competitive class. This is my up-and-down-dropper pattern, which is defined in this manner: If the last race within twenty-eight days showed a rise in class of 20% and today's race shows a drop in class of 20% or more, or to a figure of the approximate same class as the semifinal race, then do not use the last race, but rate the horse off the previous race within twenty-eight days.

6. The last race may not be representative for other reasons as well. Where a horse apparently bogged down in the mud or on a heavy track, it is permissible to use the next-to-last race, if it was within twenty-eight days of the unrepresentative race. If there was no race within that twenty-eight-day period, the horse will be rated U.

The Qualified Horse

7. A horse is entitled to a qualified, or Q, rating ordinarily if he meets any one of the following standards in his last race within twenty-eight days, or in the race in which he is rated:
    a. Up close at any two calls.
    b. Up close at one call with a class drop of 20% or more.
    c. A gain of five in either lengths or horses or both.
    d. A gain of three between two consecutive calls with a drop in class.
    e. A finish of second.
    f. Where there is not a gain or loss of more than two lengths between any two calls, or a horse is said to have run "Evenly" in the Eastern edition of the *Daily Racing Form*.

The Not-Qualified Horse

8. Horses are rated NQ in these situations:
    a. Failure to meet any one of the six standards for a Q rating.
    b. Even with meeting Q standards, a horse will be rated NQ if he is dropping 40% or more in class price, except for a gain of five or up close at two calls.
    c. When a horse's form labels him a Declining Horse, which occurs when a comparison between his last race and his previous race within twenty-eight days shows that at the first call of his last race, he was approximately the same number of lengths behind the leader as he was in the semifinal race, or farther behind, and where he finishes more than 1 length behind the leader than in his next-to-last race. This applies even if he showed one or more qualifying factors in his last race, except for a gain of five, which will always make him a Q horse.

Additional Points for Form

9. A horse will be allowed 2 form points for improvement, provided these 2 points would not exceed twice the sum of his best ability points. A horse that ran more than 1 length closer to the leader at three or more consecutive calls of his last race than in his previous race within twenty-eight days at the same class or higher is an Improving Horse.
10. A horse will be allowed 4 form points for what is known as a Big Win, which occurs when he wins his last race by more than 3 lengths, provided he was not more than 1 length ahead at the first call.

CHAPTER VIII

SELECTING THE INVESTMENT HORSE

Thus far, I have shown you how to calculate ability points, how to modify them by early-speed allowances in sprint races and races up to one mile in distance, and how to rate horses on form, with allowances for some form points. The final task now is to arrive at some final figures and from them determine how we select the horses in which to make our investments.

1. LOOKING FOR POINT ADVANTAGES

In most races, where all ability times are known and each horse has a known form rating, we will look among the first three choices in the odds for a horse that has *two or more total points* more than his nearest rival. Total points, again, are the sum of two races' ability ratings, modified by early-speed points where applicable, plus any points that may be allowed for form. A horse with an advantage of 2 points or more will be played to win and to place.

If a horse among the first three has but a 1-point advantage, we will not make a win investment, but will play this horse to place only. If two or more horses are tied in total points, we would bet to place only on the horse with the lower odds. If two of these horses that are tied in points are also tied on the odds board, or very close to it, then this is a race that we will pass altogether— not bet at all.

115

While we are looking for advantages, I have previously pointed out that if a horse has two ability times better than the best of any of his competitors, he is a *Double Advantage Horse*. This is one of the soundest investments in racing, as Double Advantage Horses win so frequently that our only regret is that there are not enough of them.

But a horse whose ability times would make him a Double Advantage Horse may slump somewhat in sprint races if he lacks early speed. Here is how we handle situations of this kind:

If a Double Advantage Horse is so deficient in early speed that he gets 0 points in that department, and there is any other horse in the race with qualified form with 6 early-speed points, then I will play the Double Advantage Horse to place only. This is regardless of the final point totals, whether or not the 6 additional early-speed points make the challenger the highest-point horse or whether the Double Advantage points are still sufficient to leave the stronger animal with a higher rating. The reason for this safety rule is that the early speedster may likely get out in front and hold on, fighting off our late-closer Double Advantage animal. As you will see, the DA horse still frequently finishes second when he is not able to win.

2. RACES NOT TO PLAY

While we hope to play every race possible, there are some races where it does not make sense to play. I have already mentioned the race where horses are tied in total points and approximately tied in odds also. We pass there because without an advantage, the race becomes a gamble, which we will avoid. Otherwise, here are some other races that we will not play:

1. Maiden special races where three or more of the entries are first-time starters will be passed, except in those races where either the favorite is a Double Advantage Horse in ability times or the favorite's only ability time is superior by two or more ticks to any of his competitors who have run previously.

2. Turf races where none of the first three favorites shows a grass race among the ten shown in his past performances, or where none shows a known qualified form rating, must be passed.

3. When none of the first three favorites shows a Q form rating, you must pass the race altogether.

3. RULES WHERE ONE OR MORE FAVORITES HAVE UNKNOWN ABILITY

When there are no races in a horse's past performances that allow you to calculate at least one ability time for him, his ability, as I earlier indicated, must be rated as underlined, which carries with it a U for form as well. When one or more of the first three favorites lacks an ability rating of any kind, you are placed back in the arena of guesswork, which can be dangerous. In these situations, we will be guided by the odds board. If the unknown-ability horse is the strong favorite, this is at least an indication that someone has high regard for that ability, about which we know nothing. We cannot play such a horse, because it constitutes an unknown gamble. Therefore, we will play the highest-rated known-ability horse to place only.

What do we mean by "strong favorite"? The unknown-ability horse, to be a strong favorite, must show on the board at least one full number advantage in the odds. An even-money favorite at 1-1 is a full point ahead of the 2-1 horse, as is the 3-2 favorite over the 5-2 second choice. But a 3-2 favorite is not a full point above the 2-1 second choice, nor is the 2-1 horse a full point ahead of the 5-2 second choice. When the odds are this closely bunched, you can be sure that the unknown-ability horse, while highly regarded, is not considered to be far enough ahead of his known-ability rivals to invoke our rule. A known-ability horse with strong credentials, who is a sound second choice in the wagering within less than one numeral of the favorite, may thus be played to win and place.

4. RULES WHERE ONE OR MORE FAVORITES HAVE UNKNOWN FORM

1. When the first favorite is a Double Advantage Horse with U form (provided his early-speed points are better than 0), and when he shows at least one recent workout, I will play him to win and place because of the potency of the Double Advantage. If he has no workouts at all, and is the favorite, I will play him to place only. If he has no workouts and is not the favorite, then he will be treated like any other unknown-form horse.

2. For U horses that are not Double Advantage, when a horse has the highest rating by 2 points or more, he should be passed and a place bet made only on the Q horse with the highest points. The unknown-form horse, because of his ability, might win, but our known-quality animal might still get second and save our investment.

3. Any unknown-form that does not have as many as 2 more points than his rivals will be passed and a win and place bet made on the qualified-form horse with the highest point rating.

5. SPECIAL HANDLING FOR LIGHTLY RACED FAVORITES

If a horse has run five times or fewer, I call him a *Lightly Raced Horse*. The significance of this is that there is not enough experience on the board to provide a full evaluation of the horse's ability. Problems in this area arise only when a Lightly Raced Horse is the favorite, but does not have the highest total points. When the Lightly Raced Horse does have the highest point rating, whether he is the actual favorite or not, bet him with great confidence.

When the Lightly Raced Horse is the favorite and does not have the highest points, you may bet him to win and place in one situation only: provided he scored a Big Win in his last race. This is a strong indication that he will do extremely well today. You can back him just to place in one situation: when he showed an improvement in his last race sufficient to merit 2 form points. This means that he is likely to do well today, but does not give us quite enough confidence in his ability to warrant full backing. But the place bet is a sound investment in this situation.

6. SPECIAL HANDLING FOR MAIDEN CLAIMERS

Maiden claiming races are somewhat different for our purposes than maiden special (or straight maiden in the Midwest and Far West) events. No matter how many first-time starters you may find in a maiden claiming event, go ahead and play the top-rated horse if he otherwise measures up. But there are still some special considerations to take into account in these kinds of races.

A horse that has gone to the post too often without winning is usually becoming a little frayed around the edges. Therefore, if a horse in a maiden claiming event has run eight times or more without winning, and there is another horse among the first three favorites that has run five times or less, making him a Lightly Raced Horse, and this second animal is within 5 total points of the runner with eight or more starts, I will pass the frequent loser and play the Lightly Raced Horse to win and place. Losing becomes a habit, and I don't like it. However, if the experienced runner is a Double Advantage Horse, then I will play him no matter what.

The second warning in maiden claiming races, and maiden specials as well, is to avoid horses with the dread disease of "seconditis." A horse that finishes second three or more times without winning in at least one-third of his races is also taking on aspects of a chronic, confirmed loser. This rule is drawn to center on horses that have run enough times to get three second-place finishes in a few races, but does not apply where a horse may have run twenty times or more with only three seconds, since we require second-place finishes in at least one-third of his efforts. Don't even bet this horse to place—pass him altogether, except for the usual rule of a Double Advantage Horse. Even if he is afflicted with seconditis, a Double Advantage may be enough to get him home first today.

7. DEALING WITH HORSES WITH ONLY ONE ABILITY TIME

In many races, particularly with lightly raced horses, or even in grass races where there is little grass experience, you will find one horse with only one ratable race while others have two or more. You could double the ability-time points based on the one performance, but I have found this somewhat unreliable. Therefore, when a horse shows only one ratable ability time, I will compare his competitors by using only the highest of their two ability times, so all of them will be compared at the same mathematical level. This is not an ideal situation, but among the choices, it seems to come out best.

8. PRACTICE EXAMPLES FOR PREPARATION

Now that all the rules are laid out for the selection of the investment horse, we shall try a few examples to prepare you to follow the next several chapters on the Big Week at Belmont. When these examples are completed, and when all the Belmont races are analyzed, you should be so familiar with the method of selection and the use of ability times, early speed, form ratings, and the like that you will be fully prepared to launch your own investment program.

Let's start with a very easy one, taken from the *Daily Racing Form* of Wednesday, April 23, 1980, in the first race at Aqueduct. Since this is a distance race, we will not use early-speed adjustments. Earlier in this book, when I discussed early speed, I pointed out that you might want to use it in races of a mile and an eighth at Aqueduct because the starting gate is so close to the first turn. But it is optional, and here we opt out. But if you do your calculations on early speed, you will find that it makes no difference in the result of this race.

We shall begin with Sturdy Knight, who shows on the tote board at 5-1 as the second choice in the wagering.

1 AQUEDUCT — 1⅛ MILES AQUEDUCT (START | FINISH)

1 ⅛ MILES. (1.47) CLAIMING. Purse $12,000. 4-year-olds and upward, 122 lbs. Non-winners of two races at a mile or over since March 15, allowed 3 lbs.; of such a race since then, 5 lbs. Claiming price $16,000; for each $1,000 to $14,000, 2 lbs. (Races when entered to be claimed for $12,500 or less not considered.)

Sturdy Knight — Own.—Bel-Sar-Ac Stable

Ch. g. 7, by Call Me Prince—Herela, by King Hairan — **$14,000** — **Br.—Ingels L R (Ky)** — **Tr.—Tufariello Frank** — 108^{5}

Turf Record	St.	1st	2nd	3rd
	4	0	0	0

	St.	1st	2nd	3rd	Amt.
1980	5	0	1	0	$2,980
1979	23	6	3	1	$50,250

10Apr80- 5Aqu	gd	7f	:22$\frac{4}{5}$	:45$\frac{4}{5}$	1:22$\frac{3}{5}$	Clm 15000	3	4	2^{1}	3^{1}	4^{10}	5^{14}	Asmussen C B	b 115	3.00	74-16	Beau Strad 114$^{5\frac{3}{4}}$ Fellow Heir 117$^{5\frac{1}{2}}$ Happy Hour 117$^{\frac{1}{2}}$	Tired	6
21Feb80- 9Aqu	fst	1$\frac{1}{16}$	⊡:47$\frac{2}{5}$	1:12$\frac{3}{5}$	1:45$\frac{3}{5}$	Clm 20000	1	1	1^{2}	1^{hd}	$2^{\frac{1}{2}}$	$4^{1\frac{1}{4}}$	Beitia E^{5}	b 112	8.10	85-18	Special Size 117no Beausy 112$^{1\frac{1}{4}}$ Wimpfybell 110^{hd}	Weakened	10
9Feb80- 1Aqu	fst	170	⊡:47$\frac{4}{5}$	1:13$\frac{2}{5}$	1:44	Clm c-16000	7	3	3^{nk}	$3^{3\frac{1}{2}}$	5^{12}	6^{18}	Dahlquist T C^{5}	b 112	*1.80	64-19	L'Arsouille 107$^{4\frac{1}{4}}$ Framarco 117$^{6\frac{3}{4}}$ Double Edge Blade 114$^{4\frac{1}{4}}$	Wide	10
1Feb80- 3Aqu	fst	6f	⊡:23	:48$\frac{2}{5}$	1:13$\frac{1}{5}$	Clm 16000	2	9	$8^{3\frac{3}{4}}$	$8^{2\frac{1}{2}}$	$3^{2\frac{1}{2}}$	2^{6}	Lopez C C^{5}	b 112	4.80	72-25	Peaceful Country 117^{6} Sturdy Knight 112^{3}PapaPia108$^{1\frac{1}{2}}$	Fin. well	10
14Jan80- 5Aqu	gd	1$\frac{1}{16}$	⊡:47$\frac{2}{5}$	1:12$\frac{4}{5}$	1:47$\frac{1}{5}$	Hcp 12500s	1	3	2^{4}	3^{5}	$5^{6\frac{1}{2}}$	$7^{6\frac{1}{4}}$	Amy J	b 120	6.60	72-23	Home By Dawn 114no Quranta Bay 113^{nk} Fellow Heir 109$^{\frac{3}{4}}$	Tired	9
31Dec79- 7Med	fst	170	:47	1:12$\frac{4}{5}$	1:44$\frac{4}{5}$	3↑Allowance	3	3	3^{8}	$4^{9\frac{1}{2}}$	4^{6}	$4^{3\frac{3}{4}}$	Gonzalez M A^{5}	b 111	*2.00	73-25	Twin Fort 116$^{\frac{3}{4}}$ John Joe 111no Balakiev 113^{3}	Evenly	8
28Nov79- 8Med	fst	170	:45$\frac{4}{5}$	1:13	1:44$\frac{3}{5}$	3↑Allowance	3	3	3^{5}	3^{3}	3^{4}	$3^{4\frac{1}{4}}$	Cordero A Jr	b 122	*1.30	74-26	General H. D. 108^{2} Ambitious Ruler 119$^{2\frac{1}{4}}$SturdyKnight122^{1}	Wide	6
19Nov79- 8Med	yl	170	Ⓣ:48$\frac{1}{5}$	1:15$\frac{4}{5}$	1:45$\frac{3}{5}$	3↑Allowance	8	3	3^{3}	$6^{4\frac{3}{4}}$	$5^{7\frac{1}{4}}$	$7^{8\frac{1}{4}}$	Fann B	b 122	9.10	54-38	Bananas Foster 116^{3} LightningLead116$^{1\frac{1}{2}}$WorthyPiper108$^{1\frac{1}{4}}$	Tired	8
8Nov79- 8Med	fst	170	:46$\frac{2}{5}$	1:12$\frac{1}{5}$	1:44$\frac{1}{5}$	3↑Allowance	1	1	1^{hd}	2^{hd}	$1^{1\frac{1}{2}}$	2^{hd}	Fann B	b 122	4.40	80-21	King of Jive 119^{hd} Sturdy Knight 122^{1} Apaway 119$^{\frac{3}{4}}$	Gamely	7
1Nov79- 8Med	fst	170	:47$\frac{1}{5}$	1:13	1:44	3↑Allowance	4	6	$4^{2\frac{1}{4}}$	$2^{\frac{1}{2}}$	$1^{1\frac{1}{2}}$	1^{3}	Fann B	b 116	*1.20	81-21	Sturdy Knight 116^{3} Emanator 108$^{1\frac{1}{2}}$ Pie 116^{7}	Driving	8

LATEST WORKOUTS Apr 7 Aqu 4f fst :50$\frac{2}{5}$ b Mar 20 Aqu 4f fst :51 b

The first inquiry is to see if he qualifies on form. In his last race he was up close, within 1 length of the leader at the first two calls, and since the race was run thirteen days previously, he qualifies on form rather easily. Now we look to see how his ability times are rated. In his next-to-last race on 21Feb80, we observe that his speed rating was high and that he ran well. The lead time, which Sturdy Knight established, was :25.1, but his first call time of 47 and change requires us to add 1 energy-adjustment point for a :25.2. Looking down the line at all his races, we can see that the 8Nov79 run at the Meadowlands reveals a :25.4 lead time which Sturdy Knight also established. There are no adjustments to be made, and we conclude that his two best ability times are :25.2 and :25.4. We will record them later along with those of the two other top choices in the betting.

The third favorite is Hasty Trial, also carrying unusually high odds on the board, almost 7-1 in the final calculation. Here is what his past performances tell us.

Hasty Trial — Dk. b. or br. c. 4, by Personality—Tryall, by Hasty Road
Own.—Blossom Cherry — $15,000 — Br.—Haggin L L III (Ky) — Tr.—Shapoff Stanley R — 115

	St.	1st	2nd	3rd	Amt.
1980	6	1	2	1	$11,150
1979	0	M	0	0	

14Apr80- 3Aqu fst 1⅛	:49⅕	1:13⅘	1:52⅕	Clm 15000	4	5	5^{6}	$5^{6\frac{1}{4}}$	$5^{3\frac{1}{4}}$	$3^{3\frac{3}{4}}$	Fell J	b 115	11.40	70–21	Sir Violet $112^{1\frac{1}{2}}$ Special Size $117^{2\frac{1}{4}}$ Hasty Trial $115^{1\frac{1}{4}}$	Rallied	5
5Apr80- 3Aqu my 1$\frac{3}{16}$	:48⅘	1:14⅘	2:00	Clm 16000	3	5	5^{4}	$5^{1\frac{3}{4}}$	$4^{6\frac{1}{2}}$	4^{9}	Fell J	b 117	11.60	53–28	Amano 117^{nk} Scamp Boy $117^{7\frac{3}{4}}$ Sir Violet 112^{1}	Even effort	7
24Mar80- 1Aqu fst 1	:46⅘	1:12⅗	1:39⅗ 3 ↑	Md 12500	3	7	$6^{4\frac{1}{2}}$	5^{5}	3^{4}	1^{1}	Castaneda M	b 126	3.70	68–24	Hasty Trial 126^{1} Sir Raja $119^{1\frac{1}{4}}$ Village Beau 122^{2}	Driving	14
5Mar80- 4Aqu fst 1$\frac{1}{16}$ ⊡	:49	1:14⅘	1:48⅕ 3 ↑	Md 18000	8	7	5^{5}	$3^{2\frac{1}{2}}$	4^{6}	$2^{6\frac{1}{2}}$	Miranda J	b 122	13.60	66–22	Lord Rumbottom $122^{6\frac{1}{2}}$ HastyTrial122^{no}ExactSam114^{hd}	Game try	10
25Feb80- 4Aqu fst 1$\frac{1}{16}$ ⊡	:50	1:16⅖	1:49⅕	Md 12500	8	5	6^{4}	6^{4}	2^{6}	$2^{8\frac{1}{2}}$	Castaneda M	b 122	12.70	59–20	Love to Love $120^{8\frac{1}{2}}$ Hasty Trial $122^{1\frac{1}{2}}$ Italitex$111^{2\frac{3}{4}}$	Shuffled back	10
14Feb80- 1Aqu fst 6f ⊡	:22⅗	:47	1:12⅗	Md 12500	3	11	11^{14}	10^{13}	9^{13}	7^{14}	McNeil T7	b 115	8.70	67–25	Quid's In $122^{3\frac{1}{2}}$ Beachois $117^{7\frac{3}{4}}$ Bold n' Great $118^{1\frac{1}{4}}$	Outrun	12

LATEST WORKOUTS Apr 2 Bel tr.t 3f fst :35⅗ h — Mar 13 Bel tr.t 4f fst :50 b — Mar 4 Bel tr.t 3f fst :37 b — Feb 23 Bel tr.t 4f my :48 h

Immediately, we can see problems with form. He was not up close in his last race at any call, and is not dropping in class, since he is running at the same $15,000 level at which he competed on 14Apr80. We now must check his running line to see if he can qualify off a sufficient gain. From the second call to the finish, he gained two in horses and 2½ lengths. This falls just short of a gain of five, which would have qualified him on form. When a horse is very close to qualifying on gain, I will take a second look usually, for if he does have strong ability times, he might be a threat to the others. But here, with his odds so high, and since he is running at the same price level as in his previous race, we will adhere to the rule and rate him as NQ, not qualified, on form.

We now come to the favorite, Debtor's Haven, who is 3-5 on the board, heavily backed by the crowd. When odds are so low on one of the top choices in the betting, it will invariabily push the odds much higher on the other contenders, as a part of the balancing of the mutuel pool. When you analyze the record of Debtor's Haven, you will readily see why he is such a heavy favorite in this race.

In form, he qualifies off his last race because he finished second. There was also a gain of five from the stretch call to the finish. But look at those ability

Debtor's Haven * Ch. h. 7, by Tom Rolfe—Due Dilly, by Sir Gaylord

Own.—Barrera O S $16,000 Br.—Meadow Stud Inc (Va) Tr.—Barrera Oscar S 117

Turf Record St. 1st 2nd 3rd 7 0 1 0

St. 1st 2nd 3rd Amt. 1980 10 1 2 1 $17,960 1979 25 5 5 4 $67,980

17Apr80- 3Aqu fst 7f :23⅖ :46⅘ 1:24⅕ Clm 18000 1 7 43½ 43½ 44½ 21 Fell J b 114 2.80 79-23 Nice Sailing 1171 Debtor's Haven 1141½Itsagoodlife112nk Gamely 7
10Apr80- 3Aqu gd 7f :23⅕ :46 1:23 Clm 15000 4 5 67 46 21½ 12 Fell J b 115 2.90 86-16 Debtor's Haven1152Laddy'sLuck1175½OutofTown117¾ Ridden out 7
2Apr80- 1Aqu fst 6f :22⅘ :46⅕ 1:11 Clm 16000 8 10 95½ 74¾ 64¾ 65 Amy J b 117 7.40 83-18 Beau Strad 112no Marsh's Robber 113nk Whiddon1082½ No threat 11
29Mar80- 5Aqu sly 1 :46⅗ 1:11⅗ 1:37⅗ Clm 19000 5 8 55 46 46 411 Amy J b 115 5.20 67-27 Arctic Service 1191¼ Pass Deceiver 1107 Caraqueno 1172¾ Tired 10
9Feb80- 2Aqu fst 6f ⊡:22⅗ :46⅕ 1:11⅕ Clm 32500 1 7 710 78½ 78¾ 67 Hernandez R b 117 6.60 81-19 Ephphatha 1134DoubleRevival115¾NiceSailing110nk Ret. bleeding 7
31Jan80- 9Aqu fst 6f ⊡:23⅖ :47⅖ 1:12⅖ Clm 32500 1 12 129¼109¼ 98¾ 98¾ Miranda J b 117 *3.60 73-25 Bold Phantom 1172 Coupon Rate 112½ Master A. J. 1173 Outrun 12
26Jan80- 2Aqu fst 170 ⊡:46⅘ 1:11⅗ 1:42⅕ Clm 47500 3 4 47 57 67 711 Amy J b 117 *1.30 80-17 Winterlock 115½ Fiddle Faddle 1174 Intercontinent 1133 Tired 7
18Jan80- 8Aqu fst 6f ⊡:22⅖ :45⅘ 1:11⅕ Allowance 5 5 56 55¾ 42¼ 2no Amy J b 115 14.10 88-19 BoldndStormy115noDebtor'sHven115noKingBoldRlity115½ Gamely 6
12Jan80- 2Aqu my 1 1/16 ⊡:47⅘ 1:12⅖ 1:45⅗ Clm 45000 9 2 1hd 1½ 21 32¼ Beitia E5 b 112 5.90 84-22 Bankers Sun 1122 YouGoFirst112nkDebtor'sHaven112½ Weakened 10
4Jan80- 8Aqu fst 1 1/16 ⊡:47⅘ 1:12⅖ 1:44⅖ Allowance 4 5 54½ 812 819 820 Montoya D b 117 7.00 72-22 Pianist 1195 Pass 'n Raise 119¾ Sir Rossel 117hd No factor 8

LATEST WORKOUTS Mar 27 Bel tr.t 4f fst :50 b

times! Both his last two races at seven furlongs were sensational. Turning to our parallel time chart to reduce them to six furlongs, in the last race we reduce the winning time of 1:24.1 at 7f to 1:11.1 for 6f. You can now compute the lead time for 6f as 1:11.1 – :46.4, or :24.2. Debtor's Haven gained 2½ lengths from the second call to the finish, allowing us to reduce his ability time by two ticks to :24.0. The second call time of :46.4 gets an addition of four ticks for lengths behind, up to :47.3, which requires us to add one tick for energy adjustment to level Debtor's Haven at :24.1.

But we have only begun. The race of 10Apr80 was even better. Again, we must convert the 7f time of 1:23.0 to the 6f time of 1:10.2. The second call lead time was :46.0, which gives us a :24.2 lead time. Debtor's Haven gained 6 lengths, allowing us to bring his ability time down by four ticks to :23.3. The second call time for Debtor's Haven gets six ticks added to the :46.0 up to :47.1, requiring an additional tick for energy to level his ability time at :23.4.

We can now make the kind of comparison chart that we will use throughout this book. Here is what it reveals:

Odds	Horse	Ability		A Pts		F	Total
.7	Debtor's Haven	:23.4	:24.1	21	19	Q	40
5.9	Sturdy Knight	:25.2	:25.4	13	11	Q	24
6.9	Hasty Trial	—	—	—	—	NQ	—

Debtor's Haven is an outstanding selection, just as the crowd easily recognized. Not only are his points far above his two weak competitors, but he is a Double Advantage Horse, almost certain to win unless some misfortune should befall him. It did not, and Debtor's Haven came home a winner, just as was expected, paying the very short price of $3.40 to win and only $2.60 to place. Many players will turn up their noses at such short prices and will pass a race like this one where a horse goes off at 3-5 odds. But it was like money in the bank, especially when one horse is so superior to his rivals in the rating method that we use.

All races are not nearly as easy as this one, as you will see when we look at another race on this same card, where lightly raced and well-bred maidens are entered. We'll begin with the favorite, Fancy Caper.

5 **AQUEDUCT**

7 FURLONGS. (1.20⅕) MAIDEN SPECIAL WEIGHT. Purse $16,000. Fillies, 3-year-olds, 121 lbs.

Fancy Caper — **Ch. f. 3, by Tom Rolfe—Capercaillie, by Native Dancer**
Own.—Buckland Farm — **Br.—Evans T M (WVa)** — **Tr.—Campo John P** — **121**

	St.	1st	2nd	3rd	Amt.
1980	2	M	2	0	$7,040
1979	4	M	0	0	

16Apr80- 6Aqu	fst 1	:46⅘	1:12⅕	1:37⅖	ⒻMd Sp Wt	10	1	1hd	2½	21½	21¾	Velasquez J	b	121	*1.90	77-17	Little Prema 1211¾ Fancy Caper1211½FriendlyFrolic1217½	Gamely	10
28Mar80- 4Aqu	fst 6f	:22⅕	:46	1:12	ⒻMd Sp Wt	2	6	64¼	46	22½	2½	Velasquez J	b	121	19.30	82-24	Thanks Eddie 121½ Fancy Caper 1214 Headwater 1215	Game try	8
11Nov79- 4Aqu	fst 7f	:23⅗	:48	1:25⅖	ⒻMd Sp Wt	7	2	62¾	41¾	36	58½	Venezia M	b	117	20.30	65-15	In Our Time 1172¼ Gloverette 1174½ On A Shoestring 1171	Tired	7
18Oct79- 2Aqu	fst 1	:47	1:12	1:38⅕	ⒻMd Sp Wt	1	1	1hd	78	716	717	Santiago A		117	33.30e	58-18	Critic's Wink 1171 Dame Du Moulin 1174¼ Rosy Riva 117½	Tired	9
30Sep79- 6Bel	sly 6½f	:22⅗	:46⅕	1:18⅗	ⒻMd Sp Wt	1	5	56¾	818	1124	1029	Santiago A		118	54.00	54-24	Cybele 1182¾ Veiled Prophet 1134¼ Madura 1189	No factor	12
19Aug79- 4Sar	sly 6f	:22⅕	:46	1:12⅗	ⒻMd Sp Wt	8	1	814	820	719	727	Maple S		117	15.10	50-21	Diorama 117¾ Fager's Fancy 1175¾ Arisen 1173	Outrun	8

LATEST WORKOUTS Apr 9 Bel tr.t 4f fst :50⅕ b Mar 26 Bel tr.t 4f gd :49 h Mar 17 Bel tr.t 4f fst :48⅖ h Mar 13 Bel tr.t 5f fst 1:02 b

We have another short-priced horse, down to almost even money. This filly has but six races on her record, which requires us to rate her in the usual manner. She qualifies on form easily off her last race. Since only her last two races in 1980 show very much, we can extract our ability times from them. In the 28Mar80 race at Aqueduct, there was a :26.0 lead time, and Fancy Caper gained 5½ lengths to allow us to reduce this by four ticks to obtain a :25.1 for her. The second call time for Fancy Caper would be 47 and change, thus picking up one tick for energy to :25.2. Then, to the last race, where there was a :25.2 lead time. She lost a half-length, which requires an additional tick to make it :25.3. Since her leading time was :46.4, there is no requirement to add anything for energy, and we can round out the time at :25.3.

You will have noted by now that this is a sprint race of seven furlongs. This means we must bring early speed into our ability calculations. Since this race is a 7f event, we will use the early-speed totals of 4, 2, and 0 where warranted.

We first look down the running lines to note that six races are listed. Only in two of the six was this young filly within 2 lengths of the lead, so she fails to win the highest early-speed points. Next we count two additional races where she was within 5 lengths of the lead, which is a medium speed rating worth 2 points. These will be added to her ability-time totals.

Our next contender, On A Shoestring, has but two races, both run in 1979. She becomes an unknown in form as we inquire into her ability times.

In the 19Nov79 effort, there was a :25.1 lead time between the first and second calls in the one-mile race. There was a gain of 2 lengths for a two-tick reduction to :24.4 for On A Shoestring. But her first call time balloons up into 48 and change and we make a two-tick addition for energy to obtain a :25.1. The

On A Shoestring Dk. b. or br. f. 3, by Quadrangle—Family Planning, by Cyane
Own.—Christiana Stable Br.—Lunger Jane duPont (Ky) Tr.—Maloney James W **121** St. 1st 2nd 3rd Amt. 1979 2 M 0 2 $3,240

19Nov79- 6Aqu fst 1 :47⅗ 1:12⅘ 1:38⅘ ⒻMd Sp Wt 3 3 45½ 43½ 42 33¼ Hernandez R 117 2.20 69–18 Espadrille 1173 Gloverette 117nk On A Shoestring 1174 Bid, hung 7
11Nov79- 4Aqu fst 7f :23⅗ :48 1:25⅖ ⒻMd Sp Wt 3 7 74¾ 77¾ 47½ 36¾ Hernandez R 117 5.40 67–15 In Our Time 1172¼ Gloverette 1174½OnAShoestring1171 Mild rally 7
LATEST WORKOUTS Apr 20 Bel 4f fst :50 b Apr 13 Bel 4f fst :49⅖ b Apr 9 Bel 4f fst :52 b

other race, of 11Nov79, was at 7f, which requires us to convert the final time of 1:25.2 to a 6f figure of 1:12.2. Off the :48.0 second call lead time, there is a lead time calculation of :24.2. There was a gain of 1 length, but for the second call time, we are at 49 and change, and add three ticks, which still leaves a final ability time of :24.4, which is very good.

We must next deal with her early-speed figures. In the two races, she was within 5 lengths of the leader in one of them, which is one-half of her starts, of course, which entitles her to 2 points for early speed.

The third choice is Lucky Ole Axe, who has just five lifetime races.

Lucky Ole Axe B. f. 3, by The Axe II—Lucky Ole Me, by Olden Times
Own.—Bohemia Stable Br.—DuPont Mrs R C (Md) Tr.—Jerkens H Allen **121** St. 1st 2nd 3rd Amt. 1980 5 M 2 3 $7,620 1979 0 M 0 0

17Apr80- 6Aqu fst 7f :23⅕ :47⅕ 1:26⅕ 3↑ⒻMd Sp Wt 8 5 74¼ 62¾ 42½ 31¼ Samyn J L 113 *2.50 69–23 Astrid's Pride 113½ Pink Supreme108¾LuckyOleAxe1132½ In close 8
4Mar80- 4Hia fst 7f :23⅕ :46⅘ 1:26⅖ ⒻMd Sp Wt 6 6 46½ 23 2hd 1½ Samyn J L 118 2.40[D] 71–24 [D]LuckyOleAxe118½NtionlPlce1181¼FrindlyFrolic1181½ Drifted dr. 10
4Mar80-Disqualified and placed second
26Feb80- 5Hia fst 1⅛ :48⅘ 1:13⅗ 1:51⅘ ⒻMd Sp Wt 7 3 35 23 23 27 Samyn J L 118 *1.40 66–22 Mia's Girl 1187 Lucky OleAxe1185Getoffofmycloud111nk 2nd best 8
19Feb80- 5Hia sly 6f :22⅖ :46⅖ 1:12⅕ ⒻMd Sp Wt 4 11 86½ 65 43½ 31¾ Samyn J L 120 *1.90 80–17 Regal Quili 120no National Palace 1201¾ Lucky OleAxe120no Wide 12
11Feb80-10Hia fst 6f :22⅘ :47 1:12⅖ ⒻMd Sp Wt 1 12 911 76½ 54½ 32½ Samyn J L 120 7.00 78–18 HappyHawaii120½SteptoTheKingdom1202LuckyOleAxe120nk Wide 12
LATEST WORKOUTS Apr 16 Bel tr.t 3f fst :39 b Apr 13 Bel tr.t 4f fst :48 h Apr 9 Bel tr.t 6f fst 1:20 b Apr 6 Bel tr.t 3f fst :38 b

This filly qualifies on form with her gain of in excess of five in her last race, four in horses and 3 lengths, as well as being up close. For ability times, the best comes in the 26Feb80 race at Hialeah, where there was a :24.4 lead time with a gain of two down to :24.2 for Lucky Ole Axe. The first call time, off 5 lengths back of a :48.5, requires a three-tick energy add-on, to bring the ability time to :25.0. The second-best ability time comes from her very first race on 11Feb80, where the lead time was :25.2. There was a gain of four, which reduces the time to :24.4 off the three-tick deduction. The energy adjustment, however, adds two ticks (:47.0 plus 7 for lengths to :48.2, which accounts for the two), which rounds it off at :25.2.

For early speed, there are five races to consider. She was just barely within 5 lengths of the lead in two of them, and since this is just short of the one-half required for a point rating, we look at her last race, which was within 5 lengths, and accordingly award her 2 points also for early speed. Here are the contenders:

Odds	Horse	Ability		A Pts		ES	F	Total
1.1	Fancy Caper	:25.2	:25.3	13	12	2	Q	27
2.9	On A Shoestring	:24.4	25.1	16	14	2	U	32
3.3	Lucky Ole Axe	:25.0	:25.1	15	14	2	Q	31

In this situation, the early-speed points did not alter the final point standing from what ability points alone would have brought. On A Shoestring, with a 1-point advantage, is a U horse in form, and thus cannot be played. Lucky Ole Axe, as the highest-rated qualifying form horse, would be our selection to win and place.

The outcome? Fancy Caper, running strongly, destroyed the field, running away to a Big Win. But Lucky Ole Axe was right there for second, thus protecting our investment somewhat, which is one of the major advantages of making place bets along with win bets.

This race illustrates several points. First is the obvious one that we can't expect our high-point selections to win every time. While Fancy Caper's speed points were no higher than the others, you may note that she was strongly to the fore in her last race, and with six starts, she could likely be expected to show improvement. She just barely missed getting 2 form points for improvement. Thus, you can see that Fancy Caper was a sound selection, although not enough under our method of play, which will demonstrate in the long run its continued effectiveness.

While we're dealing with the Aqueduct card on April 23, 1980, let's do the next race to show how some very weak performers stack up. We'll begin with Shaulah, who is another high-odds filly at 7-1 as the third choice in the betting.

6 **AQUEDUCT** START · **6 FURLONGS** AQUEDUCT · FINISH

6 FURLONGS. (1.08⅗) ALLOWANCE. Purse $24,000. Fillies and mares, 3-year-olds and upward foaled in New York State and approved by the New York State-Bred Registry which have never won a race other than maiden, claiming or starter. Weights, 3-year-olds, 113 lbs.; older, 126 lbs. Non-winners of a race other than claiming since March 15, allowed 3 lbs.; of such a race since March 1, 5 lbs.

Shaulah — **Ch. f. 3, by Chichester—Brookalina, by Bolinas Boy**
Own.—Soben Karen H — **Br.—Thomas J A (NY)** — **Tr.—Brown Tamara J** — **108**

	St.	1st	2nd	3rd	Amt.
1980	4	1	1	0	$9,400
1979	5	1	0	0	$12,000

7Apr80- 9Aqu	fst	6f	:23	:46⅗	1:13⅖	ⒻClm 18000	3	3	3^{3}	$3^{1\frac{1}{2}}$	$2^{1\frac{1}{2}}$	$1^{\frac{1}{2}}$	Miranda J	112	18.00	76–21	Shaulah $112^{\frac{1}{2}}$ Sister Rubena 111^{hd} Good Figure 113^{nk}	Driving	9
22Mar80- 3Aqu	sly	6f	:24	:48⅗	1:14⅖	3↑ Ⓕ[S]Allowance	1	2	$2^{1\frac{1}{2}}$	$3^{2\frac{1}{2}}$	3^{4}	$5^{4\frac{3}{4}}$	Beitia E	109	10.20	66–31	Miss Andrea F. $106^{1\frac{3}{4}}$ American Liberty $113^{2\frac{1}{4}}$ Where 111^{nk}	Tired	7
12Mar80- 2Aqu	fst	6f	⊡:23⅗	:49⅕	1:15⅕	ⒻClm 14000	6	1	$1^{1\frac{1}{2}}$	1^{2}	$1^{2\frac{1}{2}}$	$2^{1\frac{1}{2}}$	Graell A	112	19.20	66–20	Chicago Dancer $107^{1\frac{1}{2}}$ Shaulah $112^{\frac{1}{2}}$ Susie Toosie $107^{\frac{1}{2}}$	Gamely	7
29Feb80- 6Aqu	fst	6f	⊡:23⅕	:48⅖	1:14⅗	3↑ Ⓕ[S]Allowance	11	4	4^{nk}	$3^{1\frac{1}{2}}$	13^{22}	13^{24}	Graell A	109	80.90	47–24	Silkys Angle $123^{3\frac{1}{2}}$ AmericanLiberty$109^{2\frac{1}{2}}$MesinaJudge112^{hd}	Tired	13
26Sep79- 2Med	fst	6f	:23	:47⅕	1:13⅖	ⒻClm 16000	5	5	2^{hd}	$4^{1\frac{1}{2}}$	7^{12}	8^{20}	Blum J^{5}	113	4.50	58–19	Giggleswick 118no Northern Ripple 113^{6} Jessica Baby 118^{2}	Tired	8
16Aug79- 8Sar	fst	6f	:22⅗	:48	1:12	[S]Empire	1	2	1^{2}	3^{1}	$4^{5\frac{1}{2}}$	6^{22}	Velasquez J	119	10.10	58–20	Restrainor 119^{12} AnonymousPrince122^{3}CullodenPoint$115^{2\frac{1}{4}}$	Tired	7
5Aug79- 8Rkm	fst	6f	:21⅗	:45	1:13	ⒻCicada	7	5	4^{5}	7^{11}	10^{22}	10^{30}	Riera R Jr	110	7.10	49–22	Donna Doll 114^{4} Tinab $113^{\frac{3}{4}}$ Yankee Fashion $113^{\frac{1}{2}}$	Tired	10
23Jly79- 6Bel	fst	5½f	:23	:47⅘	1:07⅕	[S]Md Sp Wt	1	1	1^{3}	1^{3}	1^{3}	$1^{1\frac{3}{4}}$	Velasquez J	115	2.40	79–23	Shaulah$115^{1\frac{3}{4}}$SugrDottie$115^{4\frac{3}{4}}$AnonymousPrince$118^{6\frac{1}{4}}$	Ridden out	9
9Jly79- 4Bel	fst	5½f	:23	:47⅖	1:06⅗	[S]Md Sp Wt	4	2	2^{hd}	1^{hd}	$2^{1\frac{1}{2}}$	$5^{7\frac{1}{2}}$	Velasquez J	115	12.10	74–15	Restrainor$118^{6\frac{1}{4}}$DncingTrget118^{no}Summer'sFirst$115^{1\frac{1}{4}}$	Weakened	10

LATEST WORKOUTS **Apr 19 Bel tr.t 4f fst :49⅖ h** **Apr 14 Bel tr.t 4f fst :48⅕ h** **Apr 2 Bel tr.t 5f fst 1:02⅖ h** **Mar 29 Bel tr.t 4f sly :52 b**

Her poor record begins to tell you why her odds are so high. She qualifies easily on form, having won her last race. The lead time there was a slow :26.4, which we can reduce by one tick for gain to :26.3 for Shaulah. There are no further adjustments. Her best effort came back in 1979 off her first victory on 23Jly79 at Belmont. We first convert the 5½f time of 1:07.1 out to the 6f time of 1:14.0, not particularly good even for a two-year-old. The lead time thus becomes :26.1, with a required energy add-on of one more to :26.2. You will soon learn, as you make these repeated comparisons, that a horse with ability times of :26.2 and :26.3 is an extremely poor prospect to win much of anything, except against other woefully weak animals.

Since this is another sprint race, this time at 6f, we must calculate early speed again. In nine races, Shaulah has seven in which she was within 2 lengths of the lead, entitling her to 6 points for early speed.

The second choice on the board is Where, at 5-1, and again, you will see a most mediocre record.

Where — Dk. b. or br. f. 3, by Search For Gold—Hoya Sue, by Swoon's Son
Own.—Cohn S; Br.—Cohn S (NY); Tr.—Ross Chester
103 5

	St.	1st	2nd	3rd	Amt.
1980	4	0	0	2	$5,280
1979	9	1	3	0	$28,980

8Apr80- 3Aqu	fst	7f		:23	:46⅕	1:26⅕	3↑ Ⓕ S Allowance	3	5	2hd	52¾	63½	53	Rogers K L5	105	2.30	67-21	Moorea 113nk AmericanLiberty108nk SwitchUrKingdom1052¼	Tired	8
1Apr80- 5Aqu	my	7f		:23	:46⅗	1:25⅘	3↑ Ⓕ S Allowance	4	3	2hd	2hd	1½	32½	Rogers K L5	105	9.00	69-19	Screenland 1101¾ Silkys Angle 123¾ Where 1051	Weakened	6
22Mar80- 3Aqu	sly	6f		:24	:48⅗	1:14⅖	3↑ Ⓕ S Allowance	3	5	43½	45	44½	34	Martens G	111	*1.40	67-31	Miss Andrea F. 1061¾ American Liberty 1132¼ Where 111nk	Wide	7
22Feb80- 6Aqu	gd	6f	⊡	:23⅖	:47⅖	1:13	3↑ S Allowance	9	1	1hd	21	41½	53	Miranda J	109	13.30	76-19	Ray Kay 111no Bold Igloo 1131 Right Approach 106nk	Tired	10
26Dec79- 2Aqu	gd	170	⊡	:51	1:17	1:47⅗	S Allowance	2	1	1hd	2hd	43½	413	Martens G	114	3.10	51-36	Rod's Dream1172¾MyMontauk1173RightApproach1047	Weakened	7
8Dec79- 3Aqu	fst	6f	⊡	:22⅘	:47⅕	1:12⅘	S Allowance	3	3	42½	44	54	46	Martens G	114	12.30	74-13	Brazen Queen 1141½ Right Approach1172½MyMontauk1132	Evenly	7
31Oct79- 3Aqu	fst	6½f		:23	:46⅖	1:18⅖	S Allowance	5	2	42½	43	512	516	Figueroa R5	112	9.10	67-16	Can't Discount 1202 Love Is Eternal 1154¾MissArlene114½	Outrun	5
10Oct79- 3Bel	sly	6f		:23⅖	:47⅗	1:13⅗	Ⓕ S Md Sp Wt	5	1	1hd	13	15	110	Figueroa R5	113	4.10	74-26	Where 11310 Cabildo's Wish 1182 Moorea 111¾	Ridden out	9
17Sep79- 9Bel	fst	6f		:22⅗	:46⅕	1:11⅗	Ⓕ S Md Sp Wt	7	4	35½	210	214	213	Figueroa R5	113	6.60	71-21	Move It Now 11813 Where 1137¾ Ms. Naskra 1181¾	2nd best	12
29Aug79- 6Bel	sly	6½f		:22⅗	:46⅗	1:20⅗	Ⓕ S Md Sp Wt	2	4	2hd	2hd	32½	46	Cordero A Jr	117	2.80	67-15	Summer's First 1171¾ Ms. Naskra117nk MissArlene1174	Weakened	8

LATEST WORKOUTS Apr 19 Bel tr.t 4f fst :50⅕ b   Mar 29 Bel tr.t 4f sly :48⅘ h   Mar 19 Bel tr.t 4f fst :48 h   Mar 12 Bel tr.t 3f fst :36 h

She qualifies on form with two calls up close off a most unimpressive race. We have to search up and down her running lines to try to find a place to begin in seeking her best ability times. We try the big winning effort on 10Oct79 at Belmont, where she had a :26.0 lead time with one tick added for energy to give her a :26.1 rating. The next best we can do is the 8Dec79 race, where there was a :25.3 lead time with a loss of 2 lengths to give Where a :26.0. Her second call time was a flat :48.0 and the two additional energy ticks give her a :26.2.

In early speed, we have another strong candidate, with six out of ten races showing good early lick for another 6-point rating.

Now we are ready to look at the favorite, Switch Ur Kingdom, holding at even money, to see if she warrants that kind of support, even in this field of New York State–breds.

She readily qualifies on form, and as you can see, is an Improving Horse off all four calls in her last race. For our best ability time, look at 13Dec79 at Aqueduct, where the lead time was a :25.0. Our candidate gets two tacked on

Switch Ur Kingdom — B. f. 3, by Key To The Kingdom—Miss Switch, by Royal Levee
Own.—Schilling J W; Br.—DiMauro S (NY); Tr.—Picou James E
108

	St.	1st	2nd	3rd	Amt.
1980	6	1	0	2	$15,630
1979	9	M	3	2	$16,200

8Apr80- 3Aqu	fst	7f		:23	:46⅕	1:26⅕	3↑ Ⓕ S Allowance	7	2	51¾	3nk	1½	3½	Gonzalez M A5	105	4.50	69-21	Moore113nk AmricnLibrty108nk SwitchUrKingdom1052¼	Weakened	8
30Mar80- 9Key	my	6f		:22	:45⅘	1:12⅘	Ⓕ Allowance	6	5	77¾	58½	57½	65¼	Diaz J L	114	7.40	73-20	Heavenly Love 114hd Villanesian 1202 OverMission1141½	No threat	9
18Mar80- 9Key	gd	6f		:22⅗	:47⅕	1:14	Ⓕ Allowance	8	4	56	53½	32	35	Tejeira J	120	11.60	67-35	Mystic Lass 1123 HeavenlyLove1152SwitchUrKingdom120no	Wide	11
17Feb80- 2Aqu	gd	6f	⊡	:22⅘	:47⅗	1:13⅘	Ⓕ Clm 30000	3	4	52½	63¾	77	711	McNeil T7	109	9.20	64-26	Heather's Turn1181¾SharonsFareWell1163½PrittyKitty1071¼	Tired	7
20Jan80- 7Aqu	fst	170	⊡	:48⅘	1:14⅖	1:44⅗	S Handicap	6	1	11½	12	21	514	McNeil T	109	41.60	65-26	Darlin Momma 1184½ Can't Discount1175¼Rod'sDream1161½	Tired	6
3Jan80- 4Aqu	fst	6f	⊡	:23⅖	:47⅖	1:13⅗	Ⓕ S Md Sp Wt	5	2	2hd	13	13	12¾	McNeil T10	111	*1.50	76-22	SwitchUrKingdom1112¾AmericanLiberty1165½RayKy1213¾	Driving	8
24Dec79- 3Aqu	my	6f	⊡	:23	:47⅗	1:14⅘	Ⓕ S Md Sp Wt	5	2	33½	21	32	24½	Maple S	117	*1.40	65-27	Laodice1174½SwitchUrKingdom1172¼MissBeckyM.1171¾	2nd best	7
13Dec79- 2Aqu	sly	6f	⊡	:23⅕	:47⅘	1:12⅘	Ⓕ S Md Sp Wt	7	2	64½	45	37	26½	McNeil T10	107	11.80	73-20	Adlbbr1176½StchUrKngdm1072½ D WndflCndyJ.110nk	Best of rest	10
21Nov79- 5Aqu	fst	6f		:23⅕	:46⅘	1:12	Ⓕ S Md Sp Wt	5	2	31½	33	38	39½	Fell J	117	7.90	73-18	BrazenQueen117no Screenland1129½SwitchUrKingdom117½	Evenly	8
12Nov79- 8Aqu	my	7f		:23⅗	:47⅘	1:27	Ⓕ S East View	1	1	2½	44½	617	724	Fell J	114	33.60	42-34	Swirlaway 119¾ Love IsEternal1198¾RightApproach1171½	Stopped	7

LATEST WORKOUTS Apr 19 Bel 3f fst :34⅗ h   Apr 6 Bel 3f fst :37⅘ b   Mar 26 Bel tr.t 5f gd 1:03 b   Mar 16 Bel tr.t 3f fst :36 h

for loss of lengths to :25.2 and there is another two for energy add-on to wind up with a :25.4 ability time.

We next try the 20Jan80 run at Aqueduct at a mile seventy, since Switch Ur Kingdom led at the two calls we use for calculation. Lead time was :25.3 with an energy adjustment of two ticks added, for a :26.0.

As to early speed, we have the unusual situation where all three of the top betting choices wind up with 6 early-speed points, since Switch Ur Kingdom qualifies in five races out of her ten for the top point total.

We can now evaluate all three horses.

Odds	Horse	Ability		A Pts		ES	F	Total
1.0	Switch Ur Kingdom	:25.4	:26.0	11	10	6	Q1	28
5.3	Where	:26.1	:26.2	9	8	6	Q	23
7.2	Shaulah	:26.2	:26.3	8	7	6	Q	21

Switch Ur Kingdom is a Double Advantage Horse with an improving race (which gets her only 1 form point, because to allow her 2 would exceed twice the sum of her best ability time).

The major purpose of showing you this race is to illustrate that even when there are very weak contestants, you may often find a sound secure investment proposition. Double Advantage Horses even where all ability times are weak are just as powerful as in any other race. Switch Ur Kingdom, again with the short payoffs of $4 to win and $3.40 to place, was about as strong a play as you will ever want to find. Look for them in all kinds of races—profits will be your reward.

Now, I want to show you a tough grass race, and when we finish with it, I will consider that your present practice sessions are sufficient to send you forward to follow me through the Big Week at Belmont. There, a wide variety of problems will be encountered, problems you will encounter when you go to the track. But for now, let's extract from the *Daily Racing Form* of May 24, 1980, in the sixth race at Belmont, the past performances of the three leading contenders. Dauphin is a strong favorite.

The first problem is form, because Dauphin last ran on 13Apr79, over a year prior to the race under review. But we see four workouts reasonably spread out. This is a high-priced claiming race, but Dauphin did run in a stakes race in the Flamingo at Hialeah in a contest won by no less than Spectacular Bid. While Dauphin, off this one race, may not qualify as a stakes horse, he can be rated as a high-priced allowance horse, since even a $60,000 claimer is a rather

6 BELMONT

WIDENER TURF COURSE
1 1-16 MILES
BELMONT PARK
START
FINISH

1 1/16 MILES. (TURF). (1.39 1/5) CLAIMING. Purse $22,000. 4-year-olds and upward, weights, 122 lbs. Non-winners of two races at a mile or over since April 15, allowed 3 lbs. Of such a race since then, 5 lbs. Claiming price $60,000 for each $500 to $50,000 2 lbs. (Races when entered to be claimed for $45,000 or less not considered)

Coupled—Ring of Truth and Swordtail.

Dauphin
Own.—Live Oak Plantation
B. c. 4, by Majestic Prince—Fresh Start, by Prince John
$60,000 **Br.—Live Oak Stud (Ky)**
Tr.—Kelly Patrick J
117

Turf Record St.	1st	2nd	3rd		St.	1st	2nd	3rd	Amt.
1	1	0	0	1979	5	2	0	2	$12,600
				1978	4	M	2	1	$10,380

13Apr79- 9Hia	hd	*1 1/16 Ⓣ			1:41 4/5	Allowance	1	1	1^{6}	1^{8}	1^{7}	1^{3}	Solomone M	b 114	*1.10	92-13	Dauphin 114^{3} Great Cloud $114^{\frac{1}{2}}$ Mistum $114^{7\frac{1}{2}}$	Handily	8
24Mar79-10Hia	fst	1 1/8	:46	1:09 3/5	1:48 2/5	Flamingo	3	5	$5^{9\frac{1}{2}}$	4^{13}	4^{12}	5^{19}	Solomone M	b 118	12.60	71-16	Spectacular Bid 122^{12}StrikeTheMain118^{3}SirIvorAgain122^{hd}	Tired	8
12Mar79- 3Hia	fst	1 1/8	:46	1:10 3/5	1:49	Md Sp Wt	2	2	$1^{1\frac{1}{2}}$	1^{4}	1^{6}	1^{14}	Velasquez J	b 120	*1.40	87-21	Dauphin 120^{14} Hop to the Top $120^{2\frac{1}{2}}$ Rolling Stone 120^{2}	Easily	9
2Mar79- 4GP	fst	1 1/16	:47 2/5	1:12 1/5	1:45 4/5	Md Sp Wt	5	8	9^{12}	6^{11}	4^{9}	$3^{5\frac{1}{4}}$	Velasquez J	120	2.00	67-25	Bolger 120^{nk} Chungero 120^{5} Dauphin $120^{1\frac{1}{2}}$	Best others	12
7Feb79- 4GP	fst	7f	:22	:44 1/5	1:23 1/5	Md Sp Wt	2	11	$8^{8\frac{1}{4}}$	$7^{8\frac{1}{2}}$	5^{8}	$3^{2\frac{3}{4}}$	Velasquez J	120	*1.10	85-22	I Know Why $115^{1\frac{1}{4}}$ Dragon Slayer $120^{1\frac{1}{2}}$ Dauphin $120^{\frac{3}{4}}$	Stride lt.	12
10Dec78- 4Aqu	my	1 1/16 ⊡	:48	1:13 2/5	1:46	Md Sp Wt	3	9	10^{13}	6^{8}	3^{5}	3^{9}	Maple E	122	*2.40	76-16	Sandro Tasca 122^{2} Causerie 122^{7} Dauphin 122^{6}	Slow early	10
27Nov78- 8Aqu	fst	1	:47 3/5	1:13 1/5	1:38 4/5	Allowance	4	6	$2^{\frac{1}{2}}$	2^{2}	2^{6}	$2^{4\frac{1}{2}}$	Cordero A Jr	115	1.30	67-24	Crown Thy Good $115^{4\frac{1}{2}}$ Dauphin $115^{3\frac{1}{4}}$ Gist $115^{9\frac{1}{4}}$	2nd best	6
13Nov78- 4Aqu	fst	7f	:23	:46 4/5	1:25 4/5	Md Sp Wt	10	4	$2^{2\frac{1}{2}}$	3^{2}	2^{hd}	2^{hd}	Cordero A Jr	122	5.60	72-27	Sparti 122^{hd} Dauphin 122^{hd} Causerie 122^{hd}	Sharp try	13
280ct78- 3Aqu	fst	6f	:22 2/5	:45 4/5	1:12	Md Sp Wt	10	8	$10^{8\frac{1}{2}}$	10^{13}	7^{8}	$6^{6\frac{1}{2}}$	Maple E	122	17.90	76-16	Hitching Rail 122^{hd} Norge 122^{3} ⒹMansard 122^{2}	Outrun	11

LATEST WORKOUTS May 20 Bel 5f fst 1:03 b | May 16 Bel 4f fst :50 bg | ●May 8 Bel 3f sly :36 h | May 3 Bel 5f fst 1:01 1/5 h

valuable animal. With the four recent workouts, one bearing a bullet, I could say Q on form without too much difficulty.

Our next problem is what to do about ability. Since this is a grass race, we can use only grass races to rate ability. Dauphin's only effort back in 1979 was excellent, but at the "about" distance, where there are no internal times upon which to calculate our ability ratings. We are stymied—and Dauphin's ability becomes unknown.

But our difficulties are only beginning. We come to the second choice among the players, Gemmate, who likewise has not run since 1979.

Gemmate
Own.—Tartan Stable
Dk. b. or br. g. 6, by Noholme II—Brown Bud, by Vertex
$60,000 **Br.—Tartan Farms (Fla)**
Tr.—Nerud Jan H
117

Turf Record St.	1st	2nd	3rd		St	1st	2nd	3rd	Amt.
8	1	3	0	1979	12	1	3	1	$24,720
				1978	3	1	0	0	$8,100

7Dec79- 8Aqu	my	6f ⊡	:22	:45 1/5	1:10	3↑Allowance	7	7	$8^{6\frac{1}{2}}$	$8^{5\frac{1}{2}}$	$6^{6\frac{1}{2}}$	6^{6}	Foley D10	b 107	11.50e	88-18	Homeways $120^{1\frac{3}{4}}$ Royal Reasoning $120^{1\frac{1}{4}}$ ProudPocket115^{hd}	Wide	8
5Nov79- 7Aqu	sf	1 1/8 Ⓣ	:50	1:15 2/5	1:54 4/5	3↑Allowance	2	1	$2^{1\frac{1}{2}}$	3^{1}	4^{7}	6^{16}	Venezia M	b 119	10.90	54-30	Sten 117^{7} Old Crony 117^{2} Two Point Poppy 108^{nk}	Checked	10
18Oct79- 8Med	gd	1 Ⓣ	:48	1:13 3/5	1:39 4/5	3↑Allowance	3	5	$5^{3\frac{1}{2}}$	$6^{2\frac{3}{4}}$	$6^{8\frac{1}{2}}$	$7^{7\frac{1}{2}}$	Cordero A Jr	b 117	*1.80	72-26	Treatise $115^{1\frac{1}{2}}$ Bal Bay $119^{\frac{1}{2}}$ Burn $122^{\frac{3}{4}}$	In close	12
17Sep79- 4Bel	fm	1 1/16 Ⓣ	:47	1:10	1:41 3/5	3↑Allowance	3	1	$2^{2\frac{1}{2}}$	$2^{2\frac{1}{2}}$	2^{2}	1^{1}	Venezia M	117	3.10	96-09	Gemmate 117^{1} Sum Aid 115^{nk} Tusk $117^{1\frac{1}{2}}$	Driving	8
25Jly79- 5Bel	fm	1 1/16 Ⓣ	:46	1:09	1:40 3/5	3↑Allowance	7	3	3^{2}	$3^{\frac{1}{2}}$	2^{1}	$5^{2\frac{1}{4}}$	Venezia M	b 117	*1.60	91-10	Najd $117^{\frac{3}{4}}$ Serendip $116^{\frac{3}{4}}$ Ashikaga $117^{\frac{3}{4}}$	Wide	7
5Jly79- 7Bel	fm	1 1/16 Ⓣ	:47 2/5	1:11 4/5	1:41 3/5	3↑Allowance	1	1	1^{hd}	1^{hd}	2^{hd}	$2^{\frac{1}{2}}$	Venezia M	b 117	5.60	87-18	Burn $117^{\frac{1}{2}}$ Gemmate $117^{1\frac{1}{4}}$ Sandro Tasca $113^{4\frac{3}{4}}$	Gamely	10
21Jun79- 2Bel	fm	1 1/16 Ⓣ	:46 4/5	1:09 4/5	1:41 1/5	3↑Allowance	6	2	$4^{1\frac{1}{2}}$	$3^{3\frac{1}{2}}$	2^{2}	$2^{1\frac{1}{2}}$	Vasquez J	b 117	8.20	88-08	Match The Hatch$107^{1\frac{1}{2}}$Gemmate$117^{\frac{3}{4}}$CurrentRumor109^{8}	Game try	10
10Jun79- 4Bel	fm	1 1/4 Ⓣ	:46 2/5	1:35 4/5	2:00 2/5	3↑Clm 50000	7	2	2^{6}	2^{7}	5^{10}	5^{12}	Vasquez J	b 117	4.00	80-05	Texas Playboy 108^{4} Swoon's Plume 113^{4} Readjust $113^{2\frac{1}{2}}$	Tired	12
9May79- 6Aqu	fm	1 1/8 Ⓣ	:48 4/5	1:12 4/5	1:48 4/5	Allowance	5	1	1^{1}	2^{hd}	$2^{2\frac{1}{2}}$	$2^{3\frac{1}{4}}$	Vasquez J	b 117	23.10	98 —	Gristle $117^{3\frac{1}{4}}$ Gemmate $117^{1\frac{3}{4}}$ Irish Ridule 112^{1}	Best of others	9
26Apr79- 5Aqu	my	1 1/8	:49 1/5	1:13 3/5	1:51 4/5	Clm 45000	4	4	$2^{\frac{1}{2}}$	$2^{1\frac{1}{2}}$	4^{9}	5^{16}	Vasquez J	b 115	11.30	60-25	Navy Breeze 115^{6} Fiddle Faddle 117no Texas Playboy 114^{10}	Tired	5

LATEST WORKOUTS May 20 Bel 5f fst 1:01 3/5 b | May 15 Bel 5f fst 1:01 b | May 10 Bel 5f fst 1:02 b | May 5 Bel 5f fst 1:01 4/5 b

This old gelding, out for the first time in 1980, likewise shows four evenly spaced workouts. Since this is a high-priced race, and we gave Dauphin the benefit of the doubt on form, so, too, with Gemmate. And when we start to calculate ability times, there is some blinking to do. These times are remarkable. Back on 17Sep79 at Belmont, Gemmate won his race with a final time only four ticks off the track record. Between the first and second calls, the lead time was a flat :23.0, with Gemmate holding at that figure with no gain or loss.

Only one tick is added for energy, and we start with a :23.1 ability time. Take a look at 25Jly79 on the Belmont turf, where there was another :23.0 flat lead time. Gemmate gained a length off that blistering pace with times fast enough to not require any energy add-on. We have a :22.4 ability time now, a figure you will rarely see. This horse will take some beating.

The third choice is Cookie, who has qualifying form.

Cookie — B. g. 5, by Hilarious—Beau Cookie, by Beau Gar — **$60,000** — Br.—Hobeau Farm Inc (Fla) — Tr.—Voss Thomas H — **117**

Own.—Voss T H

Turf Record: St. 18, 1st 4, 2nd 1, 3rd 2

	St.	1st	2nd	3rd	Amt.
1980	2	0	0	0	
1979	11	3	0	0	$27,909

8May80-	8Pim	yl	1	Ⓣ:49⅘	1:14⅕	1:40	Allowance	1	2	42½	42¾	51¾	52¼	Torre M J	b 113	14.00	77-24	Buck's Chief 115nk Terullah 119¾ Uncle Pokey 1151	In close	8
19Apr80-	8Pim	fm	1 1/16	Ⓣ:47⅗	1:12⅗	1:44⅕	Allowance	6	2	13	1hd	58	515	Torre M J	b 113	38.40	75-14	Marquee Universal 1123½ No No Jim 114½ Advan 1191½	Weakened	8
4Nov79-	7Pen	sf	1	Ⓣ		1:39⅗	3↑Allowance	2	2	32	21	2hd	45¾	Iliescu A	b 113	2.70	66-32	Confort 1083½ Gallant Bob 113nk Frosty Honor 1132	Weakened	7
1Nov79-	6Aqu	gd	1⅜	Ⓣ:47	1:36⅘	2:17⅖	3↑Clm 55000	2	3	311	414	412	612	Cruguet J	b 116	7.00	72-18	Texas Playboy 1081½ Daranstone 122hd AudaciousFool1206½	Tired	7
5Sep79-	8Bel	fm	1¼	[T]:48⅕	1:36⅘	2:02	3↑Allowance	6	3	33½	76½	75½	63¾	Borden D A	b 117	24.00	80-16	King Green 115hd Great Neck 113½ Daranstone 1173	Tired	9
27Aug79-	6Sar	sf	1	[T]:47⅗	1:12⅕	1:37⅕	3↑Allowance	6	9	75¼	65¼	66¾	711	Vasquez J	b 117	11.40	— —	Virilify 1142 Sakara 1174½ Brave Shot II 1121½	Bothered	9
10Aug79-	5Sar	fm	1⅛	Ⓣ:47⅖	1:11⅗	1:49⅖	3↑Clm 50000	5	5	54	42	1hd	1nk	Cruguet J	b 113	6.90	80-21	Cookie 113nk Parol 1152½ Marlago 114¾	Driving	9
28Jly79-	5Bel	fm	1 1/16	[T]:45	1:08⅖	1:41⅗	3↑Allowance	5	4	48½	413	512	68	Hernandez R	b 117	12.00	88-09	Honest Moment 1116¼ Greatest Roman 113½ Sakara 117nk	Outrun	8
19Jly79-	7Del	fst	170	:46⅘	1:12	1:43	3↑Allowance	4	2	3½	67	717	719	Moseley J W	b 119	6.90	63-20	Straight Sets 1171¾ HolyMoses1171AcademicFreedom1173¼	Tired	7
1Jly79-	8Pen	sf	1 1/16	Ⓣ		1:45⅗	3↑Strohecker H	5	3	32½	31½	36	45½	Drury M A	b 110	9.00	65-29	Shy Jester 1132¾ Second Paw 1051 Pirateer 1081¾	Tired	9

1Jly79-Run in two division 6th & 8th races.

While Cookie has run well, his times do not begin to compare with those of Gemmate. Dropping down to 28Jly79, three days after Gemmate ran his grass burner, there was a strong lead time of :23.2. This was too much for Cookie, who trailed badly, and his loss of 4½ lengths gives him an add-on of five ticks for an ability time of :24.2. Because the first call time was a fast :45.0, Cookie is not penalized for energy, thus winding up with an excellent :24.2. I am always distrustful of any times registered when a horse is far back in the pack, as was Cookie here, but for the time being, we'll let it go. In the long race of 5Sep79, we have a final two-furlong measurement where the lead time was :25.1 (2:02.0 minus 1:36.4). Cookie gained 2¾ lengths in that long stretch and gets credit for a :24.4 ability time, this one surely earned. Now, let's compare the three horses.

Odds	Horse	Ability		A Pts		F	Total
1.5	Dauphin	Unknown		—		Q	—
4.9	Gemmate	:22.4	:23.1	26	24	Q	50
5.4	Cookie	:24.2	:24.4	18	16	Q	34

Since Dauphin is unknown in ability, there is no way he could be supported in this race, no matter if the crowd thought his one sparkling grass race in 1979 and his royal breeding merited the role of favorite. Now, we have a stress in our selection rules. Early in this chapter, I said that when the favorite is unknown in ability, then play the next-highest horse to place only. That would eliminate Dauphin and require us to play Gemmate to place. But I have also stressed throughout the potency of the Double Advantage Horse. Gemmate is a Double Advantage Horse only over Cookie, since we don't know about Dauphin with his unknown ability. On the other hand, Gemmate's times are downright sensational. But to play safe, which is what we do in investment situations, we will have to stick with our rule and play Gemmate to place only.

Gemmate won, of course, paying the healthy price of $11.80 up front and $5.40 for the place ticket we would have had. Poor Dauphin ran back in the crowd and Cookie could do no better than fourth. It's easy to pick Gemmate after the race is over, but that's not how we play this game.

SUMMARY OF SELECTION AND BETTING RULES

Before going on, it's time to repeat and summarize once more our selection rules for handy reference.

Races to Pass

1. There are certain races that must be passed altogether, not playable under our rules. They are:
    a. Maiden special races in which three or more horses are first-time starters, except when the favorite is a Double Advantage Horse, or when the favorite has but one ability time, which is superior by two or more to any of his competitors who have run previously.
    b. Turf races in which none of the first three favorites shows a grass race in his past performances, or none shows a Q form rating.
    c. When none of the first three favorites shows a Q form rating.
    d. When two or more of the first three betting choices are tied in point totals and are approximately equal in odds.

The Necessary Advantage

2. In races in which ability times are known and each horse has a form rating, we invest to win and place in the horse with 2 or more total points above his rivals. If the top-rated horse has but a 1-point advantage, we bet him to place. If two horses are tied in total points, we play to place on the horse with the lowest odds.

The Double Advantage Horse

3. A horse with two ability times better than the best ability times of the other two horses among the three we rate is a Double Advantage Horse. He will ordinarily have the highest point total and will be played to win and place

as the soundest investment wager in this entire method. Lack of early speed can be a weakness, however, and when he has no early-speed points and one or more of the other two competitors has 6 early-speed points, I will reduce my investment on the Double Advantage animal to place only. In addition, these other situations require some adjustment to our general rule of playing:

a. The Double Advantage Horse may have unknown form because of a layoff of more than twenty-eight days. If he is the favorite and has at least 3 early-speed points in races of six and a half furlongs or less or 2 early-speed points in seven-furlong and one-mile races, and has at least one workout, play him to win and place. If he is not the favorite and shows these necessary early-speed characteristics with one workout, play him to place only.

b. If the Double Advantage Horse has unknown form and lacks medium early speed as set forth above, pass him as an unknown-form horse, and if he shows no recent workout, also pass him.

c. If some other horse among the first three betting choices has higher total points with 6 early-speed points when the Double Advantage Horse has no early-speed points, play the Double Advantage Horse to place only.

d. In any other situation where early-speed points and additional form points may place another horse higher in point totals than the Double Advantage Horse, you will nevertheless play the Double Advantage Horse to win and place, because of the power of the Double Advantage.

e. In distance races where early-speed points are not involved, play the Double Advantage Horse to win and place if he is the favorite with a workout. If he is favored with no workouts, bet him to place. Otherwise, he is a regular U.

The Unknown-Ability Horse

4. When a horse whose ability is unknown is a strong favorite, play the highest-rated horse to place only. "Strong favorite" means that the unknown-ability horse is the betting choice by at least one full number over the second choice, such as 1-1 against 2-1, or 2-1 against 3-1.

5. When the horse whose ability is unknown is less than a strong favorite, or is not the favorite at all, play the highest-rated horse to win and place.

The Unknown-Form Horse

6. When one or more of the first three favorites has unknown form and has the highest point total by 2 or more, play the next-highest-rated horse to

place only. When the unknown-form horse has but 1 more point than the others, or the same number, or less, your investment will go on the highest-rated Q horse to win and place.

The Lightly Raced Favorite

7. A Lightly Raced Favorite (with five or fewer lifetime races) who is the favorite and has any point total less than 2 above the other two betting choices may be played to win and place only if he scored a Big Win in his last race. If he is the favorite and showed an improved running line in his last race sufficient to entitle him to 2 form points, he may be bet to place only, even if he lacks the highest point total.

Special Situations in Maiden Claiming Races

8. While maiden claiming races ordinarily present some of the soundest investment opportunities available, there are some special situations in which particular care must be taken. They are:
   a. When the highest-point-rating horse has run eight times or more without winning, and some other horse among the first three with less points has run five times or less, and the lightly raced horse is within 5 total points of the highest-rated horse, play the lightly raced horse to win and place. However, if the runner with eight or more starts is a Double Advantage Horse, he is to be played.
   b. When a horse has finished second three times or more in one-third of his races, he is afflicted with "seconditis," and should be passed, regardless of point totals, unless he is a Double Advantage Horse, in which event he may be played.

Use of One Ability Time

9. If one of the first three favorites has but one race on which an ability time can be computed, while the other horses have two, then rate all three off their best ability time only.

BIG WEEK AT BELMONT: FIRST DAY, SUNDAY, JUNE 1, 1980

On Sunday, June 1, 1980, beautiful Belmont celebrated its seventy-fifth anniversary. It was the beginning of the week of the Belmont Stakes, the last of the three Triple Crown races for three-year-olds. There was great speculation about Codex, the California horse that had defeated Genuine Risk, the filly who had won the Kentucky Derby, in a disputed Preakness. And for the opening day of this week of celebration, there were free grandstand admissions, free parking, free programs. A happy crowd of 67,107 turned out for the card. It was a marvelous birthday party, filled with excitement and anticipation for the Big Week ahead.

As we approach this week to calculate our profits, we shall use throughout this book, as we have up to now, the standard of the traditional $2 wager. It should appear obvious even to the uninitiated that wagering the traditional $2 minimum racetrack bet, even on good days, will produce profits so small that the cost of the enterprise itself would be too much to overcome. The price of a *Daily Racing Form,* transportation to the track, admission, a program, and whatever else you care to spend all add up to expenses that cannot be matched by profitable $2 bets in an investing program where, by the nature of what we're doing, we will be playing short-priced horses.

How much you wish to invest in each race is therefore up to you. Whatever it is, or whatever it was that I was investing, can be computed off the figures of the traditional $2 bet. For example, if your investment level is a $20 ticket, your return on a $2 bet can be multiplied by 10 and you can easily know what you have made. Thus, the amount of investment and the amount of return throughout our week at Belmont, and at every other track session in this book, is always given at the $2 level for illustration purposes only.

How you determine the amount of money you invest, which we usually call money management, will be dealt with later in this book when we get down to talking about some of the practical mechanics of coping with other racetrack problems.

But back to the first day of our critical test period. How well would we fare, looking at every race, applying the rules set forth in this book, tested as they were over many previous months? Belmont is indeed the big leagues, the No. 1 racetrack in all the land, the Big Apple at its finest, where the top horses, the top jockeys, the top trainers all compete. By this I do not mean to downgrade California racing, which I consider outstanding. Santa Anita and Hollywood Park now top the nation in attendance and total handle, and in a practical sense they are equally as good as Belmont. But it's in New York where it counts, and if you can't make money at Belmont, you won't be able to make it anywhere.

Let's get going with the first race. We open the *Daily Racing Form* and begin with a study of the favorite, Grand Courant, in this allowance race at a distance of a mile and one-eighth.

1 BELMONT

1⅛ MILES. (1.45⅘) ALLOWANCE. Purse $20,000. 3-year-olds and upward which have never won a race other than maiden, claiming or starter weights, 3-year-olds, 114 lbs. Older, 122 lbs. Non-winners of a race other than claiming over a mile since May 1, allowed 3 lbs. Of such a race since April 15, 5 lbs.

Grand Courant — Ch. c. 3, by Little Current—Sundestine, by Clandestine
Own.—Frasher J — Br.—Fraser J (Ohio) — Tr.—Laurin Roger — **109**

Turf Record	St.	1st	2nd	3rd		St.	1st	2nd	3rd	Amt.
	1	0	1	0	1980	8	1	6	1	$30,510
					1979	0	M	0	0	

24May80- 2Bel	fst	1	:45⅘	1:10⅖	1:36	3↑ Allowance	10	8	6⁵	2 1½	1hd	2hd	Cordero A Jr	b	113	3.60	88-17	WarofWords112hdGrandCournt113½KeyToContent114⁵	Lugged in	11
11May80- 6Aqu	gd	1⅛ Ⓣ	:49	1:14⅗	1:52	Allowance	9	10	10¹²	4 5½	3nk	2no	Cordero A Jr	b	117	3.80	84-19	Black IsBeautiful112noGrandCourant117 2¼Baladi117½	Bothered st	12
30Apr80- 9Aqu	my	1	:47⅗	1:12⅕	1:37⅖	Allowance	5	5	4¹	4¾	4nk	3 2¾	Cordero A Jr	b	122	8.80	76-21	[D]VoodooRhythm117²King'sWsh117¾GrndCournt122no	Jostled st.	8
30Apr80-Placed second through disqualification																				
21Apr80- 6Aqu	fst	1	:46⅕	1:11⅖	1:37⅘	Md Sp Wt	2	3	1¹	1³	1 1½	1 1¼	Cordero A Jr	b	122	*1.00	77-23	Grand Courant 122 1¼ Tandoor 122⁶ Residual Heat 122 6¾	Driving	8
12Apr80- 3Aqu	fst	7f	:23⅗	:46⅗	1:24⅗	Md Sp Wt	4	4	5 2½	5 2½	3 1½	3½	Beitia E⁵		117	1.80	77-19	Elegant Disguise 122½ Tandoor 122no Grand Courant117 1¾	Rallied	6
14Mar80- 3GP	fst	1 1/16	:48⅕	1:13	1:46⅕	Md Sp Wt	4	3	4¾	3 2½	2hd	2²	Cordero A Jr		120	*1.30	68-24	Orchestra Pit 115²GrandCourant120noRube'sTouch113½	Game try	8
1Mar80- 2Hia	fst	7f	:23⅕	:46	1:25	Md Sp Wt	3	4	3¹	1½	1³	2 1¼	Gonzalez M A⁵		115	*.60	77-17	Northern Grace120 1¼GrandCourant115 5½[DH]IrishNabob120½	Failed	10
18Feb80- 6Hia	fst	6f	:22⅗	:46⅘	1:11⅖	Md Sp Wt	10	2	3½	2½	2½	2no	Gonzalez M A⁵		115	5.80	86-20	Ramparts 120no GrandCourant115⁸BoldBarbizon120½	Just missed	12

LATEST WORKOUTS May 21 Bel 4f sly :48⅗ b — May 6 Bel 4f fst :50⅘ b — ●Apr 28 Bel 4f sly :47⅕ h — Apr 9 Bel 3f fst :36⅗ h

He qualified rather easily on form, off a strong performance in his last race, which was such a powerful effort that he picked up a :24.0 ability time. The lead time between the first and second calls was :24.3, and the 3½ lengths gained by Grand Courant reduces this to the :24.0 figure without any energy adjustment. Back on 18Feb80 at Hialeah, we can pick up a :24.3 without any adjustments. These are potent times, and while they will be hard to overcome, even assuming the others are good, we see a very troubling sign. This horse has run second in six of his eight lifetime races. This looks like a dangerous affliction of "seconditis." But we now have to move to the second choice in the wagering, with the name of Indeed Gallant.

Indeed Gallant — Dk. b. or br. c. 4, by Gallant Native—Dedicated Lass, by Dedicate
Br.—Penowa Farms (Md)
Own.—Sasso L P — Tr.—Bradley John M — **117**

	St.	1st	2nd	3rd	Amt.
1980	7	2	2	0	$25,980
1979	4	1	0	0	$4,620

25May80-	9Bel	fst	6f	:22⅗	:45⅗	1:10⅘	3↑Allowance	1	6	10^{10}	$8^{9\frac12}$	$5^{6\frac12}$	$2^{2\frac12}$	Martens G	b	119	44.00	85-16	Son Of Solo $113^{2\frac12}$ Indeed Gallant 119½ Dr. McGuire $112^{1\frac12}$	Rallied	11
2May80-	5Aqu	fst	1⅛	:47⅕	1:12	1:49⅖	Allowance	5	6	$5^{9\frac12}$	$4^{3\frac12}$	3^{5}	$2^{5\frac12}$	Martens G	b	117	3.80	82-19	Home By Dawn $117^{5\frac12}$ Indeed Gallant117^{hd}Ninfa'sGift112^{2}	Rallied	6
29Mar80-	2Aqu	sly	2	:48⅗	3:02⅕	3:28⅘	Hcp 12500s	3	2	9^{28}	9^{50}	—	—	Martens G	b	117	5.30	— —	FinneyFinster108^{2}FrankTalk$122^{8\frac14}$LaughandGo$114^{8\frac34}$	Stop'd eased	9
22Mar80-	5Aqu	sly	1⅛	:47⅖	1:13⅗	1:53⅗	Allowance	5	1	1^{hd}	5^{3}	$5^{8\frac12}$	5^{18}	Martens G	b	119	*2.20	49-31	Bel Baie 117^{4} Il Vagabondo $117^{1\frac34}$ Spartan Knight $117^{2\frac14}$	Tired	6
11Feb80-	5Aqu	fst	1¼	⊡:49⅖	1:41	2:07⅗	Hcp 12500s	3	2	3^{1}	1^{hd}	1^{6}	$1^{4\frac14}$	Martens G	b	112	*1.40	80-23	Indeed Gallant $112^{4\frac14}$ North Star $115^{2\frac34}$ Scamp Boy $113^{3\frac34}$	Easily	11
30Jan80-	3Aqu	fst	1$\frac{3}{16}$	⊡:48⅕	1:13⅖	1:58⅘	Hcp 12500s	1	2	$2^{1\frac12}$	1^{hd}	$1^{1\frac12}$	$1^{6\frac14}$	Montoya D	b	107	4.70	84-22	Indeed Gallant $107^{6\frac14}$ Recidian$111^{2\frac34}$LaughandGo113^{nk}	Ridden out	9
14Jan80-	5Aqu	gd	1$\frac{1}{16}$	⊡:47⅖	1:12⅘	1:47⅕	Hcp 12500s	8	7	8^{15}	9^{16}	9^{11}	$6^{3\frac14}$	Graell A	b	108	10.00	75-23	Home By Dawn 114no QurantaBay113^{nk}FellowHeir109¾	No threat	9
31Dec79-	4Aqu	fst	6f	⊡:22⅘	:46⅘	1:12⅕	3↑Md 12500	9	1	$3^{3\frac12}$	3^{4}	$1^{\frac12}$	1^{8}	Montoya D	b	120	4.40	83-19	Indeed Gallant120^{8}Taunt120½[DH]DoubleEdgeBlade120	Ridden out	9
29Nov79-	4Aqu	fst	6f	:23⅖	:48⅖	1:13⅗	3↑Md 12500	3	1	3^{2}	$4^{3\frac12}$	$3^{5\frac12}$	$4^{5\frac14}$	Montoya D		120	9.20	70-29	RulerComeBack120¾Trifusion$120^{3\frac34}$HailtheSkipper120¾	No mishap	8
24Mar79-	1Key	sly	6f	:22⅖	:46⅖	1:13⅘	Md Sp Wt	2	10	9^{14}	8^{13}	8^{17}	7^{15}	Lee R F		120	10.50	58-27	Person To Person120^{1}Mr.KnowItAll117^{1}Cabin'sPride120^{2}	Outrun	10

LATEST WORKOUTS May 23 Bel 4f fst :48⅘ h ●May 15 Bel 7f fst 1:28⅕ b Apr 30 Bel 4f sly :52⅗ b Apr 24 Bel tr.t 7f fst 1:31 b

He qualifies off a second-place finish, as well as a healthy gain. In that last race, the lead time was :25.1. We calculate Indeed Gallant's gain off a maximum of 8 lengths at the second call, leaving us with a net of 5½ lengths for a reduction in time of four ticks to :24.2. When we add the lengths behind at the second call, we are into 47 and change for a one-tick add-on for energy, giving us a final adjusted ability time of :24.3 for the race. In his previous race, on 2May80, the lead time was :24.4 between the first two calls. The gain, from 8 to 3½ lengths, was 4½, which allows us to deduct three ticks to bring the figure to :24.1. But in energy, we get up to :49.2, which requires an add-on of three ticks to make the final adjusted ability time at :24.4. These, too, are most respectable times.

The third choice on the board is Sir Kay, who immediately rates an unknown-form factor off his last race on the grass after a layoff. Here is his record.

Sir Kay — B. c. 3, by Mr Leader—Kay Emy, by Delta Judge
Br.—Nuckols Bros (Ky)
Own.—Woodside Stud — Tr.—Mondello Louis — **109**

Turf Record	St.	1st	2nd	3rd
	2	0	0	0

	St.	1st	2nd	3rd	Amt.
1980	5	1	1	2	$17,420
1979	6	M	1	1	$4,760

7May80-	2Aqu	fm	1$\frac{1}{16}$	Ⓣ:49	1:13⅕	1:44⅘	3↑Allowance	4	10	10^{7}	$8^{5\frac12}$	$8^{4\frac34}$	7^{7}	Asmussen C B	b	112	3.50	74-15	CurrentWinner$115^{4\frac12}$TestPttern114^{hd}EstrnTown109½	Lacked room	10
2Apr80-	2Aqu	fst	1⅛	:48⅘	1:13⅖	1:51⅖	Allowance	4	6	6^{6}	6^{6}	$4^{2\frac34}$	2^{nk}	Asmussen C B	b	117	*1.50	78-18	Huge Success 119^{nk} Sir Kay 117^{hd} Bold Barbizon $122^{3\frac34}$	Gaining	7
9Mar80-	6Aqu	fst	170	⊡:47⅘	1:12⅘	1:42⅗	Allowance	6	4	$3^{1\frac12}$	$2^{2\frac12}$	2^{5}	$3^{6\frac12}$	Castaneda M	b	117	7.20	82-22	Col. Frankincense $117^{5\frac14}$ Santo's Joe $117^{1\frac14}$ Sir Kay 117^{hd}	Evenly	9
16Jan80-	3Aqu	fst	1⅛	⊡:48⅕	1:13⅗	1:52⅕	Allowance	7	7	$6^{9\frac12}$	$6^{5\frac14}$	5^{7}	$3^{8\frac14}$	Martens G	b	122	4.40	77-18	Little Lenny $117^{4\frac14}$ Don Daniello 117^{4} Sir Kay 122no	Mild bid	7
9Jan80-	5Aqu	fst	1$\frac{1}{16}$	⊡:49⅖	1:14⅘	1:47⅕	Md Sp Wt	4	8	$9^{7\frac14}$	$8^{3\frac14}$	1^{hd}	1^{3}	Asmussen C B	b	122	*1.30	78-18	Sir Kay 122^{3} I'm Regal Too 122½ Bold Fencer $122^{1\frac12}$	Drew clear	9
23Dec79-	5Aqu	gd	170	⊡:48⅘	1:13⅘	1:45⅖	Md Sp Wt	4	7	6^{7}	6^{5}	3^{nk}	2^{nk}	Castaneda M	b	120	7.30	75-22	Bucksplasher 120^{nk} Sir Kay $120^{3\frac34}$ Goldenny $120^{2\frac14}$	Gamely	8
14Dec79-	6Aqu	my	1$\frac{1}{16}$	⊡:46⅖	1:11⅖	1:46	Md Sp Wt	4	8	8^{20}	6^{17}	5^{10}	$3^{3\frac34}$	Castaneda M	b	118	17.20	80-18	Prince Robair 118¾ Bucksplasher 118^{3} Sir Kay $118^{4\frac34}$	Rallied	8
30Nov79-	5Aqu	fst	7f	:23⅖	:47⅕	1:26	Md 50000	3	8	$8^{8\frac12}$	$8^{9\frac12}$	$6^{8\frac14}$	$6^{7\frac34}$	Castaneda M	b	116	26.40	63-29	I'm Vital 120^{nk} Baladi $120^{3\frac12}$ Raymond Z. $120^{2\frac14}$	No factor	8
26Jly79-	2Bel	fm	7f	Ⓣ:23⅘	:46⅗	1:25⅖	Md 40000	10	1	$7^{8\frac12}$	7^{13}	$7^{8\frac34}$	7^{5}	Hernandez R		114	38.80	72-21	Sweeten 116^{hd} Sun Party 114^{3} Pi's Guy 118¾	No threat	10
19Jly79-	4Bel	fst	6f	:22⅘	:46⅗	1:12	Md 35000	10	10	$12^{8\frac34}$	9^{11}	7^{12}	7^{15}	Velasquez J		118	34.50	67-22	SonOfADodo118^{10}AThousandMore$114^{1\frac12}$DreamCabin118^{nk}	Outrun	12

LATEST WORKOUTS May 28 Bel tr.t 6f fst 1:18 b May 24 Bel 7f fst 1:29⅗ b May 17 Bel tr.t 4f fst :49⅘ b May 6 Bel tr.t 4f fst :49⅘ b

We go ahead and compute his ability times to see if he is a real contender. The best we can come up with is :25.2 back on 23Dec79, and follow with another :25.2 on 2Apr80. These times are not sufficient to worry us as we make our comparative ratings.

Odds	Horse	Ability		A Pts		F	Total
.7	Grand Courant	:24.0	:24.3	20	17	Q	37
3.8	Indeed Gallant	:24.3	:24.4	17	16	Q	33
5.9	Sir Kay	:25.2	:25.2	13	13	U	26

Grand Courant's point lead is impressive. Despite our anxiety over his "seconditis," we must follow our rules and invest in him to win and place. I am not willing to extend rules for "seconditis" beyond maiden races. And look what happened:

FIRST RACE
Belmont
JUNE 1, 1980

1 ⅛ MILES. (1.45⅗) ALLOWANCE. Purse $20,000. 3-year-olds and upward which have never won a race other than maiden, claiming or starter weights, 3-year-olds, 114 lbs. Older, 122 lbs. Non-winners of a race other than claiming over a mile since May 1, allowed 3 lbs. Of such a race since April 15, 5 lbs.

Value of race $20,000, value to winner $12,000, second $4,400, third $2,400, fourth $1,200. Mutuel pool $189,476, OTB pool $128,555.

Last Raced	Horse	Eqt.	A.	Wt	PP	St	¼	½	¾	Str	Fin	Jockey	Odds $1
25May80 ^{9}Bel^{2}	Indeed Gallant	b	4	117	5	5	6^{2}	6^{4}	2^{4}	$1^{1\frac{1}{2}}$	$1^{4\frac{3}{4}}$	Martens G	3.80
24May80 ^{2}Bel^{2}	Grand Courant	b	3	112	8	1	$3^{1\frac{1}{2}}$	3^{3}	1^{1}	2^{6}	2^{5}	Cordero A Jr	.70
7May80 ^{2}Aqu^{7}	Sir Kay	b	3	112	4	7	8	8	$6^{\frac{1}{2}}$	3^{1}	$3^{2\frac{3}{4}}$	Asmussen C B	5.90
11May80 ^{6}Aqu^{8}	Rectory		3	109	3	6	4^{hd}	$4^{1\frac{1}{2}}$	3^{1}	$4^{1\frac{1}{2}}$	4^{3}	Santiago A	9.40
19May80 ^{7}Aqu^{9}	Crosscut	b	4	117	7	2	5^{2}	$5^{1\frac{1}{2}}$	5^{2}	5^{5}	5^{3}	Hernandez R	29.30
14May80 ^{1}Aqu^{3}	Chief Halftown	b	3	106	6	3	$1^{\frac{1}{2}}$	2^{hd}	7^{3}	$6^{\frac{1}{2}}$	$6^{2\frac{3}{4}}$	Lovato F Jr^{5}	19.30
11May80 ^{6}Aqu^{9}	Northern Grace	b	3	112	1	8	$7^{\frac{1}{2}}$	7^{hd}	8	7^{2}	$7^{5\frac{1}{4}}$	Velasquez J	14.40
25May80 ^{9}Bel^{8}	Grandiloquent Guy		3	109	2	4	2^{2}	$1^{\frac{1}{2}}$	$4^{\frac{1}{2}}$	8	8	Venezia M	23.70

OFF AT 1:05-1/2, EDT. Start good, Won ridden out. Time, :23⅘, :47⅘, 1:13, 1:38⅗, 1:51⅖ Track fast.

Official Program Numbers↘

$2 Mutuel Prices:			
5-(E)-INDEED GALLANT	9.60	3.20	2.60
8-(H)-GRAND COURANT		2.60	2.20
4-(D)-SIR KAY			2.60

This intrepid lover of second-place finishes did it again. Indeed Gallant scored an easy victory, and our day is begun with cashing a puny $2.60 place ticket. Grand Courant went back to his barn with an incredible record of seven times for second in nine races. We hope the second race will lead to better things. You see that it is a distance race on the grass and that Kiss In The Dark is the favorite (p. 136).

Our first inquiry is on form—does this filly qualify? Our second rule is *less than* 3 lengths behind the leader at various calls. What do we do with exactly 3 lengths? Line-drawing is often difficult, but to stand by a set of rules, we must do it. Despite a drop in class from allowance to a $50,000 claiming race, we have no other alternative but to disqualify this favorite off form.

The second choice in the wagering, Four A.M., has never run on the grass. Here is an unknown-ability factor, which precludes any investment in this otherwise solid animal.

When we look at Tullette, the third choice, we have the same problem.

BELMONT

WIDENER TURF COURSE
1 1-16 MILES
BELMONT PARK
START · FINISH

1 $\frac{1}{16}$ MILES. (TURF). (1.39$\frac{1}{5}$) CLAIMING. Purse $20,000. Fillies and Mares, 4-year-old, and upward, weights, 122 lbs. Non–winners of two races at a mile or over since May 1, allowed 3 lbs. Of such a race since then, 5 lbs. Claiming price $50,000 for each $5000 to $40,000 2 lbs. (Races when entered to be claimed for $35,000 or less not considered)

Kiss In The Dark

Own.—Gallo R H
$50,000

Ro. f. 4, by Al Hattab—Shining Youth, by Sir Gaylord
Br.—Gallo R H (Ky)
Tr.—Brown Tamara J

117

Turf Record					St.	1st	2nd	3rd		Amt.
St.	1st	2nd	3rd	1980	3	0	0	0		$1,140
9	3	1	1	1979	21	4	1	5		$29,104

17May80-	7Aqu fm	1$\frac{1}{16}$ ⊤:50$\frac{1}{5}$ 1:14$\frac{3}{5}$ 1:51	⑤Allowance	4 4 43 43 58 512	Miranda J	b 115	26.60	77-11 TmpusFugitII115nkRcordAcclim117$\frac{1}{2}$ChstnutSpstr119no	Steadied 7
8May80-	8Pim yl	1 ⊤:49$\frac{3}{5}$ 1:14$\frac{1}{5}$ 1:40	Allowance	8 7 79$\frac{3}{4}$ 77$\frac{3}{4}$ 62$\frac{3}{4}$ 42	Iliescu A	b 108	2.30e	77-24 Buck's Chief 115nk Terullah 119$\frac{3}{4}$ Uncle Pokey 115$\frac{1}{2}$	Rallied 8
1May80-	8Pim sly	6f :23$\frac{3}{5}$:47$\frac{3}{5}$ 1:14$\frac{1}{5}$	⑤Allowance	2 5 67$\frac{1}{2}$ 68$\frac{1}{2}$ 611 614	Kupfer T	b 112	22.20	61-26 One Ambition 112no Janet'sJustin119no ASaintSheAint115$\frac{2}{2}$	Outrun 6
1Nov79-	8Pim fst	6f :23 :46 1:11$\frac{3}{5}$ 3 ♦ ⑤Allowance	3 9 810 811 78$\frac{1}{2}$ 77$\frac{1}{2}$	Pino M G5	b 108	44.10	80-23 Spring Triple 115nk Veneralbe Lass110hdWinNona113hd	No factor 9
22Oct79-	6Med fst	1$\frac{1}{16}$:49 1:13$\frac{3}{5}$ 1:46$\frac{2}{5}$ 3 ♦ ⑤Allowance	2 4 53$\frac{1}{2}$ 511 516 529	Fann B	b 111	16.00	48-19 Forbiddnisi119$\frac{1}{2}$RichndRghtous119$\frac{1}{2}$Insubordnlc117$\frac{5}{2}$	No threat 5
21Sep79-	8Del sly	1$\frac{1}{16}$:49 1:13$\frac{1}{5}$ 1:45$\frac{3}{5}$ 3 ♦ ⑤Allowance	5 2 32 44$\frac{1}{2}$ 516 624	Kupfer T	b 112	6.90	57-20 Jamila Kadir 112$\frac{5}{2}$ Princess Ivor 117$\frac{2}{1}$ Quillascope 117$\frac{3}{2}$	Tired 6
12Sep79-	7Del fm	1$\frac{1}{16}$ ⊤:48 1:12$\frac{4}{5}$ 1:44$\frac{3}{5}$ 3 ♦ ⑤Allowance	4 6 55$\frac{1}{2}$ 34 22$\frac{1}{2}$ 12$\frac{1}{2}$	Kupfer T	b 117	*1.60	80-22 Kiss In TheDark117$\frac{2}{1}$EchoAway114$\frac{1}{2}$LetMeSleep119$\frac{5}{2}$	Ridden out 6
2Sep79-	7Pen fm	1 ⊤ 1:35$\frac{1}{5}$	⑤White Rose	7 9 84 83 81$\frac{1}{2}$ 54	Iliescu A	b 112	9.90	90-09 Euphrosyne 112$\frac{1}{2}$ Leslie J 114$\frac{1}{2}$ Keeler 116hd	Mild bid 11
27Aug79-	9Mth fm	1 ⊤:48$\frac{3}{5}$ 1:12$\frac{3}{5}$ 1:45$\frac{3}{5}$ 3 ♦ ⑤Allowance	8 7 64$\frac{1}{2}$ 31$\frac{1}{2}$ 3$\frac{1}{2}$ 35$\frac{1}{2}$	Pino M G5	b 107	6.50	67-25 T. V. Highlights119$\frac{4}{1}$FlashDouble112$\frac{4}{1}$KissInTheDark107$\frac{2}{1}$	Evenly 9
17Aug79-	8Del fm	1 ⊤:46$\frac{1}{5}$ 1:10$\frac{4}{5}$ 1:37$\frac{4}{5}$ 3 ♦ ⑤Allowance	2 6 65$\frac{1}{2}$ 24 21 11	Pino M G5	b 107	3.60	88-16 Kiss In The Dark 1071 Let Me Sleep 1145 Hi Reiko 116nk	Driving 7

LATEST WORKOUTS May 23 Bel tr.t 4f fst :51$\frac{1}{5}$ b   May 16 Bel tr.t 3f fst :38 b   Apr 23 Bow 5f gd 1:03$\frac{3}{5}$ b   Apr 19 Bow 5f gd 1:04 b

Four A.M.

Own.—Lavezzo D H Jr
$50,000

Dk. b. or br. m. 5, by Noble Table—Going Home II, by Taigo II
Br.—Lavezzo D (Fla)
Tr.—Gullo Thomas J

117

		St.	1st	2nd	3rd		Amt.
1980		3	0	2	1		$6,360
1979		6	4	0	1		$28,320

4May80-	3Aqu fst 6f :23$\frac{1}{5}$:47$\frac{3}{5}$ 1:12$\frac{3}{5}$	⑤Allowance	6 5 64 33 34 33$\frac{1}{2}$	Cordero A Jr	117	9.30	77-25 Celia Bonita 117$\frac{2}{1}$ Too Daring 1171$\frac{1}{2}$ Four A.M. 117$\frac{2}{2}$	Lugged in 8
23Jan80-	7Hia fst 6f :22$\frac{3}{5}$:46$\frac{3}{5}$ 1:12$\frac{3}{5}$	⑤Allowance	7 8 74$\frac{1}{2}$ 76$\frac{1}{4}$ 44 72$\frac{1}{2}$	Guerra W A	116	3.80	79-21 Twenty One Inch 116$\frac{2}{1}$ Four A.M.116noLiveBullet116$\frac{1}{4}$	Late speed 11
11Jan80-	9Crc fst 6$\frac{1}{4}$f :22$\frac{3}{5}$:46$\frac{3}{5}$ 1:18$\frac{3}{5}$	⑤Allowance	4 6 54$\frac{1}{2}$ 55 23 25$\frac{1}{2}$	Guerra W A	117	2.50	86-19 Golferette 1145$\frac{1}{4}$ Four A.M. 117nk Lawtonville 117$\frac{2}{1}$	Held place 8
24Dec79-	5Crc fst 7f :23$\frac{3}{5}$:47$\frac{1}{5}$ 1:27 3 ♦ ⑤Allowance		8 3 32$\frac{1}{2}$ 32 13 16	Guerra W A	114	*1.00	81-22 Four A.M. 1146 Sea Prospector 1151 Sally Lunn 113nk	Handily 8
13Dec79-	3Aqu sly 6f ⊡:22$\frac{3}{5}$:46$\frac{3}{5}$ 1:12$\frac{3}{5}$ 3 ♦ ⑤Clm 35000		5 4 59 58 33$\frac{1}{2}$ 2nk	Rocco J5	112	3.70 Ⓓ	82-20 Gladiadora 108nk ⒹFour A.M. 112$\frac{1}{2}$ All Francis 115$\frac{3}{2}$	Bore out 9
	13Dec79-Disqualified and placed ninth							
19Jly79-	7Bel fst 7f :22$\frac{3}{5}$:46$\frac{1}{5}$ 1:24$\frac{3}{5}$ 3 ♦ ⑤Allowance		5 3 31 1hd 14 3$\frac{1}{2}$	Martens G	b 117	*1.80	77-22 Jolivar 116hd Spark of Life 122$\frac{3}{4}$ Four A.M. 1173$\frac{1}{4}$	Weakened 8
8Jly79-	1Bel fst 7f :23 :46$\frac{1}{5}$ 1:24 3 ♦ ⑤Clm 50000		1 4 2hd 22$\frac{1}{2}$ 1hd 11$\frac{1}{2}$	Sullivan J5	112	2.70	82-21 Four A.M. 1121$\frac{1}{2}$ InfernalVernal1122$\frac{1}{4}$FancyHatter111$\frac{3}{4}$	Ridden out 8
28Jun79-	7Bel fst 7f :2s :46$\frac{1}{5}$ 1:24$\frac{1}{5}$ 3 ♦ ⑤Clm 25000		6 5 31$\frac{1}{2}$ 42$\frac{1}{2}$ 14 110	Gonzalez M A7	110	6.50	81-22 Four A.M. 11210 Countess Noble 114$\frac{1}{2}$ Fair Loretta 108$\frac{1}{4}$	Ridden out 8
6Jun79-	9Bel gd 7f :23 :46$\frac{1}{5}$ 1:26$\frac{3}{5}$ 3 ♦ ⑤Md 12000		2 4 12$\frac{1}{2}$ 11$\frac{1}{2}$ 16 112	Asmussen C B5	113	7.70	70-24 Four A.M. 11312 Countess Noble 1141$\frac{3}{4}$ Kiawah 114$\frac{1}{2}$	Ridden out 12
8Oct78-	9Bel fst 6f :22$\frac{3}{5}$:46$\frac{2}{5}$ 1:12 3 ♦ ⑤Md 10000		11 7 68$\frac{1}{2}$ 59$\frac{1}{2}$ 612 815	Rosado O	119	*2.00	67-19 Swifty Mollie 1192$\frac{1}{2}$ Stolen Charm 1104 Inaclinch 115$\frac{3}{4}$	Tired 11

LATEST WORKOUTS May 24 Bel 5f fst :59$\frac{3}{5}$ h   May 17 Bel tr.t 4f fst :50 b   ●May 11 Bel tr.t 1 fst 1:49$\frac{3}{5}$ b   May 1 Bel 3f fst :36 b

Tullette ✱

Own.—Cohen S
$40,000

B. f. 4, by Tom Tulle—Clarion Princess, by Viking Spirit
Br.—Ward Jay (Ky)
Tr.—Schaeffer Stephen

113

Turf Record					St.	1st	2nd	3rd		Amt.
St.	1st	2nd	3rd	1980	14	3	1	2		$33,940
2	0	1	0	1979	24	4	4	6		$32,420

21May80-	3Bel sly 7f :23 :46 1:25$\frac{3}{5}$	⑤Clm 35000	3 4 45 45 31$\frac{1}{2}$ 1nk	Venezia M	119	*1.80	75-22 Tullette 119nk Bold Ridona 117$\frac{1}{2}$ Tortoise 1178	Driving 7
8May80-	5Aqu sly 7f :23$\frac{3}{5}$:47$\frac{1}{5}$ 1:24$\frac{3}{5}$	⑤Clm 35000	2 6 65$\frac{1}{4}$ 42$\frac{1}{2}$ 22 11$\frac{3}{4}$	Venezia M	113	4.50	77-22 Tullette 1131$\frac{3}{4}$ Tortoise 113$\frac{2}{2}$ Bravo Miss 119$\frac{2}{2}$	Ridden out 7
26Apr80-	4Aqu fst 7f :22$\frac{3}{5}$:46 1:24	⑤Allowance	4 6 51$\frac{3}{5}$ 511 611 620	Asmussen C B	117	21.50	61-19 Jongleuse 1222$\frac{1}{2}$ GallantYankee117$\frac{4}{3}$MissJoyForever1122$\frac{1}{2}$	Outrun 7
16Apr80-	3Aqu fst 6f :22$\frac{3}{5}$:47$\frac{1}{5}$ 1:11$\frac{3}{5}$	⑤Allowance	3 6 67 65 54$\frac{1}{4}$ 44$\frac{1}{2}$	Venezia M	117	18.50	80-17 AfternoonDelight1172$\frac{3}{4}$Poppanesin117hdTooDring117$\frac{1}{2}$	No factor 7
3Apr80-	6Aqu fst 7f :23$\frac{3}{5}$:46$\frac{3}{5}$ 1:24$\frac{3}{5}$	⑤Clm c-30000	8 6 74 52 64$\frac{1}{4}$ 66	Miranda J	119	3.40	72-20 Honey Tree 1151$\frac{1}{2}$ Wanena 108hd Bravo Miss 1174$\frac{1}{2}$	No factor 9
22Mar80-	1Aqu sly 7f :23$\frac{1}{5}$:48$\frac{3}{5}$ 1:26$\frac{3}{5}$	⑤Clm 25000	6 8 78$\frac{1}{2}$ 54$\frac{1}{2}$ 11$\frac{1}{2}$ 15$\frac{3}{4}$	Venezia M	117	12.30	68-31 Tullette 1175$\frac{3}{4}$ PurpleShamrock117$\frac{1}{2}$SwiftPoppy117$\frac{1}{2}$	Ridden out 9
15Mar80-	4Aqu my 6f ⊡:23$\frac{3}{5}$:48$\frac{2}{5}$ 1:13$\frac{3}{5}$	⑤Clm c-20000	2 6 3$\frac{1}{2}$ 21 31$\frac{1}{2}$ 45$\frac{3}{4}$	Hernandez R	b 117	3.40	70-24 ThoughtfulCrol117nkBoldProspect1172$\frac{1}{2}$Binbuyer1082$\frac{3}{4}$	Weakened 7
12Mar80-	3Aqu fst 1$\frac{1}{16}$ ⊡:49 1:15 1:48$\frac{3}{5}$	⑤Clm 25000	3 5 4$\frac{3}{4}$ 42 514	Hernandez R	117	2.50	70-24 Hoo Ray 117nk Wanena 115$\frac{3}{4}$ Flouncy 1083$\frac{1}{2}$	Bumped, tired 5
1Mar80-	4Aqu fst 170 ⊡:48$\frac{3}{5}$ 1:14$\frac{1}{5}$ 1:44$\frac{3}{5}$	⑤Clm 27500	4 8 55$\frac{3}{4}$ 21$\frac{1}{2}$ 31$\frac{1}{2}$ 33$\frac{3}{4}$	Beitia E5	b 110	7.30	74-17 Intentional Twist 1172 Bravo Miss 1171$\frac{1}{2}$ Tullette 110$\frac{3}{4}$	Weakened 9
18Feb80-	3Aqu fst 1$\frac{1}{8}$ ⊡:48$\frac{1}{5}$ 1:13$\frac{3}{5}$ 1:54$\frac{1}{5}$	⑤Clm 32500	6 1 21 2hd 52$\frac{1}{4}$ 68$\frac{1}{2}$	Asmussen C B	b 115	5.80	66-19 Cousins Three 108$\frac{1}{2}$ LegsO'Lamb117$\frac{3}{4}$ParFortheCourse1104$\frac{1}{4}$	Tired 7

LATEST WORKOUTS Apr 20 Aqu 4f fst :52 b   Apr 14 Aqu 6f fst 1:16$\frac{3}{5}$ b   Apr 7 Aqu 5f fst 1:05 b

There are no grass races showing in the 10 listed in 1980. Once again, we are compelled to write down "Unknown" for ability, and we are confronted with this situation.

Odds	Horse	Ability		A Pts		F	Total
1.3	Kiss In The Dark	—	—	—	—	NQ	NQ
2.3	Four A.M.	Unknown		—	—	U	U
6.0	Tullette	Unknown		—	—	U	U

There is nothing here on which to base a play. We will not ever invest in situations of this kind, as the rules in the last chapter indicated. What did happen in this race? Four A.M. won it, despite a lack of prior grass experience. Kiss In The Dark, whom we disqualified on form, ran fifth in a field of seven. Horses not qualified on form seldom win, as I earlier indicated.

Perhaps we can do better in the third race, another distance run with a heavy favorite on the board.

3 BELMONT

START
1 1-16 MILES
BELMONT PARK
FINISH

1 1/16 MILES. (1.40⅖) CLAIMING. Purse $17,000. 4-year-olds and uwpard, weights, 122 lbs. Non-winners of two races at a mile or over since May 1, allowed 3 lbs. of such a race since then, 5 lbs. Claiming price $35,,000 for each $2,500 to $30,000 2 lbs. (Races when entered to be claimed for $25,000 or less not considered)

Bankers Sun — Own.—Sommer Viola — **$35,000** — Ch. c. 4, by Flag Raiser—Las Olas, by Stone Age — Br.—Stinson J R & Laverne A (Fla) — Tr.—Martin Frank — **117**

Turf Record	St.	1st	2nd	3rd
	1	0	0	0

	St.	1st	2nd	3rd	Amt.
1980	11	3	2	2	$43,700
1979	24	5	5	5	$62,715

15May80-	7Aqu	fst	1⅛		:46⅕	1:11⅘	1:51	3↑ Allowance	10	7	56½	42	67½	611	Cordero A Jr	119	14.30	69-19	AndoverRoad119¾Suznne'sStr114¾Col.Frnkincense1124¼	Bid tired	10
3May80-	2Aqu	fst	1		:45⅗	1:10	1:35⅗	Clm 50000	7	2	21½	22½	24	34¾	Asmussen C B	119	3.30	83-12	Marlago 1154¾ Fiddle Faddle 117hd Bankers Sun 1193½	Weakened	7
18Apr80-	7Aqu	fst	1⅛		:47⅖	1:11⅖	1:50⅘	Allowance	5	2	21½	21	3nk	33	Asmussen C B	117	2.30	78-24	Lean Lad 1172½ Dresden Dew 117½ Bankers Sun 117nk	Weakened	6
13Apr80-	2Aqu	fst	1⅛		:47⅕	1:11⅘	1:50⅗	Clm 40000	1	2	21	2½	11	12¼	Asmussen C B	117	*.70e	82-24	Bankers Sun 1172¼ Raise Charger1134¾GalaForecast108no	Driving	7
22Mar80-	7Aqu	sly	1		:48⅘	1:14⅘	1:40⅕	Allowance	3	4	31½	32	21½	22½	Maple E	119	*1.30	62-31	Ephphatha 1172½ Bankers Sun 1195 Silent Bid 117½	Second best	7
10Mar80-	8Aqu	fst	1 1/16	⊡	:48⅕	1:12⅗	1:44⅘	Allowance	7	4	32	32	21	2no	Rogers K L5	114	5.00[D]	90-19	Plethora 112no [D]Bankers Sun 1144¼ Raise Charger 1172	Bore in	9
10Mar80-Disqualified and placed ninth																					
21Feb80-	6Aqu	fst	1 1/16	⊡	:47⅕	1:13	1:45⅘	Allowance	8	7	77¾	45	41¾	51	Beitia E5	117	*1.40	84-18	El Kel 117nk Follow That Dream 117½ Creme Silence 122nk	Wide	9
14Feb80-	8Aqu	fst	1⅛	⊡	:49⅖	1:14⅕	1:53⅗	Allowance	4	2	11½	12	12	13¼	Asmussen C B	117	*.80	78-25	Bankers Sun 1173¼ Bye Bye Blues 117¾ Anoint 1173¾	Driving	9
2Feb80-	6Aqu	fst	1 3/16	⊡	:47⅗	1:13⅕	2:00⅕	Allowance	5	7	613	66¾	21	2nk	Asmussen C B	117	1.60	77-27	Sunny Puddles 112nkBankersSun1172SpartanKnight1222¾	Bore in	9
20Jan80-	6Aqu	fst	1 1/16	⊡	:47⅘	1:12⅗	1:45⅖	Allowance	1	1	15	14	1hd	43¼	Wacker D J5	112	*2.00	84-26	Raise A Buck 1192½ Orfanik 117¾ Dresden Dew 117no	Tired	8

LATEST WORKOUTS May 25 Bel tr.t 4f fst :48⅕ h May 11 Bel tr.t 4f fst :49⅕ b Apr 30 Bel tr.t 4f my :49 h (d) Apr 6 Bel 4f fst :48⅖ h

Bankers Sun, the heavy crowd favorite, can qualify on form by either a gain of five between the first two calls in his last race, or by an up close at one call plus a drop in class from allowance to a $35,000 claimer. In checking his ability times, the 18Apr80 race shows a :24.0 lead time, no adjustment for gain, and one tick added for energy for a solid :24.1. In the 3May80 race, the lead time was a strong :24.2, with a loss of one by Bankers Sun for an ability figure of :24.3. These are strong times, and we next turn to our "long shot" second choice to see what Turnbuckle shows us.

Looking first at form, Turnbuckle shows a Declining Horse pattern at first glance. But hold on, there is a gain of five in his top running line. It's a little shaky here, with the amount of the decline, but once having adopted a series of rules that are sound and hold up over the long haul, we're going to stick with them. Thus, Turnbuckle gets a Q for form. Now, to his ability times.

In his last race, there was a lead time of 25.0 with a gain of three to bring

Turnbuckle — Own.—Flying Zee Stable — **$32,500** — B. c. 4, by Best Turn—First Sitting, by Greek Song — Br.—Walden Education Fund (Ky) — Tr.—Martin Jose — **115**

	St.	1st	2nd	3rd	Amt.
1980	7	1	0	1	$12,720
1979	1	0	0	0	

25May80-	1Bel	fst	6f		:23⅕	:46	1:11	Clm 35000	4	9	87¼	87¾	77	54¾	Cordero A Jr		119	*2.50	82-16	Out There 1151¼ Ever Loyal 1171½ Home ByDawn1141½	No factor	9
16May80-	1Aqu	fst	7f		:23⅕	:46⅘	1:24	Clm 35000	6	4	43½	31½	2hd	1½	Cordero A Jr		117	*2.00	81-16	Turnbuckle117½AmericanRoyalty1177¾MasterMagicin117½	Driving	8
7May80-	5Aqu	fst	6f		:22⅖	:45	1:10⅘	3↑ Allowance	5	5	55½	44½	58	41¼	Cordero A Jr		119	11.10	88-20	Shekels and Pesos 113½ Towie 119hd War of Words 112¾	Mild bid	9
28Apr80-	2Aqu	sly	6f		:22⅖	:45⅗	1:10⅗	Clm 35000	2	7	56¼	49	47	35¾	Cordero A Jr		117	8.30	84-20	Coupon Rate 1102½ Ahoy Boy 1193¼ Turn Buckle 117½	Rallied	7
3Feb80-	6Aqu	fst	6f	⊡	:22⅖	:46⅖	1:10⅘	Allowance	4	7	78½	68½	514	618	Hernandez R		117	6.20	72-18	Judge Grey 11710HomeByDawn1172¼ByeByeBlues1171¼	No threat	8
24Jan80-	8Aqu	fst	170	⊡	:48⅕	1:13⅗	1:43⅗	Allowance	8	5	56	54	66	66	Hernandez R		117	8.60	78-21	Tread Lightly 1121¼ Lobsang II 117nk Anoint 117nk	No mishap	10
17Jan80-	7Aqu	fst	6f	⊡	:22⅗	:46⅕	1:11⅖	Allowance	5	4	34½	43½	35	57¼	Asmussen C B	b	117	*1.40	80-18	Zamboni 1123¼ Speedy Magreedy 1221¾ Lobsang II 117½	Tired	6
31Dec79-	9Aqu	fst	6f	⊡	:22⅘	:46⅗	1:11⅗	3↑ Allowance	3	5	2hd	2hd	53	66	Beitia E5	b	110	5.50	80-19	I'm It 1171¼ Speedy Magreedy 120hd Swordtail 117½	Tired	9
9Sep78-	3Med	fst	6f		:22⅖	:46⅕	1:12⅕	Allowance	5	6	69	59	56¼	56½	Vasquez J		114	1.30e	77-15	Our Romeo 115nk Super Hit 1091½ Ex Governor 1154	No rally	7
16Aug78-	8Sar	fst	6f		:22⅖	:46	1:10⅘	Sanford	2	5	58½	43½	34½	34¾	Vasquez J		115	27.70	81-16	Fuzzbuster 1153¾ Make a Mess 1151 Turn Buckle 115½	Wide turn	6

LATEST WORKOUTS May 23 Bel tr.t 3f fst :37⅗ h May 14 Bel tr.t 3f gd :36⅕ h May 5 Bel tr.t 3f fst :37 b Apr 26 Bel tr.t 4f fst :52 b

Turnbuckle's time down to :24.2. When we add one tick for energy, because of the second call time of 47 and change, we wind up with a :24.3. His previous race was even better, on 16May80. We convert the 1:24.0 time at 7f to 1:11.0 for 6f, and when we subtract :46.4 from that, we have a sparkling lead time of :24.1. There was a gain of one to reduce it even further, but the one tick added right back for energy winds up with a :24.1 ability time.

Almost even with Turnbuckle in the odds is Raise Charger, who hasn't run for a while.

His form is unknown, of course. But we still have to check his ability to see if he represents any threat to the strong favorite, Bankers Sun. He quickly shows a :24.4 in his last race off his own lead time of :24.2 plus two ticks for energy. In his previous race on 13Apr80, this strong front-runner has a :24.3 lead time with the one tick for energy for a second :24.4 rating. Here is how all of them now compare:

Odds	Horse	Ability		A Pts		F	Total
.8	Bankers Sun	:24.1	:24.3	19	17	Q	36
5.9	Turnbuckle	:24.1	:24.3	19	17	Q	36
6.0	Raise Charger	:24.4	:24.4	16	16	Q	32

Our two top choices are tied in total points, which requires us to make our investment to place only in Bankers Sun with the low odds.

The crowd was right in its strong backing of Bankers Sun, and while we bypassed our win ticket under the rules, we take our profit as it is and move on to the next race.

The fourth race is coming up, a one-mile event, where we see the first two betting choices looking like this:

4 BELMONT

START
1 MILE
BELMONT PARK
FINISH

1 MILE. (1.33⅗) CLAIMING. Purse $15,000. 3-year-olds, weights, 122 lbs. Non-winners of two races at a mile or over since May 1, allowed 3 lbs. Of such ar ace since then, 5 lbs. Claiming price $25,000 for each $2,500 to $20,000 2 lbs. (Races when entered to be claimed for $18,000 or less not considered)

Bolting Sam — B. g. 3, by Tentam—Bolt, by Tom Rolfe
$25,000 — Br.—Derry Meeting Fm—Crompton Mrs R III (Pa) — 1127
Own.—Sommer Viola — Tr.—Martin Frank

Turf Record	St.	1st	2nd	3rd		St.	1st	2nd	3rd	Amt.
	3	0	0	1	1980	11	4	2	2	$42,280
					1979	9	1	1	2	$17,575

24May80- 3Bel fst 1⅛ :46⅘ 1:12 1:52 Clm c-16000 3 5 58½ 43½ 41 13 Attanasio R7 b 110 *1.20 67-17 Bolting Sam 1103Willy'sWig1171½SourceOfPower1143 Ridden out 7
14May80- 1Aqu fst 1 :46 1:11⅕ 1:36⅘ Clm 20000 6 6 42½ 1½ 11½ 11½ Attanasio R7 b 110 *2.20 82-17 Bolting Sam 1101½ Littleness 1174¾ Chief Halftown 1193¾ Driving 7
5May80- 9Aqu fst 1 :46⅖ 1:11⅘ 1:38⅘ Clm 16000 10 7 52¾ 1½ 12½ 13¼ Attanasio R7 b 110 2.90 72-19 BoltingSm1103¼Willy'sWig119hdSourceOfPower117nk Ridden out 11
24Apr80- 4Aqu fst 6f :23 :46 1:11⅖ Clm 27500 7 7 73½ 75¾ 79 613 Vasquez J b 115 3.30 73-21 Native Root 112½ Private Eye 1171½ Trifecta 1174 Outrun 7
16Apr80- 9Aqu fst 7f :22⅘ :46 1:23⅘ Clm 25000 8 7 117¾ 86 56¼ 37 Cruguet J b 117 *2.00 75-17 Palace 117nk Freightliner 1176¾ Bolting Sam 1171¾ Very wide 11
24Mar80- 9Aqu fst 6f :22⅗ :46⅕ 1:11⅗ Clm 35000 10 9 63 51¼ 31½ 41¼ Fell J b 117 *2.00 84-24 Eastern Town 1171¼ Kay Kay'sKnight115noKing'sWish117no Wide 10
9Mar80- 6Aqu fst 170 ⊡:47⅘ 1:12⅘ 1:42⅗ Allowance 3 5 42 67½ 511 59¼ Beitia E5 b 112 8.60 80-22 Col. Frankincense 1175¼ Santo's Joe 1171¼ Sir Kay 117hd No rally 9
2Mar80- 3Aqu fst 6f ⊡:23⅖ :47⅕ 1:11⅘ Allowance 7 6 67 79¾ 68 37½ Beitia E5 b 112b 2.80 77-19 Dunham's Gift 1226¾ Alla Breva 117¾ DHWhat A Cut 122 Mild bid 7
2Mar80-Dead heat
17Feb80- 4Aqu gd 6f ⊡:22⅗ :46⅘ 1:12⅘ Clm 50000 4 8 85½ 54¼ 52 23 Fell J b 117 3.80 77-26 OccasionallyMonday1123BoltingSam117¾RegalRoy114¾ Went well 8
8Feb80- 7Aqu fst 6f ⊡:22⅗ :46⅘ 1:12⅘ Clm c-40000 4 7 74½ 53 52 11½ Asmussen C B 117 5.50 80-25 Bolting Sam 1171½ Budas Time 1121½ Private Eye 115hd Driving 7
LATEST WORKOUTS Apr 11 Bel 3f fst :38 b

Freightliner — Dk. b. or br. c. 3, by Cloudy Dawn—Swinging Sara, by Neartic
$25,000 — Br.—Jonabell Farm (Ky) — 117
Own.—Kimmel C P — Tr.—Toner James J

Turf Record	St.	1st	2nd	3rd		St.	1st	2nd	3rd	Amt.
	1	0	0	0	1980	9	0	2	1	$7,271
					1979	8	1	0	1	$4,405

21May80- 9Bel sly 6f :22⅗ :46 1:11⅖ Clm 30000 9 7 31½ 21½ 31½ 43¾ Fell J b 117 6.70 81-22 Dover Prince 1122¼ CoqAuVin119hdFinalAccount1171½ Weakened 9
16Apr80- 9Aqu fst 7f :22⅘ :46 1:23⅘ Clm 25000 7 6 106¾ 54½ 2hd 2nk Fell J b 117 16.20 82-17 Palace 117nk Freightliner 1176¾ Bolting Sam 1171¾ Game try 11
31Mar80- 4Aqu sly 6f :23⅕ :46⅘ 1:11 Clm 25000 7 5 53¾ 24 27 39 Fell J b 117 8.40 79-23 Lonely Guy 1178 Little Marker 1171 Freightliner 1173¾ Tired 8
24Mar80- 9Aqu fst 6f :22⅗ :46⅕ 1:11⅗ Clm 32500 5 3 52½ 61¾ 76¼ 66¾ Beitia E5 b 110 19.20 78-24 Eastern Town1171¼KayKay'sKnight115noKing'sWish117no Outrun 10
1Mar80- 9Hia sly 6f :22⅖ :45⅘ 1:11⅘ Allowance 8 1 88¼ 77½ 54 57¼ Gonzalez M A5 b 111 33.00 77-19 Ben Fab 1161½ YakimaWampum1161¼TimelessRide1163 No threat 9
18Feb80- 5Hia fst 6f :22⅖ :45⅕ 1:10⅕ Clm c-25000 3 5 41½ 46 48½ 411 Brumfield D b 116 10.80 81-20 Brilliant Prince 1113 Sweeten 1164 Rufame 1164 Tired 11
9Feb80- 5Hia fst 6f :22⅗ :46⅖ 1:13⅗ Clm 20000 6 6 51¾ 53 24 21¼ Brumfield D b 116 41.00 74-28 Double Accord 1191¼ Freightliner 1161¼ Prince Cody 116½ Rallied 10
31Jan80- 5Hia fst 1⅛ :48 1:13⅗ 1:55⅕ Clm 20000 6 3 31½ 52½ 79½ 714 Brumfield D 116 7.80 42-27 El Puncho 112½ Statee 114½ Commanding Jay 1143 Tired 8
21Jan80- 6Hia fm *1 1/16 Ⓣ 1:42 Clm 40000 9 7 812 811 99¼ 89 Morgan M R 116 31.50 82-03 No Grey Days 116hd Sun Partner 1162 Oh Daddy 1121¾ Outrun 10
6Nov79- 6CD fst 7f :22⅘ :46 1:25⅘ Allowance 2 8 76¼ 911 77 79¼ Solomone M 115 73.80 69-20 DKing Neptune 122hd Spruce Needles1173ChipRack1172½ Outrun 9
LATEST WORKOUTS May 30 Aqu 4f fst :52 b ●May 14 Aqu 5f gd 1:01 h (d) May 9 Aqu 4f my :52 b (d) Apr 14 Aqu 4f fst :49 b

Of the two horses shown above, Bolting Sam is the favorite, who qualifies easily off his strong form of the last race after three successive victories. His last race shows an adjusted ability time of :25.0 off a :25.1 lead time with a reduction of three ticks because of the gain to :24.3, but with two added right back on for energy. His 14May80 run was better, with a :25.1 lead time, two subtracted for gain, and no energy adjustment for a :24.4.

In this one-mile event, we will use early-speed points. It takes but a glance to see that Bolting Sam does not have strong early speed, but there are six races where he was within 5 lengths of the lead at the first call, which merits him 2 early-speed points.

Freightliner, the other horse shown above, likewise easily qualifies on form. His best race was his 16Apr80 race at 7f, where we reduce the final time to the 6f equivalent of 1:11.0. The lead time now becomes :25.0, and with the gain, we subtract three ticks to :24.2. Since his lengths behind leave him just short of a :47.0, we will not add an energy penalty. His next-best run was 31Mar80, where the lead time was :24.1, but Freightliner lost 5 lengths to bring him to :25.1, and with one tick more for energy, he finishes at :25.2.

Now, to early speed. Among the ten races shown, one is a turf event, which we eliminate. You can count four races where Freightliner was within 2 lengths of the lead at the first call. In cases where we are half a number short of the needed races to make one-half of the total, we look at the last race to see if it has early speed. Since it does here, we can allow Freightliner the full 4 points.

When we look at Golden Crest, the third choice in the wagering, we see that he cannot qualify on form off his very bad last race, where he not only showed nothing, but was declining all the way off a grass race, which we won't hold against him. We will not calculate his ability times when he does not qualify on form.

Golden Crest

Now that we have completed our work on the first three favorites, we can summarize their figures to see where we stand.

Odds	Horse	Ability		A Pts		ES	F	Total
2.3	Bolting Sam	:24.4	:25.0	16	15	2	Q	33
3.0	Golden Crest	—	—	—	—	—	NQ	NQ
3.9	Freightliner	:24.2	:25.2	18	13	4	Q	35

Factoring in of early speed makes the difference here, as Freightliner, the third choice, comes up with 2 more points than Bolting Sam, and is thus our investment for win and place. Look how it turned out (p. 141).

Hallelujah! We get our very first winner in this important week, and a very good one it is. Prices like $9.80 to win and $5.00 to place are what makes the world go round in our investment method, and with one good lick, we are ahead for the day. Freightliner, despite his slow start (in total lengths, he wasn't terribly far behind), came on strong, while Bolting Sam was nowhere.

140 INVESTING AT THE RACETRACK

FOURTH RACE
Belmont
JUNE 1, 1980

1 MILE. (1.33⅘) CLAIMING. Purse $15,000. 3–year–olds, weights, 122 lbs. Non–winners of two races at a mile or over since May 1, allowed 3 lbs. Of such ar ace since then, 5 lbs. Claiming price $25,000 for each $2,500 to $20,000 2 lbs. (Races when entered to be claimed for $18,000 or less not considered)

Value of race $15,000, value to winner $9,000, second $3,300, third $1,800, fourth $900. Mutuel pool $245,079, OTB pool $94,409. Quinella Pool $253,590. OTB Quinella Pool 126,890.

Last Raced	Horse	Eqt.A.Wt	PP	St	¼	½	¾	Str	Fin	Jockey	Cl'g Pr	Odds $1
21May80 9Bel⁴	Freightliner	b 3 117	9	10	10¹½	7¹½	5¹½	2³	1¹	Fell J	25000	3.90
28May80 1Bel⁷	Golden Crest	3 114	6	6	4¹½	5¹½	3½	1²	2⁴	Beitia E⁵	25000	3.00
23May80 2Bel⁵	Philanthropic	b 3 115	4	2	6¹½	6¹½	6²	4½	3⁶	Hernandez R	22500	27.20
7May80 1Aqu¹	Medford	3 119	7	8	11	11	7¹	6½	4¹½	Velasquez J	25000	35.60
18May80 4Aqu⁷	Alshain	b 3 119	3	11	7²	4¹	2¹	3ʰᵈ	5ⁿᵏ	Cordero A Jr	25000	5.20
24May80 3Bel¹	Bolting Sam	b 3 112	8	7	9½	8³	8¼	7⁵	6¾	Attanasio R⁷	25000	2.30
14May80 1Aqu²	Littleness	b 3 117	5	5	1ʰᵈ	2ʰᵈ	1ʰᵈ	5²	7¹½	Asmussen C B	25000	9.00
23May80 9Bel⁶	Star Encounter	b 3 113	2	9	8¹	10²	10⁶	9²	8²½	Martens G	20000	40.50
8May80 1Aqu¹	Needabuc	b 3 117	11	1	2ʰᵈ	1ʰᵈ	4¹	8²	9¹½	Samyn J L	25000	44.30
21May80 9Bel⁸	Page Six	b 3 117	10	3	5½	9½	11	11	10ⁿᵏ	Skinner K	25000	36.60
23May80 9Bel³	Napoleon Hill	b 3 117	1	4	3¹	3½	9²	10³	11	Rujano M	25000	14.00

OFF AT 2:57 EDT. Start good, Won driving. Time, :23⅗, :48, 1:14, 1:39⅗ Track fast.

$2 Mutuel Prices:

9–(K)–FREIGHTLINER	9.80	5.00	4.00
6–(G)–GOLDEN CREST		4.80	3.80
4–(E)–PHILANTHROPIC			7.40

$2 QUINELLA 6–9 PAID $24.60.

Golden Crest, eliminated on form, ran far better than we expected, to finish second. These NQ horses will occasionally come in second, but will not win too often.

With this pickup in our wallet and especially in our morale, we turn to the fifth race to see what beckons. The favorite is Rokeby Rose, who has but two races, making her a Lightly Raced Horse.

BELMONT

7 FURLONGS. (1.20⅖) ALLOWANCE. Purse $19,000. Fillies ane Mares, 3–year–old and upward which have never won a race other than maiden, claiming or starter weights, 3–year–olds, 114 lbs. Older, 122 lbs. Non–winners of a race other than claiming since May 1, allowed 3 lbs. Of such a race since April 15, 5 lbs.

Rokeby Rose
Own.—Rokeby Stable

B. f. 3, by Tom Rolfe—Rokeby Venus, by Quadrangle
Br.—Mellon P (Va)
Tr.—Miller Mack

114

	St	1st	2nd	3rd	Amt.
1980	2	1	0	1	$12,120
1979	0	M	0	0	

17May80– 6 Aqu fst 6f	:22⅘	:46⅖ 1:11⅛	ⒻMd Sp Wt	9 5 5² 3¹½ 1² 15¹½ Fell J	121	*1.00	84–16 Rokeby Rose 121⁵½ Hemlock 121ⁿᵏ SpeakUpNow121ʰᵈ	Ridden out 13
5May80– 4 Aqu fst 6f	:22⅗	:45⅘ 1:11⅛	ⒻMd Sp Wt	2 8 54¾ 68¼ 49½ 36¼ Fell J	121	2.30	81–19 TenCntsAKiss121⁶½ StptoThKingdom121ʰᵈ RokbyRos121ⁿᵏ	Rallied 10

LATEST WORKOUTS   May 28 Bel   5f fst 1:01 b   May 23 Bel   4f fst :50 b   May 15 Bel   3f fst :35⅘ h   May 11 Bel   4f fst :53⅗ b

Look at that Big Win off that last race! Under our rules of play, if a Lightly Raced Horse is the favorite and is coming off a Big Win, we invest to win and place, no matter what the point ratings show and no matter what speed factors may be present in the contenders. About the only kind of discomfort we could find with this rule is if another horse rated as a Double Advantage competitor, but this doesn't happen often enough to detract from the rule.

So, we'd better check ability times at least. Rokeby Rose's last good race showed a :25.2 lead time, reduced by one for gain to :25.1. Her previous effort, on 5May80, revealed a :25.2 lead time, with a gain of one counteracted by an addition of one tick for energy. We can also award 4 points for early speed off the last race.

We are now ready to look at the second choice, Utmost Celerity.

She, too, qualifies easily. In her 1May80 effort, the lead time was a sparkling

Big Week at Belmont: First Day, Sunday, June 1, 1980   141

Utmost Celerity — Ch. f. 3, by Timeless Moment—My Niche, by Fiddle Isle — Br.—Joselson S I (Ky) — Tr.—Johnson Philip G — 109
Own.—Joselson S I

	St.	1st	2nd	3rd	Amt.
1980	2	0	2	0	$9,240
1979	9	1	0	0	$7,080

15May80- 5Aqu fst 1 :47⅗ 1:12⅘ 1:38 ⒻClm 60000 2 3 41½ 3½ 2½ 2nk Castaneda M 116 *1.20 76–19 Hether'sTurn114nkUtmostCelrity1164¾DOjvn114no Wide, bumped 6
1May80- 6Aqu fst 6f :23⅕ :46⅗ 1:10⅖ ⒻClm 60000 2 7 72¾ 73¼ 32½ 2½ Castaneda M 116 74.40 90–13 Sami Sutton 111½ Utmost Celerity 1162½SarahBrown1121½ Rallied 8
8Dec79- 8Key fst 170 :48 1:13⅖ 1:44⅕ ⒻVillager 9 6 42½ 54 79 69¾ Wilson R 114 45.80 69–31 Dancing Blade 1184½ Triple A. 112no Swirlaway 1182¼ Tired 11
30Nov79- 7Med fst 170 :47⅕ 1:14 1:46⅗ ⒻAllowance 4 5 55 44 59½ 47½ Castaneda M 115 6.40 60–26 Omaha Jane 1203 HeraldPrincess1204PeaceHolder117½ No factor 7
13Nov79- 8Med sly 170 :47⅕ 1:13⅗ 1:46⅕ ⒻAllowance 8 9 611 67½ 54½ 66 Castaneda M 114 11.50 64–26 Boudicca 1142½ TwoOnOne114¾HeraldPrincess1201 Sluggish early 9
1Nov79- 2Aqu fst 6f :23⅕ :47 1:12⅗ ⒻClm 35000 7 8 85¾ 77¾ 75¾ 43½ Castaneda M 116 19.90 76–22 PttyPumpkin116hdChicgoDncer1181¼FmousTrick1162¼ No mishap 8
8Oct79- 3Bel fst 6f :23⅖ :47⅖ 1:12⅘ ⒻClm 40000 5 6 43 55 57½ 55½ Castaneda M 113 15.90 72–22 Plum's Sister 1172½ Silver Ray 117¾ Social Hill 119½ No factor 6
9Sep79- 4Bel fst 7f :23⅕ :47⅘ 1:26 ⒻMd 18000 8 9 65 44½ 11½ 18 Castaneda M 113 13.80 72–17 Utmost Celerity 1138 RiverGal1125DareToBeCaptain1172½ Driving 12
29Aug79- 4Bel sly 7f :22⅘ :46⅖ 1:26 ⒻMd 20000 8 7 47 37½ 618 618 Samyn J L 117 16.90 54–15 Ojavan 11010 Miss Prodigy 1061¼ Learning The Way 1173¾ Tired 10
2Aug79- 3Sar fst 6f :22⅗ :46⅕ 1:12 ⒻMd 35000 7 9 74½ 88 610 611 Samyn J L 117 36.10 69–16 Popachee 1172½ Sarah Brown 1151 Pretty Driver 1171½ Outrun 12
LATEST WORKOUTS May 29 Bel tr.t 4f fst :49⅕ h May 24 Bel tr.t 4f fst :51⅘ b May 11 Bel tr.t 4f fst :50⅗ b Apr 26 Bel tr.t 4f fst :51⅕ b

:23.4 and her gain allows us to subtract two ticks to a powerful :23.2, although we go back up by one to :23.3 for energy adjustment. In the last race, the lead time was :25.1, with one off for gain equaled by one up for energy. You will also note that her three successive lengths closer to the leader by more than 1 length in her last race entitles her to a bonus for improvement. There are 2 early-speed points.

The third choice, What A Year, also looks promising.

What A Year — Dk. b. or br. f. 3, by What Luck—Lyvette, by To Market — Br.—Lockridge & Sears (Ky) — Tr.—Jolley Leroy — 109[5]
Own.—Kentucky Blue Stable

	St.	1st	2nd	3rd	Amt.
1980	2	1	0	0	$10,560
1979	1	M	0	0	

11May80- 4Aqu fst 6f :22⅖ :45⅘ 1:11⅕ 3↑ⒻMd Sp Wt 4 7 43 21 1hd 11 Cordero A Jr b 114 5.70 87–14 What A Year 1141 Apple Betty 113¾ Oh Dora 1133¾ Driving 10
27Apr80- 6Aqu fst 6f :22⅕ :46 1:12 ⒻMd Sp Wt 6 1 31½ 43 42½ 41 Cordero A Jr b 121 13.50 82–21 Whenyou'resmiling 121¾ Apple Betty 121nk Moth 121no Evenly 8
1Dec79- 4Aqu fst 6f :22⅘ :46⅘ 1:13 ⒻMd Sp Wt 6 4 74¾ 89¼ 612 711 Pincay L Jr b 117 7.50 67–23 Passerine 1171¾ Kelley's Day 1172 I'm Swinging 1171¾ Outrun 11
LATEST WORKOUTS May 25 Bel 6f fst 1:17 b May 7 Bel 5f fst 1:03⅘ b ●Apr 24 Bel 5f fst 1:00⅗ hg Apr 17 Bel 5f fst 1:02 hg

Another improving youngster in the form department shows a :25.1 off the last race (lead time, :25.2, reduced by one off the gain). The 27Apr80 effort has a :26.0 lead time, a gain of two, no addition for energy, and a final :25.3 ability time. We would award 2 early-speed points here for races within 5 lengths of the lead at the first call.

We are now ready for our final evaluation, taking into account that we have a Lightly Raced Favorite.

Odds	Horse	Ability		A Pts		ES	F	Total
.9	Rokeby Rose	:25.1	:25.2	14	13	4	Q4	35
2.6	Utmost Celerity	:23.3	:25.1	22	14	2	Q2	40
3.0	What A Year	:25.1	:25.3	14	12	2	Q2	30

While Rokeby Rose does not have the highest points, if she is Lightly Raced and off a Big Win, this is not necessary. Her ability times actually compare rather well, except for the one outstanding race by Utmost Celerity. But off our rule of play, we have no hesitation in backing this young Rokeby Stable filly to win and place. And the outcome justified it fully.

FIFTH RACE
Belmont
JUNE 1, 1980

7 FURLONGS. (1.20⅖) ALLOWANCE. Purse $19,000. Fillies ane Mares, 3-year-old and upward which have never won a race other than maiden, claiming or starter weights, 3-year-olds, 114 lbs. Older, 122 lbs. Non-winners of a race other than claiming since May 1, allowed 3 lbs. Of such a race since April 15, 5 lbs.

Value of race $19,000, value to winner $11,400, second $4,180, third $2,280, fourth $1,140. Mutuel pool $233,748, OTB pool $80,797. Exacta Pool $309,736. OTB Exacta Pool $145,316.

Last Raced	Horse	Eqt.	A.Wt	PP	St	¼	½	Str	Fin	Jockey	Odds $1
17May80 6Aqu1	Rokeby Rose		3 114	1	4	2hd	31½	11½	12½	Fell J	.90
11May80 4Aqu1	What A Year	b	3 109	4	7	31	21	22	2hd	Beitia E5	3.00
15May80 5Aqu2	Utmost Celerity		3 113	3	5	6½	5hd	3½	32½	Castaneda M	2.60
5May80 2Aqu6	Social Hill		3 110	5	8	8	8	53	46	Martens G	31.90
21May80 4Bel8	Pandian	b	3 110	8	1	51	41	61	5nk	Miranda J†	73.90
5May80 2Aqu4	Astrid's Pride	b	3 111	2	6	41	72	8	63¾	Mora G	28.60
15May80 3Aqu5	Pretty Melissa		3 106	7	3	11½	1½	41	7no	Lovato F Jr5	23.40
2May80 5CD3	Dunloe Lady		3 104	6	2	76	6½	7½	8	Gonzalez M A5	15.90

OFF AT 3:30 EDT. Start good, Won ridden out. Time, :23, :46, 1:12⅘, 1:25⅘ Track fast.

$2 Mutuel Prices:				
	1-(A)-ROKEBY ROSE	3.80	2.60	2.20
	4-(D)-WHAT A YEAR		3.20	2.60
	3-(C)-UTMOST CELERITY			2.60

$2 EXACTA 1-4 PAID $11.40.

Rokeby Rose won handily. What A Year nipped Utmost Celerity by a head for second money. The heavy play on Rokeby Rose shows what was expected of her. Thus, we have another winner, still in the low-priced heavy-favorite neighborhood.

As we reach the sixth race, a run on the turf again, we blink at the board. Another very short-priced favorite is getting the heavy play from competing players. Such very low odds on winning favorites is a hard way to make money, but we must look closely to see what this race offers. Is Beech Grove, the even-money favorite, this strong a play?

The last race qualifies easily on form, as we see another improving horse. In the last race, the :24.3 lead time is reduced by three for gain and increased to :24.1 off the energy adjustment. But look what he did last August at Saratoga in his 9Aug79 performance. There was an incredible :23.2 lead time, with Beech Grove gaining 3½ lengths off that. He gets penalized two ticks for energy, but still winds up with a :23.1 ability time. You now begin to see why he is an even-money favorite.

6 **BELMONT**

WIDENER TURF COURSE
1 1-16 MILES
BELMONT PARK
START
FINISH

1 1/16 MILES. (TURF). (1.39⅕) CLAIMING. Purse $22,000. 4-year-olds and upward. Weight, 122 lbs. Non-winners of two races at a mile or over since April 15, allowed 3 lbs. Of such a race since then, 5 lbs. Claiming price $60,000; for each $5,000 to $50,000, allowed 2 lbs. (Races when entered to be claimed for $45,000 or less not considered.)

Beech Grove
Own.—Loblolly Stable

$60,000

Ch. c. 4, by Tom Tulle—Turkish Belle, by My Babu
Br.—Greathouse J W Jr & J W Sr (Ky)
Tr.—Cantey Joseph B

117

Turf Record St.	1st	2nd	3rd
7	3	1	0

	St.	1st	2nd	3rd	Amt.
1980	4	0	1	0	$4,840
1979	7	3	0	0	$31,320

24May80- 6Bel	gd	1 1/16	Ⓣ:46	1:10⅗	1:43⅕	Clm 60000	4	7	77½	53	22	2nk	Maple E	117	9.10	80-20 Gemmate 117nk Beech Grove 1173AmericanRoyalty1131¼	Bumped	11
16May80- 7Aqu	gd	1 1/16	Ⓣ:49⅘	1:13⅗	1:44⅘	3↑Allowance	8	5	32	44¼	45½	66	Maple E	119	23.00	75-15 No Neck 1191¾ El Kel 1192 Crown Thy Good 119hd	Tired	8
12Apr80- 8OP	fst	1 70	:45⅘	1:11⅗	1:42	3↑Allowance	4	10	913	109¾	913	811	Maple S	114	4.40	75-21 DringDmscus1132½HumbleHowrd1111½DyTimTudor1192	No threat	12
2Apr80- 9OP	fst	6f	:22⅖	:46⅕	1:11⅘	3↑Allowance	10	11	99½	1113	1013	99½	Maple S	114	16.40	76-19 Jackie Fires 1072½ Third And Lex 123½ Razorback 1091	No threat	11
28Sep79- 7Bel	fst	1⅛	:45⅘	1:10	1:48⅖	3↑Allowance	7	6	715	722	734	741	Velez R I	113	31.10	44-19 Causerie 1161¼ Ethnarch 1192 Pianist 114¾	Outrun	7
5Sep79- 8Bel	fm	1¼	Ⓣ:48⅕	1:36⅘	2:02	3↑Allowance	4	2	22½	56	811	814	Maple S	114	7.10	70-16 King Green 115hd Great Neck 113½ Daranstone 1173	Tired	9
9Aug79- 8Sar	fm	1 1/16	Ⓣ:47⅗	1:11	1:54⅖	3↑Allowance	8	4	46	32½	32½	52½	Maple E	117	*1.70	91-17 Sandro Tasca 114hd Rectus 114½ Burn 117½	Tired	9
29Jly79- 6Bel	fm	1⅜	Ⓣ:49⅖	1:38⅖	2:15⅖	3↑Allowance	1	1	1½	1½	14	14¾	Maple E	116	5.30	92-16 BeechGrove1164¾BrilliantProtege1174¼PetMoss1101¾	Ridden out	7
13Jly79- 3Bel	fm	1¼	Ⓣ:49	1:37⅘	2:03	3↑Allowance	5	3	31	2hd	2hd	1½	Maple E	116	*2.30	79-14 Beech Grove 116½ Audacious Fool113hdEverybodyUp1124	Driving	7
1Jly79- 4Bel	fm	1⅜	Ⓣ:48⅗	1:39⅕	2:16	3↑Md Sp Wt	2	3	35	32	21	11¼	Maple E	116	2.60	82-11 Beech Grove 1161¼ Nitroglycerin 11616 First OnLine115nk	Driving	6

LATEST WORKOUTS May 11 Bel 1 fst 1:43⅕ h May 7 Bel 6f fst 1:14⅘ h Apr 24 Bel tr.t 6f fst 1:17⅖ b

American Royalty — Dk. b. or br. g. 6, by Native Royalty—Gusellie, by One-Eyed King — $50,000 — Br.—Harbor View Farm (Fla) — Tr.—Nieminski Richard — 113
Own.—Kono Stables

	Turf Record					St.	1st	2nd	3rd	Amt.
St.	1st	2nd	3rd		1980	10	0	2	2	$12,720
30	4	3	4		1979	16	1	2	2	$24,500

24May80- 6Bel	gd	1 1/16	Ⓣ:46	1:10⅗	1:43⅕	Clm 50000	5	9	8¹²	8⁶	5⁴½	3³¼	Saumell L	113	9.00	77-20 Gemmate 117ⁿᵏ Beech Grove 117³ American Royalty113¹¼	Rallied 11
16May80- 1Aqu	fst	7f	:23⅕	:46⅘	1:24	Clm 35000	7	1	3³½	5²¼	1ʰᵈ	2½	Adams L	117	5.40	80-16 Turnbuckle117½AmericanRoyalty117⁷¾MasterMagicin117½	Gamely 8
27Apr80- 7Aqu	fst	6f	:23⅕	:46⅗	1:10⅖ 3↑	Allowance	3	2	6²½	6⁴¾	6³¼	5⁵	Saumell L	121	20.80	86-21 Reef Searcher 111¹¾ Petite Roche 114¹¾ Doney 116¹	No factor 6
17Apr80- 7Aqu	fst	6f	:22⅘	:45⅗	1:11 3↑	Allowance	5	1	5⁶½	5¹⁰	5⁹	5³½	Saumell L	121	20.70	84-23 GoldenReality118¾BrightAndBrave121¹¾DynamiteCap123¾	Outrun 6
31Mar80- 8Aqu	sly	6f	:22⅘	:46⅖	1:11⅕	Allowance	3	5	8⁸	8¹¹	8⁹	7⁸	Saumell L	117	11.20	79-23 Emperor's Key112¹¼BrightAndBrave117ⁿᵏEphphatha119²½	Outrun 8
14Mar80- 2Aqu	sly	6f	⊡:22⅘	:46	1:11	Clm 60000	1	3	4⁵	4⁶	4⁷	3⁴¾	Saumell L	117	15.10	84-25 Bold Bishop 113² Subordinate117²¾AmericanRoyalty117²¼	Evenly 7
24Feb80- 2Aqu	gd	6f	⊡:22⅗	:46	1:11⅕	Allowance	2	7	7¹¹	6¹⁰	6¹¹	6⁸¾	Saumell L	117	11.50	79-17 Judge Grey 122ⁿᵏ Emperor's Key 114ⁿᵏ Ardaluan 117½	No threat 8
20Feb80- 8Aqu	fst	6f	⊡:22⅘	:46⅕	1:11⅕	Allowance	4	1	7⁵¾	8⁷½	6⁴	6²¾	Hernandez R	115	15.00	85-19 Jim Balthrop 119¾KingBoldReality115½MasterA.J.115ⁿᵏ	No threat 9
26Jan80- 6Aqu	fst	6f	⊡:22⅘	:46⅗	1:11⅕	Allowance	10	1	10⁹¾	10⁷¼	10¹¹	7¹⁰	Saumell L	117	6.90	78-17 Contare 117³¼ Subordinate 119⁴ Carelko 117¹¼	Bore out 10
6Jan80- 7Aqu	fst	6f	⊡:23	:46⅗	1:11⅖	Allowance	3	4	6⁵½	5³	3²	2¾	Saumell L	117	6.90	86-17 Royal Reasoning 114¾AmericanRoyalty117ⁿᵒContare116ⁿᵏ	Gamely 6

LATEST WORKOUTS May 7 Bel tr.t 4f fst :51⅘ b   Apr 12 Bel 4f fst :47⅕ h

American Royalty, the second choice, has but one grass race showing on which to rate him, despite having run on the turf some thirty times.

On 24May80, the race that was won by Gemmate in our example in the last chapter, American Royalty finished behind Beech Grove. This makes Beech Grove all the more impressive, for we know what Gemmate did and what his ability times were. American Royalty faces the same :24.3 lead time that Beech Grove had, but can be credited with only 2 lengths for gain from the maximum of 8 behind, which reduces the preliminary ability time to :24.1. Two ticks must be added for energy, giving American Royalty a :24.3 ability rating.

Ring of Truth — B. g. 5, by Arts And Letters—Love Of Learning, by Hail To Reason — $60,000 — Br.—Mellon P (Va) — Tr.—Martin Frank — 117
Own.—Sommer Viola

	Turf Record					St.	1st	2nd	3rd	Amt.
St.	1st	2nd	3rd		1980	9	3	1	1	$69,406
2	0	0	0		1979	15	4	2	1	$54,520

26May80- 8Bel	fst	1	:45⅘	1:10⅖	1:35⅘ 3↑	Metropol'n H	5	1	1ʰᵈ	6³½	7¹⁰	7¹⁶	Fell J	114	10.90e	73-20 Czaravich 126ⁿᵒ State Dinner 117¹ Silent Cal 120⁴¾	Tired 8
11May80- 2Aqu	fst	1⅛	:47⅖	1:11⅖	1:49⅘	Clm 75000	1	1	1¹½	1¹	3⁶½	3¹¹	Cordero A Jr	116	*.60e	75-14 Causerie 118⁷¾ Lean Lad 118³ Ring of Truth 116¹¼	Tired 8
12Apr80- 8Aqu	fst	1¼	:48⅕	1:35⅗	2:01⅖ 3↑	Excelsior H	2	4	3²	4⁴½	7⁹¼	7¹¹	Castaneda M	b 114	10.00e	78-19 Ring of Light 114¹¼ Silent Cal 122²¼ Rivalero 118ⁿᵏ	Checked 10
29Mar80- 8Aqu	sly	1	:45⅕	1:09⅘	1:36⅘ 3↑	Westchster H	3	3	3²½	4³½	4³½	4³½	Beitia E	b 119	5.70e	78-27 Nice Catch 120ʰᵈ Ardaluan 119ⁿᵒ LarkOscillation115³½	Weakened 8
23Feb80- 8Aqu	gd	1⅛	⊡:47⅖	1:12⅕	1:50⅕ 3↑	Grey Lag H	2	7	6⁴½	6⁵	7⁷¾	10¹²	Beitia E	b 115	*.40e	83-17 I'm It 113¹¼ Causerie 113¹¾ Charlie Coast 115⁴	Stopped 10
3Feb80- 8Aqu	fst	1⅛	⊡:47⅗	1:12⅖	1:52⅕ 3↑	Stymie H	5	4	3¹½	1ʰᵈ	1²	2ʰᵈ	Beitia E	b 115	*.40e	85-18 Identical 116ʰᵈ Ring of Truth 115²¾ Charlie Coast 117³	Missed 9
25Jan80- 7Aqu	fst	1⅛	⊡:47	1:12⅘	1:49⅖	Allowance	5	2	2³	1¹½	1⁸	1⁹	Beitia E⁵	b 114	*.90	99-18 Ring of Truth 114⁹ HugableTom117¹¹YouGoFirst110⁴	Ridden out 5
12Jan80- 9Aqu	gd	170	⊡:48⅗	1:13⅕	1:42⅕	Allowance	5	1	1½	1²	1³	1³	Beitia E⁵	b 114	*2.00	91-21 Ring of Truth 114³ Salduci 108³ Lean Lad 115¹½	Ridden out 9
6Jan80- 6Aqu	fst	6f	⊡:22⅗	:46	1:10⅖	Allowance	8	6	4²½	2ʰᵈ	1¹½	1²¼	Beitia E⁵	b 112	5.20	92-17 RingofTruth112²¼KngBoldRlty115³BoldndStormy115½	Ridden out 9
28Dec79- 8Aqu	fst	6f	⊡:22⅗	:46	1:12⅕ 3↑	Allowance	1	2	1ʰᵈ	1ʰᵈ	2ʰᵈ	5¹¼	Maple E	b 119	3.80	82-26 Homeways 113¹ Hasty Tam 110ʰᵈ Hey Hey J. P. 115ⁿᵒ	Tired 8

LATEST WORKOUTS ●May 24 Bel tr.t 4f fst :46⅘ h   ●May 18 Bel tr.t 4f fst :47 h   May 7 Bel tr.t 5f fst 1:00⅘ b   May 1 Bel tr.t 4f my :48⅕ h

The third choice in the race, Ring of Truth, has run in some most impressive stakes races, but shows not a single grass race among those showing.

Ring of Truth gets an unknown for ability as we now rate the three choices.

Odds	Horse	Ability		A Pts		F	Total
1.0	Beech Grove	:23.1	:24.1	24	19	Q2	45
3.8	American Royalty	:24.3	—	17	(17)	Q	34
4.3	Ring of Truth	Unknown		—	—	U	U

Beech Grove indeed looks like an outstanding selection. He is a Double Advantage Horse as well, even giving American Royalty credit for two performances of the same caliber. Beech Grove's point total is far ahead, and we back him at the window with unhesitating confidence.

This was an easy one, but we still haven't piled up enough of a profit margin

SIXTH RACE **Belmont** JUNE 1, 1980	**1 1/16 MILES.(turf). (1.39⅘) CLAIMING. Purse $22,000. 4–year–olds and upward. Weight, 122 lbs. Non–winners of two races at a mile or over since April 15, allowed 3 lbs. Of such a race since then, 5 lbs. Claiming price $60,000; for each $5,000 to $50,000, allowed 2 lbs. (Races when entered to be claimed for $45,000 or less not considered.)**

Value of race $22,000, value to winner $13,200, second $4,840, third $2,640, fourth $1,320. Mutuel pool $247,391, OTB pool $80,428. Quinella Pool $260,390. OTB Quinella Pool $115,570.

Last Raced	Horse	Eqt.	A.	Wt	PP	St	¼	½	¾	Str	Fin	Jockey	Cl'g Pr	Odds $1
24May80 ^{6}Bel^{2}	Beech Grove		4	117	4	6	8^{3}	7^{1}	5^{3}	1^{4}	$1^{2\frac{1}{2}}$	Maple E	60000	1.00
16May80 ^{7}Aqu^{7}	Fiddle Faddle		5	114	7	9	9^{hd}	9½	8^{1}	5^{4}	2½	Fell J	50000	13.90
24May80 ^{6}Bel^{3}	American Royalty		6	113	2	7	10^{6}	10^{4}	7^{1}	2½	3^{6}	Cordero A Jr	50000	3.80
25Apr80 ^{8}Kee^{2}	Prete Khale		5	117	3	10	$7^{1\frac{1}{2}}$	6^{hd}	6½	7^{2}	4^{nk}	Santiago A	60000	24.50
25May80 ^{1}Bel^{1}	Out There	b	5	113	6	5	5½	4½	4½	4½	5no	Castaneda M	50000	21.50
24May80 ^{6}Bel^{6}	Royal Flavour		5	117	9	11	11	11	9½	6^{hd}	6^{nk}	Cruguet J	60000	17.80
25May80 ^{1}Bel^{2}	Ever Loyal	b	5	115	1	3	1½	$1^{1\frac{1}{2}}$	1^{hd}	3^{hd}	7^{9}	Velasquez J	55000	18.30
24May80 ^{6}Bel^{7}	Test Pattern		4	108	5	1	2^{2}	2^{hd}	2½	8^{5}	$8^{2\frac{3}{4}}$	Lovato F Jr^{5}	50000	48.70
26May80 ^{8}Bel^{7}	Ring of Truth	b	5	117	11	4	$4^{1\frac{1}{2}}$	$3^{1\frac{1}{2}}$	$3^{1\frac{1}{2}}$	$9^{1\frac{1}{2}}$	9^{1}	Asmussen C B	60000	4.30
29May80 ^{2}Bel^{6}	Rubla Khan		5	113	10	2	3^{1}	5^{2}	10^{6}	10^{7}	10^{8}	Skinner K	50000	43.70
8May80 ^{6}Aqu^{6}	Big Greg	b	4	113	8	8	6^{2}	8^{2}	11	11	11	Adams L	50000	46.90

OFF AT 1:09 EDT. Start good, Won driving. Time, :23⅕, :47, 1:11⅕, 1:36⅗, 1:43 Course firm.

$2 Mutuel Prices:				
	5–(D)–BEECH GROVE	4.00	3.00	2.20
	7–(H)–FIDDLE FADDLE		7.60	3.40
	3–(B)–AMERICAN ROYALTY			2.80
	$2 QUINELLA 5–7 PAID $26.20.			

to rest with any degree of ease. The seventh race, an allowance contest for some very high-class horses, is our next obstacle.

Thanks to Tony, the second choice in the betting, has been away since last December. But he does have the four workouts we require, all recently spaced. And his stakes caliber is unquestionable, off some powerful performances at the Meadowlands. Since he is of stakes caliber and has the requisite four workouts, we will rate him qualified on form.

Thanks to Tony has also strong ability times. His effort on 20Dec79 at the Meadowlands shows a :23.4 lead time, a pace at which he held without adjustment. His 24Nov79 race at Aqueduct shows a :24.3 lead time with no adjustment for Thanks to Tony, which makes him a formidable contender.

Since this is a seven-furlong race, we must apply early speed. This horse shows six races out of ten where he was within 5 lengths of the lead at the first call, entitling him to 2 early-speed points.

The favorite is I Speedup, who qualifies on form because he is an up-and-down-dropper. He ran in the Withers at Aqueduct against some pretty tough

7 **BELMONT**

7 FURLONGS. (1.20⅖) ALLOWANCE. Purse $25,000. 3–year–olds and upward which have never won four races other than maiden, claiming or starter weights, 3–year–olds, 114 lbs. Older, 122 lbs. Non–winners of two races other than maiden or claiming since April 15, allowed 3 lbs. Of such a race since then, 5 lbs.

Thanks to Tony — Own.—Sui Generis Stable

Dk. b. or br. c. 3, by Naskra—Nursey, by Run for Nurse
Br.—Mosley D F (NJ)
Tr.—Nobles Reynoldo H

111

	St.	1st	2nd	3rd	Amt.
1979	11	3	3	0	$55,015

20Dec79- 6Med fst 6f	:22⅕	:44⅘	1:08⅗	Morven	4	6	4^{4}	$3^{3\frac{1}{2}}$	$2^{1\frac{1}{2}}$	$2^{3\frac{1}{4}}$	Hernandez R	b	119	6.00	99-08	Fappiano117$^{3\frac{1}{4}}$ThankstoTony119^{2}Georgendthedrgon115^{5}	2nd best	7
12Dec79- 6Med fst 6f	:21⅘	:45⅖	1:12⅕	Saddlebrook	5	8	7^{13}	$6^{7\frac{3}{4}}$	$4^{1\frac{1}{2}}$	1¾	Hernandez R	b	113	*1.40	84-22	Thanks to Tony 113¾ Mardevar 114^{4} Royal Rollick 114¾	Driving	8
24Nov79- 8Aqu fst 1	:45⅘	1:10⅖	1:36⅖	Nashua	6	5	4^{2}	5^{2}	4^{1}	2no	Thomas D B	b	114	34.60	84-18	Googolplx117^{no}ThnkstoTony114^{hd}Comptrollr114$^{2\frac{3}{4}}$	Steadied, wide	8
16Nov79- 6Med fst 170	:47⅕	1:12⅗	1:44⅕	Allowance	3	4	4^{2}	3^{2}	2^{2}	2no	Thomas D B	b	116	2.70	80-20	Surf Club 111no Thanks to Tony116$^{7\frac{1}{2}}$Dr.Richter118^{nk}	Just missed	6
3Nov79- 6Med gd 1 1/16	:45⅖	1:11⅖	1:43	Y'ng America	13	5	$4^{3\frac{1}{2}}$	$3^{1\frac{1}{2}}$	6^{14}	8^{19}	Thomas D B	b	113	18.60	77-17	Koluctoo Bay 112$^{1\frac{1}{4}}$ Gold Stage 119^{8} Joanie's Chief 122$^{2\frac{3}{4}}$	Tired	15
9Oct79- 7Med sly 6f	:22⅖	:46	1:11⅗	Allowance	1	6	6^{6}	$7^{6\frac{1}{2}}$	$7^{6\frac{3}{4}}$	$5^{5\frac{1}{2}}$	Thomas D B	b	114	6.90	81-16	My Pal Jeff 114½ Pappa Clyde 109$^{1\frac{3}{4}}$ Surf Club 109$^{1\frac{1}{2}}$	No factor	7
24Sep79- 3Med fst 6f	:22⅗	:45⅘	1:11⅖	Allowance	5	5	$7^{3\frac{1}{2}}$	5^{6}	4^{10}	5^{13}	Lopez C		117	*1.30	75-12	I. C. Diplomat 115^{2} Sports Complex 114$^{7\frac{1}{2}}$ SurfClub112$^{2\frac{1}{2}}$	No rally	7
28Aug79- 9Mth gd 6f	:22	:45⅕	1:12⅕	[S]N J Breeders	3	7	$6^{8\frac{1}{4}}$	$5^{5\frac{1}{2}}$	4^{5}	$5^{3\frac{1}{2}}$	Lopez C		119	*.60	75-19	Table Runner 114¾ Mannerless 114^{2} Bill Wheeler 113½	Blocked	9
16Jly79- 7Mth fst 5½f	:22⅗	:45⅖	1:04⅗	Allowance	6	1	$6^{4\frac{1}{4}}$	$4^{4\frac{1}{2}}$	$3^{1\frac{1}{2}}$	$1^{2\frac{3}{4}}$	Lopez C		120	8.30	94-12	Thanks to Tony 120$^{2\frac{3}{4}}$ KnightLanding117^{nk}Ustay120^{1}	Going away	8
6Jly79- 6Mth fst 5f	:22⅕	:45⅗	:57⅖	Allowance	5	7	7^{7}	7^{7}	6^{13}	5^{15}	Lopez C		120	8.10	84-17	Antique Gold 115^{10} Sir Sizzling Nehoc 120^{3} Ustay120^{nk}	Taken up	7

LATEST WORKOUTS ●May 26 Mth 7f fst 1:29 b May 20 Mth 4f fst :49 bg May 14 Mth 6f sly 1:14⅘ b May 8 Mth 5f my 1:00⅘ b

I Speedup — B. c. 3, by Drone—Personal Charm, by Rough'n Tumble
Own.—Brookfield Farms — Br.—Isaacs H Z (Ky) — Tr.—Kelly Edward I — **109**

	St.	1st	2nd	3rd	Amt.
1980	4	1	1	0	$14,600
1979	8	3	1	3	$69,825

Entered 31May80- 7 AP

10May80- 8Aqu	fst	1	:45⅘ 1:09⅕ 1:34⅖	Withers	2	5	5 3¼	7 10	6 11	5 13	Cordero A Jr	b 126	14.20	81–13 ColonelMorn126 5½TempercHill126 4¼J.P.Brothr126½	Lacked room	7
23Apr80- 7Aqu	fst	1	:46⅖ 1:11⅖ 1:37	Allowance	5	1	1 1½	1 1½	1½	2 nk	Cordero A Jr	b 117	*1.00	81–24 Samoyed 115 nk I Speedup 117 5 Son Of A Dodo 108 1¾	Just missed	6
5Apr80- 8Aqu	gd	1	:46 1:11⅕ 1:37	Gotham	11	2	2½	3 nk	3 2½	7 6	Cordero A Jr	b 123	7.60	75–20 ColonelMorn123 noDunhm'sGift114 2¾Bucksplsher115 2¾	Weakened	12
15Mar80- 3GP	fst	6f	:22⅘ :45⅘ 1:10	Allowance	1	4	2 hd	1 1½	1 2	1 3	Cordero A Jr	b 114	*.50	89–17 I Speedup 114 3 StraightStrike114 2CreametteCity117 4	Ridden out	6
25Aug79- 8Sar	fst	6½f	:22⅕ :44⅘ 1:16⅕	Hopeful	1	12	7 5¼	5 6½	6 9½	6 10	Cordero A Jr	b 122	4.20	84–12 [D]Rockhill Native 122 6½ J. P.Brother122¾GoldStage122 1¼	In close	12
25Aug79-Placed fifth through disqualification																
15Aug79- 8Sar	fst	6f	:21⅘ :44⅘ 1:10⅖	Sanford	1	6	4 1½	4 1¼	3½	1 nk	Fell J	b 122	2.30	88–15 I Speedup 122 nk Muckraker 122 2 My Pal Jeff 117 1	Driving	7
25Jly79- 8Bel	fst	6f	:22⅘ :46⅕ 1:11⅘	Tremont	1	7	1 1	3 nk	1 hd	1 2	Cordero A Jr	b 115	4.60	83–17 I Speedup 115 2 J. P. Brother 122 no Blues Alley 122½	Driving	8
5Jly79- 4Bel	fst	5½f	:22⅖ :45⅖ 1:04⅕	Md Sp Wt	5	4	1 1½	1 2	1 6	1 8	Fell J	b 118	*2.00	94–16 I Speedup 118 8 Dusham 118 4 Rectory 118 1	Ridden out	10
25Jun79- 6Bel	fst	5½f	:22⅕ :45⅕ 1:03⅗	Md Sp Wt	6	5	5 9½	5 9	4 9	3 9	Fell J	118	4.20	88–13 Danzig 118 8½ African Water 118½ I Speedup 118 1¾	Rallied	8
7Jun79- 4Bel	fst	5½f	:22⅗ :46⅗ 1:05⅘	Md Sp Wt	2	1	3 2	4¾	3 5	3 5¾	Fell J	118	*1.50	80–27 Dr. Maguire 113 5¼ T. V. Table 118½ I Speedup 118 2¾	Lacked rally	8

LATEST WORKOUTS May 29 Bel tr.t 3f fst :37⅘ b — May 25 Bel tr.t 4f fst :48⅘ h — May 17 Bel tr.t 3f fst :37⅖ b — May 6 Bel 6f fst 1:13⅘ h

competition, and today he is dropping back into an allowance race. His 23Apr80 run is his qualifying race, where he ran strongly. His best ability time was at Gulfstream on 15Mar80, where he set the lead time of :24.1, but since it was at speedy Gulfstream, we will have to add one tick to allow for the faster surface there and give I Speedup a :24.2. He gets a :25.0 in the 23Apr80 allowance race at Aqueduct.

When we look at early speed, we sense some real competition in this race. I Speedup, in seven out of his ten races, was within 2 lengths of the lead at the first call, entitling him to 4 points. This kind of speed is always dangerous.

The third choice is Degenerate Jon, whose form is atrocious.

Degenerate Jon — Gr. c. 3, by Iron Warrior—Geala, by Bupers
Own.—Schwartz B K — Br.—King J D (Ky) — Tr.—Trovato Joseph A — **109**

	St.	1st	2nd	3rd	Amt.
1980	8	2	0	1	$84,315
1979	8	2	2	0	$56,425

10May80- 8Spt	fst	1⅛	:46⅗ 1:12⅖ 1:52	Ill Derby	1	9	10 11	7 9¼	7 12	8 13	Fires E	124	2.80	73–26 Ray'sWord124 noMightyReturn114 2½StutzBlackhwk121 1¼	Sluggish	11
3May80- 8CD	fst	1¼	:48 1:37⅗ 2:02	Ky Derby	4	9	6 4	8 8½	8 12	8 12	Hernandez R	b 126	61.70	75–11 Genuine Risk 121 1 Rumbo 126 1 Jaklin Klugman 126 4	Far back	13
19Apr80- 8Aqu	fst	1⅛	:47⅖ 1:11⅗ 1:50⅘	Wood Mem'l	7	8	5 3½	4 3½	4 7	4 5¼	Hernandez R	b 126	22.60	76–17 PluggdNckl126 1½ColonlMorn126 hdGnunRsk121 3¾	Knocked abt. st.	11
5Apr80- 8Aqu	gd	1	:46 1:11⅕ 1:37	Gotham	7	6	5 3	5 3¾	5 4	4 5½	Hernandez R	b 123	7.50	75–20 ColonelMorn123 noDunhm'sGift114 2¾Bucksplsher115 2¾	Weakened	12
8Mar80- 7GG	gd	1 1/16	:46⅘ 1:11⅕ 1:44	Cal. Derby	4	8	7 6¾	7 8¾	7 11	7 14	Hernandez R	b 117	3.30	69–25 Jaklin Klugman119 hdDoonesbury117 1½Bold'NRulling112 nk	Outrun	9
9Feb80- 8Aqu	fst	1⅛	[•]:49 1:13 1:52	Lucky Draw	1	4	3 3	2 1½	1 1½	1 1¼	Hernandez R	b 123	1.30	86–19 DegenerateJon123 1¼Googolplex121 8½DonDniello117 1½	Drew clear	5
27Jan80- 7Aqu	fst	1 1/16	[•]:47 1:11⅖ 1:44	Count Fleet	1	5	5 3½	2 hd	1 hd	1½	Amy J	b 117	10.00	94–17 Degenerate Jon 117½ Colonel Moran117 4Googolplex123 nk	Driving	7
13Jan80- 7Aqu	fst	6f	[•]:22⅖ :45⅘ 1:10⅗	Rockaway	5	5	5 4	5 2¼	4 8	3 6	Hernandez R	b 117	20.00	85–17 Colonel Moran 117 2¼ Sway 117 3½ Degenerate Jon 117 nk	Mild bid	6
11Nov79- 8Aqu	my	1⅛	:48 1:12⅖ 1:50⅖	Remsen	5	3	2 1½	2 3	6 12	7 15	Fell J	b 115	12.30	68–24 Plugged Nickle 122 4¾ Googolplex 117½ Proctor 113 4¾	Gave way	8
3Nov79- 6Med	gd	1 1/16	:45⅖ 1:11⅖ 1:43	Y'ng America	2	13	10 9¼	6 3½	7 14	6 16	Fell J	b 114	5.10	80–17 Koluctoo Bay 112 1¼ Gold Stage119 8Joanie'sChief122 2½	No threat	15

LATEST WORKOUTS May 28 Aqu 4f fst :51 b — May 23 Aqu 4f fst :47⅗ h — May 1 CD 4f fst :48⅗ b — Apr 13 Aqu 5f fst 1:01⅗ h

Since he shows none of the signs of a contending horse, we rate him not qualified, and proceed to total up.

Odds	Horse	Ability		A Pts		ES	F	Total
1.2	I Speedup	:24.2	:25.0	18	15	4	Q	37
2.3	Thanks to Tony	:23.4	:24.3	21	17	2	Q	40
3.0	Degenerate Jon	—	—	—	—	—	NQ	NQ

Even with the early-speed advantage of I Speedup, Thanks to Tony has the high points, and since we qualified him on form, he is our selection. But this time, it failed to hold up, as the chart of the race reveals.

I Speedup simply ran off and hid from the rest of the field, winning in a laugher. Thanks to Tony showed his lack of early speed by hitting the first call

Belmont

7 FURLONGS. (1.20⅖) ALLOWANCE. Purse $25,000. 3-year-olds and upward which have never won four races other than maiden, claiming or starter weights. 3-year-olds, 114 lbs. Older, 122 lbs. Non-winners of two races other than maiden or claiming since April 15, allowed 3 lbs. Of such a race since then, 5 lbs.

JUNE 1, 1980

Value of race $25,000, value to winner $15,000, second $5,500, third $3,000, fourth $1,500. Mutuel pool $226,103, OTB pool $52,867. Exacta Pool $266,323. OTB Exacta Pool $83,475.

Last Raced	Horse	Eqt.A.Wt	PP	St	¼	½	Str	Fin	Jockey	Odds $1
10May80 8Aqu5	I Speedup	b 3 111	6	2	1 1	1 4	1 4	1 6½	Cordero A Jr	1.20
21May80 5Bel5	Royal Reasoning	4 112	2	5	4 1	3 2	2 2	2 5½	Lovato F Jr5	47.70
20Dec79 6Med2	Thanks to Tony	3 113	5	4	5 1	5 ½	4 1	3 hd	Hernandez R	2.30
17May80 8Aqu7	Golden Reality	5 119	1	3	2 1	2 hd	3 2	4 2½	Maple E	7.10
10May80 8Spt8	Degenerate Jon	b 3 111	3	6	6	4 2	5 3	5 nk	Velasquez J	3.00
9May80 7Aqu3	Flashy Mac	3 104	4	1	3 1	6	6	6	Rogers K L5	15.30

OFF AT 4:43 EDT. Start good, Won ridden out. Time, :23⅕, :46⅕, 1:10⅖, 1:23⅖ Track fast.

$2 Mutuel Prices:

6-(F)-I SPEEDUP	4.40	3.00	2.40
2-(B)-ROYAL REASONING		18.80	4.20
5-(E)-THANKS TO TONY			2.60

$2 EXACTA 6-2 PAID $90.20.

point running next to last. He could never make up this kind of margin against a stronger speedster like I Speedup. Our good winning streak is broken.

Now, we come to the feature race of the day, the Edgemere Handicap on the grass, where the favorite has come from the wars in Europe.

BELMONT

INNER TURF COURSE

1¼ MILES
BELMONT PARK
START ◆ ◆FINISH

1¼ MILES. (INNER-TURF). (1.58⅘) 21st Running THE EDGEMERE HANDICAP. (Grade III). $100,000 Added. 3-year-olds and upward. By subscription of $200 each, which should accompany the nomination; $800 to pass the entry box; with $100,000 added. The added money and all fees to be divided 60% to the winner, 22% to second, 12% to third and 6% to fourth. Weights Tuesday, May 27. Starters to be named at the closing time of entries. Trophies will be presented to the winning owner, trainer and jockey and mementos to the grooms of the first four finishers. The New York Racing Association reserves the right to transfer this race to the main course. Closed with 32 nominations.

*Lyphard's Wish

Own.—Wildenstein D

B. c. 4, by Lyphard—Sally's Wish, by Sensitivo
Br.—Comte Yann de Lesguern (Fra)
Tr.—Penna Angel

122

Turf Record					St.	1st	2nd	3rd	Amt.
St. 1st 2nd 3rd				1979	8	2	2	1	$117,319
13	5	2	3	1978	5	3	0	2	$35,546

20Oct79 ◆2Newmarket(Eng) fm 1¼	2:03⅘ Ⓣ Champion Stakes(Gr.1)	4² Mercer J	122	6.50	— NorthrnBby122½ TwnAndCntry129nk HlKnght122nk	Well up, led 14
30Sep79 ◆4Longchamp(Fra) fm*1	1:38⅗ Ⓣ Prix du Moulin(Gr.1)	2½ Mercer J	123	5.25	— Irish River 123½ Lyphard's Wish 123⁴ Boitron 1231½	Well up, led 8
21Aug79 ◆3York(Eng) gd 1⅜	2:13⅖ Ⓣ Benson&HedgesGoldCup(Gr.1)	34¾ Mercer J	122	10.00	— Troy 122¾ Crimson Beau 132⁴ Lyphard Wish 122³	Well up, led 14
19Jun79 ◆2Ascot(Eng) gd 1½	2:06⅘ Ⓣ Prince of Wales StakesGr2	2¹ Mercer J	116	*2.25	— CrmsnB127¹ LyphrdsWsh116⁵ TwnndCntry127²½ Well up thruout 7
6Jun79 ◆3Epsom(Eng) gd 1½	2:36⅘ Ⓣ Derby Stakes(Gr.1)	5¹³ Mercer J	126	11.00	— Troy 126⁷ Dickens Hill 126³ Northen Baby 126¾	Led 10f 22
16May79 ◆3York(Eng) gd 1⅜	2:10½ Ⓣ Mecca Dante Stakes(Gr.3)	1¹½ Mercer J	126	3.30	— Lyphard's Wish 126¹½ Hardgreen126² LakeCity126nk	Led thruout 14
5May79 ◆3Newmarket(Eng) gd 1	1:43⅘ Ⓣ 2,000Guineas(Gr 1)	5⁷ StMartin Y	126	6.50	— Tap On Wood 126¼ Kris 126no Young Generation 126⁴	Evenly 20
17Apr79 ◆4Newmarket(Eng) gd 1	1:41⅗ Ⓣ Craven Stakes(Gr.3)	12¼ Mercer J	119	5.50	— Lyphards Wish 119²½ Tromos 126⁴ Warmington 119	Led thruout 5

LATEST WORKOUTS May 27 Bel Ⓣ 6f fm 1:14½ b   May 21 Bel 1 sly 1:39 h   May 15 Bel 5f fst :59 h   May 8 Bel 5f sly 1:04⅘ b

But Lyphard's Wish rates as a total unknown, both in ability and form. Because results from British and French races show no internal times, there is no way to compute any ability ratings, even if the tracks there were comparable, which they are not. This horse must be passed, therefore, as we turn to the second choice in the wagering.

Here is a very impressive animal. Nine times out on the turf, with seven victories and one third-place finish, with only one bad race in the lot. He came from England in the spring to run in some quality races at Pimlico. His last race was quite potent. Since we can evaluate ability time off the last two furlongs in a mile-and-a-half race, we can compute a :24.3 off Marquee Universal's lead time. This is outstanding time for the last portion of such a long race. Then, in the 19Apr80 debut at Pimlico on the grass, there is a :25.0 lead time,

Big Week at Belmont: First Day, Sunday, June 1, 1980 147

```
*Marquee Universal      Ch. c. 4, by Home Guard—Papillio, by Pampered King            Turf Record       St. 1st 2nd 3rd      Amt.
                             Br.—Ballyprior Stud (Ire)                        121   St. 1st 2nd 3rd   1980  3   2   1   0   $102,315
 Own.—Freed G                Tr.—Bullock Alec J                                      9   7   0   1    1979  6   4   0   1    $33,274
10May80- 9Pim gd 1½ (T):49⅕ 2:05 2:29⅗ 3↑Dixie H        12 1 1^2 1^1 1^3 1^4¼ Pilar H   118  2.80  89-11 MrqueeUniversl118^4¼TheVryOn113^1MtchThHtch115^no Ridden out 14
26Apr80- 9Pim sly 1 1/16 :47 1:12 1:45⅗ 3↑Riggs H        5 1 1^hd 3^2 4^2 2^2½ Pilar H  118  3.20  74-23 MtchThHtch112^2½MrqUnvrsl118^2½MornngFrlc119^1½ Steadied turn 8
19Apr80- 8Pim fm 1 1/16 (T):47⅗ 1:12⅗ 1:44⅕ Allowance     7 4 4^5 3½ 1^1½ 1^3½ Pilar H   112 *1.70  90-14 Marquee Universal 112^3½ No No Jim 114½ Advan 119^1½ Handily 8
 3Aug79♦3Goodwood(Eng) gd 1¼ 2:13⅕ (T) Extel Hcp                        9 Cauthen S    135  6.50  — — [D]Red Rufus 117¾ Lindoro 126¾ Tolstoy 113^1½ Well up,led,tired 9
21Jly79♦3Ripon(Eng) fm 1¼ 2:06 (T) Ripon Bell Ringer Hcp            1^1½ Johnson E    119  3.50  — — MrqueeUniversl119^1½ TesoroMio124½ SmokeyBr105^2 Led thruout 6
19May79♦3Thirsk(Eng) gd 1 1:42⅘ (T) Thirsk Hunt Cup Hcp              1½ Bleasdale J   124 *1.00  — — Marquee Universal 124½ Bias119^1 ParkCovert115^nk Led fnl 2 1/2f 8
28Apr79♦3Sandown(Eng) gd 1 1:51⅘ (T) Esher Cup Hcp                    1^nk Cauthen S   124  *.80  — — Marquee Universal124^nk BoldShot116½ Twickenham125^1½ All out 7
21Apr79♦2Newbury(Eng) gd 7f 1:28 (T) Greenham Stakes(Gr.3)           3^11 Cauthen S    126  7.00  — — Kris126^3 YoungGeneration126^8 MarqueeUniversl126^1½ No threat 9
 7Apr79♦1Salisbury(Eng) sf 1 1:50 (T) Grand Foods Hcp                 1^1½ Cauthen S    120 *2.25  — — MrqueeUnivrsl120^1½ Twicknhm125^6 RdRufus115^1½ Well up, drvg 7
 3Nov78♦5Newmarket(Eng) fm 6f 1:15 (T) Red Lodge Stakes(Mdn)          1¾ Street R      126 12.00  — — MrqueeUniversl126¾ AftrTomorrow126^hd ConcrtHll126^no Up late 15
  LATEST WORKOUTS   ●May 29 Pim 5f fst :58⅗ h    May 24 Pim 1 fst 1:37 h    May 17 Pim 5f fst 1:01 h    May 9 Pim 3f gd :36 h
```

reduced by three for gain, and up two for energy, to finish at :24.4. This horse is sure to be a prime contender.

The third favorite is Sten, who is not exactly a slouch.

```
Sten                         B. g. 5, by Ack Ack—Kerdassa, by Royal Vale                  Turf Record       St. 1st 2nd 3rd     Amt.
                                Br.—Pen-Y-Bryn Farm (Ky)                           119  St. 1st 2nd 3rd   1980  7   3   1   0   $99,560
 Own.—Berry M                   Tr.—DeStasio Richard T                                  15   5   1   1    1979 18   2   2   3   $70,745
18May80- 8Aqu gd 1 1/16 (T):48 1:13 1:44 Ft Marcy H          6 10 10^11 10^7¼ 6^2¾ 1^1¼ Asmussen C B 115  4.00  85-21 Sten 115^1¼ Native Courier 126^1¼ Told 113^1¼ Driving 10
 5May80- 8Aqu fm 1 1/16 (T):45⅘ 1:10 1:42⅕ Allowance         8 5 5^15 5^5½ 3^2 1^2¾ Amy J     117 12.60  94-04 Sten 117^2¾ Native Courier 122^1¼ Virilify 115^2½ Drew out 9
16Mar80- 6Aqu fst 1⅝ [.]:48⅗ 2:06⅘ 2:45⅖ Handicap           4 5 5^13 1^1 2^1½ 2^2¼ Amy J     114  8.90  89-16 Ring of Light 115^2¼ Sten 114^6¾ Identical 122^5½ 2nd best 9
 3Mar80- 8Aqu fst 1 1/16 [.]:47⅖ 1:12⅗ 1:44⅖ Allowance      5 9 9^13 9^12 8^9¾ 4^7½ Beitia E5 112  9.70  84-21 Ring of Light 117^5 Pianist 115^1¾ Favored Son 115¾ No menace 10
23Feb80- 8Aqu gd 1⅛ [.]:47⅖ 1:12⅕ 1:50⅕ 3↑Grey Lag H       10 10 9^10 10^8¾ 9^8¼ 8^9¼ Hernandez R 114 14.60 86-17 I'm It 113^1¼ Causerie 113^1¾ Charlie Coast 115^4 No threat 10
 3Feb80- 8Aqu fst 1⅛ [.]:47⅗ 1:12⅖ 1:52⅕ 3↑Stymie H         3 8 9^10 7^6¾ 6^8½ 6^6¼ Maple E   114 14.20  79-18 Identical 116^hd Ring of Truth 115^2¾ Charlie Coast 117^3 No threat 9
 6Jan80- 8Aqu fst 1⅛ [.]:49⅕ 1:13⅗ 1:51⅖ 3↑Assault H        2 2 6^3¼ 4^2¼ 3^nk 1^no Amy J      112 13.10  89-17 Sten 112^no Mr. International 118¾ Lean Lad 114^hd Stiff drive 8
15Dec79- 8Aqu fst 1⅝ [.]:48⅕ 2:04⅗ 2:43⅗ 3↑Gallant Fx H     2 5 4^7½ 4^6 4^6 4^9 Asmussen C B 110 21.80 99-15 Identical 110^6 Ethnarch 118^2½ Land of Eire 114½ Weakened 12
 1Dec79- 6Aqu fst 1 3/16 :48⅕ 1:12⅗ 1:57 3↑Allowance        5 3 3^5½ 2^4 2^5 4^7¼ Asmussen C B 115  3.90  70-23 Identical 115^6¼ Picturesque 114^1 Proud Arion 119^no Tired 6
22Nov79- 8Aqu fst 1 3/16 :48⅕ 1:12⅖ 1:56⅘ 3↑Queens Cty H    3 6 8^6¾ 7^3¼ 6^3¼ 5^3¼ Asmussen C B 111 29.00 75-20 Dewan Keys 112½ Mr. International 108^no Gallant Best116^no Wide 8
  LATEST WORKOUTS   ●May 26 Bel tr.t 1 fst 1:44⅕ b   May 17 Bel tr.t 3f fst :36⅕ b   May 3 Bel tr.t 3f fst :36 b   Apr 29 Bel tr.t 6f my 1:17⅘ b
```

Of the two turf races, his best was 5May80, where there was a lead time of :24.1. From the maximum of 8 lengths back for calculation of gain, we can give credit for two ticks, which brings a preliminary ability time of :23.4. But he gets a 48-and-change first call time to put two ticks on for energy to wind up with a solid :24.1. The 18May80 race shows a :25.0 lead time with no reduction for gain plus a four added for energy to give a :25.4.

We can now make the final tally in this fashion:

Odds	Horse	Ability		A Pts		F	Total
2.0	Lyphard's Wish	Unknown		—	—	U	U
2.5	Marquee Universal	:24.3	:24.4	17	16	Q1	34
3.2	Sten	:24.1	:25.4	19	11	Q	30

Lyphard's Wish is the favorite largely because of the respect the crowd has for his owner and trainer, who have brought some powerful horses across to this country, plus some degree of disrespect for Pimlico in Maryland.

This race, however, presents an excellent illustration of our rule requiring a "strong favorite" where ability is unknown. Lyphard's Wish is only a half-number ahead of Marquee Universal in the betting odds, and this allows us to invest in Marquee Universal to win and place. If Lyphard's Wish had been 3-2 on the board, he would have been a full number ahead, and in that event, we would have made only a place bet on Marquee Universal. Now, look at the result:

EIGHTH RACE
Belmont
JUNE 1, 1980

1 ¼ MILES.(inner-turf). (1.58⅘) 21st Running THE EDGEMERE HANDICAP. (Grade III). $100,000 Added. 3-year-olds and upward. By subscription of $200 each, which should accompany the nomination; $800 to pass the entry box; with $100,000 added. The added money and all fees to be divided 60% to the winner, 22% to second, 12% to third and 6% to fourth. Weights Tuesday, May 27. Starters to be named at the closing time of entries. Trophies will be presented to the winning owner, trainer and jockey and mementoes to the grooms of the first four finishers. The New York Raceing Association reserves the right to transfer this race to the main course. Closed with 32 nominations.
Value of race $112,800, value to winner $67,680, second $24,816, third $13,536, fourth $6,768. Mutuel pool $337,026, OTB pool $96,517.

Last Raced	Horse	Eqt.A.Wt	PP	¼	½	¾	1	Str	Fin	Jockey	Odds $1
10May80 ^{9}Pim^{1}	Marquee Universal	4 121	2	1^{1½}	1^{1}	1^{1½}	1^{1½}	1^{3}	1^{1¾}	Pilar H	2.50
10May80 ^{9}Pim^{3}	Match The Hatch	b 4 114	4	2^{hd}	2^{½}	2^{½}	2^{½}	2^{½}	2^{1¼}	Skinner K	36.20
20Oct79 ^{2}New^{4}	Lyphard's Wish	4 122	5	5^{1}	3^{1}	3^{1½}	3^{1½}	3^{2}	3^{½}	Cordero A Jr	2.00
5May80 ^{1}Aqu^{1}	Audacious Fool	4 110	7	7^{4}	7^{4}	6^{4}	6^{3}	6^{2}	4^{3}	Samyn J L	26.60
18May80 ^{8}Aqu^{2}	Native Courier	5 126	6	4^{hd}	4^{hd}	4^{1}	4^{½}	4^{hd}	5no	Maple E	3.70
18May80 ^{8}Aqu^{10}	April Axe	b 5 112	1	6^{1½}	5^{3}	5^{2}	5^{1}	4^{hd}	6^{hd}	Cruguet J	33.60
18May80 ^{8}Aqu^{1}	Sten	5 119	8	8	8	7^{1}	7^{2}	7^{4}	7^{5}	Asmussen C B	3.20
16May80 ^{7}Aqu^{3}	Crown Thy Good	4 111	3	3^{1½}	6^{hd}	8	8	8	8	Velasquez J	13.60

OFF AT 5:21 EDT. Start good, Won ridden out. Time, :24, :48, 1:11⅗, 1:35⅖, 1:58⅘ Course firm.
Equals course record.

$2 Mutuel Prices:			
2-(B)-MARQUEE UNIVERSAL	7.00	4.20	3.80
4-(D)-MATCH THE HATCH		20.00	8.00
5-(E)-LYPHARD'S WISH			4.20

This is a splendid result. You will note the words "Equals course record" just above the mutuel prices. Good horse, powerful race, and much satisfaction in the wallet.

Now, to the ninth and last race, where all we need to show you for the moment is the following.

NINTH RACE
Belmont
JUNE 1, 1980

6 FURLONGS. (1.08⅖) CLAIMING. Purse $10,500. 3-year-olds, weights, 122 lbs. Non-winners of two races since May 1, allowed 3 lbs. Of a race since then, 5 lbs. Claiming price $12,500 for each $1,000 to $10,500 2 lbs. (Races when entered to be claimed for $8,500 or less not considered)
Value of race $10,500, value to winner $6,300, second $2,310, third $1,260, fourth $630. Mutuel pool $170,839, OTB pool $77,679. Track Triple Pool $257,174. OTB Pool $336,476.

Last Raced	Horse	Eqt.A.Wt	PP	St	¼	½	Str	Fin	Jockey	Cl'g Pr	Odds $1
24May80 ^{3}Bel^{5}	Bal Breeze	3 117	12	8	5^{1}	5^{4}	3^{3}	1^{3}	Velez R I†	12500	50.30
21Apr80 ^{2}Aqu^{1}	Fays Carl	b 3 110	5	10	4^{4}	3^{1½}	2^{hd}	2^{¾}	Rogers K L^{5}	11500	6.00
16May80 ^{4}Aqu^{12}	Last Goodie	b 3 117	2	5	2^{1½}	1^{hd}	1^{hd}	3^{1½}	Rivera M A	12500	59.30
24May80 ^{3}Bel^{4}	Little Marker	b 3 117	4	2	10^{½}	9^{½}	7^{hd}	4^{2½}	Santiago A	12500	3.40
24May80 ^{3}Bel^{3}	Source Of Power	b 3 117	10	4	3^{hd}	4^{½}	5^{2}	5^{nk}	Fell J	12500	3.00
24May80 ^{3}Bel^{6}	Le Good Times	b 3 113	9	7	8^{1½}	7^{1}	8^{4}	6^{nk}	Giraldo L	10500	52.50
23May80 ^{9}Bel^{7}	Prince Robair	b 3 110	8	6	1^{hd}	2^{1½}	4^{½}	7^{½}	Lovato F Jr^{5}	11500	7.70
16May80 ^{4}Aqu^{11}	Quiet Sam	3 117	3	3	7^{½}	6^{2}	6^{½}	8^{4}	Venezia M	12500	20.10
2May80 ^{4}Key^{3}	Kim's Turn	b 3 112	11	9	12	10^{½}	9^{½}	9^{1¾}	Velasquez J	12500	22.10
5May80 ^{9}Aqu^{8}	Brookville Sport	b 3 115	6	12	9^{½}	8^{½}	10^{1½}	10^{1¼}	Maple E	11500	51.50
24May80 ^{1}Mth^{7}	Princess Deirdre	b 3 107	7	11	11^{1½}	12	12	11^{½}	Gonzalez M A^{5}	12500	68.10
23Apr80 ^{2}Aqu^{3}	Likeable	3 112	1	1	6^{½}	11^{1½}	11^{1}	12	Beitia E^{5}	12500	2.30

OFF AT 5:51 EDT. Start good, Won driving. Time, :23, :46⅘, 1:12⅗ Track fast.

$2 Mutuel Prices:			
12-(M)-BAL BREEZE	102.60	34.80	22.80
5-(F)-FAYS CARL		6.80	5.20
2-(B)-LAST GOODIE			23.20

$2 TRIPLE 12-5-2 PAID $31,802.00.

You can readily see that none of the first three betting choices even finished in the money. To show their past performances and our point ratings are of little concern, except that we will say that our selection was Source Of Power, the second choice in the wagering, who finished fifth in a crowded field. We dropped a win and place bet and are now ready to total up for the day—a pleasant task indeed. Here is our recapitulation.

Race	Selection	Invest		Return	
		Win	Place	Win	Place
1	Grand Courant	$ 2	$ 2	$ 0	$ 3.60
2	Pass	—	—	—	—
3	Bankers Sun	—	2	—	3.20
4	Freightliner	2	2	9.80	5.00
5	Rokeby Rose	2	2	3.80	2.60
6	Beech Grove	2	2	4.00	3.00
7	Thanks to Tony	2	2	0	0
8	Marquee Universal	2	2	7.00	4.20
9	Source Of Power	2	2	0	0
	Totals	$14	$16	$24.60	$21.60

Total invested $30.00
Total returned $46.20
Net profit $16.20

We are off to a splendid start, with a plain 54% return on total money invested. Out of seven win bets, we had four right on the button. Of eight place bets, six paid off, which is a good day indeed. This is a powerful example of this method of play working precisely as it should (although you cannot expect it to always do this well, particularly on those days when the first three favorites are not consistently in the money).

CHAPTER

X

BIG WEEK AT BELMONT: SECOND DAY, MONDAY, JUNE 2, 1980

Every racegoer gears up his hope at the start of a new day. The second card leads off with a long race on the turf for fillies and mares, and Wayward Lassie is the favorite.

Her best effort was back last year on 27Sep79 at Belmont, where she acquired a :24.4 (lead time :24.4, gain of one, and addition of one tick for energy). She gets a :25.3 for the preceding race on 13Sep79 (lead time :25.0, no

1 BELMONT

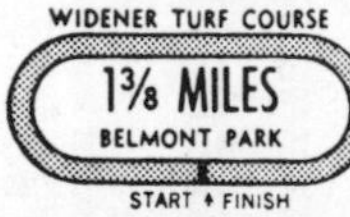
WIDENER TURF COURSE
1⅜ MILES
BELMONT PARK
START ♦ FINISH

1 ⅜ MILES. (TURF). (2.12⅗) ALLOWANCE. Purse $20,000. Fillies and Mares. 3-year-old and upward which have never won a race other than maiden, claiming or starter. Weights, 3-year-olds, 114 lbs. Older, 122 lbs. Non-winners of a race other than claiming at a mile and a furlong or over since May 1, allowed 3 lbs. Of such arace since April 15, 5 lbs. (Winners preferred)

Wayward Lassie — **Ch. f. 3, by Noholme II—Amerigo Lassie, by Prince John**
Own.—Live Oak Plantation — **Br.—Live Oak Stud (Fla)** — **Tr.—Kelly Patrick J** — **109**

Turf Record St.	1st	2nd	3rd	Year	St.	1st	2nd	3rd	Amt.
8	1	1	2	1980	3	1	0	1	$7,900
				1979	8	M	1	1	$4,760

11May80- 1Aqu	gd	1 1/16	Ⓣ:48⅘	1:13⅖	1:45⅗	3↑ ⒻAllowance	6	7	65½	74½	54½	32½	Miranda J	b	109	3.90	74-19	Passolyn 1101½ MississippiTalk1131WaywardLassie1091¾	Checked	10
13Mar80-10GP	fm	*1	Ⓣ		1:41⅕	ⒻMd Sp Wt	10	9	67½	21½	14	18½	Cordero A Jr	b	120	1.80	75-21	Wayward Lassie 1208½ FloRussell1202½I'mForBagdad1206	Handily	10
13Feb80- 6Hia	fm	1 1/16	Ⓣ		1:45⅘	ⒻMd Sp Wt	7	11	1019	812	69½	53	Gonzalez M A5	b	115	4.00	66-25	Ignite 120½ Roman Beach 1151 Miss Rebecca 120nk	Wide	12
24Nov79- 6Aqu	yl	1⅛	Ⓣ:50	1:15⅖	1:56	ⒻHandicap	1	7	73¾	65	66	66½	Samyn J L	b	110	5.40	57-38	Sparklet 1161 Cabinetta 1202¼ Verbatin Song 121nk	Outrun	7
9Nov79- 4Aqu	sf	1⅛	Ⓣ:50	1:15⅖	1:55	ⒻMd Sp Wt	7	12	128½	76¾	31	21½	Imparato J	b	117	9.40e	67-30	WalkingInRhythm1171½WaywrdLssie117½Erin'sWord117½	Bore in	12
1Nov79- 1Aqu	gd	1⅛	Ⓣ:49	1:14	1:53	ⒻMd Sp Wt	4	9	85	63½	44½	31¼	Imparato J	b	117	53.30	78-18	Tuvalu 1171 Erin's Word 117nk Wayward Lassie 117nk	Rallied	12
14Oct79- 9Bel	my	1 1/16	:48⅖	1:14⅖	1:47⅘	ⒻMd Sp Wt	12	9	73¾	910	1031	1048	Imparato J	b	118	23.70	— —	Demure 1182¾ Raise A Holme 118½ Arisen 118¾	Far back	12
27Sep79- 3Bel	gd	1 1/16	Ⓣ:47⅕	1:12	1:45⅗	ⒻMd Sp Wt	6	7	73¼	52¼	54	611	Castaneda M	b	117	33.00	57-23	Sparklet 1176 Tuvalu 1171¼ Raise A Holme 112nk	Outrun	10
13Sep79- 4Bel	fm	1 1/16	Ⓣ:46⅕	1:11⅕	1:43⅗	ⒻMd Sp Wt	1	9	915	911	911	813	Gonzalez M A7		110	22.50	65-12	Proud Barbara 117nk Suite Of Dreams 1171¼ Sparklet1176	Outrun	10
31Aug79- 5Bel	gd	1 1/16	:47⅘	1:12⅗	1:45	ⒻMd Sp Wt	5	7	78½	715	721	729	Gonzalez M A5		112	45.50	48-19	Determined Best1174¾HolidayJet117¾ClassicCurves1176	No speed	7

LATEST WORKOUTS **May 29 Bel 5f fst 1:01⅖ h** **May 23 Bel 5f fst 1:01⅗ h** **May 17 Bel 5f fst 1:04 b** **May 5 Bel 5f fst 1:03 b**

credit for gain because of being so far back in the field, and an addition of three ticks for energy adjustment because of her first call time of :49.1). She qualifies on form off her gain of more than five. As you becomc familiar with comparative ability times, you will recognize that these times are fair, not exceptional, and that you might readily find better in the race, particularly since it is an allowance event.

The second choice in the wagering, La Atrevida, is a Lightly Raced filly who won her last race on the grass in good form.

La Atrevida — B. f. 3, by Bold Bidder—Santa Quilla, by Sanctus — Br.—Manning Mr-Mrs D (Ky) — Tr.—Laurin Roger — Own.—Peters L J — 114

Turf Record	St.	1st	2nd	3rd		St.	1st	2nd	3rd	Amt.
	3	1	0	2	1980	4	1	0	2	$14,970
					1979	0	M	0	0	

25May80- 3Bel	fm	1¼	Ⓣ:47⅘ 1:38⅖ 2:02⅖	3↑ⒻMd Sp Wt	3	5	54½	3nk	12	12	Cordero A Jr	113	*1.30	82-15	La Atrevida 1132 Miss Rebecca 1137 Binomial 1133	Ridden out 12
18May80- 1Aqu	gd	1 1/16	Ⓣ:48⅕ 1:13⅗ 1:46⅖	3↑ⒻMd Sp Wt	10	7	89	46	35	33¾	Cordero A Jr	113	*2.20	69-21	Carrade 110½ Idiomatic 1133¼ La Atrevida 1132¼	Rallied 10
12May80- 9Aqu	sly	1⅛	:47⅗ 1:12⅖ 1:52⅘	3↑ⒻMd Sp Wt	8	5	69½	57½	36	44	Santiago A	113	7.00	67-19	Als Ich Kan 1131½ English Toffy 113¾ Miss Rebecca 1131¾	Wide 8
27Mar80-10GP	fm	*1 1/16 Ⓣ	1:44⅖	ⒻMd Sp Wt	5	4	47½	55½	59	310	Gonzalez M A5	115	25.70	74-16	Intendress 1201 Dominia 1209 La Atrevida 1151½	Mild bid 10

LATEST WORKOUTS May 6 Bel 5f fst 1:02⅕ b Apr 30 Bel 6f sly 1:14 h Apr 24 Bel 5f fst 1:04 b Apr 19 Bel 4f fst :52 b

In the Sunday feature of the day before, we calculated an ability time for Marquee Universal off the last two furlongs where we had a published time. We can do the same for La Atrevida, and under our rules, if the last quarter-mile time is a poor one, we can extract a better one out of the race because of the arduous nature of the long run. But you can blink when you calculate the :24.0 flat that La Atrevida gets off her last victory, as an Improving Horse. You obtain this by subtracting 1:38.2 from 2:02.2. In her other ratable race of 18May80 at Aqueduct, there is a :25.2 lead time, reduced by two for gain, but increased by four for energy adjustment to level off at a :25.4.

Before reaching any conclusions, we'd better look at the third choice, Sophisticate.

Sophisticate — B. f. 4, by Vaguely Noble—Jam Ruler, by Golden Ruler — Br.—Hunt N B (Ky) — Tr.—Imperio Leonard — Own.—Crash Geri — 117

Turf Record	St.	1st	2nd	3rd		St.	1st	2nd	3rd	Amt.
	10	1	0	2	1980	4	0	0	0	$1,605
					1979	8	1	0	2	$15,742

26May80- 7Bel	fm	1 1/16	Ⓣ:47⅘ 1:11⅘ 1:43	3↑ⒻAllowance	7	10	1012	87½	78	44½	Fell J	119	27.90	84-12	WlkingInRhythm112hdFrewellLetter1051½HiltoGlmour1193	Rallied 10
11Feb80- 5Hia	fm	1⅛ Ⓣ	1:49⅘	ⒻAllowance	2	2	22	43½	87	88	Gonzalez M A5	110	14.20	77-16	Veiled Beauty 1151¼ Diffluence 115½ Icancan 1151	Tired 9
4Feb80-10Hia	fm	*1 1/16 Ⓣ	1:44⅕	ⒻAllowance	4	4	43	41½	23	65¾	Cordero A Jr	115	3.50	74-14	Do Be Daring 115½ No Disgrace 1151¼ Veiled Beauty 1152	Tired 10
17Jan80- 7Hia	fm	1 1/16 Ⓣ	1:42⅗	ⒻAllowance	1	10	86¾	89	65¼	75½	Vasquez J	115	*2.20	79-14	King's Little Girl1151DoBeDaring1151¾What'llIDo1151½	No factor 12
13Dec79- 6Aqu	sly	6f	⊡:23⅕ :47⅖ 1:12⅘	3↑ⒻAllowance	3	8	86½	89¼	712	78	Santiago A	115	14.60	72-20	Very Distinctive 1152¼ The FourArts115nkTooDaring1151¼	Outrun 9
8Dec79- 1Aqu	fst	1 1/16	⊡:47⅗ 1:13 1:45	3↑ⒻAllowance	1	3	21½	1½	55	611	Martens G	115	5.30	78-13	Plausible Reason 1156½ Sweet Pretense 115¾ Mesabi 1152½	Tired 10
18Nov79- 6Aqu	sf	1 1/16	Ⓣ:49⅖ 1:15⅖ 1:47⅘	3↑ⒻAllowance	1	5	73½	64	56½	55¼	Santiago A	115	2.90	61-30	Ouro Verde 1151½ House Pet 117no Plausible Reason 1153¾	Tired 9
8Nov79- 4Aqu	sf	1⅛	Ⓣ:50 1:14⅘ 1:54	3↑ⒻAllowance	1	5	43	42½	1hd	32¼	Santiago A	115	13.70	72-26	Fun Worthy 1152 House Pet 115nk Sophisticate 1152	Weakened 10
17Jun79◆4Groenendael(Bel)	gd	*1⅜	2:26	Ⓣ Grand Prix de Bruxelles						46	Muyldermans J	121	3.50	— —	Shaftesbury 1235 Nikitz 117nk Lohengrin 126¾	Evenly 8
24May79◆5Longchamp(Fra)	sf	*1½	2:47⅕	Ⓣ ⒻPrix des Tuileries						57½	Lequeux A	123	*.80	— —	Yamba 1271½ MissMouse 1203 Peleocene 1233	No threat 6

LATEST WORKOUTS May 24 Bel Ⓣ 6f fm 1:17 b (d) May 16 Bel 1 fst 1:43⅗ b ●May 10 Bel 7f fst 1:23⅘ h May 3 Bel tr.t 5f fst 1:01 h

She qualifies on form with a gain in the last race. In her last race, there was a strong :24.0 lead time, which we do not reduce for gain because of lengths behind. And when we add up the first time for Sophisticate, we get a :50.1, which requires four ticks for energy adjustment to give her a :24.4. To find another grass race to calculate her times, the 8Nov79 contest at Aqueduct on a soft turf shows a good :24.4 lead time, with nothing off for gain and an add-on of four for energy to make a :25.3 and reduced one more because of soft turf to a final :25.2. We can now compare the three choices.

Odds	Horse	Ability		A Pts		F	Total
2.6	Wayward Lassie	:24.4	:25.3	16	12	Q	28
2.8	La Atrevida	:24.0	:25.4	20	11	Q2	33
4.2	Sophisticate	:24.4	:25.2	16	13	Q	29

I am always somewhat concerned when there is a wide disparity between two ability times, as La Atrevida shows. But our points stand. Since she is very Lightly Raced, and her powerful performance came in her last race in the last quarter-mile of a taxing distance, she is entered to be rated off that race at full value. This gives her a strong point lead over the other two rivals, and therefore we invest in her to win and place. Most happily indeed, as the result chart tells us.

FIRST RACE
Belmont
JUNE 2, 1980

1 ⅜ MILES.(inner-turf). (2.11⅖) ALLOWANCE. Purse $20,000. Fillies and Mares. 3-year-old and upward which have never won a race other than maiden, claiming or starter. Weights, 3-year-olds, 114 lbs. Older, 122 lbs. Non-winners of a race other than claiming at a mile and a furlong or over since May 1, allowed 3 lbs. Of such arace since April 15, 5 lbs. (Winners preferred)

Value of race $20,000, value to winner $12,000, second $4,400, third $2,400, fourth $1,200. Mutuel pool $123,142, OTB pool $145,878.

Last Raced	Horse	Eqt.	A.	Wt	PP	¼	½	¾	1	Str	Fin	Jockey	Odds $1
25May80 3Bel1	La Atrevida		3	114	2	2½	2½	1½	2½	12	1¾	Velasquez J	2.80
11May80 1Aqu3	Wayward Lassie	b	3	112	8	8½	8½	41	31	3hd	2½	Cordero A Jr	2.60
11May80 1Aqu4	Intendress	b	3	113	1	5½	5½	5½	63	2½	3¼	Rivera M A	10.90
22Apr80 2GP4	Shady Turk		3	112	9	1½	1½	3½	5hd	5½	4¼	Cruguet J	17.10
26May80 7Bel4	Sophisticate		4	117	5	103	91	7hd	4½	6½	5no	Fell J	4.20
21May80 7Bel4	Als Ich Kan		3	114	10	11	11	10½	9½	84	6hd	Montoya D	21.70
18May80 1Aqu1	Carrade	b	3	109	7	6hd	31	21	1hd	41	7¾	Delahoussaye D J	6.40
5May80 7Aqu7	Sweet Pretense		4	117	11	71	6½	6½	7½	7½	8¾	Maple E	34.00
21May80 7Bel3	Winter Romance		4	112	6	41	71	81	8½	94	94	Lovato F Jr5	30.80
21May80 7Bel5	Classic Curves		3	109	3	9½	104	94	105	103	103	Venezia M	19.10
11Apr80 8Aqu4	Diorama		3	109	4	3hd	41	11	11	11	11	Beitia E5	16.40

OFF AT 1:00, EDT. Start good, Won ridden out. Time, :24⅘, :50, 1:15, 1:39⅘, 2:04⅕, 2:16⅕, Course firm.

Official Program Numbers

$2 Mutuel Prices:

2-(B)-LA ATREVIDA	7.60	4.00	3.40
8-(H)-WAYWARD LASSIE		3.80	3.00
1-(A)-INTENDRESS			4.00

With this good one behind us, we reach the second race, a one-mile claiming event. Once more, we will omit the past performances of the first three favorites because the first two finishers were out of the long-shot ranks. Here is what the chart reveals.

SECOND RACE
Belmont
JUNE 2, 1980

1 MILE. (1.33⅗) CLAIMING. Purse $12,000. Fillies and Mares. 3-year-old and upward. Weights, 3-year-olds, 114 lbs. Older, 122lbs. Non-winners of two races at a mile or over since May 1, allowed 3 lbs. Of such a race since then, 5 lbs. Claiming price $16,000 for each $1,000 to $14,000 2 lbs. (Races when entered to be claimed for $12,500 or less not considered)

Value of race $12,000, value to winner $7,200, second $2,640, third $1,440, fourth $720. Mutuel pool $120,392, OTR pool $93,373. Track Quinella $139,823. OTB Quinella Pool $127,963.

Last Raced	Horse	Eqt.A.Wt	PP	St	¼	½	¾	Str	Fin	Jockey	Cl'g Pr	Odds $1
29May80 6Mth8	East Coast Shopper	b 4 117	4	2	2½	3¹	2½	12½	1⁴	Velasquez J	16000	14.00
23May80 1Bel4	Irish Noel	b 5 115	6	4	5⁵	4¹	4¹½	3²	2²½	Asmussen C B	15000	12.60
23May80 1Bel1	Par For the Course	4 114	7	5	6⁴	6⁵	6⁴	4²	3nk	Tejada V M Jr⁵	16000	5.40
10May80 4Aqu1	Silver Ray	3 112	1	6	3½	1hd	1hd	2¹½	4⁵	Cordero A Jr	16000	1.00
19May80 4Aqu6	Saratoga Room	4 110	5	3	4¹	5⁴	5½	6³	5¹¾	Gonzalez M A⁵	15000	9.20
19May80 4Aqu5	My Rosebud	5 117	3	1	1¹	2½	3¹½	5¹	6hd	Saumell L	16000	2.60
1May80 9Aqu1	Maraza	b 4 110	2	7	7	7	7	7	7	Beitia E⁵	15000	22.00

OFF AT 1:32, EDT. Start good, Won ridden out. Time, :24, :48, 1:14⅕, 1:40 Track fast.

$2 Mutuel Prices:				
5-(E)–EAST COAST SHOPPER		30.00	11.00	6.20
7-(G)–IRISH NOEL			9.20	6.60
8-(H)–PAR FOR THE COURSE				4.80

$2 QUINELLA 5-7 PAID $197.40.

Our choice was Silver Ray, the favorite, who couldn't hold his lead, fading back to the middle of the pack. Our investment to win and place thus went down the drain. The winner, paying $30.00, had wretched form, which is what makes long-shot payoffs. We accept this all as part of the game, and get ready for the next race.

BELMONT

INNER TURF COURSE
1⅜ MILES
BELMONT PARK
◆ START ◆ FINISH

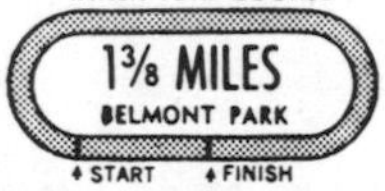

1⅜ MILES. (INNER-TURF). (2.11⅖) STARTER HANDICAP. Purse $18,000. 3-year-olds and upward which have started for a claiming price of $20,000 or less since August 1 1979. Weights, Friday, May 30. Declarations by 10:00 a.m., Saturday, May 31.

Danton King

Own.—Al Jo Stable

B. c. 3, by Danton II—Tropic Queen, by Tropic King
Br.—Caple H R (Fla)
Tr.—Garcia Efrain

112

		Turf Record	St.	1st	2nd	3rd		Amt.
		St. 1st 2nd 3rd	1980	12	4	1	4	$30,036
		7 3 0 2	1979	13	M	3	3	$4,516

23May80- 2Bel gd 1⅜ ⊤:48⅗ 1:13 1:45	Clm 40000	1 5 4³ 2¹ 1¹½ 1³¾	Velasquez J	b 117	*.80	79-21 Danton King 117³¾ Deedee's Deal 113²½ SurfClub113½	Ridden out 7
15Apr80- 9GP gd 1 ①:47⅖ 1:12⅖ 1:38⅕	Clm 35000	6 3 3⁶½ 3¹½ 2¹ 3¹⅔	Cordero A Jr	b 116	*1.50	77-22 Peaslee 112¹ Sun Partner 116⅔ Danton King 116nk	Weakened 7
7Apr80- 9GP fm 1⅜ ①:47⅖ 1:12⅗ 1:43⅗	Clm 40000	7 5 6⁵ 7³¾ 3⁶ 3⁵½	Smith A Jr	b 116	4.80	78-14 Harvest Hero 116³¼ Royal Rouge 116² Danton King 116²	Mild bid 9
22Mar80- 8GP fm 1⅜ ①:47 1:10⅗ 1:41⅗	Clm 40000	5 7 6⁶ 6⁴ 4²½ 4⁶	Cordero A Jr	b 114	4.60	87-10 Brilliant Prince113³½ JustASquare116²½ SunPartner115no	Mild, bid 11
17Mar80- 7GP fm *1⅜ ① 1:45⅗	Allowance	7 7 7⁹½ 7⁶½ 7⁷¾ 7⁸¾	Hussey C	b 117	7.60	69-22 No Bend 117⁴ Current Winner 114no Wind Change 112⅔	Wide 10
5Mar80- 2Hia fst 1⅜ :47⅖ 1:12⅗ 1:46⅗	Allowance	1 3 7⁷ 5⁴ 2⁵ 3¹¹	Velasquez J	b 115	4.50	60-26 Lights of London 115¹⁰ No Bend 119½ DantonKing115²	Bid, tired 9
21Feb80- 6Hia gd 1 ① 1:46⅖	Clm 25000	4 7 10⁵¾ 5²¼ 2¹½ 1¹	Velasquez J	b 117	*1.40	66-32 Danton King 117¹ Tony's Episode 115¹ExplodentBay115¹	Driving 12
11Feb80- 8Hia fm 1⅜ ① 1:43⅗	Clm 20000	2 9 6⁹ 2⁴ 1² 1⁸	Velasquez J	b 113	10.60	81-16 Danton King 113⁸ Ardant Ceser 113¹ Rappett 114½	Drew off 12
4Feb80- 1Hia fst 1⅛ :47⅖ 1:14⅕ 1:55⅗	Clm 12500	2 3 3³½ 3²½ 2¹½ 2²	Velasquez J	b 119	3.50	53-29 Tuck A Hummin 119² DantonKing119²½HalterQueen111no	Gamely 11
24Jan80- 2Hia fst 6f :22⅕ :46⅕ 1:13⅖	Clm c-10000	4 4 5⁶½ 5⁹ 4³½ 3²	Cordero A Jr	b 118	*2.30	74-23 London Coffee 111¹ Tight Grip 116¹ Danton King 118¹	Rallied 10

LATEST WORKOUTS   May 31 Mth 4f fst :53 b   May 29 Mth 4f fst :51 b   May 16 Mth 5f fst 1:03 b   May 10 Mth 7f fst 1:31 b

We're back on the grass with a strong-looking favorite, Danton King, coming off an impressive Big Win in his last Belmont effort. His best time was made at Gulfstream in the 22Mar80 race, with a :23.3 lead time for beginning. Danton King gained 2 lengths, but this is offset by an energy adjustment of two ticks. We add one tick for the fast Gulfstream surface, even on the grass, and get a :23.4 ability time off this race. In his last powerful run, there was a :24.1 lead time, reduced by two for gain, but when we add three for energy adjustment, we wind up with a :24.2. This horse has the figures: Would you agree with me that he couldn't lose?

The second choice, Guillermo, shows no grass races in his past performances.

Guillermo * Dk. b. or br. c. 4, by Prove Out—I Deceive, by Bagdad
Br.—Hirsch Mrs W J (Ky)
Own.—Dor-Sea Stable Tr.—Parisella John

117 Turf Record St. 1st 2nd 3rd 1 0 0 0

	St.	1st	2nd	3rd	Amt.
1980	11	4	3	0	$48,360
1979	8	2	0	1	$20,280

29May80- 2Bel fst 6f :22⅘ :45⅖ 1:10⅗ Clm 47500 4 2 32 32 43½ 21¼ Martens G b 117 4.60 88-16 Subordinate 1171¼ Guillermo 117hd Bold Voyager 117nk Gamely 7
8May80- 6Aqu sly 1 :45⅘ 1:10⅗ 1:36⅗ 3↑ Allowance 6 1 11½ 13 12½ 14¾ Martens G b 119 *1.00 83-22 Guillermo 1194¾ Cauhtemoc 1192½ Creme Silence114½ Ridden out 6
1May80- 5Aqu fst 6f :23 :46⅖ 1:10 Allowance 5 1 1hd 2hd 32½ 23 Martens G b 117 2.70 90-13 NotTomorrow1123Guillermo117hdAndoverRoad117hd Carried wide 6
19Apr80- 2Aqu fst 1 :45⅗ 1:10 1:35⅘ Clm 32500 6 1 12 1½ 12½ 13¾ Velasquez J b 115 *1.80 87-17 Guillermo 1153¾ Home By Dawn 1174¼ Coupon Rate1081¼ Driving 6
10Apr80- 2Aqu gd 1⅛ :47⅗ 1:11⅘ 1:50 Clm 25000 1 1 11 11½ 12 12 Martens G b 117 7.50 85-16 Guillermo 1172 Amano 1131¾ Super Boy 1126 Driving 6
31Mar80- 1Aqu sly 6f :23 :46⅘ 1:12 Clm 20000 6 5 52½ 41½ 1½ 1½ Martens G b 117 *2.50 83-23 Guillermo 117½ Mansard 1151¾ Right N Ready 117¾ Driving 8
13Mar80- 4Aqu fst 6f ⊡:23⅖ :47⅖ 1:12⅗ Clm 16000 1 7 11 1½ 11½ 2no Martens G b 117 6.00 81-23 Naudi 115no Guillermo 1171½ Breyer Patch 1123 Sharp try 13
28Feb80- 2Aqu fst 6f ⊡:22⅖ :45⅘ 1:10⅖ Clm 20000 1 6 31 55 915 915 Martens G b 117 9.80 77-19 Armet 1123½ Ed Cainan 1171 A. J. Raffles 112¾ Tired 11
24Feb80- 1Aqu gd 1 1/16 ⊡:47⅕ 1:12⅗ 1:45⅖ Clm 25000 6 1 21½ 24 914 812 Martens G b 117 10.00 75-17 North Star 1175¼ Lancer's Pride 117nk Gifted Leader 111½ Tired 10
9Feb80- 2Aqu fst 6f ⊡:22⅗ :46⅕ 1:11⅕ Clm 35000 7 3 13 1½ 33 55¼ Martens G b 117 11.30 83-19 Ephphatha 1134 Double Revival 115¾ Nice Sailing 110nk Tired 7
LATEST WORKOUTS May 23 Bel tr.t 4f fst :50 b

He therefore rates as an unknown horse, and since he is not the favorite, we can pass him by rather easily. The third choice in the betting is our old friend Sunny Puddles, whose last race was so poor that he cannot qualify on form.

Sunny Puddles Ch. g. 4, by Speak John—Big Puddles, by Delta Judge
Br.—Boggiano & Schwartz Mrs H (Ky)
Own.—Rockwood Stable Tr.—Campo John P

114 Turf Record St. 1st 2nd 3rd 6 0 0 1

	St.	1st	2nd	3rd	Amt.
1980	9	3	0	2	$37,380
1979	16	1	3	3	$25,140

5May80- 1Aqu fm 1⅛ Ⓣ:47 1:11⅗ 1:49⅕ 3↑ Allowance 1 2 21½ 53½ 79 612 Mena E G7 114 13.20 86-04 Audacious Fool 119¾ No Neck 1193¼ Crown Thy Good1191½ Tired 8
25Apr80- 7Aqu fst 1⅛ :48⅗ 1:13⅕ 1:51⅕ Allowance 5 1 11 1hd 1½ 11½ Mena E G10 107 7.40 79-26 SunnyPuddles1071½DresdenDew117¾SpeedyMagreedy1174 Driving 5
19Apr80- 7Aqu fst 1⅜ :48⅗ 1:38⅕ 2:18 Allowance 5 1 14 1½ 33½ 36¾ Mena E G10 106 11.40 84-17 Ivory Hunter 1152 Rabmab 1154¾ Sunny Puddles 1062¾ Tired 6
3Apr80- 9Aqu fst 1 3/16 :48 1:12⅕ 1:57⅗ Clm 30000 5 1 11½ 2hd 31 31¾ Velasquez J 117 4.30 72-20 Click Off 1171¾ Harry J. 117no Sunny Puddles 1171¾ Weakened 9
26Mar80- 2Aqu fst 1⅛ :47⅘ 1:12⅕ 1:51⅕ Clm 32500 7 4 35½ 32 44½ 43½ Hirdes J7 108 10.20 75-29 Tread Lightly 1171 Raise Charger 117½ Harry J. 1172 Weakened 8
1Mar80- 6Aqu fst 1½ ⊡:49⅕ 2:07 2:33⅕ Handicap 6 1 12 55½ 613 613 Hirdes J 109 30.00 72-17 Party Surprise 114¾ Identical 1225ProperlyPerson1161¾ Gave way 8
15Feb80- 8Aqu fst 170 ⊡:47⅕ 1:11⅘ 1:43⅕ Allowance 6 6 77½ 815 820 819 Gribcheck S B5 114 5.60 67-26 Subordinate 117hd Orfanik 1191 Psychosis 112hd No factor 8
2Feb80- 6Aqu fst 1 3/16 ⊡:47⅗ 1:13⅕ 2:00⅕ Allowance 7 1 16 15 11 1nk Gribcheck S B5 112 4.80e 77-27 Sunny Puddles 112nkBankersSun1172SpartanKnight1222¾ Driving 9
16Jan80- 6Aqu fst 1 3/16 ⊡:47⅘ 1:13 1:58⅖ Clm 18000 5 1 12 12 14 16 Hirdes J5 108 11.30 86-18 Sunny Puddles 1086 Pepysian 1121¾ DH BoldBobby112 Ridden out 10
26Dec79- 7Aqu gd 6f ⊡:23⅖ :48⅕ 1:14⅖ Clm 20000 7 6 73¼ 88 89 66¾ Santiago A 117 8.70 65-36 Lysippus 115½ Sandrito 1171¼ Rit Proud 1101 Outrun 8
LATEST WORKOUTS May 29 Bel Ⓣ 5f fm 1:00⅕ h (d) ●May 17 Bel tr.t 4f fst :47⅗ h Apr 16 Bel tr.t 4f fst :49⅖ b

With this, Danton King looks better and better as we make our comparison chart.

Odds	Horse	Ability		A Pts		F	Total
1.1	Danton King	:23.4	:24.2	21	18	Q4	43
2.9	Guillermo	Unknown		—	—	—	U
5.0	Sunny Puddles	—	—	—	—	NQ	NQ

In situations like this, you can expect an easy winner from a Double Advantage Horse off a Big Win. It looked to be the soundest investment of the day, and possibly the entire week. Watching this race might readily throw you off horses for life.

How could a horse that looked so good run so bad? Danton King trailed badly at every call, nearly out of sight, no run at all. I would readily believe that he was laboring under some grave disability, but you cannot know that when you go to the window to make your investment. We swallow our disappointment and look at the fourth race.

THIRD RACE

Belmont

JUNE 2, 1980

1 ⅜ MILES.(inner-turf). (2.11⅖) STARTER HANDICAP. Purse $18,000. 3-year-olds and uwpard which have started for a claiming price of $20,000 or less since August 1 1979. Weights, Friday, May 30. Declarations by 10:00 a.m., Saturday, May 31.

Value of race $18,000, value to winner $10,800, second $3,960, third $2,160, fourth $1,080. Mutuel pool $151,055, OTB pool $102,685. Track Exacta Pool $211,713. OTB Exacta Pool $157,892.

Last Raced	Horse	Eqt.A.Wt	PP	¼	½	¾	1	Str	Fin	Jockey	Odds $1
24May80 ^{4}Mth^{1}	Sir Violet	7 114	6	5½	5^{1½}	5^{4}	3^{3}	3^{4}	1¾	Encinas R I	9.50
29May80 ^{2}Bel^{2}	Guillermo	b 4 117	5	1^{1½}	1^{1½}	1^{1½}	1½	1½	2^{nk}	Martens G	2.90
28May80 ^{2}Bel^{7}	Hour Of Peace	3 109	3	3^{hd}	4^{3}	3^{hd}	4^{1½}	4^{5}	3^{2}	Miranda J	6.10
5May80 ^{1}Aqu^{6}	Sunny Puddles	4 114	4	2^{5}	2^{4}	2^{3}	2^{2}	2½	4^{9½}	Cruguet J	5.00
23May80 ^{5}Bel^{7}	Amano	7 120	1	4^{3}	3½	4½	5½	5½	5^{nk}	Castaneda M	10.70
23May80 ^{2}Bel^{1}	Danton King	b 3 112	2	6	6	6	6	6	6	Velasquez J	1.10

OFF AT 2:05 1/2 EDT. Start good, Won driving. Time, :23⅘, :48, 1:12⅘, 1:37, 2:01⅘, 2:14⅗, Course firm.

$2 Mutuel Prices:				
	9-(J)-SIR VIOLET	21.00	7.40	4.40
	8-(I)-GUILLERMO		4.40	3.60
	5-(F)-HOUR OF PEACE			5.20

$2 EXACTA 9-8 PAID $85.20.

4 BELMONT

5 ½ FURLONGS. (1.03) MAIDEN CLAMING. Purse $12,000. Fillies. 3-year-olds. Weights, 117 lbs. Claiming price $40,000 for each $5,000 to $30,000 2 lbs.

Coupled—Loveable Josie and Forever Agnes.

Frosty Erin

B. f. 2, by Irish Castle—College Tuition, by Rash Prince

$30,000 Br.—McLean & Minish (Ky)
Tr.—Brice Harold B Jr

Own.—Keller M **113**

St. 1st 2nd 3rd Amt.
1980 0 M 0 0

LATEST WORKOUTS May 28 Bel tr.t 4f fst :53 b May 24 Bel 4f fst :49⅖ hg May 17 Bel 5f fst :48⅕ hg May 12 Bel 4f fst :48⅕ hg

Turquoise Arrow

Ch. f. 2, by Hasty Flyer—Amazing Gem, by Amazing

$40,000 Br.—Bent Tree Farm (Fla)
Tr.—Morgan Jack B

Own.—Sahagian J **117**

St. 1st 2nd 3rd Amt.
1980 0 M 0 0

LATEST WORKOUTS May 29 Bel 5f fst 1:03⅗ h May 23 Bel tr.t 4f fst :51⅕ b May 16 Bel tr.t 3f fst :38⅖ b Apr 8 Bel 4f fst :51⅖ bg

Northern Devil

Ro. f. 2, by Barachois—Misty Devil, by Misty Day

$30,000 Br.—Binn M (NY)
Tr.—LaBoccetta Frank

Own.—Binn M **113**

St. 1st 2nd 3rd Amt.
1980 0 M 0 0

LATEST WORKOUTS May 29 Aqu 4f fst :49⅖ b May 24 Aqu 5f fst 1:05 b May 19 Aqu 5f gd 1:03⅗ b (d) May 14 Aqu 4f gd :49 hg(d)

Royal Trickster

Ch. f. 2, by Royal Saxon—Flim Flammer, by Tropical Breeze

$35,000 Br.—Nacaluso T (NY)
Tr.—Gullo Thomas J

Own.—Arkay Stable **108^{7}**

St. 1st 2nd 3rd Amt.
1980 0 M 0 0

LATEST WORKOUTS May 21 Bel tr.t 3f gd :38⅕ b May 14 Bel tr.t 4f gd :49⅖ b May 8 Bel 5f sly 1:05 b May 2 Bel 3f fst :37 hg

True Finish

Ch. f. 2, by True Knight—Big Finish, by Tronado

$40,000 Br.—Backer J W (Ky)
Tr.—DeBonis Robert

Own.—Harmonay R M **117**

St. 1st 2nd 3rd Amt.
1980 2 M 0 0

7May80- 4Aqu fst 5f :23⅗ :48⅕ 1:01 ⒻMd c-30000 6 5 2^{hd} 6^{4½} 6^{12} 6^{18} Fell J 117 7.20 62-20 [D]Ski Maid 112^{4½} Emperor's Daughter 110^{nk}Willnt112^{nk} Fell back 6

28Apr80- 4Aqu sly 4½f :22⅘ :46⅕ :52⅗ ⒻMd Sp Wt 5 8 6^{9} 5^{11} 5^{11} Skinner K 117 55.30 88-01 Sue Babe 117^{1½} Clare K. 117¾ Lady Goldberry 117^{7¾} Outrun 8

LATEST WORKOUTS May 26 Bel tr.t 4f fst :51⅕ b May 20 Bel 4f fst :53⅗ b May 14 Bel 4f gd :52 b Apr 17 Bel 4f fst :49 h

Loveable Josie

B. f. 2, by Bravest Roman—Miss Toomuch, by Uppercut

$40,000 Br.—Reynolds Mr-Mrs E (Ky)
Tr.—Barrera Luis

Own.—Gianca Stable **117**

St. 1st 2nd 3rd Amt.
1980 0 M 0 0

LATEST WORKOUTS May 29 Bel tr.t 5f fst 1:05 b May 23 Bel 5f fst 1:04 bg May 14 Bel 3f gd :37⅖ bg May 2 Bel 3f fst :36⅖ hg

Kennedy Key Doll

B. f. 2, by Kennedy Road—Laguna Doll, by Free America

$40,000 Br.—Key West Stable (Fla)
Tr.—Campo John P

Own.—Feinier I **117**

St. 1st 2nd 3rd Amt.
1980 0 M 0 0

LATEST WORKOUTS May 24 Bel 4f fst :47⅗ bg May 19 Bel 4f fst :49 hg May 15 Bel tr.t 4f fst :49⅘ b May 10 Bel tr.t 4f fst :50⅘ b

Willnt

B. f. 2, by Nostrum—Chateaurullah, by Chateaugay

$40,000 Br.—Jonabell Farm (Ky)
Tr.—Freeman Willard C

Own.—Freeman W C **117**

St. 1st 2nd 3rd Amt.
1980 2 M 1 1 $4,100

22May80- 4Bel my 5½f :23 :47⅖ 1:06⅕ ⒻMd 50000 1 2 3^{1½} 1½ 2^{hd} 3^{2¾} Cruguet J 113 *1.20 81-23 Jan Jil 117^{1} Best Flight 117^{1¾} Willnt 113^{7} Weakened 8

7May80- 4Aqu fst 5f :23⅗ :48⅕ 1:01 ⒻMd 30000 3 6 5^{3} 5^{2½} 4^{2} 3^{4¾} Gonzalez M A^{5} 112 2.70 75-20 [D]SkMd112^{4½}Empror'sDughtr110^{nk}Wllnt112^{nk} Stumbled, impeded 6

7May80-Placed second through disqualification

LATEST WORKOUTS May 30 Aqu 4f fst :51⅕ b May 19 Aqu 4f gd :53 b (d) May 6 Aqu 3f fst :39 b May 2 Aqu 4f fst :47⅗ h

Fabulous Music

Ch. f. 2, by Good Behaving—Doug's Serenade, by Royal Serenade

$40,000 Br.—Farnsworth Farms & Foxglove (Fla)
Tr.—Zito Nicholas P

Own.—Jablow M **117**

St. 1st 2nd 3rd Amt.
1980 2 M 0 0 $840

22May80- 4Bel my 5½f :23 :47⅖ 1:06⅕ ⒻMd 60000 8 7 7^{9¾} 7^{6} F^{8} 4^{9¾} Martens G 117 20.60 74-23 Jan Jil 117^{1} Best Flight 117^{1¾} Willnt 113^{7} Outrun 8

8May80- 4Aqu sly 5f :22⅘ :46⅖ :59⅕ ⒻMd Sp Wt 1 9 9^{18} 8^{19} 8^{15} 8^{13} Mena E G^{7} 110 22.70 76-22 Dandy Current117^{2¼}MadamePremier117^{2}NativeHula117^{no} Outrun 9

LATEST WORKOUTS May 17 Bel 4f fst :50 b May 2 Bel 4f fst :47⅘ h Apr 24 Bel 4f fst :49⅕ h Apr 19 Bel 4f fst :49⅘ h

Action Queen

Dk. b. or br. f. 2, by Big Bluffer—Lizabeth Action, by Ways and Means

$30,000 Br.—O'Quinn C (Fla)
Tr.—Martin Frank

Own.—Martin Charlene **113**

St. 1st 2nd 3rd Amt.
1980 1 M 0 0

22May80- 4Bel my 5½f :23 :47⅖ 1:06⅕ ⒻMd 50000 7 5 1^{hd} 2½ 4^{6} 6^{12} Asmussen C B 113 10.20 72-23 Jan Jil 117^{1} Best Flight 117^{1¾} Willnt 113^{7} Used up 8

LATEST WORKOUTS May 30 Bel tr.t 4f fst :49 b May 21 Bel tr.t 3f gd :36⅗ h May 15 Bel tr.t 3f fst :36⅖ h May 10 Bel tr.t 5f fst 1:01⅗ h

This time I have shown you the entire field, to illustrate the problems we encounter in maiden races. In our rules for making selections, I told you that in maiden special races where there were three or more first-time starters, we would pass the race unless the favorite showed outstanding credentials. But this race is a claiming event, where these two-year-old fillies are all entered for a price tag to be purchased by any operator willing to pay the bill. There are six first-time starters to lend an aura of the unknown about this event. In maiden claiming races, no matter how many first-time starters are entered, we will look to find a play, if one exists.

Here, we have a strong favorite, Willnt, at 4-5 on the board. We have to calculate her ability times by extending the short races to 6f figures. The 1:06.1 in the last race is equivalent to 1:12.3 at 6f, and with the :47.2 second call time gives a lead time of :25.1. Willnt loses three and adds one more for energy adjustment to come out with :26.0 off this race. In her other race at 5f, we extend the final time to 1:14.1 and compute a :26.0 lead time. There is another loss of 2 lengths in the running line and two more ticks to be added for energy adjustment to leave us with a :26.4.

As for early speed, while it is somewhat risky to compute in these races where so few of the horses have made any kind of record, we shall nevertheless use it, as it is still a factor. Willnt was within 2 lengths of the leader in one-half her races, that being one out of two, and thus gets 6 points.

The second choice, Loveable Josie, has not run, and with no ability time, will not figure in our ultimate consideration.

Action Queen, the third choice, has only one race, with an ability time of :27.3 off her far-back finish. However, she does get a 6 for early speed off that one race.

But remember, we also said that when a horse shows but one race on which ability time can be computed, we will use only the best ability time of the other horses among the first three favorites. We will be comparing the best time of Willnt, a :26.0, against the :27.3 of Action Queen.

Here is what we recapitulate:

Odds	Horse	Ability		A Pts		ES	F	Total
.8	Willnt	:26.0	:26.4	10	—	6	Q2	18
2.8	Loveable Josie	U	U					U
7.8	Action Queen	:27.3	—	3	—	6	Q	9

Although we are using only one race to compute ability points, you can see that Willnt's second effort was much better than the best of Action Queen, making her a Double Advantage Horse. You will have also noted the improved running line. This youthful filly, therefore, even with her low odds and even with the pile of unknowns in the race, is simply an outstanding selection, as good an investment as you will likely find.

If this were a maiden special event, as I indicated, I would quickly close my book on it. But here, Willnt is far and away the only animal in the race that shows anything at all. While a first-time starter in a claiming race occasionally scores an upset and wins, the probabilities are not sufficient to stop us.

Here is the outcome:

FOURTH RACE **5 ½ FURLONGS. (1.03) MAIDEN CLAMING. Purse $12,000. Fillies. 2-year-olds. Weights, 117 lbs. Claiming price $40,000 for each $5,000 to $30,000 2 lbs.**

Belmont

JUNE 2, 1980

Value of race $12,000, value to winner $7,200, second $2,640, third $1,440, fourth $720. Mutuel pool $131,847, OTB pool $67,792. Quinella Pool $146,724. OTB Quinella Pool $93,262.

Last Raced	Horse	Eqt.A.Wt	PP	St	¼	⅜	Str	Fin	Jockey	Cl'g Pr	Odds $1
22May80 ^{4}Bel^3	Willnt	2 117	7	4	3^{2}	$2^{1½}$	$1^{1½}$	$1^{1¾}$	Cruguet J	40000	.80
	Royal Trickster	2 108	4	1	2^{1}	$3^{1½}$	2^{2}	$2^{3¾}$	Attanasio R^7	35000	35.60
22May80 ^{4}Bel^4	Fabulous Music	2 117	8	6	4^{1}	4^{1}	$3^{½}$	$3^{½}$	Martens G	40000	10.30
	Loveable Josie	2 117	6	7	$6^{½}$	$5^{½}$	$4^{1½}$	4^{5}	Fell J	40000	2.80
22May80 ^{4}Bel^6	Action Queen	2 113	9	2	1^{2}	$1^{½}$	5^{2}	5^{3}	Asmussen C B	30000	7.80
	Frosty Erin	2 113	1	5	7^{4}	6^{4}	6^{4}	6^{nk}	Venezia M	30000	15.80
	Turquoise Arrow	2 117	2	9	8^{14}	8^{16}	7^{10}	7^{14}	Adams L	40000	31.40
7May80 ^{4}Aqu^6	True Finish	2 117	5	3	$5^{½}$	7^{2}	8^{12}	8^{10}	Cordero A Jr	40000	23.10
	Northern Devil	2 113	3	8	9	9	9	9	Rivera M A	30000	27.50

OFF AT 2:36, EDT. Start good, Won ridden out. Time, :23⅕, :47⅗, 1:00⅖, 1:07⅕ Track fast.

$2 Mutuel Prices:				
	8-(H)-WILLNT	3.60	2.80	2.60
	4-(D)-ROYAL TRICKSTER		13.80	6.60
	9-(I)-FABULOUS MUSIC			5.00
	$2 QUINELLA 4-8 PAID $53.20.			

We accept the small change, thank you, delighted to have it, and turn to the fifth race, a distance event out of the Belmont chute, where House Of Erin is the favorite.

5 BELMONT

1 1/16 MILES. (1.40⅘) CLAIMING. Purse $15,000. 4-year-olds and upward. Weight, 122 lbs. Non-winners of two races at a mile or over since May 1, allowed 3 lbs. Of such a race since then, 5 lbs. Claiming price $20,000; for each $1,000 to $18,000, 2 lbs. (Races when entered to be claimed for $16,000 or less not considered.)

House Of Erin — Ch. h. 5, by Irish Castle—Colinear, by Cohoes — **$20,000** — Br.—Stiles M (Ky) — Tr.—Martin Frank — **117**

Own.—Sommer Viola

	St.	1st	2nd	3rd	Amt.
1980	6	0	1	1	$9,480
1979	2	0	0	0	$238

18May80- 3Aqu	fst	1⅛	:48⅘	1:13⅖	1:52⅗	Clm 20000	5	3	2^{2}	2^{1}	$3^{½}$	$3^{1½}$	Rivera M A	b 117	*.90	70-19	Special Size 112^{1½} [D]Fellow Heir 110^{hd}HouseOfErin117^{2} Impeded	6
18May80-Placed second through disqualification																		
5May80- 3Aqu	fst	1	:45⅘	1:10⅕	1:36⅕	Clm 35000	4	2	$2^{½}$	$3^{1½}$	4^{4}	$4^{3¼}$	Asmussen C B	b 117	*2.00	82-19	CouponRate108^{1¼}MasterMagicin115^{1¾}PecefulCountry115^{nk} Tired	7
24Apr80- 3Aqu	fst	6f	:22⅕	:45⅕	1:10⅖	Clm 50000	5	1	4^{2}	3^{3}	3^{4}	$3^{6¼}$	Asmussen C B	b 117	7.60	85-21	Jim Balthrop 119^{5} Bold Phantom 122^{1¼}HouseOfErin117^{5½} Evenly	6
17Apr80- 7Aqu	fst	6f	:22⅖	:45⅗	1:11	3↑ Allowance	3	2	$3^{1½}$	$3^{3½}$	4^{5}	$4^{3¼}$	Asmussen C B	b 121	13.40	85-23	Golden Reality 118^{¾} BrightAndBrave121^{1¾}DynamiteCap123^{¾} Tired	6
9Apr80- 6Aqu	sly	6f	:22⅖	:46	1:10⅘	Allowance	6	4	$5^{3½}$	5^{5}	5^{10}	4^{11}	Asmussen C B	b 115	16.80	80-21	Current Rumor 115^{4½} Mr. Ed 110^{5¾} Zamboni 110^{½} Tired	6
20Mar80- 8Aqu	fst	7f	:22⅘	:46	1:23	Allowance	4	2	4^{1}	$7^{6½}$	7^{13}	7^{19}	Velasquez J	b 117	*1.70e	67-32	ClassicalBallet117^{6¾}ShantyToCastle112^{3}Emperor'sKey117^{1¾} Tired	8
10Mar79- 8Hia	fst	6f	:22	:44⅘	1:10⅗	Clm 40000	11	9	11^{14}	11^{22}	11^{15}	9^{12}	Solomone M	b 116	54.30	78-12	Drake's Dream 116^{3} Gap Knob 114^{hd} George's Duc120^{¾} No factor	12
28Feb79- 6GP	fst	6f	:21⅘	:44⅗	1:09⅗	Clm 50000	4	3	$8^{9¼}$	9^{17}	10^{18}	9^{16}	Velasquez J	b 116	36.20	75-17	Kintla's Folly 114^{2½} Old Dunk 112^{hd} GrayWillowsAce116^{hd} Outrun	10
22Jly78- 6Bel	fst	6f	:22⅗	:45⅖	1:09⅗	Clm 37500	5	4	$3^{1½}$	3^{4}	3^{5}	$5^{7½}$	Cauthen S	b 115	4.90	85-08	MgicMomentII115^{2½}SensitiveNos113^{2½}ChmpgnChppy117^{1¼} Tired	7
14Jly78- 3Bel	fst	7f	:22⅘	:46⅕	1:22⅗	Clm 40000	1	8	8^{7}	8^{7}	$5^{9½}$	4^{12}	Hernandez R	b 117	2.20	77-10	Data Link 113^{5½} Magic Moment II122^{5}NeverMind122^{1¾} No threat	8

LATEST WORKOUTS **May 27 Bel tr.t 4f fst :49 h** **May 14 Bel tr.t 3f gd :36 h** **May 2 Bel tr.t 4f fst :48 h** **Apr 8 Bel 3f fst :37⅗ b**

He qualifies on form easily from his last race. His best ability time came in the 5May80 run, where there was a :24.2 lead time with a loss of one to level at :24.3. In his last race, we get a :24.4 lead time, reduced by one for gain, but increased by three for energy to wind up with :25.1. We are now ready to look at Birkhill, the second choice at the windows.

Birkhill — B. c. 4, by Cabin—Mine Lovely, by Determine — **$18,000** — Br.—McBean P (Ky) — Tr.—Daniels Edward J Jr — **113**
Own.—Harmonay R M

Turf Record	St.	1st	2nd	3rd		St.	1st	2nd	3rd	Amt.
	1	0	0	0	1980	8	0	1	2	$5,660
					1979	19	5	5	2	$65,200

22May80- 2Bel	my	6f		:23	:46⅖	1:10⅗	Clm 20000	6	4	56	54	43	45	Cordero A Jr	b 117	3.70	84-23	Mika Song 108nk Fiveontheside 1173¾ RagingTorrent 1171	No threat	7
14May80- 9Suf	fst	6f		:22⅕	:46⅖	1:12⅗	3↑ Allowance	5	5	99¼	95	74¾	23½	Daniels W H	b 114	6.50	74-29	Westgate Brunswick 1143½ Birkhill 114nk Propaganda 1221	Rallied	9
12Apr80- 2Aqu	fst	1⅛		:49	1:13⅖	1:52⅕	Clm 20000	7	1	1hd	1hd	34½	36¼	Gonzalez M A5	b 112	*1.80	68-19	Lancer's Pride 117¾ Scamp Boy 1145½ Birkhill 1122½	Weakened	7
5Apr80- 1Aqu	my	7f		:23⅕	:46⅘	1:24⅘	Clm 25000	3	7	74	77¼	77½	54	Cordero A Jr	b 117	*1.40	73-28	Mansard 1102¾ Gifted Leader 117nk Triple Blessed 1151	Dull try	8
23Mar80- 2Aqu	my	1		:47	1:12⅕	1:37⅖	Clm 25000	5	8	63¼	64½	54½	33½	Maple E	b 117	4.20	75-25	Arctic Service 117¾ Ninfa's Gift 1172¾ Birkhill 117¾	Rallied	8
12Feb80- 4Aqu	fst	1⅛	⊡	:47⅕	1:12⅘	1:54	Clm 30000	8	3	39	35½	41	53¾	Attanasio R10	b 103	18.30	72-26	Harry J. 117hd Click Off 113¾ Adam's Pet 1171¾	Weakened	10
31Jan80- 9Aqu	fst	6f	⊡	:23⅖	:47⅖	1:12⅖	Clm 30000	11	5	107¼	1210	1115	1114	Martens G	b 115	12.50	68-25	Bold Phantom 1172 Coupon Rate 112½ Master A. J. 1173	Outrun	12
11Jan80- 6Aqu	fst	1⅛	⊡	:49⅕	1:13⅗	1:52⅖	Allowance	2	8	89¼	75¼	87¾	810	Amy J	b 117	7.40	74-19	Classical Ballet 1122¼ Orfanik 117hd El Kel 117½	No threat	9
29Dec79- 5Aqu	fst	170	⊡	:48⅖	1:13⅕	1:42⅗	Clm 37500	1	3	34	31½	24	24	Cordero A Jr	b 115	*2.20	85-19	Bankers Sun 1154 Birkhill 1152½ Harry J. 112nk	Second best	6
22Dec79- 2Aqu	gd	6f	⊡	:22⅗	:45⅗	1:11⅖	Clm 35000	3	5	44	56½	43½	1¾	Cordero A Jr	b 117	4.80	87-15	Birkhill 117¾ Strong Arm 115¾ Midnight Racer 119no	Driving	8

Our first problem here is whether the horse qualifies on form. He is not dropping in class, since the $18,000 claiming figure is obtained by the eight conditions shown on the listing of the race. He has no up-close calls, and the best gain we can obtain is four, from the first call to the stretch call. But even though the comment line doesn't use the term "Evenly," you can see that in his last race, he never gained or lost more than 2 lengths between calls. You will also see that he was much nearer the front in his last race, always a good sign. So, if you have a doubtful situation, where the horse is right on the borderline of qualifying on form or getting a discarding NQ, there is one further thing you can do to resolve any doubt you may have. Compare his last two running lines, if within the twenty-eight-day time span. If he has improved his ability time by two ticks or more, then he is more likely to be improving, and can qualify on form. In his last race, there was a :24.1 lead time, loss of 1 length, plus one tick more for energy, to give a :24.3. In his Suffolk race, there was a lead time of :26.1, less one for gain, plus one for energy, for a :26.1. The Belmont time is so superior that we must qualify Birkhill on form for this race.

Now, we can see what other ability times he has. We already have one good one, and the next best turns out to be his 11Jan80 run at Aqueduct with a :24.2

Fast and Strong — Ch. g. 7, by Olden Times—War Star, by River War — **$20,000** — Br.—Farnsworth Farm & Foxglove (Fla) — Tr.—Nash Joseph S — **117**
Own.—Schoninger B

Turf Record	St.	1st	2nd	3rd		St.	1st	2nd	3rd	Amt.
	7	0	0	2	1980	6	0	1	1	$4,105
					1979	18	4	2	4	$41,129

10May80- 2Aqu	fst	1⅜		:49⅗	1:39	2:17⅗	Clm 25000	5	5	53	31	22½	35¾	Cordero A Jr	117	8.30	87-13	Sir Gregor 108½ Mystic Era 1175¼ Fast and Strong 1171¾	Bid,tired	7
29Mar80- 2GP	fst	1⅛		:48⅕	1:12⅖	1:51⅘	Clm 20000	3	8	108¾	911	66½	46	Vasquez J	b 116	6.60	67-19	Great Reward 1161½ Pruneplum 1144½ Exaltado 116no	Rallied	10
8Mar80- 4GP	fst	1⅛		:47⅗	1:12⅕	1:51	Clm 25000	5	5	77¼	67½	68½	46½	Cordero A Jr	b 116	8.40	70-20	Jet Jumper 1091 Riley Ridge 1203 Lucky Gallant 1162½	No menace	10
9Feb80- 8Hia	fst	1⅛		:48⅖	1:13⅕	1:52⅕	Clm 25000	1	8	108	1111	916	721	Fell J	b 115	6.20	50-28	Pruneplum 1153¼ Rare Glow 1155 Kooky Monster 1141	No factor	11
29Jan80- 5Hia	fst	1⅛		:48⅖	1:13⅗	1:53⅕	Clm 20000	8	2	1hd	3nk	2hd	2nk	Fell J	b 116	8.40	66-25	Exaltado 105nk Fast and Strong 116nk Another Paris 1163	Gamely	8
19Jan80- 2Hia	fst	1⅛		:46⅘	1:12⅘	1:52⅗	Clm 20000	5	9	1014	105½	77½	612	Fell J	b 115	5.50	57-25	Three Fold 1142 Ole Pete 119hd Wet Net 1112	Outrun	12
13Dec79- 9Aqu	sly	170	⊡	:48⅕	1:13⅖	1:44⅕	3↑ Clm 25000	4	9	98	915	916	915	Encinas R I	b 117	24.20	66-20	Northen Wheys 1143 My Best Pie 1173¼ Special Size 117nk	Trailed	9
21Nov79- 7Key	fst	170		:46⅗	1:12⅖	1:43⅘	3↑ Clm 25000	5	7	710	78¾	57½	68¼	Wilson R	b 116	18.30	73-27	Cool And Noble 109¾ Forte Party 1164 LordNashua 114hd	No threat	10
11Nov79- 3Aqu	fst	1		:46⅖	1:11⅘	1:37	3↑ Clm 25000	1	8	912	911	712	713	Wacker D J5	b 112	14.10	68-15	Amano 1171¼ Debtor's Haven 119nk No Sir 1191¼	Outrun	9
12Oct79- 5Bel	sly	1⅛		:47⅕	1:12⅖	1:52⅕	3↑ Allowance	3	3	54	611	624	638	Castaneda M	b 117	13.90	28-24	Delta Leader 1144¾ Birkhill 1142¾ Dresden Dew 1143	Stopped	6

LATEST WORKOUTS May 31 Bel tr.t 3f fst :37⅗ b — May 17 Bel tr.t 4f fst :52⅖ b — May 5 Bel tr.t 1 fst 1:44⅗ b — May 1 Bel tr.t 6f my 1:17 b

lead time, a gain to reduce by three, and then a :51.0 first call time to require a five-tick add-on for energy. We finish with a healthy :24.4. The other betting choice is Fast and Strong, whose record may convince you he is neither.

He qualifies on form in his last race, with two up-close calls. His best ability effort is rated off his 8Mar80 race at Gulfstream, when we start with a :24.3 lead time, no gain in lengths, and an energy add-on of 3. When we add one more for Gulfstream's fast surface, we have a :25.2. The 29Jan80 race at Hialeah shows a :25.1 lead time with only an adjustment of two for energy to :25.3. Now, how do our three horses compare?

Odds	Horse	Ability		A Pts		F	Total
1.2	House Of Erin	:24.3	:25.1	17	14	Q	31
3.7	Birkhill	:24.3	:24.4	17	16	Q	33
4.2	Fast and Strong	:25.2	:25.3	13	12	Q	25

With a 2-point advantage, our investment choice is Birkhill. He ran strongly into the stretch and wound up getting nipped by a head by a long shot, as the chart reveals.

FIFTH RACE
Belmont
JUNE 2, 1980

1 1/16 MILES. (1.40⅗) CLAIMING. Purse $15,000. 4-year-olds and upward. Weight, 122 lbs. Non-winners of two races at a mile or over since May 1, allowed 3 lbs. Of such a race since then, 5 lbs. Claiming price $20,000; for each $1,000 to $18,000, 2 lbs. (Races when entered to be claimed for $16,000 or less not considered.)

Value of race $15,000, value to winner $9,000, second $3,300, third $1,800, fourth $900. Mutuel pool $159,023, OTB pool $110,122. Exacta Pool $217,374. OTB Exacta Pool $178,841.

Last Raced	Horse	Eqt.	A.	Wt	PP	St	¼	½	¾	Str	Fin	Jockey	Cl'g Pr	Odds $1
2Apr80 ^{1}Aqu^{11}	Crazy Chief	b	6	113	2	6	6^{1}	$5^{\frac{1}{2}}$	4^{3}	2^{5}	1^{hd}	Velasquez J	18000	14.50
22May80 ^{2}Bel^{4}	Birkhill	b	4	113	7	1	$4^{1\frac{1}{2}}$	$3^{\frac{1}{2}}$	$1^{\frac{1}{2}}$	$1^{\frac{1}{2}}$	2^{6}	Rivera M A	18000	3.70
23Apr80 ^{9}Aqu^{4}	Bee's Bay	b	4	113	5	7	$7^{\frac{1}{2}}$	$7^{\frac{1}{2}}$	$5^{\frac{1}{2}}$	$3^{\frac{1}{2}}$	3^{5}	Skinner K	18000	12.90
10May80 ^{2}Aqu^{3}	Fast and Strong	b	7	117	8	2	3^{hd}	4^{1}	6^{1}	$6^{\frac{1}{2}}$	$4^{\frac{3}{4}}$	Cordero A Jr	20000	4.20
19May80 ^{3}Aqu^{2}	House Of Erin	b	5	117	3	4	2^{1}	$2^{1\frac{1}{2}}$	3^{1}	4^{3}	$5^{1\frac{3}{4}}$	Hernandez R	20000	1.20
26May80 ^{2}Bel^{3}	Wimpfybell		4	113	1	8	8	8	7^{1}	7^{2}	6^{nk}	Borden D A	18000	6.40
18May80 ^{3}Aqu^{6}	Super Boy	b	7	113	6	3	$5^{1\frac{1}{2}}$	$6^{1\frac{1}{2}}$	8	8	$7^{1\frac{3}{4}}$	Saumell L	18000	35.20
25May80 ^{2}Bel^{9}	Ninfa's Gift		4	108	4	5	$1^{\frac{1}{2}}$	1^{1}	2^{hd}	5^{hd}	8	Gonzalez M A^{5}	18000	17.00

OFF AT 3:06 1/2 EDT. Start good, Won driving. Time, :24, :47⅗, 1:12⅘, 1:38⅕, 1:44⅘ Track fast.

$2 Mutuel Prices:

2-(B)-CRAZY CHIEF	31.00	10.80	5.40
7-(G)-BIRKHILL		5.60	3.80
5-(E)-BEE'S BAY			5.40

$2 EXACTA 2-7 PAID $198.00.

This race begins to illustrate the wisdom of place betting, which has not done too well by us up to this point. The healthy $5.60 that Birkhill paid for his second-place finish turns this race into a profit even with our loss in the win column, as place betting frequently does. We are now at the sixth race, where there are more of the usual problems that we encounter.

6 BELMONT

6 FURLONGS. (1.08⅘) ALLOWANCE. Purse $19,000. 3-year-olds and upward, which have never won two races. Weights, 3-year-olds, 114 lbs. Older, 122 lbs. Non-winners of a race other than claiming since May 1, allowed 3 lbs. Of such a race since April 15, 5 lbs.

Bailey's Beach

B. c. 4, by Graustark—Admiring, by Hail To Reason
Own.—Rokeby Stable **Br.—Mellon P (Va)** **Tr.—Miller Mack**

117

Turf Record	St.	1st	2nd	3rd
	3	0	2	1

	St.	1st	2nd	3rd	Amt.
1979	7	1	3	2	$22,760
1978	1	M	0	0	

5Nov79- 1Aqu	fst	7f	:23⅕	:46⅘	1:23⅖	3↑Md Sp Wt	5	4	5^{2¾}	3^{½}	1^{1}	1^{2½}	Fell J	b 120	*1.50	84-18	Bailey's Beach 120^{2½}CremeSilence120^{2}ArcticService120^{3¾}	Driving	8
15Oct79- 4Bel	gd	7f	:23⅗	:47⅕	1:26⅕	3↑Md Sp Wt	2	7	7^{6}	5^{6}	2^{2}	3^{1}	Fell J	b 119	*1.40	70-31	RoyalReasoning119^{no}Lionize109^{1}Bailey'sBech119^{7}	Stumbled start	8
7Oct79- 4Bel	fst	6f	:23	:46⅗	1:11⅘	3↑Md Sp Wt	2	7	8^{8¼}	8^{6}	4^{4½}	2^{1½}	Fell J	b 119	3.20	81-20	Gillotine 119^{1½} Bailey's Beach 119no Creme Silence 119^{nk}	Wide	8
13Jly79- 6Bel	fm	1 Ⓣ	:45⅘	1:10⅘	1:35⅗	3↑Md Sp Wt	6	7	7^{9}	4^{4}	4^{4}	3^{4}	Fell J	b 116	*.40	88-14	Sum Aid 116^{1¼} Fudge On 116^{2¾} Bailey's Beach 116^{3}	Wide	10
28Jun79- 6Bel	fm	1$\frac{1}{16}$ [T]	:46⅗	1:10⅘	1:43	3↑Md Sp Wt	7	6	4^{6}	2^{4}	2^{3}	2^{¾}	Velasquez J	114	*1.10	88-10	Legalese 114^{¾} Bailey's Beach 114^{1¼} Great Partner 114^{3}	Checked	10
17Jun79- 6Bel	fm	1$\frac{1}{16}$ Ⓣ	:45⅘	1:10⅕	1:41⅘	3↑Md Sp Wt	2	7	7^{12}	6^{7}	2^{2}	2^{1¼}	Velasquez J	114	*1.30	86-15	Silent Sunrise 122^{1¼} Bailey's Beach 114^{4} Dobrynin 117^{1¼}	Rallied	9
6Jun79- 2Bel	my	6f	:22⅗	:47	1:13⅖	3↑Md Sp Wt	11	10	8^{7}	5^{2¼}	5^{2½}	4^{1¾}	Velasquez J	114	9.50	73-31	Great Neck 114^{hd} Game Pride 114^{1¼} IlVagabondo122^{½}	No mishap	11
21Oct78- 1Bel	fst	6f	:23	:46⅖	1:11⅖	Md Sp Wt	2	8	8^{8¾}	7^{7}	7^{11}	6^{9¾}	Velez R I	122	22.00	75-12	Told 122^{¾} Spey 122^{1¼} Sparti 122^{5½}	No factor	8

LATEST WORKOUTS May 30 Bel 5f fst :59⅗ hg May 25 Bel 3f fst :37 b May 20 Bel 6f fst 1:15 b May 15 Bel 5f fst 1:00⅘ b

Towie

B. c. 4, by Triple Bend—Having A Ball, by Native Dancer
Own.—Happy Hill Farm **Br.—Wetherill Cortright (Ky)** **Tr.—Wright Frank I**

117

	St.	1st	2nd	3rd	Amt.
1980	1	0	1	0	$4,400
1979	5	1	0	0	$11,820

7May80- 5Aqu	fst	6f	:22⅖	:45	1:10⅘	3↑Allowance	6	4	3^{2}	2^{4}	2^{3}	2^{½}	Fell J	b 119	5.00	88-20	Shekels and Pesos 113^{½} Towie119^{hd}WarofWords112^{¾}	Just missed	9
23Aug79- 7Sar	fst	6f	:22⅕	:45⅕	1:10⅖	3↑Allowance	1	7	1^{hd}	3^{1½}	3^{1}	4^{4¼}	Amy J	b 117	8.60	84-16	Savings and Loan 114^{1½} Panzer 113^{½} Contare 113^{2¼}	Weakened	7
15Aug79- 1Sar	fst	7f	:22⅖	:44⅗	1:22⅘	3↑Allowance	4	5	3^{2}	2^{3}	4^{4½}	4^{6½}	Amy J	b 117	19.10	81-15	Priority 114^{3¼} Contare 113^{1¼} Pirate Chieftain 112^{2}	Weakened	8
26Jly79- 7Bel	fst	7f	:23	:46⅗	1:25	3↑Md Sp Wt	5	5	2^{2}	2^{½}	1^{3}	1^{nk}	Cordero A Jr	b 116	2.90	77-24	Towie 116^{nk} Princenesian 116^{3¾} Il Vagabondo 122^{¾}	Lasted	7
18Jly79- 7Bel	fst	6f	:22⅗	:46⅕	1:12	3↑Md Sp Wt	1	2	3^{3}	3^{1}	1^{½}	4^{1¼}	Amy J	116	12.30	81-23	Buckley 116^{½} Formitoo 116^{½} Treasury Bills 116^{nk}	Bore out	8
9Jly79- 6Bel	fst	6f	:22⅘	:46⅖	1:11⅗	3↑Md Sp Wt	5	8	6^{4¾}	7^{5}	6^{7½}	7^{9¾}	Amy J	116	10.20	74-15	French Colonial 122^{2} Romeo Lima 116^{2½} Game Pride116^{¾}	Outrun	12

LATEST WORKOUTS ●May 26 Bel 4f fst :46⅗ h May 20 Bel 3f fst :36⅗ b May 2 Bel 5f fst :58⅘ h Apr 25 Bel 4f fst :47⅗ hg

Bailey's Beach is the third choice in the betting, although he has not run since last November. He shows four workouts, but since he has won only one race in his life, he is not a stakes horse, and thus his form must be classed as unknown. We still must find out what his ability times show, however. His last 7f race in November can be converted to a 6f time of 1:10.4, which makes a lead time and an ability time of :24.0, very, very good. In his 7Oct79 race at Belmont, there is a lead time of :25.1, a gain of 4½ lengths to reduce it by three to :24.3, with one added for energy to give Bailey's Beach a :24.4. This unknown-form horse could be troublesome, except possibly for his lack of early speed.

There are only eight races showing in Bailey's Beach's past performances, and three of them are grass races to be ignored in computing early speed. In only one of these races was he within 5 lengths of the leader, and he thus winds up with 0 for early speed. This can be a serious deficiency if any other horse has strong early movement.

Towie, the favorite, puzzles us. His second-place finish qualifies him on form, but his ability times are weak. He gets a :25.1 off his only 1980 race where the lead time was :25.4, reduced by three for his gain. His next best figure is :25.4 off the 18Jly79 race at Belmont, where there were no adjustments. For early speed, there are six races to consider. You can readily see that in the last four, he was within 2 lengths or better of the lead at the first call, which entitles him to the full 6 points for early speed.

But now we have another factor, the second choice, Governor's Gun, who has run but one impressive race in his life.

Governor's Gun — B. g. 3, by Executioner—Hulla, by Luxemburgo — Br.—Hells Stock Farm (NJ) — Tr.—Toner John J — Own.—Kimmel C P — 114

	St.	1st	2nd	3rd	Amt.
1980	1	1	0	0	$6,720
1979	0	M	0	0	

27May80- 9Mth fst 6f :22⅘ :46 1:10⅘ 3↑Md Sp Wt 5 3 1hd 1½ 11 13 Cordero A Jr b 115 *.30 86–20 Governor's Gun 1153FascinatingJo115½AwdRock11513 Ridden out 7

LATEST WORKOUTS May 24 Aqu 4f fst :49⅕ b ●May 18 Aqu 6f fst 1:10⅗ h ●May 12 Aqu 5f fst :59⅘ h May 7 Aqu 4f fst :47⅘ hg

His only ability time was a :24.4 in his Monmouth victory, which is a true time since he set it all the way. For early speed he picks up 6 points as well, since his one race entitles him to that amount.

Let's now total up to see what we have.

Odds	Horse	Ability		A Pts		ES	F	Total
1.5	Towie	:25.1	:25.4	14	—	6	Q	20
1.6	Governor's Gun	:24.4	—	16	—	6	Q	22
4.8	Bailey's Beach	:24.0	:24.4	20	—	0	U	20

Even apart from his status as an unknown-form horse, Bailey's Beach, with his strong ability times, lacks the high total. The early-speed computation here becomes decisive. Governor's Gun's one race was markedly superior to the best that Towie could do, and Governor's Gun looks truly outstanding in this field.

SIXTH RACE
Belmont
JUNE 2, 1980

6 FURLONGS. (1.08⅘) ALLOWANCE. Purse $19,000. 3-year-olds and upward, which have never won two races. Weights, 3-year-olds, 114 lbs. Older, 122 lbs. Non-winners of a race other than claiming since May 1, allowed 3 lbs. Of such a race since April 15, 5 lbs.

Value of race $19,000, value to winner $11,400, second $4,180, third $2,280, fourth $1,140. Mutuel pool $203,741, OTB pool $106,155. Quinella Pool $187,326. OTB Quinella Pool $125,914.

Last Raced	Horse	Eqt.	A.	Wt	PP	St	¼	½	Str	Fin	Jockey	Odds $1
27May80 9Mth1	Governor's Gun	b	3	114	5	3	1hd	2 1½	1hd	1nk	Velasquez J	1.60
5Nov79 1Aqu1	Bailey's Beach	b	4	117	1	7	8½	7 1	5 3	2nk	Fell J	4.80
25May80 9Bel6	Mon Ami Gus	b	4	112	9	10	7½	6½	4hd	3 1¼	Lovato F Jr5	37.40
19Feb80 8Hia6	McCutcheon		3	113	3	1	2hd	1½	2 4	4¾	Rivera M A	15.30
7May80 5Aqu2	Towie		4	117	2	2	5 2	3½	3 1½	5 4	Cordero A Jr	1.50
4May80 9Aqu10	Wickerwork		3	104	10	4	6 2	8 4	8 1½	6 1½	Gonzalez M A5	20.00
16Mar80 2Aqu8	Little Perruader		3	114	8	9	10	10	9 4	7 2¾	Maple E	100.70
25May80 9Bel9	Pseudo Native		4	117	6	6	3½	5 3	6½	8nk	Castaneda M	72.80
20Mar80 6GP8	Lord Boyer	b	3	108	7	5	4 2	4hd	7½	9 5½	Beitia E5	10.40
11Jan80 8Hip9	Sin Boom		4	117	4	8	9 5	9 1½	10	10	Asmussen C B	63.30

OFF AT 3:38 EDT. Start good, Won driving. Time, :22⅘, :46⅖, 1:11⅖ Track fast.

$2 Mutuel Prices:			
5-(E)-GOVERNOR'S GUN	5.20	3.80	3.20
1-(A)-BAILEY'S BEACH		4.80	3.60
9-(I)-MON AMI GUS			8.60

$2 QUINELLA 1–5 PAID $16.60.

You can see that he was out of the gate early, showing his speed at the start, and had to fight off challengers, one after the other, holding on to stave off the rush of Bailey's Beach down the stretch. We are satisfied with this happy result.

Towie, as expected, was back in the middle of the field where he belonged. I am always puzzled when I see the sharp New York crowd latch onto a favorite who has almost no chance to win against some other much better horses. I can never be sure of the reason, but you will find jewels like this one over and over again. Let us hope that it continues and leave the bargains to us.

We're into the seventh race now where we can examine all three of these Lightly Raced Horses at once.

Moment Of Pleasure is the favorite off a good qualifying formful run. He is 7-5 on the board, but Mecca Road, whose one race is very poor, is being given heavy play. Mecca Road cannot qualify on form off that race, and thus we go back to Moment Of Pleasure to see what ability times he can reveal. His last race is brilliant, as he trimmed 1 length off that :24.2 lead time to rate a :24.1. His next best time, however, is only :25.3, off the 1Mar80 race at Hialeah, where the lead time was :25.2 with one tick added for energy.

Dusham is the third choice, but his only 1980 race was a grass event that places his form in the unknown category. His 1979 ability times are not likely to disturb the leaders here. His best was in the 11Aug79 race at Saratoga with a :25.0 lead time and a loss of one to :25.1. His shorter run at Belmont gets converted to a 6f final time of 1:10.2, for a :25.0 lead time. There was a loss of a length to give him another :25.1 ability time figure. Here is what we now have:

Odds	Horse	Ability		A Pts		F	Total
1.4	Moment Of Pleasure	:24.1	:25.3	19	12	Q	31
1.7	Mecca Road	—	—	—	—	NQ	NQ
3.3	Dusham	:25.1	:25.1	14	14	U	28

It is apparent that Moment Of Pleasure is our choice to win and place. As we still puzzle over how Mecca Road could be so low in the odds from his only race, we watched him score an impressive victory. Moment Of Pleasure ran third.

SEVENTH RACE
Belmont
JUNE 2, 1980

1 1/16 MILES. (1.40⅗) MAIDEN SPECIAL WEIGHT. Purse $18,000. 3-year-olds and upward. Weights, 3-year-olds, 114 lbs. Older, 122 lbs.

Value of race $18,000, value to winner $10,800, second $3,960, third $2,160, fourth $1,080. Mutuel pool $283,554, OTB pool $109,402.

Last Raced	Horse	Eqt.	A.Wt	PP	St	¼	½	¾	Str	Fin	Jockey	Odds $1
22May80 9Bel4	Mecca Road		3 114	2	4	41	3½	1hd	1½	12	Encinas R I	1.70
28May80 6Bel10	Chambersville	b	3 114	5	2	3½	44	43	33	2hd	Saumell L	5.50
10May80 5Aqu2	Moment Of Pleasure		3 115	3	3	1hd	2½	2½	21½	33½	Castaneda M	1.40
19May80 1Aqu8	Dusham		3 114	4	1	21½	1hd	3½	42	43½	Maple E	3.30
22May80 9Bel8	Waj. Jr.		3 114	1	5	5	5	5	5	5	Cruguet J	20.40

OFF AT 4:08 EDT. Start good, Won ridden out. Time, :24⅗, :48, 1:12⅗, 1:38⅖, 1:45⅕ Track fast.

$2 Mutuel Prices:			
2-(B)-MECCA ROAD	5.40	3.80	2.20
7-(G)-CHAMBERSVILLE		4.40	2.40
3-(C)-MOMENT OF PLEASURE			2.10

This is another of the mysteries of handicapping the races that one has to accept. Off the one performance showing in the *Daily Racing Form,* no one could bet Mecca Road to win. But his backers obviously knew something, as they poured in the money on their choice. These kinds of unexplainable victories do occur frequently among Lightly Raced Horses, where there is not enough of a record revealed. While this does leave us with certain hazards in playing these cards, there are far too many sound opportunities that would be neglected if we attempted to pass. Therefore, we will play them hard and close and continue to take our chances.

The eighth race, however, is a quite different matter. It is an allowance race on the grass for New York State–breds.

8 BELMONT

1 1/16 MILES. (TURF). (1.39⅘) ALLOWANCE. Purse $31,000. 3-year-olds and upward. Foaled in New York State and approved by the New York State-Bred Registry, which have never won three races other than maiden, claiming or starter. Weights, 3-year-olds, 114 lbs. Older, 122 lbs. Non-winners of two races other than maiden or claiming at a mile or over since April 15, allowed 3 lbs. Of such a race since then, 5 lbs.

When we start looking at past performances, we see that Quintessential, the favorite, has never run on the grass. That leaves him out. Quid Pro Gal, the second choice, has had grass experience but has not run since back in 1979 and lacks four workouts. This eliminates any qualifying on form, and rates an unknown. Then the third choice, Good Time Lad, has also never run on the grass. With two unknown-ability entries and one other not racing since 1979, this requires us to pass this race altogether. Investing in any one of those three would be gambling to the fullest.

But here is what did happen.

EIGHTH RACE
Belmont
JUNE 2, 1980

1 1/16 MILES.(turf). (1.39⅘) ALLOWANCE. Purse $31,000. 3-year-olds and upward. Foaled in New York State and approved by the New York State-Bred Registry, which have never won three races other than maiden, claiming or starter. Weights, 3-year-olds, 114 lbs. Older, 122 lbs. Non-winners of two races other than maiden or claiming at a mile or over since April 15, allowed 3 lbs. Of such a race since then, 5 lbs.

Value of race $31,000, value to winner $18,600, second $6,820, thi-d $3,720, fourth $1,860. Mutuel pool $151,465, OTB pool $135,180.

Last Raced		Horse	Eqt.	A.	Wt	PP	St	¼	½	¾	Str	Fin	Jockey	Odds $1
19May80	8Aqu6	Quintessential		3	109	7	4	2hd	3½	31	11½	1¾	Velasquez J	2.40
16May80	3Aqu5	Down The Drain		4	117	10	7	61	5½	63	4hd	22	Skinner K	27.80
12May80	2Aqu6	The Boy Mikey	b	4	117	8	8	4hd	41½	4½	2½	3½	Cruguet J	8.40
6Jly79	8Bel2	Quid Pro Gal		5	112	1	3	8½	61½	5½	54	41¼	Venezia M	2.90
7May80	6Aqu7	Hammertown	b	4	112	9	5	32	21½	1hd	31	51¾	Beitia E5	13.30
22May80	1Bel6	Tall Story	b	5	112	2	2	102	10½	82	6½	65	Tejada V M Jr5	59.00
15May80	3Aqu4	Troy		4	112	3	1	1½	1hd	2½	74	72	Samyn J L	6.10
22May80	5Bel4	Good Time Lad	b	6	112	6	9	7½	7½	71	86	85	Lovato F Jr5	3.80
8May80	3Aqu5	Garamar	b	5	112	4	6	5½	9hd	11	105	92	Gonzalez M A5	65.10
12May80	2Aqu7	Happy Edwardo	b	4	117	5	10	11	11	93	91	109	Asmussen C B	15.30
8May80	3Aqu7	John Roche	b	5	117	11	11	9½	82	102	11	11	Encinas R I	59.40

OFF AT 4:41 1/2; EDT Start good for all but JOHN ROCHE & HAPPY EDWARDO, Won driving. Time, :23⅖, :47⅖, 1:11⅗, 1:37, 1:43⅖ Course firm.

$2 Mutuel Prices:			
7-(G)-QUINTESSENTIAL	6.80	3.80	3.40
11-(K)-DOWN THE DRAIN		15.80	8.20
8-(H)-THE BOY MIKEY			5.20

Quintessential, the favorite, won it over a rank outsider. But in the absence of any grass record, there was no way a wager could have been made. We doff our hat to those knowledgeable enough to have confidence in Quintessential, and move on to the last race of the day to look over the maiden claimers to see if there is further hope for profit.

This campaigner down from Canada qualifies on form from his second-place finish in his first American start and picks up the role of slight favorite. The best ability time we can compute for him comes from his 15Aug79 race at Fort Erie, where there was a :26.2 lead time. Off his gain, we reduce this by three to :25.4 and give him two more for energy for a :26.1 ability time. Off his

9 **BELMONT**

7 FURLONGS. (1.20⅖) MAIDEN CLAIMING. Purse $9,000. 3-year-olds and upward. Weights, 3-year-olds, 114 lbs. Older, 122 lbs. Claiming price $14,000 for each $1,000 to $12,000 2 lbs.

Steady Rodger — Own.—Leslie R E — $13,000 — Dk. b. or br. c. 3, by Tell—Paris Dance, by Tulyar — Br.—Spears-Olsson Breeding Syndicate (Ky) — Tr.—Jerkens Steven T — 112

Turf Record: St. 2, 1st 0, 2nd 0, 3rd 1

	St.	1st	2nd	3rd	Amt.
1980	1	M	1	0	$1,980
1979	5	M	1	1	$2,252

28May80- 9Bel	fst	6f		:22⅘	:47	1:13⅘	3↑ Md 15000	4	5	36	21	2½	2¾	Encinas R I	b	111	5.10	72-24	Hivarum 111¾ Steady Rodger 111hd Taunt 1202	Gamely	11
22Sep79- 4WO	fst	170		:47	1:13⅖	1:45	Md Sp Wt	3	4	41½	42½	76¼	1110	Gomez A	b	122	9.05	68-23	Dusty Old Farmer 117hd Someolio Man 1176 LeBraconnier 1171	Tired	13
9Sep79- 4WO	fm	*5f	Ⓣ	:22⅗	:47⅘	:59⅕	Md Sp Wt	8	9	53½	35	39	311	Dittfach H		122	3.60	84-07	Lord Elgin 1147½ Rash Idea 1173 Steady Rodger 122½	Rallied	10
22Aug79- 5FE	fm	*7f	Ⓣ	:24	:47⅘	1:27⅘	Md Sp Wt	2	3	43½	44	53	43½	Dittfach H		122	2.85	77-24	Helio You 1222 Still Can Do 117no Mister Country 1171½	Evenly	6
15Aug79- 4FE	fst	6f		:23	:46⅗	1:13	Md 22500	3	8	66½	611	46	24¾	Dittfach H		122	4.15	77-17	Worth A Look 1224¾ Steady Rodger 122nk Explosive Era 1222½	Gamely	9
1Aug79- 3FE	gd	5f		:23⅕	:47	:59⅗	Md Sp Wt	7	7	53	65¼	711	711	Dittfach H		122	2.80	79-16	Triple Tara 1141¾ Sir Gordon 1171½ Aftermath 1172½		7

LATEST WORKOUTS May 15 Bel tr.t 4f fst :50 b — May 4 Bel tr.t 5f fst 1:06 b — Apr 30 Bel tr.t 3f my :38⅘ b (d) — Apr 26 Bel tr.t 4f fst :53 b

22Sep79 race at Woodbine, we have a :26.2 lead time, with one added for loss and one more for energy for an ability time of :26.4. We know that with these times, this horse will have to have some pretty slow competition to win today. But let's find out about early speed before we go any further. Of the six races shown, two are on the turf, leaving us with four to consider for early speed. In two of those, he was within 5 lengths of the lead at the first call, which entitles him to 2 points.

The second choice is Bronco Buster, and here is what he shows.

***Bronco Buster** — B. c. 4, by Busted—Aberangell, by Abernant — $12,000 — Own.—Roebling J M — Br.—Wyatt M G (Eng) — Tr.—Baeza Braulio — 1117

Turf Record	St.	1st	2nd	3rd			St.	1st	2nd	3rd	Amt.
	3	0	0	0		1980	8	M	2	1	$6,940
						1979	9	M	0	0	$4,020

8May80- 1Aqu sly 7f	:23⅕	:47	1:24⅘	3↑Md 12000	2	10	89¼	57½	33½	33¾	Attanasio R7	b	113	6.60	73–22	Needabuc 1141 Noble Side 1152¾ Bronco Buster 1139	Rallied	14
30Apr80- 1Aqu my 1	:46⅗	1:12⅖	1:39⅕	3↑Md 14000	4	5	42¼	32	43	43¾	Beitia E5	b	117	3.30	66–21	IndianDd1141¾GiftImpression114¾FisheryCouncil1151¼	Weakened	7
18Apr80- 1Aqu fst 6f	:22⅗	:46⅕	1:12⅗	3↑Md 14000	6	7	64	44	56½	42¾	Beitia E5	b	117	4.10	77–24	Royal Jove 114¾ Aerie 108¾ Gibby's Choice 1081¼	No factor	8
27Mar80- 3Aqu fst 1	:47⅕	1:12⅗	1:39⅕	3↑Md 14000	3	6	63¼	43	41	41¾	Velez R I	b	122	2.80	68–23	Bello Boy 111hd Royal Jove 1131½ Flip Phillips 112nk	Steadied	7
21Mar80- 2Aqu sly 1⅛	:50⅖	1:15⅖	1:55⅘	Clm 12500	3	2	2hd	52	819	826	Velez R I	b	117	13.90	30–32	Hospitable 1122 Back Again 114¾ Sir Violet 1105	Fin. far turn	8
23Feb80- 2Aqu gd 1⅛ ⊡	:48⅕	1:13⅘	1:53⅕	Clm 11500	8	7	76¾	52¾	42	51½	Beitia E5	b	110	7.70	78–17	Cliff Chesney 106¾ Cincelari 114nk Amano 117nk	Evenly	9
4Feb80- 3Aqu fst 1$\frac{1}{16}$ ⊡	:48⅗	1:14⅘	1:49⅕	Md 15000	3	5	43½	32	4¾	21¼	Velez R I	b	120	2.80	67–22	DoubleEdgeBlde1171¼BroncoBustr120nkOkchobRod110hd	Gamely	8
18Jan80- 3Aqu fst 1¼ ⊡	:51⅗	1:42	2:08⅕	Md 10500	4	4	41½	3½	1hd	22½	Velez R I	b	122	5.80	74–19	Boldly Yours 1222½ Bronco Buster 1225 Side Pocket 1134	Gamely	6
16Nov79- 3Aqu fst 1⅛	:48⅖	1:14⅖	1:53⅗	3↑Md 25000	7	6	56½	52¾	57½	511	Velez R I	b	120	23.10	56–26	Metro 1201 Winter Romance 1172 Nitroglycerin 1167½	No factor	7
19Oct79- 9Aqu fst 1⅛	:47⅘	1:13	1:53⅘	3↑Md 25000	2	2	2½	21	66½	610	Velez R I	b	119	5.70	56–23	ⒹMetro 1192¾ Pass The Salt 115¾ Forreko 1194	Tired	10

LATEST WORKOUTS May 29 Bel tr.t 4f fst :52 b May 25 Bel tr.t 4f fst :51 b May 6 Bel tr.t 3f fst :38 b ●Apr 28 Bel tr.t 4f sly :49⅘ h (d)

He qualifies on form because of his gain in excess of five from the first call to the stretch call in his last race. Back on 27Mar80, there was a :25.2 lead time, with no gain or loss, and one added for energy to produce a :25.3 ability time. We can find that figure on two other occasions, but his bottom-line race of 19Oct79 is enough, where there was a :25.1 lead time with a loss of one in the running line and another tick added for energy.

As for early speed, there is a reasonably good showing, as there are seven out of his ten races where he was within 5 lengths at the first call. He, too, winds up with 2 early-speed points.

Now we can turn to see what Taunt, the third choice on the board, reveals.

Taunt — Gr. c. 4, by Pontoise—Make Me Laugh, by Jester — $13,000 — Own.—Zelano J — Br.—Lever L (Ky) — Tr.—Simmons Mary Lou — 120

	St.	1st	2nd	3rd	Amt.
1980	4	M	0	1	$1,560
1979	3	M	1	0	$1,540

28May80- 9Bel fst 6f	:22⅘	:47	1:13⅘	3↑Md 14000	10	10	79	31½	1½	3¾	Suman S	b	120	15.50	72–24	Hivarum 111¾ Steady Rodger 111hd Taunt 1202	Circled horses	11
16May80- 9Aqu fst 6f	:22⅗	:46	1:11⅘	3↑Md 18000	7	8	43½	42½	810	816	Suman S	b	120	9.90	68–16	Gibby's Choice 1132 The Wiley Fox 1134½ Yacqui 1131¼	Bore out	10
28Jan80- 1Aqu fst 6f ⊡	:22⅘	:47⅕	1:14⅕	Md c-12500	2	8	1hd	12	22	58	Asmussen C B	b	122	*1.90	65–23	Limited Vision 1224 Sir Raja 1152¾ Dasht 118hd	Used up	12
10Jan80- 3Aqu fst 6f ⊡	:22⅘	:47	1:13⅖	Md 12500	2	9	63¾	44	33	43½	Rocco J5	b	117	*1.90	73–19	RidgeBlvd.118½DoubleEdgeBlde1222¾FlywheelPowr117nk	Even try	12
31Dec79- 4Aqu fst 6f ⊡	:22⅘	:46⅘	1:12⅕	3↑Md 12500	4	5	11½	13	2½	28	Maple E	b	120	2.60	75–19	Indeed Gallant 1208 Taunt120½ DH DoubleEdgeBlade120	No match	9
24Dec79- 4Aqu my 6f ⊡	:23⅕	:47⅕	1:13⅖	3↑Md 15000	3	9	5¾	2hd	21½	58¼	Maple E	b	120	5.80	69–27	Joe Montage 1093¾ Bunky 1164 Tramboline 112nk	Tired	10
28Nov79- 6Aqu gd 6f	:22⅗	:46⅖	1:12	3↑Md 20000	8	8	2hd	2hd	67	913	Maple E		120	6.60	70–17	Wheat Broker 1202¼ Peon 1221¾LordRumbottom120½	Early speed	9

LATEST WORKOUTS May 14 Bel tr.t 4f gd :49⅖ b May 10 Bel 6f fst 1:14 h May 6 Bel 5f fst 1:02 b May 2 Bel 5f fst 1:01⅕ h

He, too, qualifies on form off his last race. But his ability times are atrocious. His 10Jan80 shows a :26.2 lead time with one added for energy to give him a :26.3. His last race at Belmont carries a lead time of :26.4 with one added for energy to give him a :27.0 figure. As for early speed, among the seven races in which he has run, four of them show Taunt with excellent early foot, which entitles him to 4 points in that department.

Here is what the final ratings show:

Odds	Horse	Ability		A Pts		ES	Q	Total
2.1	Steady Rodger	:26.0	:26.4	10	6	2	Q	18
2.3	Bronco Buster	:25.3	:25.3	12	12	2	Q	26
6.4	Taunt	:26.3	:27.0	7	5	4	Q	16

This race shows why those who tell you never play maiden races are leading you into overlooking some splendid opportunities. Bronco Buster, besides being far and away ahead on total points, was a true Double Advantage Horse, one of the strongest plays in racing. The real criterion in any race is whether or not one horse is superior to another with a sufficient advantage to merit an investment. This race was one of the true gems of the week, as we invest in Bronco Buster to win and place and smile with pleasure at this result.

NINTH RACE
Belmont
JUNE 2, 1980

7 FURLONGS. (1.20⅗) MAIDEN CLAIMING. Purse $9,000. 3–year–olds and upward. Weights, 3–year–olds, 114 lbs. Older, 122 lbs. Claiming price $14,000 for each $1,000 to $12,000 2 lbs.

Value of race $9,000, value to winner $5,400, second $1,980, third $1,080, fourth $540. Mutuel pool $119,597, OTB pool $153,078. Track Triple Pool $171,969. OTB Triple Pool $317,122.

Last Raced	Horse	Eqt.	A.	Wt	PP	St	¼	½	Str	Fin	Jockey	Cl'g Pr	Odds $1
8May80 ^{1}Aqu^{3}	Bronco Buster	b	4	111	6	9	7^{2}	$6\frac{1}{2}$	$1^{1\frac{1}{2}}$	$1^{3\frac{3}{4}}$	Attanasio R^{7}	12000	2.30
29May80 ^{1}Mth^{2}	Knight Graustark	b	3	106	7	11	8^{1}	7^{4}	4^{hd}	2no	Lovato F Jr^{5}	12000	7.00
28May80 ^{9}Bel^{2}	Steady Rodger	b	3	112	3	6	1^{hd}	2^{2}	$2^{1\frac{1}{2}}$	3^{4}	Encinas R I	13000	2.10
24Apr80 ^{1}Aqu^{6}	Pat Per Chance	b	3	112	10	2	3^{hd}	$3\frac{1}{2}$	5^{3}	$4^{1\frac{1}{4}}$	Asmussen C B	12000	17.20
28May80 ^{9}Bel^{3}	Taunt	b	4	120	4	7	$4\frac{1}{2}$	$1^{1\frac{1}{2}}$	3^{2}	5^{nk}	Suman S	13000	6.40
23May80 ^{4}Bel^{9}	One for Curt	b	4	118	2	8	10^{5}	8^{hd}	$8\frac{1}{2}$	$6\frac{3}{4}$	Brocklebank J	12000	16.70
2Apr80 ^{9}Aqu^{7}	Permanent Peace		4	118	5	10	11	11	$7\frac{1}{2}$	$7^{1\frac{1}{4}}$	Mora G	12000	32.50
13Apr80 ^{3}Aqu^{7}	The Catcher	b	3	114	9	1	5^{1}	4^{1}	6^{1}	$8\frac{1}{2}$	Rivera M A	14000	7.00
24Mar80 ^{1}Aqu^{9}	Native Stand	b	3	114	1	4	$6\frac{1}{2}$	10^{1}	10^{4}	$9\frac{3}{4}$	Skinner K	14000	49.60
6May80 ^{7}GP^{8}	Expedite	b	3	114	8	5	$2^{1\frac{1}{2}}$	5^{1}	9^{3}	10^{7}	Santiago A	14000	34.40
28May80 ^{9}Bel^{5}	Rebel Lord	b	3	114	11	3	9^{1}	9^{3}	11	11	Giraldo L	14000	47.80

OFF AT 5:10 EDT. Start good, Won driving. Time, :22⅘, :46⅗, 1:12⅗, 1:26⅕ Track fast.

$2 Mutuel Prices:

6–(F)–BRONCO BUSTER	6.60	4.20	2.80
7–(G)–KNIGHT GRAUSTARK		6.60	3.60
3–(C)–STEADY RODGER			2.60

$2 TRIPLE 6–7–3 PAID $161.00.

Bronco Buster scored a Big Win, pulling away from the field as he increased his lead in the stretch. It is most pleasant to end the day on such a positive note as we recapitulate to see what our total effort for the afternoon produced.

Race	Selection	Invest		Return	
		Win	Place	Win	Place
1	La Atrevida	$ 2	$ 2	$ 7.60	$ 4.00
2	Silver Ray	2	2	0	0
3	Danton King	2	2	0	0
4	Willnt	2	2	3.60	2.80
5	Birkhill	2	2	0	5.60
6	Governor's Gun	2	2	5.20	3.80
7	Moment Of Pleasure	2	2	0	0
8	Pass	—	—	—	—
9	Bronco Buster	2	2	6.60	4.20
	Totals	$16	$16	$23.00	$20.40

Total invested $32.00
Total returned $43.40
Net profit $11.40

This has turned out to be another delightful day. Our profit off money invested is 36%, which is about what we expect on most days under this investment program. We had four winning selections out of eight playable races, and also scored a solid, although not outstanding, profit in place wagering. These are the margins we need to keep up the returns.

We now have a day off, since Belmont does not run on Tuesdays. We rest easy, gear up for the remainder of the week, and come back on Wednesday, June 4, for our third round.

CHAPTER

XI

BIG WEEK AT BELMONT: THIRD DAY, WEDNESDAY, JUNE 4, 1980

With two winning days behind us, we return for the third day, after the recess for Tuesday, with the usual degree of confidence you will soon have when you make the solid selections that our investment method reveals. We plunge into the first race, and look at the record of the favorite, Don't You Worry.

Immediately, we see a problem with form. His last effort was atrocious. There is not a single qualifying factor, and the horse is even being raised in class off a claim. He is a Declining Horse in every respect, to be shunned like the plague. We are puzzled again how a sophisticated New York crowd could

1 BELMONT

START
1⅛ MILES
BELMONT PARK
FINISH

1 ⅛ MILES. (1.45⅗) CLAIMING. Purse $15,000. Fillies, 3–year–olds. Weight, 121 lbs. Non–winners of two races over a mile since May 1 allowed 3 lbs. Of such a race since then, 5 lbs. Claiming price $25,000; for each $2,500 to $20,000, 2 lbs. (Races where entered to be claimed for $18,000 or less not considered.)

Don't You Worry — Ch. f. 3, by Raise A Cup—Island Schooner, by Herbager

$25,000 — Br.—Nuckols Bros (Ky) — Tr.—DeBonis Robert — **118**

Own.—Martin Gertrude A

	St.	1st	2nd	3rd	Amt.
1980	9	3	1	2	$30,880
1979	6	1	0	0	$6,000

25May80- 6Bel	fst	7f		:23	:46⅗	1:25⅗	ⒻClm c-20000	5	7	6^{6}	8^{10}	8^{13}	7^{21}	Rogers K L5	b 116	3.80	53-16	Singh Baby 112¾ Lorine 111^{2} Here Dear 111^{8}	No factor	9
8May80- 2Aqu	sly	1⅛		:47⅗	1:13⅖	1:53⅖	ⒻClm 25000	2	3	3^{5}	$3^{2\frac{1}{2}}$	2^{1}	1no	Miranda J	b 118	*2.70	68-22	Don't You Worry 118no Dora Star $112^{1\frac{1}{2}}$ Suzzie 111^{6}	Driving	7
17Apr80- 2Aqu	fst	1⅛		:48⅗	1:14⅗	1:54⅘	ⒻClm c-20000	4	5	5^{5}	4^{2}	1^{hd}	1^{2}	Fell J	b 116	*1.20	61-23	Don'tYouWorry116^{2}LghtUpThSky116^{1}FlghtofthS109½	Ridden out	6
10Apr80- 9Aqu	gd	1		:46⅕	1:11⅖	1:38⅗	ⒻClm 16000	5	9	7^{11}	$7^{5\frac{3}{4}}$	$5^{2\frac{3}{4}}$	$3^{\frac{3}{4}}$	Beitia E5	b 111	*2.90	72-16	Go Bananas 107¾ Dora Star 114^{hd} Don't You Worry 111½	Fin. well	11
28Mar80- 5Aqu	fst	6f		:22⅗	:46⅗	1:13⅖	ⒻClm 20000	4	7	7^{11}	6^{10}	6^{9}	$5^{4\frac{1}{2}}$	Fell J	118	3.80	71-24	McSpoodle$111^{1\frac{1}{4}}$SisterRuben$107^{1\frac{3}{4}}$GussWht'sUp116^{nk}	No menace	7
13Mar80- 2Aqu	fst	1$\frac{1}{16}$	⊡	:48⅖	1:15⅘	1:50⅗	ⒻClm 19000	6	7	7^{11}	$5^{6\frac{3}{4}}$	2^{4}	$1^{1\frac{1}{4}}$	Beitia E5	110	3.00	61-23	Don'tYouWorry$110^{1\frac{1}{4}}$MoonChild$107^{2\frac{3}{4}}$SymmtricGl114^{2}	Drew clear	8
2Mar80- 2Aqu	fst	1$\frac{1}{16}$	⊡	:48⅘	1:16	1:48⅖	ⒻClm 20000	1	5	$6^{8\frac{3}{4}}$	6^{8}	4^{7}	$3^{9\frac{3}{4}}$	Beitia E5	109	3.30	62-19	MrshmllowCrm116^{nk}DrToBCptn$117^{9\frac{1}{2}}$Don'tYoWrry$109^{4\frac{1}{2}}$	No rally	7
14Feb80- 2Aqu	fst	6f	⊡	:22⅘	:47⅖	1:15	ⒻClm 15000	5	11	10^{11}	10^{11}	$5^{3\frac{1}{4}}$	2^{nk}	Beitia E5	111	6.80	69-25	Jenne'sRuler116^{nk}Don'tYouWorry$111^{2\frac{1}{2}}$Degusttion116^{1}	Bold rush	11
27Jan80- 3Aqu	fst	6f	⊡	:22⅗	:46⅘	1:13⅕	ⒻClm 20000	6	1	$5^{6\frac{1}{2}}$	$5^{6\frac{1}{2}}$	6^{7}	$5^{6\frac{1}{2}}$	Wacker D J5	111	15.90	71-17	GlorousTms$109^{5\frac{1}{2}}$DncngDplomt116^{hd}CuttngThWnd116¾	No threat	6
26Nov79- 1Aqu	sly	6f		:22⅘	:46⅘	1:12⅘	ⒻClm 25000	4	2	6^{7}	$6^{9\frac{1}{2}}$	6^{13}	6^{22}	Pincay L Jr	117	*1.70	57-30	Bombay Veil 120^{hd}SarahBrown$117^{5\frac{1}{4}}$BlessedPrincess$112^{2\frac{1}{2}}$	Outrun	6

LATEST WORKOUTS Apr 6 Aqu 4f fst :50⅕ b

make a horse like this the favorite. You can only suppose that rumors around the backstretch took in some gullible souls. No matter what anyone may have said, this horse cannot be played off that record. In fact, we are ordinarily overjoyed when we see such a weak favorite, since it opens up fruitful opportunities for good prices on a horse that does have a chance.

The next two betting choices, Ojavan and an entry of Singh Baby and Queen So Lo, are both showing on the board at 3-1. We'll take a look at Ojavan to see what his credentials are:

Ojavan — Gr. f. 3, by Navajo—White Pine, by Woodchuck
$25,000 Br.—Williamson R (Fla) — Tr.—Jerkens Steven T
Own.—Golden R L

1115 — Turf Record: St. 1st 2nd 3rd — 1 0 0 0

	St.	1st	2nd	3rd	Amt.
1980	4	0	0	1	$4,320
1979	13	3	1	3	$33,540

29May80- 5Bel	fst	7f	:22⅘	:46⅕	1:24⅘	ⒻClm 40000	1	3	1hd	3½	48	414	Hernandez R	116	*.90	64-16	Giggleswick 1145½ Forward Girl 1147 McSpoodle 1091	No excuse	4
15May80- 5Aqu	fst	1	:47⅗	1:12⅘	1:38	ⒻClm 55000	4	2	21	1hd	32½	35	Hernandez R	114	8.60[D]	71-19	Heather's Turn 114nk Utmost Celerity1164½[D]Ojavan114no	Bore in	6
15May80-Disqualified and placed fourth																			
1May80- 6Aqu	fst	6f	:23⅕	:46⅗	1:10⅖	ⒻClm 55000	4	3	31½	52½	74½	56¼	Cruguet J	114	4.50	85-13	Sami Sutton 111½ Utmost Celerity 1162½ Sarah Brown1121½	Tired	8
9Apr80- 5Aqu	sly	6f	:22	:45⅕	1:11⅘	ⒻAllowance	3	1	54	37	38	37¾	Tejada V M Jr7	109	5.80	76-21	Donna Doll 1162½ Great Dialogue 1215¼ Ojavan 1095¼	Evenly	5
29Dec79- 9Aqu	fst	6f	⊡:22⅗	:46⅗	1:12⅗	ⒻAllowance	7	2	63¼	65½	78¼	710	Amy J	115	4.30	71-19	Inlet 115nk Darlin Momma 1155¾ Patty Pumpkin 115½	No threat	10
10Dec79- 7Aqu	fst	1 1/16	⊡:48⅗	1:13⅖	1:46⅘	ⒻAllowance	6	3	32	41¾	4¾	43½	Cruguet J	115	2.40	76-13	Demure 117no Classic Curves 115no Espadrille 1203½	Split horses	6
1Dec79- 5Aqu	fst	1	:47	1:12⅖	1:38⅖	ⒻAllowance	6	2	2hd	2hd	2½	34¼	Cruguet J	115	24.00	70-23	Going East 1153½ Turn DownTheHeat117¾Ojavan115nk	Weakened	7
21Nov79- 9Aqu	fst	7f	:23	:46⅕	1:25	ⒻClm 55000	2	7	52½	42½	45½	36	Cruguet J	114	9.00	70-18	Going East 1172½ The Wheel Turns 1163½ Ojavan 1141¼	Evenly	9
20Oct79- 1Aqu	fst	6f	:22⅘	:46⅗	1:12	ⒻClm 40000	3	4	2½	12	12	1¾	Cruguet J	117	*2.10	83-15	Ojavan 117¾ Test Tube Baby 117¾ Chicago Dancer 1154	Driving	9
7Oct79- 3Bel	fst	6f	:23	:46⅘	1:12	ⒻAllowance	4	4	54½	54	66½	516	Gonzalez M A5	108	7.50	66-20	Tash 1135½ Roma 1131½ Studio Queen 1153¾	No factor	7

LATEST WORKOUTS May 13 Bel 4f sly :48⅘ h — May 10 Bel tr.t 3f fst :38⅗ b — Apr 26 Bel tr.t 3f fst :37 b — Apr 22 Bel tr.t 3f fst :37⅗ b

He qualifies off his last race on form, and is being dropped in class after failing to win as a short-priced favorite. These are not wholesome signs as we check his ability times. Off his race of 1May80, there is a lead time of :23.4, with a loss of 4 lengths to raise Ojavan's mark to :24.3. We add one more for energy adjustment and give him a :24.4. For his next best effort, we look at the race of 15May80, where there is a lead time of :25.1 that we can reduce by one for gain and raise back up to :25.1 because of the energy adjustment.

In the entry of Singh Baby and Queen So Lo, we need only look at Singh Baby. Queen So Lo's form is so bad she should have been running in a donkey race. Anytime you confront an entry, forget a possible bargain unless one or both the horses shows the kind of credentials needed to win. Here is what Singh Baby shows:

Singh Baby — B. f. 3, by Singh—Wicked Lark, by T V Lark
$20,000 Br.—Wygod M J (Cal) — Tr.—Puentes Gilbert
Own.—Garren M M

112

	St.	1st	2nd	3rd	Amt.
1980	9	2	0	2	$18,420
1979	2	M	0	1	$1,440

25May80- 6Bel	fst	7f	:23	:46⅗	1:25⅗	ⒻClm 18000	6	8	44½	44½	3½	1¾	Martens G		112	*1.50e	74-16	Singh Baby 112¾ Lorine 1112 Here Dear 1118	Driving	9
18May80- 2Aqu	fst	7f	:23	:46⅖	1:25⅖	ⒻClm 16000	5	6	55	58	45	31	Tejada V M Jr7		109	*1.70	73-19	Sometimes Sassy 114¾ Jeanne's Ruler112nkSinghBaby1095½	Wide	7
17Apr80- 2Aqu	fst	1⅛	:48⅗	1:14⅗	1:54⅘	ⒻClm c-18000	2	3	33	52½	34	·43½	Rogers K L5		107	3.10	57-23	Don'tYouWorry1162LightUpThSky1161FlghtofthS109½	Weakened	6
8Apr80- 2Aqu	fst	6f	:22⅘	:47	1:13	3↑ⒻMd 22500	6	5	52	42¼	42	11	Borden D A		111	*1.90	78-21	Singh Baby 1111 Sally's Ifida 113nk Miss Vertee 1152½	Driving	8
24Mar80- 4Aqu	fst	7f	:23	:46⅖	1:25⅘	3↑ⒻMd 22500	7	5	42½	44	32	31¾	Borden D A		109	7.60	70-24	Zaida S. B. 1111 Somebody Super 114¾ Singh Baby 1095¾	Evenly	9
10Mar80- 4Aqu	fst	6f	⊡:22⅗	:45⅘	1:10⅘	3↑ⒻMd 30000	9	8	63½	56½	510	513	Santagata N		111	4.50	77-19	ShkeTheBet1115¼SomebodySuper1146¼PrincessArtDik106nk	Wide	12
28Feb80- 4Aqu	fst	6f	⊡:22⅗	:47⅗	1:13⅖	ⒻMd 35000	10	5	54	54½	53¾	45	Albertrani T5		116	2.80	72-19	Arbee's Charm 117¾ Maloletti 1123¼ Scarlet Stepper 1121	Evenly	11
20Feb80- 6Aqu	fst	6f	⊡:22⅘	:46⅗	1:12⅕	ⒻMd Sp Wt	8	5	41	53¾	56½	68	Dahlquist T C5		116	20.80	75-19	Mitey Lively 1211¾CountessNorfleet121noEnglishToffy1164½	Tired	12
25Jan80- 4Aqu	fst	6f	⊡:23	:47⅕	1:12⅗	ⒻMd Sp Wt	7	10	88	89¼	912	611	Saumell L	b	121	10.70	70-18	PrettyMelissa1214PureReason1213¼LeadMeHolme1211	No mishap	11
17Dec79- 6Aqu	my	6f	⊡:22⅘	:47⅘	1:14⅗	ⒻMd Sp Wt	11	8	87	1011	79½	77¾	Maple E	b	117	8.10	63-27	RoseOfMorn117¾PrettyMelissa117½VeiledProphet1171½	No threat	12

LATEST WORKOUTS Jun 1 Bel 4f fst :48 b — May 14 Bel tr.t 4f gd :49⅗ b — May 6 Bel tr.t 4f fst :48 h — May 2 Bel tr.t 5f fst 1:05 b

Her last race was good enough to qualify easily. Her best ability time comes out of her last victory also. The 7f time of 1:25.3 is converted to the 6f time of 1:12.2 to give us a lead time of :25.4. The gain of 4½ lengths gives a three-tick reduction to :25.1, with an energy add-on of one to bring the ability time up to :25.2. From the 18May80 race, we must again convert the 7f time to the 6f figure of 1:12.2 also, where we get a lead time of :26.0. The strong gain of 7 lengths allows a five-tick reduction to :25.0, but there is a two-tick add-on for energy to give us another :25.2. You will also note that in her last race, Singh Baby shows an improved running line at her last three calls to make her an Improving Horse. We can now rate the three as follows:

Odds	Horse	Ability		A Pts		F	Total
2.5	Don't You Worry	—	—	—	—	NQ	NQ
3.4	Ojavan	:24.4	:25.1	16	14	Q	30
3.4	Singh Baby	:25.2	:25.2	13	13	Q	26

Even though Singh Baby was an Improving Horse, we cannot give her credit for form points, since to do so would surpass her ability-time points off the pair of :25.2's. Remember, we can only bring an Improving Horse up to a point level represented by the best ability time, and not beyond. In any event, Ojavan has the points, including a Double Advantage, and is our selection in this race. The fourth choice in the betting, however, won the race and we are down at the beginning of the day.

FIRST RACE
Belmont
JUNE 4, 1980

1 ⅛ MILES. (1.45⅖) CLAIMING. Purse $15,000. Fillies, 3-year-olds. Weight, 121 lbs. Non-winners of two races over a mile since May 1 allowed 3 lbs. Of such a race since then, 5 lbs. Claiming price $25,000; for each $2,500 to $20,000, 2 lbs. (Races where entered to be claimed for $18,000 or less not considered.)

Value of race $15,000, value to winner $9,000, second $3,300, third $1,800, fourth $900. Mutuel pool $97,565, OTB pool $134,212.

Last Raced	Horse	Eqt.	A.Wt	PP	St	¼	½	¾	Str	Fin	Jockey	Cl'g Pr	Odds $1
20May80 ^{7}Pim^{2}	Midnight Cruise		3 116	6	8	$6^{1\frac{1}{2}}$	$5^{\frac{1}{2}}$	$3^{\frac{1}{2}}$	2^{4}	$1^{\frac{1}{2}}$	Maple E	25000	4.60
25Apr80 ^{5}Aqu^{4}	Hickory Bee		3 116	1	9	$3^{\frac{1}{2}}$	3^{1}	2^{2}	1^{hd}	$2^{4\frac{1}{4}}$	Velez R I	25000	6.00
8May80 ^{2}Aqu^{5}	Flight of the Sea		3 107	4	5	7^{hd}	8^{3}	$6^{1\frac{1}{2}}$	$4^{\frac{1}{2}}$	3^{2}	Lovato F Jr^{5}	20000	23.50
25May80 ^{6}Bel^{1}	Singh Baby		3 112	5	6	8^{3}	$6^{\frac{1}{2}}$	4^{1}	3^{2}	4^{3}	Martens G	20000	a-3.40
25May80 ^{6}Bel^{7}	Don't You Worry	b	3 118	8	2	$5^{\frac{1}{2}}$	$4^{\frac{1}{2}}$	5^{4}	6^{3}	$5^{1\frac{3}{4}}$	Fell J	25000	2.50
11May80 ^{1}Aqu^{9}	Queen So Lo		3 112	2	7	9	9	7^{4}	7^{12}	$6^{2\frac{3}{4}}$	Velasquez J	20000	a-3.40
29May80 ^{5}Bel^{4}	Ojavan	b	3 111	3	4	1^{1}	1^{5}	1^{4}	5^{1}	7^{14}	Beitia E^{5}	25000	3.70
25May80 ^{6}Bel^{5}	Good Figure		3 114	7	3	4^{1}	7^{2}	$8^{1\frac{1}{2}}$	8^{5}	$8^{6\frac{1}{2}}$	Skinner K	22500	27.50
24May80 ^{1}Bel^{10}	Light Up The Sky		3 111	9	1	2^{4}	2^{3}	9	9	9	Gonzalez M A^{5}	20000	9.70

a-Coupled: Singh Baby and Queen So Lo.

OFF AT 1:00 EDT. Start good, Won driving. Time, :23⅘, :46⅘, 1:12⅕, 1:38⅘, 1:52 Track fast.

Official Program Numbers↘

$2 Mutuel Prices:

5-(G)-MIDNIGHT CRUISE	11.20	5.00	3.80
2-(A)-HICKORY BEE		7.60	3.80
4-(E)-FLIGHT OF THE SEA			7.40

In the second race, we are back to looking at a heavy favorite.

We begin, as usual, with the problem of whether Somebody Super qualifies on form. Looking at the two top running lines, both within twenty-eight-day periods, we see this horse farther behind at every call, which is a danger signal for a Declining Horse. But look at the top line again, and you will see the gain of five from the first call to the stretch call, where four horses were passed and 2 lengths were gained. In accordance with our form rules, this gain of five is enough to make this horse a qualified form contender, so she is in.

2 BELMONT

START — 6 FURLONGS — BELMONT PARK — FINISH

6 FURLONGS. (1.08⅖) CLAIMING. Purse $11,000. Fillies, 3-year-olds. Weight, 121 lbs. Non-winners of two races since May 1 allowed 3 lbs. Of a race since then, 5 lbs. Claiming price $16,000; for each $1,000 to $14,000, 2 lbs. (Races when entered to be claimed for $12,500 or less not considered.)

Somebody Super — Ch. f. 3, by Be Somebody—Cravoke, by Crafty Admiral
Own.—Garren M M — $16,000 — Br.—Meredith Dr–Mrs G G (Md) — Tr.—Puentes Gilbert — 118

	St.	1st	2nd	3rd	Amt.
1980	11	2	3	0	$21,020
1979	0	M	0	0	

25May80-	6Bel	fst	7f	:23	:46⅗	1:25⅗	(F)Clm 20000	8	9	$8^{7\frac{3}{4}}$	$5^{6\frac{1}{2}}$	$4^{5\frac{1}{2}}$	4^{11}	Venezia M	b 118	*1.50e	63–16	Singh Baby 112¾ Lorine 111^{2} Here Dear 111^{8}	In close	9
17May80-	9Aqu	fst	6f	:22⅗	:46⅖	1:12⅕	(F)Clm 25000	1	2	1^{hd}	2½	2^{2}	$5^{6\frac{1}{2}}$	Beitia E^{5}	b 113	*1.70	75–16	Miochelle 114^{4} Gold Lease 109^{nk} Tall Coin 116¾	Used up	11
9May80-	6Aqu	gd	6f	:22⅘	:46⅗	1:12⅕	(F)Clm 20000	3	1	3^{2}	1^{1}	1^{3}	$1^{2\frac{3}{4}}$	Rogers K L^{5}	111	*1.80	82–18	Somebody Super111$^{2\frac{3}{4}}$Miochelle116$^{1\frac{3}{4}}$GloriousTimes116$^{6\frac{1}{4}}$	Driving	6
27Apr80-	9Aqu	fst	1	:47	1:12⅖	1:38	(F)Allowance	3	2	1^{hd}	2^{hd}	$10^{9\frac{1}{4}}$	11^{19}	Rogers K L^{5}	b 111	30.50	57–21	Radioactive 116^{2} Veiled Prophet 116^{4} River Gal 116$^{2\frac{1}{2}}$	Tired	12
1Apr80-	3Aqu	my	6f	:23⅕	:47	1:11⅘	3↑(F)Md 20000	6	1	3^{1}	1^{2}	1^{5}	$1^{5\frac{1}{2}}$	Rogers K L^{5}	b 108	*.80	84–19	Somebody Super108$^{5\frac{1}{2}}$ScarletStepper113$^{3\frac{3}{4}}$Quim114$^{3\frac{1}{4}}$	Ridden out	6
24Mar80-	4Aqu	fst	7f	:23	:46⅖	1:25⅘	3↑(F)Md 25000	3	2	1½	$1^{1\frac{1}{2}}$	1^{2}	2^{1}	Fell J	b 114	*.90	71–24	Zaida S. B. 111^{1} Somebody Super 114¾ Singh Baby 109$^{5\frac{3}{4}}$	Gamely	9
10Mar80-	4Aqu	fst	6f	⊡:22⅗	:45⅘	1:10⅘	3↑(F)Md 30000	2	4	1^{1}	2^{hd}	$2^{1\frac{1}{2}}$	$2^{5\frac{1}{4}}$	Fell J	b 114	10.90	85–19	ShkeTheBet111$^{5\frac{1}{4}}$SombodySupr114$^{6\frac{1}{4}}$PrincssArtDik106^{nk}	2nd best	12
28Feb80-	4Aqu	fst	6f	⊡:22⅗	:47⅗	1:13⅖	(F)Md 30000	5	1	3^{2}	$3^{2\frac{1}{2}}$	3½	$5^{5\frac{1}{2}}$	Asmussen C B	b 117	15.90	71–19	Arbee's Charm 117¾ Maloletti112$^{3\frac{1}{4}}$ScarletStepper112^{1}	Weakened	11
7Feb80-	3Aqu	fst	6f	⊡:23⅗	:49⅖	1:15⅖	(F)Md 30000	6	2	2^{hd}	3^{2}	7^{11}	7^{20}	Gribcheck S B^{5}	b 112	5.50	47–29	Heather's Turn 121$^{2\frac{1}{2}}$ Maloletti 116$^{1\frac{1}{2}}$ Hearts Again 114^{5}	Tired	7
4Feb80-	4Aqu	fst	6f	⊡:23	:48⅕	1:14⅕	(F)Md c-22500	5	2	$3^{3\frac{1}{2}}$	2^{hd}	3^{2}	$5^{5\frac{1}{2}}$	Hernandez R	119	*2.60	67–22	Jaka's Lady 116$^{2\frac{3}{4}}$ Miochelle 121^{1} High Heels 112¾	Tired	10

LATEST WORKOUTS Jun 1 Bel 3f fst :36 h May 23 Bel tr.t 4f fst :49 h May 5 Bel tr.t 5f fst 1:03 b Apr 23 Bel tr.t 4f fst :50 b

In ability times, we try the race of 1Apr80 where there was a sparkling :24.4 set by Somebody Super, with one tick added for energy adjustment. In her race of 27Apr80 at a mile, there was a :25.2 with another tick added for energy. When we turn to early speed, we see a rather dazzling record, except for the weak last race. But nonetheless in the ten races in her record, she had the highest early-speed rating in eight of them, which brings with it 6 points.

We can now turn to the second choice in the wagering, Royal Emigree, to see whether we have another contender.

There is a good form qualification as an improving horse off the last running line. But her best ability effort came at Keystone on 5Feb80, where we start with a lead time of :25.1 and have to tack on two for energy to give us a :25.3.

Royal Emigree — B. f. 3, by Stage Director—Shall Return, by Fair Ruler
Own.—Lavezzo D H Jr — $16,000 — Br.—Lavezzo D H Jr (Ky) — Tr.—Gullo Thomas J — 109^{7}

	St.	1st	2nd	3rd	Amt.
1980	10	2	1	3	$16,580
1979	8	1	0	2	$5,475

10May80-	6Key	fst	7f	:22⅖	:44⅘	1:25⅘	(F)Allowance	6	4	2^{1}	$3^{4\frac{1}{2}}$	$3^{4\frac{1}{2}}$	$4^{2\frac{3}{4}}$	Klidzia S	b 114	3.10	75–21	Gena's Deiite 117$^{2\frac{1}{4}}$ Winning Lady 114½ Jamicka 120no	Tired	9
28Apr80-	5Key	sly	6f	:22⅗	:46⅕	1:12⅖	(F)Allowance	1	3	$3^{2\frac{1}{2}}$	4^{6}	3^{11}	2^{6}	Tejeira J	b 114	2.60	74–25	Morning Jan 113^{6} RoyalEmigree114¾UsefulMiss114^{3}	Second best	6
8Apr80-	7Key	fst	7f	:22⅕	:45	1:25⅕	(F)Allowance	1	5	$8^{5\frac{3}{4}}$	8^{11}	7^{10}	5^{10}	Tejeira J	b 114	*2.20	71–24	Paris Press 117^{nk} Lt. Mary B. 117^{6} Isabella Ruth 112$^{1\frac{1}{2}}$	Outrun	9
30Mar80-	9Key	my	6f	:22	:45⅘	1:12⅘	(F)Allowance	3	6	3^{6}	$3^{5\frac{1}{2}}$	$4^{5\frac{1}{2}}$	$4^{3\frac{1}{2}}$	Tejeira J	b 114	4.40	74–20	Heavenly Love 114^{hd} Villanesian 120^{2} Over Mission 114$^{1\frac{1}{2}}$	Tired	9
7Mar80-	8Key	fst	6f	:22⅖	:46⅕	1:13	(F)Allowance	5	2	4^{4}	$4^{6\frac{1}{2}}$	3^{5}	$3^{2\frac{1}{2}}$	Tejeira J	b 114	2.10	74–27	Lealocket 115^{2} Country Bird 115½ Royal Emigree 114½	Wide	6
26Feb80-	5Key	fst	6f	:23⅖	:48	1:14⅗	(F)Allowance	2	2	$4^{4\frac{1}{2}}$	4^{6}	$4^{3\frac{1}{2}}$	$3^{1\frac{1}{2}}$	Tejeira J	b 114	5.50	67–35	Lady Empress 104$^{1\frac{1}{4}}$ Lealocket 120^{nk} Royal Emigree 114^{2}	Evenly	6
16Feb80-	5Key	sly	7f	:22⅗	:46⅕	1:26	(F)Allowance	2	3	3^{5}	$3^{2\frac{1}{2}}$	3^{2}	3^{4}	Nied J Jr	b 112	8.00	73–25	Southwillriseagain 120^{2} Lealocket 120^{2} Royal Emigree 112^{5}	Wide	8
5Feb80-	7Key	fst	6f	:23⅕	:48	1:13⅕	(F)Clm 18000	6	5	$5^{1\frac{1}{4}}$	1½	1^{1}	1^{2}	Tejeira J	b 119	*1.30	76–29	Royal Emigree 119^{2} Lady Prospector 116^{6}SisLoraine109^{2}	Driving	7
16Jan80-	8Key	fst	6f	:23	:46⅖	1:12⅗	(F)Allowance	5	3	5^{4}	6^{8}	$7^{8\frac{1}{2}}$	6^{10}	Klidzia S	b 112	12.40	69–26	Jovial Pedo 109^{1} Secret Virtue 115$^{3\frac{1}{2}}$ Fluff Stuff 114½	No threat	11
2Jan80-	6Key	fst	6f	:23⅖	:48⅕	1:14⅖	(F)Clm 17000	2	5	$4^{2\frac{1}{2}}$	4¾	2½	$1^{1\frac{1}{2}}$	Tejeira J	b 118	3.90	70–31	Royal Emigree 118$^{1\frac{1}{2}}$ Becky Bumps 116$^{2\frac{1}{2}}$SisLoraine116^{nk}	Driving	7

LATEST WORKOUTS Apr 22 Key 4f fst :49 b

After that, it falls off, as we can find several :26.2's, and nothing better. The 28Apr80 race is one and the 2Jan80 race is another. When it comes to early speed, there are eight races out of ten within 5 lengths of the lead, which awards 3 points.

For third choice in the betting, we see two horses on the board both showing at 6-1, Pillar Point and Pinot Noir. We have to take a look at both of them to see which one rates as our true third choice for comparison with the other two. We start with Pillar Point.

Pillar Point — Ch. f. 3, by Bold Monarch—Proof Requested, by Prove It

$16,000 Br.—Sears F P (Md) Tr.—Boniface J William **1097**

Own.—Sears F P Jr

	St.	1st	2nd	3rd	Amt.
1980	2	0	0	1	$539
1979	12	2	1	3	$21,510

10May80- 6Pim	fst	6f	:22⅗	:45⅘	1:10⅗	ⒻAllowance	4	1	2hd	42½	68½	616	Pino M G	b 112	11.50	77–18	Bishop's Ring 113nk Rolling Mill 11712 Chalfont Place 117¾	Tired	8
28Apr80- 6Pen	sly	6f	:22⅕	:45⅘	1:12⅘	Allowance	5	1	2½	22	23	31¼	Faine C7	b 107	2.50	79–25	Noah's Crest 113nk Final Sun 1131 Pillar Point 1071	Tired	6
20Oct79- 9CT	fst	7f	:23⅘	:47⅗	1:28⅕	Tri St. Fut	2	1	1½	11½	12	33	Grove P	b 119	*1.30	76–26	Full Crew 117½ Hasty Moment 1192½ Pillar Point119hd	Weakened	11
10Oct79- 7Lrl	my	6f	:23	:48⅖	1:15⅕	ⒻAllowance	3	1	13½	12½	12½	1no	Thornburg B	b 121	3.30	70–37	Pillar Point 121no Fair Hit 11210 Fabled Legend 114nk	All out	10
15Sep79- 8Tim	fst	*6½f	:22⅘	:47⅗	1:19⅗	ⒻⓈFrolic H	5	2	2½	2½	2hd	32½	Lloyd J S	b 113	10.80	81–18	Ernestine 1202½ Hail ToAmbition120hdPillarPoint11310	Weakened	6
7Sep79- 6Tim	fst	4f		:23	:46⅖	ⒻAllowance	5	1		21	22	23½	Lloyd J S	b 115	4.20	90–12	Still Blue 1203½ PillarPoint1151½DoubleDairya120½	Best of others	6
28Aug79- 8Del	fst	6f	:22⅕	:46⅕	1:12⅕	ⒻAllowance	5	3	11	12	2½	52	Rocco J5	b 112	11.40	82–18	Diplomatic Role120¾SunValleySally116nkPeg'sFantasy120nk	Tired	10
3Aug79- 8Bow	fst	5½f	:22⅗	:46⅘	1:06⅕	ⒻⓈAllowance	2	2	42½	45	46	47¼	Iliescu A	117	13.20	81–24	Ernestine 120nk Hail To Ambition 1172 My Aunt Ceil 1205	Tired	5
28Jly79- 7Bow	fst	5½f	:21⅘	:45⅖	1:05	ⒻⓈLuck Penny	3	5	44	48	49½	412	Iliescu A	115	22.40	82–17	Smart Angle 114nkHailToAmbition1153Salem'sNymph1229	Outrun	5
17Jly79- 5Del	fst	5½f	:22	:46⅕	1:05⅗	ⒻAllowance	4	2	55	56½	47	47	Cooke C	119	8.50	83–21	Flip's Little Girl 1195 Ivy Snow 1162HailToAmbition116hd	Evenly	7

She qualifies on form off her last race with two calls up close, as well as a drop in class. The best ability time comes out of her 3Aug79 race at Bowie, where we convert the 5½f time to a 6f figure of 1:12.2. Off the :25.3 lead time we have to add two for lost lengths for a :26.0 figure. We next use the 28Aug79 race at Delaware Park, where we add 2 lost lengths to the :26.0 lead time for a :26.2 figure. In computing early speed, there are sufficient races here for the maximum 6 points.

Now, how good is Pinot Noir?

Pinot Noir — B. f. 3, by Bold Native—My Heritage, by Independence

$14,000 Br.—Hartigan J H (Fla) Tr.—Barrera Guillermo S **112**

Own.—Harbor View Farm

	St.	1st	2nd	3rd	Amt.
1980	8	1	2	0	$12,270
1979	4	M	1	0	$2,640

10May80- 4Aqu	fst	1	:46⅖	1:11⅕	1:38	ⒻClm 14000	2	7	68½	67	36	22	Hernandez R	b 112	22.50	74–13	Silver Ray 1142 Pinot Noir 1122 Angel Dusted 111¾	Wide, bore in	10
25Apr80- 1Aqu	fst	7f	:23⅖	:47	1:25⅘ 3↑	ⒻClm 12500	5	4	54¾	57½	48	411	Hernandez R	b 114	6.80	61–26	Open Bar 1173 Lillian'sPrincess1073FourSummers1124¾	No factor	7
18Apr80- 9Aqu	fst	6f	:22⅗	:46⅖	1:12⅕	ⒻClm 16000	1	8	65	69	69½	411	Hernandez R	b 116	10.40	71–24	Tall Coin 1136¼ Antilassa 1162 Cinnamon Star 1162¾	No factor	10
29Feb80- 2Aqu	fst	6f	⊡:22⅖	:48⅕	1:15	ⒻMd 16000	9	13	911	98¼	32	11½	Hernandez R	b 121	4.30	69–24	Pinot Noir 1211½ Miss Political121nkSisterRubena112no	Drew out	14
15Feb80- 4Aqu	fst	6f	⊡:23⅕	:47⅘	1:14⅕	ⒻMd 25000	5	7	77½	66½	42½	43¼	Hernandez R	b 117	3.20	70–26	Miochelle 117½ Scarlet Stepper 1161¼ High Heels 1171½	Bid, hung	7
2Feb80- 5Aqu	fst	1 1/16	⊡:50	1:16⅗	1:49⅘	ⒻMd 25000	9	5	11½	11½	43½	713	Wacker D J5	b 116	4.20	52–27	Hickory Bee 1167¾ Miss Political 121hd Silver Glen 112¾	Tired	10
19Jan80- 1Aqu	my	1 1/16	⊡:49	1:14⅘	1:48⅖	ⒻMd 25000	2	5	21½	13	11	45¼	Hernandez R	b 117	*1.80	67–21	BelledeNaskra1164TaleFeather117½RuthlessLdy117¾	Used in lead	10
1Jan80- 4Aqu	fst	6f	⊡:22⅘	:47⅕	1:13⅖	ⒻMd 20000	2	9	1011	911	67	25½	Hernandez R	b 121	*2.40	71–18	Jolly Magec 1125½ Pinot Noir 121½ AngelDusted1214	Up for place	10
21Nov79- 1Aqu	fst	6f	:23	:47⅖	1:13⅕	ⒻMd 35000	4	6	55¼	65	65½	68¼	Hernandez R	b 117	3.80	69–18	Handmeanative 117¾ Hi Precious 1123 Lateformydate1171	Evenly	12
6Nov79- 9Aqu	fst	6f	:23	:47	1:12	ⒻMd 50000	11	1	95½	78½	814	714	Pincay L Jr	b 117	*2.90	69–17	Sierra 108hd Trickster 1175¾ Heather's Turn 115¾	Wide	11

LATEST WORKOUTS Jun 1 Bel tr.t 4f fst :49 h May 28 Bel tr.t 4f fst :50 b May 16 Bel tr.t 4f fst :49 b May 6 Bel tr.t 5f fst 1:04 b

The second-place finish in her last race qualifies on form. There is a :25.0 ability time for the last race off the lead time of :24.4, a gain of one and then two up for energy. The next best is 1Jan80, where the lead time was :26.1 with an allowable gain of 2½ lengths to reduce the time to :25.4. But the three-tick energy add-on brings the ability time to :26.2. When we look for early speed, there are only four of the ten races where Pinot Noir was within 5 lengths, so a

0 gets recorded. Her total points are 15 + 8 for 23. Pillar Point, on the other hand, has 10 + 8 and then 6 more for early speed, for 24. While there isn't much to choose between them, we'll leave Pillar Point in for our final computation. If she fails to measure up against the other two, you can be sure that Pinot Noir would hardly be a top-rated animal either.

Odds	Horse	Ability		A Pts		ES	F	Total
1.3	Somebody Super	:25.0	:25.3	15	12	6	Q	33
3.9	Royal Emigree	:25.3	:26.2	12	8	3	Q2	25
6.5	Pillar Point	:26.0	:26.2	10	8	6	Q	24

There isn't any doubt about it. Somebody Super is an easy selection off this big point margin. Could she do it? After four furlongs she was well ahead of the field and coasted on to victory.

SECOND RACE
Belmont
JUNE 4, 1980

6 FURLONGS. (1.08$\frac{2}{5}$) CLAIMIN"̃. Purse $11,000. Fillies, 3–year–olds. Weight, 121 lbs. Non–winners of two races since May 1 allowed 3 lbs. Of a race since then, 5 lbs. Claiming price $16,000; for each $1,000 to $14,000, 2 lbs. (Races when entered to be claimed for $12,500 or less not considered.)

Value of race $11,000, value to winner $6,600, second $2,420, third $1,320, fourth $660. Mutuel pool $120,740, OTB pool $96,956. Quinella Pool $125,181. OTB Quinella Pool $125,157.

Last Raced	Horse	Eqt.	A.	Wt	PP	St	¼	½	Str	Fin	Jockey	Cl'g Pr	Odds $1
25May80 ^{6}Bel^{4}	Somebody Super	b	3	118	7	2	2^{3}	1^{3}	$1^{1\frac{1}{2}}$	$1^{1\frac{3}{4}}$	Venezia M	16000	1.30
25May80 ^{6}Bel^{8}	Dosido	b	3	116	5	4	3^{1}	$2^{\frac{1}{2}}$	2^{3}	2no	Asmussen C B	16000	11.20
10May80 ^{6}Key^{4}	Royal Emigree	b	3	109	6	8	5^{hd}	4^{1}	3^{1}	$3^{4\frac{3}{4}}$	Attanasio R^{7}	16000	3.90
18May80 ^{2}Aqu^{4}	Cinnamon Star		3	113	3	6	7^{5}	6^{1}	4^{2}	$4^{2\frac{3}{4}}$	Santiago A	14000	13.60
10May80 ^{6}Pim^{6}	Pillar Point	b	3	109	1	1	1^{1}	$3^{1\frac{1}{2}}$	5^{1}	$5^{2\frac{3}{4}}$	Faine C^{7}	16000	6.50
10May80 ^{4}Aqu^{2}	Pinot Noir	b	3	112	8	7	4^{1}	7^{5}	7^{5}	6no	Rivera M A	14000	6.40
24May80 ^{3}Key^{2}	Tigger Terrible		3	107	4	3	6^{2}	5^{hd}	$6^{\frac{1}{2}}$	$7^{4\frac{1}{2}}$	Gonzalez M A^{5}	14000	7.80
10May80 ^{4}Aqu^{8}	Sticky Wicket		3	108	2	5	8	8	8	8	Tejada V M Jr^{7}	15000	25.00

OFF AT 1:28 1/2, EDT. Start good, Won driving. Time, :22$\frac{4}{5}$, :46$\frac{2}{5}$, 1:11$\frac{4}{5}$ Track fast.

$2 Mutuel Prices:			
8–(H)–SOMEBODY SUPER	4.60	3.00	2.40
6–(F)–DOSIDO		6.60	4.20
7–(G)–ROYAL EMIGREE			4.00

$2 QUINELLA 6–8 PAID $28.00.

The third race was scheduled to be run on the grass for maiden special fillies, but the rains in New York brought some soggy turf, which moved the event back to the dirt. You may thus disregard the grass listing in the conditions, as we go to the favorite, River Nile.

River Nile's form is ragged off her last race, which was on the dirt, the same surface we now have to deal with because of the rains. We can come up with a gain of four from the second call to the finish, but that falls short. A rule for a gain of five means what it says, and therefore we make the hard decision of disqualifying her on form in this race.

WIDENER TURF COURSE
1⅜ MILES
BELMONT PARK
START FINISH

3 BELMONT

1⅜ MILES. (TURF). (2.12⅖) MAIDEN SPECIAL WEIGHT. Purse $18,000. Fillies and mares, 3-year-olds and upward. Weight, 3-year-olds, 114 lbs. Older, 122 lbs.

River Nile

Dk. b. or br. f. 3, by Damascus—Up Oars, by Turn-To
Br.—Haggin L L II (Ky)
Tr.—Johnson Philip G
Own.—Kleuner R

114

Turf Record	St.	1st	2nd	3rd		St.	1st	2nd	3rd	Amt.
	1	0	0	0	1980	4	M	1	2	$7,600
					1979	3	M	0	1	$1,100

26May80- 5Bel	fst	1 1/16	:47⅗	1:12⅖	1:45⅖	3↑ ⒻMd Sp Wt	5	5	54	47½	37	34½	Skinner K	b	113	7.30	70-20	Friendly Frolic 1144½ Worthy Polly 109nk River Nile 1133	Wide	7
18May80- 1Aqu	gd	1 1/16 Ⓣ	:48⅕	1:13⅗	1:46⅖	3↑ ⒻMd Sp Wt	1	9	78½	812	712	59½	Gonzalez M A5	b	108	2.80	63-21	Carrade 110½ Idiomatic 1133¼ La Atrevida 1132¼	Blocked	10
18May80-Dead heat																				
3May80- 6Aqu	fst	7f	:23	:45⅘	1:23⅘	3↑ ⒻMd Sp Wt	5	1	21	25	31½	25½	Gonzalez M A5	b	108	4.70	76-12	PinkSupreme1085½RiverNile108¾SereneStrmr1133¾	Best of others	6
25Apr80- 6Aqu	fst	6f	:22⅗	:47	1:13	3↑ ⒻMd Sp Wt	1	4	32½	41¾	41	32	Rogers K L5	b	108	8.70	76-26	Bang The Drums 1141¼AncientMystery113¾RiverNile108nk	Evenly	8
7Nov79- 1Med	fst	6f	:22⅗	:46⅕	1:13⅕	ⒻMd Sp Wt	4	7	811	79½	511	36¼	Turcotte R L	b	118	5.70	73-24	Icy Lassie 1185 Dance Troupe 1181¼ River Nile 118nk	Rallied	10
[illegible]Sep79- 4Bel	fst	6f	:22⅖	:45⅘	1:10⅕	ⒻMd Sp Wt	11	8	76½	78	78¼	513	Velez R I		117	48.50	78-11	Naskranaut 1179¼ Critic's Wink 1172½ Shine She Will110½	Outrun	11
6Aug79-10Mth	sly	5½f	:22⅘	:47⅖	1:07⅘	ⒻMd Sp Wt	11	9	1116	1125	1123	1019	Barrera C		117	8.00	59-22	Quainty Dainty 1174McAllisterMiss117noLuxuriousGal1174	Outrun	11

LATEST WORKOUTS May 14 Bel tr.t 3f gd :37⅖ b Apr 24 Bel tr.t 3f fst :37⅘ b Apr 19 Bel tr.t 4f fst :49⅘ b Apr 14 Bel 3f fst :36⅖ hg

Miss Rebecca is the second choice, although all three in the group are closely bunched in the odds.

Miss Rebecca

Ch. f. 3, by Misty Flight—Rebecca T, by Alcide
Br.—Fink L R (Va)
Tr.—Schulhofer Flint S
Own.—Fink L R

114

Turf Record	St.	1st	2nd	3rd		St.	1st	2nd	3rd	Amt.
	5	0	1	1	1980	8	M	2	2	$10,200
					1979	2	M	0	0	

25May80- 3Bel	fm	1¼ Ⓣ	:47⅘	1:38⅖	2:02⅖	3↑ ⒻMd Sp Wt	9	8	77½	52¾	22	22	Vasquez J		113	5.40	80-15	La Atrevida 1132 Miss Rebecca 1137 Binomial1133	Best of others	12
12May80- 9Aqu	sly	1⅛	:47⅗	1:12⅖	1:52⅘	3↑ ⒻMd Sp Wt	3	7	711	47½	26	32¼	Vasquez J		113	8.50	69-19	Als Ich Kan 1131½ English Toffy 113¾ Miss Rebecca1131¾	Fair try	8
4May80- 2Aqu	fst	1⅛	:48⅕	1:13⅘	1:53⅗	ⒻMd Sp Wt	9	6	97	98½	710	58¾	Cruguet J		121	11.50	58-25	Luxcie 1211¼ Charlsie White 1212½ English Toffy 1165¼	Wide	9
27Mar80- 4GP	fm	*1 1/16 Ⓣ			1:45⅖	ⒻMd Sp Wt	4	9	1012	813	56	45½	Cruguet J		120	3.70	73-16	Taipan'sLdy1203½JoyofAces120hdCoolContess1152	Improved pos.	10
13Mar80- 4GP	fm	*1 Ⓣ			1:39⅘	ⒻMd Sp Wt	1	7	713	76¾	59½	414	Vasquez J		120	3.30	68-21	Active Voice 1205½ Roman Beach 1204½ Dominia 1204	Rallied	10
28Feb80- 6Hia	fm	1 1/16 Ⓣ			1:44⅖	ⒻMd Sp Wt	4	3	33½	32½	44	44¾	Cruguet J		118	4.50	71-16	Flight to Reality1182½FollowOrders118½Intendress1182	Weakened	10
20Feb80- 6Hia	fst	1⅛	:48⅕	1:13⅖	1:52⅖	ⒻMd Sp Wt	3	6	44	22	24	28	Cruguet J		118	2.80	62-16	RreSprkling1188MissRebcc1183½SunnyDisposition118hd	No match	11
13Feb80- 6Hia	fm	1 1/16 Ⓣ			1:45⅘	ⒻMd Sp Wt	3	9	712	710	58	31½	Cruguet J		120	20.80	67-25	Ignite 120½ Roman Beach 1151 Miss Rebecca 120nk	Rallied	12
6Nov79- 9Aqu	fst	6f	:23	:47	1:12	ⒻMd 40000	1	10	106	911	915	915	Taveras R5		108	43.10	68-17	Sierra 108hd Trickster 1175¾ Heather's Turn 115¾	Outrun	11
29Oct79- 4Aqu	fst	6f	:23	:47⅖	1:12⅘	ⒻMd 30000	9	11	85½	65	913	913	Cruguet J		117	26.20	66-25	La Zia Ninfa 117¾ Lateformydate 1162½ Maloletti 1062¼	Outrun	12

LATEST WORKOUTS Jun 2 Bel tr.t 4f fst :50⅗ b May 11 Bel tr.t 3f fst :37⅗ b May 2 Bel 4f fst :50 b Apr 26 Bel 4f fst :51⅖ b

The last race was on the grass. In looking at form, we may have to use it in some situations. But even going back to the preceding dirt race on 12May80, which is within our allowable time spans, Miss Rebecca would qualify off a sufficient gain in the running line. When you see that her last grass race was outstanding, where she ran second to La Atrevida, who won for us on Monday, we regret that we cannot use it. In the 12May80 race, however, there was a :25.0 lead time with no allowable gain, and with the three ticks for energy, we have a :25.3. The 20Feb80 race at Hialeah does a little better off a :25.1 lead time, reduced by two for gain, and increased by three for energy to wind up with a :25.2.

The third choice is Idiomatic, with only four races, which always worries us. But the last run on the grass doesn't count, either, except to qualify her on form.

Idiomatic

Dk. b. or br. f. 3, by Verbatim—Swiss Forest, by Dotted Swiss
Br.—Elmendorf Farm (Ky)
Tr.—DeBonis Robert
Own.—Harmonay R M

114

Turf Record	St.	1st	2nd	3rd		St.	1st	2nd	3rd	Amt.
	1	0	1	0	1980	1	M	1	0	$3,960
					1979	3	M	0	1	$990

18May80- 1Aqu	gd	1 1/16 Ⓣ	:48⅕	1:13⅗	1:46⅖	3↑ ⒻMd Sp Wt	7	1	14	13	11	2½	Rivera M A	b	113	9.80	72-21	Carrade 110½ Idiomatic 1133¼ La Atrevida 1132¼	Weakened	10
20Sep79- 4Bel	fst	6f	:23⅕	:47⅖	1:13⅖	ⒻMd c-37500	10	4	43	41½	2hd	31¾	Amy J		115	6.10	73-26	Sarah Brown 1131¾ River Gal108no DH BuyBackBaby117	Weakened	12
20Sep79-Dead heat																				
5Sep79- 6Bel	fst	6½f	:22⅘	:46⅗	1:19	ⒻMd Sp Wt	8	4	1110	89¾	66½	56¼	Amy J		117	84.40	75-22	Sugar And Spice1171¼Harrowing117noErin'sWord117nk	No threat	11
27Jly79- 6Mth	fst	5½f	:22⅗	:46⅕	1:06⅕	ⒻMd Sp Wt	9	11	109¼	1117	1113	1121	Solomone M		117	26.50	65-17	Santanta1171½DancingDiplomat117nkPollyannPtrick1171¼	Outrun	11

LATEST WORKOUTS May 29 Bel Ⓣ 4f fm :48 b (d) May 15 Bel 3f fst :36⅖ h May 10 Bel tr.t 4f fst :51 b May 4 Bel 4f fst :48 h

Since this filly has run but once this year on the grass, it would be unfair to disqualify her on form after her excellent race, where she ran ahead of La Atrevida. Thus, we are compelled to use this grass race to evaluate form and therefore qualify Idiomatic as a legitimate contender in today's race. Her 20Sep79 race at Belmont gave us a :26.0 lead time with no lengths adjustment, but with one tick added for energy to reach :26.1. In the 5Sep79 race at Belmont, we have to convert the 6½f time to 1:12.2 to get a :25.4 lead time. We can give no credit at all for gain because of the distance back in the field, as the gain was not completed at less than 6 lengths from the lead. We have to add two for energy and wind up with another :26.1. We are now ready to rate the three contenders.

Odds	Horse	Ability		A Pts		F	Total
1.6	River Nile	—	—	—	—	NQ	NQ
2.2	Miss Rebecca	:25.2	:25.3	13	12	Q	25
2.4	Idiomatic	:26.1	:26.1	9	9	Q	18

With River Nile out of contention, Miss Rebecca becomes a Double Advantage Horse and a sound proposition. And that's how it turns out, to our pleasure. River Nile ran well, however, and managed to finish a strong second.

THIRD RACE
Belmont
JUNE 4, 1980

1 ⅜ MILES. (2.19⅕) MAIDEN SPECIAL WEIGHT. Purse $18,000. Fillies and mares, 3-year-olds and upward. Weight, 3-year-olds, 114 lbs. Older, 122 lbs. (Originally carded to be run at 1 3/8 Miles Turf Course.)

Value of race $18,000, value to winner $10,800, second $3,960, third $2,160, fourth $1,080. Mutuel pool $157,610, OTB pool $77,911. Exacta Pool $200,308. OTB Exacta Pool $140,971.

Last Raced	Horse	Eqt.	A.	Wt	PP	¼	½	¾	1	Str	Fin	Jockey	Odds $1
25May80 ^{3}Bel^{2}	Miss Rebecca		3	114	6	6^{8}	$5^{1\frac{1}{2}}$	$3^{\frac{1}{2}}$	$2^{1\frac{1}{2}}$	$1^{1\frac{1}{2}}$	1^{2}	Vasquez J	2.20
26May80 ^{5}Bel^{3}	River Nile	b	3	114	2	$4^{\frac{1}{2}}$	6^{5}	5^{3}	3^{hd}	2^{2}	$2^{3\frac{1}{4}}$	Skinner K	1.60
25May80 ^{3}Bel^{3}	Binomial		3	114	5	$5^{\frac{1}{2}}$	4^{1}	$2^{\frac{1}{2}}$	1^{hd}	3^{3}	$3^{6\frac{1}{4}}$	Fell J	7.30
25May80 ^{3}Bel^{6}	Silver Glen		3	114	7	7	7	6^{4}	5^{4}	4^{5}	4^{8}	Martens G	26.10
24May80 ^{4}Bel^{8}	Inner Sanctum		3	109	1	3^{1}	3^{hd}	$4^{1\frac{1}{2}}$	4^{hd}	5^{13}	5^{15}	Lovato F Jr^{5}	16.40
18May80 ^{1}Aqu^{2}	Idiomatic	b	3	114	3	1^{1}	1^{5}	1^{5}	6	6	6	Rivera M A	2.40
15May80 ^{9}Aqu^{9}	Baby Doll Dina	b	3	109	4	2^{8}	2^{6}	7	—	—	—	Gonzalez M A^{5}	56.70

Baby Doll Dina, Eased.

OFF AT 2:01, EDT. Start good, Won driving. Time, :23⅕, :47⅘, 1:14⅕, 1:41⅘, 2:07⅘, 2:20⅘, Track fast.

$2 Mutuel Prices:				
	7-(G)-MISS REBECCA	6.40	2.80	2.20
	2-(B)-RIVER NILE		2.80	2.20
	5-(E)-BINOMIAL			2.60

$2 EXACTA 7-2 PAID $18.20.

We have another crowd of fillies in the fourth race, which is a seven-furlong sprint for older females. Out Of The Ground is the second choice in the betting, and we look first at her record.

4 BELMONT

7 FURLONGS. (1.20⅖) CLAIMING. Purse $15,000. Fillies and mares, 4–year–olds and upward. Weight, 122 lbs. Non–winners of two races since May 1 allowed 3 lbs. Of a race since then, 5 lbs. Claiming price $30,000; for each $2,500 to $25,000, 2 lbs. (Races when entered to be claimed for $20,000 or less not considered.)

Out Of The Ground — Ch. m. 6, by Somerset—Golden Hostess, by Royal Farmer
Own.—Southlake Stable — $30,000 — Br.—McCarron D H (NJ) — Tr.—Nobles Reynoldo H — 1125
Turf Record: St. 1st 2nd 3rd — 2 0 0 1
St. 1st 2nd 3rd Amt. — 1980 8 0 1 1 $4,760 — 1979 22 5 4 4 $67,880

8May80- 5Aqu sly 7f :23⅖ :47⅕ 1:24⅘ ⒻClm 37500 2 7 23 22 44½ 55¾ Rogers K L5 110 2.90 71-22 Tullette 1131¾ Tortoise 1132 Bravo Miss 1192 Slow start 7
14Apr80- 5Aqu fst 6f :22⅖ :46⅖ 1:11⅘ ⒻClm 30000 7 4 76¼ 53¼ 22 2½ Rogers K L5 108 9.10 83-21 Bravo Miss 117½ Out Of The Ground1081¾KageeAtkins117hd Wide 7
7Apr80- 8Key fst 7f :22⅕ :44⅖ 1:25 ⒻAllowance 2 4 47 57½ 68 74¾ Thomas D B 114 11.40 77-28 Loveliness 119nk Texette 119nk Coiled 108nk No menace 7
14Mar80- 7Aqu sly 6f ⊡:22⅘ :47⅖ 1:13⅕ ⒻClm 40000 5 6 45 43 68 58 Venezia M 113 5.10 70-25 Bold Ridona 113½ Her Angel 110no Jenni's Whistle 1073¾ Wide 7
7Feb80- 1Aqu fst 6f ⊡:24⅕ :49⅖ 1:15⅕ ⒻClm c-25000 5 4 31 32 44 63½ Miranda J 117 4.10 64-29 After The Lovin 105hd Star T. Lee 1091½ Lynco Jo 117¾ Tired 8
21Jan80- 3Aqu fst 170 ⊡:48⅕ 1:13⅖ 1:44⅕ ⒻClm 35000 6 3 3½ 41¾ 68½ 811 Hirdes J7 106 13.00 70-19 All Francis 1133½ QueenOfSt.Marys108hdMakeThatGoal113¾ Tired 9
17Jan80- 6Aqu fst 6f ⊡:22⅖ :46⅗ 1:11⅘ ⒻClm 30000 2 1 56 64½ 65¾ 68¼ Castaneda M 117 5.80 77-18 Canonization 117no Caracas 1122¾ Bravo Miss 1102½ No mishap 10
1Jan80- 5Aqu fst 6f ⊡:23⅕ :47⅕ 1:12⅕ ⒻClm 35000 3 2 42¼ 53¾ 55 33¼ Castaneda M 117 3.30 80-18 All Francis 1171¾ Bravo Miss1101½OutOfTheGround1171¼ Mild bid 8
14Dec79- 5Aqu my 170 ⊡:48⅕ 1:13⅗ 1:43⅘ 3↑ⒻClm 40000 4 2 2hd 2hd 44½ 48½ Beitia E7 106 *1.60 74-18 Hasty Snob 1141½ Jenni's Whistle 1124 Belle of theBar1113 Tired 6
LATEST WORKOUTS May 31 Mth 3f fst :36 b May 24 Mth 5f fst 1:03 b Apr 26 GS 4f fst :53⅘ b

Checking her form, there is one up-close call and a drop in class of the requisite 20%, so we can leave her in as a contender. For ability times, from the race of 14Apr80 we have a lead time of :25.2, reduced by a gain down to :25.0 and up one for energy to a :25.1. The next best effort was on 1Jan80, with a lead time of :25.0, nothing for gain or loss, and an add-on of one for energy to another :25.1 For early speed, we can award 2 points, but no more.

Now we come to the favorite, Ruhr Lil, to see what she shows.

Ruhr Lil — B. f. 4, by Mickey Mcguire—Belle of the East, by Greek Song
Own.—May–Don Stable — $30,000 — Br.—Stone W P (Ky) — Tr.—Parisella John — 119
St. 1st 2nd 3rd Amt. — 1980 9 3 3 2 $29,420 — 1979 15 M 3 0 $4,132

17May80- 4Aqu fst 1⅛ :49⅗ 1:14⅕ 1:53 ⒻClm 27500 4 4 52½ 41¾ 1hd 1½ Fell J 115 *2.10 70-16 Ruhr Lil 115½ Hoo Ray 117¾ Open Bar 1134½ Driving 7
20Apr80- 9Aqu fst 7f :22⅗ :45⅗ 1:25⅖ ⒻClm 22500 7 4 65½ 45 2½ 11½ Fell J 115 *2.20 74-16 Ruhr Lil 1151½PurpleShamrock1171Diane'sJewel1192¼ Ridden out 8
11Apr80- 2Aqu fst 1 :47 1:11⅘ 1:37⅗ ⒻClm 20000 2 3 32½ 43 43 32 Fell J 113 5.00 76-20 Flouncy 115¾ Su Noma Kathy 1121¼ Ruhr Lil 1132½ Evenly 9
27Mar80- 2Aqu fst 6f :23 :46⅗ 1:12⅕ ⒻClm 18000 4 3 73¾ 63¾ 53½ 31½ Fell J 114 9.00 80-23 Diane's Jewel1151½AfterTheLovin117noRuhrLil114nk Finished well 7
14Mar80- 3Aqu sly 1 1/16 ⊡:46⅘ 1:13⅘ 1:49⅖ ⒻClm 16000 4 6 14 79½ 42 23½ Fell J 117 8.70 63-25 Funny Nun 1173½ Ruhr Lil 1171¾ Swift Poppy 1101¾ Raced wide 7
3Mar80- 9Aqu fst 170 ⊡:48⅗ 1:14⅖ 1:46 ⒻClm c-12500 1 3 33 69½ 67 77¾ Hernandez R 117 3.30 64-21 Lillian's Princess 1124 First Motion 112hd Asli Han1101¼ Checked 9
19Feb80- 3Key fst 170 :48⅗ 1:14⅕ 1:46 ⒻClm 11000 5 3 21 1hd 2hd 2½ Black A S 116 4.00 69-24 View From The Hill 116½ Ruhr Lil 1163 Free Milady 116½ Gamely 7
5Feb80- 1Key fst 7f :23⅕ :47⅖ 1:27⅖ ⒻMd 12500 3 5 62¾ 75¼ 45½ 1no Black A S 120 *.80 70-29 Ruhr Lil 120no Ruling Hour 106¾ Like Fine Wine 109½ Just up 9
19Jan80- 1Key sl 6f :23⅖ :47⅘ 1:14 ⒻMd Sp Wt 3 5 52¼ 54½ 33½ 2no Black A S 120 6.20 72-23 Raja Magic 120no Ruhr Lil 1202½ Luck Be A Lady 1202 Sharp try 12
LATEST WORKOUTS May 31 Bel tr.t 4f fst :50 b May 15 Bel tr.t 3f fst :37⅕ b ●May 7 Bel tr.t 1 fst 1:45⅖ b May 2 Bel tr.t 4f fst :50⅘ b

She has two successive victories and qualifies easily. Her best ability time was on 11Apr80 with a :25.0 (lead time :24.4, holding even, and one added for energy). In her last good race, there was a :24.3 lead time with no allowable gain, but the slow pace puts her into the 50-and-change time period for an add-on for energy of four ticks to a :25.2. For early speed, we have another award of 2 points.

As we look to the third favorite, we are once again compelled to compare two horses. Both Very Quaint and Native Witch are showing 9-2 on the board and are very close in dollars wagered. Since Very Quaint scored a Big Win in her last race, we'll start there.

Off the qualifying Big Win, there was a :25.1 lead time which needs no adjustment, as she blistered her foes. But thereafter, we have a drop-off. Her next best time is a weak :26.2 made on 4Apr80 when she won at Aqueduct, where

Very Quaint — Ch. f. 4, by Stevward—Lonesome Highway, by Francis S — **$25,000** — Br.—Harbor View Farm (Fla) — Tr.—Campo John P — **113**

Own.—Feiner K S

	St.	1st	2nd	3rd	Amt.
1980	11	3	1	1	$23,800
1979	11	1	1	0	$6,530

19May80- 4Aqu	fst	6f		:22⅖	:45⅗	1:10⅘	ⒻClm c-15000	4	3	2hd	11½	14	14½	Vasquez J Jr		115	5.90	89–19 Very Quaint 1154½ General J. 1082¾ Miss L. And B. 113nk	Driving	8
11May80- 9Aqu	fst	6f		:22⅕	:45⅗	1:11⅘	ⒻClm 20000	1	3	3½	33½	24	57¼	Cordero A Jr		113	7.40	77–14 Asli Han 1081¼ Purple Shamrock 1173 Flouncy 1172¾	Steadied	9
2May80- 1Aqu	fst	7f		:22⅘	:46⅗	1:24⅘	ⒻClm 16000	9	1	15	14	34½	711	Vasquez J	b	119	6.30e	66–19 Asli Han 1121¼ Open Bar 1131¼ My Rosebud 1123½	Used in pace	9
20Apr80- 9Aqu	fst	7f		:22⅗	:45⅗	1:25⅖	ⒻClm 20000	2	3	11½	1hd	814	819	Albertrani T5	b	110	15.10	55–16 Ruhr Lil 1151½ Purple Shamrock 1171Diane'sJewel1192¼	Bore out	8
4Apr80- 2Aqu	sly	6f		:22⅕	:46	1:12⅖	ⒻClm 20000	6	1	14	11½	2hd	11½	Albertrani T	b	108	6.80	81–22 Very Quaint 1081½ Susie Sue 1171½ Diane's Jewel 119½	Driving	6
23Mar80- 4Aqu	my	7f		:22⅗	:46⅕	1:26	ⒻClm 16000	5	4	15	13	23	35¾	Albertrani T5	b	112	6.30	65–25 Susie Sue 1172¼ Diane's Jewel 1153½ Very Quaint 112¾	Bore out	9
14Mar80- 3Aqu	sly	1 1/16	⊡	:46⅘	1:13⅘	1:49⅖	ⒻClm 15000	2	1	14	13	31	57¾	Whitacre G10	b	107	11.40	59–25 Funny Nun 1173½ Ruhr Lil 1171¾ Swift Poppy 1101¾	Used early	7
6Mar80- 2Aqu	fst	6f	⊡	:23	:47⅗	1:14	ⒻClm 14000	8	2	2½	2hd	1½	21	Albertrani T5	b	108	8.20	73–22 Honey Tree 1171 Very Quaint 1081¼ Diane's Jewel 1171¾	Gamely	10
11Feb80- 1Aqu	fst	6f	⊡	:22⅗	:46⅘	1:12⅗	ⒻClm 16000	9	1	21½	21½	43½	45½	Albertrani T5	b	114	8.20	75–23 Lace Pillow 112½ Bright Wings 1174½ Julias Cause 108½	Tired	10

LATEST WORKOUTS Jun 1 Bel tr.t 4f fst :47⅗ h ●May 28 Bel tr.t 4f fst :48 h

she led all the way with a lead time that requires no adjustment to get the same final figure. Also off nine races, there is outstanding early speed for a full 4 points. Now we are ready to look at Native Witch, her rival in the wagering.

Native Witch — Ro. m. 6, by Banderilla—Marraldin, by Misty Day — **$30,000** — Br.—Fuller P (Ky) — Tr.—Forbes John H — **1125**

Own.—Tresvant Stable

Turf Record

St.	1st	2nd	3rd
1	0	0	0

	St.	1st	2nd	3rd	Amt.
1980	15	5	3	4	$30,590
1979	10	2	2	1	$9,310

21May80- 8Key	sly	7f	:23	:46⅕	1:25⅕	3↑ⒻAllowance	4	3	43½	46	34	22½	Terry J5	111	2.40	78–25 QueenOfTheGreen1202½NativeWitch111½RestlessGina1119	Gamely	5
7May80- 8Key	fst	6f	:22	:45	1:11	ⒻAllowance	4	6	510	49	38½	34	Terry J5	117	4.40	83–19 Love'sPleasure113hdSentimentalMiss1194NtiveWitch1172	Rallied	7
26Apr80- 8Key	fst	1 1/16	:47	1:11⅖	1:45⅖	3↑ⒻSusque'hna H	2	5	75	912	1117	914	Terry J	106	36.00	63–20 Mark 'Em Lousy 1151¼ Jay Waltzer 1112 Leslie J 1181¾	Tired	11
15Apr80- 8Key	fst	7f	:22⅘	:45⅘	1:26⅕	ⒻAllowance	6	7	64½	55½	22½	12	Terry J7	107	*2.20	76–30 Native Witch 1072 Quids Princess 114½ Betty's Right108½	Driving	8
5Apr80- 5Key	fst	6f	:23	:47⅖	1:12⅘	ⒻAllowance	3	6	66	56	35½	32	Terry J7	107	*1.90	76–30 Fly Missy Fly 113½ Just A Cop 1141½ Native Witch 1076	Wide	7
25Mar80- 7Key	my	7f	:23	:46⅖	1:24⅖	ⒻAllowance	7	1	64	42½	23	2nk	Terry J7	107	2.70	85–31 SntimntlMiss114nkNtivWitch10712Nncy'sScout1141½	Just missed	7
17Mar80- 6Key	fst	6f	:22⅖	:45⅘	1:12⅖	ⒻClm 13000	7	1	52½	32	21	13½	Terry J7	107	6.30	80–28 Native Witch 1073½ WellTurnedAnkle120½Weezeelee116no	Driving	7
11Mar80- 9Key	fst	6f	:23⅕	:47⅗	1:14	ⒻClm 10000	1	9	1112	96¾	53½	12	Black K7	107	9.30	72–33 Native Witch 1072 May Court 111nk Dottie's Gal 120nk	Drew out	12
4Mar80- 2Key	fst	170	:47⅗	1:13⅘	1:45⅕	ⒻClm c-8000	5	5	66	31½	32	33¾	Klidzia S	114	6.10	70–32 One Hour 116¾ Fly Missy Fly 1163 Native Witch 114hd	Evenly	11
24Feb80- 4Key	fst	6f	:23	:47⅖	1:13⅗	ⒻClm 8000	9	1	84	84¾	44½	32½	Klidzia S	112	*3.30	72–28 May Court 1091 One Hour 1161½ Native Witch 1122½	Rallie	

She qualifies on form off her second-place finish in a good effort at Keystone. She gets an improvement factor, too, with improved running position at every call. To search for good ability times, go back to the race of 25Mar80 at Keystone in the mud. The 7f time of 1:24.2 is converted to 1:11.2 for 6f, which gives us a lead time of :25.0. It is reduced by two for gain to :24.3 with no other adjustment required. In the 5Apr80 race at Keystone, there is a :25.2 lead time, with a reduction by three off the 4-length gain to :24.4, but with two ticks added for energy to bring us back up to :25.1. While early speed is not as strong as that of Very Quaint, in six of the ten races shown, Native Witch was within 5 lengths of the lead at the first call, and thus gets 2 points. We can now compare the two.

Very Quaint	:25.1	:26.2	14	8	4	Q4	30	total points
Native Witch	:24.3	:25.1	17	14	2	Q2	35	total points

Here the strong ability times outweigh the early speed, and since Native Witch has the higher points, she becomes our true third choice and will now be compared with the other two favorites.

Odds	Horse	Ability		A Pts		ES	F	Total
2.1	Ruhr Lil	:25.0	:25.2	15	13	2	Q	30
4.2	Out Of The Ground	:25.1	:25.1	14	14	2	Q	30
4.9	Native Witch	:24.3	:25.1	17	14	2	Q2	35

Native Witch now becomes our final selection, to win and place, because of her superior point totals. Look what happened.

FOURTH RACE
Belmont
JUNE 4, 1980

7 FURLONGS. (1.20⅗) CLAIMING. Purse $15,000. Fillies and mares, 4-year-olds and upward. Weight, 122 lbs. Non-winners of two races since May 1 allowed 3 lbs. Of a race since then, 5 lbs. Claiming price $30,000; for each $2,500 to $25,000, 2 lbs. (Races when entered to be claimed for $20,000 or less not considered.)

Value of race $15,000, value to winner $9,000, second $3,300, third $1,800, fourth $900. Mutuel pool $173,505, OTB pool $107,991. Quinella Pool $176.231. OTB Quinella Pool $150,375

Last Raced	Horse	Eqt.	A.	Wt	PP	St	¼	½	Str	Fin	Jockey	Cl'g Pr	Odds $1
21May80 ^{8}Key^{2}	Native Witch		6	112	6	9	6^{hd}	6^{hd}	3^{2}	$1^{3/4}$	Beitia E^{5}	30000	4.90
3Apr80 ^{6}Aqu^{1}	Honey Tree		4	113	10	1	4^{1}	2^{hd}	$2^{1/2}$	$2^{2 1/4}$	Maple E	25000	11.90
19May80 ^{4}Aqu^{1}	Very Quaint	b	4	113	5	2	1^{4}	1^{5}	1^{1}	$3^{1 3/4}$	Velasquez J	25000	4.80
17May80 ^{4}Aqu^{4}	Asli Han	b	4	108	3	10	10	10	$7^{1/2}$	4^{nk}	Gonzalez M A^{5}	25000	7.30
17May80 ^{4}Aqu^{1}	Ruhr Lil		4	119	4	5	$5^{1/2}$	$7^{1 1/2}$	5^{1}	5^{nk}	Fell J	30000	2.10
11May80 ^{9}Aqu^{3}	Flouncy	b	4	115	2	8	$9^{1/2}$	$9^{1/2}$	$6^{1 1/2}$	$6^{2 1/4}$	Martens G	27500	10.70
21May80 ^{3}Bel^{6}	Regaline		4	113	8	4	$3^{1 1/2}$	4^{3}	$4^{1 1/2}$	$7^{2 3/4}$	Santiago A†	25000	61.40
8May80 ^{5}Aqu^{5}	Out Of The Ground		6	117	1	7	8^{2}	$8^{1/2}$	8^{4}	$8^{5 3/4}$	Rivera M A†	30000	4.20
13Dec79 ^{3}Aqu^{6}	Tumiga's Honey	b	4	108	7	6	$7^{1 1/2}$	5^{hd}	9^{3}	$9^{3 3/4}$	Lovato F Jr^{5}	25000	29.20
11May80 ^{1}Aqu^{10}	Princess Margurite	b	4	113	9	3	$2^{1 1/2}$	3^{1}	10	10	Samyn J L	25000	42.40

OFF AT 2:34 EDT. Start good Won driving Time, :22⅘, :46, 1:12, 1:24⅘ Track fast.

$2 Mutuel Prices:			
6-(F)-NATIVE WITCH	11.80	6.40	5.00
10-(J)-HONEY TREE		9.80	7.00
5-(E)-VERY QUAINT			5.40

$2 QUINELLA 6-10 PAID $63.20.

The real choice in this race all along was between Very Quaint, with her strong early speed, and Native Witch, with her strong ability times. The chart is indeed instructive. Very Quaint was out there with her excellent speed, even building up a 6-length lead at the second call. Then Native Witch began to move. The seven-furlong distance, at which early speed is not as helpful as at the shorter six-furlong sprint, was too much for a fading Very Quaint. We are, of course, delighted with this outcome.

We're up to the fifth race now, where we look at the favorite, Chief Hilarious, in another seven-furlong sprint.

He qualifies easily on form. From his race of 17May80, he provides us with a lead time of :24.3 with no adjustments. His next best effort was on 3May80, where again he established the lead time of :25.1 with no adjustments. This was the easiest calculation you are likely to find. For early speed, we can award the full 4 points off that record. The second choice is Native Root, at 9-2.

His up-close calls qualify on form. From his powerful race of 17May80, we convert the 7f time to 1:10.2 for 6f, which gives us a lead time of :24.4. Native Root held approximately even and gets that figure for ability. Out of the

5 BELMONT — 7 FURLONGS (BELMONT PARK; START, FINISH)

7 FURLONGS. (1.20⅗) CLAIMING. Purse $18,000. 3-year-olds. Weight, 122 lbs. Non-winners of two races since May 1 allowed 3 lbs. Of a race since then, 5 lbs. Claiming price $50,000; for each $5,000 to $40,000, 2 lbs. (Races when entered to be claimed for $35,000 or less not considered.)

Chief Hilarious — B. c. 3, by Fast Hilarious—Candy Chief, by Chieftain
Own.—May-Don Stable — $50,000 — Br.—Infeld & Krebs (Fla) — Tr.—Parisella John — 114 5

	St.	1st	2nd	3rd	Amt.
1980	9	2	2	3	$32,020
1979	1	M	1	0	$2,200

28May80- 2Bel fst 1 :47⅕ 1:12⅕ 1:38⅕ Clm 62500 7 1 1hd 2½ 21 43 Beitia E5 110 1.70 74-24 Silver Sir 1131½ 🄳Give ItAChance1171½NativeRoot108hd Impeded 7
28May80-Placed third through disqualification
17May80- 5Aqu fst 1 :46⅖ 1:11 1:36⅕ Allowance 5 1 12 1hd 2hd 2¾ Beitia E5 112 6.10 84-16 Comptroller117¾ChiefHilarious112½SilverProspector1171¾ Gamely 6
3May80- 9Aqu fst 1 :45 1:10⅕ 1:36⅘ Clm c-45000 8 1 11½ 1½ 12½ 11¼ Beitia E5 110 10.60 82-12 ChiefHilarious1101¼GiveItAChance117nkHourOfPece1174¼ Driving 10
24Apr80- 2Aqu fst 6f :23 :46⅕ 1:11⅕ Clm 45000 5 2 3½ 31½ 33½ 33 Tejada V M Jr7 108 15.50🄳 84-21 Silver Sir 1171¼ Royal Rollick 1181¾🄳ChiefHilarious108nk Bore in 6
24Apr80-Disqualified and placed sixth
2Apr80- 6Aqu fst 7f :23⅕ :46⅖ 1:24⅗ 3↑ Md Sp Wt 4 1 31½ 21 1½ 1nk Tejada V M Jr7 109 3.90 78-18 ChiefHilarious109nkIrishNabob113nkElegantDisguise113hd Driving 6
16Mar80- 4Aqu fst 6f ⊡:22⅖ :46⅕ 1:12⅕ Md Sp Wt 5 8 67¼ 66¾ 66½ 66¼ Tejada V M Jr10 112 13.30 77-16 CrteBlnche1221Cesr'sWorld122nkGummoCee1221¾ Bothered start 12
8Mar80- 4Aqu fst 6f ⊡:22⅖ :45⅗ 1:10⅘ Md Sp Wt 7 1 64 57 38½ 310 Tejada V M Jr10 112 4.30 80-16 Fog A Balla 1172¼ Tandoor 1227¾ ChiefHilarious1121½ No menace 9
22Jan80- 4Hia fst 6f :22⅘ :46⅕ 1:11⅘ Md c-47500 1 6 63¾ 56½ 37 26 Samyn J L 119 *.90 78-26 RedblGroton1206ChifHilrious119hdSvnDiplomts1208 Gained place 12
14Jan80- 4Crc fst 7f :23⅗ :47⅖ 1:25⅗ Md Sp Wt 7 7 52½ 42½ 35 33½ Samyn J L 120 2.60 85-12 Mod John 1202 Exclusive Too 1201½ Chief Hilarious 1207 No rally 12
2Dec79- 4Aqu fst 6f :23⅖ :48 1:13⅕ Md 40000 3 7 43 25 24 2½ Castaneda M 120 3.00 76-29 You're My Man 120½ Chief Hilarious12010UncleLouis118¾ Gamely 7
LATEST WORKOUTS May 25 Bel tr.t 6f fst 1:17⅗ b — Apr 19 Bel tr.t 4f fst :50 b

Native Root — B. c. 3, by Princely Native—Tannis Root, by Reflected Glory
Own.—Ortiz F — $50,000 — Br.—Snowden H E Sr (Ky) — Tr.—Betancourt Eduardo — 112 5

	St.	1st	2nd	3rd	Amt.
1980	10	1	4	0	$26,180
1979	13	2	2	1	$9,032

28May80- 2Bel fst 1 :47⅕ 1:12⅕ 1:38⅕ Clm 60000 5 3 62¼ 52 41½ 33 Lovato F Jr5 b 108 16.60 74-24 Silver Sir 1131½ 🄳Give ItAChance1171½NativeRoot108hd Even try 7
28May80-Placed second through disqualification
17May80- 2Aqu fst 7f :22⅘ :45⅗ 1:23 Clm 45000 2 4 51¼ 21½ 1hd 21¾ Lovato F Jr5 b 110 11.40 84-16 Silver Sir 1221¾ Native Root 110nk Golfer 1172 Gamely 9
2May80- 3Aqu fst 1 :47⅕ 1:12⅗ 1:38⅕ Clm 35000 1 4 3nk 1hd 2hd 22 Lovato F Jr5 b 112 5.30 73-19 Golden Crest 1102 Native Root112nkPrivateEye1152¾ Saved place 6
24Apr80- 4Aqu fst 6f :23 :46 1:11⅗ Clm 30000 5 2 3nk 31½ 2½ 1½ Lovato F Jr5 b 112 5.60 86-21 Native Root 112½ Private Eye 1171¼ Trifecta 1174 Driving 7
20Apr80- 5Aqu fst 7f :22⅗ :45⅕ 1:24⅕ Clm 40000 3 2 45 43 53¾ 53¼ Lovato F Jr5 112 9.20 76-16 Silver Sir 117nk Surf Club 1132¾ Private Eye 113hd No excuse 6
12Apr80- 1Aqu fst 6f :22⅕ :45⅘ 1:11⅖ Clm 40000 6 5 41 2hd 3½ 41½ Lovato F Jr5 108 19.60 84-19 Lite Ahoy 115no Silver Sir 117nk Eastern Town 1171¼ Weakened 9
23Mar80- 9Aqu my 7f :22⅗ :45⅘ 1:25⅕ Clm 50000 2 10 99¼ 913 921 818 Saumell L b 117 48.30 57-25 Royal Rollick 1191½ Regal Roy1105½SovereignRule1192¼ No speed 10
17Feb80- 4Aqu gd 6f ⊡:22⅗ :46⅘ 1:12⅘ Clm 50000 1 6 1hd 1hd 31 55¾ Saumell L b 117 9.00 74-26 Occasionally Monday 1123 Bolting Sam 117¾ RegalRoy114¾ Tired 8
10Jan80- 2Aqu fst 6f ⊡:22⅕ :46⅕ 1:12 Clm 50000 6 3 32 43 33½ 22¼ Saumell L b 117 16.90 82-19 Regal Roy 1192¼ Native Root 117¾ Col. Frankincense1123 Gaining 8
3Jan80- 8Aqu fst 170 ⊡:48⅘ 1:13⅘ 1:43⅗ Allowance 6 2 21 43½ 612 614 Saumell L b 115 22.00 70-22 🄳Googolplex1172🄳SovereignRule1153LineEmUp1151¾ Early foot 6
LATEST WORKOUTS May 10 Bel tr.t 4f fst :48 h — Apr 18 Bel tr.t 4f fst :50 b — Apr 11 Bel tr.t 3f gd :37⅕ h — Apr 5 Bel tr.t 4f sly :48⅕ h (d)

Line Em Up — B. c. 3, by Gage Line—Celtic Lyn, by Celtic Ash
Own.—Sommer Viola — $50,000 — Br.—McDowell Farm (Ark) — Tr.—Martin Frank — 117

Turf Record	St.	1st	2nd	3rd			St.	1st	2nd	3rd	Amt.
	1	0	0	1		1980	9	1	1	0	$24,780
						1979	10	2	1	2	$20,440

28May80- 2Bel fst 1 :47⅕ 1:12⅕ 1:38⅕ Clm 65000 3 6 41¾ 62¼ 63 53¼ Cordero A Jr b 117 6.50 74-24 Silver Sir 1131½ 🄳GiveItAChance1171½NativeRoot108hd Fell back 7
18May80- 4Aqu gd 1⅛ Ⓣ:49⅘ 1:15⅕ 1:54 Clm 75000 7 5 3½ 21 22 32¼ Rivera M A b 122 5.70 72-21 King's Wish 1221½ Another Jab 107¾ Line Em Up 122nk Wide 7
18May80-Disqualified from purse money.
31Mar80- 2Aqu sly 1⅛ :46⅘ 1:11⅘ 1:51⅘ Clm c-50000 3 7 69½ 513 414 414 Fell J b 117 2.10e 62-23 Col.Frnkincense1172¼SovrignRul1151¼King'sWish11510 No factor 7
10Mar80- 7Aqu fst 1⅛ ⊡:48 1:12⅗ 1:52⅘ Handicap 3 4 32½ 32 43 42¾ Fell J b 114 18.00 79-19 Little Lenny 114no Googolplex 122no DonDaniello1192¾ Weakened 7
1Mar80- 9Bow fst 1₁⁄₁₆ :47⅕ 1:11⅘ 1:44⅖ Bowie 5 11 1015 914 89 611 Lindberg G 122 58.50 73-18 Blue Ensign1157GoldenProfit116hdPickett'sCharge1103 No threat 11
9Feb80- 9Suf fst 1 :48⅕ 1:13⅕ 1:40 Handicap 1 4 52¾ 32½ 23 21½ Caceres E 116 *2.60 75-25 GoldenProfit1201½LineEmUp116½FoolishMov1147 Altered course 10
27Jan80- 7Aqu fst 1₁⁄₁₆ ⊡:47 1:11⅖ 1:44 Count Fleet 3 7 79¼ 79½ 715 620 Santiago A 121 32.70 74-17 Degenerate Jon117½ColonelMoran1174Googolplex123nk No threat 7
12Jan80- 6Aqu gd 170 ⊡:47⅖ 1:13⅖ 1:45 Handicap 8 9 74¾ 66¼ 59½ 68½ Hernandez R 116 6.80e 68-21 Googolplex 1221 Crusader Ray K. 1081½ Sagacious 114½ Outrun 9
3Jan80- 8Aqu fst 170 ⊡:48⅘ 1:13⅘ 1:43⅗ Allowance 4 4 31 2hd 33 35 Martens G 115 3.50e 79-22 🄳Googolplex 1172 🄳SovereignRule1153LineEmUp1151¾ Impeded 6
3Jan80-Placed first through disqualification
13Dec79- 8Aqu sly 1₁⁄₁₆ ⊡:48⅖ 1:14 1:46⅗ Allowance 7 1 12 14 16 15 Cruguet J 115 10.50 81-20 Line Em Up 1155 Sun Partner 115nk Philanthropic 120hd Easily 7
LATEST WORKOUTS May 26 Bel tr.t 4f fst :49 b — May 12 Bel tr.t 5f fst 1:01⅕ h — ●May 6 Bel tr.t 6f fst 1:13⅗ h — Apr 30 Bel 6f sly 1:13⅕ h

24Apr80 race, there was a lead time of :25.1, reduced by one for gain with no further adjustment, to leave us with a :25.0. We have another early-speed horse and another 4 points here. We can now look at the third choice, Line Em Up, who has run twice against stakes competition.

Line Em Up qualifies on form, with two up-close calls and a class drop thrown in for good measure. He gets a pair of :25.0's for ability. On 10Mar80, there was a lead time of :24.3, with two added for energy. On 27Jan80, the lead time was a strong :24.2 with a healthy three ticks tacked on for energy to bring up the :25.0 final figure. But he gets only 2 early-speed points.

Now, to the comparative rating.

Odds	Horse	Ability		A Pts		ES	F	Total
.7	Chief Hilarious	:24.3	:25.1	17	14	4	Q	35
4.5	Native Root	:24.4	:25.1	16	14	4	Q	34
5.0	Line Em Up	:25.0	:25.0	15	15	2	Q	32

Chief Hilarious is a big, short-priced favorite, but he is only one point higher than Native Root. We can begin to suspect that the Chief is vastly overrated. There is not enough margin here for a win bet, but under our rules, we have to go to Chief Hilarious for a place wager. The outcome was not too surprising, when you take into account that his heavy support at the windows didn't match up with his figures.

FIFTH RACE
Belmont
JUNE 4, 1980

7 FURLONGS. (1.20$\frac{4}{5}$) CLAIMING. Purse $18,000. 3-year-olds. Weight,122 lbs. Non-winners of two races since May 1 allowed 3 lbs. Of a race since then, 5 lbs. Claiming price $50,000; for each $5,000 to $40,000, 2 lbs. (Races when entered to be claimed for $35,000 or less not considered.)

Value of race $18,000, value to winner $10,800, second $3,960, third $2,160, fourth $1,080. Mutuel pool $155,552, OTB pool $98,197. Exacta Pool $204,895. OTB Exacta Pool $160,153.

Last Raced	Horse	Eqt.	A.	Wt	PP	St	¼	½	Str	Fin	Jockey	Cl'g Pr	Odds $1
28May80 ^{8}Bow^{2}	Flying Sugar	b	3	115	6	1	$1_{\frac{1}{2}}$	1^{4}	1^{6}	$1^{1\frac{1}{2}}$	Vasquez J	40000	8.20
28May80 ^{2}Bel^{5}	Line Em Up	b	3	117	4	5	5^{1}	4^{1}	2^{3}	$2^{1\frac{1}{4}}$	Rivera M A	50000	5.00
11May80 ^{6}Aqu^{11}	Onalaska	b	3	117	8	3	8	7^{6}	4^{1}	$3^{1\frac{3}{4}}$	Brocklebank J	50000	40.60
28May80 ^{2}Bel^{2}	Native Root	b	3	112	5	4	6^{3}	5^{1}	3^{hd}	4^{11}	Lovato F Jr^{5}	50000	4.50
28May80 ^{2}Bel^{3}	Chief Hilarious		3	114	1	8	$4_{\frac{1}{2}}$	6^{2}	6^{5}	5^{nk}	Beitia E^{5}	50000	.70
25May80 ^{9}Bel^{5}	Alternating Curent		3	112	7	2	$3^{1\frac{1}{2}}$	$2^{1\frac{1}{2}}$	5^{4}	6^{11}	Gonzalez M A^{5}	50000	8.90
25May80 ^{9}FL^{5}	Royal Strings	b	3	113	2	7	2^{1}	$3_{\frac{1}{2}}$	7^{6}	$7_{\frac{3}{4}}$	Velasquez J	40000	29.00
3Sep79 ^{9}Bel^{1}	Salkahatchie		3	113	3	6	$7^{1\frac{1}{2}}$	8	8	8	Martens G	40000	55.40

OFF AT 3:02 1/2, EDT. Start good for all but CHIEF HILARIOUS, Won driving. Time, :23$\frac{1}{5}$, :46, 1:10$\frac{1}{5}$, 1:23$\frac{4}{5}$ Track fast.

$2 Mutuel Prices:

6–(F)–FLYING SUGAR	18.40	6.80	4.20
4–(D)–LINE EM UP		5.80	4.80
8–(H)–ONALASKA			9.00

$2 EXACTA 6–4 PAID $106.80.

When competing horses are closely bunched in ability points with totals not high enough to rate far above their rivals, it is not unusual to see a long-priced animal win the race. Chief Hilarious, our place selection, despite his low odds and heavy support, was never a serious contender. Our loss is not great, however, as we turn to the sixth race, where again we have a heavy favorite.

This young filly ran a strong race last out to qualify, and it is that effort that makes her the favorite today. But her best ability time came out of the 5May80 race at 7f, where we convert the final winning time to 1:11.0 for 6f. This gives us a :24.3 lead time, and Madura reduces that by four off her strong gain. The one tick added for energy leaves her with a solid :24.0 ability rating. In her last good race of 14May80, there was a lead time of :25.0, with a reduction of two for gain, offset by one for energy, to finish with a :24.4 figure. There is also improvement in the line. For early-speed points, there is a total of 2.

6 BELMONT

7 FURLONGS. (1.20⅖) ALLOWANCE. Purse $20,000. Fillies and mares, 3-year-olds and upward which have never won two races other than maiden, claiming or starter. Weight, 3-year-olds, 114 lbs. Older, 122 lbs. Non-winners of a race other than maiden or claiming since May 1 allowed 3 lbs. Of such a race since April 15, 5 lbs.

Madura — Ch. f. 3, by Graustark—Turbinia, by Hail to Reason
Own.—Darby Dan Farm — Br.—Galbreath J W (Ky) — Tr.—Rondinello Thomas L — **114**

	St.	1st	2nd	3rd	Amt.
1980	3	2	1	0	$22,180
1979	3	M	1	1	$4,660

14May80- 2Aqu fst 1 :46⅘ 1:11⅘ 1:36⅘ ⒻAllowance 1 6 44 41½ 1½ 12¾ Fell J 116 1.90 84-17 Madura 1162¾ Ten Cents AKiss1161¾ReallyMean116hd Ridden out 8
5May80- 2Aqu fst 7f :23 :46⅘ 1:24 ⒻAllowance 4 7 78 56 34½ 2½ Fell J 116 2.50 80-19 Popular Game 116½ Madura 1161¼ Bang The Drums 1214¾ Wide 8
21Jan80- 4Hia fst 6f :22⅘ :46⅗ 1:11⅘ ⒻMd Sp Wt 5 9 74½ 32 21 13¼ Fell J 120 *.90 84-26 Madura 1203¼ Accipitral 1205½ Dream Circle 1138 Handily 12
19Dec79- 4Aqu gd 6f ⊡:23⅕ :47⅕ 1:11⅘ ⒻMd Sp Wt 7 7 74¾ 84¾ 811 24¼ Fell J 117 7.70e 80-19 Delta Bid 1174¼ Madura 1171¼ English Toffy 1172¾ Second best 9
21Oct79- 2Aqu fst 6f :22⅘ :46⅗ 1:12⅕ ⒻMd Sp Wt 8 5 — — — — Velasquez J 117 *2.70 — — Tilly's Curve 117nk Island Charm 1177¼ Annecy 117¾ Pulled up 9
30Sep79- 6Bel sly 6½f :22⅘ :46⅕ 1:18⅘ ⒻMd Sp Wt 6 11 88¼ 58¼ 47 37 Cordero A Jr 118 38.10 76-24 Cybele 1182¾ Veiled Prophet 1134¼ Madura 1189 No threat 12
LATEST WORKOUTS May 31 Bel 4f fst :50⅗ b May 26 Bel 5f fst 1:02 b May 21 Bel 3f sly :38⅘ b May 12 Bel 4f fst :51 b

The second choice, Going East, has run in five stakes races, and that alone portends tough competition today.

Going East — B. f. 3, by Going Straight—Tammy Fleur, by Tim Tam
Own.—Altan Stable — Br.—Donamire Farm (Ky) — Tr.—Marcus Alan B — **109**

Turf Record	St.	1st	2nd	3rd		St.	1st	2nd	3rd	Amt.
	1	0	0	0	1980	8	0	0	4	$25,402
					1979	9	3	3	1	$41,100

14May80- 5Aqu fst 1 :46⅗ 1:11 1:35⅕ ⒻAllowance 8 4 42 3½ 34½ 35¼ Asmussen C B 116 2.80 84-17 Erin's Word 1212¾ Farewell Letter 1112¾ Going East1163¾ Evenly 8
2May80- 8Aqu fst 6f :22⅘ :45⅘ 1:10⅕ ⒻAllowance 3 6 51½ 98 86¾ 58¼ Asmussen C B 116 5.10 84-19 Punta Punta1163¼StarofAraby1163¾GlamorousNell1161¼ Bore out 9
24Mar80- 7Aqu fst 6f :22⅕ :45⅗ 1:11⅗ ⒻAllowance 5 1 63½ 64½ 64½ 42½ Velasquez J 118▲ *2.60 82-24 Tell A Secret 1141¼ Inlet 1211 Paintbrush 114nk Checked 6
24Mar80-Dead heat
1Mar80- 8Aqu fst 6f ⊡:22⅕ :46 1:11⅕ ⒻCicada 1 7 67 66½ 610 59¼ Castaneda M 114 7.60 79-17 TheWheelTurns114½DarlinMomma1214¾RemoteRuler1182¼ Outrun 8
17Feb80- 8Aqu gd 1⅛ ⊡:49⅘ 1:15 1:54 ⒻRuthless 1 3 51½ 31½ 45 44¾ Hernandez R 113 4.00 71-26 Darlin Momma 118no Triple A. 1124 Espadrille 118¾ Tired 6
2Feb80- 8Aqu fst 1⁄16 ⊡:47⅗ 1:13⅕ 1:46⅕ ⒻSearching 7 2 21½ 11½ 3½ 37¼ Maple E 113 2.40e 76-27 LuckyMyWay1124½DarlinMomma1182¾GoingEast1133¼ Weakened 10
19Jan80- 8Aqu my 1⁄16 ⊡:47⅗ 1:13⅘ 1:46⅕ ⒻBusanda 8 5 612 46½ 11 1hd Castaneda M 113 4.40Ⓓ 83-21 ⒹGoing East 113hd Espadrille 112¾ Lucky My Way 1125 Bore out 9
19Jan80-Disqualified and placed third
1Jan80- 8Aqu fst 6f ⊡:23⅘ :47⅗ 1:12⅘ ⒻRosetown 1 1 63 63¼ 42¼ 3½ Castaneda M 114 8.40 79-18 In Our Time 115nk Lucky May 114nk Going East 114½ Rallied 7
1Dec79- 5Aqu fst 1 :47 1:12⅘ 1:38⅘ ⒻAllowance 4 4 41¾ 41 3½ 13¼ Asmussen C B 115 3.40 74-23 Going East 1153¼ TurnDownTheHeat117¾Ojavan115nk Ridden out 7
21Nov79- 9Aqu fst 7f :23 :46⅕ 1:25 ⒻClm 60000 3 4 41½ 54 21 12¼ Pincay L Jr 117 *2.60 76-18 Going East 1172¼ The Wheel Turns 1163¼ Ojavan 1141¼ Driving 9
LATEST WORKOUTS May 31 Bel 5f fst 1:01⅖ b May 24 Bel 4f fst :49 b ●May 10 Bel tr.t 4f fst :47⅕ b Apr 26 Bel 4f fst :52 b

She qualifies with the necessary up-close at two calls in her last race. In that event, the lead time was :24.2, which is balanced out with a gain of one and an addition of one for energy, and that becomes the ability time. In the 2May80 race, there was a :24.2 lead time with no gain or loss, but an addition of one for energy to a :24.3. These are the kinds of ability times you would expect from a filly of the caliber of Going East. There are 4 early-speed points.

The third betting choice, Veiled Prophet, comes off an incredible victory of 15 lengths! What else does she show?

She can't get credit for a Big Win because of her early lead, but this was a very impressive performance in her last race. There was a time of :25.0 on the

Veiled Prophet — B. f. 3, by Damascus—Julia B, by Herbager
Own.—Taylor's Purchase Farm — Br.—Jones W L (Md) — Tr.—Laurin Roger — **114**

Turf Record	St.	1st	2nd	3rd		St.	1st	2nd	3rd	Amt.
	3	0	1	1	1980	6	2	2	1	$25,350
					1979	8	M	3	2	$13,920

21May80- 4Bel sly 1⁄16 :46 1:11 1:44⅘ 3↑ⒻAllowance 7 1 12 15 17 115 Cordero A Jr b 112 *.80 79-22 Veiled Prophet 11215 Adlibber 108½FantasticHigh110¾ Ridden out 11
27Apr80- 9Aqu fst 1 :47 1:12⅘ 1:38 ⒻAllowance 7 6 61¾ 4¾ 1½ 22 Cordero A Jr b 116 *1.50 74-21 Radioactive 1162 Veiled Prophet 1164 River Gal 1162½ Tired 12
25Mar80- 8GP fm *1⁄16 Ⓣ 1:45⅗ ⒻAllowance 8 4 45 41½ 12 2no Cordero A Jr b 116 3.10 78-24 Esdiev 114no Veiled Prophet 1186 Ignite 1223 Sharp 10
29Feb80- 8Hia fm 1⁄16 Ⓣ 1:43⅗ ⒻAllowance 9 1 11½ 1hd 1½ 33¼ Cordero A Jr b 116 7.90 76-25 Pepi Wiley 1141¼ Val Cyn 1142¼ Veiled Prophet 116nk Wide 12
11Feb80- 6Hia fst 6f :22⅘ :46⅗ 1:12⅗ ⒻMd Sp Wt 5 5 23 2½ 13 15 Cordero A Jr b 120 *1.90 80-18 VeiledProphet1205SquawSmoke1202Nalee'sFntsy120½ Ridden out 12
1Feb80-10Hia fm *1⁄16 Ⓣ 1:46⅗ ⒻMd Sp Wt 9 1 14 1hd 11½ 83¼ Cordero A Jr b 120 *1.60 66-21 Blissful Solitude 1201 Kinga 120nk Ignite 120nk Tired 10
17Dec79- 6Aqu my 6f ⊡:22⅘ :47⅗ 1:14⅘ ⒻMd Sp Wt 12 1 43 21½ 22 31¼ Amy J b 117 *3.50 70-27 RoseOfMorn117¾PrettyMeliss117½VeiledProphet1171¼ Weakened 12
17Nov79- 6Aqu fst 6f :22⅗ :46⅗ 1:12⅗ ⒻMd Sp Wt 5 2 31½ 32 31½ 31¾ Gonzalez M A5 b 112 2.80 78-21 TurnDownTheHet1171¼Astrid'sPride117½VeildPropht1121¾ Evenly 9
28Oct79- 9Aqu gd 7f :22⅘ :46⅗ 1:26 ⒻMd Sp Wt 2 6 64 76 66 55¼ Gonzalez M A5 b 112 *1.30 66-24 Arisen 117¾ Gloverette 1171¼ In Our Time 1172¾ Dull 9
13Oct79- 9Bel sly 6f :22⅗ :46⅘ 1:12⅗ ⒻMd Sp Wt 9 5 68 54 32½ 2¾ Gonzalez M A5 b 113 7.20 78-27 Love Sign 118¾ Veiled Prophet 1134¾ Passerine 1181¾ Wide 12
LATEST WORKOUTS Jun 2 Bel 3f fst :37 b May 19 Bel 3f fst :37 b May 12 Bel 3f fst :36⅘ b May 6 Bel 4f fst :50⅘ b

lead, with no adjustments. We have to go down to the bottom race of 13Oct79 for the next best figure. There was a lead time of :25.4, reduced by three for gain, with one added for energy, to finish with a :25.2. There is consistently strong early speed, with another 4 points here. We can now summarize.

Odds	Horse	Ability		A Pts		ES	Q	Total
.8	Madura	:24.0	:24.4	20	16	2	Q2	40
4.9	Going East	:24.2	:24.3	18	17	4	Q1	40
5.0	Veiled Prophet	:25.0	:25.2	15	13	4	Q2	34

This is a tough race, where there are three very strong contenders. Madura, tied for the point lead, has the low odds and becomes our investment to place only. Going East is indeed formidable and that last victory by Veiled Prophet scares us more than a little. But again, we must stand by our point ratings, exercise discipline, and march to the windows to back Madura to place.

SIXTH RACE
Belmont
JUNE 4, 1980

7 FURLONGS. (1.20$\frac{4}{5}$) ALLOWANCE. Purse $20,000. Fillies and mares, 3–year–olds and upward which have never won two races other than maiden, claiming or starter. Weights, 3–year–olds, 114 lbs. Older, 122 lbs. Non–winners of a race other than maiden or claiming since May 1 allowed 3 lbs. Of such a race since April 15, 5 lbs.

Value of race $20,000, value to winner $12,000, second $4,400, third $2,400, fourth $1,200. Mutuel pool $200,260, OTB pool $102,642. Track Quinella Pool $197,640. OTB Quinella Pool $132,940.

Last Raced	Horse	Eqt.	A.	Wt	PP	St	¼	½	Str	Fin	Jockey	Odds $1
21May80 ^{4}Bel^{1}	Veiled Prophet	b	3	114	2	4	1^{hd}	$1^{1\frac{1}{2}}$	1^{2}	1^{1}	Skinner K	5.50
14May80 ^{5}Aqu^{3}	Going East		3	112	4	3	$3^{\frac{1}{2}}$	2^{hd}	2^{2}	$2^{\frac{3}{4}}$	Asmussen C B	4.90
14May80 ^{2}Aqu^{1}	Madura		3	114	6	10	10^{1}	$6^{\frac{1}{2}}$	4^{1}	$3^{1\frac{1}{4}}$	Fell J	.80
25May80 ^{7}Bel^{4}	Polar Flag		4	112	10	1	$5^{1\frac{1}{2}}$	3^{2}	$3^{\frac{1}{2}}$	$4^{1\frac{3}{4}}$	Lovato F Jr^{5}	11.90
17May80 ^{7}CD^{3}	Sweetladyroll		3	113	5	11	11	9^{hd}	7^{1}	$5^{\frac{1}{2}}$	Vasquez J	8.60
22May80 ^{7}Bel^{5}	McAllister Miss	b	3	109	11	9	9^{hd}	10^{4}	8^{4}	6^{hd}	Beitia E^{5}	55.00
18May80 ^{6}Aqu^{10}	Miss Joy Forever		4	117	7	2	4^{hd}	4^{hd}	5^{1}	$7^{1\frac{1}{4}}$	Maple E†^{2}	53.30
17May80 ^{3}Aqu^{1}	Kelley's Day	b	3	114	3	6	6^{1}	8^{1}	$6^{\frac{1}{2}}$	$8^{5\frac{1}{4}}$	Rivera M A	15.30
22May80 ^{7}Bel^{3}	Higher Justice		3	106	1	5	2^{1}	$5^{1\frac{1}{2}}$	$9^{1\frac{1}{2}}$	$9^{\frac{1}{2}}$	Gonzalez M A^{5}	32.30
9May80 ^{9}Aqu^{4}	Secret Virtue	b	3	109	8	8	$8^{\frac{1}{2}}$	$7^{\frac{1}{2}}$	10^{10}	10^{18}	Miranda J	69.40
4Mar80 ^{8}Hia^{7}	Hind		4	110	9	7	7^{1}	11	11	11	Hernandez C^{7}	110.70

OFF AT 3:32 EDT. Start good, Won driving. Time, :23$\frac{2}{5}$, :46$\frac{3}{5}$, 1:10$\frac{4}{5}$, 1:23$\frac{4}{5}$ Track fast.

$2 Mutuel Prices:

2–(B)–VEILED PROPHET	13.00	5.40	3.00
4–(E)–GOING EAST		5.60	3.00
6–(G)–MADURA			2.40

$2 QUINELLA 2–4 PAID $25.60.

That 15-length win by Veiled Prophet was obviously no fluke, as she beat two very good fillies in this race. Madura was gaining in the stretch, but not enough, and finished third, as we lose our wager.

This race does present an example, however, of three very superior entries, making it an almost certain three-horse race, just as they finished.

The seventh race was also scheduled to be run on the turf, but likewise had to be shifted to the dirt because of the rains. Nonetheless, the crowd made Tromos a prohibitive favorite.

7 **BELMONT**

WIDENER TURF COURSE
START
1 MILE
BELMONT PARK
FINISH

1 MILE. (TURF). (1.33) ALLOWANCE. Purse $25,000. 3-year-olds and upward which have never won three races other than maiden, claiming or starter. Weight, 3-year-olds, 114 lbs. Older, 122 lbs. Non-winners of two races other than maiden or claiming at a mile or over since April 15 allowed 3 lbs. Of such a race since then, 5 lbs.

***Tromos** — **Ch. c. 4, by Busted—Stilvi, by Derring-Do**
Br.—Cambanis G L (Eng)
Own.—Pillar Farm — **Tr.—Howe Peter M** — **117**

	Turf Record					St.	1st	2nd	3rd	Amt.
St.	1st	2nd	3rd		1979	1	0	1	0	$5,317
4	2	1	1		1978	3	2	0	1	$74,857

17Apr79♦4Newmarket(Eng) gd 1 1:41⅕ Ⓣ Craven Stakes(Gr.3) 22½ Lynch J 126 *.30 — — LyphrdsWish1192½ Tromos1264 Wrmington119 Trailed,bid,no exc 3
20Oct78♦4Newmarket(Eng) gd 7f 1:24⅗ Ⓣ Dewhurst Stakes(Gr.1) 13 Lynch J 126 2.75 — — Tromos 1263 More Light 1261½ Warmington 126hd Led thruout 6
28Sep78♦5Ascot(Eng) fm 6f 1:16⅖ Ⓣ Clarence House Stakes 110 Lynch J 123 *2.50 — — Tromos 12310 Milford 1184 B. Foster 1233 Drew away easily 7
16Sep78♦6Doncaster(Eng) gd 6f 1:16⅕ Ⓣ Ribero Stakes 32¼ Lewis G 119 2.00 — — Indian Brave 1192 SandfordBoy123nk Tromos1193 Raced greenly 8
LATEST WORKOUTS ●Jun 3 Bel 3f fst :34⅗ b May 29 Bel Ⓣ 5f fm 1:01⅕ b (d) May 23 Bel 4f fst :47⅗ bg ●May 16 Bel 1 fst 1:39⅗ h

Once again, New York players go overboard on a favorite when there is no logical reason to do so. Tromos has never run on the dirt, and the fact that today's race was taken off the grass is not likely to help this young British colt. He has not run in more than a year, and even if his workout times are excellent, which they are indeed, his unknown ability makes him a dubious factor. At 4-5, I could never risk my money on a horse that cannot be evaluated.

The second choice is London Bells, who is also a grass campaigner, but who does have one dirt race on which he can be rated.

London Bells — **B. c. 3, by Nijinsky II—Shake a Leg, by Raise a Native**
Br.—Taylor E P (Can)
Own.—Sangster R E — **Tr.—Stephens Woodford C** — **109**

	Turf Record					St.	1st	2nd	3rd	Amt.
St.	1st	2nd	3rd		1980	5	2	1	1	$18,955
10	2	4	1		1979	6	1	3	0	$21,483

28May80- 7Bel fm 1 1/16 Ⓣ:46⅖ 1:10⅗ 1:42 3↑Allowance 5 3 34 21½ 2½ 23½ Maple E 113 *1.60 82-12 Coriander 1193½ London Bells 113hd Evasive John 1194 Gamely 7
5May80- 1Aqu fm 1⅛ Ⓣ:47 1:11⅗ 1:49⅕ 3↑Allowance 6 4 44 21 69 714 Maple E 113 *1.50 84-04 Audacious Fool 119¾ NoNeck1193¼CrownThyGood1191½ Gave way 8
6Mar80- 8GP fm 1 1/16 Ⓣ:46⅕ 1:11 1:42⅗ Allowance 6 8 66½ 31 1hd 1¾ Maple E 117 *2.80 88-07 London Bells 117¾ Raj Kapoor 1143½ Naked Sky 117¾ Driving 11
20Feb80- 4Hia fst 7f :23⅕ :45⅘ 1:24 Allowance 9 3 1hd 11 14 12¾ Maple E 116 *1.50 83-16 LondonBlls1162¾ImprssivPrnc1164PtntAppldFor1161½ Ridden out 9
8Feb80- 8Hia fm *1 1/16 Ⓣ 1:42⅖ Allowance 1 4 32 2hd 21½ 310 Maple E 115 *1.60 79-21 Proctor 1159 Naked Sky 1151 London Bells 115no Tired 10
23Aug79♦3York(Eng) gd 6f 1:15 Ⓣ Gimcrack Stakes(Gr.2) 56¾ Piggott L b 126 *2.50 — — Sonnen Gold 1261½ Lavinsky 1261½ Braughing 1263 Well up 5f 7
2Aug79♦2Goodwood(Eng) gd 7f 1:33 Ⓣ Lanson Champagne Stakes 43¼ Piggott L 123 *1.50 — — MrthonGold1262½ OnNoTrmp126hd JohnnyO'Dy126¾ Well up, led 7
4Jly79♦1Curragh(Ire) fm 6f 1:10⅗ Ⓣ Erne Plate(Mdn) 18 Murphy T 126 *.35 — — LondonBells1268 HoratioAlger1262½ Nahisk1262 Easily, led fnl 3f 14
19Jun79♦4Ascot(Eng) gd 6f 1:15⅖ Ⓣ Coventry Stakes(Gr.2) 22½ Piggott L b 123 3.50 — — Varingo 1232½ London Bells 1233 Final Straw 1233 Away slowly 18
2Jun79♦2Leopardst'n(Ire) gd 5f 1:01⅖ Ⓣ Kilpedder Plate(Mdn) 2no Piggott L 126 *.30 — — JyBird123no LondonBells1266 TieAnchor126n· With pace thruout 15
LATEST WORKOUTS Jun 3 Bel 4f fst :49 b May 27 Bel 3f fst :35⅖ b May 24 Bel 7f fst 1:29 b May 15 Bel 6f fst 1:15 b

He certainly qualifies on form after his last good effort, even though it was on the grass. The only dirt race we can use comes from the 20Feb80 effort at Hialeah, where we first have to convert a strong winning 7f time down to 1:11.0 for 6f. We have a :25.1 lead time with no changes, but London Bells has demonstrated he knows how to win on the dirt. Off that race, we would allow 4 points for early speed.

Bucksplasher, son of an illustrious father, is the third choice.

His miserable form was demonstrated in two stakes races, and he is back in an easier allowance race today. But despite the high quality of the races in which he ran, this horse must be an NQ on form.

From the three favorites, we have two that show no ratings, Tromos because of unknown ability and Bucksplasher because of NQ form. This leaves only London Bells to consider. Since Tromos is the favorite with unknown ability, we have to pass him and thus are allowed to invest only in the next rated horse

Bucksplasher — Ch. c. 3, by Buckpasser—Victoria Star, by Northern Dancer
Br.—Kilroy W S (Ky)
Own.—Ken-Mort Stable — Tr.—Marcus Alan B — **109**

	St.	1st	2nd	3rd	Amt.
1980	9	2	1	4	$44,243
1979	5	1	1	1	$13,820

10May80- 8Aqu	fst	1	:45⅘	1:09⅕	1:34⅖	Withers	4	6	67¼	59½	7 12	7 15	Fell J	b 126	17.60	79–13	Colonel Moran 1265½TemperenceHill1264¼J.P.Brother126½	Outrun	7
19Apr80- 8Aqu	fst	1⅛	:47⅖	1:11⅗	1:50⅘	Wood Mem'l	5	4	42½	54	9 16	10 19	Castaneda M	b 126	35.30	62–17	Plugged Nickle 1261½ ColonelMoran126hdGenuineRisk1213¾	Tired	11
5Apr80- 8Aqu	gd	1	:46	1:11⅕	1:37	Gotham	9	11	74¼	42¼	42½	32¾	Vasquez J	b 115	14.00f	78–20	Colonel Moran123noDunham'sGift1142¾Bucksplasher1152¾	Rallied	12
27Mar80- 8Aqu	fst	7f	:22⅗	:45⅖	1:23⅕	Allowance	5	3	32½	2½	15	13¾	Fell J	b 117	4.10	85–23	Bucksplsher1173¾BrDexter1192¾SirSizzlingNhoc1172¾	Ridden out	7
27Feb80- 8Aqu	fst	1 1/16 ⊡	:47	1:11⅘	1:45⅕	Whirlaway	6	3	42	52½	43½	35¼	Castaneda M	b 117	23.10	83–17	Don Daniello 117½ Googolplex 1214¾ Bucksplasher 117½	Even try	6
20Feb80- 5Aqu	fst	1 1/16 ⊡	:47⅘	1:13	1:45⅘	Allowance	5	4	42½	32	35½	37½	Dahlquist T C5	b 117	5.10	77–19	Little Lenny 122no Sagacious 1197½ Bucksplasher 1175½	Tired	5
9Feb80- 5Aqu	fst	1 1/16 ⊡	:49⅖	1:14⅘	1:47	3↑ Allowance	2	1	1½	1½	11	1nk	Asmussen C B	b 119	*.90	79–19	Bucksplasher 119nk Bar Dexter 1171¾ Santo's Joe 112¾	Driving	8
27Jan80- 5Aqu	fst	1 70 ⊡	:48⅕	1:13⅕	1:43	Allowance	8	7	65	62¾	32	36¾	Asmussen C B	b 119	*.80	80–17	Don Daniello 1175 Self Pressured 1171¾ Bucksplasher 1191¾	Wide	8
7Jan80- 6Aqu	fst	1 70 ⊡	:48	1:13⅕	1:43⅗	Allowance	3	3	21	21	21½	23¼	Maple E	b 122	3.30	81–22	Sagacious 1173¼ Bucksplasher 1223 Don Daniello 117hd	2nd best	8
23Dec79- 5Aqu	gd	1 70 ⊡	:48⅘	1:13⅘	1:45⅖	Md Sp Wt	6	1	1½	11	1hd	1nk	Maple E	b 120	*.80	75–22	Bucksplasher 120nk Sir Kay 1203¾ Goldenny 1202¼	Driving	8

LATEST WORKOUTS May 31 Bel 5f fst 1:01⅖ b May 24 Bel 4f fst :48 h May 8 Bel 4f sly :48 b ●May 3 Bel 4f fst :47 h

to place, which is London Bells. Since this is a mile race, we would have computed the early-speed factor had it been necessary. But we rested with a place bet on London Bells and saw this result.

SEVENTH RACE
Belmont
JUNE 4, 1980

1 MILE. (1.33⅗) ALLOWANCE. Purse $25,000. 3-year-olds and upward which have never won three races other than maiden, claiming or starter. Weight, 3-year-olds, 114 lbs. Older, 122 lbs. Non-winners of two races other than maiden or claiming at a mile or over since April 15 allowed 3 lbs. Of such a race since then, 5 lbs. (Originally carded to be run at 1 Mile Turf Course.)

Value of race $25,000, value to winner $15,000, second $5,500, third $3,000, fourth $1,500. Mutuel pool $201,182, OTB pool $118,147. Exacta Pool $221,620. OTB Exacta Pool $147,293.

Last Raced	Horse	Eqt.	A.	Wt	PP	St	¼	½	¾	Str	Fin	Jockey	Odds $1
27May80 8Key3	Bold Pretender	b	4	117	8	1	61	41½	21½	1½	1¾	Fell J	23.60
28May80 7Bel2	London Bells		3	113	2	9	8½	71	4½	33	21¾	Maple E	5.60
25May80 8Bel8	Col. Frankincense		3	105	3	3	12	12	1½	21	32	Attanasio R7	10.20
26May80 9Bel8	Great Neck	b	4	117	4	2	2hd	3½	3½	41	4hd	Cordero A Jr	12.20
10May80 8Aqu7	Bucksplasher	b	3	113	9	6	9	6hd	52	54	55½	Vasquez J	6.10
18May80 7Aqu5	Shanty To Castle	b	5	117	6	4	7hd	9	61	61½	62	Adams L	38.70
18May80 7Aqu3	Doney		5	112	5	7	51	5hd	83	7½	7¾	Beitia E5	12.00
28May80 7Bel7	French Cut		3	113	1	8	4½	2hd	71½	85	85	Rivera M A	16.30
17Apr79 4New2	Tromos		4	117	7	5	3hd	8½	9	9	9	Velasquez J	.80

OFF AT 4:05 1/2 EDT. Start good, Won driving. Time, :23⅖, :46⅖, 1:11, 1:36⅗ Track fast.

$2 Mutuel Prices:				
	10–(N)–BOLD PRETENDER	49.20	13.00	5.80
	3–(E)–LONDON BELLS		5.40	3.80
	4–(F)–COL. FRANKINCENSE			5.20

$2 EXACTA 10–3 PAID $182.00.

While another long shot won the race, London Bells did get a solid second, making us a nice profit for this one. I don't want to sound out an "I told you so" routine, but look at poor Tromos, struggling home last with a lot of money on his back going down the drain. Bucksplasher, too, off his terrible form, was predictably back in the crowd where he belonged. Incidentally, the winner, Bold Pretender, paying a handsome $49.20, had ability times that were extremely strong, demonstrating the power of that method. But no matter how good he or any other horse may look, we will not violate our rule to limit all investments to one of the three top choices in the betting.

But with this profit at hand, we come to the eighth and feature race, the Domino Stakes for two-year-old fillies.

We have something very unusual at the outset, a three-horse entry thrown into the race by trainer Roger Laurin. This entry rates as the second favorite, but we can back it only if one or more of its members shows adequate ability.

8 BELMONT

5 ½ FURLONGS. (1.03) 2nd Running DOMINO. $50,000 Added. Fillies, 2-year-olds. Weight, 119 lbs. By subscription of $100 each which should accompany the nomination; $400 to pass the entry box, with $50,000 added. The added money and all fees to be divided 60% to the winner, 22% to second, 12% to third and 6% to fourth. Non-winners of a race other than maiden or claiming allowed 3 lbs. Maidens, 6 lbs. Starters to be named at the closing time of entries. Trophies will be presented to the winning owner, trainer and jockey. Closed Wednesday, May 21, 1980 with 24 nominations.

Coupled—Demurely, Madame Premier and Sue Babe; Lady Goldberry and Ski Maid.

Demurely — B. f. 2, by Majestic Prince—A Charm, by Nashua
Br.—David Mrs H N (Ky)
Own.—Phillips N F — Tr.—Laurin Roger — **116**

	St.	1st	2nd	3rd	Amt.
1980	1	1	0	0	$10,200

16May80- 6Aqu fst 4½f :22⅕ :46⅗ :53⅕ ⒻMd Sp Wt 6 2 3^{3}½ 4^{6}½ 1½ Venezia M 117 18.90 96-04 Demurely 117½ Shut Up 117½ Famous Partner 1171½ Driving 10
LATEST WORKOUTS Jun 1 Bel 5f fst 1:01⅕ b May 26 Bel 4f fst :50⅕ b May 14 Bel 3f gd :39⅘ b May 8 Bel 4f sly :48⅗ h

Sue Babe — B. f. 2, by Mr Prospector—Sleek Dancer, by Northern Dancer
Br.—Kaskel H (Fla)
Own.—Regent Farm — Tr.—Laurin Roger — **116**

	St.	1st	2nd	3rd	Amt.
1980	1	1	0	0	$9,600

28Apr80- 4Aqu sly 4½f :22⅘ :46⅕ :52⅗ ⒻMd Sp Wt 1 1 1hd 1^{1}½ 1^{1}½ Martens G 117 *2.20 99-01 Sue Babe 1171½ Clare K. 117¾ Lady Goldberry 1177¾ Ridden out 8
LATEST WORKOUTS ●May 29 Bel 5f fst 1:00⅕ h May 24 Bel 5f fst 1:00⅘ h May 20 Bel 4f fst :47⅖ b May 15 Bel 4f fst :49⅖ b

Madame Premier — B. f. 2, by Raja Baba—Hail Hail, by Hail To Reason
Br.—Greathouse W (Ky)
Own.—Taylor's Purchase Farm — Tr.—Laurin Roger — **116**

	St.	1st	2nd	3rd	Amt.
1980	2	1	1	0	$13,720

26May80- 6Bel fst 5½f :23 :46⅗ 1:05⅖ ⒻMd Sp Wt 7 3 2hd 1½ 1^{1} 1½ Skinner K 117 2.40 88-20 Madame Premier 117½ Shalomar 117^{3} Clare K. 117^{4} Driving 10
8May80- 4Aqu sly 5f :22⅘ :46⅖ :59⅕ ⒻMd Sp Wt 2 2 4^{5} 5^{6}½ 5^{5}½ 2^{2}¼ Skinner K 117 *1.70 87-22 Dandy Current 1172¼ Madame Premier117^{2}NativeHula117^{no} Wide 9
LATEST WORKOUTS May 23 Bel 4f fst :47⅖ h May 17 Bel 3f fst :35⅘ h May 4 Bel 4f fst :47 h

Sue Babe has not run since April, and that was in a four-and-a-half-furlong sprint, which we are unable to rate because of inadequate internal times. So this one gets an immediate unknown rating. And Demurely likewise falls into the same category off her short-sprint victory. But you notice that Sue Babe's effort was only one tick short of the track record at that unusual distance.

But we are left to Madame Premier for any serious play. We see that she is fully qualified and then convert the 5½f race to 6f for measuring purposes, where we have 1:11.3. This produces a good :25.0 lead time for two-year-old fillies, with no adjustment required. Her other time is computed by expanding the 5f time to 1:11.3 also, for a :25.1 lead time. Off the gain, we can subtract three and then add one for energy to wind up with an extremely impressive :24.4. We would also award 6 points for early speed off the last race.

As we look over the other contenders, we see that in this two-year-old event, none has more than two ratable races. Accordingly, we are entitled to ignore the early speed factor, since there is not enough before us to have representative data on which to compute.

Despite the strong three-horse entry, the crowd has made Dandy Current the favorite off her one impressive victory.

Her 5f time must be extended to a comparable 6f figure, where we get another 1:11.3. The lead time thus becomes :25.1, and with no adjustment that is the ability time.

Dandy Current — B. f. 2, by Little Current—Groton's Dandy, by Groton
Br.—Oxford Stable (Ky)
Own.—Oxford Stable — Tr.—Hirsch William J Jr — **116**

	St.	1st	2nd	3rd	Amt.
1980	1	1	0	0	$9,600

8May80- 4Aqu sly 5f :22⅘ :46⅖ :59⅕ ⒻMd Sp Wt 3 1 1hd 2hd 1½ 1^{2}¼ Vasquez J 117 3.30 89-22 DandyCurrent1172¼MadmePremier117^{2}NtiveHul117^{no} Ridden out. 9
LATEST WORKOUTS Jun 3 Bel 3f fst :35⅘ b May 30 Bel 4f fst :47⅘ h May 26 Bel 5f fst 1:01⅗ b May 20 Bel 4f fst :49 b

Bend The Times, the third selection, has not run in more than a month and shows only two recent workouts.

Bend The Times Dk. b. or br. f. 2, by Olden Times—Bend An Ear, by Never Bend
Br.—Pin Oak Farm (Ky)
Tr.—Rieser Stanley M
Own.—Carrion J **116**

	St.	1st	2nd	3rd	Amt.
1980	3	1	1	1	$15,077

3May80- 6CD	fst	5f	:22⅖	:45⅘	:58⅗	ⒻDebutante	3	2	4$4\frac{1}{2}$	45	3$4\frac{1}{2}$	34	Romero R P	119	1.30	92-11	ExcitableLady119$2\frac{3}{4}$MstersDrem119$1\frac{1}{4}$BendTheTimes119$3\frac{1}{2}$	Evenly 7
23Apr80- 7Kee	fst	$4\frac{1}{2}$f	:22⅖	:46⅖	:53	Lafayette	7	1		2hd	1hd	2$1\frac{1}{2}$	Romero R P	116	*.40	88-12	Firm Boss 122$1\frac{1}{2}$ BendTheTimes116$\frac{1}{2}$SilverDollarBoy122$4\frac{1}{4}$	Gamely 7
8Apr80- 3Kee	sly	$4\frac{1}{2}$f	:22⅖	:45	:51	ⒻMd Sp Wt	8	4		14	1$1\frac{1}{2}$	13	Romero R P	117	5.50	100 —	BendTheTimes1173PlinSpeking117$3\frac{3}{4}$MstersDrem1179	Ridden out 10

LATEST WORKOUTS ●May 31 Mth 5f fst 1:00 h May 26 Mth 5f fst 1:00⅖ h ●Apr 28 CD 5f sly 1:01⅗ h ●Apr 19 Kee 4f fst :47 h

While you may want to argue that this is not too serious for a young filly, experience has brought me to the rule of four recent workouts. Anything less than that, as I have seen over and over again, makes a horse weak on qualifying form, even with a bullet workout, which is shown here for the latest workout as well as the two back in April. Therefore, I will be compelled to place a U in the form column for this obviously capable young runner. And since there is only one first-time starter in the entire field, we are now ready to total up to see who gets our support.

Odds	Horse	Ability		A Pts		F	Total
1.4	Dandy Current	:25.1	—	14	(14)	Q	28
1.5	Madame Premier	:24.4	:25.0	16	(16)	Q1	33
	Demurely	Unknown					U
	Sue Babe	Unknown					U
3.7	Bend The Times	—	—			U	U

EIGHTH RACE
Belmont
JUNE 4, 1980

5 ½ FURLONGS. (1.03) 2nd Running DOMINO. $50,000 Added. Fillies, 2-year-olds. Weight, 119 lbs. By subscription of $100 each which should accompany the nomination; $400 to pass the entry box, with $50,000 added. The added money and all fees to be divided 60% to the winner, 22% to second, 12% to third and 6% to fourth. Non-winners of a race other than maiden or claiming allowed 3 lbs. Maidens, 6 lbs. Starters to be named at the closing time of entries. Trophies will be presented to the winning owner, trainer and jockey. Closed Wednesday, May 21, 1980 with 24 nominations. Value of race $56,800, value to winner $34,080, second $12,496, third $6,816, fourth $3,408. Mutuel pool $190,125, OTB pool $102,935.

Last Raced	Horse	Eqt.	A.	Wt	PP	St	¼	⅜	Str	Fin	Jockey	Odds $1
28Apr80 4Aqu1	Sue Babe		2	116	7	6	22	24	1$\frac{1}{2}$	1$3\frac{1}{2}$	Martens G	a-1.50
16May80 6Aqu1	Demurely		2	116	1	1	7$1\frac{1}{2}$	6$1\frac{1}{2}$	43	2nk	Venezia M	a-1.50
26May80 6Bel1	Madame Premier		2	116	3	3	41	41	32	3$\frac{1}{2}$	Skinner K	a-1.50
3May80 6CD3	Bend The Times		2	116	4	2	11	1$1\frac{1}{2}$	25	4$8\frac{1}{2}$	Cordero A Jr	3.70
	Minnesota Belle		2	113	8	8	8	8	6$1\frac{1}{2}$	5$3\frac{1}{4}$	Beitia E	54.30
8May80 4Aqu1	Dandy Current		2	116	5	5	6$1\frac{1}{2}$	7$1\frac{1}{2}$	7$1\frac{1}{2}$	6$1\frac{1}{2}$	Velasquez J	1.40
5May80 3CD1	Seed the Cloud	b	2	116	2	4	3$\frac{1}{2}$	3$\frac{1}{2}$	52	72	Fell J	10.30
30Apr80 7Spt1	Enchanted Lady		2	119	6	7	53	52	8	8	Bailey J D	10.20

a-Coupled: Sue Babe, Demurely and Madame Premier.
OFF AT 4:37 1/2 EDT. Start good, Won ridden out. Time, :22⅗, :45⅘, :58⅕, 1:04⅘ Track fast.

$2 Mutuel Prices:

1-(G)-SUE BABE (a-entry)	5.00	4.00	3.00
1-(A)-DEMURELY (a-entry)	5.00	4.00	3.00
1-(C)-MADAME PREMIER (a-entry)	5.00	4.00	3.00

Dandy Current, even though lightly raced, is so close in the odds to the three-horse entry that they are in effect co-favorites. Since she lacks any of the commanding factors for a Lightly Raced Horse, and since Madame Premier stands out as a Double Advantage animal, we go to Madame Premier to win and place. We are betting the entry, of course, but only because of Madame Premier. And what a powerhouse entry it turned out to be!

The entry swept the board, with both Sue Babe and Demurely, as unknown factors, beating their formidable stablemate. This does no harm at all to our pocket and we proceed to the ninth and last race.

9 BELMONT

START / 6 FURLONGS / BELMONT PARK / FINISH

6 FURLONGS. (1.08⅖) CLAIMING. Purse $11,000. 4-year-olds and upward. Weight, 122 lbs. Non-winners of two races since May 1 allowed 3 lbs. Of a race since then, 5 lbs. Claiming price $16,000; for each $1,000 to $14,000, 2 lbs. (Races when entered to be claimed for $12,500 or less not considered.)

Marsh's Robber — Own.—Mesco Stable

B. h. 5, by No Robbery—Blue Madam, by Revoked — **$14,000** — **Br.—Gentry T (Ky)** — **Tr.—LaBoccetta Frank** — **113**

	St.	1st	2nd	3rd	Amt.
1980	10	0	4	1	$10,560
1979	26	5	4	3	$48,370

26May80-	3Bel	fst	7f	:23	:46⅕	1:25	Clm 12500	5	1	1hd	1hd	1½	2no	Beitia E5	b 112	4.80	77–20	Pompini114noMrsh'sRobber112nkProspector'sJoy117hd	Lugged in	6
27Apr80-	2Aqu	fst	6f	:23	:46⅘	1:11⅖	Clm 15000	4	1	21	1hd	2hd	33¼	Adams L	b 115	4.70	83–21	Siwash Chief 119no Naudi 1173¼ Marsh's Robber 1152	Tired	7
18Apr80-	2Aqu	fst	6f	:22⅖	:45⅖	1:11⅘	Clm 15000	1	3	2½	3nk	41	95¼	Adams L	b 115	*3.10	79–24	Siwash Chief 117¾ Naudi 1171¾ At The Crease 117¾	Tired	11
2Apr80-	1Aqu	fst	6f	:22⅘	:46⅕	1:11	Clm 14000	5	2	2hd	11	1hd	2no	Santagata N	b 113	*2.40	88–18	Beau Strad 112no Marsh's Robber 113nk Whiddon 1082½	Nosed	11
23Mar80-	1Aqu	my	6f	:22⅘	:46⅘	1:12	Clm 12500	8	1	3½	2hd	1hd	2nk	Santagata N	b 117	4.60	83–25	Snow Alert 117nk Marsh's Robber 1172¾ Jilting Jim 107¾	Sharp	8
2Mar80-	9Aqu	fst	6f	⊡:23⅕	:47⅘	1:13⅗	Clm 14000	10	3	64¾	84¼	55½	79¼	Santagata N	b 117	8.90	67–19	Breyer Patch 110¾Dobi'sKnight117nkSlowtoAnger1081¾	No threat	10
22Feb80-	9Aqu	gd	6f	⊡:23⅕	:47	1:12⅕	Clm 16000	7	5	53	31½	22	55	Asmussen C B	b 117	*3.50	78–19	Island Nymph 1171¾ Gorizpa 1132 Joe Montage 111½	Weakened	12
15Feb80-	5Aqu	fst	6f	⊡:22⅗	:46⅖	1:12⅗	Clm 20000	10	4	52¾	74½	1110	1011	Saumell L	b 117	16.10	70–26	Peaceful Country 117nk Hamoud 117hd A. J.Raffles112nk	Stopped	12
7Feb80-	9Aqu	fst	6f	⊡:23	:47	1:12⅗	Clm 25000	8	6	76	98¾	914	1012	Saumell L	b 117	15.40	69–29	Silver Screen 1171 Orgullo Solo 119hd ChieftainBob1171¼	Bore in	11
12Jan80-	3Aqu	my	6f	⊡:22	:46⅗	1:12⅗	Clm c-20000	8	1	32½	21½	1hd	2¾	Martens G	b 119	6.80	80–22	Orgullo Solo 117¾ Marsh's Robber 119¾StarRights1121¾	Held well	11

LATEST WORKOUTS May 23 Aqu 3f fst :36⅗ h — May 19 Aqu 5f gd 1:01⅘ h (d) — May 13 Aqu 4f sly :53 b (d) — May 6 Aqu 5f fst 1:03 b

Marsh's Robber is the favorite, and after qualifying on form, we can extract from the race of 2Apr80 a :24.4 lead time with no adjustments. The next best was on 23Mar80 at :25.1, also with no adjustments. There are the full 6 points for early speed.

Space Wars is right behind Marsh's Robber in the wagering, as the crowd is apparently concentrating on the exotic bets.

Space Wars — Own.—Allegretti V V

Dk. b. or br. g. 4, by Triple Bend—Delp Space, by Princequillo — **$16,000** — **Br.—Weakly P (Ky)** — **Tr.—Corbellini William R** — **117**

Turf Record	St.	1st	2nd	3rd
	1	0	0	1

	St.	1st	2nd	3rd	Amt.
1980	11	0	3	2	$10,080
1979	10	1	4	0	$15,605

22May80-	2Bel	my	6f	:23	:46⅖	1:10⅗	Clm 18000	5	5	76¾	44	53¼	55¾	Fell J	b 114	4.60	83–23	Mika Song 108nkFiveontheside1173¾RagingTorrent1171	No threat	7
9May80-	5Pim	fst	6f	:23⅕	:47⅖	1:12⅘	Allowance	2	4	46	43	32	31	Baker C J	b 112	4.60	81–22	Fully Loaded 1121 Poppi Joe 113no Space Wars 112¾	Mild rally	6
1May80-	7Pim	sly	6f	:23⅕	:46⅗	1:12⅗	Allowance	3	5	57½	66¾	66	75¾	Baker C J	b 112	7.50	77–26	Sound The Chimes 117¾ Ben Bolt 115no Polar Point 119½	Tired	7
24Apr80-	8Pim	fm	5f	Ⓣ:22⅕	:46	:58⅗	Allowance	8	5	69½	611	35½	34	Baker C J	b 112	6.40	89–15	Hear Hear 112½ Spectacular Choice 1193½ SpaceWars112¾	Rallied	8
4Apr80-	5Pim	my	6f	:23	:46⅘	1:13	Allowance	5	3	46½	45½	25	23½	Baker C J	b 112	4.00	77–23	Chrisangle 1193½ Space Wars 112hd Fully Loaded 112hd	Fin. well	7
25Mar80-	7Pim	gd	6f	:23⅖	:47⅖	1:13⅕	Allowance	1	4	44	42½	3nk	41¾	Baker C J	b 112	*1.70	78–26	Propose a Toast 119no Fully Loaded 1121 Zulla 115¾	Weakened	8
14Mar80-	7Bow	gd	6f	:22⅘	:46	1:12⅘	Allowance	8	1	45½	34½	43½	21	Baker C J	b 112	5.00	75–31	Crow's Nest 1121 Space Wars 112¾ Chrisangle 119nk	Gaining	9
4Mar80-	7Bow	fst	6f	:22⅘	:46⅗	1:12⅖	Allowance	6	3	46	45	22	2no	Baker C J	b 112	14.00	78–27	EasternBazaar112noSpaceWars112nkGallantHeron119no	Sharp try	7
24Jan80-	8Bow	fst	6f	:22⅖	:45	1:09⅗	Allowance	4	7	89½	811	810	75	Baker C J	b 112	24.40	87–14	BrilliantCounty112nkSoundTheChimes1151½BigVision109½	Outrun	8
15Jan80-	8Bow	fst	7f	:23	:46	1:25⅕	Allowance	7	1	1hd	33	63½	77¾	Baker C J	b 112	5.50	71–31	Buckley 1082½ Polar Point 1151 Oaklawn 1092½	Tired	9

LATEST WORKOUTS ●Apr 15 Bow 5f gd 1:02⅗ b

We are not happy about his form, but there is indeed a gain of five between the first and second calls, which is enough. If you worry about his lengths behind as compared to his 9May80 race at Pimlico, a quick calculation of ability times will change the picture. Out of the last race, we have a :24.4 (lead time of :24.1, loss of two, plus one more for energy). In the Pimlico race, there was a

:25.2 lead time, with two off for gain, but two more added right back for energy to finish at a :25.2. Thus, you are in reality seeing an Improving Horse, although we won't give form credit for it in the absence of being closer to the lead in the last race. While we're still on ability times, drop down to the 24Jan80 run at Bowie, where we began with a lead time of :24.3 and get a reduction of three for gain to :24.0. There is only one to be added for energy and we have :24.1 as the final ability time. Yes, indeed, Space Wars is not to be overlooked, except that early speed is so poor that he gets 0.

For third choice, we have two horses both showing at 5-1, with almost identical dollars in the win pool on their behalf. Since we must rate them both, we will include them in the final calculation after we find out what they offer.

Ed Cainan — B. h. 5, by Olden Times—Lady Marguery, by Tim Tam — $16,000 — Br.—Runnymede Farm & Noonan (Ky) — Tr.—DeBonis Robert — 1107
Own.—Martin Gertrude A

	St.	1st	2nd	3rd	Amt.
1980	11	2	3	1	$25,080
1979	10	0	5	1	$14,920

26May80- 3Bel	fst	7f		:23	:46⅕	1:25	Clm c-12500	2	2	2hd	2hd	2½	61	Asmussen C B	b 119	*.50	76-20	Pompini114noMrsh'sRobber112nkProspector'sJoy117hd	Weakened	6
17May80- 1Aqu	fst	7f		:22⅘	:45⅖	1:23⅖	Clm c-10000	5	4	11½	14	18	19¾	Asmussen C B	b 117	*1.00	84-16	Ed Cainan 1179¾ Shed Shy 113nk Gorizpa 1171	Driving	14
11May80- 3Aqu	fst	6f		:22⅖	:45⅘	1:11⅕	Clm 25000	6	6	42	3½	42	43	Asmussen C B	b 117	*1.50	84-14	Cumulo Nimbus 112¾ Siwash Chief 1151¾ Disco Count 108½	Tired	7
16Apr80- 1Aqu	fst	6f		;22⅗	:46	1:11	Clm 30000	3	2	3nk	2hd	11½	21	Asmussen C B	b 117	*2.30e	87-17	IslandNymph1191EdCainan1171¼CumuloNimbus108½	Second best	11
27Mar80- 5Aqu	fst	6f		:22⅖	:45⅘	1:10⅖	Clm c-22500	3	3	62½	42½	32	32¾	Asmussen C B	b 117	*2.10	88-23	IslandNymph1192¾CumuloNimbus110noEdCainan1176	Wide, hung	8
9Mar80- 2Aqu	gd	6f	⊡	:22⅘	:46⅘	1:11⅘	Clm 20000	6	2	2hd	1½	14	13½	Asmussen C B	b 117	*1.90	85-22	Ed Cainan 1173½ Island Nymph 1132¼ Williamstown 117nk	Driving	9
28Feb80- 2Aqu	fst	6f	⊡	:22⅖	:45⅘	1:10⅖	Clm 20000	10	5	74½	65	45½	23½	Asmussen C B	b 117	16.10	88-19	Armet 1123½ Ed Cainan 1171 A. J. Raffles 112¾	Gaining	11
4Feb80- 2Aqu	fst	6f	⊡	:22⅘	:46⅗	1:11⅕	Clm 20000	4	4	22	33½	36½	410	Santiago A	117	7.60	78-22	Ephphatha 1175 Armet 1171½ Prospector's Joy 1193½	Weakened	7
25Jan80- 9Aqu	fst	6f	⊡	:22⅕	:46	1:11⅗	Clm 25000	4	7	76¼	76	85¾	95	Hernandez R	117	8.40	81-18	Il Vagabondo 117no Pleasure Ban 1171 Williamstown 1171	Outrun	9
14Jan80- 7Aqu	gd	6f	⊡	:22⅗	:46⅖	1:12⅗	Clm 27500	6	7	85¼	64	55¼	52½	Martens G	115	6.50	78-23	Ruler Come Back 1121¾MidnightRacer119hdMansard117hd	Outrun	10

LATEST WORKOUTS ●May 6 Bel tr.t 5f fst 1:01⅕ h Apr 30 Bel 4f sly :51 b Apr 23 Bel tr.t 4f fst :48⅘ h Apr 12 Bel tr.t 6f fst 1:14⅕ h

This one qualifies on form. He gets a good :24.3 out of the race of 27Mar80 off that lead time with no adjustments. On 9Mar80, there is a :25.0 lead time with no adjustments either. Strong early speed merits 6 points here. Now, we can turn to Pokie Joe, the other 5-1 choice.

Pokie Joe — B. g. 4, by Jean-Pierre—Cornisara, by Cornish Prince — $16,000 — Br.—Niblick Stable (Ky) — Tr.—Puentes Gilbert — 117
Own.—Garren M M

Turf Record	St.	1st	2nd	3rd		St.	1st	2nd	3rd	Amt.
	3	0	1	0	1980	12	1	6	1	$18,950
					1979	26	2	6	7	$42,763

18May80- 9Aqu	fst	7f		:22⅘	:45⅗	1:24⅕	Clm 14000	2	8	75¼	56	4¾	2nk	Venezia M	b 113	10.10	80-19	Pruneplum 119nk Pokie Joe 113¾ Mika Song 1122¾	Wide	8
7May80- 9Aqu	fst	6f		:22⅗	:46	1:11⅗	Clm 10000	7	4	31½	33	34½	22	Gonzalez M A5	b 112	4.10	83-20	Bahama Lark 1122 Pokie Joe 112½ Debrett 1171¼	Fin well	10
30Apr80- 2Aqu	my	7f		:23⅕	:46⅘	1:24⅘	Clm 10500	1	8	1hd	1½	1hd	2hd	Gonzalez M A5	b 108	5.90	77-21	Ace's Harlequin 117hd Pokie Joe 1084¼ Ernie's Lad 1175	Sharp	8
20Apr80- 3Aqu	fst	6f		:23	:46⅕	1:11⅘	Clm 12500	7	6	44¼	55	55½	65¼	Beitia E5	b 112	*2.20	79-16	Paso Flores 117¾ Caraqueno 1171 Sandrito 1151¾	Tired	7
14Apr80- 2Aqu	fst	6f		:23	:46⅘	1:11⅖	Clm 12500	5	3	44½	47½	44	23½	Beitia E5	b 112	5.50	82-21	Siwash Chief 1173½PokieJoe112½CornCountry113½	Up for second	7
5Apr80- 2Aqu	my	6f		:23⅖	:47⅗	1:12⅘	Clm 12500	4	3	21	33½	35½	33½	Beitia E5	b 112	3.60	75-28	Snow Alert 119nk Breyer Patch 1103¼ Pokie Joe 1123¾	Weakened	6
26Mar80- 3Aqu	fst	7f		:23⅖	:48⅖	1:25⅘	Clm c-10000	5	5	31½	41¾	23	2¾	Asmussen C B	b 119	*2.00	71-29	Wartyme 112¾ Pokie Joe 1192 Dark Vadar 1062¼	Gamely	8
9Mar80- 9Aqu	fst	6f	⊡	:22⅗	:47	1:13⅖	Clm 10000	6	7	911	98¼	86½	22¾	Asmussen C B	b 117	7.60	74-22	Whiddon 1192¾ Pokie Joe 1171¼ Dark Vadar 113nk	Went well	12
24Feb80- 9Aqu	gd	6f	⊡	:22⅖	:46⅖	1:13⅖	Clm 7500	7	9	78½	48	33	1½	Asmussen C B	b 117	3.60	77-17	Pokie Joe 117½ Bill Campbell 117¾ Shed Shy 112nk	Driving	11
15Feb80- 3Aqu	fst	6f	⊡	:23⅕	:47⅘	1:13⅗	Clm 12500	9	9	76¼	98¾	85¼	66	Asmussen C B	b 117	*2.70	70-26	Gorizpa 117nk Ernie's Lad 1142 Wilford 1091½	No threat	11

LATEST WORKOUTS May 31 Bel tr.t 4f fst :47⅘ h ●May 25 Bel tr.t 4f fst :48 h ●Apr 27 Bel tr.t 4f fst :48 h ●Apr 12 Bel tr.t 3f fst :35 b

He qualifies on form also with his strong drive in the last race. Back on 14Apr80, there is a lead time of :24.3, reduced by three because of the gain of 4 lengths, and then brought up to :24.2 by the energy add-on of two ticks. His next best comes out of his last good race, where we convert the 7f time to 1:11.1

to obtain a :25.3 lead time. His gain lops off four ticks to :24.4, and since there is no energy adjustment, that is his figure. His early speed is not quite as strong, but he easily gets 3 points for a medium showing.

Comparing Ed Cainan with Pokie Joe, the first of the two has ability times of :24.3 and :24.4 for ability points of 17 and 16, or 33, with another 6 for early speed for a total of 39. Pokie Joe has :24.2 and :24.4 for 18 and 16, or a good 34, with 3 for early speed, giving him a total of 37. Early speed is the prevailing force and we can now compare Ed Cainan with the other two betting choices, as his 2-point advantage eliminates Pokie Joe.

Odds	**Horse**	**Ability**		**A Pts**		**ES**	**F**	**Total**
3.3	Marsh's Robber	:24.4	:25.1	16	14	6	Q	36
3.6	Space Wars	:24.1	:24.4	19	16	0	Q	35
5.2	Ed Cainan	:24.3	:24.4	17	16	6	Q	39

Ed Cainan comes out on top in the point comparison, and we back him to win and place. Space Wars had the best ability times, but early speed moved both his rivals ahead in the point department. But look who won the race. But, as you can see, Ed Cainan, because of his healthy odds, paid a nice $6.40 for his second-place finish, which, of course, turned a profit for the race. Space Wars showed surprising speed in this effort to beat Ed Cainan by a struggling nose.

NINTH RACE
Belmont
JUNE 4, 1980

6 FURLONGS. (1.08⅖) CLAIMING. Purse $11,000. 4–year–olds and upward. Weight, 122 lbs. Non–winners of two races since May 1 allowed 3 lbs. Of a race since then, 5 lbs. Claiming price $16,000; for each $1,000 to $14,000, 2 lbs. (Races when entered to be claimed for $12,500 or less not considered.)

Value of race $11,000, value to winner $6,600, second $2,420, third $1,320, fourth $660. Mutuel pool $120,063, OTB pool $187,200. Triple Pool $192,565. OTB Triple Pool $401,404.

Last Raced		Horse	Eqt.	A.	Wt	PP	St	¼	½	Str	Fin	Jockey	Cl'g Pr	Odds $1
22May80	^{2}Bel^{5}	Space Wars	b	4	117	6	8	6^{1½}	3^{hd}	1^{hd}	1no	Fell J	16000	3.60
26May80	^{3}Bel^{6}	Ed Cainan	b	5	110	7	6	5½	4^{3}	2^{4}	2^{5}	Attanasio R^{7}	16000	5.20
18May80	^{9}Aqu^{2}	Pokie Joe	b	4	117	5	10	8½	7^{hd}	6^{3}	3½	Venezia M	16000	5.20
26May80	^{1}Bel^{1}	Pet the Jet	b	4	113	2	2	4^{hd}	5^{1½}	5½	4^{2½}	Cruguet J	14000	9.00
24May80	^{2}Bel^{10}	Exotic Bet	b	4	117	10	5	2½	1^{hd}	4½	5¾	Asmussen C B	16000	10.50
10Apr80	^{3}Aqu^{6}	DH Bold Palette		6	117	4	7	10	10	8^{1½}	6	Adams L	15000	10.60
26May80	^{3}Bel^{2}	DH Marsh's Robber	b	5	113	9	4	1^{hd}	2^{hd}	3^{hd}	6^{nk}	Rivera M A	14000	3.30
27Mar80	^{5}Aqu^{5}	Stylistic		4	112	1	1	9^{hd}	9^{2}	7½	8^{2½}	Lovato F Jr^{5}	16000	11.80
21May80	^{1}Bel^{9}	Ace's Harlequin		7	115	8	3	3^{1½}	6^{hd}	10	9^{hd}	Encinas R I	15000	17.00
28Jun79	^{6}Pim^{8}	Imthebest	b	5	117	3	9	7^{hd}	8½	9^{hd}	10	Cordero A Jr	16000	26.30

DH—Dead heat.

OFF AT 5:05 EDT. Start good, Won driving. Time, :22⅘, :46⅘, 1:11⅖ Track fast.

$2 Mutuel Prices:			
6–(F)–SPACE WARS	9.20	5.60	3.40
7–(G)–ED CAINAN		6.40	3.60
5–(E)–POKIE JOE			3.20

Now, let's add up this entire day.

Race	Selection	Invest		Return	
		Win	Place	Win	Place
1	Ojavan	$ 2	$ 2	$ 0	$ 0
2	Somebody Super	2	2	4.60	3.00
3	Miss Rebecca	2	2	6.40	2.80
4	Native Witch	2	2	11.80	6.40
5	Chief Hilarious	—	2	—	0
6	Madura	—	2	—	0
7	London Bells	—	2	—	5.40
8	Madame Premier entry	2	2	5.00	4.00
9	Ed Cainan	2	2	0	6.40
	Totals	$12	$18	$27.80	$28.00

Total invested $30.00
Total returned $55.80
Net profit $25.80

This turned out to be a remarkable day, bounteous indeed. Out of six win bets, there were four successes, highlighted by the big $11.80. On the place side, with a play in every race, we scored in six out of nine. But what was remarkable was that on a day when the profits in the win column were actually outstanding, we made excellent money betting to place. This is accounted for by two unusually large place prices, which do not ordinarily occur. In addition, there were two other good ones, as any place price of $4.00 and up in this method of play is considered highly salutary.

With a beautiful day like this behind us, our week is rolling, as we look ahead to Thursday's card.

CHAPTER

XII

BIG WEEK AT BELMONT: FOURTH DAY, THURSDAY, JUNE 5, 1980

After three successive days of profits, we approach Thursday's card with more anticipation. Can we keep it up, or will the profit picture collapse under a deluge of long shots? Here's the first race, with North Star the heavy favorite.

This one is hard to believe, again. Such atrocious form leads to an immediate disqualification on that ground. The New York punters, always keen on the class displayed by a horse, too often equate fancy claiming prices with

1 BELMONT

1 ⅝ MILES. (2.40⅘) STARTER HANDICAP. Purse $17,000. 3–year–olds and upward which have started for a claiming price of $12,500 or less since January 1, 1979. Weights, Monday, June 2. Declarations by 10:00 a.m. Tuesday, June 3.

North Star — **B. g. 7, by Bold Destroyer—Easy Kate, by Misty Day or King Hairan**
Own.—Lebowitz J — **Br.—Lotze E L Jr (Ky)** — **Tr.—LaBoccetta Frank** — **124**

Turf Record St.	1st	2nd	3rd		St.	1st	2nd	3rd	Amt.
				1980	10	5	1	1	$52,320
2	0	0	0	1979	6	4	0	0	$27,480

11May80-	2Aqu	fst	1⅛		:47⅖	1:11⅖	1:49⅘	Clm 75000	6	8	8^{19}	8^{19}	8^{15}	4^{12}	Hernandez R	b	113	15.40	74-14	Causerie $118^{7\frac{3}{4}}$ Lean Lad 118^{3} Ring of Truth $116^{1\frac{1}{4}}$	No threat 8
24Apr80-	7Aqu	fst	1⅛		:48⅘	1:13	1:51⅖	Allowance	3	5	$5^{9\frac{1}{2}}$	$5^{8\frac{1}{2}}$	$5^{5\frac{3}{4}}$	$5^{2\frac{1}{2}}$	Hernandez R	b	115	8.10	75-21	Hugable Tom $116^{\frac{3}{4}}$ Tunerup $115^{\frac{1}{2}}$ Contare 114^{1}	No mishap 5
16Apr80-	2Aqu	fst	1⅝		:49⅖	2:06⅖	2:46⅖	3↑ Hcp 12500s	3	6	$6^{9\frac{3}{4}}$	3^{5}	2^{2}	$1^{1\frac{3}{4}}$	Hernandez R	b	122	*1.10	70-17	North Star $122^{1\frac{3}{4}}$ Might HaveBeen$113^{\frac{1}{2}}$FrankTalk120^{hd}	Drew clear 7
5Apr80-	9Aqu	gd	1⅛		:47⅗	1:12⅖	1:51⅕	Allowance	4	9	9^{16}	9^{11}	$5^{6\frac{1}{2}}$	$3^{3\frac{1}{4}}$	Hernandez R	b	115	9.90	76-20	Addison $115^{1\frac{3}{4}}$ Next Frontier $115^{1\frac{1}{2}}$ North Star 115^{hd}	Wide late 9
15Mar80-	6Aqu	gd	$1\frac{1}{16}$	⊡	:48⅕	1:13⅗	1:45⅖	Clm 37500	8	8	7^{9}	$4^{5\frac{1}{2}}$	$2^{1\frac{1}{2}}$	$1^{\frac{3}{4}}$	Hernandez R	b	115	3.30	87-18	North Star $115^{\frac{3}{4}}$ Paris Station $114^{6\frac{1}{4}}$ Click Off $115^{1\frac{1}{4}}$	Ridden out 8
24Feb80-	1Aqu	gd	$1\frac{1}{16}$	⊡	:47⅕	1:12⅗	1:45⅖	Clm 22500	2	7	6^{10}	4^{8}	1^{2}	$1^{5\frac{1}{4}}$	Hernandez R	b	117	*2.90	87-17	North Star $117^{5\frac{1}{4}}$ Lancer's Pride 117^{nk} Gifted Leader $111^{\frac{1}{2}}$	Easily 10
11Feb80-	5Aqu	fst	1¼	⊡	:49⅖	1:41	2:07⅗	Hcp 12500s	6	6	9^{10}	$5^{6\frac{1}{4}}$	2^{6}	$2^{4\frac{1}{4}}$	Hernandez R	b	115	8.00	76-23	Indeed Gallant $112^{4\frac{1}{4}}$ North Star $115^{2\frac{3}{4}}$ Scamp Boy$113^{3\frac{3}{4}}$	2nd best 11
30Jan80-	3Aqu	fst	$1\frac{3}{16}$	⊡	:48⅕	1:13⅖	1:58⅘	Hcp 12500s	9	9	$9^{9\frac{3}{4}}$	$9^{9\frac{3}{4}}$	7^{12}	7^{14}	Amy J	b	117	*1.60	70-22	Indeed Gallant $107^{6\frac{1}{4}}$ Recidian $111^{2\frac{3}{4}}$ Laugh and Go 113^{nk}	Dull try 9
20Jan80-	2Aqu	fst	$1\frac{3}{16}$	⊡	:48⅗	1:13⅕	2:00	Clm 20000	7	7	7^{15}	5^{11}	2^{3}	$1^{\frac{1}{2}}$	Amy J	b	114	*2.00	78-26	North Star $114^{\frac{1}{2}}$ Itsagoodlife $110^{2\frac{3}{4}}$ Gifted Leader $117^{2\frac{1}{2}}$	Driving 7
13Jan80-	1Aqu	fst	1⅛	⊡	:47⅖	1:12⅖	1:52⅘	Clm 12500	4	7	7^{9}	$5^{7\frac{1}{2}}$	$1^{1\frac{1}{2}}$	$1^{7\frac{1}{2}}$	Amy J	b	119	*2.10	82-17	North Star $119^{7\frac{1}{2}}$PassDeceiver$114^{1\frac{3}{4}}$CliffChesney119^{nk}	Ridden out 12

LATEST WORKOUTS Jun 3 Aqu 3f fst :36⅗ b May 29 Aqu 4f fst :50 b May 25 Aqu 6f fst 1:14⅘ h May 20 Aqu 4f fst :48⅗ h

quality. Form and ability are what count, and when either one is lacking, the horse won't do it, no matter how high he has been running. We throw out North Star immediately and go on to the high-priced second and third choices, both showing 6-1 on the board. We start with Pruneplum.

Pruneplum — Dk. b. or br. g. 6, by Olden Times—Plum Plum, by On-And-On
Own.—Boland P | Br.—Schmidt C E Jr (Fla) | Tr.—Paley Herb | **110**

Turf Record	St.	1st	2nd	3rd			St.	1st	2nd	3rd	Amt.
	4	0	0	0		1980	12	6	1	1	$30,740
						1979	3	1	0	0	$9,000

26May80- 6Mth	fst	6f	:22⅖	:46	1:10⅗	Clm 18500	2	7	87¾	76	55	48½	Thornburg B	119	4.80	78-19	Ready Axe 1135 Flying Duck 1163 Rough Angle 116½	Rallied	9
18May80- 9Aqu	fst	7f	:22⅘	:45⅗	1:24⅕	Clm 16000	1	7	53¾	66	3½	1nk	Cordero A Jr	119	2.50	80-19	Pruneplum 119nk Pokie Joe 113¾ Mika Song 1122¾	Driving	8
5May80- 6GP	fm	1 1/16 Ⓣ	:46⅗	1:10⅕	1:41⅘	Clm 20000	7	5	59	912	912	98¾	Guerra W A	112	5.60	83-16	Poking 116no To His Credit 1161½ Dauntless Prince 116hd	Tired	9
25Apr80- 6GP	fst	7f	:22⅖	:45⅖	1:23⅖	Clm 16000	6	8	106	73¾	3nk	13	MacBeth D	120	*2.70	87-23	Pruneplum 1203 Creme De La Fete 111hd Domastyle 1123	Driving	10
14Apr80- 8GP	sly	1 1/16	:47⅘	1:12⅗	1:45⅖	Clm 19000	8	6	52¾	23	32	32½	MacBeth D	114	*.90	71-17	No Niagaras 1202½ Pierre's King 116no Pruneplum 1141	Bid, hung	8
29Mar80- 2GP	fst	1⅛	:48⅕	1:12⅖	1:51⅘	Clm 19000	10	3	41½	2hd	2hd	21½	Cordero A Jr	114	*.70	71-19	Great Reward 1161½ Pruneplum 1144½ Exaltado116no	Second best	10
15Mar80- 2GP	fst	1⅛	:48⅖	1:13⅘	1:52⅘	Clm 16000	2	3	33½	31½	12	14	Cordero A Jr	120	*1.80	68-17	Pruneplum 1204 Exaltado 1131 Mister Parky 1163	Ridden out	10
1Mar80- 4Hia	sly	1⅛	:47⅘	1:12⅘	1:51⅖	Clm c-12500	6	2	2½	1hd	12	11½	Cordero A Jr	122	*1.00	75-19	Pruneplum 1221½ Chockablock 1161½ Dr. Dodd 116½	Ridden out	8
25Feb80- 5Hia	fst	1⅛	:48⅖	1:13⅕	1:51⅘	Clm 28000	7	3	32½	31½	55½	57	Cordero A Jr	113	*1.40	66-22	Tipp Town 1082¾ Rare Glow 115hd Kingofthemountain115nk	Tired	7
9Feb80- 8Hia	fst	1⅛	:48⅖	1:13⅕	1:52⅕	Clm 25000	8	3	52	2hd	11	13¾	Cordero A Jr	115	*2.40	71-28	Pruneplum 1153¾ Rare Glow 1155 Kooky Monster 1141	Driving	11

LATEST WORKOUTS Jun 2 Mth 6f fst 1:15 b — May 17 Mth 4f fst :49⅖ b — May 2 GP 5f fst 1:02⅖ b — Apr 24 GP 4f fst :49⅗ b

While his form is not altogether wholesome, there is the requisite gain of five from the first call to the stretch call, and that will serve to qualify Pruneplum. For ability, we can see at Gulfstream in his 29Mar80 run there was a lead time of :24.1, which he lowered by one with a gain. But two ticks have to be added for energy plus one for GP (Gulfstream Park), and we get a :24.3 ability time. (This is the first time in the Big Week that we have had to allow for track speeds. See Chapter V if you've forgotten the method.) Another good effort came at Gulfstream in the 25Apr80 race at 7f, where we convert the final time to a 6f figure of 1:10.3. The lead time thus becomes :25.1, and we have reduced that by three because of gain to :24.3 and when we add the necessary one-tick penalty for GP's fast surface, we have a :24.4.

There are actually two more horses showing at 6-1, but Conspirator is so poor that we will skip him for the moment and show you what the other contender, Might Have Been, reveals.

Might Have Been — Dk. b. or br. h. 5, by Hail To Reason—Evening Primrose, by Nashua
Own.—Broadfield | Br.—Galbreath J W (Ky) | Tr.—King W Preston | **113**

Turf Record	St.	1st	2nd	3rd			St.	1st	2nd	3rd	Amt.
	9	0	1	1		1980	11	2	4	0	$40,300
						1979	13	2	0	0	$15,150

15May80- 2Aqu	fst	1½	:49	2:05⅗	2:31⅘	3↑ Hcp 10000s	7	2	2hd	11½	2hd	2nk	Martens G	b	114	2.50	72-19	Come On In 110nk MightHaveBeen1143¼Conspirator1221¼	Gamely	7
10May80- 2Aqu	fst	1⅜	:49⅗	1:39	2:17⅗	Clm 25000	6	4	43	1½	44	47½	Martens G		117	*2.20	85-13	Sir Gregor 108½ Mystic Era 1175¼ Fast and Strong 1171¾	Tired	7
16Apr80- 2Aqu	fst	1⅝	:49⅖	2:06⅖	2:46⅖	3↑ Hcp 12500s	1	2	2hd	12	12	21¾	Martens G	b	113	7.10	68-17	North Star 1221¾ Might Have Been113½FrankTalk120hd	Game try	7
29Mar80- 2Aqu	sly	2	:48⅗	3:02⅕	3:28⅘	Hcp 12500s	8	5	43½	48½	417	522	Asmussen C B	b	115	2.90	30-27	Finney Finster 1082 Frank Talk 1228¼ Laugh and Go 1148¾	Tired	9
19Mar80- 3Aqu	fst	2	:50⅕	3:02⅖	3:28⅕	Hcp 10000s	2	1	11½	11½	2hd	1no	Martens G	b	114	*1.90	55-32	MightHaveBeen114noConspirator1229½PrideofNaskr1176½	Driving	7
12Mar80- 6Aqu	fst	1¾ ⊡	:50⅘	2:35⅖	3:01⅖	Hcp 12500s	6	1	1½	2hd	23	22¾	Martens G	b	115	17.90	92-20	Bay Laurel 1182¾ MightHaveBeen1152½FrankTalk12310	Weakened	8
3Mar80- 6Aqu	fst	1¾ ⊡	:48	2:38⅖	3:04⅕	Hcp 10000s	8	3	32	86	817	823	Martens G	b	116	4.70	58-21	Conspirator 1133¾ Bay Laurel 1214¾ Coup Stick 1088	Stopped	11
18Feb80- 9Aqu	fst	1½ ⊡	:50	2:07	2:35⅕	Hcp 10000s	4	2	42½	12	15	14	Martens G	b	111	20.90	75-19	Might HaveBeen1114BayLaurel120½CaliforniaPrince122nk	Driving	10
4Feb80- 6Aqu	fst	1¼ ⊡	:49⅘	1:40⅖	2:06⅖	Hcp 10000s	2	3	32½	47	513	517	Hernandez R	b	114	5.10e	69-22	Recidian 1158 Conspirator 1151½ Fellow Heir 1151¾	In tight	9
30Jan80- 2Aqu	fst	1⅛ ⊡	:48⅘	1:14⅖	1:54⅗	Clm 16000	3	3	2hd	12	2hd	2½	Creighton R L	b	117	10.30	72-22	FellowHeir112½MightHveBeen117¾BluBottlGlss1158½	Held gamely	8

LATEST WORKOUTS May 28 Bel tr.t 5f fst 1:05 b — May 25 Bel 5f fst 1:01⅗ b — May 3 Bel 5f fst 1:00 h — Apr 8 Bel tr.t 5f fst 1:04⅗ b

Might Have Been qualifies on form off his last race, but his ability times bring some difficulty because of the long races involved. This one is a real marathon runner, and horses at stretched-out mileage usually don't move too fast. He should be right at home in today's event at a mile and five-eighths, however, enough to test the stamina of any competitor. But let's try to extract something from this mess of figures. Look at 10May80, where we can at least try to measure from the first two calls. There was a lead time of :49.2 for the four furlongs involved, and we can now break that into two pieces. The gain of three is more than offset by the slow time and we wind up with a :49.3. We can put a faster time on the front end and give the horse a :24.3 without being too far out of line. But beyond that, we run into more difficulty. Drop down to 30Jan80, where he ran the comparatively short distance of a mile and one-eighth at Aqueduct. Lead time was :25.3 and the energy add-on brings it up to :26.0. But we can do better than that in the two-miler on 19Mar80, where there is a last quarter time of :25.4, not quite so far off.

Here is what we now have.

Odds	Horse	Ability		A Pts		F	Total
1.3	North Star	—	—	—	—	NQ	NQ
6.1	Pruneplum	:24.3	:24.4	17	16	Q	33
6.5	Might Have Been	:24.3	:25.4	17	11	Q	28

With North Star out of consideration, Might Have Been is the only threat to Pruneplum, who indeed is a decisive choice. We invest in him with great confidence, especially pleased with the price if we prevail.

FIRST RACE
Belmont
JUNE 5, 1980

1 5/8 MILES. (2.40 4/5) STARTER HANDICAP. Purse $17,000. 3-year-olds and upward which have started for a claiming price of $12,500 or less since January 1, 1979. Weights, Monday, June 2. Declarations by 10:00 a.m. Tuesday, June 3.

Value of race $17,000, value to winner $10,200, second $3,740, third $2,040, fourth $1,020. Mutuel pool $113,301, OTB pool $180,667.

Last Raced	Horse	Eqt.	A.	Wt	PP	1/4	1/2	1	1 3/8	Str	Fin	Jockey	Odds $1
26May80 6Mth4	Pruneplum		6	111	3	5 2	5 2	1 hd	1 1/2	1 1 1/2	1 5	Cordero A Jr	6.10
31May80 7Suf5	Sword Bearer	b	5	119	8	3 1	3 hd	3 hd	3 2	3 3	2 1/2	Carrasco B	18.90
23May80 5Bel6	Come On In	b	5	114	2	2 1 1/2	1 2	2 1	2 1/2	2 hd	3 1 3/4	Fell J	14.70
26May80 2Bel4	Cincelari	b	5	114	5	6 1/2	6 2	6 3	4 2	4 2	4 1 1/2	Adams L	12.50
11May80 2Aqu4	North Star	b	7	124	9	9	9	9	7 1 1/2	6 2	5 3/4	Hernandez R	1.30
15May80 4Pim2	Laugh and Go	b	5	112	7	8 3	8 1 1/2	7 2	5 2	5 hd	6 3 3/4	Asmussen C B	11.20
15May80 2Aqu2	Might Have Been	b	5	113	4	1 hd	2 1/2	4 1/2	6 1/2	7 8	7 12	Martens G	6.50
29May80 3Bel2	Haltung		6	109	6	7 1 1/2	7 3	8 1/2	9	8 2	8 6	Beitia E	8.40
15May80 2Aqu3	Conspirator		4	118	1	4 1/2	4 hd	5 2	8 1 1/2	9	9	Mora G	6.60

OFF AT 1:01 EDT. Start good, Won ridden out. Time, :24 4/5, :50, 1:41 3/5, 2:07 4/5, 2:33 3/5, 2:46 4/5, Track fast.

Official Program Numbers

$2 Mutuel Prices:			
3-(C)-PRUNEPLUM	14.20	7.80	5.00
8-(H)-SWORD BEARER		13.60	7.60
2-(B)-COME ON IN			8.80

What a splendid way to begin a new day, with the best winning price we have received yet! I still cannot understand how the crowd could make North Star the favorite. Pruneplum won by 5 big lengths, going away. I also want to point out the importance of the qualifying form factor of the gain of five, since that's how we allow Pruneplum in our calculations. In yesterday's race, Somebody Super was also a winner off that form signal. It is usually a sound and reliable indicator of a horse's readiness to run, as these races demonstrate.

The second race is a maiden special event with two Lightly Raced contenders in this New York State–bred affair getting the most play. We can expect some pretty weak ability times as we take a look.

Rowell attracts the heavy play at the windows. He qualifies in form, but his last race shows a :26.3 lead time and his loss of nearly 5 lengths brings him up to :27.3. In his previous race on 17Mar80, there was a lead time of :26.2 and his loss of 9 lengths requires a jump to :28.1, plus another for energy, to give a :28.2 ability time. It is one of the slowest you have seen in this book. And yet this horse is showing 3 to 5 on the board! This is simply incredible. We can allow him 6 points for early speed, however.

Resuscitator, the second choice, looks much better. In his last race, he set the lead time of :25.4 and gets only one added on for energy, to give him an almost respectable :26.0. In his sprint race on 19May80, there was a :26.3 lead time, and his being far back in the field gets three more added for energy to a :27.1 figure. We also award 6 points for early speed and then turn to the third choice, Navarino.

This poor creature has run fifteen times without winning. That alone disqualifies him against Lightly Raced Horses unless he possesses ability times good enough to make him a Double Advantage Horse. But here, Navarino won't even qualify on form off his last race, since he fails to show a single one of the six form factors that would allow him to qualify. A Double Advantage Horse that is not qualified on form cannot be considered. So, out with Navarino.

This returns us to our point totals, which look like this.

Odds	Horse	Ability		A Pts		ES	F	Total
.7	Rowell	:27.3	:28.2	2	0	6	Q	8
2.9	Resuscitator	:26.0	:27.1	10	4	6	Q	20
4.4	Navarino	—	—	—	—	—	NQ	NQ

An investment in Resuscitator doesn't inspire us, but there is enough showing to indicate that we should go ahead under our rules. We almost got away with it, and even showed a profit on the race.

SECOND RACE **6 FURLONGS. (1.08⅖) MAIDEN SPECIAL WEIGHTS. Purse $23,00[illegible] 3-year-olds and upward foaled in New York State and approved by the New York Stat[illegible] weights, 3-year-olds, 114 lbs. Older, 122 lbs.**

Belmont

JUNE 5, 1980

Value of race $23,000, value to winner $13,800, second $5,060, third $2,760, fourth $1,380. Mutuel pool $122,570, OTB pool $79,008. Quinella Pool $97,818. OTB Quinella Pool $96,598.

Last Raced	Horse	Eqt.A.Wt	PP	St	¼	½	Str	Fin	Jockey	Odds $1
19May80 ^{9}Aqu^{6}	Palio Limani	3 114	2	1	3^{3}	3^{2}	2^{3}	$1^{1\frac{1}{2}}$	Skinner K	8.00
28May80 ^{4}Bel^{5}	Resuscitator	b 3 115	3	5	1^{hd}	1^{hd}	1^{2}	2^{6}	Hernandez R	2.90
28May80 ^{4}Bel^{3}	Navarino	b 3 114	1	3	5^{3}	4^{2}	$3^{\frac{1}{2}}$	3^{4}	Martens G	4.40
28May80 ^{4}Bel^{6}	Whiglet's Pride	b 3 109	4	4	6	6	$5^{\frac{1}{2}}$	4^{2}	Beitia E^{5}	17.20
19May80 ^{9}Aqu^{3}	Rowell	3 114	5	6	2^{2}	2^{2}	4^{4}	$5^{2\frac{1}{2}}$	Asmussen C B	.70
28May80 ^{4}Bel^{9}	Winter Bird	3 109	6	2	4^{hd}	$5^{1\frac{1}{2}}$	6	6	Lovato F Jr^{5}	36.20

OFF AT 1:33 1/2 EDT. Start good, Won driving. Time, :23⅖, :47⅘, 1:13⅗ Track fast.

$2 Mutuel Prices:				
	3-(D)-PALIO LIMANI	18.00	6.60	4.20
	4-(E)-RESUSCITATOR		4.80	3.40
	2-(C)-NAVARINO			3.20

I'll take place prices any day when they bring black ink in the race before us. This wasn't much, but the horse had a real chance to win, of course, in this extremely weak field. Poor Rowell, again showing how the crowd does select some wretched animals as favorites, ran about the way we would expect.

The third race is on the turf at a mile and a sixteenth. We have a couple of co-favorites at 5-2, and we'll start with Tell She's Irish off an amazing 20-length victory.

But the problem here is that Tell She's Irish has never run on the grass, and thus becomes an unknown-ability horse. Western Isle is the other co-favorite.

3 BELMONT

INNER TURF COURSE
1 1-16 MILES
BELMONT
FINISH START

1 1/16 MILES. (INNER–TURF). (1.40⅘) CLAIMING. Purse $17,000. Fillies, 3–year–olds. Weight, 121 lbs. Non–winnners of two races at a mile or over since May 1 allowed 3 lbs. Of such a race since then, 5 lbs. Claiming price $40,000 for each $2,500 to $35,000, 2 lbs. (Races when enterd to be claimed for $30,000 or less not considered.)

Tell She's Irish *

Own.—Martin Gertrude A

Dk. b. or br. f. 3, by Tell—Budir, by Bupers
$37,500 Br.—Arnold & Sledd (Ky)
Tr.—DeBonis Robert

114

	St.	1st	2nd	3rd	Amt.
1980	9	4	0	0	$18,780
1979	5	M	1	0	$2,130

Entered 4Jun80- 1 BEL

5May80- 3Key	fst	1 70	:47 1:12⅗ 1:44	ⒻClm c-14000	7	1	1½	16	112	120	Cantagallo G J5	114	*1.80	80–22	Tell She's Irish 11420 Pation 116½ Shy Samantha 1093½	Easily	9
16Apr80- 2Key	fst	1 70	:48⅖ 1:15⅕ 1:46⅘	ⒻClm 14000	6	1	12	11	1hd	11	Cantagallo G J5	111	*2.30	66–30	Tell She's Irish 1111 Full Strength 116½ War Branch 1144	Driving	8
4Apr80- 5Key	sly	1 70	:47⅖ 1:14⅖ 1:46⅘	ⒻClm 11000	2	1	18	17	16	15	Cantagallo G J5	111	*2.00	66–26	TellShe'sIrish1115Patrician'sGlory112nkWrBrnch1147	Ridden out	7
21Mar80- 7Key	sly	6f	:22⅖ :46 1:13⅘	ⒻClm 14000	6	1	42	23	53½	53¾	Cantagallo G J5	111	10.40	69–27	Heal Over 114nk Dancer's Line 1161½ Flip A Penny 1202	Tired	7
11Mar80- 3Kev	fst	7f	:23 :47⅖ 1:28⅘	ⒻClm 14000	2	—	—	—	—	—	Rodriguez J J5	113	23.20	— —	Winning Lady 1202 Dancer'sLine1165SassyStudent1162	Lost rider	7
17Feb80- 3Key	gd	6f	:23⅕ :47⅗ 1:14	ⒻClm 14000	4	1	51¾	65¾	59	56¼	Black A S	119	6.10	66–25	HopesandDreams1162½Dncer'sLine1071½OverMission116½	No rally	8
5Feb80- 7Key	fst	6f	:23⅕ :48 1:13⅕	ⒻClm 18000	7	1	3nk	51½	58½	611	Black A S	116	6.90	65–29	Royal Emigree 1192 Lady Prospector 1166 Sis Loraine 1092	Tired	7
27Jan80- 7Key	fst	6f	:22⅖ :46⅕ 1:12⅖	ⒻAllowance	3	6	97¼	910	913	815	Black A S	114	30.10	65–21	Secret Virtue 1154½ Entitlement 1082½Gail'sMouse1141	No threat	10
7Jan80- 3Key	fst	6f	:23 :47⅗ 1:14⅘	ⒻMd 14000	7	1	1½	11½	11½	13	Black A S	120	4.00	68–30	Tell She's Irish 1203 Loose IntheCabooz1202Lotainfo1204	Driving	7
30Dec79- 1Key	fst	6f	:23⅖ :48⅖ 1:15	ⒻMd 15000	1	4	41	79	612	610	Black A S	120	4.90	57–27	Callaloo Carol 116no Rush to The Front 1205CrockPot120no	Tired	9

LATEST WORKOUTS May 30 Bel 5f fst 1:01⅕ h   May 24 Bel tr.t 4f fst :49⅗ b   May 18 Bel tr.t 4f fst :51 b   Apr 26 Key 4f fst :49 b

Western Isle

Own.—Classic Two Stable

Dk. b. or br. f. 3, by The Axe II—Fair Wind, by Distinctive
$40,000 Br.—Woodcrest Farm (Ky)
Tr.—Worswick Douglas J

116

Turf Record St.	1st	2nd	3rd
1	0	1	0

	St.	1st	2nd	3rd	Amt.
1980	8	2	2	0	$23,080
1979	2	M	0	0	$225

24May80- 1Bel	gd	1 1/16 Ⓣ	:48 1:12⅖ 1:45	ⒻClm 45000	4	7	53¾	22	22	22	Vasquez J	b	114	3.60	77–20	Antilassa 1112 Western Isle 114no Loving Lady 116¾	Held second	10
2May80- 2Aqu	fst	1	:47 1:12⅘ 1:39⅕	ⒻClm 45000	1	5	46	23	23	2¾	Vasquez J	b	115	3.10	69–19	Light Bulb 107¾ Western Isle 1152¾ Arbee's Charm 114¾	Gamely	7
13Apr80- 9Aqu	fst	7f	:23 :46⅘ 1:25⅕	ⒻClm 40000	5	10	1013	106¼	47½	48	Vasquez J	b	116	34.80	67–24	Sami Sutton 1135¾ Sarah Brown 116½PerfectPoppy1161¾	Late bid	10
8Mar80- 5Aqu	fst	1 70 ⊡	:47⅗ 1:13⅕ 1:44⅖	ⒻAllowance	10	10	912	1017	1016	918	Albertrani T5	b	111	45.40	62–16	Mitey Lively 1167¾ Appropriate 116nk ExclusiveBeach111¾	Outrun	10
15Feb80- 2Aqu	fst	1 70 ⊡	:49 1:15⅖ 1:46⅘	ⒻClm c-25000	6	7	43½	31	2hd	13½	Venezia M	b	116	9.30	68–26	WesternIsle1163½DareToBeCptin114½UsefulMiss1131¼	Ridden out	9
4Feb80- 1Aqu	fst	1 1/16 ⊡	:48 1:14⅗ 1:48⅕	ⒻClm 30000	5	7	57	42¼	24	44¾	Martens G	b	116	16.40	68–22	SamiSutton1114UsefulMiss113½MarshmllowCrem114nk	Weakened	8
24Jan80- 6Aqu	fst	1 1/16 ⊡	:48⅕ 1:13⅖ 1:47⅕	ⒻAllowance	3	8	79½	66½	814	816	Venezia M	b	116	24.70	62–21	Popachee 1161¼ Broken Home 121hd Cinto Tora 1161½	Outrun	9
11Jan80- 4Aqu	fst	1 1/16 ⊡	:48⅗ 1:15⅖ 1:51	ⒻMd 18000	7	6	58	2hd	13	1¾	Amy J	b	122	*1.90	59–19	Western Isle 122¾ Nosey Flahe 113¾DonnaE.Bello1175	Ridden out	9
31Dec79- 1Key	fst	6f	:23 :47 1:13⅖	ⒻMd Sp Wt	8	6	74¾	68	68¾	57¾	Shuk N	b	120	29.30	67–25	Pt'sSurprise1202½Gil'sMouse120nkSouthwillrisegin1204	No factor	9
12Dec79- 2Key	fst	6f	:22⅖ :46⅖ 1:12⅗	ⒻMd Sp Wt	2	8	811	711	620	623	Barreira A M7	b	113	10.30	56–23	ConnieKnows1202½Gail'sMouse1207TwentyTwoKrt1203	No factor	9

LATEST WORKOUTS May 19 Bel 5f fst 1:01 h   Apr 27 Bel tr.t 5f fst 1:04 b   Apr 5 Aqu 5f sly 1:03⅖ b (d)

This filly has but one race on the grass, from which she qualifies on form out of her last run. She picked up an excellent ability-time figure off a :24.2 lead time, a gain of one with an add-on for energy of two, which comes out at :24.3. We must now consider Ortona, the third choice on the board.

*Ortona

Own.—Malmstrom I W

Ch. f. 3, by Canisbay—Oga, by Molvedo
$40,000 Br.—A A Razz Di S Vivaldo (Italy)
Tr.—DeStasio Richard T

116

Turf Record St.	1st	2nd	3rd
1	0	0	0

	St.	1st	2nd	3rd	Amt.
1980	8	2	0	0	$15,000
1979	0	M	0	0	

24May80- 1Bel	gd	1 1/16 Ⓣ	48 1:12⅖ 1:45	ⒻClm 45000	1	10	109	98¼	57	42¾	Cruguet J	114	12.70	76–20	Antilassa 1112 Western Isle 114no Loving Lady 116¾	Rallied	10
2May80- 2Aqu	fst	1	47 1:12⅘ 1:39⅕	ⒻClm 47500	6	7	69	44	55	57¼	Maple E	114	13.20	63–19	Light Bulb 107¾ Western Isle 1152¾ Arbee's Charm114¾	No factor	7
20Apr80- 1Aqu	fst	6f	22⅘	46⅕ 1 11⅘	ⒻClm 40000	2	6	79¾	68½	69½	69¾	Maple E	116	9.10	74–16	ⒹSarahBrown116nkPerfectPoppy1161½IllgottenGins1073¾	Outrun	7
11Apr80- 8Aqu	fst	1⅛	48⅕ 1 12⅘ 1 50	ⒻAllowance	5	7	88¾	85¾	513	522	Maple E	116	20.80	63–20	Erin's Word 1168¾ Passolyn 1162 Exclusive Beach1118¼	No factor	8
22Mar80- 2Aqu	sly	7f	23⅗ 48⅗ 1 28⅘	ⒻClm 30000	2	8	87¾	87¾	32	1nk	Maple E	116	17.90	57–31	Ortona 116nk Warm Tamale 1193 Lorine 1112¾	Driving	8
24Feb80- 4Aqu	fst	1 1/16 ⊡	48⅗ 1:14⅖ 1 48	ⒻAllowance	1	3	88	97½	813	817	Miceli M	116	44.10	57–17	Cinto Tora 1168¼ Frankincense 1111¼ Forward Girl 1112¾	Tired	9
12Feb80- 6Aqu	fst	6f ⊡	:23 :47⅘ 1:14⅕	ⒻAllowance	11	11	1112	1115	1013	911	Hernandez R	116	64.20	62–26	Chuckle 1162¼ Electric Chair 113nk Right Approach 116¾	Outrun	11
25Jan80- 2Aqu	fst	6f ⊡	:23⅗ :48⅕ 1:14	ⒻMd 30000	2	9	3nk	32½	21½	1hd	Asmussen C B	121	35.90	74–18	Ortona 121hd ⒹArbee's Charm 112nk Heather's Turn 1212	Driving	11

LATEST WORKOUTS May 21 Bel tr.t 5f gd 1:03 b   May 15 Bel tr.t 6f fst 1:18 b   May 9 Bel tr.t 5f sly 1:04⅖ b   Apr 28 Bel tr.t 5f sly 1:04⅘ b (d)

This one likewise has but a single turf race, finishing behind Western Isle on 24May80. Off the same :24.2 lead time there is no allowable gain and there is a four-tick add-on for energy to bring the lone ability time to :25.1. Let's now see what we have.

Odds	Horse	Ability		A Pts		F	Total
2.5	Tell She's Irish	Unknown		—	—	U	U
2.5	Western Isle	:24.3	—	17	(17)	Q	34
4.4	Ortona	:25.1	—	14	(14)	Q	28

Tell She's Irish worries us because of this last outstanding race on the dirt, but without any grass performances, she cannot be supported. When we dealt with unknown-ability horses in our rules of selection, we were concerned about how to deal with favorites. Since Tell She's Irish is no more than a co-favorite, with no clear-cut support at the windows over Western Isle, we need not invoke our rules but can look for regular play situations. While we don't like to rate any horse off one performance, a second-place finish is a very positive sign. Also, Ortona, the third choice, who qualified on form because of her gain, has but one race and she was behind Western Isle. Therefore, we now invest in Western Isle to win and place.

THIRD RACE **Belmont** **JUNE 5, 1980** — **1 $\frac{1}{16}$ MILES.(inner-turf). (1.40⅘) CLAIMING. Purse $17,000. Fillies, 3-year-olds. Weight, 121 lbs. Non-winnners of two races at a mile or over since May 1 allowed 3 lbs. Of such a race since then, 5 lbs. Claiming price $40,000 for each $2,500 to $35,000, 2 lbs. (Races when enterd to be claimed for $30,000 or less not considered.)**

Value of race $17,000, value to winner $10,200, second $3,740, third $2,040, fourth $1,020. Mutuel pool $150,163, OTB pool $116,858. Exacta Pool $222,830. OTB Exacta Pool $181,345.

Last Raced	Horse	Eqt.A.Wt	PP	St	¼	½	¾	Str	Fin	Jockey	Cl'g Pr	Odds $1
24May80 ^{1}Bel^{2}	Western Isle	b 3 116	6	7	6^{3}	$4^{1\frac{1}{2}}$	2^{hd}	1^{1}	1^{5}	Vasquez J	40000	2.50
5May80 ^{3}Key^{1}	Tell She's Irish	3 114	3	1	1^{4}	1^{5}	1^{4}	2^{3}	$2^{\frac{1}{2}}$	Cordero A Jr	37500	2.50
26May80 ^{7}Bel^{9}	Mischievous Saint	b 3 116	4	4	$4^{\frac{1}{2}}$	3^{2}	3^{2}	4^{5}	3^{hd}	Samyn J L	40000	8.80
21May80 ^{4}Bel^{11}	Cabinetta	3 116	7	6	5^{1}	$6^{1\frac{1}{2}}$	5^{4}	$3^{1\frac{1}{2}}$	4^{4}	Rivera M A	40000	5.00
21May80 ^{7}Bel^{6}	Tale Feather	b 3 112	1	2	7^{4}	8	8	7^{5}	5^{3}	Velasquez J	35000	17.90
24May80 ^{1}Bel^{4}	Ortona	3 116	8	8	8	7^{4}	$6^{\frac{1}{2}}$	$5^{1\frac{1}{2}}$	6^{3}	Cruguet J	40000	4.40
24May80 ^{1}Bel^{5}	Blessed Princess	b 3 116	2	3	2^{2}	2^{1}	4^{1}	$6^{\frac{1}{2}}$	$7^{3\frac{1}{4}}$	Fell J	40000	9.00
25May80 ^{6}Bel^{9}	Dora Star	b 3 109	5	5	3^{1}	$5^{1\frac{1}{2}}$	7^{5}	8	8	Beitia E^{5}	35000	22.70

OFF AT 2:05 EDT. Start good Won ridde out. Time, :22⅘, :46⅗, 1:11, 1:36⅕, 1:42⅖ Course firm.

$2 Mutuel Prices:			
6-(H)-WESTERN ISLE	7.00	3.20	2.60
3-(E)-TELL SHE'S IRISH		4.00	3.60
4-(F)-MISCHIEVOUS SAINT			4.60

$2 EXACTA 6-3 PAID $31.60.

A happy outcome indeed. Western Isle ran away from the others with a Big Win of 5 lengths, demonstrating the power of a good second-place finish in her last race off an excellent ability time. Thus far, this day is going exactly the way we like it. In the fourth race, we are back to dealing with maiden claimers, two-year-olds who are all lightly raced.

Again, we approach this mass of unknown factors with great care. This one is to be played only if we can find something that stands out. The favorite is Corbeil, a first-time starter, who thus rates a total unknown. Bagdad Island, the second choice, was not close enough in his last race to qualify on form, and thus he is eliminated from consideration. The third horse in the wagering is

4 BELMONT

START
5½ FURLONGS
BELMONT PARK
FINISH

5½ FURLONGS. (1.03) MAIDEN CLAIMING. Purse $12,000. 2-year-olds. Weight, 118 lbs. Claiming price $40,000; for each $5,000 to $30,000, 2 lbs.

Tournament Tested — Ch. c. 2, by Barachois—Crowned Abroad, by Going Abroad
$35,000 Br.—Cashman E (Fla) Tr.—Jacobs Eugene — **116**
Own.—Barberino P
St. 1st 2nd 3rd Amt. — 1980 2 M 0 0
23May80- 6Bel fst 5½f :23 :46⅖ 1:05⅕ Md 25000 6 4 44½ 36 48½ 514 Santiago A b 118 43.30 75-16 Fleet Falcon 11811 Bell Run 1151¼ Northern Barbi 1131¼ Tired 8
12May80- 4Aqu sly 5f :22⅘ :46⅖ :59⅕ Md 40000 6 8 66½ 713 715 714 Santiago A b 118 39.10 75-19 Adams Buddy1181¼DistinctiveKing1185BagdadIsland1182½ Outrun 8
LATEST WORKOUTS Jun 3 Bel tr.t 4f fst :51 b May 30 Bel tr.t 4f fst :51 b May 20 Bel tr.t 5f fst 1:04⅘ b May 11 Bel tr.t 3f fst :38 b

Our Celtic Heir — Ch. c. 2, by Bold Hour—Princess Weird, by Swoons Son
$40,000 Br.—Congleton & Courtney (Ky) Tr.—Jensen Kay E — **118**
Own.—Keogh G J
St. 1st 2nd 3rd Amt. — 1980 2 M 0 0
14May80- 4Aqu fst 5f :22⅘ :46⅖ :58⅘ Md 55000 6 4 45½ 511 816 820 Moreno H E 116 13.60 72-17 Bara Prince 1131½ Beneficiary 1186 R. Zweily 118½ Tired 8
1May80- 1Aqu fst 5f :23 :46⅘ :59 Md Sp Wt 4 3 42¾ 44½ 66 77¼ Moreno H E 118 28.40 83-13 Lockjaw 118nk Buffalo Luck 118no PerfectShot1181¼ Early speed 7
LATEST WORKOUTS Jun 4 Bel tr.t 3f gd :38 b (d) May 31 Bel 5f fst 1:02⅖ b May 10 Bel tr.t 4f fst :49 h Apr 26 GP 4f fst :49 bg

Bagdad Island — Ch. c. 2, by Bagdad—Island Trade, by Neptune
$40,000 Br.—Timberlawn Farm Inc (Ky) Tr.—Barrera Luis — **118**
Own.—Tel-Kay Stable
St. 1st 2nd 3rd Amt. — 1980 1 M 0 1 $1,440
12May80- 4Aqu sly 5f :22⅘ :46⅖ :59⅕ Md 40000 4 3 34½ 48½ 39 36¼ Rivera M A b 118 5.00 83-19 Adams Buddy1181¼DistinctiveKing1185BagdadIsland1182½ Evenly 8
LATEST WORKOUTS Jun 1 Bel tr.t 4f fst :48⅘ h May 27 Bel tr.t 4f fst :49⅕ h May 21 Bel tr.t 4f gd :49⅗ b May 11 Bel tr.t 3f fst :37⅗ b

Nosey's Pride — Dk. b. or br. c. 2, by Shecky Greene—Entraineuse, by Dance To Market
$40,000 Br.—Chibcha Farm (Fla) Tr.—Dunham Bob G — **118**
Own.—Boaz Mary A
St. 1st 2nd 3rd Amt. — 1980 1 M 0 0
14May80- 4Aqu fst 5f :22⅘ :46⅖ :58⅘ Md 50000 3 3 817 820 714 511 Venezia M 114 14.80 81-17 Bara Prince 1131½ Beneficiary 1186 R. Zweily 118½ No threat 8
LATEST WORKOUTS Jun 4 Aqu 3f gd :37⅘ b (d) May 31 Aqu 5f fst 1:02 h ●May 21 Aqu 4f gd :48 h (d) May 12 Aqu 3f fst :40 b

Daren Did It — Ch. c. 2, by Irish Ruler—Light Behind, by Roman Line
$40,000 Br.—M & M Bloodstock Agency (Fla) Tr.—Zito Nicholas P — **118**
Own.—Jablow Andrea
St. 1st 2nd 3rd Amt. — 1980 1 M 0 0 $840
25May80- 4Bel fst 5½f :22⅘ :46⅘ 1:05⅘ Md 60000 6 5 57 54½ 43¼ 48 Martens G 118 21.20 78-16 NativeGunner1164DistinctiveKing1182½TresureHunter1181½ Tired 7
LATEST WORKOUTS Jun 3 Bel 3f fst :36 h May 23 Bel 3f fst :35 h May 17 Bel 4f fst :49 h May 14 Bel tr.t 4f gd :49⅕ h

Corbeil — B. c. 2, by Jacinto—Epergne, by Round Table
$40,000 Br.—Perry Mrs W H (Ky) Tr.—Whiteley Frank Y — **118**
Own.—Perry Mrs W H
St. 1st 2nd 3rd Amt. — 1980 0 M 0 0
LATEST WORKOUTS Jun 3 Bel tr.t 4f fst :52⅘ b May 29 Bel 4f fst :49⅖ bg May 23 Bel 4f fst :49⅗ bg May 16 Bel 4f fst :50⅗ b

Northern Barbi — Dk. b. or br. c. 2, by Northern Native—Now Barbi, by Barbizon
$40,000 Br.—Swan C S (Okla) Tr.—Campo John P — **113 5**
Own.—Ginger Red Stable
St. 1st 2nd 3rd Amt. — 1980 1 M 0 1 $1,320
23May80- 6Bel fst 5½f :23 :46⅖ 1:05⅕ Md 25000 3 1 34 46½ 38 312 Lovato F Jr5 113 7.00e 77-16 Fleet Falcon 11811 Bell Run 1151¼ Northern Barbi 1131¼ Evenly 8
LATEST WORKOUTS Jun 1 Bel tr.t 4f fst :51 b May 22 Bel 3f sly :36⅖ bg May 19 Bel tr.t 5f fst 1:02⅖ h May 18 Bel 3f fst :36 hg

Bid For The Bank — Ch. c. 2, by Raise A Bid—Banksia, by Blue Prince
$40,000 Br.—Hutchens Barbara B (Fla) Tr.—Esposito J L — **118**
Own.—Zimmerman S
St. 1st 2nd 3rd Amt. — 1980 1 M 0 0 $720
12May80- 4Aqu sly 5f :22⅘ :46⅖ :59⅕ Md 35000 2 4 88 59 510 48¾ Nunez A10 104 20.50 80-19 AdamsBuddy1181¼DistinctiveKing1185BagddIslnd1182½ No factor 8
LATEST WORKOUTS May 22 Aqu 3f sly :36 h ●May 18 Aqu 3f fst :36⅗ h May 9 Aqu 6f my 1:16 bg(d) May 4 Aqu 4f fst :51 bg

R. Zweily — B. c. 2, by Mississipian—Miss Snow Goose, by Nearctic
$40,000 Br.—Seleven B E & Doree (Fla) Tr.—Martin Frank — **118**
Own.—Lehmann R N
St. 1st 2nd 3rd Amt. — 1980 2 M 0 1 $1,680
25May80- 4Bel fst 5½f :22⅘ :46⅘ 1:05⅘ Md 60000 1 1 1½ 2hd 53¼ 511 Asmussen C B 118 3.90 75-16 NtiveGunner1164DistinctiveKing1182½TresureHunter1181½ Outrun 7
14May80- 4Aqu fst 5f :22⅘ :46⅖ :58⅘ Md 60000 1 1 13 11½ 22 37½ Asmussen C B 118 3.00e 84-17 Bara Prince 1131½ Beneficiary 1186 R. Zweily 118½ Tired 8
LATEST WORKOUTS Jun 2 Bel 3f fst :40 bg May 21 Bel tr.t 4f gd :48⅘ h May 10 Bel tr.t 5f fst 1:01⅘ h May 2 Bel tr.t 5f fst 1:03⅗ b

Active Stock — Ch. c. 2, by Torsion—Eden's Apple, by Promised Land
$40,000 Br.—Aronow Stable (Fla) Tr.—Morgan Jack B — **118**
Own.—Sahagian J
St. 1st 2nd 3rd Amt. — 1980 0 M 0 0
LATEST WORKOUTS Jun 3 Bel 4f fst :49⅗ b May 28 Bel 5f fst 1:05 b May 23 Bel 4f fst :49 bg May 15 Bel 3f fst :38⅕ b

Daren Did It, and he can't qualify either on form, even though he was close, but not quite, to a gain of five. With one unknown-ability horse and two others not qualified on form, here is the perfect race to pass, which we do.

We'll show you the chart to reveal the odds and how they finished. Bagdad Island almost won it, with Corbeil, the favorite, losing the rider. But almost is not enough, and this one you can have.

FOURTH RACE 5½ FURLONGS. (1.03) MAIDEN CLAIMING. Purse $12,000. 2-year-olds. Weight, 118 lbs. Claiming price $40,000; for each $5,000 to $30,000, 2 lbs.

Belmont

JUNE 5, 1980

Value of race $12,000, value to winner $7,200, second $2,640, third $1,440, fourth $720. Mutuel pool $158,050, OTB pool $105,087. Track Quinella Pool $158,309. OTB Quinella Pool $117,749.

Last Raced		Horse	Eqt.	A.	Wt	PP	St	¼	⅜	Str	Fin	Jockey	Cl'g Pr	Odds $1
14May80	4Aqu5	Nosey's Pride		2	118	4	7	8	5½	3½	1no	Venezia M	40000	7.40
12May80	4Aqu3	Bagdad Island	b	2	118	3	3	11½	14	13	23½	Rivera M A	40000	2.40
23May80	6Bel3	Northern Barbi		2	113	7	4	2½	2hd	21	32½	Lovato F Jr5	40000	18.30
25May80	4Bel4	Daren Did It		2	118	5	5	62	4½	53	4no	Martens G	40000	4.40
12May80	4Aqu4	Bid For The Bank		2	118	8	6	51	32	41½	55½	Maple E	40000	4.90
23May80	6Bel5	Tournament Tested	b	2	116	1	1	7½	8	64	65	Santiago A	35000	71.30
		Active Stock		2	118	9	8	41	71	71	74¼	Adams L	40000	31.90
14May80	4Aqu8	Our Celtic Heir	b	2	118	2	2	3hd	61	8	8	Cruguet J	40000	17.40
		Corbeil		2	118	6	9	—	—	—	—	Vasquez J	40000	2.30

Corbeil, Lost rider.

OFF AT 2:37 1/2 EDT. Start good, Won driving. Time, :23⅕, :47⅗, 1:00⅖, 1:07 Track fast.

$2 Mutuel Prices:			
4-(D)-NOSEY'S PRIDE	16.80	8.00	5.20
3-(C)-BAGDAD ISLAND		3.60	3.20
7-(G)-NORTHERN BARBI			6.20

The fifth race brings us back to our preferred distance, six furlongs, where we first take a look at the favorite, Two Cents Extra.

5 BELMONT

6 FURLONGS. (1.08⅖) CLAIMING Purse $14,000. Fillies, 3-year-old, weights, 121 lbs. Non-winners of two races since May 1, allowed 3 lbs. Of a race since then, 5 lbs. Claiming price $25,000 for each $2,500 to $20,000 2 lbs. (Races when entered to be claimed for $18,000 or less not considered).

Two Cents Extra — Gr. f. 3, by Fast Hilarious—Two Time, by Tompion

Own.—Double Cee Stable — **$25,000** Br.—Murrell J (Fla) Tr.—Zito Nicholas P — **116**

Turf Record						St.	1st	2nd	3rd	Amt.
St.	1st	2nd	3rd		1980	5	0	0	2	$8,400
1	0	1	0		1979	10	3	1	1	$30,060

9Apr80- 5Aqu sly 6f	:22	:45⅕	1:11⅘	ⒻAllowance	4	5	43½	59	512	413	Gonzalez M A5		111	2.20	71-21	Donna Doll 1162½ Great Dialogue 1215¼ Ojavan 1095¼	Bled	5
2Apr80- 7Aqu fst 7f	:22⅗	:45⅕	1:23⅖	ⒻAllowance	1	3	11	1½	2½	36¾	Martens G		116	7.60	77-18	Cybele 1166 Paintbrush 116¾ Two Cents Extra 1161½	Tired	5
13Mar80- 5Aqu fst 6f	⊡:23⅕	:47⅖	1:13	ⒻClm 60000	4	4	3nk	3½	41	44¾	Martens G	b	116	*.60	74-23	Sarah Brown1122¼Arbee'sCharm1122½StoneRock113hd	Weakened	6
5Mar80- 7Aqu fst 6f	⊡:22⅖	:46⅕	1:11⅗	ⒻAllowance	5	1	32½	3½	32	43	Martens G		116	1.80	83-22	Dolly By Golly 116½ Full Tigress 1162 Ray Kay 121½	Tired	6
21Feb80- 8Aqu fst 6f	⊡:22⅗	:46⅗	1:12	ⒻAllowance	2	4	41¼	32½	32½	32¾	Dahlquist T C5		113	17.60	81-18	Inlet1161½TheWheelTurns1181¼TwoCentsExtr1131¼	No solid rally	7
21Nov79- 9Aqu fst 7f	:23	:46⅕	1:25	ⒻClm 60000	6	2	21	31½	59½	712	Fell J		116	3.70	64-18	Going East 1172½ The Wheel Turns 1163½ Ojavan 1141¼	Tired	9
15Nov79- 5Aqu fst 6f	:22	:45⅕	1:09⅘	ⒻAllowance	3	3	32	43½	49½	514	Fell J		117	11.40	80-15	Damask Fan 1153½ Rio Rita 1154¾ Loaded Gun 1173½	Tired	5
3Nov79- 8Key sly 6f	:22⅕	:45⅗	1:11⅕	ⒻSchuylkill	8	10	86½	89¾	89¾	814	Moseley J W		118	23.60	72-23	Nuit D'Amour 1211½ Dancing Blade 1183½ LoadedGun1154	Outrun	11
26Oct79- 6Aqu fst 7f	:23⅕	:46⅘	1:25⅖	ⒻAllowance	4	3	1½	32	54	67¾	Pincay L Jr		120	5.60	66-24	Dancing Blade 120½ Tash 120½ Tell A Secret 1171¾	Tired	8
12Oct79- 4Bel sly 1	:46⅖	1:11⅘	1:39⅕	ⒻAllowance	4	1	11½	1½	22	35½	Martens G		115	3.90	66-24	Bold'NDetermined1155TllAScrt115½TwoCntsExtr11511	Weakened	5

LATEST WORKOUTS May 31 Bel tr t 4f fst :49⅕ h — May 24 Bel 4f fst :47 h — May 17 Bel 4f fst :48⅗ h — May 3 Bel 4f fst :49⅕ b

The first problem question is: Does this filly qualify on form? Her last wretched race was run in April, so ostensibly she would rate as unknown. But look at that drop in class down to $25,000. How do we know whether this meets our 40% class drop disqualifying rule or not?

When a horse is dropping from an allowance race back into a claiming event, the only way you can equate a monetary drop in class is to go back to the last claiming race in the past performances to see what dollar value it carried. Here, in the third race from the top, that of 13Mar80, Two Cents Extra ran with a $60,000 tag. Since she ran her next two efforts in allowance company, you can assume the allowance race was of a high enough class to at least equal the $60,000 claimer. Therefore, you can put a $60,000 value on the last allowance race. By these standards, Two Cents Extra is dropping nearly out of sight, all the way down to $25,000, more than 50%. Any further questions? This one, therefore, gets not a U for form, but a flat NQ because of the class drop.

We are now ready to look at the second choice, Roman Beach, at 5-2 on the board.

Roman Beach — B. f. 3, by Proudest Roman—Beach Picnic, by Petare — **$25,000** — Br.—Don Dee Farm (Fla) — Tr.—Pascuma James J Jr — **118**

Own.—Baer S M

Turf Record	St.	1st	2nd	3rd	Amt.
St. 1st 2nd 3rd					
7 0 2 0					
1980	12	1	2	2	$13,230
1979	4	M	2	0	$2,504

24May80- 1Bel	gd	1 1/16 Ⓣ	:48	1:12⅖	1:45	ⒻClm 40000	9	5	$7^{4\frac14}$ $4^{4\frac12}$ 4^{7} 7^{10}	Maple E	b 114	12.50	69-20	Antilassa 111^{2} Western Isle 114no Loving Lady $116^{\frac34}$	No factor 10
15May80- 9Aqu	fst	6f	:22	:45⅖	1:11⅖	3↑ⒻMd 27500	7	1	$3^{2\frac12}$ $3^{\frac12}$ 1^{4} 1^{8}	Cordero A Jr	b 113	8.60	86-19	RomanBeach113^{8}QueenofWax111^{1}ScrletStepper$109^{1\frac34}$	Ridden out 9
9May80- 5Aqu	gd	1	:46⅗	1:12⅕	1:38⅕	3↑ⒻMd 25000	3	1	2^{hd} 4^{3} 4^{8} 4^{15}	Cordero A Jr	b 113	*2.00	60-18	Fantastic High 113^{6} Sally's Ifida $113^{2\frac34}$ Yellow Ribbon$104^{5\frac34}$	Tired 6
21Apr80- 1GP	yl	*1 1/16 Ⓣ			1:48⅘	3↑ⒻMd 25000	5	1	1^{1} 1^{hd} $8^{5\frac12}$ 8^{14}	MacBeth D	b 114	3.70	48-28	Gleaming Cap103^{1}Penny'sHoney$120^{1\frac14}$SensitivElizabeth$112^{\frac34}$	Tired 9
10Apr80-10GP	my	1 1/16	:47⅕	1:12⅗	1:45⅕	ⒻMd Sp Wt	4	2	2^{6} 4^{11} 4^{11} 4^{16}	Milner J A^{7}	b 113	4.60	59-24	Bubbling Dancer 120^{2} Dominia 120^{5} Brekke $120^{8\frac12}$	Tired 8
3Apr80- 4GP	fm	*1 Ⓣ			1:40⅘	ⒻMd Sp Wt	10	4	$3^{1\frac12}$ 3^{4} 7^{12} 8^{15}	Perret C	120	6.60	62-23	Joy of Aces 120^{2} Cool Contessa $115^{1\frac12}$ Follow Orders 120no	Tired 10
27Mar80-10GP	fm	*1 1/16 Ⓣ			1:44⅖	ⒻMd Sp Wt	4	2	$2^{1\frac12}$ 1^{3} 3^{4} 4^{12}	Cordero A Jr	120	5.50	72-16	Intendress 120^{1} Dominia 120^{9} La Atrevida $115^{1\frac12}$	Tired 10
13Mar80- 4GP	fm	*1 Ⓣ			1:39⅘	ⒻMd Sp Wt	7	1	1^{3} $1^{1\frac12}$ 2^{1} $2^{5\frac12}$	Cordero A Jr	120	3.00	76-21	Active Voice $120^{5\frac12}$ Roman Beach $120^{4\frac12}$ Dominia 120^{4}	2nd best 10
22Feb80- 6Hia	gd	1 1/16 Ⓣ			1:48	ⒻClm c-25000	5	1	$1^{\frac12}$ $1^{\frac12}$ 2^{hd} 5^{5}	Ashcroft D C^{7}	108	4.00	53-35	Blue Time $111^{\frac12}$ Fast Tracie $108^{\frac12}$ Blissful Solitude $118^{3\frac12}$	Used up 10
13Feb80- 6Hia	fm	1 1/16 Ⓣ			1:45⅘	ⒻMd Sp Wt	9	1	1^{4} 1^{4} 1^{4} $2^{\frac12}$	Long B^{5}	115	18.20	68-25	Ignite $120^{\frac12}$ Romàn Beach 115^{1} Miss Rebecca 120^{nk}	Tired 12

LATEST WORKOUTS Jun 2 Aqu 4f fst :49⅗ b May 5 Mth 4f fst :51 b ●Apr 8 Hia 4f my :48 hg

Her last race was on the grass and need not be used as a qualifying test. She is also an up-and-down-dropper off a good race of 15May80, which easily qualifies her on form. In that race, she gets an ability time of :26.0 off the same lead time with no adjustments. Since most of her races are on the turf, we are limited in the races from which to extract other ability times, but we have to use the 9May80 effort at Aqueduct. There was a lead time of :25.3 with a loss of three, which comes out to a :26.1. For early speed, we can award but 3 points off three dirt races. We are now at the third choice, McSpoodle, showing 4-1 on the board.

McSpoodle — Ch. f. 3, by Twist the Axe—Quick Dynasty, by Dynastic — **$25,000** — Br.—Dundee Barbara & J (Ky) — Tr.—Nadler Herbert — **111^{5}**

Own.—Lauren Sybil L

	St.	1st	2nd	3rd	Amt.
1980	6	2	0	1	$16,320
1979	5	1	0	0	$6,300

29May80- 5Bel	fst	7f	:22⅘	:46⅕	1:24⅘	ⒻClm 35000	4	2	$3^{1\frac12}$ $2^{\frac12}$ 3^{7} 3^{13}	Beitia E^{5}	109	7.50	65-16	Giggleswick $114^{5\frac12}$ Forward Girl 114^{7} McSpoodle 109^{1}	Weakened 4
9May80- 9Aqu	fst	7f	:23⅕	:47	1:24⅘	ⒻClm 35000	4	4	$4^{2\frac12}$ 3^{2} 8^{12} 8^{16}	Beitia E^{5}	110	8.30	61-18	Handmeanative $116^{2\frac14}$ Antilassa $109^{1\frac12}$ Arbee's Charm $116^{5\frac14}$	Tired 10
10Apr80- 6Aqu	gd	7f	:23	:46⅕	1:24⅘	ⒻClm 25000	6	2	$2^{\frac12}$ 3^{1} 1^{hd} $1^{1\frac14}$	Beitia E^{5}	113	*2.00	77-16	McSpoodle $113^{1\frac14}$ Dosido $111^{\frac34}$ Queen So Lo 116no	Drew clear 7
28Mar80- 5Aqu	fst	6f	:22⅗	:46⅗	1:13⅖	ⒻClm 20000	6	6	3^{3} $3^{1\frac12}$ $3^{2\frac12}$ $1^{1\frac14}$	Beitia E^{5}	111	5.00	76-24	McSpoodle $111^{1\frac14}$ SisterRubena$107^{1\frac34}$GuessWhat'sUp116^{nk}	Driving 7
13Mar80- 5Aqu	fst	6f	⊡:23⅕	:47⅖	1:13	ⒻClm 60000	5	6	$5^{3\frac34}$ $6^{8\frac12}$ 6^{9} 6^{11}	Ortega J A^{10}	b 107	29.00	68-23	Sarah Brown $112^{2\frac14}$ Arbee's Charm $112^{2\frac12}$ StoneRock113^{hd}	Outrun 6
12Feb80- 6Aqu	fst	6f	⊡:23	:47⅘	1:14⅕	ⒻAllowance	5	7	$6^{5\frac34}$ $8^{7\frac12}$ [illegible] $6^{5\frac34}$	Gribcheck S B^{5}	111	104.30	67-26	Chuckle $116^{2\frac14}$ Electric Chair 113^{nk} Right Approach $116^{\frac34}$	Outrun 11
21Dec79- 7Med	fst	6f	:22⅘	:46⅕	1:11⅖	ⒻAllowance	2	5	$2^{\frac12}$ 4^{2} 7^{9} $6^{9\frac12}$	McCauley W H	120	6.90	78-14	Pink Panties $115^{\frac12}$ Creme Count $120^{2\frac12}$ GumballMachine120^{3}	Wide 7
8Dec79- 2Aqu	fst	6f	⊡:22	:46⅕	1:12⅖	ⒻAllowance	2	2	2^{4} $4^{4\frac12}$ 6^{9} 7^{8}	Gonzalez M A^{5}	115	34.30	74-13	Tea Sipper $115^{1\frac14}$ Inlet $115^{1\frac14}$ Social Hill $115^{\frac12}$	Tired 7
26Nov79- 3Med	sly	6f	:22⅗	:46⅗	1:13⅗	ⒻMd Sp Wt	3	1	1^{5} 1^{3} 1^{3} 1^{nk}	Gomez M A	118	3.80	77-23	McSpoodle 118^{nk} Hustlin' Harriet 118^{hd} Creme Count118^{4}	Lasted 7
15Nov79- 9Med	fst	6f	:22⅗	:46⅘	1:14	ⒻMd Sp Wt	4	3	1^{hd} 2^{hd} $3^{2\frac12}$ 5^{4}	Gomez M A	118	34.40	71-25	Starry Salute $118^{\frac12}$ La Kamika $118^{1\frac12}$ Acute 118^{2}	Tired 12

LATEST WORKOUTS May 1 Bel tr.t 3f my :37⅕ h

This one qualifies easily on form off the last race. To obtain ability times, we take the winning effort of 10Apr80, convert the 7f time to a 6f equivalent of 1:12.3, and get a lead time of :26.2. We can reduce it by one tick for gain to an ability time of :26.1. The 28Mar80 run at Aqueduct shows a lead time of :26.4, and with a gain of one, this comes down to :26.3. McSpoodle has good early speed, and gets 6 points in this department. We can now compare the contenders for a final point rating.

Odds	Horse	Ability		A Pts		ES	F	Total
1.2	Two Cents Extra	—	—				NQ	NQ
2.5	Roman Beach	:26.0	:26.1	10	9	3	Q	22
4.1	McSpoodle	:26.1	:26.3	9	7	6	Q	22

With Two Cents Extra out on NQ form because of class drop, we see that Roman Beach and McSpoodle are tied in total points. Roman Beach has the ability and McSpoodle comes up on early speed, although you will see that Roman Beach had considerable front speed in her turf races. But because of the tie in points, we make a place bet only on Roman Beach because of her lower odds. You will not be surprised at the result, as our two "tigers" ran first and second.

FIFTH RACE
Belmont
JUNE 5, 1980

6 FURLONGS. (1.08$\frac{4}{5}$) CLAIMING Purse $14,000. Fillies, 3–year–old, weights, 121 lbs. Non–winners of two races since May 1, allowed 3 lbs. Of a race since then, 5 lbs. Claiming price $25,000 for each $2,500 to $20,000 2 lbs. (Races when entered to be claimed for $18,000 or less not considered).

Value of race $14,000, value to winner $8,400, second $3,080, third $1,680, fourth $840. Mutuel pool $149,207, OTB pool $103,138. Exacta Pool $199,703. OTB Exacta Pool $165,360.

Last Raced	Horse	Eqt.A.Wt	PP	St	¼	½	Str	Fin	Jockey	Cl'g Pr	Odds $1
24May80 ^{1}Bel^{7}	Roman Beach	b 3 118	3	2	$2\frac{1}{2}$	1^{hd}	$1^{1\frac{1}{2}}$	$1^{1\frac{1}{2}}$	Cordero A Jr	25000	2.50
29May80 ^{5}Bel^{3}	McSpoodle	3 111	7	5	$3\frac{1}{2}$	3^{2}	$3^{1\frac{1}{2}}$	2no	Beitia E^{5}	25000	4.10
17May80 ^{9}Aqu^{7}	Illgotten Gains	3 116	1	1	5^{1}	5^{3}	$4\frac{1}{2}$	$3^{2\frac{1}{4}}$	Martens G	25000	16.10
9Apr80 ^{5}Aqu^{4}	Two Cents Extra	3 116	4	3	4^{2}	4^{1}	5^{3}	$4\frac{1}{2}$	Velasquez J	25000	1.20
9May80 ^{6}Aqu^{6}	Sister Rubena	b 3 111	6	4	$1^{1\frac{1}{2}}$	2^{1}	$2\frac{1}{2}$	5no	Lovato F Jr^{5}	25000	16.30
25May80 ^{6}Bel^{2}	Lorine	b 3 111	5	6	6^{4}	6^{2}	6^{4}	$6^{6\frac{1}{2}}$	Gonzalez M A^{5}	25000	10.70
9May80 ^{9}Aqu^{7}	Yar Jesting	3 116	2	7	7	7	7	7	Samyn J L	25000	10.90

OFF AT 3:07 EDT. Start good, Won driving. Time, :22$\frac{3}{5}$, :46$\frac{2}{5}$, 1:11$\frac{3}{5}$ Track fast.

$2 Mutuel Prices:			
4–(D)–ROMAN BEACH	7.00	4.20	3.20
8–(I)–MCSPOODLE		4.80	3.60
1–(A)–ILLGOTTEN GAINS			4.40

Roman Beach was good enough to win, showing the best early speed. We are secure with our place bet, however. One of the big lessons from this race is how Two Cents Extra fared against fillies she should have beaten easily if in good form. The precipitate class drop, as we earlier indicated, is almost a sure sign that a horse may not do well today (except for those occasional trainers who are more concerned about a victory than a sale).

The sixth race presents another heavy favorite in Friendly Frolic, which we will now examine.

The last Big Win was impressive, and it merits a qualifying four in the form department. The lead time in that race was :24.4, but we have to add one for energy to bring us up to :25.0. In the 19Feb80 race at Hialeah, we get a :25.2 ability time off a lead time of :25.3, less three for gain and with two more added for energy, back up to :25.2.

6 BELMONT

1⅛ MILES
BELMONT PARK
START
FINISH

1⅛ MILES. (1.45⅖) ALLOWANCE. Purse $20,000. Fillies and mares, 3-year-olds and upward which have never won two races. Weight, 3-year-olds, 114 lbs. Older, 122 lbs. Non-winners of a race other than claiming over a mile since May 1 allowed 3 lbs. Of such a race since April 15, 5 lbs.

Friendly Frolic

Dk. b. or br. f. 3, by Best Turn—Bing Bang, by Nearctic
Br.—Calumet Farm (Ky)
Tr.—Veitch John M
Own.—Calumet Farm

114

	St.	1st	2nd	3rd	Amt.
1980	5	1	1	3	$18,680
1979	3	M	0	0	$960

26May80- 5Bel	fst	1 1/16	:47⅗	1:12⅖	1:45⅖	3↑ Ⓕ Md Sp Wt	6	1	1½	14	15	14¼	Fell J	b 114	*.50	75-20 Friendly Frolic 1144¼ Worthy Polly109nkRiverNile1133	Ridden out 7
24Apr80- 5Aqu	fst	1	:47⅕	1:12⅗	1:38⅘	3↑ Ⓕ Md Sp Wt	2	4	32	41¾	2hd	2no	Fell J	114	*.70	72-21 Darby Dame 114no Friendly Frolic 1145½ Shelia 109½	Gamely 7
16Apr80- 6Aqu	fst	1	:46⅘	1:12⅕	1:37⅖	Ⓕ Md Sp Wt	7	6	33	32½	32½	33¼	Fell J	121	5.60	76-17 Little Prema 1211¾ Fancy Caper 1211½FriendlyFrolic1217½	Evenly 10
4Mar80- 4Hia	fst	7f	:23⅕	:46⅘	1:26⅖	Ⓕ Md Sp Wt	1	7	77½	66¾	42	31¾	Fell J	118	4.90	69-24 [D]LuckyOleAxe118½NationalPlce1181¼FriendlyFrolic1181½	Gaining 10
19Feb80- 6Hia	sly	6f	:22⅗	:46⅘	1:12⅖	Ⓕ Md Sp Wt	11	10	86¾	79	57	35¼	Fell J	120	19.30	76-17 Squaw Smoke 1204½ Third Jewel 120¾ Friendly Frolic120½	Rallied 12
5Oct79- 6Bel	fst	1	:46⅕	1:11⅖	1:37⅖	Ⓕ Md Sp Wt	3	8	811	811	612	418	Velasquez J	118	11.10	63-21 Spruce Pine 11810 Nijit 1187 Erin's Word 118¾	No threat 8
30Sep79- 6Bel	sly	6½f	:22⅗	:46⅕	1:18⅗	Ⓕ Md Sp Wt	9	8	1111	1120	615	619	Velasquez J	118	29.10	64-24 Cybele 1182¾ Veiled Prophet 1134¼ Madura 1189	No factor 12
15Sep79- 4Bel	fst	6f	:22⅖	:45⅘	1:10⅕	Ⓕ Md Sp Wt	6	6	1011	1014	812	816	Velasquez J	117	12.50	75-11 Naskranaut 1179¼ Critic's Wink 1172½ Shine She Will110½	Outrun 11

LATEST WORKOUTS Jun 4 Bel 3f fst :35⅘ h Jun 1 Bel 3f fst :37⅕ b May 25 Bel 3f fst :37⅖ b May 21 Bel 4f sly :53 b

Luxcie

Dk. b. or br. f. 3, by Executioner—Lawn, by Herbager
Br.—Whitney T P (Ky)
Tr.—Johnson Philip G
Own.—Whitney T P

114

	St.	1st	2nd	3rd	Amt.
1980	4	1	1	0	$15,560
1979	9	M	1	1	$6,000

21May80- 7Bel	sly	1¼	:49⅗	1:40⅗	2:06⅗	3↑ Ⓕ Allowance	5	1	13	13	12	2½	Samyn J L	108	2.90	66-22 Karand 113½ Luxcie 1083¾ Winter Romance 1141	Failed 7
4May80- 2Aqu	fst	1⅛	:48⅕	1:13⅘	1:53⅗	Ⓕ Md Sp Wt	5	2	1hd	2hd	1½	11¼	Castaneda M	121	10.30	67-25 Luxcie 1211¼ Charlsie White 1212¼ English Toffy 1165¼	Driving 9
17Apr80- 6Aqu	fst	7f	:23⅕	:47⅕	1:26⅕	3↑ Ⓕ Md Sp Wt	3	7	31	52¾	53½	43¾	Castaneda M	114	23.20	66-23 Astrid's Pride113½PinkSupreme108¾LuckyOleAxe1132½	Weakened 8
29Mar80- 7FD	sly	5½f	:22⅗	:46⅖	1:05⅗	Ⓕ N Table Vis	7	10	94¾	77¾	712	614	DePass R	b 115	9.80	79-18 Wampum 1137 HitchHike1161½Anchorwoman1131½	Steadied early 10
15Nov79- 9Med	fst	6f	:22⅗	:46⅘	1:14	Ⓕ Md Sp Wt	5	9	55½	53¾	65¼	96	Castaneda M	b 118	3.10	69-25 Starry Salute 118½ La Kamika 1181½ Acute 1182	Tired 12
5Nov79- 6Aqu	fst	6f	:22⅘	:46⅕	1:11	Ⓕ Md Sp Wt	1	4	11½	2hd	42½	69¾	Castaneda M	b 117	14.50	78-18 Tax Holiday 1172¾ Chain Bracelet 1172¼ Harrowing1171¾	Used up 12
30Sep79- 6Bel	sly	6½f	:22⅗	:46⅕	1:18⅗	Ⓕ Md Sp Wt	7	6	3nk	46½	919	929	Castaneda M	118	20.40	54-24 Cybele 1182¾ Veiled Prophet 1134¼ Madura 1189	Tired 12
15Sep79- 9Bel	fst	6f	:22⅖	:46⅕	1:11⅖	Ⓕ Md Sp Wt	2	8	1011	97¼	910	67	Gonzalez M A7	110	21.10	78-11 Virginia Reef 117½ Passerine 1173½ Last Embrace 1171½	Outrun 11
5Sep79- 4Bel	fst	6½f	:22⅕	:45⅘	1:19⅖	Ⓕ Md Sp Wt	11	4	45½	46	43	66	Gonzalez M A7	110	17.00	73-22 MissHatchet117¾DameDuMoulin117nkBishop'sCounter1171¼	Tired 12
20Jly79- 6Bel	fst	6f	:22⅘	:46⅘	1:11⅗	Ⓕ Md Sp Wt	5	6	44	45	513	719	Asmussen C B	117	8.40	65-21 Damask Fan 1174¼ Lovin' Lass 1178½ Miss Hatchet 1171¾	Tired 11

LATEST WORKOUTS Jun 1 Bel tr.t 3f fst :37 b May 18 Bel tr.t 4f fst :47⅗ h

Luxcie, a promising daughter of Executioner, is the second choice at 5-2. She qualifies after a good effort from the long mile and a quarter on 21May80. Her best ability time was back on 15Sep79 at Belmont, where we start with a lead time of :25.1, no adjustment for gain or loss, and one added for energy to give us a :25.2. Her next best is not so good, off the 4May80 race, where there is a :25.3 lead time compiled by Luxcie, to which two ticks for energy are added to bring her up to :26.0.

The third candidate is Darby Dame.

Darby Dame

B. f. 3, by His Majesty—Stealaway, by Olympia
Br.—Galbreath J W (Ky)
Tr.—Rondinello Thomas L
Own.—Darby Dan Farm

111

	St.	1st	2nd	3rd	Amt.
1980	3	1	0	1	$13,500
1979	4	M	0	0	$1,560

25May80- 2Bel	fst	1 1/16	:49⅕	1:13⅕	1:44⅕	3↑ Ⓕ Allowance	6	4	53¼	57	38	38½	Rivera M A	113	*2.20	72-16 Really Mean 1081 Bang The Drums 1137½DarbyDame11311	Rallied 6
24Apr80- 5Aqu	fst	1	:47⅕	1:12⅗	1:38⅘	3↑ Ⓕ Md Sp Wt	1	6	64¾	63¾	4nk	1no	Rivera M A	114	4.40	72-21 Darby Dame 114no Friendly Frolic 1145½ Shelia 109½	Driving 7
14Apr80- 6Aqu	fst	6f	:22⅘	:47	1:12⅕	Ⓕ Md Sp Wt	1	5	88¼	67¼	54	43½	Fell J	121	8.50	78-21 [D]AncientMystery1211¼Headwater1211¼IcingOntheCake1161	Wide
26Nov79- 4Aqu	sly	7f	:23	:46⅗	1:26⅕	Ⓕ Md Sp Wt	5	1	78½	610	510	45½	Venezia M	117	*1.40e	64-30 SutOfDrms1071½Tddlypom1174FblosProspct112hd	Loose bandage 7
11Nov79- 4Aqu	fst	7f	:23⅗	:48	1:25⅖	Ⓕ Md Sp Wt	1	6	42¼	55¾	58½	47¾	Cordero A Jr	117	18.60	66-15 In Our Time 1172¼ Gloverette1174½OnAShoestring1171	Early foot 7
28Oct79- 9Aqu	gd	7f	:22⅘	:46⅖	1:26	Ⓕ Md Sp Wt	9	1	74	66	913	910	Venezia M	117	39.40	61-24 Arisen 117¾ Gloverette 1171¼ In Our Time 1172¾	Outrun
30Sep79- 4Bel	sly	6½f	:22⅗	:45⅖	1:18	Ⓕ Md Sp Wt	11	10	1117	820	818	722	Cordero A Jr	118	13.80	64-24 Genuine Risk 1181¾ Remote Ruler 11813 Espadrille 1181¾	Outrun

LATEST WORKOUTS Jun 1 Bel 4f fst :51 b May 24 Bel 3f fst :37 b May 20 Bel 5f fst 1:03 b May 14 Bel 4f gd :50 b

Her form last out is simply too poor to qualify. While she did finish third, she was far back throughout, and this is not good enough to warrant support at the windows. We are now ready to make our comparison chart.

Odds	Horse	Ability		A Pts		F	Total
.9	Friendly Frolic	:25.0	:25.2	15	13	Q4	32
2.6	Luxcie	:25.2	:26.0	13	10	Q	23
4.3	Darby Dame	—	—	—	—	NQ	NQ

On the figures, Friendly Frolic's odds are justified. She has a strong lead in points with her Big Win in her last race. But, as you have seen by now, what looks so good on paper doesn't always produce on the track.

SIXTH RACE
Belmont
JUNE 5, 1980

1 1/8 MILES. (1.45⅘) ALLOWANCE. Purse $20,000. Fillies and mares, 3 year olds and upward which have never won two races. Weight, 3-year-olds, 114 lbs. Older, 122 lbs. Non-winners of a race other than claiming over a mile since May 1 allowed 3 lbs. Of such a race since April 15, 5 lbs.

Value of race $20,000, value to winner $12,000, second $4,400, third $2,400, fourth $1,200. Mutuel pool $192,442, OTB pool $99,411. Quinella Pool $180,826. OTB Quinella Pool $129,084.

Last Raced	Horse	Eqt.A.Wt	PP	St	¼	½	¾	Str	Fin	Jockey	Odds $1
14May80 2Aqu8	Miss Hatchet	3 113	6	5	61	5hd	4½	23	13½	Saumell L	16.70
25May80 2Bel3	Darby Dame	3 113	5	4	5hd	61½	6½	53	21½	Rivera M A	4.30
26May80 5Bel1	Friendly Frolic	b 3 114	1	7	46	3½	1½	1½	3no	Fell J	.90
15May80 5Aqu5	Frankincense	3 109	2	6	7	7	7	4½	44½	Borden D A	9.90
21May80 4Bel3	Fantastic High	b 3 110	7	1	31½	47	33	3½	5½	Miranda J	23.00
10May80 8Crc2	Lalim	b 3 112	3	2	1½	2½	53	6½	64	Velasquez J	17.30
21May80 7Bel2	Luxcie	3 114	4	3	2½	1hd	22	7	7	Samyn J L	2.60

OFF AT 3:37 EDT. Start good, Won driving. Time, :23, :46⅗, 1:11⅗, 1:38⅘, 1:51⅘ Track fast.

$2 Mutuel Prices:			
7-(G)-MISS HATCHET	35.40	11.60	3.20
6-(F)-DARBY DAME		5.60	2.60
1-(A)-FRIENDLY FROLIC			2.20

Friendly Frolic was a big disappointment. She reached the lead by the time she had run six furlongs, but began to fade thereafter and wound up a badly beaten third. We have to forget a race like this and go on to the next one, where you will find the highest-priced claiming race you are ever likely to see. We start with another strong favorite, Causerie.

While you can see below that the claiming price is $100,000, you will also see

7 BELMONT — START — 7 FURLONGS — BELMONT PARK — FINISH

7 FURLONGS. (1.20⅖) CLAIMING. Purse $25,000. 4-year-olds and upward. Weight, 122 lbs. Claiming price $100,000; for each $5,000 to $75,000, 2 lbs.

Causerie *
Own.—Sommer Viola
B. c. 4, by Verbatim—belle Biz, by Crimson Satan
$75,000 **Br.—Runnymede Farm (Ky)**
Tr.—Martin Frank
112

Turf Record									
St.	1st	2nd	3rd		St.	1st	2nd	3rd	Amt.
4	0	0	1	1980	6	3	1	0	$71,373
				1979	21	6	1	4	$86,497

26May80- 8Bel	fst	1		:45⅘	1:10⅖	1:35⅘	3 ↑ Metropol'n H	8	5	62¼	53	65	68¼	Cordero A Jr		112	10.90e	81-20	Czaravich 126no State Dinner 1171 Silent Cal 1204¾	Gave way 8
11May80- 2Aqu	fst	1⅛		:47⅖	1:11⅖	1:49⅘	Clm 90000	3	3	42½	21	16	17¾	Asmussen C B	b	118	*.60e	86-14	Causerie 1187¾ Lean Lad 1183 Ring of Truth 1161¼	Driving 8
22Mar80- 6Aqu	sly	7f		:24	:47⅘	1:26⅕	Allowance	3	2	2½	41½	75¼	65¼	Asmussen C B		122	*1.00e	65-31	Hotspur 122¾ Contare 110no Lark Oscillation 1192¼	Tired 7
23Feb80- 8Aqu	gd	1⅛	⊡	:47⅖	1:12⅕	1:50⅕	3 ↑ Grey Lag H	3	1	11½	1hd	2hd	21¼	Venezia M		113	*.40e	94-17	I'm It 1131¼ Causerie 1131¾ Charlie Coast 1154	No excuse 10
10Feb80- 6Aqu	fst	1¼	⊡	:50⅕	1:40	2:05⅗	Handicap	6	3	2hd	13	15	11¼	Beitia E		116	*1.30	90-20	Causerie 1161¼ Pass 'n Raise 1142¾ Properly Person 1183	All out 7
19Jan80- 7Aqu	my	1 1/16	⊡	:47⅗	1:12⅘	1:45⅗	Allowance	5	3	21½	12	14	14	Beitia E5		114	2.10	86-21	Causerie 1144 Imperialism 115nk Hitching Rail 1152	Easily 8
24Dec79- 7Aqu	my	170	⊡	:47⅖	1:12⅘	1:44⅗	Allowance	3	2	21	21½	34½	38½	Castaneda M		122	*1.40	70-27	Tulsarullah 1153¼ Current Melody 1155¼ Causerie 1221¼	Tired 5
16Dec79- 6Aqu	gd	170	⊡	:47⅘	1:12⅘	1:43	3 ↑ Allowance	2	6	3½	2hd	3½	45	Castaneda M		115	4.50e	82-20	WisePhilip115hdLarkOscillation1173MusicalPhntsy1152	Weakened 8
Aqu	fst	6f	⊡	:22	:45	1:09⅗	3 ↑ Allowance	7	1	55	33½	33	32	Pincay L Jr		120	6.10	94-15	Tim the Tiger 1131¼ Norge 113¾ Causerie 1202	Evenly 8
3Aqu	gd	1⅛		:48	1:12⅕	1:48	Discovery H	1	1	11½	1½	43½	511	Castaneda M		113	7.60e	84-18	Belle's Gold 1214 Smarten 1222¾ Gallant Best 1152½	tired

LATEST WORKOUTS ●**May 25 Bel tr.t 3f fst :35⅖ h** **May 19 Bel tr.t 6f fst 1:16 b** ●**May 6 Bel tr.t 1 fst 1:46⅖ b** **Apr 30 Bel 6f sly 1:13⅕ h**

that Causerie is entered for $75,000. Does this mean there is a drop in class? Not at all, since you must always look at the actual claiming price of the race to determine the class price of the race. Thus, our next question is: Does Causerie qualify on form? Anytime a horse drops from a stakes race into a claiming race, even as fancy a claimer as this one, you can call this a class drop. With that in hand, Causerie qualifies on form because of one call up close plus class drop.

As you might expect, ability times are good. In the 11May80 race, there was a :24.0 lead time, subtract one for gain, add one for energy, and you have your :24.0 figure. Back on 6Dec79, there is a :24.3 lead time with a gain of one to provide an ability time of :24.2. For early speed, this horse is really good, meriting 6 points off several races. This one will be tough, but now let's see what Isella, the second choice, presents.

Isella — Ch. h. 5, by Peace Corps—Gallamar, by Royal Dorimar — **$100,000** — 122

Own.—Blusiewicz L — Br.—Cavanaugh Jr & Mulcahy (Fla) — Tr.—Blusiewicz Leon

Turf Record St.	1st	2nd	3rd	Year	St.	1st	2nd	3rd	Amt.
1	0	0	0	1980	9	2	4	1	$48,778
				1979	8	4	1	0	$72,950

24May80-	9Pim	gd	1 1/16	:45⅗	1:09⅘	1:42⅕	3↑ Cty Balt H	4	1	1½	1hd	2hd	36½	Franklin R J	b 110	2.20	87-16	Crow's Nest 109½ T. V. Hill 1146 Isella 110nk	Tired	4
24May80-Run in Two Divisions: 8th & 9th Races.																				
17May80-	6Pim	fst	1 1/16	:46	1:10⅖	1:42⅘	Allowance	1	2	24½	21½	42½	57¾	Franklin R J	b 112	3.40	84-12	T. V. Hill 1192 Skipper's Friend 119no Zoot Alors 1192¾	Tired	8
20Apr80-	7Aqu	fst	6f	:21⅘	:44⅕	1:09⅘	3↑ Bold Ruler	2	4	21½	34	45½	57	Franklin R J	b 119	4.50	87-16	Dave's Friend 1232¾ Tilt Up 1211½ Double Zeus 121¾	Tired	6
5Apr80-	7Pim	fst	6f	:23	:45⅗	1:10⅗	3↑ J E Hoover H	3	2	11	16	17	111	Franklin R J	b 116	2.50	93-19	Isella 11611 Ambitious Ruler 1101½ Dave's Friend 125no	Handily	4
22Mar80-	7Pim	fst	6f	:23⅖	:46⅖	1:11⅕	Allowance	1	4	2hd	12	13	13¾	Bracciale V Jr	b 116	*.80	90-21	Isella 1163¾ Quill's Turn 1191 Northern Baron 119¾	Ridden out	7
16Feb80-	9Bow	fst	1 1/16	:48⅕	1:11⅘	1:45⅕	3↑ Natv D'ncr H	2	2	2hd	34½	68½	516	Kurtz J	113	10.70	64-21	Pole Position 1253 The Cool Virginian 1175 Telly Hill 1161½	Tired	6
3Feb80-	8Aqu	fst	1⅛ ⊡	:47⅘	1:12⅖	1:52⅕	3↑ Stymie H	2	1	1hd	43	48	87½	Passmore W J	113	15.20	78-18	Identical 116hd Ring of Truth 1152¾ Charlie Coast 1173	Tired	9
26Jan80-	8Bow	fst	1 1/16	:47⅖	1:11⅖	1:44⅘	Allowance	1	4	45	21½	23	25	Kupfer T	112	3.20	78-21	Pole Position 1155 Isella 1122 T. V. Hill 1171¾	Second best	8
12Jan80-	9Bow	gd	6f	:22⅘	:45⅘	1:11	3↑ S Maryland H	1	4	2hd	32½	33	22½	Fann B	115	5.60	83-33	Dave's Friend 1182½ Isella 115¾ Shelter Half 118¾	Up for place	8
20Dec79-	8Lrl	fst	6f	:23	:46⅘	1:11⅘	3↑ Allowance	3	4	44½	44	31	12	Fann B	115	*.80	88-23	Isella 1152 Take The Pledge 1101 Coastal Call 115¾	Driving	7

LATEST WORKOUTS May 16 Pim 3f fst :35⅘ h — May 6 Pim 7f fst 1:27¾ h — May 3 Pim 4f my :49 b — Apr 15 Aqu 5f sly :59⅗ h

This one, too, qualifies off the last race. And look at those splendid ability times! In his last race at Pimlico, Isella made the lead time of :23.4 with no adjustment. To demonstrate his consistency, he came up with the same figure on 17May80, in his previous race at Pimlico. There was a :24.2 lead time, and his gain of three lengths reduces his figure to :23.4, with no adjustment for energy. We see some more good early speed, and once more, we award 6 points. Also, notice an improvement factor out of the last race, moving up from an allowance to a stakes race. Very impressive!

How about the third horse, Chop Chop Tomahawk?

Chop Chop Tomahawk * — Dk. b. or br. h. 5, by Noholme II—Nell Girl, by I Appeal — **$100,000** — 122

Own.—Daybreak Farm — Br.—Daybreak Farm (Fla) — Tr.—Fernandez Floreano

Turf Record St.	1st	2nd	3rd	Year	St.	1st	2nd	3rd	Amt.
3	0	0	0	1980	4	1	0	1	$23,400
				1979	18	1	2	4	$53,926

9May80-	8Aqu	fst	7f	:22⅘	:46	1:23⅕	Allowance	6	1	21½	1hd	2hd	1hd	Cordero A Jr	115	3.70	85-18	ChopChopTomhwk115hdBoldVoygr1152BldndStrmy117no	Driving	6
30Apr80-	7Aqu	my	1	:45⅗	1:10⅖	1:36⅗	Allowance	7	3	33½	42¾	31	32½	Cordero A Jr	115	7.50	80-21	Soldr'sLrk1151¼DoublZus1151¼ChopChopTomhwk1153½	Went well	7
20Apr80-	8Aqu	fst	6f	:22⅕	:45	1:10⅖	Allowance	4	4	52	41½	41	53½	Lovato F Jr5	112	10.00	86-16	Psychosis 1121½ Coup De Chance 122¾ BoldandStormy119½	Tired	8
1Mar80-	7SA	fst	6½f	:21⅘	:44⅕	1:15⅖	Allowance	1	8	95¾	99½	911	911	Delahoussaye E	116	27.10	82-09	Priority 117¾ Moduno 114½ Known Presence 120nk	Outrun	9
24Nov79-	7Aqu	fst	1	:47⅖	1:11⅗	1:36⅖	3↑ Allowance	3	1	1hd	54½	69	618	Cruguet J	117	4.40	66-18	Charlie Coast 115½ Rivalero 114noMusicalPhantasy1178½	Stopped	6
13Oct79-	7Bel	sly	7f	:23⅖	:47⅕	1:24⅗	3↑ Allowance	1	2	12	11½	1hd	31¾	Cordero A Jr	117	5.00	77-27	GllntBest119nkDewnKeys1191½ChopChopTomhwk1177	Weakened	5
23Sep79-	7Bel	my	7f	:22⅗	:45⅖	1:21⅘	3↑ Allowance	4	5	31	31½	24	35½	Cruguet J	117	8.00	87-19	Topsider1155Prfontin116½ChopChopTomhwk117no	Lacked a rally	7
16Sep79-	7Bel	fst	6f	:23⅕	:46	1:09⅗	3↑ Allowance	4	2	2½	2½	1hd	1nk	Cruguet J	115	9.40	94-13	ChopChopTomhwk115nkDoubleZeus1191½Prefontine1171¾	Driving	5
26Aug79-	6Sar	fst	6½f	:22	:44⅖	1:15⅕	3↑ Allowance	5	2	21	43	47	47¾	Cruguet J	115	10.60	91-12	Fanny's Fox 1176¼ Proud Arion 1151 Sorry Lookin 115½	Tired	9
4Aug79	8Det	fst	1 40	:48	1:13⅖	1:42⅕	3↑ Handicap	5	1	1hd	13	11	21⅓	Catalano W	117	1.70	98-29	Win Bill 1201⅓ Chop Chop Tomahawk 1176 Stole The Show 110¾		6

LATEST WORKOUTS Jun 2 Bel 4f fst :48 b — May 25 Bel 5f fst 1:01 b — May 17 Bel 4f fst :49 b — Apr 18 Bel 4f fst :47⅘ hg

He qualifies easily on form. He has some excellent times, but has never run against the kind of competition that Causerie and Isella present. For example, his 16Sep79 race at Belmont shows a remarkable :23.3 with no adjustment involved. His next best, however, falls off considerably to :24.4, which, in ordinary company, is pretty good. That figure was compiled at least three times, with the 30Apr80 race providing the last example. Early speed again, and another 6 points here. Here is what our comparison chart now shows:

Odds	Horse	Ability		A Pts		ES	F	Total
1.1	Causerie	:24.0	:24.2	20	18	6	Q	44
3.0	Isella	:23.4	:23.4	21	21	6	Q	48
3.7	Chop Chop Tomahawk	:23.3	:24.4	22	16	6	Q2	46

These are very high point totals for some of the best sprinters in the East. Our New York friends don't give Isella enough credit for his fine Maryland efforts. And look what he did to them, as we back him to win and place most positively.

SEVENTH RACE **7 FURLONGS. (1.20⅖) CLAIMING. Purse $25,000. 4-year-olds and upward. Weight, 122 lbs. Claiming price $100,000; for each $5,000 to $75,000, 2 lbs.**

Belmont

JUNE 5, 1980

Value of race $25,000, value to winner $15,000, second $5,500, third $3,000, fourth $1,500. Mutuel pool $158,376, OTB pool $103,171. Exacta Pool $192,766. OTB Exacta Pool $155,221.

Last Raced	Horse	Eqt.	A.	Wt	PP	St	¼	½	Str	Fin	Jockey	Cl'g Pr	Odds $1
24May80 ^{9}Pim^{3}	Isella	b	5	122	5	2	1^{1}	1^{1}	1^{3}	1^{4}	Vasquez J	100000	3.00
1Jun80 ^{7}Bel^{2}	Royal Reasoning	b	4	117	6	3	2^{1}	$2^{1\frac{1}{2}}$	2^{2}	2^{3}	Lovato F Jr^{5}	100000	11.80
26May80 ^{8}Bel^{6}	Causerie		4	112	3	1	6^{4}	$5^{\frac{1}{2}}$	3^{1}	$3^{3\frac{1}{4}}$	Asmussen C B	75000	1.10
23Apr80 ^{8}Aqu^{7}	Navy Chaplain		5	114	4	5	7	7	4^{3}	4^{3}	Skinner K	80000	13.80
9May80 ^{8}Aqu^{1}	Chop Chop Tomahawk		5	122	1	6	$3^{\frac{1}{2}}$	$4^{\frac{1}{2}}$	5^{hd}	5^{hd}	Cordero A Jr	100000	3.70
26May80 ^{9}Bel^{10}	Not Tomorrow	b	4	117	7	4	4^{1}	3^{hd}	$6^{1\frac{1}{2}}$	$6^{5\frac{3}{4}}$	DelhoussyDJ^{5}	100000	9.50
26May80 ^{9}Suf^{3}	Zamboni	b	4	109	2	7	$5^{\frac{1}{2}}$	6^{2}	7	7	Beitia E^{5}	75000	19.50

OFF AT 4:07 1/2 EDT. Start good, Won ridden out. Time, :23, :46⅕, 1:10, 1:22⅘ Track fast.

$2 Mutuel Prices:				
	5-(E)-ISELLA	8.00	4.80	2.60
	6-(F)-ROYAL REASONING		7.80	3.20
	3-(C)-CAUSERIE			2.40

$2 EXACTA 5-6 PAID $55.00.

It feels good to get back to the cashier's window again. Isella scored a Big Win, finishing 7 lengths ahead of the favorite, Causerie. He led from wire to wire, as befitting a strong front-running horse with excellent credentials. This was one of the more powerful bets in the entire week, and the payoff was pleasantly high. If we could regularly rake in winners paying $8.00, we would have a hefty pile of profits.

But on to the eighth and feature race, an allowance event on the turf.

8 BELMONT

WIDENER TURF COURSE
START
1 MILE
BELMONT PARK
FINISH

1 MILE. (TURF). (1.33) ALLOWANCE. Purse $35,000. Fillies and mares, 3-year-olds and upward which have not won three races of $15,000 over a mile in 1979–80. Weight, 3-year-olds, 114 lbs. Older, 122 lbs. Non-winners of a race of $15,000 at a mile or over since May 1 allowed 3 lbs. Of such a race since April 1, 5 lbs. Of two such races in 1979–80, 7 lbs. (Maiden, claiming and starter races not considered.)

Tweak — Dk. b. or br. f. 4, by Secretariat—Ta Wee, by Intentionally
Br.—Tartan Farms (Fla)
Own.—Tartan Stable — Tr.—Nerud Jan H — **115**

Turf Record	St.	1st	2nd	3rd		St.	1st	2nd	3rd	Amt.
	1	0	1	0	1980	1	0	0	0	$1,920
					1979	11	4	2	0	$69,203

23May80- 8Bel fst 7f :22⅘ :46 1:23⅖ 3↑ⒻAllowance 1 4 2hd 3 1½ 4 1½ 4 2¾ Foley D10 107 5.00 82-16 Sub Rosa 117¾ Fall Aspen 124¾ Back To Stay 116 1¼ Tired 6
7Dec79- 7Aqu my 6f ⊡:22⅗ :46⅕ 1:11⅖ 3↑ⒻAllowance 2 4 2hd 2½ 2hd 1 1¾ Cordero A Jr 115 *1.20 87-18 Tweak 115 1¾ Cornish Runner 108no Back To Stay 117hd Driving 5
21Nov79- 6Med fst 1 1/16 :47⅗ 1:12⅖ 1:45⅗ 3↑ⒻM. Liberty H 8 5 45 4 3½ 59 5 4¾ Thomas D B 113 6.00 78-25 Skipat 120nk Six Crowns 116¾ Water Malone 117³ Wide 8
8Nov79- 6Med fst 1 1/16 :47⅗ 1:12⅕ 1:45 ⒻHoney Bee H 8 4 31 3½ 1½ 2¾ Thomas D B 114 15.60 85-21 Heavenly Ade 115¾ Tweak 114³ Jameela 121² Lost whip 9
13Oct79- 8Key gd 1 1/16 :48 1:12⅕ 1:43⅘ ⒻCotillion 6 4 5 2¾ 5 2½ 4 5½ 4 9¼ Thomas D B 118 2.40 76-18 Alada 116 1¼ Too Many Sweets 116no Heavenly Ade 116⁸ Wide 6
1Oct79- 6Med sly 170 :46⅗ 1:11⅖ 1:41⅘ ⒻFair Lawn 3 2 3½ 2hd 1 1½ 1 3¼ Thomas D B 115 1.60 92-16 Tweak 115 3¼ Mumkin 115⁴ Leslie J 113 5½ Drew out 5
13Sep79- 8Med fm 1 1/16 Ⓣ:46⅘ 1:10 1:41 ⒻBoiling Sp H 6 3 35 34 23 21 Thomas D B 113⁴ 9.70 96-06 Gala Regatta 122¹ DH Record Acclaim 114 DH Tweak 113⁴ Gamely 6
13Sep79-Dead heat
13Sep79-Run in Two Divisions 6th & 8th Races.
23Aug79- 9Mth fst 1 :47⅗ 1:12⅕ 1:37⅘ 3↑ⒻAllowance 4 5 4 4½ 31 1 1½ 13 Thomas D B 115 1.60 84-16 Tweak 115³ Highland Gypsy 114² Phebe B. 116⁵ Ridden out 8
11Aug79-10Mth fst 1 1/16 :47 1:11⅘ 1:43⅗ 3↑ⒻAllowance 10 6 3 1½ 3nk 1 1½ 1 1½ Thomas D B 113 3.20 86-10 Tweak 113 1½ Champagne Party 112² Cat Song 108½ Driving 12
25Jly79- 9Mth fst 6f :21⅘ :44⅘ 1:09⅘ 3↑ⒻAllowance 6 11 11 8¾ 11 11 10 13 4 4¼ Thomas D B 113 14.00 87-14 LdyDrrington114 2½WillowBottomMiss114¹NeverBbble110¾ Rallied 12
LATEST WORKOUTS May 31 Bel 4f fst :47⅘ b ●May 20 Bel tr.t 4f fst :48 h May 15 Bel 4f fst :48 b May 10 Bel 5f fst 1:01⅗ b

Tweak, a daughter of Secretariat and the brilliant sprinter Ta Wee, last ran on the dirt. She has not been on the grass since last September, in her only lifetime effort. Do we rate her qualified off her dirt race? Ordinarily, we do, since it demonstrates a willingness to run. And where there is successful or promising grass experience, a horse that ran well on the dirt in its last effort is likely to do well on the grass, if the ability is there. For that reason, we would rate Tweak as qualified on form.

There is only one race on the turf which can be rated, back on 13Sep79 at the Meadowlands. There was a blistering :23.1 ability time, with one length gained off that, balanced by a one-tick addition for energy. This :23.1 becomes the only ability time we have, and it is simply sensational.

Since this is a race of one mile, we will use early-speed points. Tweak must be rated off her one grass race to determine how well she gets moving in the early phases. The 5 lengths back she showed on 13Sep79 gives her 2 early-speed points.

We next look at Just A Game II, one of the truly top grass fillies in the country, who is the big favorite today. You can see that she has never lost on the

***Just A Game II** — Dk. b. or br. f. 4, by Tarboosh—Hobby, by Falcon
Br.—Rathvale Stud (Ire)
Own.—Brant P — Tr.—Whiteley David A — **119**

Turf Record	St.	1st	2nd	3rd		St.	1st	2nd	3rd	Amt.
	16	7	2	2	1980	5	3	0	0	$109,095
					1979	2	0	1	0	$1,496

5Apr80- 9GP fm 1 1/16 Ⓣ:46⅕ 1:10⅕ 1:40⅖ 3↑ⒻOrchid H 5 3 3 2½ 21 13 1¾ Brumfield D 119 *.70 99-07 Just A Game II 119¾ LaSoufriere115 2½LaRouquineII114hd Driving 10
12Mar80- 9GP fm 1 Ⓣ:47⅕ 1:10⅗ 1:35⅕ 3↑ⒻS'wnee R'vr 3 2 2hd 1 1½ 15 15 Brumfield D 117 *1.70 94-13 Just AGameII117⁵LaSoufriere113 4½LaVoyageuse120no Ridden out 10
12Mar80-Run in Two Divisions 8th & 9th Races.
25Feb80- 9Hia fm 1 1/16 Ⓣ 1:42⅗ ⒻAllowance 2 2 21 12 15 1 6½ Brumfield D 115 4.10 85-17 Just A Game II 115 6½ Ball Gate 115noLaSoufriere115⁴ Ridden out 7
18Feb80- 7Hia fst 6f :22⅕ :45⅖ 1:10⅗ ⒻAllowance 8 6 7 6½ 77 6 5¾ 5 6½ Vasquez J 115 4.40 83-20 Hill Billy Dancer 117² Yoka 115³ Guimauve 115½ No mishap 9
29Jan80- 9Hia fst 6f :22 :45⅖ 1:10⅗ ⒻAllowance 5 4 31 2½ 2½ 98 Vasquez J 116 4.20 82-25 SilverOaks116¹HillBillyDancer116¹SisterRosmund116hd Gave way 10
9Jun79♦3Epsom(Eng) yl 1½ 2:43⅗ Ⓣ ⒻOaks Stakes(Gr.1) 10 25 Shoemaker W 126 20.00 – – Scintillate 126³ Bonnie Isle 126¹ Britannias Rule 126⁴ Prom 6f 14
2Jun79♦4Leopardst'n(Ire) gd 1⅛ 1:58⅖ Ⓣ Kilmacanogue Hcp 2¾ Piggott L 131 4.00 – – Mississippi133¾ JustAGm131no OisinDubh134 2½ Set pace, gamely 8
7Oct78♦4Curragh(Ire) gd 1 1:42⅘ Ⓣ Beresford Stakes(Gr.2) 1hd Carberry T 123 50.00 – – Just A Game 123hd SandyCreek126⁴ Accomplice126¾ Bid,led,held 5
30Sep78♦5PhoenixPk(Ire) gd 5f :58⅘ Ⓣ Maher Nursery Hcp 5 4¼ Coogan B 130 8.00 – – Feathers Lad 126nk Lattygar 107³ Sun's Image 102hd [illegible] well 10
[illegible]Sep78♦3PhoenixPk(Ire) gd 7f 1:21 Ⓣ ⒻPark Stakes(Gr.3) 2² Morgan J 126 10.00 – – Solar 126² Just A Game 126hd Sister Jinks 11[illegible] Well up thruout 9
LATEST WORKOUTS Jun 4 Bel 3f fst :36 b ●May 30 Bel 5f fst :59⅕ b May 25 Bel 4f fst :47 b May 20 Bel 4f fs :46⅗ h

grass in this country after coming over from Ireland, beating La Soufriere, the other top betting choice, in each of the three times they have met on the turf.

After her successful Florida campaign, she has been out of competition since early April, but the four workouts at the bottom of her past performances shows that she is ready, fully qualified on form as a legitimate stakes runner. She also has plenty of early speed, and will get a 4-point figure here. From her last race at Gulfstream, there was a :24.0 lead time, reduced by one for gain, but offset by one for the fast GP surface, and we have the ability time at that figure. In the 12Mar80 race, there is a lead time of :23.2, with one added for energy and one for GP's surface, and we wind up with a :23.4 ability time.

La Soufriere, a gallant old mare, is formidable also, but has been repeatedly beaten by Just A Game II. Here is her record.

```
La Soufriere            Ch. m. 5, by Explodent--Golden Way, by Diplomat Way                  Turf Record        St. 1st 2nd 3rd      Amt.
                        Br.--Ocala Stud Farms Inc & Swanson (Fla)               115    St. 1st 2nd 3rd   1980  7   1   2   3    $46,410
  Own.--Allen H         Tr.--Jacobs Eugene                                             34   8   7   6    1979 17   2   2   3    $78,719
 5Apr80- 9GP  fm 1 1/16 T :46 1/5 1:10 1/5 1:40 2/5 3+ F Orchid H   2 6 6 8½ 4 1½ 2 3 2 ¾ Cruguet J  115 10.40  98-07 Just A Game II119¾LaSoufriere1152½LaRouquineII114hd 2nd best 10
26Mar80- 8GP  fm *1 1/16 T            1:43         F Allowance    2 3 3 5 3 1½ 2 1½ 1½ Cordero A Jr  114 *1.00  91-13 La Soufriere 114½ Champagne Shower1143½BallGate1142½ Driving 10
12Mar80- 9GP  fm 1 T :47 1/5 1:10 3/5 1:35 1/5 3+ F S'wnee R'vr  6 6 5 2 4 3 3 5½ 2 5 Cordero A Jr  113 9.10  89-13 JustAGameII1175LaSoufriere1134½LaVoygeuse120no Second best 10
      12Mar80-Run in Two Divisions 8th & 9th Races.
25Feb80- 9Hia fm 1 1/16 T             1:42 3/5     F Allowance    7 5 4 2½ 3 3 3 5½ 3 6½ Vasquez J  115 2.70  78-17 Just A Game II 1156½ Ball Gate 115no La Soufriere 1154  Tired 7
18Feb80- 9Hia yl 1 1/16 T             1:44 3/5 3+ F ColumbianaH 9 5 7 3¾ 7 3½ 8 6¼ 10 9 Cruguet J  112 12.70e  66-25 Producer 1223 Tempus Fugit II 1162 Ouro Verde 1111  No threat 12
31Jan80- 8Hia fm *1 1/16 T            1:42 4/5     F Allowance    7 3 1½ 1 1 1hd 3 2 Vasquez J  114 3.90  85-19 TempusFugitII1141½SpringInDeepse119½LSoufrir114no Weakened 9
21Jan80- 9Hia fm *1 1/16 T            1:40 2/5     F Allowance    4 6 6 2¾ 6 3¼ 3 1½ 3 2¼ Cruguet J  115 *2.70  97-03 Spring In Deepsea 1181¼ Titre 1151 La Soufriere 1154  Mild rally 8
29Dec79- 7Crc fm *1⅛ T                1:50 2/5 3+ F Allowance    1 3 3 1½ 2 1½ 2 1½ 3 1½ Vasquez J  120 *1.40  69-32 Highland Gypsy 116½ Eavesdrop 1091 La Soufriere 1205  Tired 6
 3Nov79- 7Aqu sly 1⅛   :47 4/5 1:13 2/5 1:52 1/5 3+ F Allowance    3 3 3 4½ 4 2½ 4 6½ 5 20 Venezia M  115 10.70  54-23 English Trifle 1105 Pleasing Star 1133½ Shukey 1151¾  Tired 6
11Oct79- 6Med gd 1¼    :49  1:38 2/5 2:03 2/5 3+ F Q'n Chrl'e H 4 1 1 1 3½ 5 6 6 13 Venezia M  112 25.10  78-15 Water Malone 117hd Six Crowns 1122¼ Flitalong 1085  Tired 7
  LATEST WORKOUTS    Jun 4 Bel tr.t 3f gd :36 1/5 b (d)    May 31 Bel tr.t 7f fst 1:29 b    ● May 26 Bel tr.t 5f fst 1:00 3/5 h    May 20 Bel tr.t 4f fst :49 4/5 b
```

She has run thirty-four times on the grass and finished in the money on twenty-one of those occasions. She too has not run since her April defeat by Just A Game II at Gulfstream, where she lost by only three-quarters of a length. She too has four recent workouts and qualifies on form. Her ability times, as you might expect, are very strong. In her last race, even though she was beaten by Just A Game, she has a better ability time by virtue of her gain. Off the :24.0 lead time, she gets credit for 6½ lengths for four ticks reduction to :23.1, with only one more added for energy and one for GP's surface, to give her a :23.3. Her other measurable time was on 12Mar80, when there was a :23.2 lead time, with a loss of one and one more added for Gulfstream, plus one more for energy, to wind up with :24.0. Her early speed is sufficient for 2 points.

We can now make our comparison chart to see what we have.

Odds	Horse	Ability		A Pts		ES	F	Total
.5	Just A Game II	:23.4	:24.0	21	—	4	Q	25
3.7	Tweak	:23.1	—	24	—	2	Q	26
4.7	La Soufriere	:23.2	:24.0	23	—	2	Q	25

This race troubles me very much. On our point-rating method, we are compelled to bet on Tweak to place only, as she is 1 point ahead of the other two based on her one strong race, which she might not be able to repeat. Here is where handicapping knowledge of any veteran player will cry out and tell you that Tweak was most unlikely to beat Just A Game II. And even though Just A Game II is only tied in total points with La Soufriere, you can be sure that a horse that has beaten a rival three times in a row is going to do it again.

Off good solid handicapping, therefore, one could hardly go wrong playing Just A Game II to win and place. But we have prescribed rules in this book for sound investment over a long period of time. They are intended to replace handicapping judgment, no matter how good it may be, because handicapping judgment alone has not been enough to make investment profits for hardly anyone. Therefore, even when we know better (and whose judgment is always right?), we will stick to our rules of play in this book. There is simply no room for deviation based upon "handicapping knowledge" any more than one should deviate on a hunch. Thus we put down our money on Tweak to place.

The outcome was just what could have been expected. Just A Game II led wire to wire, merely toying with this field. The other two didn't even finish in the money. We leave this race, thankful we had only a place bet to lose.

EIGHTH RACE
Belmont
JUNE 5, 1980

1 MILE.(turf). (1.33) ALLOWANCE. Purse $35,000. Fillies and mares, 3-year-olds and upward which have not won three races of $15,000 over a mile in 1979–80. Weight, 3-year-olds, 114 lbs. Older, 122 lbs. Non-winners of a race of $15,000 at a mile or over since May 1 allowed 3 lbs. Of such a race since April 1, 5 lbs. Of two such races in 1979–80, 7 lbs. (Maiden, claiming and starter races not considered.)

Value of race $35,000, value to winner $21,000, second $7,700, third $4,200, fourth $2,100. Mutuel pool $173,922, OTB pool $141,903.

Last Raced	Horse	Eqt.A.Wt	PP	St	¼	½	¾	Str	Fin	Jockey	Odds $1
5Apr80 ^{9}GP^{1}	Just A Game II	4 119	2	2	1^{hd}	1^{hd}	$1\frac{1}{2}$	1^{5}	1^{4}	Brumfield D	.50
17May80 ^{7}Aqu^{3}	Chestnut Speester	6 117	5	3	4^{3}	3^{1}	3^{1}	3^{hd}	2no	Samyn J L	9.80
19May80 ^{6}Aqu^{8}	Karin Jones	6 115	3	5	6	6	6	5^{1}	3^{nk}	Asmussen C B	30.20
23May80 ^{8}Bel^{4}	Tweak	4 115	1	4	$3^{1\frac{1}{2}}$	4^{1}	4^{1}	$4^{1\frac{1}{2}}$	$4^{1\frac{1}{4}}$	Velasquez J	3.70
5Arr80 ^{9}GP^{2}	La Soufriere	5 115	4	1	2^{1}	$2^{2\frac{1}{2}}$	2^{2}	$2\frac{1}{2}$	5^{4}	Cordero A Jr	4.70
23May80 ^{8}Bel^{5}	Peaceful Banner	4 115	6	6	5^{3}	5^{5}	5^{2}	6	6	Montoya D	30.10

OFF AT 4:40 1/2 EDT. Start good Won ridden out. Time, :23, :46⅕, 1:10⅘, 1:35⅗ Course firm.

$2 Mutuel Prices:			
2-(B)-JUST A GAME II	3.00	2.80	2.20
5-(G)-CHESTNUT SPEESTER		5.20	3.20
3-(C)-KARIN JONES			3.80

We start to get ready for the ninth and final race, a sprint race at six furlongs, where three horses are not only bunched closely in the odds, but are so high on the board that it is obvious the crowd likes nobody. Let's start with Peaceful Country.

Peaceful Country shows 9-2 in a race where you could almost say there is no favorite. He is tied for second in the win pool with Ephphatha, who will be surveyed shortly. Peaceful Country's form is questionable off two very long grass races as he drops back into a six-furlong sprint. Now notice that he is a Declining Horse off these races, having run further back at every call. Aside

9 BELMONT

START
6 FURLONGS
BELMONT PARK
FINISH

6 FURLONGS. (1.08⅖) CLAIMING. Purse $16,000. 4-year-olds and upward. Weight, 122 lbs. Non-winners of two races since May 1 allowed 3 lbs. Of a race since then, 5 lbs. Claiming price $35,000; for each $2,500 to $30,000, 2 lbs (Races when entered to be claimed for $25,000 or less not considered.)

Peaceful Country — B. g. 5, by Hold Your Peace—Out of Doors, by Bimelech — **$35,000** — Br.—Meadowbrook Farm Inc (Fla) — Tr.—Zito Nicholas P — Own.—Wright Mrs E B — **117**

Turf Record: St. 4, 1st 0, 2nd 1, 3rd 0

	St.	1st	2nd	3rd	Amt.
1980	15	3	3	2	$37,300
1978	10	1	0	1	$10,950

31May80-	2Bel	fm	1⅜	T	:47⅘	1:37	2:15⅗	Clm 40000	3	3	33	3nk	33	43¼	Martens G	117	3.00	76-19	Bel Baie 1142¾ Burn 117nk Adam's Pet 117nk	Weakened	6
12May80-	1Aqu	sf	1½	Ⓣ	:51	2:11⅕	2:37⅕	Clm 35000	6	2	3½	14	1½	2nk	Martens G	113	5.00	55-45	Amano 113nk Peaceful Country 11310 Back Again 1082½	Gamely	6
5May80-	3Aqu	fst	1		:45⅘	1:10⅕	1:36⅕	Clm 32500	2	6	76½	55	54½	33	Fell J	115	3.50	82-19	CouponRate1081¼MasterMgicin1151¾PecefulCountry115nk	Railied	7
26Apr80-	1Aqu	fst	7f		:22⅘	:45⅗	1:24⅕	Clm 25000	1	5	74¾	76¼	3½	1½	Fell J	117	5.70	80-19	PecefulCountry117½HomByDwn117nkCumuloNimbus112nk	Driving	9
20Apr80-	2Aqu	fst	1⅛		:48⅗	1:12⅘	1:51⅖	Clm 25000	1	2	2hd	1hd	2hd	22	Cordero A Jr	117	3.60	76-16	Scamp Boy 1132PeacefulCountry1171ParisStation1124	Weakened	7
3Apr80-	9Aqu	fst	1 3/16		:48	1:12⅕	1:57⅗	Clm 30000	8	5	33½	65½	54½	56¾	Hernandez R	117	19.30	67-20	Click Off 1171¾ Harry J. 117no Sunny Puddles 1171¾	Tired	9
26Mar80-	2Aqu	fst	1⅛		:47⅘	1:12⅕	1:51⅕	Clm 35000	6	3	49½	76¼	58½	56	Hernandez R	117	7.10	73-29	Tread Lightly 1171 Raise Charger 117½ Harry J. 1172	Tired	8
10Mar80-	8Aqu	fst	1 1/16	⊡	:48⅕	1:12⅗	1:44⅘	Allowance	6	7	89½	79	69	57¼	Hernandez R	117	15.20	83-19	Plethora 112no [D]Bankers Sun 1144¼ Raise Charger 1172	Outrun	9
10Mar80-Placed fourth through disqualification																					
3Mar80-	2Aqu	fst	1⅛	⊡	:47⅘	1:13⅕	1:52⅗	Clm 30000	3	4	33½	31½	3½	2hd	Asmussen C B	117	5.80	83-21	Click Off 117hd Peaceful Country117noRaiseCharger1172½	Gamelv	10
20Feb80-	2Aqu	fst	6f	⊡	:22⅗	:45⅘	1:11⅕	Clm 25000	11	4	97¾	98½	86	32¾	Miceli M	119	9.60	85-19	Mika Song 1122 Sal's Dream 117¾ Peaceful Country 119hd	Rallied	12

LATEST WORKOUTS May 28 Bel 4f fst :47⅘ h — May 23 Bel 4f fst :50 b — ●Apr 18 Bel 3f fst :34⅘ h — Apr 14 Bel 4f fst :48⅘ h

from our rule that we will now follow, what does this tell you? A distance grass runner is dropping back to a sprint on the dirt after falling off in form. While we would not normally want to disqualify a horse in a dirt race off poor form on the grass, we are dealing here with a decline based on two successive grass races. Peaceful Country is a Declining Horse, and that is enough to NQ him right now.

We next come to Flighty Jim, who has an almost insignificant margin in the odds to become the technical favorite.

Flighty Jim * — Ch. c. 4, by Jim J—Misty Dana, by Misty Flight — **$30,000** — Br.—Leary Mrs J E (Va) — Tr.—Forbes John H — Own.—Tresvant Stable — **1085**

	St.	1st	2nd	3rd	Amt.
1980	10	2	3	1	$18,500
1979	15	4	1	3	$34,611

26May80-	7Key	fst	170	:46⅘	1:11⅗	1:41⅘	3↑ Clm 32000	4	1	1½	2½	31½	33¼	Terry J5	b	113	4.10	88-15	Ba Ba Blue 118nk Split Deck 1183 Flighty Jim 1134	Weakened	6
11May80-	8Key	fst	170	:46⅖	1:11⅖	1:42	Allowance	6	1	11½	1½	2½	2hd	Terry J5	b	107	13.60	90-20	Steelwood 113hd Flighty Jim 1072 Elevate 122¾	Sharp	8
29Apr80-	7Key	my	6f	:22⅖	:45⅗	1:11	Clm c-25000	1	4	32	32½	32	21¼	Wilson R	b	116	*.50	86-21	Great Estate 1191¼ Flighty Jim 1161¾TimeForJustice115¾	Gamely	6
20Apr80-	7Key	fst	6f	:22⅕	:45⅖	1:10⅖	Clm 22500	4	1	13	12	11½	2nk	Wilson R	b	117	2.60	90-24	Woodfly 116nk Flighty Jim 1173 Orgullo Solo 1195	Gamely	7
7Apr80-	7Key	fst	6f	:22⅖	:45⅖	1:11⅖	Clm c-17500	5	2	1hd	16	15	11½	Wilson R	b	119	*1.20	85-28	Flighty Jim 1191½ Jay's Win 119nk Tip His Hat 1162½	Ridden out	9
23Mar80-	7Key	gd	6f	:22⅗	:45⅘	1:10	Allowance	4	5	42¼	32½	55	513	Sayler B	b	115	21.90	79-20	Great Boone 1144½ Cheating Arthur 1152½ Spunky 114½	Tired	7
15Mar80-	7Key	gd	6f	:23	:46⅖	1:12	Clm 20000	5	1	11	12	11½	13½	Wilson R	b	114	8.20	82-28	Flighty Jim 1143½ Uno Cinco 114no Great Estate 1163	Driving	8
18Feb80-	7Key	fst	6f	:22⅘	:46	1:11⅖	Allowance	4	8	83	84¼	87¾	89¼	Gomez M A	b	116	23.10	76-24	Jiva Coolit 114nk Ornithologist 1162 Bossy Noble 116no	Wide	8
23Jan80-	7Key	gd	7f	:22⅘	:46⅘	1:24⅘	Clm 30000	3	3	1hd	2hd	31½	67¼	Sayler B	b	116	6.40	76-24	Hail By Jove 1134½ Sunsaka 1201½ Forte Party 118hd	Bore in	8
9Jan80-	8Key	fst	6f	:22⅕	:45⅖	1:11	Allowance	4	4	32½	64¼	77	67¾	Klidzia S	b	112	18.40	79-26	Super Who 121½ Real Terror 113¾ Mug Hunter 1143	Tired	7

LATEST WORKOUTS May 24 Key 4f fst :50 b — ●Apr 16 Key 4f fst :48 h

All his races have been run at Keystone, where he has racked up some excellent performances. He qualifies on form off the last race, where his ability time comes out to :25.0 off the lead time plus one. In the preceding race we get the same figure, and that is it. For early speed, we can readily establish 6 points.

Also close in the odds is Bye Bye Blues, who is an NQ, so we skip him and show you Ephphatha, who does have some strong efforts.

While we don't like to see any running line as far back as the last one, this horse does qualify on our gain-of-five rule. Even in that last race, there is a :24.3 lead time, and with a gain of 3½, we can shave that by three down to

:24.0. Only one must be added for energy, and Ephphatha gets a :24.1 off this effort. Back on 4Feb80, there was a :24.3 lead time, lowered by a gain of one down to a :24.2 ability time. In five races of the ten shown, Ephphatha was within 2 lengths of the lead at the first call, and therefore also gets 6 points for early speed.

What do we have now?

Odds	Horse	Ability		A Pts		ES	F	Total
4.3	Flighty Jim	:25.0	:25.0	15	15	6	Q	36
4.7	Peaceful Country	—	—				NQ	NQ
4.7	Ephphatha	:24.1	:24.2	19	18	6	Q	43

Ability times of Ephphatha are strong enough to make him a Double Advantage Horse, and even though his last race is not too good, he has qualified on form and gets our money to win and place. But it was Flighty Jim who came on to win and close out our day.

Big Week at Belmont: Fourth Day, Thursday, June 5, 1980   211

We can now start to total up.

Race	Selection	Invest		Return	
		Win	Place	Win	Place
1	Pruneplum	$ 2	$ 2	$14.20	$ 7.80
2	Resuscitation	2	2	0	4.80
3	Western Isle	2	2	7.00	3.20
4	Pass	—	—	—	—
5	Roman Beach	—	2	—	4.20
6	Friendly Frolic	2	2	0	0
7	Isella	2	2	8.00	4.80
8	Tweak	—	2	—	0
9	Ephphatha	2	2	0	0
	Totals	$12	$16	$29.20	$24.80

Total invested	$28.00
Total returned	$54.00
Net profit	$26.00

This was a most healthy day in the pocketbook, with half our win bets producing and five of the eight place bets turning into money. While the price bonanza on Pruneplum was the big event of the afternoon, you will get numbers like that every so often among one of the first three betting choices. But anytime you score 50% winners up front and five out of eight place bets, you are going to turn in a profit for the day. This is one more illustration of the strength of our method of play, despite the omission of an almost sure winner like Just A Game II in the eighth race.

CHAPTER XIII

BIG WEEK AT BELMONT: FIFTH DAY, FRIDAY, JUNE 6, 1980

I went to the track early on Friday, June 6, on one of the early Belmont racetrack specials out of Pennsylvania Station. It was a comfortable and pleasant ride, not too crowded, with the players so absorbed in the *Racing Form* that there was little conversation, even among those who seemed to know each other. Excitement had begun to build for Saturday's big event, the Belmont itself. But the Friday card presented the same array of challenges that we would meet every day, although the first race, at seven furlongs, looked rather promising as I studied the favorite, Kens Bishop.

1 BELMONT

7 FURLONGS. (1.20⅘) CLAIMING. Purse $10,500. 4–year–olds and upward. Weight, 122 lbs. Non–winners of two races since May 1, allowed 3 lbs. Of a race since then, 5 lbs. Claiming price $10,000; for each $500 to $9,000, allowed 2 lbs. (Races when entered to be claimed for $8,000 or less not considered.)

Kens Bishop — **Ro. h. 5, by King's Bishop—Lucky Jo Jo, by Mito**
Own.—Natiss H D — **$10,000** — **Br.—Greathouse J W Jr & J W Sr (Ky)** — **Tr.—Toscano John T Jr** — **115**[7]

	St.	1st	2nd	3rd	Amt.
1980	9	3	3	0	$24,320
1978	9	0	3	0	$6,430

26May80- 2Bel	fst	1⅛		:47⅖	1:13⅕	1:52⅗	Clm 16000	3	4	$7^{3¾}$	$9^{8¼}$	$9^{8¾}$	10^{13}	Asmussen C B		117	7.50	51–20	Il Vagabondo 117^{nk} Ernie's Lad 115^{3} Wimpfybell 115^{hd}	Tired	12
10May80- 1Aqu	fst	1		:46⅗	1:11	1:36⅗	Clm 12500	7	6	$2^{1½}$	$2^{½}$	$1^{½}$	1^{hd}	Tejada V M Jr[7]		112	3.00	83–13	Kens Bishop 112^{hd} Recidian $119^{1½}$ Prospector's Joy $117^{½}$	Driving	8
4May80- 4Aqu	fst	1		:47	1:13	1:38⅖	Clm 10000	7	8	3^{2}	2^{1}	$2^{½}$	1^{nk}	Beitia E[5]		112	*1.10	74–25	Kens Bishop 112^{nk} Hive 117^{12} Gorizpa 117^{1}	Driving	8
24Apr80- 9Aqu	fst	1⅛		:49	1:14	1:53⅗	Clm 10000	3	6	$5^{4¼}$	3^{2}	1^{1}	$2^{1½}$	Beitia E[5]		114	5.20	65–21	GayPlume$118^{1½}$KensBishop114^{5}LordRumbottom113^{2}	Second best	10
12Apr80- 9Aqu	fst	1⅛		:47⅗	1:12⅕	1:52	Clm 12500	8	5	$5^{8½}$	4^{3}	$4^{6½}$	5^{11}	Santagata N		117	4.70	64–19	Cincelari 119^{4} Hamoud $117^{4¼}$ Nashuma 112^{1}	Poor start	10
29Mar80- 3Aqu	sly	1⅛		:48⅖	1:13⅖	1:54⅕	Clm 8500	6	3	2^{2}	2^{hd}	1^{3}	$1^{3¾}$	Santagata N		117	*3.50	64–27	Kens Bishop$117^{3¾}$SeminoleWarrior117^{hd}Christoforo$115^{5½}$	Driving	7
20Mar80- 2Aqu	fst	7f		:23⅕	:46⅖	1:25⅖	Clm 7500	2	4	$3^{1½}$	$3^{3½}$	2^{2}	$2^{½}$	Fell J		117	*1.70	73–32	OSayRubiayat$110^{½}$KensBishop117^{hd}BillCampbell$117^{6½}$	Drifted out	9
9Mar80- 9Aqu	fst	6f	⊡	:22⅗	:47	1:13⅖	Clm 10000	11	5	7^{7}	6^{5}	7^{6}	$8^{6¾}$	Saumell L	b	117	4.40	70–22	Whiddon $119^{2¾}$ Pokie Joe $117^{1¼}$ Dark Vadar 113^{nk}	Wide	12
28Feb80- 9Aqu	fst	6f	⊡	:23	:47⅕	1:13	Clm 7500	7	1	$3^{1½}$	$3^{½}$	$3^{1½}$	$2^{½}$	Gribcheck S B[5]	b	112	6.10	78–19	News $112^{½}$ Kens Bishop $112^{¾}$ Shed Shy 112no	Gamely	12
12Aug78- 7Sar	sly	7f		:22	:44⅘	1:21⅗	3 ↑ Allowance	1	5	4^{9}	5^{12}	4^{18}	4^{25}	Graell A	b	110	24.30	72–18	Seattle Slew 119^{6} Proud Birdie $115^{2¾}$ Capital Idea 115^{16}	Outrun	5

Off his last race, you might think Kens Bishop was going nowhere. But there was a big up-and-down drop in class. He had been raised from $12,500 to compete at $16,000, and had done very badly. His trainer was bringing him back down today at a more realistic price of $10,000, where he had run extremely well. On form, therefore, because of the rise and drop in class, we could use the second-to-last race of 10May80 and see that Kens Bishop does indeed qualify on form.

Having passed the form hurdle, I now go to ability times, and see that in the good race of 10May80, there was a lead time of :24.2, shaved by one on a gain to give Kens Bishop a :24.1 ability time. On 12Apr80, there is a :24.3 lead time with an allowable gain of five, for a four-tick reduction down to :23.4. This must be increased by two for energy and we finish with another :24.1 ability time, which is extremely good for any $10,000 horse. For our speed calculation, there are 2 points for medium speed.

The second choice in the wagering is one of those typical come-from-behind horses, an aged ten-year-old gelding named Pompini.

***Pompini** B. g. 10, by Hawaian Lad—Pregonera, by The Rabbi
Own.—Gangel Roni J $9,000 Br.—Haras Las Ortigas (Arg) Tr.—Cotter Mary M **115**

Turf Record					St.	1st	2nd	3rd	Amt.
St.	1st	2nd	3rd	1980	10	1	1	1	$12,110
2	0	0	1	1979	14	1	2	0	$12,150

26May80-	3Bel	fst	7f	:23	:46⅕	1:25	Clm 10500	6	5	6^{14}	6^{16}	$67\frac{1}{2}$	1no	Fell J	114	16.20	77–20	Pompini 114no Marsh'sRobber112^{nk}Prospector'sJoy117^{hd}	Driving	6
17May80-	1Aqu	fst	7f	:22⅘	:45⅖	1:23⅖	Clm 9000	13	8	13^{11}	13^{14}	8^{16}	5^{12}	Fell J	114	16.50	72–16	Ed Cainan $117^{9\frac{3}{4}}$ Shed Shy 113^{nk} Gorizpa 117^{1}	No factor	14
4May80-	1Aqu	fst	1	:48⅖	1:13⅘	1:39⅗	Clm 9000	7	4	4^{2}	4^{2}	3^{1}	$2\frac{1}{2}$	Fell J	114	3.50	67–25	Recidian $117\frac{1}{2}$ Pompini $114^{1\frac{3}{4}}$ Prospector's Joy $117^{1\frac{1}{4}}$	Gamely	8
27Apr80-	1Aqu	fst	7f	:23⅗	:47	1:25⅖	Clm 9000	1	9	7^{4}	$64\frac{1}{2}$	$45\frac{1}{2}$	$33\frac{1}{2}$	Miranda J	113	6.60	70–21	Hiv. $117\frac{1}{2}$ Bunky 117^{3} Pompini 113^{1}	Mild bid	9
11Apr80-	3Aqu	fst	7f	:23	:45⅘	1:24⅖	Clm 9000	4	8	9^{18}	9^{17}	7^{9}	$42\frac{1}{2}$	Venezia M	113	10.00	76–20	Jara 117^{nk} [D]Sandrito 113no Sailing High $106^{2\frac{1}{4}}$	Late bid	9
26Mar80-	3Aqu	fst	7f	:23⅖	:48⅖	1:25⅘	Clm 9000	8	1	6^{10}	$65\frac{1}{4}$	5^{5}	4^{5}	Venezia M	113	8.00	67–29	Wartyme $112\frac{3}{4}$ Pokie Joe 119^{2} Dark Vadar $106^{2\frac{1}{4}}$	Evenly	8
20Mar80-	6Aqu	fst	7f	:23⅕	:46⅗	1:25⅘	Clm 7500	10	1	7^{14}	7^{12}	$59\frac{1}{2}$	$46\frac{1}{2}$	Venezia M	117	5.30	65–32	Sandrito 117^{5} Our Charlie G. $117\frac{3}{4}$ Jara $119\frac{3}{4}$	Rallied	10
8Mar80-	1Aqu	fst	170	[•]:48	1:13⅕	1:44⅗	Clm 7500	6	8	7^{13}	7^{16}	7^{14}	6^{13}	Venezia M	117	9.90	66–16	Royal Tuffie $117\frac{1}{2}$ Judge Root 117^{2} Spring Lodge 117^{2}	Outrun	10
26Jan80-	1Aqu	fst	1⅛	[•]:48⅘	1:13⅗	1:53⅗	Clm 8000	7	9	9^{10}	$66\frac{1}{2}$	$54\frac{3}{4}$	7^{14}	Venezia M	113	9.40	64–17	Conspirator $117^{1\frac{1}{4}}$ All Our Hopes $115^{3\frac{3}{4}}$ Searing 119^{nk}	Outrun	10
17Jan80-	1Aqu	fst	170	[•]:48	1:13⅘	1:44⅗	Clm 8000	2	10	8^{12}	8^{10}	$43\frac{1}{4}$	$45\frac{3}{4}$	Martens G	113	6.80	73–18	Bb'sBetloBoy$117\frac{1}{2}$AllOurHopes109^{nk}Rumncoke112^{5}	No real threat	10

LATEST WORKOUTS Jun 4 Bel 3f fst :37 b May 15 Bel 3f fst :37⅕ b Apr 25 Bel 4f fst :50 b Apr 19 Bel 4f fst :52 h

Because he won his last race, coming from somewhere around Brooklyn, he qualifies on form. In computing ability times, the 7f figure is adjusted to 1:12.0, which gives a :25.4 lead time. Here is where our line-drawing at allowable lengths for gain is best illustrated. Pompini came from 16 lengths back at the second call to barrel home a winner. I refuse to allow any gain from beyond 8 lengths, and that's all he gets here. This requires a six-tick adjustment off the lead time down to a :24.3. Now, we can use the 16 lengths back to rate his second call time at :49.2, which requires a three-tick add-on for energy, to round out the ability time for this race at :25.1. If we had given Pompini credit for the full gain of 16 lengths, and allowed a twelve-tick subtraction from the lead time of :25.4, we would have wound up with a :23.2, and no ten-year-old gelding running at $8–10,000 claiming prices could possibly navigate that fast. You will also note at this point that Pompini has won but two races in twenty-four starts shown in his current record, which tells you how inconsistent these late-chargers usually are. His last race was one of the rare victories he will score now and then. His other ability rating comes in his race of 11Apr80, where he once again rallied from the next county, 17 lengths behind, to close to within 2½ lengths of the winner. The 7f final time is adjusted down to 1:11.2 to get a lead time of :25.3. Using the maximum 8 lengths of gain, with a six-tick subtraction, Pompini's ability time goes down to :24.2, to which three ticks are added off the :49.1 second call time, to finish with a :25.0 figure.

For early speed, it is easy to see that this horse gets nothing.

For the third choice, Hive and Recidian are shown on the board at 5-1, respectable enough. Both horses fail to qualify on form, but I will reproducc Hive to show you another look at a true Declining Horse.

Hive Ch. g. 6, by Dr Fager—Quilting, by Princequillo
Own.—Rafsky J K **$9,000** Br.—Tartan Farms (Fla) Tr.—Donato Robert A **117**

Turf Record	St.	1st	2nd	3rd	Amt
1980	11	2	2	0	$19,370
1979	16	0	2	2	$11,628
Turf	2	0	0	0	

26May80- 1Bel	fst	6f	:23⅕	:47	1:12⅕	Clm 10000	2	1	34	44¼	47	44¾	Saumell L	119	4.10	76-20 Pet the Jet 1171¼ Royaldate 117no Bravo's Flame1083½	No excuse 11
4May80- 4Aqu	fst	1	:47	1:13	1:38⅖	Clm 10000	3	3	2½	11	1½	2nk	Saumell L	117	3.60	74-25 Kens Bishop 112nk Hive 11712 Gorizpa 1171	Gamely 8
27Apr80- 1Aqu	fst	7f	:23⅗	:47	1:25⅖	Clm 10000	2	4	31½	21½	21	1½	Saumell L	117	*2.00	74-21 Hive 117½ Bunky 1173 Pompini 1131	Driving 9
19Apr80- 1Aqu	fst	6f	:22⅗	:45⅘	1:12⅕	Clm 10000	2	7	96½	812	67	52½	Saumell L	117	16.80	79-17 Patty D'Baker 114½ Ace's Harlequin117½SailingHigh110¾	Late bid 10
3Apr80- 1Aqu	fst	6f	:23	:46⅘	1:11⅖	Clm 10000	2	4	2hd	31½	52¾	53¾	Castaneda M	117	5.60	82-20 Patty D'Baker 112¾ Senor Riddle 115½ Jara 1171¾	Tired 8
23Mar80- 1Aqu	my	6f	:22⅘	:46⅘	1:12	Clm 11500	7	6	41	54¼	85¼	75¾	Castaneda M	115	7.20	77-25 Snow Alert 117nk Marsh's Robber 1172¾ Jilting Jim 107¾	Tired 8
3Mar80- 1Aqu	fst	6f	⊡:23⅖	:47⅘	1:13	Clm 14000	2	5	2hd	2hd	33	47½	Castaneda M	115	4.80	71-21 At The Crease 117no True Chronicle 1153¾ Snow Alert1113¾	Tired 9
22Feb80- 9Aqu	gd	6f	⊡:23⅕	:47	1:12⅕	Clm 14000	12	1	42	63¾	99	1214	Castaneda M	115	8.30	69-19 Island Nymph 1171¾ Gorizpa 1132 Joe Montage 111½	Brief foot 17
10Feb80- 2Aqu	fst	6f	⊡:23⅖	:47⅘	1:13⅖	Clm 15000	1	2	2hd	1hd	2hd	1nk	Castaneda M	115	8.90	77-20 Hive 115nk Siwash Chief 119½ Limited Vision 112½	Driving 9
16Jan80- 1Aqu	fst	6f	⊡:23	:47⅖	1:13	Clm 16000	3	6	75¼	74¼	43½	23	Castaneda M	117	7.30	76-18 Siwash Chief 1133 Hive117nkWheatBroker1121	Returned bleeding 11

LATEST WORKOUTS May 17 Aqu 3f fst :35⅗ h May 13 Aqu 5f sly 1:06 b (d) ●Apr 15 Aqu 4f sly :49 h

Despite this form, enough money was pumped in on Hive to bring his odds down to 5-1. This was money truly thrown away, as you will see in another moment. There is no form signal in his running line. At every call in his last race, at the same $10,000 price at which he ran on 4May80 in his semifinal race, he was farther back in the pack. Horses that fall farther behind at every call at the same class price would require a miracle to win their next race; they are the poorest bets in racing. Back in the second chapter of this book, I said that in many races, from among the three top betting choices, one would often have no chance at all. This is Exhibit A. Hive, off that record, had, in my view, no chance whatsoever.

Since there is only one qualified horse among the three favorites, Kens Bishop, we will skip our comparison chart and invest to win and place. But the ability times we've already calculated show that Kens Bishop, on top of everything else, is a Double Advantage Horse in this crowd.

Even so, Kens Bishop dawdled a bit himself and just managed to nip the two leaders at wire. But the bottom line is what counts—a winner by a nose pays just as much at the windows as if he won by 30 lengths. Note that old Pompini was up to his usual tricks, last in a field of ten at the start, last at the first call, last at the second call, moving up in the stretch to seventh, and closing nicely to finish fifth, less than 5 lengths from the lead. This is what these traditional

FIRST RACE
Belmont
JUNE 6, 1980

7 FURLONGS. (1.20⅘) CLAIMING. Purse $10,500. 4-year-olds and upward. Weight, 122 lbs. Non-winners of two races since May 1, allowed 3 lbs. Of a race since then, 5 lbs. Claiming price $10,000; for each $500 to $9,000, allowed 2 lbs. (Races when entered to be claimed for $8,000 or less not considered.)

Value of race $10,500, value to winner $6,300, second $2,310, third $1,260, fourth $630. Mutuel pool $101,079, OTB pool $178,901.

Last Raced	Horse	Eqt.A.Wt	PP	St	¼	½	Str	Fin	Jockey	Cl'g Pr	Odds $1
26May80 2Bel10	Kens Bishop	5 115	5	8	81	61	33	1nk	Tejada V M Jr7	10000	2.20
26May80 2Bel12	Recidian	5 119	1	4	31½	2hd	2hd	2¾	Venezia M	10000	5.90
26May80 1Bel3	Bravo's Flame	b 4 108	7	5	21½	1½	1½	33½	Lovato F Jr5	9000	12.70
26May80 1Bel4	Hive	6 117	9	2	4hd	5½	51	4½	Saumell L	9000	5.80
26May80 3Bel1	Pompini	10 115	6	10	10	10	7½	5no	Fell J	9000	4.70
26May80 1Bel10	Gorizpa	b 5 113	4	3	72	84	6½	62	Maple E	9000	15.20
26May80 1Bel6	Jara	5 116	10	1	51	3½	4hd	71¼	Castaneda M	9000	13.80
1Jun80 7Pen8	Lucky Cajun	b 4 117	3	9	6hd	7½	85	84¼	Encinas R I	10000	11.70
4May80 1Aqu7	Our Charlie G.	b 4 114	2	7	94	9½	10	91½	Asmussen C B	9000	23.10
26May80 1Bel5	Patty D'Baker	6 117	8	6	1½	41	91	10	Ho G	10000	7.70

OFF AT 1:00 EDT. Start good, Won driving. Time, :23, :47, 1:12⅕, 1:25⅕ Track fast.

Official Program Numbers↘

$2 Mutuel Prices:			
5-(F)-KENS BISHOP	6.40	4.40	3.60
1-(A)-RECIDIAN		6.00	4.60
7-(H)-BRAVO'S FLAME			5.60

late-runners usually do, and few of them will ever again find my money supporting their chances.

With that wholesome beginning, the second race is a very long grass event for maiden special runners. The slight favorite is Romeo Lima.

2 BELMONT

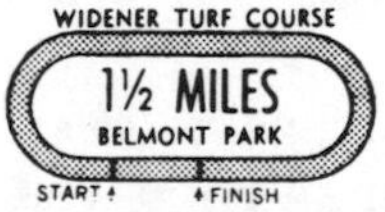

1 ½ MILES. (TURF). (2.24⅘) MAIDEN SPECIAL WEIGHT. Purse $18,000. 3-year-olds and upward. Weights, 3-year-olds, 114 lbs. Older, 122 lbs.

Romeo Lima — **B. c. 4, by Buckpasser—Respected, by Round Table**
Own.—Brant P — **Br.—Claiborne Farm (Ky)** — **Tr.—Whiteley Frank Y Jr** — **122**

	St.	1st	2nd	3rd	Amt.
1980	2	1	1	0	$2,700
1979	5	M	1	0	$6,060

12Apr80- 1SoP fm *1⅞	S'chase		3:31	3↑Md Sp Wt	6	2	1½	14½	18	116	Fishback J	147		— —	Romeo Lima 14716 Too Few Stripes 1472 Hillish 15110		6
29Mar80- 1Cam gd *1¾	S'chase		3:20⅖	3↑Md Sp Wt	3	3	35	21	2nk	21	Witham R	142		— —	Winter Wonderland 1551 Romeo Lima 14218 Hillish 145	Gamely	3
26Jly79- 7Bel fst 7f	:23	:46⅗	1:2.5	3↑Md Sp Wt	2	6	53¾	33½	45	44¾	Hernandez R	116	2.80	72-24	Towie 116nk Princenesian 1163¾ Il Vagabondo 122¾	Off slowly	7
9Jly79- 6Bel fst 6f	:22⅘	:46⅖	1:11⅗	3↑Md Sp Wt	9	4	3nk	11	12	22	Vasquez J	116	11.50	82-15	French Colonial 1222 Romeo Lima 1162½GamePride116¾	2nd best	12
11May79- 9Aqu fst 6f	:22⅖	:46	1:11⅗	3↑Md Sp Wt	8	1	21½	41¾	55½	58¾	Vasquez J	113	2.80	76-19	Guillermo 1131¼ Silver Blaze 1131½ Tsuba 1133¼	Tired	12
22Apr79- 4Aqu fst 1	:45⅗	1:10⅖	1:36⅘	3↑Md Sp Wt	5	2	21	21	23½	49	Vasquez J	114	3.20	73-11	Council Rock 1131¾ Chungero 1096 Sunny Puddles 1081¼	Tired	9
12Apr79- 6Aqu fst 6f	:21⅘	:45⅖	1:11⅕	3↑Md Sp Wt	3	7	55½	58½	58	56¾	Vasquez J	113	*2.10	80-19	Dapper Escort 1131¾ Happy Hour 1143 Tellurite 109.1	Hit by whip	8

12Apr79-Placed fourth through disqualification

LATEST WORKOUTS **Jun 5 Bel (T) 4f fm :49⅕ b (d)** **May 29 Bel (T) 5f fm 1:02 b (d)**

This looks like a good steeplechase horse, where his win by 16 lengths in his jump race in April still leaves him a maiden on the flat surfaces. But he cannot be rated off his jump races and there are no other grass events showing. His ability is thus classed as unknown, and his form likewise gets this same doubtful category, since he has had but two workouts since his April effort over the jumps. We had better see what the second choice, Gleaming Rose, looks like.

His last turf race, where there was a good second-place finish, qualifies him for form. In that race, we have the difficulty of calculating ability times off odd distances, such as a mile and three-eighths where the second call time is posted at the one-mile mark. We compute a 4f time of :50.4 for the lead figures, giving

Gleaming Rose B. c. 4, by Gleaming—Guelder Rose, by Sir Gaylord
Br.—Nickerson & Wygod (Ky)
Own.—Wygod M J Tr.—Nickerson Victor J
122 Turf Record St. 1st 2nd 3rd: 3 0 1 1
St. 1st 2nd 3rd Amt.
1980 2 M 1 0 $3,960
1979 5 M 0 1 $1,680

28May80- 6Bel fm 1⅜ Ⓣ:46⅘ 1:37⅗ 2:14⅕ 3↑Md Sp Wt 13 12 129½ 65 24 23 Asmussen C B b 124 13.70 83-12 Good Bid 1133 Gleaming Rose 1245¼ Bolshoi 124hd Lacked room 14
25Apr80- 7Aqu fst 1⅛ :48⅗ 1:13⅕ 1:51⅕ Allowance 4 4 44½ 58½ 517 529 Asmussen C B b 117 24.40 50-26 Sunny Puddles 1071½DresdenDew117¾SpeedyMagreedy1174 Tired 5
30Nov79- 9Aqu fst 1 :48⅕ 1:13⅖ 1:38⅘ 3↑Md Sp Wt 8 8 912 917 923 926 Castaneda M b 120 18.00 46-29 Triple Blessed 120½ Creme Silence1207LittleKingdom120¾ Outrun 9
20Nov79- 8Med yl 1 Ⓣ:48⅖ 1:14⅘ 1:42⅕ 3↑Allowance 8 7 711 87¼ 68¾ 64½ Castaneda M b 114 3.90 63-24 Fillu 114nk Majestic Leader 1111 Balakiev 119¾ No threat 8
31Oct79- 5Aqu gd 1 Ⓣ:48⅕ 1:13⅘ 1:39⅗ 3↑Md Sp Wt 1 8 810 76¾ 45 31½ Castaneda M b 119 41.70 80-17 Test Pattern 1191 Sword Game 116½ Gleaming Rose 1192 Rallied 10
19Oct79- 9Aqu fst 1⅛ :47⅘ 1:13 1:53⅘ 3↑Md 25000 4 5 59 913 1018 1021 Castaneda M 119 18.50 45-23 ⒹMetro 1192¾ Pass The Salt 115¾ Forreko 1194 Tired 10
1Oct79- 4Bel sly 7f :23 :47 1:27⅖ 3↑Md 25000 1 9 912 913 913 814 Castaneda M 119 10.50 51-25 Flying Straight1102GallantO.119½Prospector'sJoy1193¾ Slow start 9
LATEST WORKOUTS ●May 25 Aqu 5f fst 1:01 h May 14 Aqu 1 gd 1:49 b (d) May 7 Aqu 4f fst :52 b May 2 Aqu 3f fst :37⅕ b

Gleaming Rose a credit of three for gain down to :50.1, divide it in half, take the lesser figure, and have a :25.0 ability time before adjustment for energy. That adds two more to wind up with a :25.2 for this effort.

The other grass races are easier to rate, since we have the standard first two calls at the 4f and 6f distances. Back on 31Oct79 at Aqueduct, there is a :25.3 lead time with an allowable gain to one to reduce to :25.2. But there is a four for energy to push the ability time up to :26.1. In the Meadowlands race on 20Nov79, the lead time is :26.2, no allowable gain, and another four for energy to go out of sight at :27.1. Thus we use the last-race figure of :25.2 and the :26.1 at Aqueduct.

The third choice is Bolshoi, appropriately named out of Nijinsky II.

Bolshoi B. c. 4, by Nijinsky II—Gallant Demand, by Gallant Man
Br.—Lufkin D W (Ky)
Own.—Greene Nona Lou Tr.—Kay Michael
122 Turf Record St. 1st 2nd 3rd: 4 0 1 1
St. 1st 2nd 3rd Amt.
1980 1 M 0 1 $2,160
1979 4 M 2 0 $7,285

28May80- 6Bel fm 1⅜ Ⓣ:46⅘ 1:37⅗ 2:14⅕ 3↑Md Sp Wt 6 10 108½ 108½ 67½ 38¼ Fell J 124 3.00 78-12 Good Bid 1133 Gleaming Rose 1245¼ Bolshoi 124hd Rallied 14
8Oct79- 5Bel sf 1⅜ Ⓣ:49⅕ 1:42 2:20⅗ 3↑Md Sp Wt 3 6 59¼ 411 411 213 Fell J 119 4.00 41-38 Great Partner 11913 Bolshoi 119no Allez VouzEn119no Up for 2nd 7
17Jun79- 6Bel fm 1 1/16 Ⓣ:45⅘ 1:10⅕ 1:41⅘ 3↑Md Sp Wt 4 5 46 44½ 66 46½ Martens G 114 5.60 80-15 Silent Sunrise 1221¼ Bailey's Beach 1144Dobrynin1171¼ No factor 9
4Jun79- 2Bel sly 1 1/16 :46⅕ 1:11⅘ 1:46⅖ 3↑Md Sp Wt 7 4 36 45½ 34 26 Martens G 114♦ 4.20 64-24 Csnov'sCup1146 DH Herbgr'sFinst117 DH Bolshoi1145½ Lacked rally 7
4Jun79-Dead heat
3Apr79- 2Hia fm *1 1/16 Ⓣ 1:42⅕ Md Sp Wt 9 8 1022 — — — Rivera M A 120 12.10 — — Bends Me Mind 1201½ Shadowbrook 115½ Mallard 1202 Eased 10
LATEST WORKOUTS May 23 Bel 1 fst 1:42 hg May 12 Bel 6f fst 1:13⅘ h May 7 Bel 4f fst :49⅕ h Apr 27 Bel 6f fst 1:16⅘ h

This one, a Lightly Raced Horse, ran in the same long race on 28May80 as did Gleaming Rose. We can get a gain of five out of the running line even though any gain was made too far back as far as lengths are concerned. Bolshoi passed seven horses, or half the field of fourteen, to finish third. You will recall our rule for allowable gain, in that a gain must be finished within less than 6 lengths of the lead. But that pertains to lengths, not horses, and here we barely get a qualifier. Passing five or more horses in any race is a difficult task, much more so than gaining in lengths. Now we have to struggle with ability times. Back on 17Jun79 at Belmont, there was a :24.2 lead time, reduced by one for gain and increased by two for energy to come out with a :24.3, which is pretty good. Now, we can return to the last race, where, with Gleaming Rose, we noted the lead time as :50.4 for four furlongs. There is no allowable gain for Bolshoi, but one-half of this figure is :25.2, and since we will always revert to a lower portion, we can use :25.1. But we still have an energy tack-on of two to bring us back up to :25.3.

Here is what we come up with on the comparison chart.

Odds	Horse	Ability		A Pts		F	Total
2.2	Romeo Lima	Unknown		—	—	U	U
2.4	Gleaming Rose	:25.2	:26.1	13	9	Q	22
4.3	Bolshoi	:24.3	:25.3	17	12	Q	29

At this point, you must recall our rule about unknown-ability horses as favorites, where we are allowed to invest for place when the unknown-ability horse is a "strong" favorite. Romeo Lima lacks the one-number advantage over Gleaming Rose, and in fact, from the closeness of the odds, you can see that Romeo Lima is only barely ahead of Gleaming Rose in the wagering. Under this situation, we can bypass the lukewarm unknown-ability favorite and invest in the animal with the strongest credentials. This happens to be Bolshoi by a wide margin, and he gets our money to win and place.

SECOND RACE 1 ½ MILES.(turf). (2.24⅘) MAIDEN SPECIAL WEIGHT. Purse $18.000. 3-year-olds and upward. Weights, 3-year-olds, 114 lbs. Older, 122 lbs.

Belmont

JUNE 6, 1980

Value of race $18,000, value to winner $10,800, second $3,960, third $2,160, fourth $1,080. Mutuel pool $137,084, OTB pool $130,092. Quinella Pool $133,323. OTB Quinella Pool $155,315.

Last Raced	Horse	Eqt.	A.	Wt	PP	¼	½	1	1¼	Str	Fin	Jockey	Odds $1
28May80 6Bel3	Bolshoi	b	4	122	9	2^{4}	$2^{1\frac{1}{2}}$	$3^{1\frac{1}{2}}$	$1^{\frac{1}{2}}$	1^{1}	$1^{1\frac{1}{4}}$	Fell J	4.30
28May80 6Bel2	Gleaming Rose	b	4	122	6	10^{4}	$8^{\frac{1}{2}}$	1^{hd}	2^{2}	$2^{2\frac{1}{2}}$	$2^{2\frac{1}{4}}$	Asmussen C B	2.40
22May80 9Bel5	Raise A Crown	b	3	114	3	3^{hd}	4^{1}	4^{2}	3^{hd}	3^{5}	$3^{6\frac{1}{4}}$	Cordero A Jr	5.50
7May80 1Aqu7	Spruce It Up		3	114	2	$7^{\frac{1}{2}}$	6^{hd}	$8^{\frac{1}{2}}$	5^{hd}	4^{2}	4no	Martens G	26.70
28May80 6Bel6	Johnny's Redman		3	114	7	$8^{\frac{1}{2}}$	9^{2}	6^{2}	7^{3}	6^{2}	5^{hd}	Encinas R I	38.20
28May80 6Bel9	Glendevon		3	114	1	$4^{1\frac{1}{2}}$	3^{1}	5^{hd}	$6^{\frac{1}{2}}$	$5^{\frac{1}{2}}$	6^{4}	Skinner K	37.30
28May80 6Bel11	Exact Sam		3	114	11	11	11	11	$10^{\frac{1}{2}}$	$9^{\frac{1}{2}}$	7^{nk}	Cruguet J	23.40
2May80 6Aqu5	B. Worthy		3	109	8	$9^{\frac{1}{2}}$	10^{4}	10^{3}	11	10^{3}	$8^{\frac{3}{4}}$	Delahoussaye D J5	9.20
28May80 6Bel14	Winabit	b	3	114	10	6^{1}	7^{1}	7^{hd}	$8^{\frac{1}{2}}$	$8^{\frac{1}{2}}$	$9^{3\frac{1}{4}}$	Santiago A	78.00
12Apr80 1SoP1	Romeo Lima		4	122	5	$1^{\frac{1}{2}}$	1^{hd}	2^{hd}	4^{3}	7^{2}	10^{2}	Vasquez J	2.20
22May80 3Bel2	Nippy The Great		3	114	4	5^{5}	5^{2}	9^{2}	9^{2}	11	11	Brocklebank J	41.10

OFF AT 1:28 EDT Start good, Won ridden out. Time, :24, :49⅖, 1:15⅖, 1:39⅗, 2:04⅘, 2:30, Course firm.

$2 Mutuel Prices:			
9-(K)-BOLSHOI	10.60	4.20	2.80
6-(H)-GLEAMING ROSE		3.60	2.60
3-(C)-RAISE A CROWN			3.40

Bolshoi held on nicely to beat Gleaming Rose and provide a splendid payoff. Look where Romeo Lima finished. I had not the slightest hesitation in making my investment on Bolshoi, and with the day barely begun, we have two nice winners with good returns.

In the third race, we're back to a bunch of maidens with very little promise, although the best thing that can be said for them is that they are Lightly Raced in the middle of their three-year-old season. The favorite is Visualization, at 3-2 on the board, with but one race in her record.

Her last race barely qualifies on form, based on a class drop from maiden special down to a $40,000 claimer, plus an up-close at the first call in the only effort. We have but one ability time to study, where there is a :26.0 lead time, a loss of one and one tick added for energy to produce a :26.2 ability time. Early speed off this one race picks up the maximum 6 points. I might as well show

3 BELMONT

6 FURLONGS. (1.08⅖) MAIDEN CLAIMING. Purse $12,000. Fillies and Mares. 3-year-olds and upward. Weights, 3-year-olds, 114 lbs. Older, 122 lbs. Claiming price $40,000; for each $2,500 to $35,000, allowed 2 lbs.

Visualization — B. f. 3, by Native Royalty—Lalibela, by Cohoes — $40,000 — Br.—Parke B (Fla) — Tr.—Barrera Guillermo S — 114
Own.—Harbor View Farm

	St.	1st	2nd	3rd	Amt.
1980	1	M	0	0	$1,020
1979	0	M	0	0	

31May80- 6Bel fst 6f :23 :46⅘ 1:12⅘ 3↑ⒻMd Sp Wt 3 5 4^{2} 3^{5} $3^{4\frac{1}{2}}$ $4^{5\frac{1}{2}}$ Hernandez R 113 11.50 72-16 Hemlock$113^{2\frac{1}{4}}$AncientMystry$113^{2\frac{3}{4}}$CupCompnion$113^{\frac{1}{2}}$ No menace 8
LATEST WORKOUTS May 28 Bel tr.t 5f fst 1:04 b May 20 Bel tr.t 4f fst :48⅖ b ●May 11 Bel tr.t 6f fst 1:17 b May 2 Bel 5f fst 1:00 hg

you three fillies together to see what else is available. Cheering Section is the second choice with the crowd, while A Woman Scorned and Soaring Sea, both 6-1 on the board, are basically tied for third and fourth favorites and, therefore, must be compared also.

A Woman Scorned — Dk. b. or br. f. 3, by Cornish Prince—Rebecca M, by King of the Tudors — $40,000 — Br.—McIntire & Trimble Mmes (Ky) — Tr.—Dunham Bob G — 114
Own.—Southlake Stable

	St.	1st	2nd	3rd	Amt.
1980	3	M	0	2	$4,020
1979	1	M	0	0	

2Feb80- 4Aqu fst 6f ⊡:23⅕ :48⅗ 1:15 ⒻMd Sp Wt 9 3 5^{5} $5^{3\frac{3}{4}}$ 3^{4} $3^{4\frac{3}{4}}$ Venezia M 121 3.50 64-27 Illgotten Gains121^{nk}HurryImp$121^{4\frac{1}{2}}$AWomanScorned$121^{2\frac{1}{2}}$ Rallied 12
25Jan80- 6Aqu fst 6f ⊡:23 :47⅗ 1:13⅘ ⒻMd Sp Wt 4 7 8^{4} $5^{2\frac{3}{4}}$ $5^{1\frac{1}{2}}$ 4^{3} Borden D A 121 21.90 74-18 Karand $121^{1\frac{3}{4}}$ Campfire Gal121^{hd}Damariscotta$121^{1\frac{1}{4}}$ No solid rally 12
13Jan80- 4Aqu fst 6f ⊡:22⅘ :47⅕ 1:14 ⒻMd 35000 2 8 $8^{6\frac{3}{4}}$ $7^{6\frac{3}{4}}$ $5^{3\frac{1}{2}}$ 3^{2} Borden D A 117 73.60 72-17 Winning Bend $121^{\frac{1}{2}}$ Miochelle $117^{1\frac{1}{2}}$AWomanScorned117^{3} Rallied 12
28Dec79- 4Aqu fst 6f ⊡:23⅘ :49 1:15 ⒻMd 30000 4 4 $4^{1\frac{1}{2}}$ 6^{3} $9^{6\frac{3}{4}}$ 9^{11} Sipus E J^{5} 112 22.50 58-26 Sami Sutton 117^{2} Miss Political 115^{2} Maloletti $112^{3\frac{3}{4}}$ Tired 11
LATEST WORKOUTS Jun 3 Aqu 4f fst :49 b ●May 29 Aqu 5f fst 1:01⅖ h May 23 Aqu 5f fst 1:02 h May 17 Aqu 4f fst :49⅘ b

Cheering Section — Dk. b. or br. f. 3, by Pass Catcher—Iron Cleaver, by Iron Ruler — $37,500 — Br.—October House Farm (Fla) — Tr.—Baeza Braulio — 107^{5}
Own.—Entremont Farm

	St.	1st	2nd	3rd	Amt.
1980	4	M	0	1	$1,476
1979	0	M	0	0	

15May80- 9Aqu fst 6f :22 :45⅘ 1:11⅘ 3↑ⒻMd 30000 8 4 $2^{1\frac{1}{2}}$ 2^{hd} $3^{4\frac{1}{2}}$ 4^{11} Fell J 114 8.30 75-19 RomanBeach113^{8}QueenofWax111^{1}ScrletStepper$109^{1\frac{3}{4}}$ Weakened 9
23Apr80- 6Pim fst 6f :23⅘ :47⅕ 1:13⅖ 3↑ⒻMd 23500 6 1 $1^{\frac{1}{2}}$ 1^{hd} 2^{hd} $3^{1\frac{1}{2}}$ Imparato J 114 7.90 77-25 Toy Boat 112^{1} No Yen To $107^{\frac{1}{2}}$ Cheering Section 114^{5} Weakened 8
12Apr80- 5Pim fst 6f :22⅘ :46⅘ 1:13⅖ 3↑ⒻMd Sp Wt 1 4 3^{nk} $1^{\frac{1}{2}}$ 1^{hd} 8^{10} Imparato J 114 5.30 69-20 Arch Miss 112^{2} Bold Tango $112^{1\frac{3}{4}}$ Drawn Blank $106^{1\frac{1}{2}}$ Tired 10
18Mar80- 9Pim fst 6f :23 :46⅗ 1:12⅘ 3↑ⒻMd Sp Wt 5 2 2^{hd} 2^{hd} 3^{3} $9^{8\frac{1}{2}}$ Guerra W A 112 7.60 73-22 Dancing Dame $113^{\frac{3}{4}}$ Fagers Charisma 122^{4} Clinician 112no Tired 12
LATEST WORKOUTS Jun 5 Bel tr.t 3f fst :35 h May 31 Bel tr.t 4f fst :47⅗ h May 26 Bel tr.t 4f fst :49 h May 12 Bel tr.t 4f fst :49 h

Soaring Sea — Ch. f. 3, by Naskra—Steady Wind, by Sea-Bird — $40,000 — Br.—Meadowhill (Ky) — Tr.—Johnson Philip G — 114
Own.—Meadowhill

Turf Record: St. 2, 1st 0, 2nd 0, 3rd 0

	St.	1st	2nd	3rd	Amt.
1980	5	M	0	0	$2,190
1979	1	M	0	0	

25May80- 3Bel fm 1¼ Ⓣ:47⅘ 1:38⅘ 2:02⅘ 3↑ⒻMd Sp Wt 7 2 3^{2} $4^{\frac{3}{4}}$ 3^{6} 4^{12} Samyn J L b 113 9.50 70-15 La Atrevida 113^{2} Miss Rebecca 113^{7} Binomial 113^{3} Tired 12
18May80- 1Aqu gd $1\frac{1}{16}$ Ⓣ:48⅕ 1:13⅗ 1:46⅖ 3↑ⒻMd Sp Wt 3 6 $5^{7\frac{1}{2}}$ $6^{7\frac{3}{4}}$ $5^{6\frac{1}{2}}$ 4^{6} Samyn J L 113 14.60 67-21 Carrade $110^{\frac{1}{2}}$ Idiomatic $113^{3\frac{1}{4}}$ La Atrevida $113^{2\frac{1}{4}}$ No factor 10
24Apr80- 5Aqu fst 1 :47⅕ 1:12⅗ 1:38⅘ 3↑ⒻMd Sp Wt 5 3 $4^{2\frac{1}{2}}$ $5^{3\frac{1}{2}}$ $6^{5\frac{1}{2}}$ 6^{11} Asmussen C B 113 11.70 61-21 Darby Dame 114no Friendly Frolic $114^{5\frac{1}{2}}$ Shelia $109^{\frac{1}{2}}$ Tired 7
17Apr80- 6Aqu fst 7f :23⅕ :47⅕ 1:26⅕ 3↑ⒻMd Sp Wt 7 1 $8^{4\frac{1}{4}}$ $7^{4\frac{1}{2}}$ 7^{6} $7^{6\frac{3}{4}}$ Asmussen C B 113 17.40 63-23 Astrid's Pride $113^{\frac{1}{2}}$ Pink Supreme $108^{\frac{3}{4}}$LuckyOleAxe$113^{2\frac{1}{2}}$ Outrun 8
29Mar80- 1FD sly 6f :21⅗ :45⅘ 1:12⅖ Allowance 5 7 7^{10} $7^{7\frac{3}{4}}$ $6^{8\frac{1}{2}}$ $6^{4\frac{1}{2}}$ DePass R 115 4.40 78-18 Magic Run 113^{1} Flying Cloud Nine115^{1}NoTimetoPlay$115^{\frac{1}{2}}$ Outrun 9
15Oct79- 6Bel gd 6f :23⅗ :47⅘ 1:13⅕ ⒻMd Sp Wt 2 6 6^{4} $5^{4\frac{1}{2}}$ 7^{7} 7^{12} Castaneda M 118 18.10 64-31 NewAndImprovd$118^{3\frac{1}{2}}$MidnightFrolic$118^{3\frac{1}{2}}$Whitst$118^{1\frac{1}{4}}$ No threat 9
LATEST WORKOUTS Jun 5 Bel tr.t 3f fst :37⅗ b May 16 Bel tr.t 4f fst :49⅗ b May 11 Bel tr.t 4f fst :51⅖ b May 6 Bel tr.t 4f fst :51 b

Off our rules for form, A Woman Scorned, idle since February, rates an unknown. She gets an ability time of :26.1 for her 25Jan80 race off a :25.4 lead time and an addition of two for energy. Her other rating comes out of the 11Jan80 effort, where there was a lead time of :26.4, a gain to reduce it by three, then an addition of two to round off at :26.3. She gets 3 points for early speed out of three of her four races.

Cheering Section's best rating comes out of the 23Apr80 run at Pimlico, where there was a :26.1 lead time, a loss of two in lengths and one more for energy to give us a :26.4 completed ability time. The other races are rather atrocious, but out of the 18Mar80 effort, there was a lead time of :26.1, with a loss of nine, nothing added for energy, and a final of :28.0. Plenty of early speed here merits 6 points.

And then to Soaring Sea, whose last two races were on the grass. Where there is sufficient qualifying form on the grass, and the horse is returning to the dirt today, we'll allow the turf runs for form, and Soaring Sea therefore qualifies. For ability times, the 24Apr80 race at Aqueduct shows a :25.2 lead time, a loss of one in lengths, and an add-on of one for energy to come up with a :25.4, by far the best you will see in this crowd. Out of the Florida Downs race on 29Mar80, there is a :26.3 lead time, reduced by three for gain, with one added back for energy to come up with a :26.1. This one has medium speed and gets 3 points accordingly.

Now, let's try to compare all four of these.

Odds	**Horse**	**Ability**		**A Pts**		**ES**	**F**	**Total**
1.5	Visualization	:26.2	—	8	—	6	Q	14
4.4	Cheering Section	:26.1	:28.0	9	—	6	Q	15
6.5	A Woman Scorned	:26.1	:26.3	9	—	3	U	12
6.5	Soaring Sea	:25.4	:26.1	11	—	3	Q	14

Since Visualization as the favorite shows but one race, we use only the best race of the other three to add up ability points. Visualization does not have the highest rating but is a Lightly Raced Favorite. Since this is a maiden race, there is obviously no Big Win, and likewise, no improvement off a previous race, since there was none. Therefore, we have to look elsewhere for a place bet only, since under our rule for Lightly Raced Favorites, we go to a place bet on the next-highest-qualified animal.

Cheering Section, because of her early speed, comes out 1 point ahead in this closely rated pack. This fits our usual rule of betting to place only when the top-rated horse has but a 1-point advantage over the others. Therefore, we invest on Cheering Section to place and sit back to see how she does. Here is the chart of the race:

THIRD RACE
Belmont
JUNE 6, 1980

6 FURLONGS. (1.08⅘) MAIDEN CLAIMING. Purse $12,000. Fillies and Mares. 3-year-olds and upward. Weights, 3-year-olds, 114 lbs. Older, 122 lbs. Claiming price $40,000; for each $2,500 to $35,000, allowed 2 lbs.

Value of race $12,000, value to winner $7,200, second $2,640, third $1,440, fourth $720. Mutuel pool $143,185, OTB pool $95,996. Exacta Pool $203,294. OTB Exacta Pool $166,700.

Last Raced	Horse	Eqt.	A.	Wt	PP	St	¼	½	Str	Fin	Jockey	Cl'g Pr	Odds $1
31May80 6Bel4	Visualization		3	114	6	2	2½	21½	25	11¼	Hernandez R	40000	1.50
15May80 9Aqu4	Cheering Section		3	108	2	1	11	11½	11	26¾	Beitia E5	37500	4.40
25Oct79 4Aqu5	Ballet Mistress		3	105	7	9	41	4½	4½	3¾	Gonzalez M A5	35000	21.70
24Apr80 5Aqu7	Ruthless Lady	b	3	114	4	7	11	103	7½	4nk	Adams L	40000	40.30
18May80 1Aqu9	Golden Gift	b	3	114	10	3	33	32	31	51	Cruguet J	40000	19.30
	T. V. Party		3	114	8	8	9½	7hd	5hd	6¾	Asmussen C B	40000	15.60
24Mar80 4Aqu5	Item One		3	110	11	11	6½	6½	96	71¼	Venezia M	35000	14.90
1Mar80 6Bow7	Sweet Foot		3	114	5	4	5½	51	6½	8½	Fell J	40000	8.40
2Feb80 4Aqu3	A Woman Scorned		3	114	1	5	8hd	91	8½	97¾	Borden D A	40000	6.50
	Granny's Here		3	104	9	10	101½	11	11	10	Gervais R10	40000	58.80
25May80 3Bel4	Soaring Sea	b	3	114	3	6	71½	8½	10½	—	Samyn J L	40000	6.50

Soaring Sea, Bled.

OFF AT 2:01 1/2, EDT. Start good, Won driving. Time, :22⅘, :47, 1:12⅕ Track fast.

$2 Mutuel Prices:

6-(F)-VISUALIZATION	5.00	3.80	3.00
2-(B)-CHEERING SECTION		4.80	3.80
7-(G)-BALLET MISTRESS			8.40

Visualization showed why it is important to deal with care when approaching Lightly Raced Favorites with lower total points than other horses. There wasn't enough evidence to build a program on, and that's why we passed. But Cheering Section, off that good early speed, was right up there on the lead until Visualization passed her in the stretch. Our place ticket was worth a good $4.80, as we watched Soaring Sea pull up as a bleeder.

The fourth race brings another maiden effort, this time with two-year-old fillies at five and a half furlongs in a maiden special event. I will show you the field here, and you can see four first-time starters, which brings us to the rule for passing the race entirely. Three other entries with one effort behind them ran at the short sprint distance of four and a half furlongs, which does not allow for a rating here. You can readily see there is nothing here; if there were at least one with a strong showing, we might find an investment. Look at Sea Explorer, Irish Toy, and Musical Eagle, and at every turn, this race requires looking the other way.

4th Belmont

5 ½ FURLONGS. (1.03) MAIDEN SPECIAL WEIGHT. Purse $17,000. Fillies. 2-year-olds. Weight, 117 lbs.

Coupled—Musical Eagle, Sea Explorer and Dark Reality.

Dar El Qamar
Gr. f. 2, by Grey Dawn II—Class It Out, by Outing Class
Own.—Franzheim K II   117   Br.—Franzheim K II (Ky)   1980   1 M 0 0
Tr.—Freeman Willard C
16May80-6Aqu   4½f :221 :463 :531ft   15 117   5   77½1017 99½ Cruguet J7   ⒻMdn 87 Demurely, ShutUp, FamousPartner 10
Jun 5 Aqu 3f ft :37 b   Jun 1 Aqu 4f ft :473 h   May 28 Aqu 4f ft :474 h   May 24 Aqu 4f ft :483 b

Coprincess
Dk. b. or br. f. 2, by Cornish Prince—Thimbleful, by Needles
Own.—Willwynee Stable   1107   Br.—Williams Mr-Mrs J S (Ky)   1980   1 M 0 0 $1,020
Tr.—DiMauro Stephen
16May80-6Aqu   4½f :221 :463 :531ft   41 117   8   44 36 42½ Cordero A Jr8   ⒻMdn 93 Demurely, ShutUp, FamousPartner 10
Jun 5 Bel 3f ft :36 h   Jun 2 Bel 4f ft :48 b   May 28 Bel 4f ft :473 h   May 23 Bel 4f ft :472 h

Haley
Ch. f. 2, by Unconscious—Cozumel, by T V Lark
Own.—Lehmann R N   117   Br.—Madden P (Ky)   1980   0 M 0 0
Tr.—Martin Frank
May 30 Bel 4f ft :502 bg

Musical Eagle
B. f. 2, by Stop The Music—Running Eagle, by Bald Eagle
Own.—Buckland Farm   117   Br.—Evans T M (Va)   1980   1 M 0 0 $540
Tr.—Lee P O'Donnell
27May80-3Mth   5f :23 :48 1:002ft   7½e 117   42½ 64 47 416 Brumfield D6   ⒻMdn 68 Cavort, SurePrincess, MissyMcGrew 9
Jun 2 Bel tr.t 4f ft :50 b   May 22 Bel 6f sy 1:16 b   May 15 Bel 4f ft :502 bg   Apr 26 Bel 4f ft :511 b

Irish Toy
Ch. f. 2, by Irish Ruler—Mechanical Toy, by Red Fox
Own.—Win Pat Stable   117   Br.—Smith P P (Fla)   1980   3 M 0 0 $225
Tr.—Poole George T
26May80-6Bel   5½f :23 :463 1:052ft   24 117   99½1018 1027 926 Maple E4   ⒻMdn 62 MadamePremier, Shalomar, ClareK. 10
3May80-6CD   5f :222 :454 :583ft   25 114   57½ 510 510 511 CrdrAJr4   ⒻDebutante 85 ExcitbleLdy, MstersDrm, BndThTims 7
24Apr80-3Kee   4½f :22 :46 :522ft   67 119   4 57 49½ 49¼ Day P5   ⒻMdn 83 ExcitableLdy, Brin'sBbe, BoldEscpe 11
 424Apr80—Dead heat
Jun 3 Aqu 4f ft :482 h   ●May 23 Aqu 4f ft :472 h   Apr 23 Kee 3f ft :371 bg   Apr 19 Hia 4f ft :49 b

Mawgrit
B. f. 2, by Hoist The Flag—Spring Sunshine, by Nashua
Br.—Calumet Farm (Ky) 1980 0 M 0 0
Own.—Calumet Farm 117 Tr.—Veitch John M
Jun 4 Bel 4f ft :47³ hg May 31 Bel 6f ft 1:15 b May 26 Bel 5f ft 1:00¹ hg May 21 Bel 4f sy :48⁴ b

My Princess Royale
Dk. b. or br. f. 2, by Native Royalty—Austerity, by Citation
Br.—Allen H (Fla) 1980 0 M 0 0
Own.—Allen H 117 Tr.—Jacobs Eugene
May 27 Bel 5f ft 1:00 h

Sea Explorer
Ch. f. 2, by Little Current—Candalita, by Olympia
Br.—Galbreath J W (Ky) 1980 1 M 0 0
Own.—Buckland Farm 117 Tr.—Lee P O'Donnell
27May80-3Mth 5f :23 :48 1:00²ft 7½e117 8⁶¾ 8⁵¾ 6⁹ 6¹⁹ Asmussen CB² ⒻMdn 65 Cavort, SurePrincess,MissyMcGrew 9
Jun 2 Bel tr.t 4f ft :50 b May 22 Bel 6f sy 1:16 h May 15 Bel 4f ft :50² bg May 10 Bel tr.t 4f ft :50 b

Dark Reality
Dk. b. or br. f. 2, by In Reality—Dark Legend, by Round Table
Br.—Evans T M (Va) 1980 0 M 0 0
Own.—Buckland Farm 112⁵ Tr.—Campo John P
Jun 1 Bel tr.t 5f ft 1:02² h May 28 Bel 4f ft :48⁴ hg May 20 Bel tr.t 5f ft 1:03¹ b May 14 Bel 3f gd :36² hg

Gold Ticket
Ch. f. 2, by Mr Prospector—Polly B, by Green Ticket
Br.—Cavanaugh Jr & Mulcahy (Fla) 1980 1 M 0 0
Own.—Kimmel C P 117 Tr.—Toner James J
16May80-6Aqu 4½f :22¹ :46³ :53¹ft *2 117 4 6⁷ 5⁸ 7⁴½ Maple E⁵ ⒻMdn 91 Demurely, ShutUp,FamousPartner 10
●Jun 1 Aqu 5f ft 1:01 b May 26 Aqu 5f ft 1:03 b May 12 Aqu 4f ft :52³ b May 7 Aqu 4f ft :47⁴ hg

We're up to the fifth race now, a seven-furlong sprint with some reasonably decent animals. Mika Song and Nice Sailing are practically co-favorites, with Mika Song having a few more dollars in the win pool when they come out of the gate.

5 BELMONT

START
7 FURLONGS
BELMONT PARK
FINISH

7 FURLONGS. (1.20⅖) CLAIMING. Purse $14,000. 4-year-olds and upward. Weight 122 lbs. Non-winners of two races since May 1, allowed 3 lbs. Of a race since then, 5 lbs. Claiming price $20,000; for each $1,000 to $18,000, allowed 2 lbs. (Races when entered to be claimed for $16,000 or less not considered.)

Mika Song
Dk. b. or br. h. 5, by Big Brave—Mimika, by Greek Song
$20,000 Br.—Country Life Farm (Md)
Own.—Twin Bee Stable Tr.—LaBoccetta Frank
114⁵

Turf Record	St.	1st	2nd	3rd		St.	1st	2nd	3rd	Amt.
	2	0	0	0	1980	11	2	1	2	$23,400
					1979	21	3	3	4	$25,782

22May80- 2Bel my 6f :23 :46⅖ 1:10⅗ Clm 18000 4 7 6⁶¼ 6⁴¼ 2½ 1ⁿᵏ Beitia E⁵ b 108 4.30 89-23 Mika Song 108ⁿᵏ Fiveontheside 1173¾ RagingTorrent117¹ Driving 7
18May80- 9Aqu fst 7f :22⅘ :45⅗ 1:24⅕ Clm 16000 3 4 4³¼ 4⁴½ 2½ 3¹ Beitia E⁵ b 112 6.90 79-19 Pruneplum 119ⁿᵏ Pokie Joe 113¾ Mika Song 1122¾ Weakened 8
27Apr80- 2Aqu fst 6f :23 :46⅘ 1:11⅖ Clm 16000 6 7 6²¼ 6⁴½ 5³¼ 4⁵¼ Amy J b 117 2.70 81-21 Siwash Chief 119ⁿᵒ Naudi 1173¼ Marsh's Robber 115² Mild bid 7
23Mar80- 2Aqu my 1 :47 1:12⅕ 1:37⅖ Clm 25000 7 1 1¹ 1½ 3³ 4⁴¼ Amy J b 117 7.50 75-25 Arctic Service 117¾ Ninfa's Gift 1172¾ Birkhill 117¾ Tired 8
27Feb80- 1Aqu fst 6f ⊡:22⅖ :45⅘ 1:10⅘ Clm 35000 9 6 6³¾ 3³ 9⁷¾ 9⁸½ Venezia M b 117 *3.40 81-17 SilverScreen1072¾CouponRate117ʰᵈHomeByDawn1171¼ Gave way 10
20Feb80- 2Aqu fst 6f ⊡:22⅗ :45⅘ 1:11⅕ Clm c-25000 2 8 3¹ 2ʰᵈ 1½ 1² Beitia E⁵ b 112 5.40 88-19 Mika Song 112² Sal's Dream 117¾ Peaceful Country119ʰᵈ Driving 12
9Feb80- 2Aqu fst 6f ⊡:22⅗ :46⅕ 1:11⅕ Clm 32500 6 2 4⁴½ 4⁴ 6⁵¾ 4⁵ Beitia E⁵ b 110 14.90 83-19 Ephphatha 113⁴ Double Revival 115¾ Nice Sailing 110ⁿᵏ Evenly 7
3Feb80- 9Aqu fst 1 1/16 ⊡:47⅖ 1:13⅖ 1:46⅘ Clm 35000 1 1 1½ 1½ 4⁴ 6⁶¼ Beitia E⁵ b 110 16.00 74-18 Party Surprise 115½ Plethora 110¾ General H. D. 1083¾ Tired 8
20Jan80- 2Aqu fst 1 3/16 ⊡:48⅗ 1:13⅕ 2:00 Clm c-25000 4 4 4⁷ 6¹¹ 7¹⁰ 6⁷½ Lopez C C⁵ b 112 7.70 71-26 North Star 114½ Itsagoodlife 1102¾ Gifted Leader 1172½ Tired 7
9Jan80- 3Aqu fst 1 1/16 ⊡:47⅘ 1:13⅕ 1:46⅕ Clm c-20000 9 2 3¹½ 2ʰᵈ 1ʰᵈ 3ⁿᵏ Saumell L b 117 4.40 83-18 Crazy Chief 110ʰᵈ No Sir 118ʰᵈ Mika Song 117½ Weakened 10
LATEST WORKOUTS May 15 Aqu 4f fst :49⅘ h May 11 Aqu 4f fst :51 h May 5 Aqu 4f fst :50⅘ h Apr 17 Aqu 5f fst 1:01⅗ h

Mika Song qualifies easily on form. His last race on 22May80 in the mud is almost too good to be true. The lead time was :24.1 and his gain of four allows for a three-tick reduction down to :23.3, with only one more added for energy. This gives us an unusually good :23.4 ability time. On 27Apr80, there was a :24.3 lead time, with one added for loss and one for energy to come up with :25.0. Mika Song gets 2 points in the early-speed department. Now, let's see how Nice Sailing, the other low-odds horse, shapes up.

Nice Sailing
Own.—Lunetta J

$20,000

Ch. g. 4, by Sail On–Sail On—Nice To Us Kids, by Mighty Fennec
Br.—Curley Mollie A (Md)
Tr.—Shamshoian Michael

117

Turf Record					St.	1st	2nd	3rd	Amt.
St.	1st	2nd	3rd	1980	11	1	0	2	$13,840
1	0	0	0	1979	9	2	2	0	$20,040

3Jun80- 7Mth	fst	1 1/16		:47	1:12	1:44 4/5	3 ↑ Allowance	7	3	1hd	2½	33½	411	Bracciale V Jr	118	3.40	70–18	Apaway 113nk Kettle Kin 11210 Seeds and Stems 110¾	Weakened	8
26May80- 5Mth	fst	6f		:22 3/5	:45 3/5	1:10	3 ↑ Allowance	1	6	51¼	33½	35	38	Bracciale V Jr	117	5.00	82–19	Pitch Game 1092 Lambent 1186 Nice Sailing 1173	Evenly	6
25Apr80- 1Aqu	fst	7f		:22 4/5	:45 3/5	1:24 1/5	Clm 25000	3	6	53¼	55½	43	41	Skinner K	119	8.00	79–19	PecfulCountry117½HomByDwn117nkCumuloNimbus112nk	Mild bid	9
17Apr80- 3Aqu	fst	7f		:23 2/5	:46 4/5	1:24 1/5	Clm 20000	4	4	31½	32	12	11	Skinner K	117	11.20	80–23	Nice Sailing 1171 Debtor's Haven 1141½ Itsagoodlife112nk	Driving	7
3Apr80- 9Aqu	fst	1 3/16		:48	1:12 1/5	1:57 3/5	Clm 25000	3	3	53¾	78½	711	89½	Skinner K	114	33.80	64–20	Click Off 1171¾ Harry J. 117no Sunny Puddles 1171¾	Tired	9
26Mar80- 2Aqu	fst	1⅛		:47 4/5	1:12 1/5	1:51 1/5	Clm 32500	8	5	610	66	812	810	Skinner K	115	19.60	69–29	Tread Lightly 1171 Raise Charger 117½ Harry J. 1172	No threat	8
16Mar80- 9Aqu	fst	6f	⊡	:22 3/5	:46 1/5	1:11 4/5	Clm 30000	11	7	107¾	85¼	89¾	84½	Skinner K	117	23.50	80–16	Williamstown 113no Snowline 1121 Silver Screen 109no	No threat	11
27Feb80- 1Aqu	fst	6f	⊡	:22 2/5	:45 4/5	1:10 4/5	Clm 32500	3	9	97¼	87¼	77	66½	Hernandez R	b 115	8.70	83–17	SilverScreen1072¾CouponRate117hdHomeByDawn1171¼	No threat	10
21Feb80- 6Aqu	fst	1 1/16	⊡	:47 1/5	1:13	1:45 4/5	Allowance	7	6	67¾	78	65¾	77½	Hernandez R	117	10.20	77–18	El Kel 117nk Follow ThatDream117½CremeSilence122nk	No factor	9
9Feb80- 2Aqu	fst	6f	⊡	:22 3/5	:46 1/5	1:11 1/5	Clm 32500	3	6	67	67	55½	34¾	Dahlquist T C5	110	4.20	83–19	Ephphatha 1134 Double Revival 115¾ Nice Sailing110nk	Mild rally	7
3Feb80- 5Aqu	fst	6f	⊡	:22 2/5	:46 2/5	1:11 3/5	Allowance	3	6	68½	68½	57½	47½	Fell J	117	14.00	78–18	BrightAndBrve1174½ExoticTrveler112hdMidnightRcr1173	No rally	7
8Sep79- 9Rkm	fst	140		:46 2/5	1:12 1/5	1:41 1/5	3 ↑ Allowance	5	6	65¾	1hd	1hd	12	Nicolo P	114	*1.80	86–23	Nice Sailing 1142 Hitch A Rina 1143½ Standing Room1131	Driving	7

LATEST WORKOUTS Jun 1 Mth 4f fst :50 b May 22 Mth 5f sly 1:03 b May 10 Mth 6f fst 1:19 b Apr 24 Bel 5f fst 1:01 1/5 h

This one is running back in three days off a distance race at Monmouth, where he qualifies easily on form. We get some good ability times here, too. Back on 17Apr80, in his 7f run at Aqueduct, the converted 6f final time becomes 1:11.1, which gives us a :24.2 lead time. The gain of two offset partially by one for energy produces a final :24.1 figure. In the 26Mar80 race, there was another :24.2 lead time, with an allowable gain of two, plus an energy add-on of three, to provide a :24.3 ability time. We have another 2 points for early speed.

Two other horses are showing at 9-2 on the board, although Pub, an old campaigner with one 1980 race after being idle since 1978, shows a few more dollars in the win pool than Need More Time, the other competitor.

Pub
Own.—Mohan A

$20,000

Ch. h. 7, by Prince John—Having A Ball, by Native Dancer
Br.—Wetherill Cortright (Ky)
Tr.—Walsh Thomas M

117

Turf Record					St.	1st	2nd	3rd	Amt.
St.	1st	2nd	3rd	1980	1	0	0	0	$116
2	0	0	0	1978	6	1	0	1	$12,060

30May80- 6RD	fst	6f		:22 3/5	:46 3/5	1:13	3 ↑ Allowance	7	4	32	76	511	67¾	Cooksey P J5	114	10.00	70–29	Pete's First 1191½ Bluff Garden 1995 Winged Rascal 119nk		9
8Sep78- 7Bel	fst	1		:46	1:10 3/5	1:35 4/5	3 ↑ Allowance	5	2	3½	43½	610	614	Cauthen S	b 117	2.50	75–20	Squire Ambler 1132¼ MorningFrolic1133¼BoldVoyager1132¼	Tired	7
26Aug78- 6Sar	fst	7f		:22 4/5	:45 3/5	1:22 4/5	3 ↑ Allowance	1	1	12½	1hd	12	13½	Velasquez J	b 117	2.40	91–12	Pub 1173½ Thin Slice 1133½ Siwash Chief 1122½	Driving	5
7Aug78- 6Sar	gd	7f		:22 1/5	:44 3/5	1:22	3 ↑ Allowance	2	6	51½	52	33½	32¾	Velasquez J	b 117	5.80	92–10	Bold Voyager 114no Thin Slice 1142¾ Pub 1179	In close	6
14Jly78- 8Bel	fm	1 1/16	Ⓣ	:47	1:10 3/5	1:42	3 ↑ Allowance	8	6	610	76¼	96¾	96¾	Amy J	117	8.00	79–11	Daranstone 116nk Pepysian 117½ Chance To Go 117hd	No menace	10
7Jly78- 7Bel	fst	1 1/16		:46 3/5	1:10 4/5	1:42 4/5	3 ↑ Allowance	7	9	912	97¾	55¾	44¾	Turcotte R	117	3.00	83–20	Dredger 112nk Squire Ambler 1112¼ Raiswin 1112¼	Mild bid	9
25Jun78- 7Bel	fst	6f		:22 1/5	:44 4/5	1:08 4/5	3 ↑ Allowance	2	6	87¼	810	712	49½	Turcotte R	117	10.90	88–14	Nice Catch 1174 Coffee 1171¼ Damocles 1144¼	Late gain	8
5Dec77- 6Aqu	fst	1 1/16	⊡	:47 3/5	1:12 3/5	1:43 3/5	3 ↑ Allowance	2	3	46½	31½	21½	2½	Maple E	122	3.40	96–15	Bywayofchicago 115½ Pub 12213 Ess 'n Eff 1156	2nd best	6
29Nov77- 8Aqu	sly	1⅛		:49 2/5	1:14 1/5	1:51 4/5	3 ↑ Allowance	2	3	42½	31½	1hd	11	Cauthen S	117	3.10	76–16	Pub 1171 Right Number 110¾ Social Seeker 117¾	Driving	6
17Nov77- 7Aqu	sly	7f		:22	:45 1/5	1:23 3/5	3 ↑ Allowance	3	3	59	46½	24	25½	Maple E	117	3.20	77–20	ComeAwayWithMe1205½Pub1172¼PretenseRoyal117¾	Second best	6

The first question on Pub is whether he qualifies on form. He has one up-close call in his last race at River Downs in Cincinnati. You will note that it was in an allowance race, and today he is running in the $20,000 claiming ranks. Any allowance race at Aqueduct is a higher-class event than a medium claimer, but River Downs is a small track with low purses; an ordinary allowance there would not be nearly as high in class as a $20,000 claiming race at Aqueduct. This is one situation where it is important to know the value of the various tracks around the country. Accordingly, Pub is not dropping in class in today's race, but is actually rising in class. He does not qualify on form. In addition, his ratable New York races all occurred back in 1978, and we cannot go back that far in looking for ability times. Thus, out he will go in our consideration. We can now study the record of Need More Time.

Need More Time — B. g. 4, by Duck Dance—Miskodeed, by Needles — $18,000 — Br.—Dudley & Heath (Fla) — Tr.—Brown Steven R — 1105

Own.—Tresvant Stable

Turf Record	St.	1st	2nd	3rd
	3	0	0	0

	St.	1st	2nd	3rd	Amt.
1980	6	1	0	2	$9,085
1979	23	2	2	2	$28,410

24May80-	6Key fst	1 70	:45⅗	1:11⅕	1:42⅘	3↑ Allowance	2	3	33½	1hd	12	1½	Terry J5	b	112	2.70	86-14	Need More Time 112½ Goldstone 112nk Apaway 1213	Driving 6
13May80-	8Key fst	1 1/16	:47⅗	1:12⅖	1:45⅘	Allowance	4	3	2hd	3nk	22	32½	Terry J5	b	108	5.20	72-25	El Chicoon 114no Mrs.K.'sBirthday1222½NeedMoreTime1082	Tired 5
5May80-	6Key fst	6f	:23	:46⅖	1:11⅕	Clm c-17500	3	4	41¼	43	42½	32¾	Thomas D B	b	116	5.70	83-22	AttaBoyPres1191½BlueFlagDy1071¼NeedMoreTime1161¼	Steadied 6
20Apr80-	7Key fst	6f	:22⅕	:45⅖	1:10⅖	Clm 25000	6	7	710	710	611	510	Thomas D B	b	116	24.40	80-24	Woodfly 116nk Flighty Jim 1173 Orgullo Solo 1195	No threat 7
5Apr80-	1Aqu my	7f	:23⅕	:46⅘	1:24⅘	Clm 25000	7	2	22	22½	89	88½	Fell J	b	117	10.10	68-28	Mansard 1102¾ Gifted Leader 117nk Triple Blessed 1151	Tired 8
7Mar80-	9Aqu fst	6f	⊡:22⅘	:45⅗	1:10⅘	Clm 25000	2	8	63¾	78¼	913	1012	Miceli M	b	117	27.30	78-19	Armet 1144¼ Cumulo Nimbus 1101 MidnightRacer117no	No threat 11
22Dec79-	6Med fst	6f	:22⅖	:46⅕	1:11⅗	3↑ Clm 25000	5	7	56½	53½	42½	1nk	Gonzalez M A5	b	109	5.00	87-18	NeedMoreTime109nkBossyNoble1111¼StrwberryWin1191¼	Driving 7
10Dec79-	8Med fst	1 70	:47⅕	1:12⅕	1:42⅗	3↑ Allowance	6	5	41	54½	615	720	Nied D	b	113	5.20	68-20	Ambitious Ruler 1167WorthyPiper108noRileyRidge1166	Poor start 7
30Nov79-	4Aqu fst	1	:47⅕	1:12⅖	1:38	Clm 35000	3	3	21	2½	4¾	32¾	Fell J		114	14.60	73-29	Ransack 117½ Fun Hour 1152¼ Need More Time 114no	Weakened 7
Nov79-	8Med yl	1 70	Ⓣ:48⅕	1:15⅘	1:45⅗	3↑ Allowance	2	2	2½	3nk	34	56	Rogers K L5		108	15.20	56-38	Bananas Foster 1163 LightningLead1161½WorthyPiper1081¼	Tired 8

This traveler up from Keystone qualifies on form off his last race victory. His best ability time came from his 22Dec79 race at the Meadowlands, where there was a lead time of :25.2 and a gain sufficient to knock off three ticks to provide a :24.4 ability time. In his last race at Keystone, there was a :25.3 lead time, reduced by three for gain, with no further adjustment, and a :25.0 final figure. There is enough early speed here to pick up 4 points. We can now total up on our three contenders.

Odds	Horse	Ability		A Pts		ES	F	Total
2.1	Mika Song	:23.4	:25.0	21	15	2	Q	38
2.2	Nice Sailing	:24.1	:24.3	19	17	2	Q	38
4.8	Need More Time	:24.4	:25.0	16	15	4	Q	35

This is a beautiful example of what I mean by horses being tied in total points and in odds as well. Mika Song and Nice Sailing are even-steven. While total dollars in the win pool show a slight edge to Mika Song, the board numbers show both of them at 2-1. The dollar edge is insignificant, and this invokes our safety rule of passing the race altogether. The chart makes this look good.

FIFTH RACE
Belmont
JUNE 6, 1980

7 FURLONGS. (1.20⅖) CLAIMING. Purse $14,000. 4-year-olds and upward. Weight, 122 lbs. Non-winners of two races since May 1, allowed 3 lbs. Of a race since then, 5 lbs. Claiming price $20,000; for each $1,000 to $18,000, allowed 2 lbs. (Races when entered to be claimed for $16,000 or less not considered.)

Value of race $14,000, value to winner $8,400, second $3,080, third $1,680, fourth $840. Mutuel pool $169,983, OTB pool $122,964. Exacta Pool $222,677. OTB Exacta Pool $184,447.

Last Raced	Horse	Eqt.A.Wt	PP	St	¼	½	Str	Fin	Jockey	Cl'g Pr	Odds $1
24May80 6Key1	Need More Time	b 4 110	4	8	3½	2hd	1hd	1½	Gonzalez M A5	18000	4.80
22May80 2Bel7	Disco Count	4 108	1	4	11	11½	24	21¼	Lovato F Jr5	18000	17.20
30May80 1Bel3	Escapulario	4 117	6	3	43	44	3½	34½	Giraldo L	20000	7.00
3Jun80 7Mth4	Nice Sailing	4 117	3	6	5hd	61	52	4nk	Velasquez J	20000	2.20
30May80 6RD6	Pub	7 117	5	1	2½	32	44	51¼	Skinner K	20000	4.50
22May80 2Bel1	Mika Song	b 5 114	7	7	61	5½	66	66¾	Beitia E5	20000	2.10
2Jun80 8Bel11	John Roche	5 117	8	2	8	75	7½	71¼	Venezia M	20000	25.90
20Apr80 9Aqu5	Coley's Gift	5 114	2	5	7½	8	8	8	Brocklebank J	20000	50.60

OFF AT 3:02, EDT. Start good, Won driving. Time, :23, :46⅕, 1:11⅕, 1:24⅗ Track fast.

$2 Mutuel Prices:

4-(D)-NEED MORE TIME	11.60	7.00	4.40
1-(A)-DISCO COUNT		14.20	7.00
6-(F)-ESCAPULARIO			5.00

I am going to omit the sixth race in the interest of time and space. It was another maiden special event with more than three first-time starters, and once more I am required to pass. Today's program is becoming a little fretful with so many passed and dubious opportunities. But in the seventh, we are back to horses with sufficient records and a heavy favorite in Suzanne's Star.

7 BELMONT

1⅛ MILES. (1.45⅖) ALLOWANCE. Purse $21,000. 3-year-old: and upward which have never won two races other than Maiden, Claiming or Start: . Weights 3-year-olds, 114 lbs. Older, 122 lbs. Non-winners of a race other than maiden or claiming over a mile since May 1, allowed 3 lbs. Of such a race since April 15, 5 lbs.

Suzanne's Star — Ro. c. 3, by Son Ange—Game Maid, by Greek Game
Own.—Daly J R
Br.—Daly J R (Ky)
Tr.—Healy Paul A
111

	St.	1st	2nd	3rd	Amt.
1980	5	2	1	1	$33,936
1979	5	M	0	1	$2,580

25May80- 8Bel	fst	1⅛	:45⅘	1:10⅗	1:49⅕	Peter Pan	8	5	$6^{8\frac{1}{2}}$	$5^{2\frac{1}{4}}$	2^{2}	$3^{4\frac{1}{4}}$	Vasquez J	114	18.70	77-16	Comptroller $114^{1\frac{1}{4}}$ Bar Dexter 117^{3} Suzanne's Star$114^{2\frac{1}{4}}$	Bid,tired	9
15May80- 7Aqu	fst	1⅛	:46⅕	1:11⅘	1:51	3↑ Allowance	7	9	9^{12}	5^{4}	4^{2}	$2^{\frac{3}{4}}$	Vasquez J	114	8.70	79-19	AndoverRoad$119^{\frac{3}{4}}$Suzanne'sStr$114^{\frac{3}{4}}$Col.Frnkincense$112^{4\frac{1}{4}}$	Blocked	10
23Apr80- 9Aqu	fst	1	:47	1:12	1:38⅕	Allowance	3	6	6^{6}	$5^{3\frac{1}{2}}$	$4^{2\frac{1}{2}}$	1^{nk}	Vasquez J	122	11.50	75-24	Suzanne's Star 122^{nk} SunnyWinters117^{nk}King'sWish$117^{2\frac{3}{4}}$	Driving	9
14Apr80- 4Aqu	fst	1	:48	1:13⅗	1:38⅖	Md Sp Wt	1	4	$5^{2\frac{1}{2}}$	$3^{1\frac{1}{2}}$	$2^{\frac{1}{2}}$	$1^{1\frac{3}{4}}$	Martens G	122	2.00	74-21	Suzanne's Star $122^{1\frac{3}{4}}$ Globe $122^{6\frac{1}{2}}$ Alshain 117^{2}	Driving	7
4Apr80- 4Aqu	sly	6f	:22⅗	:45⅘	1:11	Md Sp Wt	6	3	6^{8}	5^{11}	5^{12}	$4^{7\frac{3}{4}}$	Martens G	122	24.50	80-22	I'ma Hellraiser $122^{4\frac{1}{4}}$ WindRiverMan$122^{2\frac{3}{4}}$GoodBid$117^{\frac{3}{4}}$	No threat	8
3Dec79- 4Aqu	fst	6f	:22⅘	:46⅖	1:12⅗	Md Sp Wt	2	6	6^{16}	6^{14}	5^{13}	5^{10}	Asmussen C B	118	27.00	70-22	McCutcheon118^{hd}ColonelMorn118^{4}MomentOfPlesur$118^{2\frac{1}{4}}$	Evenly	8
20Oct79- 4Aqu	fst	6f	:22⅖	:45⅗	1:10⅘	Md Sp Wt	3	4	4^{5}	$4^{6\frac{1}{2}}$	$4^{8\frac{1}{2}}$	$4^{8\frac{1}{4}}$	Vasquez J	118	21.00	81-15	Torsional$118^{2\frac{1}{4}}$Dr.Johnson118^{2}MomentOfPleasure118^{4}	No mishap	12
22Sep79- 9Bel	sly	7f	:23	:46⅖	1:24⅗	Md Sp Wt	8	4	$7^{3\frac{1}{4}}$	6^{5}	6^{13}	6^{16}	Asmussen C B	120	7.80	63-15	ImpressivePrince120^{3}DegenerateJon$120^{4\frac{3}{4}}$I'mReglToo120^{2}	Outrun	8
14Sep79- 4Bel	fst	6f	:22⅘	:46⅘	1:12⅕	Md Sp Wt	4	9	$10^{9\frac{1}{2}}$	8^{10}	$6^{9\frac{3}{4}}$	$3^{8\frac{1}{2}}$	Fell J	118	12.60	72-17	Speed City 118^{5} ImpressivePrince$118^{3\frac{1}{2}}$Suzanne'sStar118^{2}	Rallied	11
3Sep79- 4Bel	fst	6½f	:23	:46⅘	1:18⅖	Md Sp Wt	1	12	$10^{9\frac{1}{2}}$	$10^{7\frac{3}{4}}$	10^{11}	10^{10}	Vasquez J	118	8.00	74-17	Koluctoo Bay 118^{2} War of Words118^{hd}RaiseACrown113^{nk}	Outrun	13

LATEST WORKOUTS Jun 5 Bel 3f fst :35⅗ h May 22 Bel 5f sly 1:00 h May 10 Bel 6f fst 1:14⅕ h Apr 30 Bel 7f sly 1:30 b

This horse qualifies in form off his last race in the Peter Pan, and picks up a good ability time in the process. The lead time was :24.4, and the allowable gain gets a reduction of four down to :24.0, which is increased by one due to energy to wind up with a :24.1 ability time. In the race of 23Apr80, there was a lead time of :25.0, reduced by two off a gain, and counterbalanced by an increase of two for energy to wind up with a :25.0 ability time.

Huge Success is the second favorite and looks like this:

Huge Success — Ch. c. 3, by Native Heritage—Lifelong Friend, by Stevward
Own.—Harbor View Farm
Br.—Harbor View Farm (Ky)
Tr.—Barrera Guillermo S
111

	St.	1st	2nd	3rd	Amt.
1980	8	2	2	0	$31,840
1979	0	M	0	0	

25May80- 8Bel	fst	1⅛	:45⅘	1:10⅗	1:49⅕	Peter Pan	1	3	$3^{2\frac{1}{2}}$	$6^{3\frac{1}{4}}$	$5^{5\frac{1}{4}}$	6^{7}	Hernandez R	b 114	48.80	74-16	Comptroller $114^{1\frac{1}{4}}$ Bar Dexter 117^{3} Suzanne's Star $114^{2\frac{1}{4}}$	Tired	9
30Apr80- 8Aqu	my	1⅛	:48⅖	1:12⅗	1:49⅗	Handicap	7	5	5^{3}	$6^{4\frac{1}{4}}$	$5^{6\frac{1}{2}}$	$4^{9\frac{3}{4}}$	Hernandez R	114	6.60	77-21	Bar Dexter $112^{3\frac{3}{4}}$ Little Lenny $115^{1\frac{3}{4}}$ Don Daniello $118^{4\frac{1}{4}}$	Evenly	7
17Apr80- 5Aqu	fst	1	:46⅘	1:11⅗	1:36⅕	Allowance	7	4	$4^{2\frac{1}{2}}$	4^{2}	$3^{1\frac{1}{2}}$	$2^{1\frac{3}{4}}$	Hernandez R	122	21.50	83-23	Speed City $112^{1\frac{3}{4}}$ Huge Success $122^{\frac{1}{2}}$ Bar Dexter $117^{\frac{1}{2}}$	Gamely	7
2Apr80- 2Aqu	fst	1⅛	:48⅘	1:13⅖	1:51⅖	Allowance	2	1	$1^{\frac{1}{2}}$	1^{hd}	2^{hd}	1^{nk}	Hernandez R	119	6.00	78-18	Huge Success 119^{nk} Sir Kay 117^{hd} Bold Barbizon $122^{3\frac{3}{4}}$	Driving	7
13Mar80- 6Aqu	fst	1^{70}	⊡:48⅘	1:14⅕	1:43⅘	3↑ Md Sp Wt	3	1	2^{3}	$2^{\frac{1}{2}}$	1^{hd}	1^{nk}	Hernandez R	114	*1.10	83-23	Huge Success 114^{nk} Rebel Blade $115^{1\frac{1}{4}}$ BoldBarbizon114^{5}	Driving	7
3Mar80- 3Aqu	fst	1^{70}	⊡:48	1:14	1:44⅗	Md Sp Wt	3	4	$8^{7\frac{3}{4}}$	9^{12}	4^{11}	$2^{7\frac{3}{4}}$	Hernandez R	122	2.90	71-21	RedMThNms$122^{7\frac{3}{4}}$HugSuccss122^{nk}RblBld122^{nk}	Bumped, bore out	9
25Feb80- 6Aqu	gd	6f	⊡:22⅖	:46⅖	1:11⅗	Md Sp Wt	2	4	1^{hd}	6^{4}	$5^{5\frac{1}{2}}$	$4^{5\frac{1}{2}}$	Hernandez R	122	15.90	80-20	Alternating Curent $117^{\frac{3}{4}}$ BirthdaySong122^{hd}FogABalla$117^{4\frac{3}{4}}$	Tired	9
18Feb80- 4Aqu	fst	6f	⊡:22⅕	:45⅘	1:11⅘	Md Sp Wt	4	9	8^{7}	8^{12}	7^{13}	4^{10}	Dahlquist T C^{5}	117	41.70	75-19	Dunham'sGift$122^{2\frac{1}{4}}$Caesr'sWorld122^{5}AceGreenberg$117^{2\frac{3}{4}}$	Mild bid	12

LATEST WORKOUTS Jun 2 Bel tr.t 4f fst :49⅘ b May 20 Bel 6f fst 1:16⅗ b May 16 Bel tr.t 3f fst :37⅘ b ●May 10 Bel 5f fst 1:00 h

This horse also qualifies on form because of the up-close at the first call and a drop from a stakes race, the same Peter Pan event where Suzanne's Star ran third, into an allowance race. For ability times, there are several ratings of :25.0. In the Peter Pan, there was the same :24.4 lead time that confronted Suzanne's Star, with a loss of one to make the :25.0 here. In the previous race on 30Apr80, there was a :24.1 lead time, increased by one after the loss of a length, and increased three more on energy. The two races before that one also come up with the same :25.0 figure.

The third choice is Imaromeo, at 6-1 in the odds.

Imaromeo — Dk. b. or br. c. 3, by Gallant Romeo—Irealize, by Chieftain
Br.—Isaacs H Z (Ky)
Tr.—Kelly Edward I
Own.—Brookfield Farm

104 5

	St.	1st	2nd	3rd	Amt.
1980	3	1	0	1	$9,300
1979	4	1	0	2	$13,680

23May80-	7Bel	fst	6f	:22⅖	:44⅘	1:09⅘	3↑ Allowance	7	6	77¼	79¼	58½	35¼	Lovato F Jr5	b	105	7.40	88–16 I'ma Hell Raiser 1132¾ Caphal 1142½ Imaromeo 105½	Mild bid	7
21Apr80-	3Aqu	fst	6f	:22⅗	:45⅘	1:11⅕	Allowance	3	5	52	53	44	42¼	Cordero A Jr	b	122	2.00	85–23 Lite Ahoy 117¾ Sir Sizzling Nehoc 1171TonyMack117½	No excuse	6
22Mar80-	2GP	fst	6f	:22⅗	:45⅘	1:12	Allowance	6	8	75½	43½	23	1no	Cordero A Jr	b	114	*.90	79–21 Imaromeo 114no Rufame 1144½ Hadden Hall 1142	Driving	9
6Oct79-	5Bel	fst	6f	:22⅗	:45⅗	1:10⅘	Allowance	2	7	54½	35	35½	33½	Velasquez J	b	115	8.20	84–21 Speed City 1151½ Plugged Nickle 1102 Imaromeo 1151½	Bumped	7
14Sep79-	6Bel	fst	7f	:22⅗	:45⅘	1:24	Allowance	5	5	73½	86	78¼	43¼	Velasquez J	b	115	7.30	79–17 Storm Wave 117hdStraightStrike1203KoluctooBay120nk	Late foot	9
28Jly79-	4Bel	fst	6f	:22⅘	:47⅕	1:12⅕	Md Sp Wt	8	4	21½	11	16	14¾	Velasquez J	b	118	*.60	81–19 Imromeo1184¾CurrentWinner118¾ChmpgnMood1187¼	Ridden out	8
5Jly79-	6Bel	fst	5½f	:22⅖	:45⅕	1:04	Md Sp Wt	6	5	54¼	46	35½	34½	Velasquez J		118	41.30	90–16 African Water 1183¼ Speed To Spare 1181¼Imaromeo118¾	Rallied	10

LATEST WORKOUTS   May 30 Bel 5f fst 1:00⅕ h   May 20 Bel tr.t 5f fst 1:03 b   May 15 Bel tr.t 5f fst 1:02⅖ b   May 10 Bel 4f fst :51 b

This one qualifies on form because of the gain in excess of five in the last race. There was a :25.0 lead time in that race, with an allowable gain of 2¾ lengths to reduce the figure to :24.3, without any further addition for energy. For the next rating, we go back to 6Oct79 to a :25.1 lead time reduced by one for gain to :25.0. We can now summarize on these three.

Odds	Horse	Ability		A Pts		F	Total
.7	Suzanne's Star	:24.1	:25.0	19	15	Q	34
5.8	Huge Success	:25.0	:25.0	15	15	Q	30
6.0	Imaromeo	:24.3	:25.0	17	15	Q	32

Suzanne's Star, heavily played, does not have enough of a point advantage to warrant such a discrepancy in odds between his two main opponents. But the 2-point margin is enough here to justify a win and place bet, much to my ultimate displeasure.

SEVENTH RACE
Belmont
JUNE 6, 1980

1⅛ MILES. (1.45⅗) ALLOWANCE. Purse $21,000. 3-year-olds and upward, which have never won two races other than Maiden, Claiming or Starter. Weights, 3-year-olds, 114 lbs. Older, 122 lbs. Non-winners of a race other than maiden or claiming over a mile since May 1, allowed 3 lbs. Of such a race since April 15, 5 lbs.

Value of race $21,000, value to winner $12,600, second $4,620, third $2,520, fourth $1,260. Mutuel pool $173,059, OTB pool $122,923. Exacta Pool $240,872. OTB Exacta Pool $192,420.

Last Raced		Horse	Eqt.	A.	Wt	PP	St	¼	½	¾	Str	Fin	Jockey	Odds $1
25May80	8Bel6	Huge Success	b	3	113	4	4	2½	3½	21	1hd	1nk	Hernandez R	5.80
25May80	8Bel3	Suzanne's Star		3	113	3	5	65	66	68	23	27¾	Vasquez J	.70
24May80	8Suf3	Peace For Peace		3	109	6	1	4½	52	4½	32	32¾	Samyn J L	7.60
23May80	7Bel3	Imaromeo	b	3	105	7	2	53	4½	5½	41½	41¾	Lovato F Jr5	6.00
15May80	7Aqu4	Dresden Dew	b	4	117	2	3	11	11½	1½	52	52½	Velasquez J	9.70
28May80	2Bel4	Give It A Chance	b	3	109	1	7	31	2hd	3hd	67	67	Venezia M	22.20
22May80	1Bel1	John's Slash		3	111	5	6	7	7	7	7	7	Skinner K	10.20

OFF AT 4:01 EDT. Start good, Won driving. Time, :23⅗, :46⅖, 1:11⅕, 1:36⅗, 1:49⅘ Track fast.

$2 Mutuel Prices:

4–(D)–HUGE SUCCESS	13.60	5.40	4.20
3–(C)–SUZANNE'S STAR		2.80	2.40
6–(F)–PEACE FOR PEACE			3.80

Huge Success won by a neck and Suzanne's Star failed to make it, finishing second. Since I have talked a great deal about early speed in this book, you may note that Suzanne's Star's lengths behind at the first call in her races amounted to a bundle. Because I do not use early-speed computations in distance races, we didn't factor it in, and will not. My purpose in bringing it up here is to point out how early speed can sometimes play a role in distance races as well, particularly those run out of a chute.

In the eighth and feature race, an allowance event with a hefty $25,000 purse, there is another strong favorite in Euphrosyne, which will give us some new problems when we get to summarizing our choices.

8 BELMONT

INNER TURF COURSE
1⅜ MILES
BELMONT PARK
START FINISH

1 ⅜ MILES. (INNER-TURF). (2.11⅖) ALLOWANCE. Purse $25,000. Fillies and Mares. 3-year-olds and upward, which have never won three races other than Maiden, Claiming or Starter. Weights, 3-year-olds, 114 lbs. Older, 122 lbs. Non-winners of two races other than maiden or claiming over a mile and a furlong since April 15, allowed 3 lbs. Of such a race since then, 5 lbs.

Euphrosyne — Dk. b. or br. f. 4, by Judger—Sys Superstar, by Sea-Bird
Own.—Templeton Stable
Br.—Templeton Stables (Ky)
Tr.—Smithwick D Michael
117

Turf Record	St.	1st	2nd	3rd		St.	1st	2nd	3rd	Amt.
	9	3	3	0	1980	1	0	0	0	$60
					1979	13	3	3	2	$60,988

26May80-	8Fai	fm	*1⅛ Ⓣ			2:16	3↑Allowance	7	12	56½	62	55¾	418	Rengert K3	145	*1.70	— —	Mc Adam 1463½ Last Waterloo 1532 Pala Mountain 14112		14
10Nov79-	6Aqu	yl	1⅛	Ⓣ:49⅘	1:14⅗	1:54	3↑ⒻAllowance	4	3	21	21	21½	21	Cruguet J	115	*1.50	73–24	Whodatorsay 1171 Euphrosyne 115hd Hey Babe 1101¼	Gamely	8
17Oct79-	8Aqu	gd	1 1/16	Ⓣ:47⅘	1:13	1:45⅖	ⒻLamb Chop H	8	6	66	77	64	24	Cruguet J	112	11.70	74–22	Record Acclaim 1144 Euphrosyne 1121 SweptAway1121¾	Blocked	12
11Oct79-	7Bel	sly	1	:46⅗	1:11⅖	1:38	3↑ⒻAllowance	1	5	511	411	49	38¼	Cruguet J	116	2.20	70–27	Sharp Zone 114no Clown's Doll 1148¼ Euphrosyne 116¾	Wide	5
1Oct79-	8Bel	sly	1¼	:47⅘	1:39⅖	2:05⅗	ⒻAthenia H	8	8	812	613	619	524	Cruguet J	112	37.70	48–25	Poppycock 114hd Fourdrinier 1149½ Six Crowns 11410	Wide	10
12Sep79-	2Bel	fm	1 1/16	Ⓣ:47⅖	1:11⅖	1:42⅘	3↑ⒻAllowance	5	8	75½	84¾	34	2nk	Shoemaker W	115	*1.10	82–15	Lancastera 110nk Euphrosyne 1153 Festival Day 117hd	Lugged in	10
2Sep79-	7Pen	fm	1 Ⓣ			1:35⅕	ⒻWhite Rose	6	11	107	72½	5¾	11½	Cooke C	112	12.70	94–09	Euphrosyne 1121½ Leslie J 114½ Keeler 116hd	Drew out	11
15Jly79-	8Bel	fm	1¼	Ⓣ:48⅖	1:36⅗	2:01	ⒻGarden Cty H	8	5	53¼	86¼	64½	56¼	Velasquez J	114	18.70	83–15	Hey Babe 113no Record Acclaim 1121¾ Swept Away 1151¾	Wide	11
7Jly79-	4Bel	fm	1¼	Ⓣ:49	1:39⅘	2:03⅘	3↑ⒻAllowance	2	7	719	64	53	43¾	Cruguet J	116	3.20	71–14	Record Acclaim 112hd March Time 1173½ Golferette 111nk	Rallied	7
24Jun79-	5Bel	fst	1⅛	:48⅗	1:14	1:51⅕	3↑ⒻAllowance	5	6	66½	61	42½	54	Cruguet J	114	6.30	67–19	Poppycock 109nk March Time 1222¾ MillieAndMe122nk	Very wide	6

When we begin our first task to check recent action to see what kind of form we will encounter, we immediately run into a situation so unusual that it could not possibly be covered in the rules of play in this book. Euphrosyne, who has competed successfully in stakes races, opened her 1980 season at Fair Hill, Maryland, which is primarily a steeplechase track and runs only an occasional non-hurdle race. Note that in the weight column, this filly carried 145 pounds, a total that you will never see at any regular race meet in the United States. She ran on the flat, however, and showed a 4½-length gain between the first and second calls. A race of this kind was no more than a workout for the return to Belmont, where Euphrosyne was back at a competitive 117 pounds, ridden by Jean Cruguet, a regular jockey, not by one of the heavy steeplechase riders as in the Fair Hill event. At the very worst, we could call her form unknown.

Now to the computation of ability times, where we are compelled to look at 1979 efforts for some excellent runs. In the 7Jly79 race at Belmont, at a mile and a quarter, we can compute the last quarter time, where there was a :24.0 lead time with no gain or loss. This, as I have indicated earlier, is very special in a long-distance race. Trying the same technique again, the 15Jly79 run in the Garden City Handicap produces a :24.2 lead time with no gain or loss, and since we don't adjust for energy after a horse has run a mile, we get that ability-time figure.

Endicotta, another four-year-old filly who has only recently turned to the grass, is the second choice in the wagering.

Endicotta — B. f. 4, by Roberto—Miss Devereux, by Spy Song
Br.—Forest Retreat Farms Inc (Ky)
Own.—Davison E P — Tr.—Hertler John O — **117**

Turf Record: St. 1st 2nd 3rd — 2 0 1 1
St. 1st 2nd 3rd Amt. — 1980 10 1 2 1 $28,180 — 1979 8 2 1 2 $25,410

29May80- 1Bel hd 1 1/16 Ⓣ:45⅕ 1:09 1:40⅖ 3↑ⒻAllowance 1 4 35½ 44 43½ 33½ Venezia M 119 7.40 90–10 Free Again 1161½ Island Charm 1132 Endicotta 1191½ Evenly 10
19May80- 5Aqu gd 1⅛ Ⓣ:49 1:14 1:52 3↑ⒻAllowance 2 3 21½ 1hd 11½ 2hd Venezia M 119 17.80 84–14 Esdiev 113hd Endicotta 1192 Double Dial 1132¼ Just failed 8
14Apr80- 7Aqu fst 1 :46⅗ 1:11⅕ 1:36⅗ 3↑ⒻAllowance 5 5 53½ 57 410 410 Gonzalez M A5 118 4.80 73–21 Fager's Fancy 1032¾ What'll IDo1233¾MakeThatGoal1183½ Evenly 6
29Mar80- 7Aqu sly 6f :22⅘ :46⅘ 1:12⅗ ⒻAllowance 5 6 67½ 65¾ 53 44¾ Venezia M 117 9.20 75–27 SuperbeAffir109¾VeryDistinctive1122½RestlssRiddl1101½ Steadied 6
7Mar80- 2Aqu fst 1 1/16 ⊡:48 1:13⅗ 1:46⅖ ⒻAllowance 8 6 75¼ 86½ 75½ 66¼ Saumell L 119 12.80 76–19 Skagerrak 1172¾ Cousins Three 112½ Marchpane 1172¾ No threat 8
22Feb80- 7Aqu gd 170 ⊡:49⅘ 1:15⅕ 1:44⅘ ⒻAllowance 6 3 31½ 3nk 41 43¾ Saumell L 119 *1.50 74–19 Gueniviere 117¾ Restless Riddle 117½ Marchpane1192½ Weakened 6
7Feb80- 7Aqu fst 170 ⊡:49 1:15⅗ 1:46 ⒻAllowance 5 5 53½ 31½ 2½ 1¾ Saumell L 117 2.50 72–29 Endicotta 117¾ Legs O' Lamb 117nk Make That Goal 1122 Driving 8
28Jan80- 8Aqu fst 1 1/16 ⊡:48 1:13⅘ 1:46⅕ ⒻAllowance 2 4 63¾ 41 2hd 2½ Saumell L 117 8.90 82–23 I'll Be Around 117½ Endicotta 117½ Legs O' Lamb 1178¾ Checked 10
20Jan80- 5Aqu fst 1⅛ ⊡:49⅘ 1:15⅕ 1:54⅖ ⒻAllowance 7 4 43 32½ 43 44¼ Saumell L 117 7.20 70–26 Marchpane 1221½ I'll Be Around 1122 Legs O' Lamb 117¾ Evenly 7
9Jan80- 7Aqu fst 6f ⊡:22⅗ :46⅕ 1:11⅘ ⒻAllowance 6 5 54 66 63¾ 54 Saumell L 122 3.60 81–18 RestlessRiddle1121½SpecilReport117½VeryDistinctive117¾ No rally 8
LATEST WORKOUTS ●May 15 Aqu 6f fst 1:13 h — May 10 Aqu 6f fst 1:15⅘ b — May 2 Aqu 3f fst :35⅘ b — Apr 7 Aqu 1 fst 1:45 b

Since her last two races were on the grass, we can compare them for form. Note that in her last effort, she obtained the comment "Evenly," which would otherwise serve to qualify her, based on her running line. But you will also see a classic pattern of a Declining Horse, farther behind the lead at every call at the same class. Since we throw out all Declining Horses except where there is a gain of five in the last race, Endicotta has got to go as NQ on form. That leaves us with one other competitor, Double Dial, to study, to see how she looks after her one grass effort at Aqueduct, where she ran behind Endicotta.

Double Dial — B. f. 3, by Tom Tulle—Once Double, by Double Jay
Br.—Stevens L T (Ky)
Own.—Lofton W A — Tr.—Cantey Joseph B — **114**

Turf Record: St. 1st 2nd 3rd — 1 0 0 1
St. 1st 2nd 3rd Amt. — 1980 5 3 1 1 $29,700 — 1979 1 M 0 0

19May80- 5Aqu gd 1⅛ Ⓣ:49 1:14 1:52 3↑ⒻAllowance 8 1 11½ 2hd 21½ 32 Maple E 113 4.40 82–14 Esdiev 113hd Endicotta 1192 Double Dial 1132¼ Weakened 8
9Apr80- 7OP fst 170 :46⅕ 1:13⅖ 1:44⅘ 3↑ⒻAllowance 2 4 43½ 21½ 11 14 Maple S 111 *.90 72–24 Double Dial 1114 Bobbi Admiral 1103 Demolished 1133½ Easily 6
31Mar80- 8OP fst 170 :47⅕ 1:13⅘ 1:44⅗ 3↑ⒻAllowance 4 4 31½ 1½ 12½ 13½ Maple S 114 2.30 73–26 Double Dial 1143½ My Aunt 114¾Knight'sDamsel1231¾ Ridden out 11
17Mar80- 6OP gd 6f :22⅗ :47⅖ 1:13⅘ 3↑ⒻAllowance 9 7 78½ 55½ 22 2¾ Maple S 114 5.50e 75–29 Sweetladyroll 113¾ Double Dial 1141¾ Plum's Sister 1134½ Gamely 9
10Mar80- 3OP fst 6f :23⅖ :48⅘ 1:15⅗ 3↑ⒻMd Sp Wt 9 12 72¾ 2hd 11½ 1no Maple S 114 5.60 67–30 Double Dial 114no Poker Happy 1142 Nimble Neva 112nk Driving 12
26Aug79- 2Sar fst 6½f :22⅖ :45⅖ 1:17⅕ ⒻMd Sp Wt 5 10 1213 1118 817 722 Maple E 117 33.10 67–12 Fager's Fancy 1178½ Show Notice 1173½TeaSipper1172¼ No factor 12
LATEST WORKOUTS May 29 Bel tr.t 5f fst 1:01⅘ h — ●May 12 Bel tr.t 1 fst 1:47⅕ b — ●May 2 Bel tr.t 1 fst 1:44⅖ h — Apr 26 Bel 6f fst 1:17 b

Double Dial qualifies on form with her string of up-close calls. In that 19May80 race, she gets a lead time of :25.0, which is boosted by three ticks for energy to give her a :25.3. We can now compare to see what we have.

Odds	Horse	Ability		A Pts		F	Total
1.0	Euphrosyne	:24.0	:24.2	20		U	20
2.4	Endicotta	—	—	—	—	NQ	NQ
4.3	Double Dial	:25.3	—	12		Q	12

With Endicotta's form removing her as a contender, Euphrosyne looks far away to be the best filly in the race. She is the favorite with unknown form, and her recent effort at Fair Hill with 145 pounds on her back may readily be treated as a workout. Under our rules of play, as a Double Advantage Horse with a workout, and as a strong favorite, we can invest without hesitation, as I did when I marched to the window and plunked down for win and place. The payoff was not large, but was most welcome.

EIGHTH RACE
Belmont
JUNE 6, 1980

1 ⅜ MILES.(inner-turf). (2.11⅗) ALLOWANCE. Purse $25,000. Fillies and Mares. 3-year-olds and upward, which have never won three races other than Maiden, Claiming or Starter. Weights, 3-year-olds, 114 lbs. Older, 122 lbs. Non-winners of two races other than maiden or claiming over a mile and a furlong since April 15, allowed 3 lbs. Of such a race since then, 5 !bs.

Value of race $25,000, value to winner $15,000, second $5,500, third $3,000, fourth $1,500. Mutuel pool $201,539, OTB pool $128,934.

Last Raced	Horse	Eqt.A.Wt	PP	¼	½	¾	1	Str	Fin	Jockey	Odds $1
26May80 8Fai4	Euphrosyne	4 117	6	51½	51½	5½	51	32	11½	Cruguet J	1.00
29May80 1Bel3	Endicotta	4 117	3	31½	31	21½	21½	2hd	2½	Venezia M	2.40
29May80 1Bel9	Fun Worthy	b 4 117	4	6	6	6	6	54	3nk	Montoya D	9.90
19May00 5Aqu3	Double Dial	3 114	5	12	12	11½	1½	1½	43¾	Maple E	4.30
29May80 1Bel6	Keep Off II	3 109	1	43	42	31	31	4½	53¾	Samyn J L	12.90
14May80 5Aqu5	Demure	3 112	2	21	2hd	41½	4½	6	6	Velasquez J	10.90

OFF AT 4:33 1/2, EDT. Start good, Won handily. Time, :24⅕, :49⅖, 1:14⅕, 1:38⅖, 2:02⅕, 2:15⅖, Course firm.

$2 Mutuel Prices:				
	7-(G)-EUPHROSYNE	4.00	3.00	2.40
	3-(C)-ENDICOTTA		3.00	2.40
	4-(D)-FUN WORTHY			2.80

Euphrosyne didn't have much difficulty in beating this field. Endicotta ran better than we expected, to finish second, but the point again is that a horse whose form is declining may possibly hold on for second money but will not win if there is anything else in the field to hold sway. It is now time for the ninth race, in which the favorite, Ernie's Lad, becomes our first subject.

9 BELMONT

1 1/16 MILES. (1.40⅖) CLAIMING. Purse $12,000. 4-year-olds and upward. Weight, 122 lbs. Non-winners of two races at a mile or over since May 1, allowed 3 lbs. Of such a race since then, 5 lbs. Claiming price $16,000; for each $1,000 to $14,000, 2 lbs. (Races when entered to be claimed for $12,500 or less not considered.)

Ernie's Lad — **Dk. b. or br. g. 5, by Banderilla—Surfaced, by Tom Stone**
Own.—Baer S M — **$15,000** — **Br.—Heyer Mrs E (Md)** — **Tr.—Pascuma James J Jr** — **117**

Turf Record	St.	1st	2nd	3rd		St.	1st	2nd	3rd	Amt.
	5	1	0	0	1980	12	1	3	2	$18,790
					1979	19	1	2	4	$12,996

26May80- 2Bel	fst	1⅛	:47⅖	1:13⅕	1:52⅗	Clm 15000	8	7	63¼	43	1½	2nk	Cordero A Jr	b 115	10.30	64-20	Il Vagabondo 117nk Ernie's Lad 1153 Wimpfybell 115hd	Sharp	12
19May80- 2Aqu	fst	1⅛	:49	1:13⅕	1:51⅘	Clm 12500	1	4	31	1hd	12	1½	Cordero A Jr	b 117	*1.70	76-19	Ernie's Lad 117½ Haltung 1134¾ Return For Glory 112hd	Driving	6
10May80- 1Aqu	fst	1	:46⅗	1:11	1:36⅗	Clm 12500	2	4	52¾	53	53½	42	Cordero A Jr	b 117	7.00	81-13	Kens Bishop 112hd Recidian 1191½ Prospector's Joy 117½	Evenly	8
30Apr80- 2Aqu	my	7f	:23⅕	:46⅘	1:24⅘	Clm 12500	4	6	72¾	65	54¼	34¼	Cordero A Jr	b 117	8.80	73-21	Ace's Harlequin 117hd Pokie Joe 1084¼ Ernie's Lad 1175	Rallied	8
10Apr80- 3Aqu	gd	7f	:23⅕	:46	1:23	Clm 14000	7	3	55½	67	47	48¼	Cordero A Jr	b 114	5.40	78-16	Debtor's Haven 1152 Laddy'sLuck1175½OutofTown117¾	No factor	7
29Mar80- 5Aqu	sly	1	:46⅗	1:11⅗	1:37⅗	Clm 18000	1	4	33	56½	59	513	Saumell L	b 114	17.50	65-27	ArcticService1191¼PassDeceiver1107Crqueno1172¾	Tired after 1/2	10
22Mar80- 9Aqu	sly	7f	:23⅖	:47⅗	1:26⅖	Clm 16000	3	7	78	76½	46	47¾	Velasquez J	b 117	3.80	61-31	Amano 1172 Prospector's Joy 1075½ Gorizpa 108nk	Wide	9
8Mar80- 2Aqu	fst	170	⊡:48	1:13⅗	1:44⅘	Clm 15000	4	4	53	42	2hd	2nk	Castaneda M	b 115	*3.00	78-16	HappyHour117nkErnie'sLad1153¼PssDeceiver1173	Fought gamely	9
29Feb80- 3Aqu	fst	1 1/16	⊡:48	1:14⅕	1:46⅘	Clm 15000	6	7	78	63¼	52½	33	Castaneda M	b 115	4.30	77-24	Quranta Bay 1172¾ Irish Lament 117nk Ernie's Lad 115hd	Rallied	10
22Feb80- 9Aqu	gd	6f	⊡:23⅕	:47	1:12⅕	Clm 15000	1	8	97¼	97¼	66½	44¼	Saumell L	b 115	10.90	79-19	Island Nymph 1171¾ Gorizpa 1132 Joe Montage 111½	Rallied	12

LATEST WORKOUTS May 7 Aqu 4f fst :49⅗ b Apr 27 Aqu 4f fst :51⅗ b Apr 22 Aqu 5f fst 1:05⅖ b ● Apr 8 Aqu 3f fst :36 h

Ernie's Lad qualifies on form off his strong last race. Back in his effort on 19May80, there was a lead time of :24.1, with a gain of one erased by an add-on of three for energy, which winds up at :24.3 for an ability time. We get the same figure again out of the 10May80 race, where the lead time was :24.2, no gain or loss, plus one for energy. The second favorite is Crazy Chief.

```
Crazy Chief                Dk. b. or br. g. 6, by Chieftain—Trick Chick, by Prince John           Turf Record          St. 1st 2nd 3rd    Amt.
                           $16,000  Br.—Shoshone Farm (Fla)                          119   St. 1st 2nd 3rd   1980  6   2   0   1   $18,330
Own.—Mintzer J B                    Tr.—Ferriola Peter                                      3   0   0   0    1979 15   3   4   1   $38,490
2Jun80- 5Bel fst 1 1/16    :47 3/5 1:12 4/5 1:44 4/5       Clm 18000    2 6 54 41½ 2½ 1hd Velasquez J      b 113 14.50  78-24 Crazy Chief 113hd Birkhill 1136 Bee's Bay 1135            Driving 8
2Apr80- 1Aqu fst 6f        :22 4/5 :46 1/5 1:11            Clm 16000    10 7 74¼ 1111 1115 1113 Velasquez J  b 117 10.80  75-18 Beau Strad 112no Marsh's Robber 113nk Whiddon1082½    No factor 11
14Mar80- 1Aqu sly 1⅛ [•]:47     1:12 3/5 1:52 2/5          Clm 20000    6 3 33 53½ 816 924 Maple E          b 115  9.20  60-25 Il Vagabondo 119nk Bel Baie 11710 Lancer's Pride 1151      Wide 9
30Jan80- 6Aqu fst 170 [•]:48 1/5 1:13 4/5 1:43 3/5         Allowance    9 4 52½ 52¾ 99¼ 813 Dahlquist T C5 b 112 23.10  71-22 Orfanik 1171¾ I'm It 1173½ Lean Lad 117no                  Tired 9
25Jan80- 8Aqu fst 6f  [•]:22 2/5 :45 4/5 1:10 3/5          Allowance    5 12 129 107¾ 56¾ 38½ Dahlquist T C5 b 112• 40.40 82-18 Empror'sKy1173½BrghtAndBrv1175[DH]SlntBd117  Pinched back st. 12
      25Jan80-Dead heat
9Jan80- 3Aqu fst 1 1/16 [•]:47 4/5 1:13 1/5 1:46 1/5       Clm c-20000  5 3 2½ 1hd 2hd 1hd McNeil T7        b 110  3.80  83-18 Crazy Chief 110hd No Sir 118hd Mika Song 117½             Driving 10
27Dec79- 2Aqu gd 170 [•]:49     1:15 1/5 1:46 1/5 3↑ Clm 20000     1 2 2½ 1hd 2½ 22¾ Castaneda M       b 117 10.30  68-33 Debtor's Haven 1172¾ Crazy Chief 1173¾ No Sir 1153      No match 8
16Dec79- 7Aqu gd 1 1/16 [•]:49 3/5 1:15 1/5 1:46 3/5 3↑ Clm 20000  6 6 43½ 21 33 45¾ Castaneda M        b 117  8.30  75-20 Plethora 1171¼ Hive 1124½ Framarco 117hd                    Wide 7
2Dec79- 9Aqu fst 1⅛        :48 4/5 1:14 3/5 1:54 2/5 3↑ Clm 16000  6 3 33 3½ 1hd 1nk Castaneda M         b 117 19.20  63-29 Crazy Chief 117nk First Return 1171¾ Mad Spring 1171¾   Driving 10
25Nov79- 2Aqu fst 1⅛       :48 2/5 1:13 3/5 1:51 4/5 3↑ Clm 20000  8 5 511 79 819 824 Pincay L Jr        b 117  4.90  52-21 North Star 1133¼ Debtor's Haven 1175 BufferState1103  No factor 8
 I ATEST WORKOUTS    Mav 30 Bel  5f fst 1:00 2/5 hg        May 26 Bel  4f fst  :48   h
```

This horse qualifies off his last race, just four days ago when he shocked the field with a $31 payoff, beating Birkhill, our selection, by a head. But the lead time in that race was a :25.1, which Crazy Chief reduced by two off his gain but which must pick up two more for energy, leaving us with the same :25.1 with which we began our calculations. Out of the 25Jan80 race there was a lead time of :24.4, to which we add one for loss in lengths and one more for energy to wind up with :25.1 once again. We can now look at Royaldate, the third choice.

```
Royaldate                  B. c. 4, by Royal Saxon—Matesdate, by Sailor                              Turf Record          St. 1st 2nd 3rd    Amt.
                           $15,000  Br.—Fenway Farm (Fla)                          1085  St. 1st 2nd 3rd   1980  2   0   1   0    $2,310
Own.—Weiner K                       Tr.—Gullo Thomas J                                      1   0   0   0    1979 35   3   6   4   $44,760
26May80- 1Bel fst 6f       :23 1/5 :47 1:12 1/5            Clm 10000    9 7 65¼ 34½ 35½ 21¼ Cordero A Jr      117  7.50  80-20 Pet the Jet 1171¼ Royaldate 117no Bravo's Flame 1083½           Wide 11
9Jan80- 9Aqu fst 1⅛ [•]:47 1/5 1:11 3/5 1:53 1/5           Clm c-16000  4 9 1115 910 1014 911 Asmussen C B    117  5.60  69-18 Jack's Pet 110hd Pepysian 1171¾ Slow to Anger 117½          Outrun 11
24Dec79- 2Aqu my 170 [•]:49 1/5 1:15 1/5 1:47 1/5          Clm 16000    6 6 67¾ 58 55 23 Venezia M           113  4.30  63-27 Ha'Penny Moon 1133Royaldate113nkHappyHour1171¼  Best others 6
16Dec79- 9Aqu gd 1⅛ [•]:49 3/5 1:14 2/5 1:54 1/5           Clm 17000    7 10 911 810 713 716 Fell J          115 *2.30  59-20 Searing 113½ Nashuma 1146½ Stuttgart 1172½                 Dull try 10
7Dec79- 3Aqu my 170 [•]:47 4/5 1:13 2/5 1:44 2/5           Clm 18000    6 5 74 64¾ 32½ 3¾ Asmussen C B       113 *2.00  79-18 Tellurite 113¾ Our Charlie G. 115hd Royaldate 113hd            Wide 7
26Nov79- 2Aqu sly 1⅛       :49 3/5 1:14 2/5 1:56           Clm 16000    4 5 66½ 66½ 65 3hd Asmussen C B       117  3.20  55-30 Dance Scout117noNotimeforgoodbye115noRoyaldate117nk  Rallied 6
5Nov79- 2Aqu fst 1⅛        :48 4/5 1:13 2/5 1:51 1/5       Clm 25000    1 8 811 810 811 89¾ Asmussen C B      113 *2.20e 69-18 General H. D.112nkSal'sDream1194¾FollowThatDream117¾  Outrun 8
24Oct79- 6Aqu fst 1⅛       :48 1:13 3/5 1:54 3/5           Clm 22500    7 8 712 63½ 52 32¼ Fell J             115  5.00  60-28 Beautiful Contest 1191½ [D]Wimpfybell 110¾ Royaldate1153½  Wide 8
      24Oct79-Placed second through disqualification
10Oct79- 2Bel sly 1        :46 4/5 1:11 2/5 1:40 1/5       Clm 20000    3 5 56 58 36 2½ Fell J                119  3.70  66-26 Bankers Sun 117½ Royaldate 1193¾ HereComesHerbert1171½  Wide 7
26Sep79- 4Bel fst 7f       :24 :47 2/5 1:24 3/5            Clm 20000    6 8 84¼ 63¾ 25 26½ Fell J             119  3.80  72-20 Pokie Joe 1126½ Royaldate 119hd Bankers Sun 1172¾             Wide 8
LATEST WORKOUTS   ●Jun 2 Bel tr.t 5f fst 1:01  h      May 23 Bel tr.t 3f fst :37  b      May 3 Bel tr.t 5f fst 1:03  b
```

There was an easy qualification out of the last good race, where the lead time was :25.1, reduced by three for gain, with only one added back for energy to give us a healthy :24.4 ability time. The next best comes out of the 9Jan80 race, where the lead time was :24.2, no credit at all for gain, since the horse was so far back, and four added for energy, to wind up with :25.1. We now rate the three horses.

Odds	Horse	Ability		A Pts		F	Total
2.7	Ernie's Lad	:24.3	:24.3	17	17	Q	34
3.1	Crazy Chief	:25.1	:25.1	14	14	Q	28
6.4	Royaldate	:24.4	:25.1	16	14	Q	30

NINTH RACE
Belmont
JUNE 6, 1980

$1\frac{1}{16}$ MILES. ($1.40\frac{4}{5}$) CLAIMING. Purse $12,000. 4–year–olds and upward Weight, 122 lbs. Non–winners of two races at a mile or over since May 1, allowed 3 lbs. Of such a race since then, 5 lbs. Claiming price $16,000; for each $1,000 to $14,000, 2 lbs. (Races when entered to be claimed for $12,500 or less not considered.)

Value of race $12,000, value to winner $7,200, second $2,640, third $1,440, fourth $720. Mutuel pool $130,027, OTB pool $221,291. Track Triple Pool $221,261. OTB Triple Pool $416,816.

Last Raced	Horse	Eqt.	A.	Wt	PP	St	¼	½	¾	Str	Fin	Jockey	Cl'g Pr	Odds $1
2Jun80 5Bel1	Crazy Chief	b	6	119	5	6	5^{1}	2^{hd}	1^{hd}	1^{1}	$1^{1\frac{1}{4}}$	Velasquez J	16000	3.10
26May80 2Bel7	Caraqueno		5	115	6	8	$10^{\frac{1}{2}}$	$9^{\frac{1}{2}}$	$7^{\frac{1}{2}}$	$4^{\frac{1}{2}}$	$2^{\frac{3}{4}}$	Martens G	15000	18.00
2Jun80 5Bel5	House Of Erin	b	5	117	4	7	8^{hd}	8^{2}	5^{hd}	$3^{\frac{1}{2}}$	3no	Rivera M A	16000	8.80
26May80 3Bel4	Californian Star	b	4	112	9	2	$1^{\frac{1}{2}}$	1^{hd}	3^{1}	2^{1}	$4^{\frac{3}{4}}$	Gonzalez MA†5	16000	21.60
26May80 2Bel2	Ernie's Lad	b	5	117	11	3	7^{3}	6^{1}	6^{2}	6^{2}	$5^{\frac{1}{2}}$	Cordero A Jr	15000	2.70
2Jun80 3Bel5	Amano		7	119	8	4	$4^{\frac{1}{2}}$	$5^{\frac{1}{2}}$	4^{hd}	5^{1}	6no	Castaneda M	16000	8.10
16Apr80 2Aqu5	Finney Finster	b	8	115	1	12	12	12	12	8^{hd}	$7^{1\frac{3}{4}}$	Borden D A	15000	17.30
26May80 2Bel5	Buffer State	b	5	112	2	11	6^{hd}	7^{1}	$8^{1\frac{1}{2}}$	7^{1}	$8^{\frac{3}{4}}$	Beitia E5	16000	17.20
26May80 1Bel2	Royaldate		4	108	10	9	$11^{1\frac{1}{2}}$	11^{3}	10^{1}	9^{2}	$9^{3\frac{1}{4}}$	Attanasio R5	15000	6.40
26May80 2Bel8	Wartyme		6	113	3	10	$9^{1\frac{1}{2}}$	10^{1}	$11^{1\frac{1}{2}}$	10^{1}	$10^{2\frac{1}{4}}$	Asmussen C B	14000	14.80
26May80 2Bel6	Fellow Heir	b	7	117	12	1	2^{hd}	3^{1}	$2^{\frac{1}{2}}$	11^{2}	11^{nk}	Fell J	16000	16.90
17May80 3Suf4	Testimony	b	4	117	7	5	3^{1}	$4^{\frac{1}{2}}$	$9^{\frac{1}{2}}$	12	12	Santiago A	16000	29.60

OFF AT 5:04 EDT. Start good, Won driving. Time, $:23\frac{2}{5}$, $:46\frac{3}{5}$, $1:11\frac{1}{5}$, $1:37\frac{4}{5}$, $1:44\frac{3}{5}$ Track fast.

$2 Mutuel Prices:				
	5–(E)–CRAZY CHIEF	8.20	5.40	4.60
	6–(G)–CARAQUENO		14.40	9.00
	4–(D)–HOUSE OF ERIN			6.20

Our choice has to be Ernie's Lad off his 4-point margin. But look what Crazy Chief did to us.

Crazy Chief proved that his last race four days ago was no fluke. You will note that he had come back from a long layoff, and it would appear that some of his probable aches and pains of the past had been cured during his vacation. This is something we are not yet able to do anything about but accept, since on the record that we had to use, we could not have rated Crazy Chief any higher. With this one behind us, here is how we fared for the entire day.

		Invest		Return	
Race	Selection	Win	Place	Win	Place
1	Kens Bishop	$ 2	$ 2	$ 6.40	$ 4.40
2	Bolshoi	2	2	10.60	4.20
3	Cheering Section	—	2	—	4.80
4	Pass	—	—	—	—
5	Pass	—	—	—	—
6	Pass	—	—	—	—
7	Suzanne's Star	2	2	0	2.80
8	Euphrosyne	2	2	4.00	3.00
9	Ernie's Lad	2	2	0	0
	Totals	$10	$12	$21.00	$19.20

Total invested	$22.00
Total returned	$40.20
Net profit	$18.20

Well, the day wasn't so bad, after all. Net profit was easily above the 50% return mark, far more than enough to sustain any investor over any period of time. The power came in the first two races, and after that, there was a big fall-off, but this too can happen. There were only three winners for the day, but five place tickets helped the cause. The bottom line looked pale only after the splendid profit of the day before, but this indeed was another successful afternoon. I went back to Manhattan on the train with the crowd, quite content, looking forward to the final big day of Belmont week when the big race would be run and my crucial test period would be at an end. It was already enormously successful, with the only thing remaining being whether I could make a clean sweep and a profit every afternoon.

BIG WEEK AT BELMONT: SIXTH DAY, SATURDAY, JUNE 7, 1980

As I came to Belmont day itself, the last test run of the week selected, I approached it with some trepidation. When I selected the week as the crucial test of all my fully developed methods, I was almost certain there would be a profit every day, even though I knew how imposing such an outcome would be. With five days behind me, and one to go, what if the steady run of profits folded and there was a losing day? What if the first three betting choices in the races on the card picked today were to go off their form and run as miserably as is possible? But I was confident, for on stakes days, there is usually a high-quality card where favorites ordinarily run well. Now, I wanted this day's profit very badly.

The first race was an extremely high-priced claimer, with Hugable Tom, a five-year-old gelding, holding as the favorite.

Off his last race, you might be most unforgiving. But it was on the grass, where Hugable Tom apparently does not run well. So I could look back at his previous race on the dirt. It, too, was not inspiring, and there is no way we can qualify him on form out of these two efforts. Thus, our first study produces an NQ on form. When we come to the second choice in the wagering, Bold Phantom, we look to see if he can qualify on form.

We can make it here rather easily on two counts, the first of which is an "Evenly" race. While there was some mild zigzagging in the running line, this is a rather classic illustration of the "even" effort. Likewise, there are two of the

1 BELMONT

START

7 FURLONGS

BELMONT PARK

FINISH

7 FURLONGS. (1.20⅘) CLAIMING. Purse $18,000. 4-year-olds and upward. Weight, 122 lbs. Non-winners of two races since May 1 allowed 3 lbs.; of a race since then, 5 lbs. Claiming price $50,000; for each $5,000 to $40,000, 2 lbs. (Races when entered to be claimed for $35,000 or less not considered.)

Hugable Tom ✻ — B. g. 5, by Tom Rolfe—Hugable, by Warfare — **$50,000** — Br.—Calumet Farm (Ky) — Tr.—Lake Robert P — Own.—Gir-Sto Stable — **117**

Turf Record: St. 1st 2nd 3rd — 3 0 0 0

	St.	1st	2nd	3rd	Amt.
1980	11	4	1	1	$74,460
1979	17	5	5	3	$94,634

24May80- 6Bel	gd	1$\frac{1}{16}$ Ⓣ	:46 1:10⅗ 1:43⅕	Clm 60000	11	6	$6^{3½}$	7^{5}	7^{10}	8^{13}	Castaneda M	119	9.90	67–20 Gemmate 117^{nk} BeechGrove117^{3}AmericanRoyalty$113^{1½}$	No factor 11
11May80- 2Aqu	fst	1⅛	:47⅖ 1:11⅖ 1:49⅘	Clm 100000	7	7	6^{8}	$6^{6½}$	7^{12}	8^{15}	Castaneda M	122	4.10	71–14 Causerie $118^{7¾}$ Lean Lad 118^{3} Ring of Truth $116^{1¼}$	No factor 8
24Apr80- 7Aqu	fst	1⅛	:48⅘ 1:13 1:51⅖	Allowance	5	4	$4^{1½}$	$3^{1½}$	1^{hd}	$1^{¾}$	Castaneda M	116	2.40	78–21 Hugable Tom 116¾ Tunerup 115½ Contare 114^{1}	Driving 5
8Apr80- 7Aqu	fst	7f	:23⅕ :45⅖ 1:22⅘	Allowance	3	5	$5^{3½}$	$4^{4½}$	3^{3}	1^{hd}	Castaneda M	117	5.30	87–21 Hugable Tom 117^{hd}LarkOscillation$119^{2½}$BoldVoyager117¾	Driving 7
1Apr80- 1Aqu	my	1	:45⅘ 1:10⅖ 1:36⅖	Clm 75000	2	2	$4^{6½}$	2^{4}	2^{3}	$1^{2¼}$	Fell J	122	*1.60	84–19 Hugable Tom $122^{2¼}$ Roman Tea 122^{2} Tantivy $118^{1½}$	Ridden out 6
13Mar80- 8Aqu	fst	1$\frac{1}{16}$ ⊡	:48⅖ 1:13⅗ 1:44⅘	Allowance	4	5	5^{3}	$3^{1½}$	3^{2}	$4^{2¼}$	Fell J	117	3.20	87–23 Bold Josh 117¾ Weth Nan $117^{1¼}$ Rabmab 117¾	Weakened 7
25Feb80- 2Aqu	gd	1$\frac{1}{16}$ ⊡	:48⅕ 1:13 1:45⅕	Clm c-50000	6	6	$7^{7¼}$	7^{6}	$3^{½}$	1^{1}	Beitia E5	112	*1.50	88–20 Hugable Tom 112^{1} Party Surprise119^{no}TreadLightly$119^{2¼}$	Driving 7
16Feb80- 6Aqu	sly	1$\frac{1}{16}$ ⊡	:47⅖ 1:13⅕ 1:47⅖	Allowance	6	7	6^{6}	$5^{7½}$	5^{9}	5^{12}	Asmussen C B	b 117	*2.00	65–29 LrkOscilltion119^{nk}Michel'sEdge$115^{5½}$RingofLight$110^{3½}$	No excuse 8
25Jan80- 7Aqu	fst	1⅛ ⊡	:47 1:12⅘ 1:49⅖	Allowance	4	3	3^{5}	$2^{1½}$	2^{8}	2^{9}	Asmussen C B	b 117	2.20	90–18 Ring of Truth114^{9}HugableTom117^{11}YouGoFirst110^{4}	Second best 5
21Jan80- 7Aqu	fst	6f ⊡	:22⅗ :46 1:10⅘	Allowance	2	5	$5^{4½}$	$5^{3¾}$	4^{5}	$4^{3¾}$	Asmussen C B	b 115	4.10	86–19 Hotspur 115¾ Double Zeus 122^{hd} Ring of Light 115^{3}	Evenly 6

LATEST WORKOUTS Apr 18 Aqu 6f fst 1:15⅘ b

Bold Phantom — B. g. 6, by Bold and Brave—Phanem, by Gray Phantom — **$45,000** — Br.—Woodard R B (Ky) — Tr.—Weymouth Eugene E — Own.—Woodard R B — **115**

Turf Record: St. 1st 2nd 3rd — 1 0 0 1

	St.	1st	2nd	3rd	Amt.
1980	9	3	1	2	$31,200
1979	7	2	1	2	$23,170

30May80- 8Key	fst	7f	:22⅕ :44⅗ 1:22⅖	Allowance	6	4	2^{3}	$3^{2½}$	$3^{3½}$	$3^{2¾}$	Castaneda J A	118	3.10	92–15 Surprise Bidder 115^{2} Ornithologist115¾BoldPhantom$118^{1¼}$	Evenly 7
16May80- 2Aqu	fst	6f	:22⅖ :45⅘ 1:10⅖	Clm 50000	4	2	4^{5}	4^{5}	$4^{3½}$	$3^{2½}$	Castaneda M	117	10.50	88–16 Mr. Ed $117^{1¼}$ Bold Voyager $117^{1¼}$ Bold Phantom 117^{hd}	Mild bid 8
6May80- 8Key	fst	6f	:22⅕ :45 1:10⅖	Allowance	6	6	$6^{5¾}$	$6^{8½}$	$6^{6½}$	$5^{4¼}$	Rodriguez J J5	114	4.60	86–20 Virrac $116^{1¼}$ Ornithologist 119^{1} Fast Consent 122½	No menace 8
24Apr80- 3Aqu	fst	6f	:22⅕ :45⅕ 1:10⅖	Clm 50000	3	4	3^{2}	2^{3}	2^{4}	2^{5}	Castaneda M	122	4.00	86–21 JimBlthrop119^{5}BoldPhntom$122^{1¼}$HouseOfErin$117^{5½}$	Second best 6
13Apr80- 8Key	fst	6f	:22⅖ :45⅘ 1:11	Allowance	4	4	$3^{2½}$	2^{1}	3^{1}	1no	Tejeira J	119	8.80	87–26 Bold Phantom 119no PrinceHagley108^{hd}HangingTree113^{3}	Driving 9
7Apr80- 2Aqu	fst	6f	:22⅗ :45⅕ 1:10⅗	Clm 40000	2	6	$4^{3½}$	3^{6}	2^{4}	$1^{½}$	Castaneda M	117	2.80	90–21 Bold Phantom 117½ Armet 117no See The World 112^{2}	Driving 6
16Mar80- 7Key	fst	6f	:22⅖ :45⅗ 1:11	Allowance	7	7	$5^{2¼}$	$4^{2¼}$	8^{4}	$8^{3¼}$	Black A S	115	3.90	84–21 Simon Bee 114^{nk} Mug Hunter 115^{1} Ornithologist 118^{nk}	Tired 9
31Jan80- 9Aqu	fst	6f ⊡	:23⅖ :47⅖ 1:12⅖	Clm 35000	2	9	$4^{1¾}$	2^{hd}	2^{hd}	1^{2}	Montoya D	117	6.40	82–25 Bold Phantom 117^{2} Coupon Rate 112½ MasterA.J.117^{3}	Drew clear 12
17Jan80- 9Aqu	fst	6f ⊡	:21⅘ :45 1:10⅘	Clm 45000	4	8	$5^{3¾}$	5^{6}	$8^{9¾}$	7^{6}	Graell A	117	14.20	84–18 Bold Bishop $117^{1½}$ Jim Balthrop 117½ Judge Grey 112¾	No factor 11
16Dec79- 7Key	fst	6f	1:11⅗	3↑Allowance	2	—	—	—	—	$4^{3¾}$	Black A S	122	*1.50	80–21 Anothergambler 115^{2} Double Craps 107¾ M. A.'s Date 122^{1}	Fog 6

LATEST WORKOUTS May 24 Key 5f fst 1:00 h — May 13 Key 3f my :37 b — May 2 Key 4f my :48⅖ h

four calls up close. For ability, the 16May80 race shows a :24.3 lead time, reduced by two for gain, for a :24.1. On 7Apr80, there was a :25.2 lead time, with the gain of four ticks bringing us to :24.3, with nothing added for energy.

The third choice in the wagering is Raise A Buck.

Raise A Buck — B. g. 4, by Raise A Bid—Skyblue Pink, by My Babu — **$45,000** — Br.—Diamond C Farm Inc (Fla) — Tr.—Parisella John — Own.—May-Don Stable — **115**

Turf Record: St. 1st 2nd 3rd — 4 0 0 1

	St.	1st	2nd	3rd	Amt.
1980	5	2	0	1	$27,680
1979	25	2	6	6	$57,900

29May80- 2Bel	fst	6f	:22⅘ :45⅖ 1:10⅗	Clm 50000	6	7	7^{6}	$5^{6½}$	$5^{7½}$	$5^{3¾}$	Lovato F Jr5	b 112	18.80	85–16 Subordinate $117^{1¼}$ Guillermo 117^{hd} Bold Voyager 117^{nk}	No factor 7
9Feb80- 7Aqu	fst	170 ⊡	:47⅗ 1:12⅘ 1:43⅖	Allowance	6	6	$6^{7½}$	$5^{3½}$	$5^{2½}$	$4^{4½}$	Martens G	b 122	*1.80	80–19 Ransack 119½ Lark Oscillation $119^{3¼}$ RoyalReasoning112¾	Dull try 6
31Jan80- 7Aqu	fst	1$\frac{1}{16}$ ⊡	:49⅕ 1:14⅗ 1:46⅗	Allowance	2	1	$1^{½}$	1^{hd}	$1^{½}$	$1^{1¼}$	Martens G	b 119	*1.60	81–25 RaiseABuck$119^{1¼}$HitchingRail117^{hd}PerfectBidder117^{1}	Drew clear 7
20Jan80- 6Aqu	fst	1$\frac{1}{16}$ ⊡	:47⅘ 1:12⅗ 1:45⅖	Allowance	3	3	3^{7}	2^{4}	2^{hd}	$1^{2½}$	Martens G	b 119	4.60	87–26 Raise A Buck $119^{2½}$ Orfanik 117¾ Dresden Dew 117no	Drew out 8
1Jan80- 7Aqu	fst	1$\frac{1}{16}$ ⊡	:47 1:12⅘ 1:45⅖	Allowance	4	5	$3^{2½}$	$4^{1½}$	$3^{2½}$	$3^{1¼}$	Martens G	b 122	*1.10	86–18 Roman Tea 117^{hd} Dresden Dew $112^{1¼}$ Raise A Buck 122^{10}	No rally 6
24Dec79- 8Aqu	sly	1⅛ ⊡	:49 1:14⅖ 1:54⅘	3↑Allowance	5	2	2^{hd}	2^{hd}	2^{hd}	2^{nk}	Martens G	b 120	8.80	73–27 Imitating 115^{nk} Raise A Buck $120^{3¾}$ Minimal Art 117^{nk}	Wide 8
10Dec79- 6Aqu	fst	1⅛ ⊡	:48 1:11⅗ 1:51	3↑Allowance	2	3	$4^{¾}$	$4^{1¾}$	2^{1}	1^{nk}	Fell J	b 115	2.60	91–13 Raise A Buck 115^{nk} Princenesian 115^{hd} Big Greg $115^{3¼}$	Driving 7
12Nov79- 2Aqu	my	1⅛	:49⅘ 1:15⅕ 1:52⅗	3↑Allowance	4	3	$3^{1½}$	$4^{1½}$	3^{2}	$3^{1¼}$	Fell J	b 115	*1.80	70–34 Harry J. 115^{nk} Pull A Cutie $115^{1¼}$ Raise A Buck 115^{3}	Evenly 6
31Oct79- 6Aqu	fst	6f	:22⅕ :45⅖ 1:10⅖	3↑Allowance	3	8	$7^{6½}$	7^{10}	6^{6}	$4^{5½}$	Fell J	b 114	5.50	85–16 Royal Reasoning119^{2}TwelveViolines$119^{2¾}$Contare114¾	No menace 9
21Oct79- 5Aqu	fst	1⅛	:48⅖ 1:12⅕ 1:51⅖	Clm c-50000	7	1	1^{1}	$1^{1½}$	2^{hd}	$2^{½}$	Maple E	b 117	3.10	77–16 ProperlyPerson117½RaiseABuck117^{hd}MdeleineBehve115½	Gamely 7

LATEST WORKOUTS May 25 Bel tr.t 4f fst :50 b — May 21 Bel tr.t 4f gd :50⅖ b — May 2 Bel tr.t 4f fst :50⅖ b — Apr 28 Bel tr.t 4f sly :53 b (d)

Form is again our problem, and this one just can't make it. He was never close in his last race. The only basis for considering him would be if there was a decent gain of the required five. He passed two horses but the 2¼ lengths picked up from the first call is not quite enough. Because we cannot bend our rules at every close call, we have to place the NQ tag on this one also.

With both Hugable Tom and Raise A Buck eliminated on form, there is no need to do a comparison chart, as long as we have one qualified animal for our win and place investment. Bold Phantom didn't look bad at all off his good ability times, and I was rather hopeful as I gave him my support. But this time I was dead wrong.

FIRST RACE
Belmont
JUNE 7, 1980

7 FURLONGS. (1.20⅗) CLAIMING. Purse $18,000. 4-year-olds an' upward. Weight, 122 lbs. Non-winners of two races since May 1 allowed 3 lbs.; of a race since then, 5 lbs. Claiming price $50,000; for each $5,000 to $40,000, 2 lbs. (Races when entered to be claimed for $35,000 or less not considered.)

Value of race $18,000, value to winner $10,800, second $3,960, third $2,160, fourth $1,080. Mutuel pool $222,071, OTB pool $123,414.

Last Raced	Horse	Eqt.A.Wt	PP	St	¼	½	Str	Fin	Jockey	Cl'g Pr	Odds $1
24May80 6Bel^{8}	Hugable Tom	5 117	3	6	3½	2^{hd}	1^{hd}	12¾	Fell J	50000	1.10
1Jun80 6Bel^{7}	Ever Loyal	5 115	5	3	1^{3}	1^{1}	2^{2}	2^{3}	Velasquez J	45000	12.70
29May80 2Bel^{5}	Raise A Buck	b 4 115	1	2	2½	3^{3}	3^{6}	36½	Cordero A Jr	45000	4.30
30May80 8Key^{3}	Bold Phantom	6 115	6	5	4½	5^{1}	5^{1}	4^{hd}	Montoya D	45000	3.90
29May80 2Bel^{7}	Beekman Hill	5 117	7	1	5½	6^{2}	6^{10}	51½	Saumell L	50000	12.00
1Jun80 6Bel^{5}	Out There	b 5 115	2	7	6^{2}	4½	4^{2}	6^{19}	Castaneda M	45000	7.50
24May80 2Bel^{7}	Tahitian Tempo	4 113	4	4	7	7	7	7	Vasquez J	40000	12.40

OFF AT 1:03 1/2. Start good, Won ridden out. Time, :23, :46⅘, 1:11⅕, 1:24⅘ Track sloppy.

Official Program Numbers↘

$2 Mutuel Prices:			
4-(D)-HUGABLE TOM	4.20	3.40	2.60
6-(F)-EVER LOYAL		8.40	4.60
1-(A)-RAISE A BUCK			2.80

My effective form rules let me down. It was bound to happen, as it will every now and then, as I told you in the chapter on form. Hugable Tom justified the crowd's faith and won rather handily. Bold Phantom was a disappointment, and thus Belmont day gets off to a not-so-good beginning.

We have some expensive and well-bred fillies in the second race at seven furlongs.

2 BELMONT

7 FURLONGS. (1.20⅗) HANDICAP. Purse $35,000. Fillies and mares, 3-year-olds and upward. Weights Wednesday, June 4. Declarations by 10:00 A.M., Thursday, June 5.

Jedina — **Dk. b. or br. f. 4, by What A Pleasure—Killaloe, by Dr Fager**
Br.—Nerud J A (Fla)
Own.—Nerud J A — **Tr.—Nerud Jan H** — **117**

	St.	1st	2nd	3rd	Amt.
1980	1	1	0	0	$15,000
1979	9	4	1	0	$65,308

23May80- 3Bel	fst	6f	:23	:46⅕	1:09⅘	3↑ⒻAllowance	5	1	2^{hd}	11½	11½	12½	Cordero A Jr	119	2.50	94-16	Jedina 1192½ Damask Fan 108^{8} Clown's Doll 119^{hd}	Ridden out	6
27Dec79- 6Med	fst	6f	:23⅕	:47⅕	1:12	ⒻHalfmoon H	6	3	52¼	6^{6}	58½	4^{12}	Cordero A Jr	117	2.90	73-23	Olden Charade 119^{5} Sexy 116^{6} Syncopating Lady 122½	No threat	7
23Nov79- 8Aqu	fst	6f	:22⅖	:45⅘	1:10⅕	ⒻDark Mirage	7	1	2^{hd}	3½	2^{hd}	2^{3}	Cordero A Jr	116	5.20	89-20	Misty Gallore 118^{3} Jedina 116^{2} Clown's Doll 1161¾	No match	7
2Nov79- 8Aqu	fst	6½f	:22⅕	:45	1:17	ⒻHigh Voltage	3	3	55½	52½	11½	1^{hd}	Cordero A Jr	115	6.30	90-22	Jedina 115^{hd} Sexy 114^{2} Needle Me On 112¾	Driving	8
13Oct79- 5Bel	sly	6f	:22⅘	:46⅗	1:12⅖	3↑ⒻAllowance	7	7	66½	7^{10}	6^{11}	69½	Velasquez J	116	7.90	70-27	Cry Wolf 117¾BackToStay1173¾CornishRunner116^{nk}	Broke slowly	7
3Sep79- 7Bel	fst	7f	:23⅕	:46⅘	1:24⅖	3↑ⒻAllowance	4	2	21½	2^{hd}	1^{hd}	1¾	Velasquez J	115	7.40	80-17	Jedina 115¾ Lady Darrington 115^{hd} Star Invader 1171½	Driving	5
20Aug79- 9Sar	my	7f	:22⅘	:45⅘	1:24⅕	3↑ⒻAllowance	5	3	2½	32½	2^{2}	1no	Cordero A Jr	117	4.20	81-18	Jedina 117no Sexy 1131½ Cornflower 110^{hd}	Driving	10
6Aug79- 7Sar	fst	6f	:22⅘	:46⅕	1:11⅕	3↑ⒻMd Sp Wt	8	3	11½	1^{3}	1^{3}	11¼	Cordero A Jr	117	8.60	84-20	Jedina 1171¼ Caesar's Dish 1173¾ O'Connell Street 117^{nk}	Driving	10
8Jly79- 4Bel	fst	6f	:22⅘	:46⅘	1:12⅕	3↑ⒻMd Sp Wt	8	3	32½	3½	32½	5^{7}	Vasquez J	116	6.60	74-21	Spark of Life 1151¼ Nasty Jay 122½ O'Connell Street 116^{4}	Tired	9
29Jun79- 3Bel	fst	7f	:23	:46⅖	1:25⅕	3↑ⒻMd Sp Wt	4	6	86½	8^{11}	77¼	79¾	Vasquez J	114	7.90	66-23	Jolivar 114½ Peaceful Snow 114^{4} Caesar's Dish 114^{1}	No factor	8

LATEST WORKOUTS Jun 5 Bel 4f fst :47⅕ b May 31 Bel 4f fst :50 b May 20 Bel 5f fst :59⅗ h May 15 Bel 5f fst :58⅘ h

Jedina is the favorite off an excellent win in her last race, after a long layoff since last winter. The lead time, set by Jedina, was a blazing :23.2 with no adjustments of any kind, as she set the clock figures. This is a brilliant performance. We have to drop down to 3Sep79 at Belmont to get the next best time.

The 7f time in this race is converted to 1:11.2 for 6f, which gives us a :24.3 lead time with no adjustments of any kind. There is sufficient early speed to pick up 4 points here. While Jedina looks very good, there is some other talent in this race. Ball Gate is the second choice.

***Ball Gate** — B. m. 5, by Snow Ball—Free Gate, by Cross Petition
Own.—Ring G — Br.—Haras Los Robles (Arg) — Tr.—Garcia Carlos A — **118**

Turf Record	St.	1st	2nd	3rd			St.	1st	2nd	3rd	Amt.
	3	0	2	1		1980	7	2	2	1	$46,020
						1979	2	0	1	0	$11,913

19May80- 6Aqu	fst	6f	:22⅕	:45⅗	1:10⅘	ⒻAllowance	6	3	43½	53½	1hd	12¾	Velasquez J	122	2.40	89–19	Ball Gate 1222¾ Bill's Fancy 115nk Celia Bonita 110no	Ridden out	8
1May80- 8Aqu	fst	7f	:23⅖	:46⅗	1:22⅘	ⒻAllowance	2	3	3nk	11	12½	1¾	Velasquez J	115	7.60	87–13	Ball Gate 115¾ One I Love 1172 Sub Rosa 1171¼	Driving	7
26Mar80- 8GP	fm	*1 1/16 Ⓣ			1:43	ⒻAllowance	8	1	11	1hd	33	34	MacBeth D	114	2.50	87–13	La Soufriere 114½ Champagne Shower 1143½ Ball Gate1142½	Tired	10
12Mar80- 6GP	fm	1 1/16 Ⓣ	:48⅗	1:12⅕	1:43⅖	ⒻAllowance	4	6	42¼	61¾	1½	21	Velasquez J	114	5.30	83–13	Solo Haina 1141 Ball Gate 1141½ La Rouquine II 114¾	2nd best	10
25Feb80- 9Hia	fm	1 1/16 Ⓣ			1:42⅗	ⒻAllowance	4	1	11	22	25	26½	Maple E	115	16.10	78–17	Just A Game II 1156½ Ball Gate 115noLaSoufriere1154	Held place	7
24Jan80- 9Hia	fst	6f	:22⅖	:46	1:10⅖	ⒻAllowance	3	7	75¼	85¾	73¼	611	Encinas R I	115	26.20	80–23	Pradera 1193 Jameela 1226 Lawdy Miss Clawdy 1221¼	No threat	8
15Jan80- 8Hia	fst	6f	:22⅖	:45⅘	1:10⅕	ⒻAllowance	5	3	117½	76¼	56	610	Encinas R I	115	31.40	82–15	Pradera 1193½ Conga Miss 1152½ Gentle Touch 115nk	No threat	12
10Feb79- 6Aqu	fst	6f	⊡:22⅖	:46	1:11⅕	ⒻHandicap	1	5	75¼	710	711	58¾	Hernandez R	120	*.70	79–14	Misty Native 1153 Akita 113nk Cycylya Zee 1133¼	Outrun	7
13Jan79- 8Aqu	sly	6f	⊡:22⅘	:47	1:12⅕	3↑ⒻInterboro H	1	3	43½	75¾	49	24½	Moseley J W	119	3.60	78–19	Gladiolus 1224½ Ball Gate 1194 Dr. Penny Binn 1132¼	Checked	9
6Aug78♦9LaPlata(Arg)	my	*1			1:43⅕	ⒻGrPr d'Potrancas(Gr.1)						12	Gorrais I	123	*.50	— —	Ball Gate 1232 Alegria Real 1231 Aletta 1231½	Well pl.,easily	9

LATEST WORKOUTS Jun 4 Bel 4f fst :47⅖ h — May 28 Bel 3f fst :34⅘ h — May 14 Bel 4f gd :48 b — May 10 Bel 3f fst :37⅖ b

This mare from Argentina has won her last two races with keen efforts. In her race of 1May80, we convert the 7f time of 1:22.4 down to 1:10.2 for 6f, which gives us a :23.4 lead time, which requires no adjustments to become the ability time. In her last race, there was a lead time of :25.1, reduced by three off her gain, and with no reduction for energy, we have a :24.3. This one can move also. She lacks strong early speed, but has enough to get 2 points.

The third choice in the wagering, Belladora, is up from a campaign in Florida.

Belladora — B. f. 4, by Stage Door Johnny—Prayer Bell, by Better Self
Own.—Spring Hill Stable — Br.—Evans E P (Va) — Tr.—Kelly Thomas J — **116**

Turf Record	St.	1st	2nd	3rd			St.	1st	2nd	3rd	Amt.
	2	1	0	0		1980	3	1	0	0	$9,343
						1979	3	3	0	0	$70,976

26Mar80- 9GP	fst	7f	:22⅕	:44⅗	1:23	3↑ⒻPromise	6	10	86	88¼	913	813	Cruguet J	122	*2.50	76–18	Mimi J 114½ Blitey 1221½ Impetuous Gal 1172½	Slow st. stumbled	11
12Mar80- 8GP	fm	1	Ⓣ:47⅗	1:11⅗	1:37⅕	3↑ⒻS'wnee R'vr	9	3	36½	32½	74¾	53¼	Velasquez J	118	*.60	81–13	Ouro Verde 112nk No Disgrace 1103 AnnaYrrahD.112hd	Weakened	10
12Mar80-Run in Two Divisions 8th & 9th Races.																			
25Feb80- 6Hia	fm	5½f Ⓣ			1:05	ⒻAllowance	6	6	84¼	62½	31½	1nk	Velasquez J	115	2.70	86–17	Belladora115nkWinston'sSapphire1191OurGallntLdy109hd	Driving	9
28Apr79-11Hia	fst	1⅛	:47⅖	1:12⅕	1:50⅗	ⒻPoinsetta	1	3	2½	21	12	110	Velasquez J	114	*.40	79–21	Belladora 11410 Speier's Hope 112no MaybeTheBest1122¼	Handily	11
4Apr79-11Hia	fst	7f	:22⅘	:46	1:24⅘	ⒻHibiscus	3	6	54½	66	52¼	12¾	Velasquez J	112	*.30	79–29	Belladora 1122¾ Too ManySweets117hdSpeier'sHope1121½	Driving	7
22Mar79- 3Hia	fst	7f	:22⅖	:45⅗	1:22⅘	ⒻAllowance	8	1	24	22	13	17½	Velasquez J	114	*2.30	89–18	Belladora 1147½ Allison's Gal 1143 Speier's Hope 122hd	Easily	8
18Nov78- 8Aqu	sly	1⅛	:46⅗	1:11⅖	1:50	ⒻDemoiselle	7	6	59¼	64¾	44½	33½	Miranda J	112	4.70	81–14	Plankton 112nk Distinct Honor 1133¼ Belladora 1121¾	Steadied	9
26Oct78- 6Aqu	fst	7f	:22⅖	:45⅗	1:24⅘	ⒻAllowance	8	9	86¼	88½	53	1¾	Miranda J5	114	2.40	77–19	Belladora 114¾ Polar Flag 1193¼ Cornish Runner 119nk	Driving	12
5Oct78- 3Bel	my	6f	:23	:46⅘	1:11⅘	ⒻMd Sp Wt	8	7	67½	510	34½	11¼	Miranda J7	112	10.10	83–22	Belladora 1121¼ Gisela's Pleasure 1194 Retroactive 1193½	Driving	9

LATEST WORKOUTS Jun 3 Bel 6f fst 1:13⅘ b — May 25 Bel 5f fst 1:00 h — May 17 Bel tr.t 5f fst 1:04⅖ b — May 10 Bel 4f fst :50 b

While she has not run since late March, this filly, with an excellent record, has had four recent workouts, and as a stakes competitor, qualifies on form. Note that she won the Poinsetta at Hialeah in 1979 by 10 full lengths. In her race of 22Mar79, the 7f time is converted to 1:10.2 for a :24.4 lead time. This is reduced by two for gain down to a :24.2 ability time. The best we can do otherwise is :25.1 for an ability time off the 28Apr79 victory in the Poinsetta. The lead time was :24.4, but we have to add one because of the loss of a half-length, and then put on one more for energy to get the :25.1 figure. She is weak in early speed, however, and gets a 0 here.

With this, we can make our comparison chart.

Odds	Horse	Ability		A Pts		ES	F	Total
1.3	Jedina	:23.2	:24.3	23	17	4	Q	44
3.7	Ball Gate	:23.4	:24.3	21	17	2	Q	40
4.6	Belladora	:24.2	:25.1	18	14	0	Q	32

While Jedina and Ball Gate were reasonably close on ability points, with Jedina having a 2-point advantage, the early-speed factor swung heavily in her favor. Jedina was out in front from the gate and led all the way in excellent time to win.

SECOND RACE
Belmont
JUNE 7, 1980

7 FURLONGS. (1.20⅘) HANDICAP. Purse $35,000. Fillies and mares, 3-year-olds and upward. Weights Wednesday, June 4. Declarations by 10:00 A.M., Thursday, June 5.

Value of race $35,000, value to winner $21,000, second $7,700, third $4,200, fourth $2,100. Mutuel pool $254,939, OTB pool $122,752. Track Quinella Pool $227,857; OTB Quinella Pool $166,979.

Last Raced	Horse	Eqt.A.Wt	PP	St	¼	½	Str	Fin	Jockey	Odds $1
23May80 3Bel1	Jedina	4 117	5	1	11½	1½	11	1½	Cordero A Jr	1.30
31May80 8Bel4	Miss Baja	5 113	2	7	4½	31½	33	22¾	Maple E	8.10
19May80 6Aqu1	Ball Gate	5 118	1	3	3½	21½	21	31¼	Velasquez J	3.70
26Mar80 9GP8	Belladora	4 116	7	2	61½	6½	42	45½	Shoemak' W	4.60
24May80 7Bel1	Mongo Queen	b 4 123	4	5	51	51½	612	52	Fell J	5.60
23May80 3Bel3	Clown's Doll	b 4 112	6	6	7	7	5½	6	Martens (	27.80
23May80 8Bel2	Fall Aspen	4 116	3	4	2hd	4hd	7	—	Velez R I	8.70

Fall Aspen, Eased.

OFF AT 1:36, EDT. Start good, Won driving. Time, :23⅕, :46⅗, 1:11, 1:23⅗ Track sloppy.

$2 Mutuel Prices:

5-(F)-JEDINA	4.60	3.40	2.60
2-(B)-MISS BAJA		6.40	4.60
1-(A)-BALL GATE			3.40

You might also note that an unusually good place price of $3.40 was racked up here, because an outsider came in second. You will occasionally get these good place prices on a horse with odds as low as those of Jedina, and when you do, it is a bargain indeed. Now, to the third race, where we have some lightly raced colts for this time of year.

3 BELMONT

1 MILE. (1.33⅗) ALLOWANCE. Purse $20,000. 3-year-olds and upward, Which have never won two races. Weights, 3-year-olds, 114 lbs.; older, 122 lbs. Non-winners of a race other than claiming at a mile or over since May 15 allowed 3 lbs.; of such a race since May 1, 5 lbs.

Key To Content — B. c. 3, by Forli—Key Bridge, by Princequillo — **109**
Own.—Rokeby Stable — Br.—Mellon P (Va) — Tr.—Miller Mack

	St.	1st	2nd	3rd	Amt.
1980	3	1	0	1	$12,000
1979	1	M	1	0	$2,860

24May80- 2Bel	fst 1	:45⅘	1:10⅖	1:36	3↑Allowance	6	1	2hd	11½	2hd	3½	Fell J	b 114	*.90e	87-17	WarofWords112hdGrandCournt113½KeyToContent1145	Weakened 11
17May80- 5Aqu	fst 1	:46⅖	1:11	1:36⅕	Allowance	3	4	44½	42½	42½	63½	Fell J	117	2.50	82-16	Comptroller 117¾ Chief Hilarious112½SilverProspector1171¾	Tired 6
26Apr80- 9Aqu	fst 6f	:22⅕	:45⅘	1:12	3↑Md Sp Wt	4	2	32	41½	21½	13¼	Fell J	113	5.60	83-19	Key To Content 1133¼ Tentation 1141¼ Waj. Jr. 114¾	Drew out 11
3Dec79- 6Aqu	fst 6f	:22⅗	:46⅗	1:12⅗	Md Sp Wt	8	4	55½	54	32	24¼	Fell J	118	9.30	76-22	VoodooRhythm1184¼KeyToContent118hdCretivPln1183	Game try 8

LATEST WORKOUTS ●Jun 5 Bel 4f fst :46⅗ h — May 30 Bel 4f fst :50 b — May 23 Bel 3f fst :35⅕ h — May 15 Bel 4f fst :47⅖ h

Key To Content is the favorite and qualifies off his last good race. The lead time is :24.3, and as is frequent with good horses, no adjustment is necessary to get that same ability time. In the previous race of 17May80, there was a :24.3 lead time, reduced by two for gain, but one gets placed back on for energy to finish with an excellent :24.2. He also gets a full 4 points for early speed.

Bold Barbizon is the second favorite, fairly well backed.

Bold Barbizon Dk. b. or br. c. 3, by Ward McAllister—Lady Barbizon, by Barbizon
Own.—Reynolds D P Br.—Reynolds D (Ky) Tr.—Kelly Thomas J **109**
St. 1st 2nd 3rd Amt.
1980 7 1 0 5 $18,860
1979 0 M 0 0
30Apr80- 9Aqu my 1 :47⅗ 1:12⅕ 1:37⅖ Allowance 7 3 3½ 2hd 3nk 42¾ Fell J b 119 6.30 76–21 [D]VoodooRhythm1172King'sWsh117¾GrndCournt122no Weakened 8
30Apr80-Placed third through disqualification
2Apr80- 2Aqu fst 1⅛ :48⅘ 1:13⅖ 1:51⅖ Allowance 5 4 31½ 31½ 3nk 3nk Fell J 122 2.00 78–18 Huge Success 119nk Sir Kay 117hd Bold Barbizon 1223¾ Held well 7
23Mar80- 6Aqu my 1 :46⅘ 1:12⅗ 1:38⅗ Md Sp Wt 7 5 42 12½ 15 17½ Fell J 122 *1.30 73–25 Bold Barbizon 1227½ Tandoor 122nk Bold Fencer1223¾ Ridden out 9
13Mar80- 6Aqu fst 170 [•]:48⅘ 1:14⅕ 1:43⅘ 3↑Md Sp Wt 5 5 34 31½ 33 31½ Fell J 114 3.20 81–23 Huge Success 114nk Rebel Blade 1151¼ Bold Barbizon 1145 Wide 7
5Mar80- 6Aqu fst 6f [•]:22⅖ :45⅘ 1:12⅕ 3↑Md Sp Wt 8 9 77½ 79½ 39 45¼ Beitia E5 109 6.40 78–22 Bypasser 126nk Caesar's World 1123 Tombouctou 1142 Wide 9
18Feb80- 6Hia fst 6f :22⅗ :46⅘ 1:11⅖ Md Sp Wt 11 7 62¾ 32 46 38 Solomone M 120 4.40 78–20 Ramparts 120no Grand Courant 1158BoldBarbizon120½ Weakened 12
2Feb80- 4Hia fst 6f :22⅗ :46⅕ 1:11⅘ Md Sp Wt 8 11 99 86¾ 54 39½ Solomone M 120 11.10 74–23 Wickerwork 1153 Ramparts 1206½ Bold Barbizon 1202½ Rallied 12
LATEST WORKOUTS Jun 4 Bel tr.t 4f gd :48⅖ h (d) ●May 28 Bel 6f fst 1:13⅖ h May 17 Bel tr.t 4f fst :49 b ●May 12 Bel 3f fst :35 h

This horse has not run since 30Apr80, more than the 28 days we allow. He is not a stakes horse off his record, and therefore the four recent workouts still leave him with an unknown form rating. In that last race, there was a lead time of :24.3, with one added for energy to wind up with a :24.4 ability time. In the 2Apr80 race, there was a :24.3 lead time also, nothing for gain or loss, but three added for energy to ring up a :25.1 ability time. There is enough good early speed to justify 4 points also, because of the last-race effort.

The third choice, Operable, has been drifting upward in the odds, and when you look at his record you can see why.

Operable Dk. b. or br. c. 3, by Dr Fager—The Hand, by Intentionally
Own.—Tartan Stable Br.—Tartan Farms (Fla) Tr.—Nerud Jan H **111**
St. 1st 2nd 3rd Amt.
1980 2 1 0 0 $10,200
1979 1 M 0 0
24May80- 2Bel fst 1 :45⅘ 1:10⅖ 1:36 3↑Allowance 8 7 75½ 1014 1019 921 Velasquez J 113 5.40 67–17 War of Words 112hd Grand Courant 113½KeyToContent1145 Wide 11
10May80- 5Aqu fst 1 :46 1:10⅖ 1:36⅖ Md Sp Wt 3 1 1hd 11 1½ 12½ Velasquez J 113 6.60 84–13 Operable1132½MomentOfPleasure1135½Irishtocrt1132½ Ridden out 7
3Dec79- 6Aqu fst 6f :22⅗ :46⅗ 1:12⅗ Md Sp Wt 5 7 88¼ 812 812 713 Velasquez J 118 8.90 67–22 VoodooRhythm1184¼KeyToContent118hdCreativePlan1183 Outrun 8
LATEST WORKOUTS Jun 4 Bel tr.t 4f gd :48 h (d) May 5 Bel 4f fst :48⅘ b Apr 30 Bel 5f sly 1:00 h Apr 25 Bel 5f fst 1:02⅕ b

Off the wretched form of the last race, Operable fails to qualify as a contender in this race, and out he goes. Now, to our comparison.

Odds	Horse	Ability		A Pts		ES	F	Total
.8	Key To Content	:24.2	:24.3	18	17	4	Q1	40
2.0	Bold Barbizon	:24.4	:25.1	16	14	4	Q	34
6.8	Operable	—	—	—	—		NQ	NQ

We have a Double Advantage Horse, which we always like. Key To Content's low odds reflect what he should have done. Note how badly Bold Barbizon ran, while Operable, off his poor form, rehabilitated himself with a second-place effort.

THIRD RACE
Belmont
JUNE 7, 1980

1 MILE. (1.33⅘) ALLOWANCE. Purse $20,000. 3-year-olds and upward, Which have never won two races. Weights, 3-year-olds, 114 lbs.; older, 122 lbs. Non-winners of a race other than claiming at a mile or over since May 15 allowed 3 lbs.; of such a race since May 1, 5 lbs.

Value of race $20,000, value to winner $12,000, second $4,400, third $2,400, fourth $1,200. Mutuel pool $276,611, OTB pool $82,848. Exacta Pool $383.856. OTB Exacta Pool $180,539.

Last Raced	Horse	Eqt.	A.	Wt	PP	St	¼	½	¾	Str	Fin	Jockey	Odds $1
24May80 ^{2}Bel^{3}	Key To Content	b	3	113	6	1	1½	1½	1½	1^{2}	1^{2¼}	Fell J	.80
24May80 ^{2}Bel^{9}	Operable		3	114	3	2	2^{1½}	2^{2}	2^{5}	2^{4}	2^{5}	Cordero A Jr	6.80
28May80 ^{1}Bel^{5}	Gummo Cee		3	109	1	5	4^{hd}	4½	3^{1½}	3^{3}	3^{1}	Borden D A	32.90
24May80 ^{2}Bel^{5}	Prince Dandy	b	4	112	2	4	5^{4}	6	5½	4½	4^{2¼}	Beitia E^{5}	17.50
24May80 ^{2}Bel^{4}	Sunny Winters	b	3	112	4	6	6	5^{hd}	4½	5^{6}	5^{10}	Cruguet J	8.20
30Apr80 ^{9}Aqu^{3}	Bold Barbizon	b	3	112	5	3	3^{4}	3^{5}	6	6	6	Velasquez J	2.00

OFF AT 2:16 1/2 EDT. Start good Won ridden out. Time, :23, :45⅘, 1:10⅗, 1:36⅘ Track sloppy.

$2 Mutuel Prices:

7-(H)-KEY TO CONTENT	**3.60**	**2.60**	**2.40**
3-(C)-OPERABLE		**4.20**	**3.00**
1-(A)-GUMMO CEE			**5.00**

Two solid victories in a row uplift us somewhat as we look at a long mile-and-a-quarter race on the grass. Farewell Letter rates as the favorite.

Farewell Letter — **B. f. 3, by Arts And Letters—Tower Of London, by Quadrangle**
Own.—Rokeby Stable — **109** — **Br.—Mellon P (Va)** — **Tr.—Miller Mack**

1980	3	0	2	0	$9,240
1979	7	2	0	1	$19,290
Turf	2	0	1	1	$6,150

26May80-7Bel	1$\frac{1}{16}$ [T]	:47^{4}	1:11^{4}	1:43 fm	3½	105^{5}	2½	2^{hd}	2^{hd}	2^{hd}	Lovato F Jr^{5}	ⒻAlw	89	WlkngInRhythm,FrllLtr,HltGlmr	10
14May80-5Aqu	1	:46^{3}	1:11	1:35^{1}ft	5¾	111^{5}	?1	2½	2^{3}	2^{2¾}	Beitia E^{1}	ⒻAlw	87	Erin'sWord,FrewellLetter,GoingEst	8
2May80-8Aqu	6f	:22^{3}	:45^{4}	1:10^{1}ft	27	111^{5}	9^{5}	8^{6½}	7^{5¾}	6^{8½}	Beitia E^{8}	ⒻAlw	83	PuntaPunt,StrofArby,GlmorousNell	9
5Nov79-8Aqu	1	:46	1:10^{2}	1:36 ft	28	114	9^{4}	7^{8½}	6^{9½}	5^{8}	AsmssnCB^{8}	ⒻTemptd	78	GenuineRisk,StreetBllet,TellASecrt	9
26Oct79-6Aqu	7f	:23^{1}	:46^{4}	1:25^{2}ft	5	120	5^{3}	6^{4}	6^{7}	5^{6¾}	Fell J^{1}	ⒻAlw	67	Dancing Blade, Tash, Tell A Secret	8
5Oct79-5Bel	1$\frac{1}{16}$	:46^{4}	1:11^{2}	1:44^{2}ft	*8-5	115	2^{1}	1½	1^{5}	1^{9½}	Fell J^{3}	ⒻAlw	80	FarewellLetter,Cabinetta,Swirlaway	6
20Sep79-2Bel	1$\frac{1}{16}$ [T]	:47	1:11	1:42^{4}fm	12	113	6^{4}	6^{5¼}	3^{2½}	3^{1} ♦	Fell J^{3}	ⒻAlw	89	ProudBarbar,Cbinett,FrewellLetter	8
♦20Sep79—Dead heat															
7Sep79-1Bel	7f	:23^{1}	:47	1:25^{3}ft	3¾	117	2½	1^{hd}	1^{2}	1^{2¾}	Cruguet J^{2}	ⒻM40000	74	FarewellLetter,SarhBrown,Rionnde	8

Jun 5 Bel 4f ft :47 h **Jun 2 Bel 4f ft :51 b** **May 25 Bel 3f ft :37^{1} b** **May 20 Bel 4f ft :47 h**

This past performance is taken from the West Coast edition of the *Daily Racing Form.*

This filly's last race produced a :24.1 ability time off a lead time of :24.0 with an addition of one for energy. Her other grass race was back on 20Sep79, where there was another :24.0 lead time with a loss of one and an additional add-on of one for energy for a :24.2. This is why Farewell Letter is the favorite. The second choice is Passolyn, who has won her only grass race.

Passolyn ✻ B. f. 3, by Fast Passer—Carolyn's World, by Misty Flight

Br.—Ritzenberg M (Va)

Own.—Ritzenberg M Tr.—Turner William H Jr

109 Turf Record St. 1st 2nd 3rd 1 1 0 0 | St. 1st 2nd 3rd Amt. | 1980 8 2 1 2 $28,465 | 1979 0 M 0 0

22May80- 7Bel gd 1 1/16 :47 4/5 1:12 1:42 2/5 3↑Ⓕ Allowance 4 4 3 2½ 2 3 3 6½ 4 14 Borden D A 113 10.10 76-11 Little Prema 113 11 Distinct Honor 114 2 Higher Justice 108 1 Tired 6

11May80- 1Aqu gd 1 1/16 Ⓣ:48 4/5 1:13 2/5 1:45 3/5 3↑Ⓕ Allowance 4 8 8 9 5 2½ 2 ½ 1 1½ Borden D A 110 9.00 77-19 Passolyn 110 1½ MississippiTalk 113 1 WaywardLssie 109 1¾ Ridden out 10

27Apr80- 9Aqu fst 1 :47 1:12 2/5 1:38 Ⓕ Allowance 1 11 10 3¾ 10 4 9 9 8 13 Borden D A 121 5.30 63-21 Radioactive 116 2 Veiled Prophet 116 4 River Gal 116 2½ Tired 12

11Apr80- 8Aqu fst 1 1/8 :48 1/5 1:12 4/5 1:50 Ⓕ Allowance 1 4 5 2¼ 4 2 2 6 2 8¾ Borden D A 116 3.60 76-20 Erin's Word 116 8¾ Passolyn 116 2 Exclusive Beach 111 8¼ Steadied 8

29Mar80- 4Aqu sly 1 :46 4/5 1:12 3/5 1:40 Ⓕ Md Sp Wt 7 3 2 3 1 ½ 1 3 1 4¾ Borden D A 121 5.20 66-27 Passolyn 121 4¾ Ruthless Lady 121 1¾ SummerTown 121¾ Ridden out 11

11Mar80- 4GP fst 6f :22 2/5 :46 1/5 1:11 4/5 Ⓕ Md Sp Wt 10 7 7 4¼ 3 2 3 4 3 3 Cruguet J 120 6.80 77-24 My Gallant Gypsy 120 2½ SilvertipMtn. 113½ Passolyn 120 3 Bid, hung 12

27Feb80- 6Hia fst 6f :22 3/5 :46 1/5 1:11 Ⓕ Md Sp Wt 4 11 8 8 6 7½ 4 8½ 3 11 Maple E 118 5.30 77-17 Star of Araby 118 9½ Silvertip Mtn. 111 1¼ Passolyn 118 2 In close 12

15Feb80- 4Hia gd 6f :22 1/5 :45 2/5 1:10 4/5 Ⓕ Md 30000 6 9 8 6¾ 3 4½ 4 7 6 8½ Long B5 109 5.30 80-15 Flash McAllister 118 3 Searcy 118 3 CampDavidMiss 114 nk Dwelt start 9

LATEST WORKOUTS Jun 2 Bel tr.t 4f fst :48 3/5 h May 17 Bel tr.t 5f fst 1:01 4/5 b May 10 Bel tr.t 3f fst :37 3/5 b Apr 25 Bel tr.t 4f fst :48 4/5 h

While the last race might not qualify on form, it occurred on the dirt and may not be held against this young filly. Thus, the 11May80 race serves both as a form qualifier and the only race from which we can extract an ability time. There was a :24.3 lead time, from which we can allow a reduction of four for the sizeable gain involved, bringing us down to :23.4. But the :48.4 first call time goes up for Passolyn to a :50.3 when her 9 lengths behind are added, and this restores the four ticks to wind up with :24.3. The third choice in the betting, Mississippi Talk, comes off two excellent turf distance races.

Mississippi Talk B. f. 3, by Mississipian—Chit I Chat, by Round Table

Br.—Schiff J M (Ky)

Own.—Schiff J M Tr.—Kelly Thomas J

109 Turf Record St. 1st 2nd 3rd 2 1 1 0 | St. 1st 2nd 3rd Amt. | 1980 6 2 1 0 $20,300 | 1979 2 M 0 0

27May80- 7Mth fm 1 Ⓣ:48 3/5 1:14 1:39 3/5 3↑Ⓕ Allowance 3 5 5 3½ 2 hd 1 1 1 1¼ MacBeth D 114 *1.30 77-23 Mississippi Talk 114 1¼ Peg'sFantasy 112 8 MyAunt 114 1½ Drew clear 9

11May80- 1Aqu gd 1 1/16 Ⓣ:48 4/5 1:13 2/5 1:45 3/5 3↑Ⓕ Allowance 2 2 1 hd 1 1 1 ½ 2 1½ Fell J 113 5.10 75-19 Passolyn 110 1½ Mississippi Talk 113 1 WaywardLassie 109 1¾ Gamely 10

8Mar80- 9Aqu fst 1 70 ⊡:47 4/5 1:13 2/5 1:43 4/5 Ⓕ Allowance 5 10 8 10 6 5½ 6 8¾ 6 9 Martens G 121 8.90 74-16 TurnDownThHt 116 2¼ Hthr'sTurn 116 2¾ McAllstrMss 116 nk No factor 10

18Feb80- 1Aqu fst 1 1/16 ⊡:47 3/5 1:14 1:47 4/5 Ⓕ Md Sp Wt 8 8 8 10 5 5½ 2 ½ 1 3½ Martens G 121 4.90 75-19 MississippiTalk 121 3½ Astrid'sPride 121 hd SilverGlen 121 5 Ridden out 10

28Jan80- 6Aqu fst 1 1/16 ⊡:48 2/5 1:15 1/5 1:48 4/5 Ⓕ Md Sp Wt 9 4 4 1 4 1 4 6 5 9¾ Martens G 121 8.30e 60-23 Frankincense 121 7¾ Instinctive Ms. 114½ River Gal 121 1½ Wide 9

7Jan80- 4Aqu fst 1 70 ⊡:48 3/5 1:14 1:46 3/5 Ⓕ Md Sp Wt 9 — — — — — Martens G 121 6.10 — — Exclusive Beach 121 nk Frankincense 121 2 RiverGal 116 2¼ Lost rider 10

19Dec79- 4Aqu gd 6f ⊡:23 1/5 :47 1/5 1:11 4/5 Ⓕ Md Sp Wt 3 8 8 5¼ 7 4¼ 9 13 6 10 Martens G 117 18.90 75-19 Delta Bid 117 4½ Madura 117 1½ English Toffy 117 2¾ Outrun 9

1Dec79- 4Aqu fst 6f :22 4/5 :46 4/5 1:13 Ⓕ Md Sp Wt 11 7 8 9¾ 9 9¾ 7 13 6 11 Gonzalez M A5 112 39.40 67-23 Passerine 117 1¾ Kelley's Day 117 2 I'm Swinging 117 1¾ Outrun 11

LATEST WORKOUTS Jun 4 Bel 4f fst :53 b May 2 Bel 7f fst 1:28 h Apr 23 Bel 6f fst 1:15 4/5 hg ●Apr 16 Bel tr.t 6f fst 1:14 2/5 h

While she qualifies on form, her ability times won't measure up with those of the other two. From the 11May80 race, there was a lead time of :24.3 with an add-on of two for energy to a flat :25.0. In the last race at Monmouth, the lead time was :25.2, reduced by three off a gain to :24.4, but with a three added right back on for energy to finish with :25.2. Here is the wrap-up.

Odds	Horse	Ability		A Pts		F	Total
1.8	Farewell Letter	:24.1	:24.2	19	—	Q	19
4.1	Passolyn	:24.3	—	17	—	Q	17
5.3	Mississippi Talk	:25.0	:25.2	15	—	Q	15

Farewell Letter stands out enough to get a Double Advantage rating, as we place a win and place bet with our usual degree of confidence. But after leading in the stretch, she was beaten by a rank outsider and all we can salvage is second-place money.

FOURTH RACE
Belmont
JUNE 7, 1980

1 ¼ MILES.(inner-turf). (1.58⅘) ALLOWANCE. Purse $21,000. Fillies and mares, 3-year-olds and upward, Which have never won two races other than maiden, claiming or starter. Weights, 3-year-olds, 114 lbs.; older, 122 lbs. Non-winners of a race other than maiden or claaming at a mile and a furlong or over since May 15 allowed 3 lbs.; of such a race since May 1, 5 lbs.

Value of race $21,000, value to winner $12,600, second $4,620, third $2,520, fourth $1,260. Mutuel pool $306,156, OTB pool $126,125. Quinella Pool $327,998. OTB Quinella Pool $177,330.

Last Raced	Horse	Eqt.	A.	Wt	PP	¼	½	¾	1	Str	Fin	Jockey	Odds $1
26May80 ^{7}Bel^6	Proud Barbara		3	113	2	11	11	10^2	7^2	$2\frac{1}{2}$	$1\frac{1}{2}$	Maple E	14.70
26May80 ^{7}Bel^2	Farewell Letter	b	3	109	11	4^1	4^1	4^2	$3^{1\frac{1}{2}}$	$1^{1\frac{1}{2}}$	2^3	Encinas R I	1.80
27May80 ^{7}Mth^1	Mississippi Talk		3	109	10	2^1	$2^{1\frac{1}{2}}$	3^1	4^2	$4\frac{1}{2}$	3^{nk}	Shoemaker W	5.30
26May80 ^{7}Bel^7	Lady Hardwick		3	113	8	7^2	8^{hd}	$9\frac{1}{2}$	9^2	7^1	$4\frac{1}{2}$	Vasquez J	19.50
22May80 ^{7}Bel^4	Passolyn		3	109	3	$10^{1\frac{1}{2}}$	10^3	$8^{1\frac{1}{2}}$	$5\frac{1}{2}$	$6^{1\frac{1}{2}}$	$5^{2\frac{1}{2}}$	Borden D A	4.10
26May80 ^{7}Bel^5	Sham on You	b	4	112	9	6^3	5^1	2^1	$2\frac{1}{2}$	$3\frac{1}{2}$	6^1	Gonzalez M A^5	30.20
17May80 ^{7}Aqu^7	Diffluence		4	117	5	$8\frac{1}{2}$	$7\frac{1}{2}$	$7\frac{1}{2}$	6^1	8^5	$7^{1\frac{1}{4}}$	Fell J	17.30
28Apr80 ^{8}Aqu^9	Virginia Reef	b	3	112	1	$1^{1\frac{1}{2}}$	1^2	1^{hd}	$1\frac{1}{2}$	$5\frac{1}{2}$	$8^{1\frac{1}{4}}$	Asmussen C B	43.80
22May80 ^{7}Bel^2	Distinct Honor		4	117	6	$5\frac{1}{2}$	$6^{1\frac{1}{2}}$	11	11	10^4	$9^{2\frac{1}{4}}$	Cruguet J	8.20
26May80 ^{7}Bel^3	Hail to Glamour		4	117	4	$9^{1\frac{1}{2}}$	$9\frac{1}{2}$	$5\frac{1}{2}$	$8\frac{1}{2}$	9^1	10^8	Venezia M	7.40
21May80 ^{7}Bel^1	Karand		3	114	7	3^1	3^{hd}	$6\frac{1}{2}$	10^3	11	11	Hernandez R	19.40

OFF AT 2:56 EDT. Start good, Won driving. Time, :24, :48⅕, 1:13⅘, 1:37⅘, 2:03⅕ Course soft.

$2 Mutuel Prices:				
	3-(B)-PROUD BARBARA	31.40	12.00	5.60
	11-(K)-FAREWELL LETTER		4.20	3.20
	10-(J)-MISSISSIPPI TALK			4.60

$2 QUINELLA 3-11 PAID $49.80.

The fifth race has some remarkable talent on this day filled with able animals. Winter's Tale, from whom we will hear much later in the season, has not yet run in his first stakes race, as he rates the favorite's role here.

5 BELMONT

1 MILE. (1.33⅗) ALLOWANCE. Purse $35,000. 3-year-olds and upward, Which have not won two races of $15,000 in 1979-80. Weights, 3-year-olds, 114 lbs.; older, 122 lbs. Non-winners of two races of $12,000 at a mile or over since March 1 allowed 3 lbs.; of two such races in 1979-80, 5 lbs.; of two races of $15,000 at any distance in 1979-80, 7 lbs. (Maiden, claiming and starter races not considered.)

Winter's Tale — B. g. 4, by Arts And Letters—CHristmas Wind, by Neartic
Own.—Rokeby Stable — Br.—Mellon P (Va) — Tr.—Miller Mack — **115**

	St.	1st	2nd	3rd	Amt.
1980	1	1	0	0	$13,800
1979	4	3	0	0	$25,200

26May80- 9Bel	fst	7f	:22⅘	:46	1:23⅖	3↑ Allowance	3	10	$7^{4\frac{1}{2}}$	$6^{3\frac{1}{2}}$	3^1	$1^{2\frac{1}{2}}$	Fell J	119	3.60	85-20	Winter's Tale119$^{2\frac{1}{2}}$RainPrince112$\frac{1}{2}$DynamicMove114^{hd}	Ridden out	10
3Dec79- 7Aqu	fst	1	:46⅗	1:11⅗	1:37⅖	3↑ Allowance	2	4	$5^{4\frac{3}{4}}$	$7^{5\frac{3}{4}}$	5^7	$5^{8\frac{1}{4}}$	Fell J	115	*.60	70-22	Lark Oscillation117^{3}Pianist115$^{1\frac{3}{4}}$WaveForever117$^{2\frac{1}{2}}$	Lacked room	8
19Nov79- 8Aqu	fst	7f	:23	:45⅘	1:22⅖	3↑ Allowance	1	4	3^5	2^2	2^{hd}	$1^{4\frac{1}{2}}$	Fell J	120	*.80	89-18	Winter's Tale 120$^{4\frac{1}{2}}$RoyalReasoning120^{hd}TermPaper117$^{2\frac{1}{4}}$	Handily	5
8Nov79- 7Aqu	fst	7f	:23	:45⅘	1:23⅘	3↑ Allowance	6	7	5^4	$4^{3\frac{1}{2}}$	$1\frac{1}{2}$	$1^{3\frac{1}{4}}$	Fell J	120	*1.50	82-19	Winter's Tale 120$^{3\frac{1}{4}}$ Contare 115$^{1\frac{1}{4}}$ Mon AmiGus115^{no}	Ridden out	7
26Oct79- 4Aqu	fst	6f	:23	:47⅕	1:12	3↑ Md Sp Wt	8	7	4^4	$3^{1\frac{1}{2}}$	2^{hd}	$1^{2\frac{1}{2}}$	Fell J	119	2.20	83-24	Winter'sTle119$^{2\frac{1}{2}}$LordOfTheSe119$\frac{1}{2}$SpeedyMgrdy119$^{4\frac{1}{2}}$	Ridden out	9

LATEST WORKOUTS Jun 1 Bel 4f fst :49 b — May 23 Bel 5f fst :59 hg — May 17 Bel 6f fst 1:13⅘ h — May 12 Bel 5f fst 1:00⅘ h

Winter's Tale has won four of his five lifetime starts, with only one weak race. In his last race on 26May80, we convert the 7f time to 1:10.3 for 6f to get a lead time of :24.3. Three ticks are subtracted for gain and we have a :24.0 ability time. Back on 19Nov79, in another 7f event, the conversion to a 6f time gives a speedy 1:10.0 for a lead time of :24.1, and that is reduced by a gain of two to :23.4, even better than the other race. Early speed is only medium, and we get 2 points here. But this race is loaded with impressive horses, as we look at Son Of A Dodo, the second choice, who scored a Big Win in his last race.

This one has been running against some of the top three-year-olds in the East, as he ran second in the Bay Shore to Colonel Moran in one of his better races. In the impressive last race, there was a lead time of :24.1, reduced by one

Son Of A Dodo — Ch. g. 3, by Son Ange—Dodo S, by Nagea
Br.—Ridgeley Farm (Ky)
Own.—Carl Suzanne F — Tr.—DiMauro Stephen — **107**

Turf Record	St.	1st	2nd	3rd		St.	1st	2nd	3rd	Amt.
	1	0	1	0	1980	9	2	1	2	$54,265
					1979	7	3	1	1	$38,751

21May80- 5Bel	sly	6f	:22⅘	:46⅕	1:10⅖	3↑Allowance	3	6	54½	21	11½	13½	Cordero A Jr		113	*1.70	90-22	SonOfADodo1133½SpyChrger1171½Intercontinent117¾	Ridden out	7
7May80- 7Aqu	fst	7f	:23⅕	:46	1:23	3↑Allowance	2	4	52½	52¼	2hd	12	Cordero A Jr		112	1.60	86-20	Son Of A Dodo 1122 Restless Run1213¼Zamboni116hd	Ridden out	7
23Apr80- 7Aqu	fst	1	:46⅖	1:11⅖	1:37	Allowance	1	4	45½	68¼	47	35¼	Whitacre G7		108	4.20	76-24	Samoyed 115nk I Speedup 1175 Son Of A Dodo 1081¾	Evenly	6
12Apr80- 5Aqu	fst	1	:45⅕	1:09⅘	1:36⅕	Handicap	5	6	611	65½	31½	61¼	Cruguet J		114	*1.20	84-19	Occasionaly Monday116nkRainPrince118nkDonDaniello118no	Hung	7
5Apr80- 8Aqu	gd	1	:46	1:11⅕	1:37	Gotham	2	1	64	86¼	75½	97¾	Fell J		114	8.70	73-20	ColonelMoran123noDunhm'sGift1142¾Bucksplsher1152¾	Fell back	12
23Mar80- 8Aqu	my	7f	:23⅕	:46⅖	1:23⅘	Bay Shore	5	2	52	42¼	21½	21¼	Cordero A Jr	b	115	8.70	81-25	ColonelMoran1211¼SonOfADodo1151¾Dunhm'sGift1146	Went well	7
10Mar80- 9GP	fst	7f	:22⅗	:45⅖	1:22⅗	Hutcheson	3	2	43	63¾	56	48	Cordero A Jr	b	112	3.80	83-27	Plugged Nickle 1227 Execution's Reason 122½ One Son114½	Tired	6
26Feb80- 9Hia	fst	6f	:22	:45⅖	1:09⅘	Allowance	1	3	44½	43½	43	34¾	Fell J	b	115	7.20	89-22	Gold Stage 1224 Plugged Nickle 122¾ Son Of A Dodo1154	Evenly	7
15Feb80- 7Hia	gd	6f	:22	:44⅘	1:09⅘	Allowance	8	6	32	21	22	42¾	Fell J	b	116	6.50	91-15	Antique Gold 116¾ClassicJoker116nkReefSearcher1181¾	Rid, tired	11
14Oct79- 8Bel	my	1	:46⅗	1:12⅖	1:38⅕	Champagne	7	3	33	52¾	66¾	611	Pincay L Jr	b	122	9.70	66-25	Joanie's Chief 1221¾ Rockhill Native 1222 Googolplex 1224¼	Tired	8

LATEST WORKOUTS May 29 Bel tr.t 4f fst :48 h — May 20 Bel 3f fst :36 b — ●May 14 Bel tr.t 5f gd 1:01⅖ b — May 2 Bel tr.t 4f fst :48⅕ h

off a gain down to a :24.0 ability time. In the previous race at 7f, we convert the time to the 6f figure of 1:10.2 for a :24.2 lead time, reduced by two for gain, and we have another :24.0 figure. Once more, we have an early-speed point total of 2. And now for the third choice, Fool's Prayer, who likewise is formidable.

Fool's Prayer — B. h. 5, by Roberto—Beautiful Morning, by Graustark
Br.—Galbreath J W (Ky)
Own.—Darby Dan Farm — Tr.—Rondinello Thomas L — **116**

Turf Record	St.	1st	2nd	3rd		St.	1st	2nd	3rd	Amt
	25	4	3	1	1980	6	2	0	1	$40,9[illegible]
					1979	11	1	2	0	$14,674

24May80- 5Bel	fst	1⅛	:46⅗	1:10	1:48	3↑Allowance	5	5	52½	44½	21½	12	Rivera M A		117	2.60	87-17	Fool's Prayer 1172 Doc Sylvester 1214¾ Tunerup 1122	Ridden out	7
3May80- 7Aqu	fst	1 5/16	:48⅘	1:37	2:07⅘	Handicap	3	4	37½	31½	33	32½	Rivera M A		117	4.30	103-12	Ring of Light 122¾ Pianist 1161¾ Fool's Prayer 1174¼	Evenly	5
12Apr80- 8Aqu	fst	1¼	:48⅕	1:35⅗	2:01⅖	3↑Excelsior H	3	6	84¾	55½	56	54¼	Rivera M A		115	8.40	85-19	Ring of Light 1141¼ Silent Cal 1222¼ Rivalero 118nk	Evenly	10
22Mar80- 9GP	fst	1¼	:47⅕	1:36⅖	2:01⅖	3↑Gulf Park H	7	6	62½	41¾	3nk	41¾	Rivera M A		113	14.50	87-21	Private Account 119½ Lot O' Gold 1201 Silent Cal 118nk	Hung	7
15Mar80- 8GP	fst	1 1/16	:47⅘	1:11⅘	1:43	Allowance	6	4	42½	42½	3½	11¼	Rivera M A		114	19.00	86-17	Fool's Prayer 1141¼ Roscoe Blake 114noBigBulldozer109½	Driving	10
23Feb80- 9Hia	fm	1 1/16 Ⓣ			1:43	Allowance	10	3	31½	21	66½	77¼	Rivera M A		115	48.20	76-22	Morning Frolic 1223¼ Poverty Boy 115nk Soldier Boy 115½	Tired	11
27Oct79◆2Newbury(Eng)	sf	1½			2:46⅕	Ⓣ St. Simon Stakes(Gr.3)						710	Matthias J		126	25.00	— —	Main Reef 1222 Bonnie Isle 116½ Beggar's Bridge 126nk	Trailed	7
4Oct79◆2Newmarket(Eng)	fm	1½			2:33⅘	Ⓣ Southfield Hcp						616	Matthias J		146	14.00	— —	Goblin 135¾ Falls of Lora 1382½ Len Ashurst 1175	Well pl, tired	7
25Sep79◆4Lingfield(Eng)	fm	1½			2:36⅕	Ⓣ Upham Stakes						1nk	Eddery P		126	10.00	— —	Fool's Prayer 126nk Galaxy Libra115nk Valour14025	Well up drvg	4
19Sep79◆2Ayr(Scot)	gd	1⅜			2:35	Ⓣ Doonside Cup						617	Matthias J	b	119	14.00	— —	TownandCountry1192½ GalaxyLibr1103 MoveOff1196	Prom to str	6

LATEST WORKOUTS Jun 5 Bel 4f fst :47⅗ b — May 31 Bel 4f fst :52 b — May 20 Bel 6f fst 1:17⅖ b — May 15 Bel 4f fst :49⅕ b

This one also scored an impressive victory in his last race. The lead time there was a stunning :23.2, but the loss of two lengths and one tick added for energy winds up with another :24.0 ability time, quite common with these horses. The next effort, however, came at Gulfstream on 15Mar80, where the lead time was :24.0, nothing on or off for gain, but two ticks get added for energy and one more for the GP surface to give us a :24.3 ability time. As with the other two horses, early speed amounts to 2 points. We can now compare this most unusual group of outstanding competitors. Anytime you have three horses all coming off excellent victories, you will see a stirring event.

Odds	Horse	Ability		A Pts		ES	F	Total
1.9	Winter's Tale	:23.4	:24.0	21	20	2	Q	43
2.9	Son Of A Dodo	:24.0	:24.0	20	20	2	Q4	46
3.5	Fool's Prayer	:24.0	:24.3	20	17	2	Q	39

Son Of A Dodo comes up with the high point total because of his Big Win. But Winter's Tale, with only five races, is a Lightly Raced Favorite and is a strong favorite indeed. He can't quite qualify for a Big Win off his last excellent race, and we can't score for improvement because his last run was his first of the season. But off his victory, we cannot put anyone ahead of him, and therefore, we back Son Of A Dodo to place only, fully aware that this is somewhat risky. But once again, we are applying the necessary discipline to stay with these rules, for we are indeed lost without them. The result of the race was astonishing.

FIFTH RACE
Belmont
JUNE 7, 1980

1 MILE. (1.33⅘) ALLOWANCE. Purse $35,000. 3-year-olds and upward, Which have not won two races of $15,000 in 1979–80. Weights, 3-year-olds, 114 lbs.; older, 122 lbs. Non-winners of two races of $12,000 at a mile or over since March 1 allowed 3 lbs.; of two such races in 1979–80, 5 lbs.; of two races of $15,000 at any distance in 1979–80, 7 lbs. (Maiden, claiming and starter races not considered.)

Value of race $35,000, value to winner $21,000, second $7,700, third $4,200, fourth $2,100. Mutuel pool $374,184, OTB pool $131,539. Exacta Pool $

Last Raced	Horse	Eqt.A.Wt	PP	St	¼	½	¾	Str	Fin	Jockey	Odds $1
29May80 8Bel3	Thin Slice	5 115	2	5	1½	1½	1¹	12½	15½	Hernandez R	6.70
26May80 9Bel1	Winter's Tale	4 115	7	4	5½	6⁴	5hd	21½	2²	Fell J	1.90
21May80 5Bel1	Son Of A Dodo	3 112	1	3	7	5½	3hd	3½	3hd	Cordero A Jr	2.90
10May80 7Aqu2	Lark Oscillation	b 5 114	4	6	6hd	4½	4½	4³	4⁴	Beitia E5	3.60
24May80 5Bel1	Fool's Prayer	5 116	3	7	2hd	2hd	2hd	6⁸	5¾	Rivera M A	3.50
22May80 8Bel5	Delta Leader	4 119	5	1	4hd	3½	6⁶	5½	6¹⁰	Castaneda M	38.30
16May80 3Aqu8	Liberty Legend	b 5 115	6	2	3hd	7	7	7	7	Maple E	40.40

OFF AT 3:36 1/2 EDT. Start good, Won ridden out. Time, :23⅗, :46⅖, 1:10⅘, 1:35⅗ Track sloppy.

$2 Mutuel Prices:				
	3–(C)–THIN SLICE	15.40	5.60	4.20
	8–(I)–WINTER'S TALE		3.60	2.80
	1–(A)–SON OF A DODO			3.00

An outsider named Thin Slice destroyed this sparkling field, running away with a 5½-length victory, with Winter's Tale finishing well ahead of Son Of A Dodo. While I won't show you his past performances, Thin Slice had far and away the best point rating, with ability times of :23.0 and :23.4, which would have made him our selection if we were not bound to stay with the first three favorites. Thin Slice deserved to win this race against outstanding competition, but despite his point advantage, I insist on sticking with the rule of investing in the first three betting choices only, no matter how good some other horse looks.

With a double loss in this tough race, we're on to the sixth, where there is another long turf event before us. The odds-on favorite is Current Winner.

The first big issue concerns form. Does Current Winner qualify? He would not make it insofar as gaining lengths is concerned, because we won't count any that are not completed within 6 lengths of the leader. But he did pass seven horses—and that is a lot of horses. Thus, off his gain of five, we must leave him in. For ability, in his last race, there was a good lead time of :24.2, but we add three for energy to get a :25.0. In the prior race, off a :24.1 lead time, we wind up with :24.4, nothing especially outstanding.

6 BELMONT

WIDENER TURF COURSE
1½ MILES
BELMONT PARK
START FINISH

1 ½ MILES. (TURF). (2.24⅘) HANDICAP. Purse $40,000. 3-year-olds. Weights Wednesday, June 4. Declarations by 10:00 A.M., Thursday, June 5.

Current Winner — Ch. c. 3, by Little Current—Simple Beauty, by Vaguely Noble
Own.—Darby Dan Farm
Br.—Galbreath Mrs J W (Ky)
Tr.—Rondinello Thomas L
112

Turf Record	St.	1st	2nd	3rd		St.	1st	2nd	3rd	Amt.
	8	2	3	1	1980	6	1	2	0	$17,355
					1979	9	1	2	2	$26,167

26May80- 4Bel fm 1⅛ Ⓣ:46⅘ 1:10⅘ 1:42	3↑Allowance	10	11	11¹⁶	9¹⁴	67¼	47	Saumell L	b	113	3.00e	79-12	Lunar Ray 1135 Cauhtemoc 1191½ Dressage 114¾	Rallied 12
7May80- 2Aqu fm 1⅛ Ⓣ:49 1:13⅕ 1:44⅘	3↑Allowance	5	6	84	64	2hd	14½	Cordero A Jr	b	115	*2.20	81-15	CurrentWinner1154½TestPttern114hdEsternTown109½	Ridden out 10
17Mar80- 7GP fm *1⅛ Ⓣ 1:45⅗	Allowance	8	9	913	88½	54½	24	Cordero A Jr	b	114	*2.20	74-22	No Bend 1174 Current Winner114noWindChange112¾	Forced wide 10
18Feb80- 8Hia fst 1⅛ :46⅘ 1:11⅗ 1:43⅕	Allowance	10	10	106½	98¾	812	816	Cordero A Jr	b	115	3.50	71-20	Naked Sky 115¾ Mod John 1191 Diogenes 1152½	No factor 10
1Feb80- 2Hia fm *1⅛ Ⓣ 1:43⅘	Allowance	1	5	54½	42½	25	21½	Cordero A Jr	b	115	*1.90	81-21	Acromion 1151½ Current Winner 115¾ Diogenes 115½	Drifted out 10
17Jan80- 8Hia fm 1⅛ Ⓣ 1:42⅗	Allowance	12	8	86¾	66½	67	65½	Cordero A Jr	b	115	*.80	80-14	JustASqure115¾RoylRouge115½Longdistncerunner115½	No excuse 12
19Nov79- 7Aqu sf 1⅛ Ⓣ:50⅘ 1:16 1:48⅕	Allowance	8	4	33½	32½	42	32¾	Cordero A Jr	b	115	*1.70	61-36	PruneDew115nkGrndiloquentGuy1152½CurrentWinner1151	Evenly 8
11Nov79- 8Aqu my 1⅛ :48 1:12⅗ 1:50⅘	Remsen	7	7	816	816	817	817	Cordero A Jr	b	113	11.20	66-24	Plugged Nickle 1224¾ Googolplex 117½ Proctor 1134¾	Outrun 8
29Oct79- 6Aqu yl 1⅛ Ⓣ:47 1:13 1:53	Pilgrim	3	4	37½	33	1½	2hd	Cordero A Jr	b	114	5.00	79-16	Freeo 115hd Current Winner 114¾ French Cut 1174½	Gamely 7

29Oct79-Run in Two Divisions 6th & 8th Races.

14Oct79- 8Bel my 1 :46⅗ 1:12⅘ 1:38⅕	Champagne	3	8	811	78½	78¾	712	Venezia M	b	122	6.50e	65-25	Joanie's Chief 1221¾ Rockhill Native1222Googolplex1224½	Outrun 8

LATEST WORKOUTS Jun 6 Bel 4f fst :51 b Jun 2 Bel 4f fst :52 b May 24 Bel 4f fst :50 b May 14 Bel 4f gd :50⅘ b

The second choice in the wagering is Don Daniello, who has but one grass effort to his credit.

Don Daniello — Ch. c. 3, by Irish Ruler—Atom Princess, by Prince John
Own.—Huntdale Stable
Br.—Natoli D & Dinae & Pascuma (Fla)
Tr.—Pascuma James J Jr
122

Turf Record	St.	1st	2nd	3rd		St.	1st	2nd	3rd	Amt.
	1	0	0	1	1980	10	2	1	6	$68,033
					1979	6	1	0	2	$9,000

25May80- 8Bel fst 1⅛ :45⅘ 1:10⅗ 1:49⅕	Peter Pan	5	9	916	99¾	87¾	57	Fell J	b	117	8.00	74-16	Comptroller 1141½ Bar Dexter 1173 Suzanne'sStar1142½	No factor 9
7May80- 8Aqu fm 1⅛ Ⓣ:48 1:12⅕ 1:43⅖	Hill Prince	6	8	78½	88½	75½	3¾	Fell J	b	117	13.40	87-15	Ben Fab 126¾ Vatza 113no Don Daniello 117nk	Finished wide 8
30Apr80- 8Aqu my 1⅛ :48⅗ 1:12⅗ 1:49⅗	Handicap	1	4	41½	3½	32½	35½	Fell J	b	118	3.80	81-21	Bar Dexter 1123¾ Little Lenny 1151¾ Don Daniello 1184½	Evenly 7
12Apr80- 5Aqu fst 1 :45⅕ 1:09⅘ 1:36⅕	Handicap	4	5	36½	54	63½	3½	Saumell L	b	118	5.40	84-19	OccsionlyMondy116nkRnPrnc118nkDonDnllo118no	Finished strong 7
10Mar80- 7Aqu fst 1⅛ ⊡:48 1:12⅗ 1:52⅘	Handicap	6	7	79	67½	64	3hd	Saumell L	b	119	5.60	82-13	Little Lenny 114no Googolplex122noDonDaniello1192¾	Raced wide 7
27Feb80- 8Aqu fst 1⅛ ⊡:47 1:11⅘ 1:45⅕	Whirlaway	5	6	57	42	1hd	1½	Saumell L	b	117	9.70	88-17	DonDniello117½Googolplex1214¾Bucksplsher117½	Long hard drive 6
9Feb80- 8Aqu fst 1⅛ ⊡:49 1:13 1:52	Lucky Draw	3	5	511	511	411	39¾	Saumell L	b	117	11.70	76-19	Degenerate Jon 1231½ Googolplex 1218½ DonDaniello1171½	Rallied 5
27Jan80- 5Aqu fst 170 ⊡:48⅕ 1:13⅕ 1:43	Allowance	2	6	76½	74½	2½	15	Saumell L	b	117	5.70	87-17	DonDaniello1175SelfPressured1171¾Bucksplsher1191¾	Drew clear 8
16Jan80- 3Aqu fst 1⅛ ⊡:48⅕ 1:13⅗ 1:52⅕	Allowance	1	3	33	3nk	22	24½	Saumell L	b	117	7.30	81-18	Little Lenny 1174½ Don Daniello 1174 Sir Kay 122no	Second best 7
7Jan80- 6Aqu fst 170 ⊡:48 1:13⅕ 1:43⅗	Allowance	8	8	811	42½	33½	36½	Saumell L	b	117	38.00	78-22	Sagacious 1173½ Bucksplasher 1223 Don Daniello117hd	Held show 8

LATEST WORKOUTS ●May 20 Aqu 7f fst 1:30 b May 15 Aqu 4f fst :48 h Apr 29 Aqu 3f sly :36 b (d) Apr 24 Aqu 6f fst 1:17⅗ b

His last dirt race in the Peter Pan would not qualify him, but it is the grass race we are concerned about, where his form qualifies easily off his gain. In that race, there was a :24.1 lead time with no gain or loss, but a hefty three ticks for energy brings us up to :24.4.

The third choice in the betting is a filly out of Secretariat, who has a most impressive turf record, having won four times in eight starts, with only one

Esdiev — Dk. b. or br. f. 3, by Secretariat—Day Line, by Day Court
Own.—Snyder H I
Br.—Gaines & Johnson (Ky)
Tr.—DiMauro Stephen
114

Turf Record	St.	1st	2nd	3rd		St.	1st	2nd	3rd	Amt.
	8	4	1	2	1980	5	3	0	2	$31,560
					1979	10	1	1	1	$22,576

19May80- 5Aqu gd 1⅛ Ⓣ:49 1:14 1:52	3↑ⒻAllowance	1	4	43½	31	32	1hd	Cordero A Jr	113	*1.50	84-14	Esdiev 113hd Endicotta 1192 Double Dial 1132½	Driving 8
4Apr80- 9GP fm *1⅛ Ⓣ 1:45⅕	ⒻAllowance	5	7	66	35½	21	1hd	Cruguet J	122	*1.50	80-22	Esdiev 122hd Pepi Wiley 1224½ Snuggle Bunny 12211	Driving 7
25Mar80- 8GP fm *1⅛ Ⓣ 1:45⅗	ⒻAllowance	9	9	710	53	32½	1no	Cruguet J	114	*1.20	78-24	Esdiev 114no Veiled Prophet 1186 Ignite 1223	Driving 10
6Feb80- 5Hia fm *1⅛ Ⓣ 1:43⅗	ⒻAllowance	8	7	87½	75½	45	32¾	Fell J	114	*1.10	80-16	Critic's Wink 114nk Champagne Ginny 1142½ Esdiev 1142	Rallied 9
29Jan80- 8Hia fm *1⅛ Ⓣ 1:50	ⒻAllowance	4	7	75	54½	52¾	32½	Fell J	114	*1.20	80-12	Arisen 1141½ Erin's Word 1181 Esdiev 1143½	Rallied 9
17Nov79- 8Aqu fst 1⅛ :48⅕ 1:13⅕ 1:51⅕	ⒻDemoiselle	5	7	63½	51½	68¾	511	Maple E	113	41.50	68-21	Genuine Risk 116no Smart Angle 1216¾ Spruce Pine 1123¾	Tired 7
29Oct79- 8Aqu yl 1⅛ Ⓣ:49 1:14⅗ 1:52⅗	Pilgrim	8	4	44½	43½	42	41¾	Asmussen C B	112	6.00	80-16	I Take All 115½ Prune Dew 1141½ Dressage 119no	Evenly 10

29Oct79-Run in Two Divisions 6th & 8th Races.

7Oct79- 8Bel fst 1 :47 1:12⅗ 1:38⅕	ⒻFrizette	6	11	11¹⁵	11¹⁴	915	722	Hernandez R	119	51.60	55-20	Smart Angle 1191¾ Royal Suite 11911 Hardship 1195	Broke slowly 11
17Sep79- 8Bel fm 7f Ⓣ:23 :46⅕ 1:24	Cascade	2	7	85½	64½	32	23	Asmussen C B	110	7.00	81-09	War of Words 1133 Esdiev 1102½ Bing 113¾	2nd best 10

17Sep79-Run in Two Divisions 6th & 8th Races.

7Sep79- 8Bel st 1⅛ :47⅘ 1:13 1:46⅕	ⒻAllowance	3	6	56½	54½	44	47½	Saumell L	113	3.40	64-20	LadyHardwick1181½Popchee1133½DeterminedBest1182¾	No factor 6

LATEST WORKOUTS Jun 1 Bel 4f fst :48⅘ b May 26 Bel 4f fst :49 b May 14 Bel tr.t 5f gd 1:03 b May 7 Bel tr.t 4f fst :49⅗ b

finish out of the money. She is in tough today, with no showing that she has ever defeated colts.

Esdiev, off three successive victories, qualifies on form. Because of the series of Florida races, we are having difficulty in finding ability times, but the last race at Aqueduct is good enough. The lead time is :25.0, reduced by two for gain but increased by three ticks on energy to wind up with a :25.1. Back on 17Sep79 at Belmont, in a 7f sprint on the grass, we convert final time to a 6f equivalent of 1:11.0 and get a :24.4 lead time. The gain of one is offset by an energy adjustment of one and we finish with an ability time of :24.4. Here is how they add up.

Odds	Horse	Ability		A Pts		F	Total
.8	Current Winner	:24.4	:25.0	16	(15)	Q	16
3.0	Don Daniello	:24.4	—	16		Q	16
6.3	Esdiev	:24.4	:25.1	16	(14)	Q	16

The whole town is tied. Relying on one race for comparison, we have a triple heat in points, and without extending it too much farther, we go to Current Winner to place only because of the odds. I didn't even worry about the inquiry sign when it went up, because I had a sure collectable ticket no matter what was decided as the official winner. Since my place ticket was good either way, and the price didn't change, it was all academic for our bottom line. I could only sympathize for the poor punters who had Don Daniello on top, since on many a day I have suffered the same fate, having my winner dropped back to second on a foul claim. Someday maybe I'll get even on that score myself.

SIXTH RACE
Belmont
JUNE 7, 1980

1 ½ MILES.(turf). (2.24⅘) HANDICAP. Purse $40,000. 3-year-olds. Weigh's, Wednesday, June 4. Declarations by 10:00 A.M. Thursday, June 5. Closed Wednesda

Value of race $40,000, value to winner $24,000, second $8,800, third $4,800, fourth $2,400. Mutuel pool $449,415, OTB pool $122,490. Quinella Pool $361,275. OTB Quinella Pool $156,765.

Last Raced	Horse	Eqt.	A.Wt	PP	¼	½	1	1¼	Str	Fin	Jockey	Odds $1
25May80 ^{8}Bel^5	[D]Don Daniello		3 122	5	4^4	$4\frac{1}{2}$	$1\frac{1}{2}$	$1\frac{1}{2}$	$1\frac{1}{2}$	1no	Pincay L Jr	3.00
26May80 ^{4}Bel^4	Current Winner	b	3 113	8	$8^{1\frac{1}{2}}$	$8^{1\frac{1}{2}}$	$2\frac{1}{2}$	2^1	2^5	2^7	Cordero A Jr	a-.80
28May80 ^{6}Bel^1	Good Bid		3 110	1	7^4	7^2	$5\frac{1}{2}$	$3\frac{1}{2}$	3^2	3^5	Samyn J L	7.80
26May80 ^{4}Bel^1	Lunar Ray		3 117	4	6^1	6^{hd}	7^6	$5\frac{1}{2}$	4^2	$4^{2\frac{3}{4}}$	Rivera M A	a-.80
19May80 ^{5}Aqu^1	Esdiev		3 114	9	9	9	$6^{1\frac{1}{2}}$	6^5	$5\frac{1}{2}$	$5^{2\frac{1}{2}}$	Cruguet J	6.30
26May80 ^{4}Bel^5	Sulcus	b	3 113	3	3^3	$3^{1\frac{1}{2}}$	$4\frac{1}{2}$	4^1	6^{14}	6^{18}	Fell J	26.90
18May80 ^{4}Aqu^1	King's Wish	b	3 112	7	$2^{1\frac{1}{2}}$	2^5	$3^{1\frac{1}{2}}$	7^8	7^{12}	7^{10}	Asmussen C B	28.00
26May80 ^{8}Key^7	Little Lenny		3 116	2	$5\frac{1}{2}$	5^1	9	8^6	8^{12}	8^{15}	Velasquez J	12.80
29May80 ^{7}Bel^2	Reactant	b	3 111	6	1^{hd}	1^{hd}	8^1	9	9	9	Moreno H E	34.20

[D]–Don Daniello Disqualified and placed second.
a–Coupled: Current Winner and Lunar Ray.
OFF AT 4:16 1/2, EDT. Start good, Won driving. Time, :23⅘, :48⅖, 1:15, 1:41⅕, 2:07⅗, 2:32⅖, Course soft.

$2 Mutuel Prices:				
	1–(I)–CURRENT WINNER (a–entry)	3.60	2.40	2.20
	6–(F)–DON DANIELLO		3.40	2.60
	3–(B)–GOOD BID			3.40

Things are getting a little sticky by now as we look at the seventh race, where once again we have an outstanding field of good older stakes horses running for a purse of $40,000 in an allowance race that is far superior to many stakes at most other tracks. Dewan Keys is the strong favorite.

7 **BELMONT**

1¼ MILES. (2.00) ALLOWANCE. Purse $40,000. 3–year–olds and upward, Which have not won two races of $15,000 at a mile and a furlong or over in 1979–80. Weights, 3–year–olds, 114 lbs.; older, 122 lbs. Non–winners of two races of $15,000 at a mile or over since April 5 allowed 3 lbs.; of two such races since January 1, 5 lbs.; of such a race in 1979–80, 7 lbs. (Maiden, claiming and starter races not considered.)

Dewan Keys — Ch. h. 5, by Dewan—Eleven Keys, by Royal Union
Own.—Morrissey J O Jr — Br.—Keyes F (Fla) — Tr.—Johnson Philip G
117 — Turf Record: St. 2, 1st 0, 2nd 0, 3rd 1

	St.	1st	2nd	3rd	Amt.
1980	3	1	0	0	$21,000
1979	13	3	6	2	$136,816

22May80-	8Bel	gd	1 1/16	:46⅖	1:11	1:42	3↑ Allowance	3	4	3^4	2^4	2^2	1^{hd}	Skinner K	121	1.60	92-11	Dewan Keys 121^{hd} Lucy's Axe $119^{5\frac12}$DamascusSilver$121^{7\frac12}$	Driving	7
3May80-	8Aqu	fst	7f	:22⅘	:45⅕	1:21	3↑ Carter H	4	6	6^5	6^6	$6^{8\frac34}$	$6^{8\frac12}$	Castaneda M	113	25.70	87-12	Czaravich 126^{nk} Tanthem 122^{hd} Nice Catch 120^{nk}	Trailed	6
20Apr80-	7Aqu	fst	6f	:21⅘	:44⅕	1:09⅘	3↑ Bold Ruler	5	5	6^{14}	6^{17}	6^{12}	$6^{8\frac34}$	Asmussen C B	119	15.50	85-16	Dave's Friend $123^{2\frac34}$ Tilt Up $121^{1\frac12}$ Double Zeus $121^{\frac34}$	Outrun	6
22Nov79-	8Aqu	fst	1 3/16	:48⅕	1:12⅖	1:56⅘	3↑ Queens Cty H	4	3	3^2	$3^{\frac12}$	2^{hd}	$1^{\frac12}$	Maple E	112	3.90	78-20	Dewan Keys $112^{\frac12}$ Mr. International108^{no}GallantBest116^{no}	Driving	8
15Nov79-	6Med	fst	1⅛	:47	1:11⅘	1:51⅕	3↑ J'ky Holow H	2	5	$5^{4\frac14}$	$6^{1\frac34}$	$3^{\frac12}$	2no	Maple E	114	13.10	77-25	Silent Cal 118no Dewan Keys $114^{1\frac14}$ Smarten $122^{8\frac12}$	Jostled	7
3Nov79-	8Aqu	sly	1⅛	:47⅘	1:12⅖	1:50⅖	3↑ Stuyvesant H	1	4	$3^{1\frac12}$	$3^{\frac12}$	1^{hd}	3^{hd}	Maple E	112	5.50	83-23	Music of Time 114no What A Gent 111^{hd}DewanKeys112^2	In close	6
27Oct79-	7Aqu	fst	1	:45⅘	1:10⅘	1:36	3↑ Allowance	3	4	4^8	4^6	3^7	$2^{6\frac12}$	Shoemaker W	115	5.00	79-22	Dr. Patches $115^{6\frac12}$ Dewan Keys 115^{hd} TimtheTiger114^2	Up for 2nd	6
13Oct79-	7Bel	sly	7f	:23⅖	:47⅕	1:24⅗	3↑ Allowance	3	4	4^4	$4^{3\frac12}$	2^{hd}	2^{nk}	Maple S	119	3.80	79-27	GallantBest119^{nk}DewanKeys$119^{1\frac12}$ChopChopTomhwk117^7	Gamely	5
1Oct79-	7Bel	sly	1	:46⅘	1:11	1:36⅕	3↑ Allowance	1	1	2^{hd}	$2^{\frac12}$	2^{hd}	2^2	Maple S	115	2.10	85-25	Trimlea 115^2 Dewan Keys 115^9 Prefontaine [illegible]	Second best	5
11Sep79-	6Med	fst	6f	:22⅕	:45	1:10⅕	3↑ Jrsy Blues H	4	8	8^{12}	$7^{7\frac14}$	6^9	$5^{5\frac14}$	Maple E	121	4.70	89-15	King'sFshion118^3Whtsyourplesure122^{nk}Fn[illegible]Fox115^{no}	Late foot	8

LATEST WORKOUTS Jun 5 Bel tr.t 4f fst :48⅕ h May 30 Bel [illegible] 4f fst :49⅕ b ● May 16 Bel tr.t 6f fst 1:13⅗ h ● May 11 Bel [illegible] 3f fst :35⅕ h

This versatile animal has been traveling in some impressive company. He ran on 3May80 in the prestigious Carter Handicap at seven furlongs, trailing some speed burners like Czaravich and Tanthem, but still picking up a :24.0 ability time. The 1:21.0 final time for the Carter is off our conversion chart, but extending comparable times up the scale leads us to a 6f time of 1:08.4, which is championship form in New York. This provides a :23.3 lead time with the loss of lengths bringing it up to :24.1 for ability. From the 13Oct79 Belmont race, we convert the 7f time again to get a 6f figure of 1:11.3. This provides a lead time of :24.2 with a gain of three down to :23.4, which is increased by one to :24.0 by the energy adjustment.

The second choice is Lucy's Axe, trained by Joe Cantey, who is soon to have his day fulfilled in the Belmont Stakes.

Lucy's Axe qualifies on form off the last race. His best ability time was back on 27May79 where the unadjusted lead time was :24.1. On 16May80, there was

Lucy's Axe * — B. c. 4, by The Axe II—Lucy Grey, by Turn-To
Own.—Close Lucy H — Br.—Hackman W M (Md) — Tr.—Cantey Joseph B
117 — Turf Record: St. 4, 1st 1, 2nd 1, 3rd 1

	St.	1st	2nd	3rd	Amt.
1980	2	0	1	0	$9,620
1979	11	3	3	2	$119,101

22May80-	8Bel	gd	1 1/16	:46⅖	1:11	1:42	3↑ Allowance	5	2	1^1	1^4	1^2	2^{hd}	Martens G	b 119	*1.50	92-11	Dewan Keys 121^{hd} Lucy's Axe $119^{5\frac12}$ Damascus Silver$121^{7\frac12}$	Failed	7
16May80-	8Aqu	fst	6f	:22⅖	:44⅗	1:09⅖	Allowance	3	4	$6^{4\frac14}$	$5^{6\frac12}$	5^6	$4^{4\frac14}$	Maple E	b 119	15.60	92-16	King'sFashion$119^{1\frac34}$PrinceAndrew119^{no}Dr.Patches$119^{2\frac12}$	No factor	6
22Jly79-	9Del	fm	1⅛	Ⓣ:48⅖	1:12⅗	1:50⅘	L Richards	3	1	$1^{2\frac12}$	$1^{2\frac12}$	$1^{2\frac12}$	1^1	Gilbert R B	b 126	2.40	— —	Lucy's Axe 126^1 Buck's Chief 114^5 Idle Jack 113no	Ridden out	8
14Jly79-	8Atl	hd	1⅛	Ⓣ:48⅖	1:11⅘	1:48⅖	Leon Levy H	4	3	5^2	$3^{3\frac12}$	$3^{2\frac12}$	3^3	Maple E	b 118	*1.10	91-09	Flying Dad 113^3 Commadore C. 114^{no}Lucy'sAxe118^{nk}	Wide, hung	7
30Jun79-	8Mth	gd	1 1/16	Ⓣ:48⅕	1:13⅖	1:47	Lampli'ter H	4	10	10^{11}	$10^{7\frac14}$	$6^{3\frac14}$	2^{nk}	Maple E	b 121	6.40	66-31	QuietCrossing121^{nk}Lucy'sAxe121^{no}GretNck112^3	Taken up sharply	12
24Jun79-	8Bel	fm	1	Ⓣ:44⅖	1:08⅗	1:34⅖	Saranac	5	5	$7^{8\frac12}$	10^{11}	$8^{8\frac14}$	$8^{7\frac34}$	Perret C	123	4.70	90-08	Told $114^{1\frac34}$ Crown Thy Good $114^{\frac12}$ Quiet Crossing $123^{1\frac14}$	Dull try	10
2Jun79-	8Pim	sly	1 1/16	:47⅗	1:12⅖	1:45⅖	Annapolis H	2	2	$2^{2\frac12}$	$2^{1\frac12}$	2^1	1^{hd}	Gilbert R B	120	*.70	78-21	Lucy's Axe 120^{hd} Buck's Chief $113^{4\frac12}$ Ply The Sea 107^7	Driving	4
27May79-	8Bel	fst	1⅛	:46⅕	1:10⅖	1:47	Peter Pan	3	1	$1^{\frac12}$	2^{hd}	2^6	2^{13}	Maple E	123	7.20	79-20	Coastal 120^{13} Lucy's Axe $123^{1\frac14}$ Pianist $117^{4\frac14}$	No match	6
12May79-	8Aqu	fst	1	:46	1:11	1:35⅗	Withers	7	8	8^8	7^7	6^{12}	6^{15}	Maple E	126	14.50	73-13	Czaravich $126^{\frac34}$InstrumentLanding$126^{1\frac14}$StrikeTheMain$126^{3\frac14}$	Wide	9
14Apr79-	9OP	fst	1⅛	:47⅗	1:11⅗	1:50	Ark Derby	10	5	$4^{3\frac12}$	$4^{3\frac12}$	5^5	$5^{8\frac12}$	Maple E	123	3.70	84-23	Golden Act 126^{nk} Smarten 120^6 Strike The Main 115^{nk}	No threat	10

LATEST WORKOUTS Jun 6 Bel 3f fst :36⅕ b ● Jun 1 Bel 6f fst 1:12⅗ h ● May 13 Bel 6f sly 1:13 h ● May 9 Bel 5f sly 1:00⅘ h (d)

a :24.4 lead time, less two for gain, for a :24.2 ability figure. This, too, is a good horse. And the third choice, Ivory Hunter, is a stalwart on the grass, which may not count today.

Ivory Hunter B. h. 6, by Sir Ivor—Style, by Traffic Judge
Br.—Webster R N (Ky)
Own.—Webster R N Tr.—Laurin Roger 117

	St.	1st	2nd	3rd	Amt.
Turf Record	31	4	4	7	
1980	9	1	1	2	$47,878
1979	10	0	2	3	$29,398

25May80- 5Bel fm 1½ Ⓣ:48⅖ 2:02⅘ 2:27⅕ 3↑Handicap 2 4 46½ 3½ 11½ 14¾ Cordero A Jr b 114 3.10Ⓓ 88-15 ⒹIvory Hunter 1144¾ Xmas Box 111hd No Neck 112no Bore in 8
25May80-Disqualified and placed fourth
10May80- 9Pim gd 1½ Ⓣ:49⅕ 2:05 2:29⅗ 3↑Dixie H 5 12 1214 104½ 76¾ 55¾ Venezia M b 115 36.60 83-11 MarqueeUniversl1184¾TheVeryOne1131MtchTheHtch115no Outrun 14
19Apr80- 7Aqu fst 1⅜ :48⅗ 1:38⅕ 2:18 Allowance 4 5 610 65 11½ 12 Cordero A Jr b 115 5.10 91-17 Ivory Hunter 1152 Rabmab 1154¾ Sunny Puddles 1062¾ Driving 6
12Apr80- 9GP fm 1½ Ⓣ:46⅖ 2:02⅗ 2:28⅖ 3↑Pan Amer. H 1 12 1217 1216 810 55¾ Guerra W A b 112 22.00 76-25 Flitalong 1101 Morning Frolic 1191½ Novel Notion 117nk Rallied 12
29Mar80- 7GP fm 1½ Ⓣ:47 2:00 2:25⅕ Allowance 2 7 717 67½ 35 33½ Brumfield D b 115 6.40 94-06 Novel Notion 1223½ Young Bob 114no Ivory Hunter 1152½ Rallied 8
23Feb80-10Hia fm 1½ Ⓣ 2:29⅖ 3↑Turf Cup H 7 7 913 52½ 44½ 35½ Maple E b 111 142.50 78-22 John Henry 122½ Dancing Master 1135 Ivory Hunter 111hd Rallied 10
9Feb80- 9Hia fm 1⅛ Ⓣ 1:47 Allowance 5 9 922 916 913 78 Maple E 115 31.80 91-12 MorningFrolic1224HeDzzlesToo1151OnceOverLightly115nk Outrun 9
25Jan80- 9Hia fm *1$\frac{1}{16}$ Ⓣ 1:40⅗ Allowance 9 9 76 75¾ 45½ 47 Maple E 115 14.10 91-06 Dargelo 1151½ Imitating 115½ Bananas Foster 1155 Mild bid 9
14Jan80- 7Crc fm *1⅛ Ⓣ 1:48 Allowance 4 7 715 713 57½ 24½ Maple E 114 5.70 78-23 Three Grandson's 1174½ Ivory Hunter 1142½ Dargelo 117hd Rallied 7
31Dec79- 9Crc fm *1⅛ Ⓣ 1:51⅕ 3↑Allowance 6 6 610 77½ 56½ 55¼ Solomone M 114 7.10 62-33 Ice Cool 1143 Friendly Sword 113¾ Dargelo 112hd No threat 6
LATEST WORKOUTS May 21 Bel 3f sly :35⅗ b May 8 Bel 3f sly :36⅘ b ●May 3 Bel tr.t 4f fst :47⅘ h Apr 8 Hia 4f my :50 b

While Ivory Hunter scored a Big Win in his last grass race, all we can allow for this effort is a qualification on form, since we do not rate ability times and other serious factors out of turf events when today's race is on the dirt. We have but one dirt race from which to obtain a rating, the 19Apr80 event at a difficult distance. All we can do is to obtain a reading between 4f and a mile to obtain a four-furlong time of :49.3. We allow three ticks off for gain to bring it down to :49.0. The division in half, with the lesser portion for credit, leaves us with a :24.2 as the only ability rating on the dirt.

Here is the comparative rating.

Odds	Horse	Ability		A Pts		F	Total
1.2	Dewan Keys	:24.0	:24.1	20	19	Q	39
2.8	Lucy's Axe	:24.1	:24.2	19	18	Q	37
4.1	Ivory Hunter	:24.2	—	18	(18)	Q	36

SEVENTH RACE
Belmont
JUNE 7, 1980

1 ¼ MILES. (2.00) ALLOWANCE. Purse $40,000. 3-year-olds and upward, Which have not won two races of $15,000 at a mile and a furlong or over in 1979–80. Weights, 3-year-olds, 114 lbs.; older, 122 lbs. Non-winners of two races of $15,000 at a mile or over since April 5 allowed 3 lbs.; of two such races since January 1, 5 lbs.; of such a race in 1979–80, 7 lbs. (Maiden, claiming and starter races not considered.)

Value of race $40,000, value to winner $24,000, second $8,800, third $4,800, fourth $2,400. Mutuel pool $237,645, OTB pool $103,389. Exacta Pool $244,276. OTB Exacta Pool $168,661.

Last Raced	Horse	Eqt.	A.	Wt	PP	¼	½	¾	1	Str	Fin	Jockey	Odds $1
22May80 8Bel1	Dewan Keys		5	117	2	2	24	24	22	11	14	Skinner K	1.20
22May80 8Bel2	Lucy's Axe	b	4	117	5	1hd	12	12	1½	22	2½	Maple E	2.80
28May80 3Bel4	Knight's Tale	b	6	117	1	4½	4hd	4hd	4½	41	3nk	Pincay L Jr	14.90
25May80 5Bel4	Ivory Hunter	b	6	117	6	31½	35	34	31½	52	4hd	Cordero A Jr	4.10
24May80 9Pim2	T. V. Hill		5	117	4	6	6	6	51	3hd	5¾	Hinojosa H	4.20
2May80 6CD4	Rabmab	b	5	117	3	55	54	53	6	6	6	Velasquez J	15.90

OFF AT 4:55, EDT Start good, Won ridden out. Time, :24⅗, :48⅕, 1:12⅘, 1:38, 2:02⅗ Track muddy.

$2 Mutuel Prices:			
2–(B)–DEWAN KEYS	4.40	2.60	2.40
6–(F)–LUCY'S AXE		3.00	2.60
1–(A)–KNIGHT'S TALE			4.20

While these horses are closely bunched in their rating, Dewan Keys has the necessary 2-point advantage for a win and place bet. It wasn't even too difficult, as he ran away from second-place Lucy's Axe in the stretch to post a Big Win, even though the payoff was low. But we're back on the winning level at last.

Now, we come to what we've been waiting for all week, the Belmont Stakes, the last of the three big Triple Crown races for three-year-olds. By this time, I am a little week-weary, but still excited over what promises to be a thriller. Can Genuine Risk, the filly who has become America's favorite at this point, come back after her controversial defeat by Codex in the Preakness? Will Codex be able to handle the Belmont mud today? The track has become increasingly muddier as the day has progressed.

At this point, my handicapper's instinct had taken hold, which made me resolve to pass the race. During the week I had been asked several times by friends for my choice in the Belmont. "I don't know," was my constant answer, followed by the advice, "Don't bet this race; it's too tough." And I did not make any wager on the Belmont in 1980. I am sure every reader will indulge me in my "handicapper's instinct," but I will count this race nevertheless in my compilation for the day. There is no allowance in this book for "handicapper's instinct," since the methods here are meant to work day in and day out by steady application of the rules that you have read thus far. There have been several races in the past chapters where my handicapper's instinct went against my point ratings, but if handicapping instinct controlled us, then we could forget all the investment advice in this work. We stick by our rules, and here is what we have.

8 BELMONT

1½ MILES. (2.24) 112th Running THE BELMONT (Grade I). $200,000 Added. 3-year-olds. By subscription of $100 each to accompany the nomination; $1,000 to pass the entry box; $2,000 to start. A supplementary nomination of $5,000 may be made on Wednesday, June 4 with an additional $15,000 to start, with $200,000 added of which 60% to the winner, 22% to second, 12% to third and 6% to fourth. Colts and geldings 126 lbs.; Fillies 121 lbs. Starters to be named at the closing time of entries. The winning owner will be presented with the August Belmont Memorial Cup to be retained for one year, as well as a trophy for permanent possession and trophies will be presented to the winning trainer and jockey and mementoes to the grooms of the first four finishers. Closed Friday, February 15, 1980 with 247 nominations. Supplementary nominees Pikotazo and Temperence Hill.

Genuine Risk — **Ch. f. 3, by Exclusive Native—Virtuous, by Gallant Man**
Own.—Firestone Mrs B R — **Br.—Humphrey Mrs G W Jr (Ky)** — **Tr.—Jolley Leroy**

121

	St.	1st	2nd	3rd	Amt.
1980	5	3	1	1	$339,210
1979	4	4	0	0	$100,245

17May80- 9Pim	fst	1 3/16	:47⅘	1:11⅕	1:54⅕	Preakness	5	6	4^{4}	$4^{3¼}$	2^{1}	$2^{4¾}$	Vasquez J	121	*2.00	94-12	Codex $126^{4¾}$ Genuine Risk $121^{3¼}$ColonelMoran126^{7}	Bothered turn	8
3May80- 8CD	fst	1¼	:48	1:37⅗	2:02	Ky Derby	10	7	$7^{4¼}$	$1^{1½}$	1^{2}	1^{1}	Vasquez J	121	13.30	87-11	Genuine Risk 121^{1} Rumbo 126^{1} Jaklin Klugman 126^{4}	Driving	13
19Apr80- 8Aqu	fst	1⅛	:47⅖	1:11⅗	1:50⅘	Wood Mem'l	3	3	3^{2}	$3^{1½}$	3^{2}	$3^{1½}$	Vasquez J	121	8.20	79-17	PluggedNickle$126^{1½}$ColonelMorn126^{hd}GenuinRisk$121^{3¾}$	Game try	11
5Apr80- 7Aqu	gd	1	:46⅘	1:12	1:38⅗	ⒻHandicap	4	4	3^{2}	$1^{1½}$	1^{1}	$1^{2¼}$	Vasquez J	124	*.20	73-20	Genuine Risk $124^{2¼}$ TellASecret$115^{3¼}$SprucePine113^{11}	Ridden out	4
19Mar80- 7GP	fst	7f	:22	:44⅘	1:22⅗	ⒻAllowance	3	5	4^{4}	$3^{2½}$	$1^{½}$	$1^{2½}$	Vasquez J	113	*.40	91-20	Genuine Risk $113^{2½}$ Sober Jig $112^{3½}$ Peace Bells$115^{1½}$	Ridden out	6
17Nov79- 8Aqu	fst	1⅛	:48⅕	1:13⅕	1:51⅕	ⒻDemoiselle	6	4	$3^{½}$	2^{hd}	2^{hd}	1no	Pincay L Jr	116	1.20	79-21	Genuine Risk 116no Smart Angle $121^{6¾}$ Spruce Pine $112^{3¾}$	Driving	7
5Nov79- 8Aqu	fst	1	:46	1:10⅖	1:36	ⒻTempted	4	5	$5^{1¼}$	$1^{1½}$	1^{2}	1^{3}	Vasquez J	114	*.90	86-18	Genuine Risk 114^{3} Street Ballet$117^{½}$TellASecret$114^{4½}$	Ridden out	9
18Oct79- 6Aqu	fst	1	:47	1:11⅘	1:36⅖	ⒻAllowance	6	2	2^{1}	2^{hd}	1^{2}	$1^{7¼}$	Vasquez J	115	*.60	84-18	Genuine Risk $115^{7¼}$ Going East 117^{5} Cinto Tora $115^{4½}$	Ridden out	6
30Sep79- 4Bel	sly	6½f	:22⅗	:45⅖	1:18	ⒻMd Sp Wt	8	11	4^{5}	$4^{6½}$	2^{3}	$1^{1¾}$	Vasquez J	118	*3.10	86-24	Genuine Risk $118^{1¾}$ Remote Ruler 118^{13} Espadrille $118^{1¾}$	Driving	11

LATEST WORKOUTS **Jun 4 Bel 5f fst 1:00⅘ h** **May 28 Bel 6f fst 1:14⅖ b** **●May 14 Pim 5f fst :59 h** **●Apr 30 CD 5f sl 1:02⅖ b**

Codex — Ch. c. 3, by Arts and Letters—Roundup Rose, by Minnesota Mac
Br.—Tartan Farms (Fla)
Own.—Tartan Stable — Tr.—Lukas D Wayne — **126**

	St.	1st	2nd	3rd	Amt.
1980	7	4	0	1	$509,000
1979	7	2	2	0	$25,576

17May80- 9Pim fst 1 3/16 :47⅘ 1:11⅕ 1:54⅕ Preakness 3 3 32 1hd 11 14¾ Cordero A Jr 126 2.70 99-12 Codex1264¾GenuineRisk1213¼ColonelMoran1267 Wide, ridden out 8
13Apr80- 8Hol fst 1⅛ :45⅖ 1:10 1:47⅖ Hol Derby 8 6 76¼ 63 2hd 12 Delahoussaye E 122 4.30 95-19 Codex 1222 Rumbo 1221¼ Cactus Road 1225½ Drew clear 11
30Mar80- 8SA fst 1⅛ :46⅕ 1:10 1:47⅗ S A Derby 9 4 31 3nk 12½ 1nk Valenzuela P A 25.30 91-13 Codex 120nk Rumbo 1207½ Bic's Gold 1203 Lasted 9
16Mar80- 5SA fst 1 1/16 :46⅘ 1:11 1:42 Allowance 2 1 11½ 1½ 12½ 15½ Valenzuela P A5 111 5.70 91-12 Codex 1115½ Egg Toss 120no Jihad 1203½ Easily 9
2Feb80- 6SA fst 1 1/16 :46⅕ 1:10⅗ 1:41⅗ Allowance 2 4 43 31½ 42 41¼ Valenzuela P A5 113 6.30 92-09 Rumbo 114½ Score Twenty Four 116nk Proven Jewel 120½ Evenly 7
19Jan80- 4SA sl 1 :47⅘ 1:13⅗ 1:39⅘ Allowance 1 2 31½ 66 613 622 Hawley S 116 2.10 50-30 Bold 'N Rulling 1097ScoreTwentyFour1185ProvenJewel1168 Tired 6
9Jan80- 6SA sly 1 :45⅗ 1:10⅘ 1:37⅕ Allowance 4 4 33 52¾ 46 36¼ Shoemaker W 118 *2.10 77-18 Dandy Wit 1141 Moorish Star 1205¼ Codex 118no Even try 7
28Oct79- 8SA fst 1 1/16 :46⅕ 1:09⅘ 1:41⅗ Norfolk 4 7 74 69 611 57¾ Hawley S 118 9.50e 85-13 The Carpenter 118hd Rumbo 1182 Idyll 1182¼ Wide 8
14Oct79- 7SA fst 1 1/16 :46⅖ 1:11⅖ 1:42⅘ Allowance 6 3 3nk 3nk 1½ 1¾ Hawley S 115 3.90 87-09 Codex 115¾ Halpern Bay 115¾ Rumbo 1182½ Driving 7
21Sep79-11Pomfst 6f :21⅕ :44⅗ 1:11⅖ Beau Brummel 3 3 44½ 58½ 69 4¾ Ramirez R 114 *.60 88-17 Marimia's Son 114hd DLe Caporal114½StormyPrince114hd Rallied 7
LATEST WORKOUTS Jun 2 Bel 5f fst 1:00⅘ b May 27 Bel 5f fst 1:00⅗ b ●May 10 Hol 5f fst :58⅗ h May 2 Hol 5f fst :59⅖ h

Rumbo * — Dk. b. or br. c. 3, by Ruffinal—Irreproachable, by Windy Sands
Br.—Westerly Stud Farms (Cal)
Own.—GaynoStable&BellBloodstockCo — Tr.—Bell Thomas R Jr — **126**

	St.	1st	2nd	3rd	Amt.
1980	7	3	3	1	$269,275
1979	5	1	2	1	$52,310

24May80- 8Hol fst 1 1/16 :45⅖ 1:09⅘ 1:40⅗ Golden State 5 6 510 2½ 1½ 15 Shoemaker W 17 *.30 92-11 Rumbo 1175 The Carpenter 1241¾ Score Twenty Four115no Easily 6
3May80- 8CD fst 1¼ :48 1:37⅗ 2:02 Ky Derby 9 13 1210 56 33½ 21 Pincay L Jr 126 4.00 86-11 Genuine Risk 1211 Rumbo 1261JaklinKlugman1264 Swerved, wide 13
13Apr80- 8Hol fst 1⅛ :45⅖ 1:10 1:47⅖ Hol Derby 9 9 810 85½ 43¾ 22 Pincay L Jr 122 *1.80e 93-19 Codex 1222 Rumbo 1221¼ Cactus Road 1225½ Wide late 11
30Mar80- 8SA fst 1⅛ :46⅕ 1:10 1:47⅗ S A Derby 1 8 88 88¾ 58½ 2nk Pincay L Jr b 120 4.70 91-13 Codex 120nk Rumbo 1207½ Bic's Gold 1203 Finished strong 9
15Mar80- 8SA fst 1 1/16 :46⅖ 1:11 1:41⅗ San Felipe H 2 5 58½ 63¾ 66¾ 33½ Pincay L Jr b 119 3.20 89-15 Raise A Man 1191½ The Carpenter 1232 Rumbo 119¾ Rallied 7
20Feb80- 8SA sly 1 1/16 :47⅖ 1:12⅕ 1:44⅗ S Catalina 5 3 3½ 3½ 1½ 13 Shoemaker W b 117 *1.20 78-26 Rumbo 1173 Idyll 114no Bold 'N Rulling 117½ Driving 6
20Feb80-Run in two divisions 7th & 8th races.
2Feb80- 6SA fst 1 1/16 :46⅕ 1:10⅖ 1:41⅗ Allowance 7 5 54 41¾ 3½ 1½ Shoemaker W 114 *.80 93-09 Rumbo 114½ Score Twenty Four 116nk Proven Jewel 120½ Driving 7
28Oct79- 8SA fst 1 1/16 :46⅕ 1:09⅘ 1:41⅗ Norfolk 5 8 89 79½ 45 2hd Shoemaker W 118 10.30 93-13 The Carpenter 118hd Rumbo 1182 Idyll 1182¼ Gamely 8
14Oct79- 7SA fst 1 1/16 :46⅖ 1:11⅖ 1:42⅘ Allowance 1 6 63¾ 51¾ 32 31½ Toro F 118 5.60 85-09 Codex 115¾ Halpern Bay 115¾ Rumbo 1182½ Mild bid 7
12Sep79- 3Dmr fst 1 :46⅕ 1:11⅖ 1:36⅗ Md Sp Wt 7 6 62¾ 33½ 2½ 1½ Pincay L Jr 118 *1.30 85-13 Rumbo 118½ Dandy Wit 1183½ Blazingalong 1185 Driving 8
LATEST WORKOUTS ●May 20 SA 5f fst :58⅗ h May 2 CD 3f fst :36⅖ b Apr 26 SA 1 fst 1:39⅕ h Apr 8 SA 6f fst 1:13⅕ h

The first three choices were beaten by the outsider Temperence Hill, as you will recall from television and newspaper accounts. Codex, the high-point horse, who would rate as our selection under the investment method in this book, was helpless in the mud and finished out of it. Otherwise, sparing the bloody details, here is how our point ratings came out.

Odds	Horse	Ability		A Pts		F	Total
1.9	Codex	:23.2	:24.0	23	20	Q4	47
2.1	Genuine Risk	:23.3	:24.1	22	19	Q	41
1.6	Rumbo	:23.3	:24.2	22	18	Q4	44

Both Codex and Rumbo were off Big Wins. Even adjusting their California times, they still looked good, as did Genuine Risk. We shall put this one in the loss column for both win and place, and move on to the ninth and last race of our week.

We need a final victory badly. To maintain the pace of winning every day, it is essential to score in the last race, or else we're down the drain. And despite the sogginess in the air, we're back on the grass again with another distance event, where Le Notre, who hasn't run since July of 1979, rates as the favorite.

This Lightly Raced colt shows four workouts, and the fact that he last ran in a stakes race allows us to qualify him on form. Every one of his races has been

9 BELMONT

INNER TURF COURSE — 1⅜ MILES — BELMONT PARK — START — FINISH

1⅜ MILES. (INNER-TURF). (2.11⅖) ALLOWANCE. Purse $20,000. 3-year-olds and upward, Which have never won a race other than maiden, claiming or starter. Weights, 3-year-olds, 114 lbs.; older, 122 lbs. Non-winners of a race other than claiming over a mile and a furlong since May 15 allowed 3 lbs.; of such a race since May 1, 5 l;bs. (Winners Preferred)

Le Notre — **B. c. 4, by Herbager—Open Hearing, by Court Martial**
Own.—Phipps 0 — **Br.—Phipps 0 (Ky)** — **Tr.—Penna Angel** — **117**

Turf Record					St.	1st	2nd	3rd	Amt.
St.	1st	2nd	3rd	1979	5	1	1	0	$15,380
5	1	1	0	1978	0	M	0	0	

29Jly79- 8Bel	fm	1¼	[T]:49	1:38	2:02⅖	Lexington H	4	3	43½	75	912	813	Fell J	113	5.10	69-16	Virilify 1081¾ T. V. Series 113¾ Crown Thy Good 1145	Tired	11
22Jly79- 7Bel	fm	1⅜	[T]:48	1:36⅘	2:13⅗	3↑Allowance	7	5	43	32	2½	2hd	Fell J	113	*1.00	101-15	Rightful Ruler 116hd Le Notre 1136 Sunny Puddles 1121½	Missed	7
24Jun79- 2Bel	fm	1⅜	[T]:45⅘	1:37	2:15	3↑Allowance	6	9	911	64	35½	46¼	Fell J	114	*.70	88-08	Rectus 112hd Argold 1146 Parol 117nk	Lost whip	9
15Jun79- 7Bel	fm	1¼	[T]:46⅖	1:36⅕	2:02⅖	3↑Allowance	8	11	1119	65¾	53½	4nk	Cruguet J	109	*.60	82-14	Scouting Party 109no Coriander 112no Serendip 109nk	Gaining	12
29May79- 6Bel	gd	1⅜	(T):47⅘	1:40	2:18⅖	3↑Md Sp Wt	6	6	68	12	14	12½	Cruguet J	113	*1.20	70-28	Le Notre 1132½ Great Partner 1133¾ Argold 1135¼	Easily	11

LATEST WORKOUTS Jun 2 Bel 4f fst :48 b ●May 27 Bel [T] 5f fm 1:01 b May 21 Bel 5f sly 1:01 b May 15 Bel 5f fst 1:00⅗ h

on the turf, as you can see. These difficult distances cause some calculation problems, but let's have at it.

In the 22Jly79 race, there is a :48.4 lead time between the 4f and one-mile points. This can be reduced by one for gain, with an add-on of two for energy to come up to :49.0. We now divide in half and use the lesser portion, or :24.2, as the ability time out of this race. For another effort, the last race on 29Jly79 shows a :49.0 lead time, with a loss of 2 lengths to make it :49.2 for Le Notre. Three more must be added as an energy adjustment to bring the figure to :50.0. We again divide in half, reduce the half to a lesser portion, and get a :24.4 as the ability figure.

The second choice in the betting is Argold, another offspring of my old favorite from the past, Al Hattab.

Argold — **Ro. g. 4, by Al Hattab—For Sparkles, by Forli**
Own.—Giboney Stable — **Br.—Bloom H J (Ky)** — **Tr.—Kay Michael** — **117**

Turf Record					St.	1st	2nd	3rd	Amt.
St.	1st	2nd	3rd	1980	3	0	0	1	$950
8	1	2	4	1979	10	1	2	3	$21,890

25May80- 5Bel	fm	1½	(T):48⅖	2:02⅘	2:27⅕	3↑Handicap	3	5	57½	53½	54	56	Samyn J L	112	7.20	82-15	[D]Ivory Hunter 1144¾ Xmas Box 111hd No Neck 112no	Hung	8
10May80- 3Aqu	fst	1⅛	:47⅗	1:11⅗	1:50⅕	3↑Allowance	1	5	511	611	69½	58¾	Velasquez J	119	12.10	75-13	PreferredList1084VoodooRhythm1113HourOfPece113½	No threat	7
8Mar80- 7GP	fm	1 1/16	(T):47⅗	1:11⅖	1:43⅕	Allowance	1	8	86¾	63½	52½	32½	Samyn J L	114	14.50	82-12	Oak Table 1142 El Bark 114½ Argold 1141	Rallied	12
24Jun79- 2Bel	fm	1⅜	[T]:45⅘	1:37	2:15	3↑Allowance	4	8	79	53½	2½	2hd	Velasquez J	114	8.70	94-08	Rectus 112hd Argold 1146 Parol 117nk	Led, missed	9
16Jun79- 2Bel	fm	1½	(T):47	2:03	2:27⅕	3↑Md Sp Wt	10	7	68	32½	11	14	Velasquez J	114	*2.30	88-01	Argold 1144 Sarawan 1091 Great Partner 1142¼	Ridden out	10
28May79- 6Bel	gd	1⅜	(T):47⅘	1:40	2:18⅖	3↑Md Sp Wt	1	11	1116	812	311	36¼	Velasquez J	113	1.50	64-28	Le Notre 1132½ Great Partner 1133¾ Argold 1135¼	Rallied	11
17May79- 5Aqu	gd	1½	(T):48⅗	2:07⅖	2:32⅕	3↑Md Sp Wt	3	6	43	1½	1hd	2nk	Cruguet J	113	*1.60	105-02	Audacious Fool 113nkArgold1134¼HoptotheTop1144¾	Held gamely	11
29Apr79- 2Aqu	my	1 3/16	:49	1:14⅕	2:01⅖	3↑Md Sp Wt	7	7	64¼	53¼	54	46	Cruguet J	113	8.50	49-25	Dresden Dew 1152½ Metro 109½ Testimony 1143	Evenly	8
10Apr79- 4Hia	hd	*1⅛	(T)		1:48⅘	Md Sp Wt	3	9	813	611	46½	37	Solomone M	120	1.70	84-12	Rectus 1206½ Marirv 120½ Argold 120nk	Up for show	10
3Apr79- 1Hia	fm	*1 1/16	(T)		1:42⅗	Md Sp Wt	2	9	922	718	59	34¼	Ussery R A10	110	42.50	84-10	Proud Relic 120nk Chungero 1204 Argold 110no	In close, bobbled	9

LATEST WORKOUTS Jun 2 Bel 5f fst 1:01 b May 18 Bel 4f fst :48⅕ h May 5 Bel 5f fst 1:02 b Apr 27 Bel 6f fst 1:16⅘ b

My sentiment for the money put in my pocket by Al Hattab's brilliant efforts in my earlier years of following racing cannot obscure the fact that Argold cannot qualify on form. While he gained 4 lengths between the first and second calls, he could not sustain it and began to fall back. There are no qualifying factors here, and out he must go, accordingly, with an NQ label.

The third choice is Worth A Bet, although his name won't influence our judgment even in the slightest. What do his points show?

Worth A Bet qualifies off his last race by virtue of his gain in excess of five. We have to do some of the same extended calculations that we used on Le Notre to get our ability times here. From the last race, there is a lead time of :48.3, very good indeed. There is no allowance for gain because of the lengths

Worth A Bet — B. c. 4, by Twice Worthy—Betsy Be Good, by Pretendre
Own.—Zantker E — Br.—Zantker E (Ky) — Tr.—Conway James P — 117

Turf Record	St.	1st	2nd	3rd
	6	1	0	1

	St.	1st	2nd	3rd	Amt.
1980	3	0	0	1	$2,400
1979	12	1	1	1	$17,020

29May80- 7Bel	hd	1¼	[T]:47⅗	1:36⅕	2:01⅗	3↑Allowance	12	10	10^{15}	$9^{8\frac{1}{2}}$	6^{7}	$3^{4\frac{3}{4}}$	Montoya D	b	119	22.30	81–10	Valiant Order 108^{1} Reactant $108^{3\frac{3}{4}}$ Worth A Bet 119^{nk}	Wide	12
10May80- 3Aqu	fst	1⅛	:47⅗	1:11⅗	1:50⅕	3↑Allowance	3	7	7^{20}	7^{25}	7^{26}	7^{22}	Montoya D	b	119	32.00	62–13	Preferred List 108^{4} VoodooRhythm111^{3}HourOfPeace$113^{\frac{1}{2}}$	Trailed	7
6Jan80- 9FG	fst	1¼	:50⅘	1:41⅗	2:07	Handicap	1	4	4^{6}	6^{7}	6^{12}	6^{16}	DelahoussyeDJ	b	111	8.10	60–19	Swap Or Trade 112no Pool Court $117^{\frac{3}{4}}$ Prince Freddie $113^{1\frac{3}{4}}$	Tired	7
30Dec79- 5FG	gd	1^{40}	:47⅕	1:13⅘	1:43⅗	3↑Allowance	2	7	7^{15}	7^{13}	$7^{7\frac{1}{4}}$	$2^{2\frac{1}{2}}$	DelhoussyeDJ^{5}	b	114	4.50	72–22	Au Courant $119^{2\frac{1}{2}}$ Worth A Bet $114^{1\frac{1}{2}}$WhiteLark$119^{\frac{1}{2}}$	Belated rally	7
6Nov79- 2Aqu	sf	1½	Ⓣ:49⅖	2:11⅘	2:37⅗	3↑Allowance	3	6	7^{19}	6^{11}	5^{12}	5^{12}	Montoya D	b	115	17.10	61–31	ProperlyPerson117^{1}KingOfMardiGrs$115^{1\frac{1}{2}}$GretPrtner$115^{8\frac{3}{4}}$	Outrun	7
30Sep79- 3Bel	sly	1¼	:48	1:40⅖	2:06⅘	3↑Allowance	5	6	6^{15}	6^{11}	6^{14}	4^{12}	Montoya D	b	118	10.40	54–24	Properly Person 108^{7} Back Again 117^{2} Adam'sPet114^{3}	No threat	6
2Sep79- 2Bel	gd	1¼	[T]:49⅗	1:40	2:06⅗	3↑Md Sp Wt	5	4	$4^{2\frac{1}{2}}$	$2^{1\frac{1}{2}}$	2^{1}	1no	Montoya D	b	118	4.40	61–30	Worth A Bet 118no Great Partner $118^{6\frac{3}{4}}$ Koru 122^{9}	Just up	6
20Aug79- 4Sar	gd	1½	[T]:51	2:06⅖	2:31⅕	3↑Md Sp Wt	3	7	$7^{5\frac{1}{2}}$	5^{4}	5^{8}	$4^{6\frac{1}{4}}$	Montoya D	b	117	5.50	— —	King OfMardiGras$117^{2\frac{1}{4}}$KeytoReason117^{nk}LittleRoba$117^{3\frac{3}{4}}$	Rallied	9
10Aug79- 2Sar	fm	1⅛	Ⓣ:48⅕	1:13⅖	1:50⅘	3↑Md Sp Wt	9	9	$7^{4\frac{1}{2}}$	4^{4}	$4^{7\frac{1}{2}}$	4^{3}	DelhoussyeDJ^{5}	b	112	*1.80e	70–21	NorthernGenrl117^{hd}QuickDnc117^{3}KingOfMrdiGrs117^{no}	Wide turn	10
21Jly79- 4Bel	fm	1	Ⓣ:47⅕	1:11⅖	1:36⅖	3↑Md Sp Wt	9	10	$9^{5\frac{1}{4}}$	5^{9}	$4^{7\frac{1}{2}}$	$4^{7\frac{1}{4}}$	DelhoussyeDJ^{5}	b	111	32.30	81–14	Nataniel$116^{1\frac{1}{4}}$MarchingMrine$116^{5\frac{1}{4}}$NorthernGenerl$116^{\frac{3}{4}}$	Very wide	12

LATEST WORKOUTS Jun 4 Bel 5f fst 1:01⅕ h May 27 Bel 4f fst :50 b May 23 Bel 1 fst 1:43 b May 17 Bel 4f fst :50 b

behind, and four ticks have to be added for energy to bring the figure up to :49.2. We divide that in half, using the lesser portion, and obtain a :24.3 figure. Because the last race was on a hard surface, we add one tick to wind up with a :24.4 figure. The next best we can find comes out of the bottom race on 21Jly79 at Belmont, where there was a :24.1 lead time, with four added for lost lengths and two more ticks for energy adjustment to come up with a final :25.2.

Here is the comparison chart for our last race.

Odds	Horse	Ability		A Pts		F	Total
1.3	Le Notre	:24.2	:24.4	18	16	Q	34
2.8	Argold	—	—	—	—	NQ	NQ
5.7	Worth A Bet	:24.4	:25.2	16	13	Q	29

With Argold out on form, Le Notre is a solid selection on ability times. The fact that he was a Lightly Raced Horse was also a plus factor. We invest in Le Notre to win and place and root hard for this one, for we need it. And look at the most happy result.

NINTH RACE Belmont JUNE 7, 1980

1 ⅜ MILES.(inner–turf). (2.11⅘) ALLOWANCE. Purse $20,000. 3–year–olds and upward, Which have never won a race other than maiden, claiming or starter. Weights, 3–year–olds, 114 lbs.; older, 122 lbs. Non–winners of a race other than claiming over a mile and a furlong since May 15 allowed 3 lbs.; of such a race since May 1, 5 l;bs. (Winners Preferred)

Value of race $20,000, value to winner $12,000, second $4,400, third $2,400, fourth $1,200. Mutuel pool $346,708, OTB pool $189,084. Track Triple Pool $387,414; OTB Triple Pool $464,928.

Last Raced	Horse	Eqt.	A.	Wt	PP	¼	½	¾	1	Str	Fin	Jockey	Odds $1
29Jly79 ^{8}Bel^{8}	Le Notre		4	117	10	8^{1}	$8^{1\frac{1}{2}}$	6^{1}	3^{hd}	4^{2}	1^{nk}	Encinas R I	1.30
25May80 ^{5}Bel^{5}	Argold		4	117	1	4^{1}	4^{hd}	$3^{\frac{1}{2}}$	4^{2}	2^{hd}	$2^{\frac{3}{4}}$	Velasquez J	2.80
29May80 ^{8}Bel^{5}	Nataraja	b	4	112	4	3^{1}	$3^{\frac{1}{2}}$	5^{1}	6^{1}	5^{3}	3^{hd}	Gonzalez M A^{5}	43.70
29May80 ^{7}Bel^{5}	Rebel Blade		3	113	5	$2^{\frac{1}{2}}$	$2^{1\frac{1}{2}}$	1^{hd}	1^{hd}	$3^{\frac{1}{2}}$	4^{1}	Maple E	15.80
29May80 ^{7}Bel^{9}	Torrential		4	117	2	1^{1}	1^{hd}	2^{1}	2^{hd}	1^{hd}	$5^{2\frac{1}{2}}$	Skinner K	8.70
11May60 ^{6}Aqu^{3}	Baladi		3	112	3	7^{1}	$7^{\frac{1}{2}}$	$7^{\frac{1}{2}}$	7^{2}	6^{hd}	6no	Cruguet J	7.80
29May80 ^{7}Bel^{3}	Worth A Bet	b	4	117	6	$9^{\frac{1}{2}}$	9^{1}	9^{1}	9^{2}	$8^{\frac{1}{2}}$	$7^{1\frac{3}{4}}$	Montoya D	5.70
29May80 ^{7}Bel^{6}	Santo's Joe	b	3	109	7	10	10	10	8^{hd}	$7^{1\frac{1}{2}}$	8^{2}	Venezia M	26.10
29May80 ^{7}Bel^{7}	Parmetti	b	3	112	9	$5^{\frac{1}{2}}$	5^{1}	4^{hd}	5^{hd}	8^{8}	9^{14}	Cordero A Jr	52.60
19May80 ^{7}Aqu^{7}	Longdistancerunner		3	112	8	$6^{\frac{1}{2}}$	6^{hd}	8^{2}	10	10	10	Santiago A	37.20

OFF AT 6:19–1/2, EDT. Start good, Won driving. Time, :24⅗, :49⅘, 1:15⅖, 1:40, 2:04⅕, 2:16⅘, Course soft.

$2 Mutuel Prices:			
11–(K)–LE NOTRE	4.60	3.40	3.00
1–(A)–ARGOLD		3.20	3.00
4–(D)–NATARAJA			9.40

Argold made a fight of it, but it was Le Notre down the stretch, passing three horses to win by a neck. A few palpitations, sure, but ah, the cashier cares not. With this final victory in our pockets, we can calculate the entire day.

Race	Selection	Invest		Return	
		Win	**Place**	**Win**	**Place**
1	Bold Phantom	$ 2	$ 2	$ 0	$ 0
2	Jedina	2	2	4.60	3.40
3	Key To Content	2	2	3.60	2.60
4	Farewell Letter	2	2	—	4.20
5	Son Of A Dodo	—	2	—	0
6	Current Winner	—	2	—	2.40
7	Dewan Keys	2	2	4.40	2.60
8	Codex	2	2	0	0
9	Le Notre	2	2	4.60	3.40
	Totals	$14	$18	$17.20	$18.60

Total invested $32.00
Total returned $35.80
Net profit $ 3.80

Did I say profit? At least you can't call it a loss. It was our worst day of the Belmont Big Week, of course, and this is normally what I mean by a "bad day." We had four winners, which is about our usual expectation, but with rock-bottom prices, it is hard to make money. With nothing paying more than $4.60 to win and $4.20 to place, you have to hit an awful lot of winning horses to come out ahead. But I repeat, this is a profit, and that is still what we are seeking.

The vagaries of this last day will be encountered time and time again. But it was a beautiful week indeed, and we'll move forward to recapitulate it in summary form and demonstrate what has been accomplished.

ANALYZING THE BIG
WEEK AT BELMONT

After the wondrous week was finished, making a profit every single day, flushed with the great success of Thursday's pile of prices, I undertook to do the kind of statistical summary that I usually do to find out how the results unwind.

Before we go further, let's come back to the question: How typical was this week? If I said, "Oh, shucks, typical like always, that's what you can expect," that wouldn't be quite right. Provided you play hard and tough with the rules of selection, and whenever the first three favorites run within a reasonable range of expectation, you're going to do almost as well. Prices in New York tend to run a little low, as the big money flocks to the favorites. The returns on Belmont Day itself were so low that you would hardly expect to see consistent prices like that for winners.

As you will see in the next chapter, when we come to results at other tracks, there will be losing days. So, winning six days in a row cannot be said to be typical. What I have said, and will repeat again here, is that you will rarely find two successive losing days, but it can happen—see the next chapter. Three days in a row I simply cannot imagine, and the thesis of this book is that in any given three successive racing days, playing with the instructions set forth herein, you will make money. And that is sound investment, indeed.

But back to Belmont. To see what has been accomplished, let's run through the days in detail, day by day. Here they are:

Date	Win Bets	Cost	Won	Return	Win Profit
June 1	7	$14	4	$24.60	$10.60
June 2	8	16	4	23.00	7.00
June 4	6	12	4	27.80	15.80
June 5	6	12	3	29.20	17.20
June 6	5	10	3	21.00	11.00
June 7	7	14	4	17.20	3.20
The Week	39	78	22	142.80	64.80

In adding up all the money poured through the windows, the total was $174, combining the amount of win bets with the amount of place bets. The total profit, or net return on wagers, was $101.40. This comes out to 57.6% return on money invested for the entire week!

And, once again, I must ask, where else in the world could you get such a return on money in one week?

But, in actuality, you need not have brought $174 with you to the racetrack (still talking in terms of the $2 bet). Once you get ahead, you are churning the money the track has turned over to you for your superiority over other race-goers. For example, on our first day at Belmont, there was no break into the profit column until the fourth race.

We began the first day with a $4 investment in the first race. The return was $3.60 (remember Grand Courant, the horse that loved to run second?), giving us a loss of $0.40. We passed the second race, and wagered only $2 in the third race, losing that. Our investment was at that point only $2.40. Then, in the fourth race, we invested $2 to win and $2 to place on Freightliner, which made our total investment for the day only $6.40. From that point on, we never once fell below the net profit line.

Thus, the only money we were forced to take out of our pocket was the sum of $6.40. It was used over and over again throughout the week, as all our investments were made out of profits after the fourth race ticket on June 1 was cashed. The $6.40 out of pocket grew to $101.40 profit, and with the $6.40, we were up to $107.80. When you calculate it this way, the actual return on money used was somewhere around 1584%, a figure to stagger the imagination.

You can see that there was a great deal of action. Out of fifty-four total races over the six racing days, we had thirty-nine win bets, an average of 6.5 per day. And that is what you may expect, and perhaps even more. Actually, because of

Pl Bets	Cost	Pl	Return	Pl Profit	Total Profit
8	16	6	21.60	5.60	$ 16.20
8	16	5	20.40	4.40	11.40
9	18	6	28.00	10.00	25.80
8	16	5	24.80	8.80	26.00
6	12	5	19.20	7.20	18.20
9	18	6	18.60	.60	3.80
48	96	33	132.60	36.60	101.40

the influx of two-year-olds, with no racing records, we had to pass more races than usual. Grass racing doesn't begin much earlier than this, and here again, we will have races to pass where none of the contenders can qualify.

As you would expect, we made more bets to place than to win under our selection rules. There were forty-eight place bets, which came out to an average of eight per day, which is plenty of action for everyone. This should occur, under our rules, at every track in the country, day after day, on an average.

In the Belmont week, look at the wholesome winning percentage! Of the thirty-nine bets made, twenty-two of them turned into winners, a rather remarkable 56%. I will concede here and now that this number of winners is higher than you may ordinarily expect, since in midyear, with warm weather conditions, at the height of the New York season, the public betting choices seem to do somewhat better than in the early and late months of the year. But I still strive for 50% winners as a realistic goal. I might add that in the week behind us, there were flocks of low-priced winners which tended to hold down profits.

Place prices, of course, are much lower, and you must hit a steady run of success to make a profit. Here, there was a 68.6% figure on our thirty-three good tickets out of forty-eight bets. This is sound and secure. The lower the risk, the lower the return. But you should see by now why I love place betting.

The old question always arises: If win betting is so much more profitable than place betting, why bother with place at all? I will assure you that win betting is almost always more profitable than place betting, simply because there is a good return on win bets with higher prices. But I believe place betting, with its reliability, is a wholesome supplement to win betting, and particularly for a person who cannot go to the track every day.

There will be days when your high-point selections, for whatever reason, just don't seem to be able to win. But they'll be right there in the second slot, time after time. In the summer of 1980, after my week at Belmont, I was visiting a Western track, pouring my usual win and place bets through the windows. For five races in a row, frustrating as it was, my selection ran second. Those five place tickets had enough in them to almost exactly balance out my profit-and-loss sheet. I had not won anything, but I had not lost either. Then, on the sixth selection, my horse came roaring home at a nice $9.80 price and I was in clover for the afternoon. My place ticket in that race, too, was over $5.00.

Successes like that happen again and again. A series of second-place finishes, if you are not backing up for place, can destroy your morale, affect your judgment, tear you apart with frustration. I still have difficulty in persuading one of my sharp handicapping sons of the wisdom of place betting, and I have seen him suffer for it time and time again. Of course, on his good days, he far outstrips me in dollar winnings, but I'm the guy who grinds out the steady profits.

Let's look also to see how our Double Advantage Horses fared. This little chart shows you what happened there.

DOUBLE ADVANTAGE HORSES

Date	Race	Horse	Win Result	Place Result
1Jun80	6Bel	Beech Grove	$ 4.00	$ 3.00
2Jun80	3Bel	Danton King	0	0
	4Bel	Willnt	3.60	2.80
	9Bel	Bronco Buster	6.60	4.20
4Jun80	1Bel	Ojavan	0	0
	3Bel	Miss Rebecca	6.40	2.80
	8Bel	Madame Premier	5.00	4.00
5Jun80	2Bel	Resuscitator	0	4.80
6Jun80	1Bel	Kens Bishop	6.40	4.40
	8Bel	Euphrosyne	4.00	3.00
	9Bel	Ernie's Lad	0	0
7Jun80	3Bel	Key To Content	3.60	2.60
	4Bel	Farewell Letter	0	4.20
	9Bel	Le Notre	4.60	3.40
		Totals	$44.20	39.20

Total win bets	14 at	$28
9 won, returned		$44.20
Profit		$16.20 (58%)

Total place bets	14 at	$28
11 placed, returning		$39.20
Profit		$11.20 (40%)

Total invested	$56.00
Total returned	$83.40
Net profit	$27.40 (49%)

The only one you might want to question is Madame Premier on June 4, 1980, in the eighth at Belmont. This filly was a part of the three-horse entry that trainer Laurin ran in that race. Madame Premier defeated all the others in the race except her two stablemates, both of whom were unknown in ability. It is the payoff that counts, and the entry, which embraced Madame Premier, swept the board.

Thus, there were fourteen Double Advantage Horses in six days, slightly better than two per day, which is almost precisely in line with what I have found at other tracks on other days. This is your most bountiful bonanza indeed.

But what if you invested in Double Advantage Horses only? On days when you might not find any, or only one, you would become very restless. But when you see that the other selections are still very profitable without Double Advantage investments, there is no reason not to follow the entire program at its fullest.

This summary shows where it comes out.

Total win bets	39 for $78	Returning	$142.80
Subtract DA Horses	14 for $28	Returning	$ 44.20
Remaining bets	25 for $50	Returning	$ 98.60

In those twenty-five bets where there was not a Double Advantage Horse, there were thirteen winners, or more than 50%, with a profit of $48.60, which is around 97% on your money spent. This profit rate was even better than Double Advantage at Belmont because of the prices involved.

But in this respect the Belmont week was not typical at all. Ordinarily, Double Advantage Horses will be the backbone of your investment program, and will produce a higher return than other selections. Their winning and place

percentages across the country are higher and their prices better than at Belmont, where again, the crowd dearly loves to load up on favorites. As you have seen from the Belmont week's display, some of those favorites are very unwise selections indeed. But betting on Double Advantage Horses (whether the crowd knows they are Double Advantage or not) is almost like investing in Fort Knox.

Should you try to tailor an entire investment program to Double Advantage Horses? If you have the patience and forbearance, which few people do, yes, and you will do splendidly. One of the problems in it is that if you find none in an entire racing day, you tend to get frustrated. And if you should find but one, and for some reason he falls below expectations and runs out of the money, your unhappiness will grab you pretty hard. It seems to me that the only person who could adopt an investment program based solely on Double Advantage Horses would be someone who goes to the track every day, is blessed with unusual patience, and would never miss out on investing in one of those infrequent opportunities. Those of us who cannot go to the track every day both deserve and demand more action than relying on Double Advantage plays would give us. The higher payoffs on the other selections also help provide an answer for us.

When we go through the other tracks in the next chapter and show you the various fluctuations in winning patterns and how the procedure works over other successive days, you will have a better appreciation of the entire program of investing. We can now leave the wonderful Big Week at Belmont to cast our advantages elsewhere.

INVESTING AT OTHER TRACKS
AROUND THE COUNTRY

After completion of the Big Week at Belmont, with its overwhelming success, the question quite naturally arose: How about other tracks? Belmont is only a part of the racing scene, and players throughout the United States and at some of the very good Canadian tracks have every right to ask how this method of play will work for them.

It was decided then to demonstrate the method at all other major tracks *that were running at the same time as Belmont,* and apply the rules exactly as during the Big Week. I followed this method of play for three successive days at each of these tracks. Since I had never found three successive days at any track that failed to show a profit, I contend that this test is sufficient to indicate that the procedure was as effective as at Belmont.

The first task was to acquire the necessary copies of the *Daily Racing Form.* Back issues were purchased from the newspaper's plants in New Jersey for the East, in Chicago for the Midwest, and in Los Angeles for the West Coast.The tracks chosen for study were Suffolk Downs in Boston and Monmouth Park in northeastern New Jersey for the East, Arlington Park in Chicago and Churchill Downs in Louisville for the Midwest, and Hollywood Park and Golden Gate Fields in California for the Far West. These were the most important U.S. tracks in operation during the first week in June 1980, and if a profit could be recorded at each and every one of them for a successive three-day period, my point would be made and all skeptics impressed.

Then began the work. The first three favorites were extracted from the charts and their form, ability points, early speed, and final totals were computed. The races that had to be passed were passed, and play was always in accordance with the rules, even if my own handicapping told me otherwise (just as I would not play the Belmont Stakes itself, but used the results as a part of my final computation).

Let's take the results, one by one:

1. Suffolk Downs

Suffolk Downs, in the Boston area, runs on Sunday, just as do Belmont and Hollywood Park in California. The horses at Suffolk won't measure up to those at the bigger tracks, but there is a representative variety of races, including turf events. Here are my selections for the ten-race card, and how they fared for the first day.

Sunday, June 1, 1980

		Invest		Return	
Race	Selection	Win	Place	Win	Place
1	Kimble County	$ 2	$ 2	$ 5.20	$ 3.40
2	Really Confusing	2	2	4.40	3.80
3	Turn for the Best	2	2	0	4.40
4	Skip Row	—	2	—	0
5	Unto This Day	—	2	—	0
6	Banging Bill	2	2	0	0
7	Shore Route	2	2	0	0
8	Pass (turf)	—	—	—	—
9	Royal Hangover	2	2	6.40	4.60
10	Pass (all unknown)	—	—	—	—
	Totals	$12	$16	$16.00	$16.20

Total invested	$28.00
Total returned	$32.20
Net profit	$ 4.20

Thus, our first day at Suffolk started slowly, but it was a profit nevertheless. You will note that Suffolk's card consisted of ten races, allowing for a little more action than usual. Now, let's see how we do on Monday, the next racing day.

Monday, June 2, 1980

Race	Selection	Invest Win	Invest Place	Return Win	Return Place
1	Rusty G's Pleasure	$ 2	$ 2	$ 0	$ 0
2	Union Line	2	2	0	0
3	Wright Big Jest	2	2	4.20	3.20
4	Albano	2	2	0	0
5	Sharp Bluffer	2	2	0	0
6	Royal Impression	2	2	6.20	4.20
7	Kaiago	2	2	0	0
8	Snow Person	2	2	4.40	3.00
9	Ice Jammer	2	2	0	0
10	Call Me Proud	2	2	14.80	7.20
	Totals	$20	$20	$29.60	$17.60

Total invested	$40.00
Total returned	$47.20
Net profit	$ 7.20

Here was your maximum-action day—ten races, ten win bets, ten place bets, grappling with every race on the card. Four winners out of ten helped turn a profit because of one big price in the very last race of the day. We were slightly under the line in place betting, but once again, for the second day in a row, there is a profit, not too great, to be sure, but the black ink we must have.

Because of Sunday racing, Suffolk Downs is dark on Tuesdays, just as in New York at Belmont. Wednesday is the next racing day as we try to make it three profit afternoons in a row.

Race	Selection	Invest		Return	
		Win	Place	Win	Place
1	Shade the Best	$ 2	$ 2	$ 7.00	$ 4.20
2	Good Syntax	2	2	0	0
3	Ski Pants	2	2	0	2.40
4	All Nair	2	2	13.80	9.20
5	Pass	—	—	—	—
6	Pass	—	—	—	—
7	Skippers Best	2	2	0	0
8	Martian Dancer	2	2	3.20	2.40
9	Gallant Buzz	—	2	—	3.60
10	Satan's Thunder	2	2	5.00	3.00
	Totals	$14	$16	$29.00	$24.80

Total invested	$30.00
Total returned	$53.80
Net profit	$23.80

A very good day indeed, the third profitable outing in succession, which is what we like to see. Our total profit for the three days was $35.20, off $98 poured into the windows. Out of our twenty-three win bets, we scored on eleven, falling just slightly under the 50% mark. In place wagering, we had twenty-six bets with fourteen successes, not nearly as good as we would like. But in the three days, we did make a profit on place betting, as the $52 we put into it brought us a return of $58.60, which is still pretty good for a safety device.

2. Monmouth Park

Beautiful Monmouth park on the northeast Jersey coast is another of my favorite tracks in the country. I don't get there as often as I would like, but the ocean atmosphere and the lovely surroundings make it a pleasant place to go to the races. Let's start with the first day; I have already written extensively about the first race on that occasion.

Monday, June 2, 1980

		Invest		Return	
Race	Selection	Win	Place	Win	Place
1	Jaohar	$ 2	$ 2	$13.40	$ 7.60
2	Road to Mecca	2	2	0	0
3	Natural Dancer	2	2	3.00	3.00
4	Stentorious	2	2	0	0
5	Critias	2	2	0	0
6	Red Mirage	—	2	—	3.20
7	Flatter	2	2	0	0
8	Hill Billy Dancer	2	2	5.20	3.60
9	Potential	—	2	—	4.00
	Totals	$14	$18	$21.60	$21.40

Total invested $32.00
Total returned $43.00
Net profit $11.00

We had seven win bets on the nine-race card and a place wager in every race. Our three winners produced a profit, and the place betting, scoring on five of the eight bets, also turned a small gain. Once again, we had one excellent price with Jaohar in the first race, which put the day off to a rousing beginning.

Tuesday, June 3, 1980

Race	Selection	Invest		Return	
		Win	Place	Win	Place
1	Emory B	$ 2	$ 2	$ 5.80	$ 3.40
2	Yard Marker	2	2	0	0
3	Verna's Pride	2	2	0	3.20
4	Pass	—	—	—	—
5	Dance D'Espoir	—	2	—	0
6	Double Zeus	2	2	0	2.60
7	Apaway	2	2	7.20	3.40
8	Foretake	2	2	0	3.40
9	My Aunt	2	2	8.80	4.40
	Totals	$14	$16	$21.80	$20.40

Total invested	$30.00
Total returned	$42.20
Net profit	$12.20

The second day is also profitable by the steady margin that we like. We again had three winning selections out of the seven we played, and this time had six place playoffs out of eight, which is very good, for a profit in both columns. The $7.20 and $8.80 payoffs on two of the winners represent the usual bread-and-butter returns that you should regularly find, and they make up for the low $4.20 prices on outstanding favorites. And when you get a big one, like Jaohar the day before, you can begin to total up the profits.

But before we get too overconfident, I must tell you there is some rough water ahead, as we go into our third day at Monmouth.

Wednesday, June 4, 1980

Race	Selection	Invest		Return	
		Win	**Place**	**Win**	**Place**
1	Jack Shelley	$ 2	$ 2	$ 0	$ 5.20
2	Facinating Jo	2	2	4.80	3.20
3	Pass	—	—	—	—
4	Pass	—	—	—	—
5	Last Volley	2	2	0	0
6	The Dennis Bay	2	2	0	0
7	Betty's Right	—	2	—	5.80
8	Pass	—	—	—	—
9	Olympic Ticket	2	2	0	0
	Totals	$10	$12	$ 4.80	$14.20

Total invested	$22.00
Total returned	$19.00
Net LOSS	$ 3.00

What's this? Our very first losing day is staring us in the face. On the win list, it was a disaster. We made but five bets and could win but one at the very short price of 4.80. Now you may see what I have been saying about playing to place. Our excellent return on place betting saved the day from being a disgrace. We had but six plays there, but three of them returned, with two for good prices. We spent $22 and returned $19, for a loss of only $3 for the day. And let me tell you, on your bad losing days, if you could hold your losses this low at all times, you would be in sound position indeed.

Because I don't like to leave on a losing day, I decided to extend Monmouth one day further, and because all the races were worked out, I will now show you the fourth day in a row.

Thursday, June 5, 1980

Race	Selection	Invest		Return	
		Win	Place	Win	Place
1	Hawiian Gild	$ 2	$ 2	$ 9.40	$ 4.60
2	Flip a Penny	2	2	0	0
3	Watauga	2	2	3.80	2.60
4	Berean	—	2	—	4.40
5	Swooned	2	2	6.80	4.20
6	Addy Girl	2	2	0	0
7	Hotter Than Hades	2	2	0	5.00
8	Snuggle Bunny	—	2	—	5.80
9	Abe's Jest	2	2	0	0
	Totals	$14	$18	$20.00	$26.60

Total invested	$32.00
Total returned	$46.60
Net profit	$14.60

Ah, this is much better. Out of seven win bets, we had the usual three winners, but the profit was there. Once more, place betting was a jewel, as we made more there than in the win column, wagering nine times and scoring with six of them.

While our first three days did produce a profit, even with the losing card, we wound up with three winning days in four attempts with a total profit of $34.80 off $116 total in the investment column. We had twenty-six win selections over the four days, with only ten of them paying off, which is under the 40% we believe is necessary to maintain a steady profit. But even with that low percentage of return, there was still a profit in the win column. In place investing, out of thirty-two plays, we scored with twenty, which is 62.5%, good enough for almost anyone. The Monmouth trial was a sparkling success, too.

3. ARLINGTON PARK

Arlington Park is Chicago's major track, running in the prime summer months. Despite some ups and downs, with 1981 and 1982 looking like strong years, it is still the leading track between New York and California. Our three days of play here were most instructive, and let's start with an unhappy one.

Monday, June 2, 1980

Race	Selection	Invest Win	Invest Place	Return Win	Return Place
1	Pass	—	—	—	—
2	Bold Herald	$ 2	$ 2	$ 0	$ 0
3	Medroso	2	2	0	0
4	Pass	—	—	—	—
5	Razorback	2	2	0	0
6	Native Pet	2	2	5.40	3.40
7	Hudson	—	2	—	0
8	Satin Ribera	2	2	6.00	3.60
9	Penn Peg	2	2	0	0
	Totals	$12	$14	$11.40	$ 7.00

Total invested	$26.00
Total returned	$18.40
Net LOSS	$ 7.60

This was really a bad day, the very worst I have ever seen. What caused it? First of all, out of the nine races, only four were won by one of the first three favorites. Since our nationwide, long-term percentage expectancy is 67%, or two out of three, whenever the first three betting choices fail to this degree, we are going to have trouble. We could avoid it only by hitting some good-priced animals, but here our highest return was $6.00. We were perhaps lucky (I don't like to use that word) to find only six plays on the win card and seven to place. The first race, for example, was filled with first-time starters, and we passed the fourth because none of the top three was qualified on form. In the seventh race, our selection, Hudson, was only one point above the next horse, which warranted only a place bet.

With this truly tough day behind us, what can we do next?

Tuesday, June 3, 1980

Race	Selection	Invest		Return	
		Win	**Place**	**Win**	**Place**
1	Pass	—	—	—	—
2	Milyon Dolar	$ 2	$ 2	$ 0	$ 0
3	Peachblow	2	2	8.60	5.20
4	Pass	—	—	—	—
5	Son Gallant	2	2	0	0
6	Extractor	2	2	7.20	4.40
7	Vitz	—	2	—	3.80
8	Conga Miss	2	2	5.80	3.20
9	Go Go Teresa	2	2	11.60	7.80
	Totals	$12	$14	$33.20	$24.40

Total invested	$26.00
Total returned	$57.60
Net profit	$31.60

This one started so slowly that I began to wonder what was going on at Arlington Park. But, oh, what a finish. Out of six win bets, we had four on top, and for seven place wagers, five of them paid off. We had a bountiful day, almost comparable to the big one at Belmont. From the $26 in bets, we returned $57.60, a lovely profit of $31.60. And in the ninth race, Go Go Teresa was a Double Advantage Horse that paid $11.60, almost the highest price I have ever seen for a horse of this caliber. The $7.80 place price was almost unbelievable, as you seldom expect prices like that in the middle. This day made up for the previous day's downfall, which is usually the case after a losing day. We are now ready for the third day.

Wednesday, June 4, 1980

Race	Selection	Invest		Return	
		Win	Place	Win	Place
1	Mighty Brian	$ 2	$ 2	$ 0	$ 0
2	Dancing Belle	2	2	0	0
3	Pass	—	—	—	—
4	Triple Rhythm	2	2	0	0
5	Avenging Lad	2	2	9.20	3.60
6	Pass	—	—	—	—
7	My Princess Pride	—	2	—	4.40
8	Flying Target	2	2	7.20	4.20
9	Triple Power	2	2	0	0
	Totals	$12	$14	$16.40	$12.20

Total invested $26.00
Total returned $28.60
Net profit $ 2.60

Meager as meager can be, like our last day at Belmont, but a profit is a profit is a . . . Out of six win bets, we had only two on top, and here was our profit. Out of our seven place bets, only three came in, producing a slight loss in place betting. But for the three days, our overall profit was $26.60 off $78 invested, slightly better than 33%, which we will accept over and over again.

Our success level was relatively low. There were only eighteen win bets, averaging six per day, with only eight winners. Actually, one more winner would have made a 50% figure, so we're not terribly far off. Place betting didn't do as well as usual, either, since of the twenty-one bets we made, only ten were returned with money. But once again, the real test comes from three successive days, and Arlington, too, provides the profits we expect.

4. CHURCHILL DOWNS

Historic Churchill Downs, renowned for the Kentucky Derby, provided our next test. Here is how it went.

Monday, June 2, 1980

Race	Selection	Invest		Return	
		Win	Place	Win	Place
1	The Assyrian	$ 2	$ 2	$ 9.80	$ 6.40
2	Holloway's Mistake	—	2	—	3.40
3	Crawchief	—	2	—	0
4	Pass	—	—	—	—
5	Allie's Tune	2	2	5.60	4.40
6	Pass	—	—	—	—
7	Fee Dee	2	2	0	0
8	Sky Light Princess	2	2	0	0
9	Bordeaux Native	2	2	0	0
	Totals	$10	$14	$15.40	$14.20

Total invested	$24.00
Total returned	$29.60
Net profit	$ 5.60

This was a close day also, with fewer win plays than we would ordinarily expect to see. First-time starters in the fourth and a totally not-qualified field in the sixth wiped out those races, and in others, the margins were so small that only place bets were warranted. But two of the five win bets paid off, and that is enough to show the necessary profit. Place betting, with three out of seven hitting, was two dimes over the break-even point. But again, there will be many marginal days like this as we wait for the big bonanzas to make our investment program worthwhile. They come along with enough frequency, as you saw at Belmont and in the one outstanding day at Arlington, to pile up the dollars when needed.

Tuesday, June 3, 1980

Race	Selection	Invest		Return	
		Win	**Place**	**Win**	**Place**
1	Pretty Pistol	$ 2	$ 2	$ 0	$ 0
2	Sham Castle	2	2	5.60	3.80
3	Cathy's Roman	2	2	0	0
4	Socking	2	2	0	5.60
5	Extra Turn	—	2	—	0
6	Bill for Florida	2	2	0	4.40
7	Cabinook	2	2	0	0
8	Great Balance	—	2	—	0
9	I'm Snake Bit	2	2	5.00	3.80
	Totals	$14	$18	$10.60	$17.60

Total invested $32.00
Total returned $28.20
Net LOSS $ 3.80

Once more, the first three favorites yielded the day to long-shot horses. Only four of the first three favorites won, and only six of them managed to get second. A day when only six of the first three betting choices can come in second is extremely unusual, bordering on the kind of disaster that you will seldom see. We had seven win bets with only two producing for a pronounced loss there. Place betting, with a play in every race, almost made it, but fell slightly short with four returns for a $0.40 loss. On the day, with $32 going into the windows, the return was only $28.20, for a net loss of $3.80.

But here I want to emphasize with some pride the strength of our method of play, even on this disagreeable afternoon. When we limit our play to only the first three favorites, and only four can win on a nine-race card, and where only six of them can do as well as second, and we wind up losing $3.80 off $32 wagered, this indeed demonstrates how tough you can be in the demanding competitive world at the racetrack. You won't find too many days when only four of the first three favorites win. And when you encounter dark afternoons like that, and still wind up losing only $3.80 off a $2 range, then you can be sure that the good days that are also inevitable will put you well up in the investment profit department.

This illustrates one of our themes in this book: On your very worst days, you will lose very little. On your very good days, you will win a great deal. On the days in between, you will usually win in varying amounts, and that, in the end, will result in steady, consistent profits.

Wednesday, June 4, 1980

Race	Selection	Invest		Return	
		Win	Place	Win	Place
1	Tudor T Bird	$ 2	$ 2	$ 6.80	$ 4.20
2	Tom Lancan	—	2	—	4.80
3	Man It Be	2	2	0	0
4	Smoke de Judge	2	2	6.40	4.20
5	Lou's Shadow	2	2	0	6.00
6	Green Connection	2	2	7.40	4.80
7	Black George	2	2	0	0
8	Pet Streak	2	2	0	5.60
9	Amber Banta	2	2	0	0
	Totals	$16	$18	$20.60	$29.60

Total invested	$34.00
Total returned	$50.20
Net profit	$16.20

This is the day I have been waiting for to make my case for place betting. It was an excellent day all told, with three winners out of eight win selections showing a profit. But look at the list for place. Nine times to the windows, with six good place returns. Again you see three winners with only medium price produced a profit and I don't have to keep licking my chops over the place returns.

Off $34 invested, the return was $50.20 to make this a very good day at Churchill, the kind we expect, with total profit at $16.20. Here's how the three days compare:

June 2,	net profit	$ 5.60
June 3,	net LOSS	(3.80)
June 4,	net profit	16.20
	Total net profit	$18.00

So far, this is our weakest performance, but still a good profit. If you averaged that figure for all your days, securely, you would be well off indeed. Note also that in twenty races, we had but seven winners, a percentage so poor that we should be ashamed, but not ashamed of profits. On the place ledger, out of twenty-five wagers, we were successful on thirteen, only slightly better than 50%, which is very poor for place betting.

Therefore, I will make my point again for the last time. Even when you hit a poor streak and the method is weak, you will still win money, as Churchill Downs demonstrates. We had only 35% winners, the poorest we can ever expect to do over a three-day period, and yet showed an overall net profit in the win betting of $6.60. And here, for three days, place betting returned a greater profit than win betting.

5. HOLLYWOOD PARK

When you fly across the country into Los Angeles International Airport, your plane glides down right over Hollywood Park. Even when the track is not running, I like to look out the window at the palm trees, the infield, the splendid oval with the architectural beauty of an arch by Saarinen. Hollywood Park, along with Santa Anita, provides the biggest crowds, the biggest attendance, and sharp players surely as knowledgeable as the New York crowd that frequents Belmont and Aqueduct. I have had the pleasure of attending many races at Hollywood Park, and I constantly look forward to doing it again and again. But this time, I extracted my profits on paper, as I began the three-day comparison study for the first week in June 1980. Let's start right out with the first Sunday program.

Sunday, June 1, 1980

Race	Selection	Invest		Return	
		Win	Place	Win	Place
1	Lady's Career	—	$ 2	—	$ 0
2	Mascadoll	$ 2	2	$ 3.20	3.00
3	Ack Ack Attack	2	2	5.40	3.80
4	Gold Prince	2	2	5.40	3.40
5	Pass	—	—	—	—
6	Pass	—	—	—	—
7	Guarantee	2	2	0	0
8	Kinderboun	2	2	0	0
9	Truco	2	2	0	8.60
	Totals	$12	$14	$14.00	$18.80

Total invested $26.00
Total returned $32.80
Net profit $ 6.80

A strange day, indeed. After three successive winners early in the day, the fifth race was a turf event with three unknowns and the sixth was loaded with first-time starters. Then the losing started, but finished off with an incredible place payoff of $8.60 on a horse that was only 5-1 on the board. We wound up with three winners in six selections for a very slight profit there, and on the place side, buoyed by the big one, we hit four out of seven and made money. Off $26 invested, the return was $32.80, for a short $6.80 profit. Rather thin, we admit, but as long as we're scoring in black ink, we're going to stay constantly ahead.

But what was extremely significant, the first three favorites, who usually do pretty well in Southern California, won only four of the nine races on the card, again an incredibly low performance. But we had three of those four, and with having to forgo win bets in three races, we managed a slight profit. Anytime you make a profit when there are only four winners among the first three favorites, you are doing well indeed.

Wednesday, June 4, 1980

Race	Selection	Invest Win	Invest Place	Return Win	Return Place
1	Pass	—	—	—	—
2	You're Welcome	$ 2	$ 2	—	$ 6.20
3	Dazzingly	2	2	$ 9.00	5.40
4	Pashanat Reb	—	2	—	3.40
5	Delude	2	2	0	2.80
6	Pass	—	—	—	—
7	Card Game	—	2	—	4.60
8	Splendid Girl	2	2	0	0
9	She's a Swope	2	2	4.60	3.20
	Totals	$10	$14	$13.60	$25.60

Total invested $24.00
Total returned $39.20
Net profit $15.20

An excellent day at Hollywood Park, after two days of inactivity. With Sunday racing, Hollywood Park and Santa Anita both take Monday and Tuesday off, as they maintain the five-day week. Again, there was an outstanding day in the place pool, as six of seven wagers resulted in profits. Six of the nine among the first three favorites won, and on a day like this, you have to make money.

Thursday, June 5, 1980

Race	Selection	Invest		Return	
		Win	Place	Win	Place
1	Pass	—	—	—	—
2	Banker John	$ 2	$ 2	$ 6.40	$ 3.60
3	Greater Knight	—	2	—	3.20
4	Pass	—	—	—	—
5	Two Wars	—	2	—	3.00
6	Classic Dawn	—	2	—	0
7	Dreamy Louise	2	2	0	2.40
8	Borzoi	2	2	5.00	2.80
9	Poems and Promises	2	2	0	0
	Totals	$ 8	$14	$11.40	$15.00

Total invested $22.00
Total returned $26.40
Net profit $ 4.40

Again, we were stunned with how few win bets we were able to make. Hollywood Park runs a lot of short two-year-old sprints at this time of year, such as the first race, where three first-time starters at five furlongs required us to pass. The fourth race found no qualified form horse, and in the third, fifth, and sixth races, the point totals were so close that no horse could show a sufficient advantage to warrant a win bet. There went five races for win, but we were able to have seven plays for place.

With only $22 invested for the second successive day, our total return came out to $26.40, a very slender day, but like the others, another winner. Here are how the three days measured up:

June 1	net profit	$ 6.80
June 4	net profit	15.20
June 5	net profit	4.40
	Total net profit	$26.40

While we had the lowest number of plays at any of the tracks, the return percentage was very high. Out of fifteen win bets, we had seven winners for 47%. And on the place side, out of twenty-one wagers, fifteen were successful, for a beautiful 71%, the best we have obtained. But with a 47% win percentage, the profits were low because the prices were down even below the Belmont range, and in the entire three days, there was only one price above $6.40, and that was $9.00. The California players like to support their favorites, too. On the other hand, some of the place prices were surprisingly high, as long shots came home in front to boost up the prices in the middle.

But lest you think the returns were like hooking a minnow so small that it should be thrown back in the water, put your calculator to work and you will find a 37% return on your investment. That is a most happy return.

6. GOLDEN GATE FIELDS

Outside San Francisco, across the Bay in Alameda County, stands Golden Gate Fields. My few experiences there tell me you will likely freeze to death if you don't stay inside to hover around the mutuel windows. But I always freeze in San Francisco anyway. We selected GG as our last track, and as you will now see, we ran into some heavy trouble.

Tuesday, June 3, 1980

Race	Selection	Invest		Return	
		Win	Place	Win	Place
1	Galomine	$ 2	$ 2	$ 0	$ 0
2	With My Sister	2	2	0	0
3	Neva More	2	2	0	6.80
4	My Sunshine	—	2	—	4.40
5	Frank's Idea	2	2	0	0
6	Ima Sidewinder	2	2	7.00	4.40
7	Kapalua's Native	—	2	—	0
8	Logarythm	2	2	0	0
9	Grampy Allison	—	2	—	0
	Totals	$12	$18	$ 7.00	$15.60

Total invested	$30.00
Total returned	$22.60
Net LOSS	$ 7.40

This was a day you would like to forget, and quickly. In the nine races, five were won by one of the first three favorites, but our selections fell off badly. A day with only one winner is a disgrace for us, and here it was. Of $12 on the win board, our lone winner gave us $7.00, while making a place bet in every race returned a little better, but still a loss there, too. We wound up investing $30 and returning the slim sum of $22.60, for a $7.40 setback, another extremely bad day. Let's bury this one and go on to the next.

Wednesday, June 4, 1980

		Invest		Return	
Race	Selection	Win	Place	Win	Place
1	Instant Whip	$ 2	$ 2	$ 0	$ 0
2	Melulate	2	2	0	0
3	Pencils and Pens	2	2	5.80	4.20
4	Wink an Eye	—	2	—	3.20
5	Barbizon Jay	2	2	0	0
6	Fair Shasta	2	2	5.60	4.20
7	Charger Ruler	2	2	0	0
8	Mission Gem	—	2	—	3.20
9	Pass	—	—	—	—
	Totals	$12	$16	$11.40	$14.80

Total invested $28.00
Total returned $26.20
Net LOSS $ 1.80

We finally found out it was possible to lose two days in a row. This is the first time I have found it and the only occasion in all the research and work I have done with this method of play. I was sure it would happen somewhere and somehow, and this is it. And actually, the horses were not running too badly, as six races were won by one of the first three favorites, and seven place finishes were recorded. One of the big problems I encountered on this day was that many of the contenders simply had no early speed at all in sprint races, and thus there were few real advantages showing. It was almost like drawing winners out of a hat, as the close margins sufficient to support weren't good enough to come through.

Another interesting phenomenon occurred which warrants comment outside our usual rules. In the sixth race, Fair Shasta was a first-time starter, but had workouts that were faster than the racing times of her competitors. This is so unusual that I didn't try to make a rule to cover it, but when you see any first-time starter in a race with workout times faster than any horse with a record has actually run, dash to the seller's window and load on. This is even better than a Double Advantage.

But even so, the loss for the day was not all that bad. There was $28 invested and a return of $26.20 for a loss of $1.80. We can live with setbacks like that if we can find our big days. We'd better have one quickly at GG, or else we're going to wind up in the three-day loss column for the first time.

Thursday, June 5, 1980

I have to tell you this before I show you the results. Five—yes, five—Double Advantage Horses showed up on this card. I have never seen that happen before, or anything near to it. And let me tell you most happily that all five—yes, all five—came home in front, and these were our winners for the day. Sweet profit indeed, and GG finally capitulated. The three days were beautiful.

Race	Selection	Invest		Return	
		Win	Place	Win	Place
1	Fast Pocket	—	$ 2	—	$ 3.60
2	Indian Curry	$ 2	2	$ 0	0
3	Solis Noche	2	2	3.80	2.60
4	Above the Stars	2	2	3.20	2.60
5	Mr. Daunt Jillov	2	2	11.00	4.60
6	Pass	—	—	—	—
7	Watch Wendy	2	2	5.00	3.40
8	Pass	—	—	—	—
9	Gummo Joe	2	2	4.40	2.80
	Totals	$12	$14	$27.40	$19.60

Total invested	$26.00
Total returned	$47.00
Net profit	$21.00

Out of six win bets, five produced to roll up the profits. We had seven place bets with six returns, adding up to a much smaller profit, but black ink nevertheless. From $26, we brought back $47, for a clear $21 profit, enough to turn the three days into what we had believed would happen—a net profit.

Here is how they rate:

June 3	net LOSS	$(7.40)
June 4	net LOSS	(1.80)
June 5	net profit	21.00
Total net profit		$11.80

We had six win bets every day, and of these eighteen, there were but eight winners, again one less than 50%. On the place side, we had twenty-four tickets with thirteen returning good paper, for 53%. Golden Gate was tough, but our rash of Double Advantage Horses on the third day turned it around. And my point is, as all these results show, that these good days do come along and make up for the occasional weak efforts you will find.

SUMMARY

What did we accomplish at these six racetracks, scattered around the country, for three days in June, paralleling the Big Week at Belmont? First of all, we scored a net profit at every one for the same period in which we were rolling up big returns in New York. If we had extended the test for an entire week, the result would have been the same, I am certain. But you will surely agree this is a substantial test. Out of nineteen racing cards, only five produced no profit. Only two of those five really hurt. And the big days were there to make up for the losers, time and time again.

Obviously, our percentage of returns did not run as high as at Belmont. Out of 120 win bets, we had fifty-one good ones, at 42%. No one doubts that if you return 40% winners or more, you will make money at the racetrack. On the place side, there were 149 selections, with eighty-five coming in at a 57% rate, which, while under our expectancy, is still a steady, profitable enterprise. Under this method, even if you had only 50% place returns, you would make a small margin of profit. But you will indeed make more than that.

How did we do overall in those nineteen days at six different racetracks? As well as showing a profit for every period, our totals showed win profits of $95.20 for a return on total money invested in win bets as 39.6%. Does anyone want to disparage that rate of return?

With place betting, we had 149 opportunities with a net profit of $57.60, which calculates to a 19% return on investment. Sure, we'd like to make more, but I'm positive that any investor in the United States would accept a steady 19% return on his money, day in and day out. None of this takes into account limiting the initial investment and earning money thereafter out of profits.

And, overall, despite the final bottom line being much less than we have every right to expect, your total net profit comes out to a 28% return on all money put through the windows.

Doubters, you may now step aside. The investors are ready to go to work.

XVII

THE PRACTICAL SIDE OF MAKING IT WORK

All handicapping theory and knowledge is useless if it can't be implemented properly. The real test is at the windows, getting there in time with the right amount of money on the right horse, with the discipline and determination that are required to make it work. In other words, piling it up on paper doesn't count.

Special guidelines transform good theory into sound practice. Here are those that I have found most helpful, in four important areas, which we'll take one by one.

1. GETTING READY FOR THE RACE ITSELF

How do you know which horses will turn out to constitute the first three favorites? And how are you able to compare total points to know which one will be your selection in the race?

Here is what I do. As soon as I have my copy of the *Daily Racing Form,* whether on the day before or the morning of the races or even upon arriving at the track, I start writing out names of horses for my comparison charts before I even look at a single past performance. I start this by looking at the selections in the *Form* and writing down the names of the three horses that are chosen in the Consensus column. This does not mean that they will turn out to be the first three favorites, but at least it is a starting point. After I do this, I glance briefly over the past performances of the horses that are entered to seek out some other likely animal, and if I see a strong last race or heavy earnings in the consistency box in the upper right-hand portion of the horse's record, I can at least surmise that this horse might be among the first three betting choices.

Then I begin the process of looking at each horse's record, checking his form first of all, and then working on ability times. I like to write all this in a loose-leaf notebook, although you may find some other procedure more useful. Like most other players, I will mark up my *Racing Form* considerably, writing ability times on the paper itself for later copying in my notebook. I also apply early-speed computations where appropriate and record my point computation there also. All this is done before I know what the odds will be.

When I arrive at the track, my first step is to check the program for the day, looking at the morning-line odds as given, or, where program selections are made, using that standard. I will check my list of probable contenders from the *Form* against what the program tells me, and if there are any omissions (which is frequent), I will then write in the names of those horses from the program to the list I have already accumulated. By this time, I will usually have the names and ratings of five horses, although in smaller fields where there are strong entries, I may never have to deal with more than three at any time.

After all this is done, one must next watch the tote board. In many situations, the favorite is obvious. Ordinarily, the lines to watch are those which may determine the third and fourth choices in the betting. For many races, if not the majority, your own final point totals will be more important than the actual finishing odds, since if there is a definite high-point horse with totals above any of the others, you are sure to invest in him despite how the odds turn out, as long as he is one of the first three favorites, which is where you will usually find him.

A strong example is a Double Advantage Horse. These horses are almost always among the first three favorites, frequently first or second in the betting odds. When you have such a selection, it doesn't matter very much who will wind up as third or fourth choice, since you're going to play the Double Advantage animal anyway (or a very high-point horse as well in other situations).

However, there may be a competing horse whose ability times are close enough to wipe out the Double Advantage for the horse you are watching. If the competing horse falls back in the odds to where he is not among the first three favorites, the Double Advantage may spring to life among the top three in the wagering, for that is where the Double Advantage counts.

The real crunch comes when horses are closely bunched in total points and also closely bunched in the odds. This happens once or more on almost every card, and is especially critical when potential third and fourth choices are strong in the total-points department. A mistake in one single race on the card can sometimes determine whether your day develops a profit or a loss. This brings me to the next vital area, which may be the most important of all.

2. DISCIPLINE AND DETERMINATION

This part of the investment program comes down to the sermon for the day. We start throwing words around like "discipline" and "determination," and you wonder if we're drifting off into "God, mother, country, and home." But these tired old words will surely control your handicapping destiny, and if you're not prepared to take them seriously, then file this book on a shelf somewhere and forget trying to make money at the racetrack.

I said above that this may be the most important part of all in this whole program. Sure, you have to know what to do and how to do it, but if you can't apply it, it simply won't work.

This means that you have to be so tough and so self-disciplined that you resist all other temptation—and there is plenty of that. Another of my bright handicapping sons, whose knowledge of this game is truly remarkable, still insists on playing exactas, particularly in races where there is a strong favorite. He's really trying to determine who will run second. Sometimes he does, and his returns are sometimes bountiful. But he tears up tickets time and time again in races where I quietly go back to the window to receive good green bills in exchange for my winning tickets.

Thus, the rule I gave you early in this book must remain inviolate. You will not play daily doubles, exactas, trifectas, quinellas, or anything else except WIN and PLACE only. It's easy to say, but you'll find yourself torn again and again over a "sure thing" daily double or exacta. *Don't.* I am happy for my son when he hits a big exacta payoff, but let him have it. I think I know what I am doing, and it works.

The exotic bets are only one booby trap. More important to me (since I have been able to truly conquer the temptation on the gambling wagers) is to stay faithfully with the first three betting choices and the high-point horse. I know there are many good-looking animals that pay good money to win who are not up there in the odds or the points. But even worse is the horse with high points who is not one of the first three favorites. He looks so-o-o good, doesn't he? Play him, you will surely be saying to yourself, you can beat the system, he's bound to be there when the finish line is reached. Don't listen to old debbil

Temptation. *Do not play him.* Back in March, April, and even into May of 1980, when I had almost fully developed my whole program, I still experimented with high-point horses who were not among the first three betting choices. I suffered for it.

Therefore, when your calculations have provided a high-point horse who is not among the first three favorites, think of Double-D, Discipline and Determination. This book provides an investment method to make money at the racetrack—its goal is not to eventually own the grandstand. The steady profits you will make (remember the two losing days at GG, followed by a big winner) will be enough for anyone. If you're behind when the ninth race rolls around and that strong-looking fifth choice in the betting has the high points and a price that will put you ahead for the day, forget it. Accept today's red ink gracefully, with full knowledge that tomorrow will almost surely bring the profits that will make your program a success.

This kind of preachment could go on and on, with plenty of specific examples, but I've said enough. If you really must deviate from the program set forth here, in the final analysis, you will do it. But don't blame this book and this author. Look in the mirror.

3. HOW NOT TO GET SHUT OUT

The most perplexing practical problem, assuming you've done all your homework, your careful arithmetical computations, and conquered all the evil of temptation, is how to get your money through the window before the bell rings. "Getting shut out," in terms of the regular racegoers, is a thing to be feared in this program.

Again, when there is one outstanding selection, and his odds are sufficiently strong to allow you to know that he will be one of the first three choices, regardless of what the play is on any other animal, your problem is minimal. You can bet early. For much of a race card, this situation will usually exist. In most races, even the early money on the board will demonstrate a trend, and by the time of about five minutes before post, most of the odds are reasonably well established.

But every racing day, you will encounter some races where you cannot be certain who will be the second, third, fourth, or fifth choices. Closely bunched odds will fluctuate as money keeps coming in, right until the time the bell rings and the horses spring out of the starting gate. You can look at your figures in front of you and know that your ultimate selection depends on how those odds go, since the heart of our program is to stay with the first three favorites.

I have developed a practical method that has worked at every track where I have attended. The problem is acute at the big tracks, such as in New York and California, where there are large crowds and especially long lines at the windows. With the advent of the modern pari-mutuel machines that enable the person behind the windows to cash all kinds of bets, if you get in line less than five minutes before post, you may be shut out. Even a short line can sometimes do you in, as some little old lady in front of you has about fifteen exacta combinations at $2 each, all slowly called out to an impatient teller, causing delay all back up the line.

First, early in the day, I try to make a judgment on the length of the lines at the windows. If there are any substantial lines at all, I know that I have to be there early enough to make sure my money goes in the till, and long before the final odds are established. I therefore go to a line at a window where I can always see an odds board. Most of the tracks have them inside, and many show odds on the TV monitors above the back of the windows, easily visible.

As I move slowly to the head of the line, I keep watching the board and especially the minutes remaining to post time. If the odds are stable enough to permit an early decision, I make my bet as soon as possible and return to my seat. But suppose the third and fourth choices are closely bunched and odds are constantly shifting. Late money can make substantial changes that produce at the last flash a pattern quite different from the one that existed when the early bettor bought his ticket.

Here is how I cope with that situation. When I get close enough to the window, about third in line, and the odds are still unsettled, I quietly and politely ask the person behind me to change places. No one objects to moving ahead in the line. When the line is ready to move again, and the odds are still unsettled, I invite the next person to move ahead of me. I constantly maintain my third position in line, until post time nears, when I move it into the second position, always ready to have the person behind me step ahead if the clock warrants it.

I will not wait beyond the last half-minute. If the odds change after that time—and they sometimes do—it is something that I will have to live with. Sometimes, on the way back to my seat, the last flash may do me in, but by then it is too late and I will have to stay with my point selection, whatever it may be.

But this is a method that works and positively solves the problem, except for those rare occasions that I have just mentioned, when the very last flash makes a substantial change. It is also exceptionally easy to apply, offends no one, and gives you the maximum amount of protection for your investment program. I have never been shut out once since I adopted this program of getting in line early enough not to be left out, and having people move ahead of me until the odds are fixed for my purposes.

4. MONEY MANAGEMENT

At last, we come to how you handle your money. This, too, comes along as a part of the Double-D's, Discipline and Determination, and if you don't handle this one right, the whole investment program will collapse. For me, it isn't nearly as difficult as maintaining the discipline of staying with the first three favorites, no matter what. But without a money plan, you won't make it, either.

The first cardinal rule, as inviolate as the rule not to make exotic bets, is to bet the same amount every time to win and place, all within a framework of a money level. By that I mean that because a horse is a 3-5 favorite and will return practically nothing is no reason to load more on him than the 9-2 third choice in another race who may look like far less of a sure thing. This rule holds even if your outstanding selection will pay only $2.10 to place. Money is money, and remember, the low payoff comes with the low risk. But once you load up on a favorite because you feel it's the only way you're going to make money, you're already in deep trouble and in danger of wiping out a sound program.

Therefore, you must, steadily and consistently, throughout every race on the card, wager exactly the same amount to win and place, no matter what the odds may be. My sons still sneer at the 3-5 favorite, and would never make a place bet on such a horse. I'll still take the money.

Now that we've settled the issue of betting the same amount in every situation, the next big question is: How much?

As I have told you earlier, the $2 figure used in this book is only for illustration and calculation. You cannot expect to make money at the racetrack by betting $2 to win and place on every race, because the profits you will inevitably make will yield to the expense of your operation. You must, therefore, adopt some other amount of money for regular play, and follow a certain program for it.

You not only need a determined amount for each race, but you need a capital figure from which to draw. Losing three or four races in a row will sober your expectations with dramatic intensity. Thus you must have enough to confidently weather any adverse run, even as bad as the one at Golden Gate Fields.

My belief is that whatever your capital investment is, this program is safe enough that you can invest 10% in every race. Let's asume you have the modest sum of $100. Since 10% of that figure is $10, you invest $10 in a race by putting $5 to win and $5 to place on your selection. That becomes your betting figure.

But what if, in this 10% level, you have only a place bet under our rules? This happens over and over again, as you have seen from all the playing days in this book. Your base bet is still $5 as an integral portion of your 10% allotment for each race. If you bet more than $5 to place on your selection, you would be violating the iron rule of playing the same amount of money on every race.

What if you lose three races in a row, for example, with a loss of $30 out of your $100 capital, leaving you with only $70 in your investment bank? Does the 10% rule require you to reduce your bet size down to $7 for both win and place? If you did, your money would obviously last a great deal longer.

No. You will stay with your base bet of $5 as long as there is money in your till. To lower the total wagered per race would again be shifting the amount. If you go four or five races without cashing a ticket under this program, something is drastically wrong. If you tap out on a program of wagering 10% of your capital per race, you have either lost the Double-D, misunderstood this book, or run into incomprehensible misfortune (which is not likely to happen).

But, of course, a $100 reserve with $5 bets to win and $5 bets to place won't make very much money either. If you have $200 to invest, and want to start with $10 to win and $10 to place, you're getting a little closer.

Let's build a program on that basis. You have $200 (which even the least affluent among us can probably put together). You follow every rule in this book, as you must. And profits begin to come in, just like the man said. What do you do about making some better money?

I would recommend doing it this way. Retain your profits and pay your expenses out of pocket money, the way you would ordinarily do when you go to the track. As soon as your $200 builds to a quantum of $300, you would consider this as the next higher rung in your investment block. Having arrived at a designated figure, which in this case would be $300 (or it could be $400, or anything else depending upon your starting capital), you would then adjust your bets again at the same 10% level and keep them there throughout your program, until you either advance to a higher money level or tap out (which is not going to happen). Your 10% of $300 would be $30 and you would divide this into win bets of $15 and place bets of $15.

You will then begin to escalate. If your next money level is fixed at $400 for capital, as soon as you reach it, raise your 10% betting level to $40 with $20 on top and $20 in the middle.

You can carry this along as far as you wish. You may want to retain half your profits for investment capital and spend the other half. You may feel uncomfortable with 10% as too high, and may feel much better with 5% (a $400 portfolio with $10 to win and $10 to place, for example). I would not recommend a higher percentage than 10 in any event. I think 5% is small, but it is vitally important that each of you invest in complete comfort and confidence, or else you'll make errors in both arithmetic and application of rules that do get a little sticky at times.

Therefore, you will always use a fixed percentage based upon an established level of capital. You may raise your level of capital whenever you accumulate enough profits to establish it. You will *always* continue to invest the same amount of money to win and place at whatever investment level you are using, adjusting amounts upward only as your capital grows sufficiently to reach a new established money rung, or level.

With a sound program like this, the only thing you need is the certainty that the program itself works. That is what this book is all about. No matter whether you are new to racing or whether you have been playing the horses for years (always losing more than you win, of course), you should not start a program, even on a low modest capital amount, until you thoroughly understand everything in this book. Now go back and read most of it again, especially the selection rules.

When you are thoroughly ready, you may begin. See you in Saratoga!

If horse is "loseing ground", the actual beaten length should be used, not reduced to 8.

1.

1. ^{10}200 — 60

2. ^{10}260 — 78

3. ^{20}338 —

	40	66
	26.40	11.80
	Profet	Bank

1. 10 — — $\frac{132}{59}$ = 191 + 200 = 391

2. 20 — — 264 + 118 = 382 + 391 = 773

3. 40 — — 528 + 236 = 764 + 773 = 1537

4. 40   764 + 1537 = 2301

5. 60   792 + 354 = 1146

      100   = 1910 / 1500 per week